The Law of Investor Protection

AUSTRALIA
LBC Information Services
Sydney

CANADA and USA
The Carswell Company
Toronto

NEW ZEALAND
Brooker's
Auckland

SINGAPORE and MALAYSIA
Thomson Information (S.E. Asia)
Singapore

The Law of Investor Protection

by

JONATHAN FISHER
B.A., LL.B. (Cantab.), of Gray's Inn, Barrister
Senior Visiting Fellow, City University Business School (PVM)

and

JANE BEWSEY
M.A. (Cantab.), of Inner Temple, Barrister

Published in 1997 by
Sweet and Maxwell Ltd of
100 Avenue Road, Swiss Cottage,
London NW3 3PF
Laserset by LBJ Enterprises Ltd
Aldermaston and Chilcompton.
Printed and bound in Great Britain by
Hartnolls Ltd, Bodmin

No natural forests were destroyed to
make this product: only farmed
timber was used and re-planted.

ISBN 0 421 54630 1

A catalogue record for this book is
available from the British Library

All rights reserved. U.K. statutory material in this publication is acknowledged as Crown copyright.
No part of this publication may be reproduced or transmitted, in any form or by any means, or stored in any retrieval system of any nature, without prior written permission, except for permitted fair dealing under the Copyright, Designs and Patents Act 1988, or in accordance with the terms of a licence issued by the Copyright Licensing Agency in respect of photocopying and/or reprographic reproduction. Application for permission for other use of copyright material including permission to reproduce extracts in other published works shall be made to the publishers.
Full acknowledgment of author, publisher and source must be given.

All Securities and Investments Board Rules and Principles are reproduced by kind permission.

© Sweet & Maxwell Ltd
1997

Preface

The last 15 years have witnessed a change in our attitude towards the use of money. Whereas during the years of high inflation people came to the view that it was sensible to spend money on consumer goods before inflation ravaged the value of their money, the contemporary attitude towards money is quite different. Successive Conservative administrations have encouraged people to save money, through a variety of investment schemes. Investment opportunities have multiplied and often these have been laced with tax incentives. Thrift has become a fashionable virtue.

Associated with the growth of investment opportunities, the Thatcher years witnessed a revolution in the provision of financial services, as "Big Bang" in the City heralded a new era of the small investor in which the ordinary and the meek were invited to accumulate wealth by prudent investment in the financial markets. New types of investment vehicles developed, as small shareholders were encouraged to participate in capital ventures. The size of the world shrank, as computer technology enabled money to be transferred across international boundaries instantaneously at the press of a button. The time of the financial entrepreneur had arrived. Instead of acting as the intermediary between capital and labour, which was the role ascribed to the entrepreneur in classical Marxist theory, the entrepreneur acted as the intermediary between capital and investor. The investor varied in degrees of sophistication from the City meritocrat who was investing his large annual profit bonus to the ordinary man on the Clapham omnibus who had some money to invest but was uneducated in the skills of financial investment.

Legal headlines in the past 15 years have been dominated by the casualties of the changes and innovations which have occurred in the investment world, as Parliament and the Courts have struggled to protect the interests of investors. Investors lost money which they had invested, sometimes at the hands of dishonest men who set out to defraud their victims of their savings, but more often at the hands of the incompetent or the reckless, who were trying to accumulate wealth for themselves and their clients by taking risks which the more prudent could not justify. Barlow Clowes, the Levitt Group, BCCI, the Lloyd's insurance market, and more recently Barings Bank, have become household names associated with the dishonest or reckless loss of investor's money.

It was unfortunate, though perhaps inevitable, that before sponsoring this change in attitude in favour of saving and investment the Government did not ensure that there were sufficient legal protections in place to protect the investor. In order to afford investors some protection the courts have sought to rely upon the traditional common law principles enshrined in the law of contract and the law of tort. In some areas the courts have successfully assimilated the changes and innovations within the boundaries of established legal norms and principles, but in other areas the task has been too great. Parliament has responded to investor related problems by amending existing post-war legislation in some areas and enacting fresh legislation in others, and different Acts of Parliament apply to different spheres of investment activity. A burgeoning jurisprudence is developing in each of these spheres of activity, as cases under the new statutory regimes, such as the Financial Services Act 1986, the Pensions legislation and the new Company and Insolvency legislation have started to come through the courts, with increasing frequency in recent years.

There is no shortage of written material on each of these areas, and there are good texts on the subject matter of each area which is covered in this book. The problem lies not with the absence of comprehensive texts on each subject, but rather in the fact that the statutory and non-statutory systems for investor protection, together with the established areas of criminal and civil law, are so unwieldy and fragmented that it is difficult to take an overall view. There is no book which pulls together the disparate threads into one readable and coherent text.

It is the object of this book to undertake this somewhat Herculean task and provide readers with a coherent account of the law which protects investors and regulates those involved in the investment industry. At the present time the law of investor protection is not a recognised subject in its own right. We hope that this book will stimulate interest in the development of this area of the law in academic as well as legal circles.

Notwithstanding the depth of the recession, investment activity has continued. New challenges continue to confront the legal system. We hope that in meeting these challenges this book will, by drawing together disparate strands and presenting an overall approach to the subject, provide a useful companion to legal practitioners, compliance officers and all those who work in the field of investment.

Above all, we hope that the production of a coherent text which concerns itself with an overall picture of investor protection will assist in efforts to improve the present state of the existing law. There can be little doubt that fragmentation of investor protection and regulation has hindered the development of the law in this area.

Similar problems have arisen in other jurisdictions, not just in Europe, the United States, Canada and Australia, but also in Pacific Rim countries and countries which have seen a rapid growth in investment markets. Experiences in former Commonwealth countries, the East European countries, and the Middle East, particularly in Israel, come to mind. We hope that this book will also be of interest and assistance to legislators, legal practitioners and academic lawyers in these jurisdictions.

Preface

In undertaking this work we have not sought to analyse investor protection in jurisprudential or socio-economic terms. Our focus is confined to a consideration of the provisions of the substantive law.

There are bound to be errors and omissions in a book of this kind. We hope that readers will point them out to us, for correction in the next edition. We also hope readers will let us know where they would like to see changes in content or scope. We have avoided the use of footnotes in the hope that the text will flow more freely.

The book deals with the law relating to England and Wales. The law is stated as at July 31, 1996.

The idea to write this book arose from the need to provide a text for Masters degree students who study Investment Law at City University Business School (PVM). Jonathan Fisher would like to thank all at City University for their encouragement with this work.

Both authors wish to acknowledge with grateful thanks the support they have received from their families, their clerks, and our publishers, Sweet and Maxwell, at all times during the writing of this book.

Jonathan Fisher
Jane Bewsey
5 King's Bench Walk
Inner Temple
London

July 31, 1996

Contents

	page
Preface	v
Table of Cases	xvii
Table of Statutes	xxxix
Table of Statutory Instruments	lvii
Table of Rules of the Supreme Court	lix
Table of Treaties and Conventions	lxi
Table of E.C. Directives	lxiii

PART 1 — INTRODUCTION

1. **Investor Protection in Context**	3
Definition of an Investor	3
Recognition of Investor Interests	5

PART 2 — THE FINANCIAL SERVICES ACT 1986

2. **Overview**	13
Framework	16
Promotion and Advertising Restrictions	22
Jurisdiction	24
3. **Implementation**	25
Direct Authorisation	25
Authorisation by an SRO	26
Recognised Professional Bodies	28
Europe	28
The Three Tiers	29
Separation of Client Accounts and Dealings with Client Moneys	31
Suitability of Investment	33
Understanding of Risk	35
The Customer Agreement	36
Advertising Standards	38
Financial Resources and Solvency	39

4. **Enforcement and Sanctions** 43
   Unauthorised Trading 43
   Injunctions and Restitution Orders 44
   Monitoring, Inspection and Discipline 47
   Compensation and Complaints 54

5. **Personal Pensions** 63

PART 3 — THE PENSIONS ACT 1995

6. **Overview** 71
   The Scheme of the Pensions Act 1995—OPRA 74
   Conclusion 80

7. **Duties and Powers** 83
   Trustee Appointment and Removal 83
   Minimum Funding Requirement and the Collection of Contributions 87
   Investment 90
   Administration 96
   Receipts by Trustees: Separate Bank Accounts 98
   Ongoing Surplus 98
   Transfer Values 100
   Communication 101
   The Modification of Schemes: Amendment 101
   Benefits 103

8. **Ancillary Provisions** 105
   Contracting out of the Act: State Pensions 105
   Divorce 108
   Equal Treatment 110
   Money Purchase Schemes 113

9. **Disputes and Compensation** 117
   Dispute Resolution 117
   Occupational Pensions Advisory Service (OPAS) 117
   The Pensions Ombudsman 118
   The Pensions Compensation Board 121
   Industrial Tribunals 123

PART 4—STATUTORY AND NON-STATUTORY SYSTEMS FOR THE REGULATION OF INVESTMENT

10. **The Insurance Companies Act 1982** — 127
    The Scheme of the Insurance Companies Act 1982 — 127
    Supervision and Regulation of Insurance Companies — 131
    The Conduct of Insurance Business — 136
    The Overlap Between the Financial Services Act 1986 and Life Insurance — 137
    Insurance Ombudsman Bureau — 138

11. **Lloyd's of London** — 141
    History — 142
    The Structure of Lloyd's — 142
    Lloyd's and the Financial Services Act 1986 — 144
    The Regulation of Lloyd's — 144
    Other Lloyd's Boards — 146
    Lloyd's Regulatory Plan 1996 — 148
    Equitas — 151
    Judicial review — 152

12. **The Stock Exchange** — 155
    Structure of the Stock Exchange — 157
    The Rules of the London Stock Exchange — 159
    Judicial Review — 163
    Listing Requirements — 164
    Unlisted Securities—Alternative Investment Market — 173
    Companies Act 1985 — 177
    Remedies for False, Misleading or Incomplete Statements in Connection with Offers of Securities — 178
    Conclusion — 179

13. **The Panel on Take-overs and Mergers** — 181
    A Common Law Vacuum — 182
    Europe — 183
    Definition of Terms — 183
    The Panel on Take-overs and Mergers — 183
    Judicial Review — 185
    The City Code on Take-overs and Mergers — 187
    Substantial Acquisitions Rules — 196
    Conclusion — 198

14. The Banking Act 1987	201
Scheme of Banking Act 1987	202
Authorisation	205
Changes in Control	211
Impact of Single Market—Second Banking Co-ordination Directive	213
Procedural Proprieties	213
Unauthorised Deposit Taking	214
Supervisory Controls	216
Information and Investigation	217
Role of Auditor in Policing Banks	221
Appeals	222
Compensation	223
Common Law Remedies	224
Supervision in Practice	226
Relationship Between Banking Act and other Supervisory Regimes	228
The Future	229
15. Building Societies	231
The Building Societies Act 1986	232
The Proposed Legislation	237

PART 5—INVESTOR PROTECTION IN CRIMINAL LAW

16. Theft Act offences	241
Theft Act 1968	242
Property by deception	253
False Accounting	257
Valuable Securities	259
Theft Act 1978	259
Forfeiting and Counterfeiting Act 1981	261
Jurisdiction	262
Conclusion	263
17. Fraudulent Trading	265
The Legislative History	265
The Criminal Offence	266
If any Business of a Company is Carried On	266
A Party to the Carrying On of a Business	267
With Intent to Defraud Creditors . . . or for any Fraudulent Purpose	268

18. Conspiracy	271
Statutory Conspiracy	271
Conspiracy to Defraud	273
Jurisdiction	276
Reform of the Law of Conspiracy to Defraud	276
19. Companies Act offences	277
Restrictions on Directors Taking Financial Advantage	277
Allotment of Shares	280
Other Offences in Part IV of the Companies Act 1985	281
Consent to Prosecute	282
Accounting Records	282
Company Investigations	284
The Efficacy of Companies Act Regulation	285
20. Market Manipulation	287
Insider Dealing	288
Inducing an Investment	297
21. A Company's Purchase of its Own Shares	303
The Fundamental Prohibition on the Acquisition by a Company of its Own Shares	303
Provision by a Company of Financial Assistance for the Acquisition of its Own Shares	305
Section 151 in Practice and Calls for Reform	314
22. Directors' Disqualification	315
Disqualification on Conviction for an Indictable Offence	315
Disqualification for Persistent Breach of Companies Legislation	318
Disqualification for Unfitness	318
Disqualification in the Public Interest	320
Disqualification Following a Declaration of Fraudulent or Wrongful Trading	320
Disqualification where an Undischarged Bankrupt Acting as a Director	320
The Consequences of Contravention of an Order for Disqualification	321
Register of Disqualification Orders	321

Contents

23.	**Confiscation of Assets and Compensation**	323
	Confiscation Orders	323
	Restraint Orders and Charging Orders	330
	Compensation Orders	331
	Restitution Orders	334
	Deprivation Orders	334
24.	**Money Laundering**	335
	Assisting Another to Retain the Benefit of Criminal Conduct	335
	Acquisition, Possession or Use of the Proceeds of Criminal Conduct	338
	Concealing or Transferring the Proceeds of Criminal Conduct	338
	Tipping Off	339
	The Money Laundering Regulations 1993	340
	Money Laundering in Practice	343
25.	**Investor Protection and the Criminal Process**	345
	The Serious Fraud Office	345
	Reviewing a Decision not to Prosecute	350
	Reviewing a Decision not to Commence Disciplinary Proceedings or an Investigation	352

PART 6—INVESTOR PROTECTION IN CIVIL LAW

26.	**Investor Protection in Company Law**	355
	Directors' Duties	355
	Minority Shareholders Actions	362
	The Rule in Foss v. Harbottle	363
	Unfair Prejudice	365
	Just and Equitable Winding-up	369
	Fraudulent Trading	370
	Powers of the DTI to Investigate Companies	370
	The Privilege Against Self-incrimination	373
	Disclosure of Transcripts and Documents Obtained During the Course of Investigations	375
27.	**Investor Protection in Trust Law**	377
	Investor's Funds Held on Trust	378
	Knowing Receipt and Knowing Assistance in Breach of Trust	381
	Tracing Remedies	387

28. Investor Protection at Common Law	393
Deceit	393
Misrepresentation	395
Conspiracy	397
Conversion	399
Money Had and Received	399
Illegal Transactions	401
29. Negligent Advice and Negligent Financial Information	403
Hedley Byrne	404
Liability for Negligent Investment Advice or Conduct	405
Negligent Statements in Accounts	412
Auditing Standards	414
Overlap Between Claims for Negligent Advice or Misrepresentation and Breach of Contract	415
30. Parties to a Civil Action	417
Personal Liability of Directors	417
31. Pre-emptive Civil Remedies	425
The Mareva and Anton Piller Jurisdiction	425
Privilege Against Self-Incrimination	432
Bankers Trust Orders	436
Summary Judgment	441

PART 7—CONCLUSION

32. The Future	445
The Need for Reform	445
A Co-ordinated Approach	446
Strengthening the Policing Role of Auditors	447
Enforcement	447

PART 8—APPENDICES

Appendix 1	Regulatory structure for Financial Services in the United Kingdom	451
Appendix 2	Schedule 1 of the Financial Services Act 1986	452

Appendix 3	The Securities and Investment Board's Statements of Principle	473
Appendix 4	The Core Conduct of Business Rules	477
Appendix 5	General Principles of the Panel for Takeovers and Mergers	492
Appendix 6	Schedule 24 of the Companies Act 1985 (as amended)	494

Index 515

Table of Cases

A. v. B. Bank (Bank of England Intervening) [1993] Q.B. 311; [1992] 3 W.L.R. 705; [1992] 1 All E.R. 778; (1991) 135 S.J. 11; *Financial Times*, May 15, 1991; *The Times*, May 16, 1991 14–081
A. v. C. (Note) [1981] Q.B. 956 .... 31–008, 31–009
ADT v. Binder Hamlyn, December 6, 1995 (unreported) 29–047
AT & T Istel Ltd v. Tully [1993] A.C. 45; [1992] 3 W.L.R. 344; [1992] 3 All E.R. 523; [1992] 136 S.J.L.B. 227; (1992) 142 N.L.J. 1088; *The Independent*, July 21, 1992; *The Times*, July 24, 1992, H.L.; reversing [1992] Q.B. 315; [1992] 2 W.L.R. 112; [1992] 2 All E.R. 28; (1992) 142 N.L.J. 88; [1992] *Gazette*, January 15, 32; *The Times*, November 18, 1991, C.A. 31–036, 31–037, 31–045
Aaron's Reefs Ltd v. Twiss [1896] A.C. 273 20–044
Acatos & Hutcheson plc v. Watson [1995] 1 B.C.L.C. 218; [1995] B.C.C. 446; *The Times*, December 30, 1994, Ch.D. 21–009
Adams v. Queen, The [1995] 1 W.L.R. 52; [1995] 2 Cr.App.R. 295; [1995] 2 B.C.L.C. 17; [1995] B.C.C. 376; [1995] Crim.L.R. 561; (1995) 92 L.S.Gaz. 33; (1995) 139 S.J.L.B. 13; *The Times*, November 4, 1994; *The Independent*, January 9, 1995 (C.S.) P.C.; affirming ... 18–018, 20–052
Agip (Africa) Ltd v. Jackson [1991] Ch. 547; [1991] 3 W.L.R. 116; [1992] 4 All E.R. 451; (1991) 135 S.J. 117; *The Times*, January 9, 1991; *Financial Times*, January 18, 1991, C.A.; affirming [1990] Ch. 265; [1989] 3 W.L.R. 1367; [1992] 4 All E.R. 385; (1990) 134 S.J. 198; [1989] L.S.Gaz., January 17, 34 28–023
Aiken v. Stewart Wrightson Members Agency [1995] 1 W.L.R. 1281; [1995] 3 All E.R. 449; [1995] 2 Lloyd's Rep. 618; *The Times*, March 8, 1995, Q.B.D. 29–021, 29–050
Al-Nakib Investments (Jersey) Ltd v. Longcroft [1990] 3 All E.R. 321; [1990] B.C.C. 517; [1991] B.C.L.C. 7; (1990) 140 N.L.J. 741; *The Times*, May 4, 1990 29–042
Al Saudi Banque v. Clark Pixley (a firm) [1990] Ch. 313; [1990] 2 W.L.R. 344; [1989] 3 All E.R. 361; [1990] B.C.L.C. 46; 1989 Fin.L.R. 353; (1989) 5 B.C.C. 822; 1989 P.C.C. 442; (1989) 139 N.L.J. 1341; [1990] L.S.Gaz., March 14, 36 29–040
Allied Arab Bank Ltd v. Hajjar [1988] Q.B. 787; [1988] 22 W.L.R. 942; (1988) 132 S.J. 659; [1987] 3 All E.R. 739; [1987] 1 F.T.L.R. 455 31–016
Allied Maples Group Ltd v. Simmons & Simmons [1995] 1 W.L.R. 1602; [1995] 4 All E.R. 907; [1995] N.P.C. 83; (1995) 145 N.L.J. Rep. 1646, C.A. 29–025
Alpine Investments BV v. Minister van Financien (C384/93) [1995] All E.R. (E.C.) 543; [1995] 2 B.C.L.C. 214; *The Times*, June 16, 1995 .. 2–010
Anthony v. Wright [1995] 1 B.C.L.C. 236; [1995] B.C.C. 768; *The Independent*, September 27, 1994, Ch.D. 29–029

TABLE OF CASES

Arab Bank plc v. Mercantile Holdings Ltd [1994] Ch. 71; [1994] 2 W.L.R. 307; [1994] 2 All E.R. 74; [1993] B.C.C. 816; [1994] 1 B.C.L.C. 330; (1995) 69 P. & C.R. 410; (1994) 91 (12) L.S.Gaz. 37; [1993] E.G.C.S. 164; [1993] N.P.C. 130; *The Times*, October 19, 1993; *The Independent*, October 11, 1993 (C.S.), Ch.D. 21–025
Arab Monetary Fund v. Hashim (1994) 6 Admin.L.R. 348; *The Times*, May 4, 1993; *The Independent*, April 30, 1993; C.A.; affirming [1989] 1 W.L.R. 565; [1989] 3 All E.R. 466; (1989) 133 S.J. 749; *The Times*, January 16, 1989, Ch.D. 31–039, 31–040
—— v. —— (No. 5) [1992] 2 All E.R. 911 31–010
Armour Hick Northern Ltd v. Whitehouse [1980] 1 W.L.R. 1520; (1980) 124 S.J. 864; *sub nom.* Armour Hick Northern v. Armour Trust [1980] 3 All E.R. 833 21–021
Arrows (No. 4), *Re.*; *sub nom.* Hamilton v. Naviede and Director of the Serious Fraud Office [1995] 2 A.C. 75; [1994] 3 W.L.R. 656; [1994] 3 All E.R. 814; [1995] 1 Cr.App.R. 95; [1994] B.C.C. 641; [1994] 2 B.C.L.C. 738; (1994) 144 N.L.J. Rep. 1203; *The Times*, July 26, 1994; *The Independent*, July 26, 1994, H.L.; affirming [1993] Ch. 452; [1993] 3 W.L.R. 513; [1993] 3 All E.R. 861; [1993] B.C.C. 473; [1993] B.C.L.C. 1222, C.A. 26–082, 31–027
Atlantic Computers, *Re*. May 23, 1996 (unreported) 26–085
Attorney-General's Reference (No. 1 of 1980) [1981] 1 W.L.R. 34; (1980) 124 S.J. 881; [1981] 1 All E.R. 366; (1980) 72 Cr.App.R. 60; [1981] Crim.L.R. 41, C.A. 16–058
—— (No. 2 of 1982) [1984] Q.B. 624; [1984] 2 W.L.R. 447; (1984) 128 S.J. 221; [1984] 2 All E.R. 216; (1984) 78 Cr.App.R. 131; [1985] Crim.L.R. 241; (1984) 81 L.S.Gaz. 279, C.A. 16–008
—— (No. 1 of 1995), *The Times*, January 30, 1996 14–060
Att.-Gen. of Hong Kong v. Nai-Keung [1987] 1 W.L.R. 1339 16–052
—— v. Reid [1994] 1 A.C. 324; [1993] 3 W.L.R. 1143; [1994] 1 All E.R. 1; (1993) 137 S.J.L.B. 251; [1993] N.P.C. 144; (1993) 143 N.L.J. 1569; *The Times*, November 12, 1993; *The Independent*, November 24, 1993, P.C. 26–016
August Investments Pty Ltd v. Poseidon Ltd and Samin Ltd [1971] 2 S.A.S.R. 71 21–011

Bank Fur Handel und Effekten v. Davidson & Co. Ltd [1975] D.L.R. (3d) 303 29–029
Bank of Credit and Commerce International SA (9), *Re.* [1994] 2 B.C.L.C. 636, C.A.; [1994] 3 All E.R. 764 31–005
Bank of Crete SA v. Koskotas (No. 2) [1992] 1 W.L.R. 919; [1993] 1 All E.R. 748; *The Times*, June 30, 1992 25–018
Bank of England v. Riley [1992] Ch. 475; [1992] 2 W.L.R. 840; [1992] 1 All E.R. 769; *The Times*, November 1, 1990, C.A. 14–080, 31–037
Bankers Trust Co. v. Shapira [1980] 1 W.L.R. 1274; (1980) S.J. 480; [1980] 3 All E.R. 353, C.A. 31–011
Bankers Trust International plc v. PT Dharmala Sakti Sejahtera, December 1, 1995 (unreported) 29–033
Banque Bruxelles Lambert SA v. Eagle Star Insurance, March 22, 1996 (unreported) 29–019

TABLE OF CASES

Banque Financiere de la Cite SA v. Westgate Insurance Co.; *sub nom.*
Banque Keyser Ullman SA v. Skandia (U.K.) Insurance Co. [1991] 2
A.C. 249; [1990] 3 W.L.R. 364; [1990] 2 All E.R. 947; [1990] 2
Lloyd's Rep. 377; 91990) 134 S.J. 1265; (1990) 140 N.L.J. 1074;
[1990] L.S.Gaz., October 3, 36, H.L.; affirming [1990] 1 Q.B. 665;
[1989] 3 W.L.R. 25; (1989) 133 S.J. 817; [1988] 2 Lloyd's Rep. 513;
[1989] 2 All E.R. 952; 1989 Fin.L.R. 1, C.A.; reversing .. 28–013, 29–050
Barber v. Guardian Royal Exchange Assurance Group (C-262/88) [1991] 1
Q.B. 344; [1991] 2 W.L.R. 72; [1990] 2 All E.R. 660; [1990] I.C.R.
616; [1990] I.R.L.R. 240; [1990] E.C.R. I–1889; [1990] 2 C.M.L.R.
513; (1990) 140 N.L.J. 925, E.C.J. 8–027
Barclays Bank v. Khaira [1993] 1 F.L.R. 343; [1993] Fam. Law 124, C.A.;
reversing [1992] 1 W.L.R. 623; [1991] N.P.C. 141; *The Times*,
December 19, 1991 29–031
Barclays Bank plc v. Quince Care Ltd [1992] 4 All E.R. 363 27–025
Barclays Bank Ltd v. Quistclose Investments Ltd [1970] A.C. 567; [1968] 3
W.L.R. 1097; 112 S.J. 903; [1968] 3 All E.R. 651, H.L.; affirming *sub
nom.* Quistclose Investments v. Rolls Razor (in liquidation) [1968]
Ch. 540; [1968] 2 W.L.R. 478; *sub nom.* Quistclose Investments v.
Rolls Razor (in voluntary liquidation) [1968] 1 All E.R. 613; [1967]
C.L.Y. 514 .... 27–008, 27–009, 27–012, 27–026
Barclays Bank plc v. Willowbrook International Ltd, *The Times*, February
5, 1987 27–010
Barlow Clowes Gilt Managers Ltd, *Re.* [1992] Ch. 208; [1992] 2 W.L.R. 36;
[1991] 4 All E.R. 385; [1991] B.C.C. 608; [1991] B.C.L.C. 750; [1991]
N.P.C. 73; (1991) 141 N.L.J. 999; *The Times*, June 13, 1991; *Financial
Times*, June 18, 1991; *The Independent*, June 25, 1991 .... 25–017, 26–082
Barlow Clowes International Limited (in liquidation) v. Vaughan [1994] 4
All E.R. 22; [1992] B.C.L.C. 910, C.A. 27–033
Barnes v. Addy [1874] L.R. 9, Ch.App. 244 .... 27–013, 27–018
Barrett v. Duckett [1995] 1 B.C.L.C. 243; [1995] B.C.C. 362; *The Independent*, August 15, 1994 (C.S.) C.A.; reversing [1993] B.C.C. 778;
[1995] 1 B.C.L.C. 73, Ch.D. 26–039
Bartlett v. Barclays Bank Trust Co. Ltd (No. 1) [1981] 1 Ch. 515; [1980] 2
W.L.R. 430; (1979) 124 S.J. 85; [1980] 1 All E.R. 139 7–038
Bater v. Bater [1951] P. 209 28–007
Bayer AG v. Winter (No. 2) [1986] 1 W.L.R. 540; (1985) 130 S.J. 373;
[1986] 2 All E.R. 43 .... 31–014, 31–024, 31–025
A. J. Bekhar & Co. Ltd v. Bilton [1981] 1 Q.B. 923; [1981] 2 W.L.R. 601;
(1981) 125 S.J. 203; [1981] 2 All E.R. 565; [1981] 1 Lloyd's Rep. 491;
[1981] Com.L.R. 50, C.A. 31–008
Belmont Finance Corporation v. Williams Furniture Ltd (No. 2) [1980] 1
All E.R. 393, C.A. 21–020, 21–028
Bird Precision Bellows, *Re.* [1986] Ch. 658; [1986] 2 W.L.R. 158;
(1986) 130 S.J. 51; [1985] 3 All E.R. 523; (1986) 83 L.S.Gaz. 36;
[1986] P.C.C. 25, C.A.; affirming [1984] Ch. 419; [1984] 2 W.L.R.
869; (1984) 128 S.J. 348; [1984] 3 All E.R. 444; (1984) 81 L.S.Gaz.
187 26–052
Bishopsgate Investment Management v. Homan [1995] 1 W.L.R. 31 (Pet.
dis.), H.L.; [1995] Ch. 211; [1994] 3 W.L.R. 1270; [1995] 1 All E.R.
347; [1994] B.C.C. 868; (1994) 91 (36) L.S.Gaz. 37; (1994) 138
S.J.L.B. 176; *The Times*, July 14, 1994; *The Independent*, September
26, 1994 (C.S.), C.A. 27–035, 27–036

TABLE OF CASES

Blair v. Canada Trust Co. [1986] 32 D.L.R. (4th) 515 29–031
Blake, *Re.* (1885) 29 Ch.D. 913 7–002
Blunt v. Park Lane Hotel [1942] 2 K.B. 253 31–029
Boardman v. Phipps [1967] 2 A.C. 46; [1966] 3 W.L.R. 1009; 110 S.J. 853; [1996] 3 All E.R. 721; [31 Conv. 63] H.L.; affirming *sub nom.* Phipps v. Boardman [1965] Ch. 992; [1965] 2 W.L.R. 839; 109 S.J. 197; [1965] 1 All E.R. 849; [29 Conv. 233; 28 M.L.R. 587], C.A.; affirming [1964] 1 W.L.R. 993; 108 S.J. 619; [1964] 2 All E.R. 187; [114 L.J. 815; 28 Conv. 310; 98 K.T. 275]; [1964] C.L.Y. 3345; [1965] C.L.Y. 3575 7–020
Borden (U.K.) Ltd v. Scottish Timber Products Ltd and McNicol Brownlie [1981] Ch. 25; [1979] 3 W.L.R. 672; (1979) 123 S.J. 688; [1979] 3 All E.R. 961; [1980] 1 Lloyd's Rep. 160, C.A.; reversing [1979] 2 Lloyd's Rep. 168; (1978) 122 S.J. 825 27–036
Boscawen v. Bajwa Abbey National plc v. Boscawen [1995] 4 All E.R. 769; (1995) 70 P. & C.R. 391; (1995) 139 S.J.L.B. 111; (1995) 92 (21) L.S.Gaz. 37; [1995] N.P.C. 67; *The Times*, April 25, 1995; *The Independent*, May 23, 1995, C.A. 27–037, 27–038
Bovey Hotels, *Re.*, July 31, 1981 (unreported) 26–043
Bowden, *ex p.* [1994] 1 W.L.R. 17 4–050
Brady v. Brady [1989] A.C. 755; [1988] B.C.L.C. 579 .. 21–030, 21–031, 21–034
Brinks Ltd v. Abu-Saleh and others [1995] 1 W.L.R. 1478; [1995] 4 All E.R. 65; *The Times*, January 30, 1995; *The Independent*, March 6, 1995 (C.S.), Ch.D. 31–062
—— v. —— (No. 2) [1995] 1 W.L.R. 1487; [1995] 4 All E.R. 74; *The Times*, May 12, 1995; *The Independent*, June 5, 1995 (C.S.), Ch.D.   31–063
Brinks Limited (formerly Brinks Mat Ltd) v. Kamal Hassan Abu-Saleh, October 10, 1995 (unreported) 27–028
British and Commonwealth Holdings (Joint Administrators) v. Spicer and Oppenheim, *sub nom.* British and Commonwealth Holdings (Nos. 1 & 2), *Re.* [1993] A.C. 426; [1992] 3 W.L.R. 853; [1992] 4 All E.R. 876; [1992] B.C.C. 977; [1993] B.C.L.C. 168; (1992) 142 N.L.J. 1611; *The Times*, November 3, 1992, H.L.; affirming [1992] Ch. 342; [1992] 2 W.L.R. 931; [1992] 2 All E.R. 801; [1992] B.C.C. 165 and [1992] B.C.C. 172; [1992] B.C.L.C. 641; *The Times*, December 31, 1991, C.A.; reversing [1991] B.C.C. 651 and [1991] B.C.C. 658; [1992] B.C.L.C. 306 and [1992] B.C.L.C. 314; *Financial Times*, November 6, 1991; *The Times*, November 8, 1991; *Financial Times*, August 6, 1991 26–083
British and Commonwealth Holdings v. Barclays Bank [1996] 1 All E.R. 381 21–023
British Thomson-Houston Co. Ltd v. Sterling Accessories [1924] 2 Ch. 33; [1924] All E.R. 294 30–010
Brown v. City of London Corporation [1996] 22 E.G. 118 17–016
Brown v. KMR Services; Sword-Daniels v. Pitel [1995] 4 All E.R. 598; 2 Lloyd's Rep. 2; Lloyd's Rep. 1; *The Times*, July 26, 1995; *The Independent*, September 13, 1995; Lloyd's List, October 3, 1995 (I.D.), C.A.; affirming [1994] 4 All E.R. 385; *The Independent*, April 19, 1994; *The Guardian*, April 22, 1994, Q.B.D. ... 29–014, 29–015, 29–019
Burland v. Earle [1902] A.C. 83 26–033

CBS United Kingdom Ltd v. Lambert [1983] Ch. 37; [1982] 3 W.L.R. 746; (1982) 126 S.J. 691; [1982] 3 All E.R. 237; (1983) 80 L.S.Gaz. 36; [1983] F.L.R. 127, C.A. 31–013

Table of Cases

CBS United Kingdom Ltd v. Perry [1985] F.S.R. 421 31–019
Candler v. Crane, Christmas & Co. [1951] 2 K.B. 164; [1951] 1 T.L.R. 371; 95 S.J. 171; [1951] 1 All E.R. 426; [106 L.J. 115; 67 L.Q.R. 466; 32 Can. Bar.R. 638; 14 M.L.R. 345; 15 M.L.R. 160; 18 M.L.R. 398; 67 L.Q.R. 173], C.A. 29–002, 29–005
Caparo Industries plc v. Dickman [1990] 2 A.C. 605; [1990] 2 W.L.R. 358; [1990] 1 All E.R. 568; (1990) 134 S.J. 494; [1990] B.C.C. 164; [1990] B.C.L.C. 273; [1990] E.C.C. 313; [1990] L.S.Gaz., March 28, 42; [1990] L.S.Gaz., September 26, 28; [1991] J.B.L. 36; (1990) 140 N.L.J. 248, H.L.; reversing [1989] Q.B. 653; [1989] 2 W.L.R. 316; (1989) 133 S.J. 221; [1989] 1 All E.R. 798; (1989) 5 B.C.C. 105; [1989] B.C.L.C. 154; 1989 P.C.C. 125, C.A.; reversing in part ... 29–037, 29–043
Carecraft Construction Co. Ltd, *Re.* [1994] 1 W.L.R. 172; [1993] 4 All E.R. 499; [1993] B.C.C. 336; [1993] B.C.L.C. 1259 .... 22–023, 22–024
Carreras Rothman's v. Freeman Mathews Treasure [1985] Ch. 207; [1984] 3 W.L.R. 1016; (1984) 128 S.J. 614; [1985] 1 All E.R. 155; (1984) 81 L.S.Gaz. 2375; 1985 P.C.C. 222 27–009
Cavendish Funding Ltd v. Henry Spencer & Sons Ltd, March 20, 1996 (unreported) 29–027
Century Life Plc v. The Pensions Ombudsman [1995] P.L.R. 135; *The Times*, May 23, 1995, Q.B.D. 9–008
Chan Man-Sin v. Att.-Gen. of Hong Kong [1988] 1 W.L.R. 196; (1988) 132 S.J. 126; [1988] 1 All E.R. 1; (1988) 86 Cr.App.R. 303; [1988] Crim.L.R. 319; (1988) 85 L.S.Gaz. 36, P.C. 16–027, 16–049
Charterhouse Investment Trust Ltd v. Tempest Diesels Ltd [1985] 1 B.C.C. 99544; *Financial Times*, June 28, 1985 21–024
Chetwynd's settlement, *Re.* [1902] 1 Ch. 692 7–002
Chief Constable of Hampshire v. A Ltd [1985] Q.B. 132; [1984] 2 W.L.R. 954; (1984) 128 S.J. 279; [1984] 2 All E.R. 385; (1984) 79 Cr.App.R. 30; [1984] 81 L.S.Gaz. 1212, C.A. 23–041
Chief Constable of Kent v. V [1983] Q.B. 34; [1982] 3 W.L.R. 462; (1982) 126 S.J. 536; [1982] 3 All E.R. 36, C.A. 23–041
Chief Constable of Leicestershire v. M and another [1989] 1 W.L.R. 20; [1988] 3 All E.R. 1015; (1988) 138 New L.J. 295 23–041
Chief Constable of Surrey v. A and another, *The Times*, October 27, 1988 23–041
Churchill v. Walton [1967] 2 A.C. 224, H.L.; [1967] 2 W.L.R. 682; 131 J.P. 277; 111 S.J. 112; [1967] 1 All E.R. 497; 41 Cr.App.R. 212; [83 L.Q.R. 325], H.L.; reversing *sub nom.* R. v. Churchill [1967] 1 Q.B. 190; [1966] 2 W.L.R. 1116; 110 S.J. 526; [1966] 2 All E.R. 215; [1966] C.L.Y. 2175; C.C.A. 21–043
City Equitable Fire Insurance Co. Ltd, *Re.* [1995] Ch. 407 26–019
City Index v. Leslie [1992] Q.B. 98; [1991] 3 W.L.R. 207; [1991] 3 All E.R. 180; [1991] B.C.L.C. 643; (1991) 141 N.L.J. Rep. 419; *The Times*, March 21, 1991; *The Independent*, April 5, 1991; *Financial Times*, March 19, 1991, C.A.; affirming (1990) 140 N.L.J. Rep. 1572; *The Independent*, August 3, 1990, D.C. 2–017
Clayton's Case [1817] 1 Mer. 572 27–033
Cloverbay Ltd (joint administrators) v. Bank of Credit and Commerce International SA [1991] Ch. 90; [1990] 3 W.L.R. 574; [1991] 1 All E.R. 894; [1991] B.C.L.C. 135, C.A. 31–019
Clowes and another [1994] 2 All E.R. 316 16–036

TABLE OF CASES

Coca-Cola v. Gilbey [1995] 4 All E.R. 711; (1995) 145 N.L.J. Rep. 1688; *The Times*, November 28, 1995; *The Independent*, October 10, 1995, Ch.D. 31–059
Coloroll Pension Trustees v. Russell (C–200/91) [1995] All E.R. (E.C.) 23; [1995] I.C.R. 179; [1994] I.R.L.R. 586; [1994] O.P.L.R. 179; [1994] I.R.L.R. 586; [1994] I.R.L.R. 602; [1994] I.R.L.R. 617; *Financial Times*, October 4, 1994; *The Times*, November 30, 1994, ECJ 8–028, 8–034
Company, A, *Re.* [1985] B.C.L.C. 333 30–008
——, [1986] B.C.L.C. 376 26–049
——, [1986] B.C.L.C. 382 .... 26–045, 26–049
——, [1986] 1 W.L.R. 281; (1985) 130 S.J. 202; [1986] 2 All E.R. 253; (1986) 83 L.S.Gaz. 1058 26–049
Company's Application, A, *Re.*, *The Times*, February 13, 1989 4–025
Continental Assurance Company of London plc, *Re.*, June 14, 1996 (unreported) 22–020
Cooper (Gerald) Chemical Limited, *Re.* [1978] Ch. 262; [1978] 2 W.L.R. 866; (1977) 1215 S.J. 848; [1978] 2 All E.R. 49 .. 17–007, 17–012, 17–017
Cornish (formerly Humes) v. Midland Bank plc [1985] 3 All E.R. 513; 1985 F.L.R. 298; (1985) 135 New L.J. 869, C.A. 29–031
Cossens, *ex p.*, In the matter of Warrall [1820] Cases in Bankruptcy 53   31–044
Cowan de Groot Properties Ltd v. Eagle Trust plc [1992] 4 All E.R. 700; [1991] B.C.L.C. 1045 27–020
Cremieux v. France [1993] 16 E.H.R.R. 357, E.C.H.R. 31–028
Crest Homes plc v. Marks [1987] A.C. 829; [1987] 3 W.L.R. 293; (1987) 131 S.J. 1003; [1987] 2 All E.R. 1074; [1988] R.P.C. 21; (1987) 137 New L.J. 662; (1987) 84 L.S.Gaz. 2362, H.L.; affirming [1987] 3 W.L.R. 48; [1987] F.S.R. 305; (1987) 137 New L.J. 318; (1987) 84 L.S.Gaz. 2048, C.A. 31–050

DHN Food Distributors v. Tower Hamlets L.B.C.; Bronze Investments v. Same; DHN Food Transport v. Same; [1976] 1 W.L.R. 852; 120 S.J. 215; [1976] J.P.L. 363; 74 L.G.R. 506; *sub nom.* DHN Food Distributors v. London Borough of Tower Hamlets [1976] 3 All E.R. 462; *sub nom.* DHN Food Distributors (in liquidation) v. Tower Hamlets L.B.C.; Bronze Investments (in liquidation) v. Same; DHN Food Transport (in liquidation) v. Same (1976) 32 P. & C.R. 240, C.A.; reversing *sub nom.* DHN Food Distributors, Bronze Investments and DHN Food Transport v. L.B.C. of Tower Hamlets (Ref. Nos. 36, 37 and 38/1974 (19750 30 P. & C.R. 251, Lands Tribunal 30–009
Daniels v. Daniels [1978] Ch. 406; [1978] 2 W.L.R. 73; [1978] 2 All E.R. 89; (1977) 121 S.J. 605 26–034
Darby and Brougham, *Re.* [1911] 1 K.B. 95 30–004
De Berenger Case 3 M & S 66; 105 E.R. 536 12–004
Depositors Protection Fund v. Barclays Bank; *sub nom.* Deposit Protection Board v. Dalia [1994] 2 A.C. 367; [1994] 2 W.L.R. 732; [1994] 2 All E.R. 577; [1994] 2 B.C.L.C. 277; (1994) 138 S.J.L.B. 123; [1994] *Gazette*, 29 June 30; *The Times*, May 20, 1994; *The Independent*, May 31, 1994, H.L.; reversing [1994] 1 All E.R. 539; (1993) 137 S.J. (L.B.) 143; (1993) 143 N.L.J. 781; *The Times*, May 1, 1993; *The Independent*, May 18, 1993, C.A.; affirming [1993] Ch. 243; [1992] 3 W.L.R. 945; [1994] 1 B.C.L.C. 510; [1992] N.P.C. 90; *The Times*, July 9, 1992; *Financial Times*, July 16, 1992; *The Independent*, August 12, 1992 14–097

TABLE OF CASES

Derby & Co. Ltd v. Weldon (Nos. 3 & 4) [1990] Ch. 65; [1989] 2 W.L.R. 412; (1989) 133 S.J. 83; (1989) 139 N.L.J. 11, C.A.; affirming (1989) 133 S.J. 1446; (1988) 138 N.L.J. 339 31–004
Derry v. Peek [1889] 14 App. Cas. 337 .... 28–004, 28–005, 28–014
D.P.P. v. McCabe (1993) 157 J.P. 443; [1992] Crim.L.R. 885; [1993] C.O.D. 15; (1993) 157 J.P.N. 122, D.C. 16–031
D'Jan of London Ltd, Re. [1993] B.C.C. 646 26–020
Doyle v. Olby (Ironmongers) Ltd [1969] 2 Q.B. 158; [1969] 2 W.L.R. 673; 113 S.J. 128; [1969] 2 All E.R. 119; [32 M.L.R. 556]; C.A. 28–008
Dunford and Elliott Ltd v. Johnson and Firth Brown Ltd (1976) 121 S.J. 53; [1977] 1 Lloyd's Rep. 505; [1978] F.S.R. 143, C.A. 13–005
Durn [1973] 3 All E.R. 715 16–029

EVTR Ltd, Gilbert v. Barker, Re., *The Times*, June 24, 1987 27–010
Eagle Star Insurance Co. Ltd and Eagle Star Life Assurance Co. Ltd, Re., *The Times*, December 7, 1990 10–016
Eagle Trust v. SBC Securities; Eagle Trust v. SBCI Bank Corp. Investment Banking [1995] B.C.C. 231; *The Independent*, September 28, 1994 29–029
East v. Maurer [1991] 1 W.L.R. 461; [1991] 2 All E.R. 733 28–011
Ebrahimi v. Westbourne Galleries [1973] A.C. 360; [1972] 2 W.L.R. 1289; 116 S.J. 412; [1972] 2 All E.R. 492, H.L.; reversing *sub nom.* Westbourne Galleries, Re. [1971] Ch. 799; [1971] 2 W.L.R. 618; (1970) 115 S.J. 74; [1971] 1 All E.R. 56, C.A.; reversing [1970] 1 W.L.R. 1378; 114 S.J. 785; [1970] 3 All E.R. 374 .... 26–053, 26–055
Edginton v. Fitzmaurice [1885] 29 Ch.D. 459 28–003
Edwards v. Toombs [1983] Crim.L.R. 43; (1983) 80 L.S.Gaz. 93, D.C. ... 16–057
El Ajou v. Dollar Land Holdings plc [1994] 2 All E.R. 685; [1994] B.C.C. 143; [1994] 1 B.C.L.C. 464; [1993] N.P.C. 165; *The Times*, January 3, 1994, C.A.; reversing [1993] 3 All E.R. 717; [1993] B.C.L.C. 735; [1993] B.C.C. 698 27–040
—— v. —— (No. 2) [1995] 2 All E.R. 213; *The Times*, January 3, 1995, Ch.D. 27–040
Elderkin v. Merrill Lynch Royal Securities Ltd [1977] 80 D.L.R. (3d) 313 29–031

Fallon v. Securities and Investments Board, May 5, 1994, C.A. (unreported) 4–014
Felton v. Callis [1969] 1 Q.B. 200; [1968] 3 W.L.R. 951; 112 S.J. 672; [1968] 3 All E.R. 673 31–015
Fibrosa Spolka Akcyjina v. Fairbairn Lawson Combe Barbour Ltd [1943] A.C. 32 28–021
Finnegan and Brand, October 13, 1995 (unreported) 14–065
Firedart Limited, Official Receiver v. Fairall, Re. [1994] 2 B.C.L.C. 340 22–016
First Interstate Bank of California v. Cohen Arnold & Co. [1995] E.G.C.S. 188; *The Times*, December 11, 1995, C.A. 29–026
First National Commercial Bank plc v. Humberts, *The Times*, January 27, 1995 29–028
Foss v. Harbottle (1843) 2 Hare 461; [106 L.J. 611; [1957] C.L.J. 194; [1958] C.L.J. 93; 74 S.A.L.J. 443; 35 M.L.R. 318; 49 A.L.J. 134; 40 Conv. 51] 26–030, 26–031, 26–035, 26–037, 26–041, 26–049

TABLE OF CASES

Fuji Finance Inc. v. Aetna Life Insurance Co. Ltd [1995] Ch. 122; [1994] 3 W.L.R. 1280; [1994] 4 All E.R. 1025; (1995) 92 (02) L.S.Gaz. 35; *The Times*, July 21, 1994; *The Independent*, September 15, 1994, Ch.D. 10–016, 10–024
Funke v. France (1993) 16 E.H.R.R. 297 31–028

Galoo Ltd (in liquidation) v. Bright Grahame Murray (a firm) [1995] 1 All E.R. 16 29–043
Gilford Motor Co. v. Horne [1933] Ch. 935 30–007
Ginora Investments Ltd v. James Capel & Co. Ltd, February 10, 1995 (unreported) 29–035
Goldcorp Exchange Ltd (in receivership), *Re.*, *sub nom.* Kensington v. Unrepresented Non-Allocated Claimants [1994] 3 W.L.R. 199; [1994] 2 All E.R. 806; (1994) 138 (LB) 127; (1994) Tr.L.R. 434; (1994) 144 N.L.J. 792, D.C. 27–036, 27–037
Goose v. Wilson & Sandford, April 1, 1996 (unreported) 27–027
Graff v. Shawcross, Macdonald and Frazer, October 10, 1980 (unreported) 13–019
Grayan Building Service Ltd (in liquidation) *Re.* [1995] Ch. 241; [1995] 3 W.L.R. 1; [1995] B.C.C. 554, C.A. 22–020
Great Western Assurance Co., *Re.*, July 31, 1996 (unreported) 10–014
Guiness plc v. Saunders, *sub nom.* Guiness v. Ward [1988] 1 W.L.R. 863; (1988) 132 S.J. 820; (1988) 4 B.C.C. 377; [1988] 2 All E.R. 940; 1988 P.C.C. 270; (1988) 138 New L.J. 142; [1988] B.C.L.C. 607, C.A.; affirming [1988] B.C.L.C. 43 19–003
—— v. —— [1990] 2 A.C. 663; [1990] 2 W.L.R. 324; (1990) 134 S.J. 457; [1990] 1 All E.R. 652; [1990] B.C.C. 205; [1990] B.C.L.C.402; [1990] L.S.Gaz., March 7, 42, H.L.; affirming 26–014
Gurney v. Womersley [1854] 4 E & B 133 28–022

H and others, *Re.* [19964] 2 All E.R. 391 30–005
Haley v. Northington Archives Ltd, November 15, 1995 (unreported) .. 30–012
Hedley Byrne & Co. v. Heller & Ptnrs [1964] A.C. 465; [1963] 3 W.L.R. 101; 107 S.J. 454; [1963] 2 All E.R. 575; [1963] 1 Lloyd's Rep. 485, H.L.; affirming [1962] 1 Q.B. 396; [1961] 3 W.L.R. 1225; 105 S.J. 910; [1961] 3 All E.R. 891; [1961] C.L.Y. 518, C.A.; affirming, *The Times*, December 21, 1960; [1960] C.L.Y. 186 ... 29–005, 29–011, 29–048
Henderson v. Merrett Syndicates; Hallam-Eames v. Same; Hughes v. Same; Arbuthnott v. Feltrim Underwriting Agencies; Deeny v. Gooda Walker (in liquidation) [1995] 2 A.C. 145; [1994] 3 W.L.R. 761; [1994] 3 All E.R. 506; [1994] 2 Lloyd's Rep. 468; (1994) 144 N.L.J. Rep. 1204; *The Times*, July 26, 1994; *The Independent*, August 3, 1994, H.L.; affirming, *The Times*, December 30, 1993; *The Independent*, December 14, 1993, C.A.; affirming, *The Times*, October 20, 1993 .... 29–008, 29–014, 29–050
Herrington v. Kenco Mortgage & Investments Ltd [1981] 125 D.L.R. (3d) 377 29–031
Hillsdown Holdings plc v. The Pensions Ombudsman, July 12, 1996 (unreported) 9–011
Hoechst United Kingdom Ltd v. Chemiculture Ltd [1993] F.S.R. 270 .. 25–018
Hogg v. Cramphorn; Same v. Same [1967] Ch. 254; [1996] 3 W.L.R. 995; 110 S.J. 887; [1996] 3 All E.R. 420; [1963] C.L.Y. 397 ... 26–011, 26–036

TABLE OF CASES

Horcal Ltd v. Gatland [1984] B.C.L.C. 549; [1984] I.R.L.R. 288, C.A.;
affirming [1983] I.R.L.R. 459; (1983) 133 New L.J. 1133 26–016
Hornal v. Neuberger Products Ltd [1957] 1 Q.B. 247 28–008
House of Spring Gardens Ltd v. Waite [1985] F.S.R. 173 ..... 31–017, 31–020,
31–024, 31–025
Howard Marine and Dredging v. A. Ogden & Sons (Excavations) [1978]
Q.B. 574; [1978] 2 W.L.R. 515; (1977) 122 S.J. 48; [1978] 2 All E.R.
1134; [1978] 1 Lloyd's Rep. 334; (1977) 9 Build.L.R. 34, C.A. 28–011
Hughes and others v. Asset Manager plc [1995] 3 All E.R. 669; *The
Independent*, June 13, 1994 (C.S.), C.A. 2–005
Hydrodam (Corby) Ltd (in liquidation), *Re.* [1994] 2 B.C.L.C. 180; [1994]
B.C.C. 161; *The Times*, February 19, 1994, Ch.D. 30–020

IBM United Kingdom Ltd v. Prima Data International Ltd [1994] 1
W.L.R. 719; [1994] 4 All E.R. 748 31–034
Industrial Development Consultants v. Cooley [1972] 1 W.L.R. 443; (1971)
116 S.J. 255; [1972] 2 All E.R. 162 26–015
Infante v. Charman, July 31, 1996, unreported 30–014
Inland Revenue Commissioners v. Desoutter Brothers [1946] 1 All E.R.
58 1–004
—— v. Rolls Royce Ltd [1994] 2 All E.R. 340 1–003
Inquiry under the Company Security (Insider Dealing) Act, An, [1988] 1
All E.R. 203 4–026

James McNaughton Papers Group Ltd v. Hicks, Anderson & Co. (a firm)
[1991] 2 Q.B. 113; [1991] 2 W.L.R. 641; [1991] 1 All E.R. 134;
[1990] B.C.L.C. 235; (1990) 140 N.L.J. 1311; *The Independent*,
September 11, 1990, C.A. 29–039
Jeffrey S. Levitt Ltd, *Re.* [1992] Ch. 457; [1992] 2 W.L.R. 975; [1992] 2 All
E.R. 509; [1992] B.C.C. 137; [1992] B.C.L.C. 250; *The Times*,
November 6, 1991 31–052
Jones v. Lipman [1962] 1 W.L.R. 832; 106 S.J. 531; [1962] 1 All E.R.
442 30–007

K, *Re.* [1990] 2 W.L.R. 1224 23–038
Kayford Ltd, *Re.* [1975] 1 All E.R. 604 27–010
Kettlewell v. Refuge Assurance Co. [1908] 1 K.B. 545 28–024
Khan v. Khan [1982] 2 All E.R. 60 31–047

Lawrence v. Metropolitan Police Commissioner [1972] A.C. 626; [1971] 3
W.L.R. 225; 115 S.J. 565; 55 Cr.App.R. 471; *sub nom.* Lawrence v.
Commissioner of Police for the Metropolis [1971] 2 All E.R. 1253;
[[1971] C.L.J. 185]; H.L.; affirming *sub nom.* R. v. Lawrence (Alan)
[1971] 1 Q.B. 373; [1970] 3 W.L.R. 1103; *sub nom.* R. v. Lawrence
114 S.J. 864; [1970] 3 All E.R. 933; 55 Cr.App.R. 73, C.A. 16–005,
16–042
Learoyd v. Whitely (1887) 12 App.Cas. 727 7–038
Levin, *Re.*, March 1, 1996 (unreported) 16–057

TABLE OF CASES

Liggett v. Kensington [1993] 1 N.Z.L.R. 257 27–036
Lion Nathan Ltd v. CC Bottlers Ltd, May 14, 1996 (unreported) 29–024
Lipkin Gorman (a firm) v. Cass, *The Times*, May 29, 1985 31–010
—— v. Karpnale Ltd [1991] A.C. 548; [1991] 3 W.L.R. 10; [1992] 4 All E.R. 512; (1991) 135 S.J.L.B. 36; (1991) 141 N.L.J. 815; *The Times*, June 7, 1991; *The Independent*, June 18, 1991; *Financial Times*, June 11, 1991; *The Guardian*, June 13, 1991, H.L.; reversing [1989] 1 W.L.R. 1340; [1992] 4 All E.R. 409; [1989] Fin.L.R. 137; [1989] B.C.L.C. 756; (1990) 134 S.J. 234; [1990] L.S.Gaz., January 31, 40; (1989) 139 N.L.J. 76, C.A. 27–025
Little Olympian Each-Ways Ltd (No. 3), *Re.* [1995] 1 B.C.L.C. 26–048
Lo-Line Electric Motors Ltd, *Re.*, Companies Act 1985, *Re.* [1988] Ch. 477; [1988] 3 W.L.R. 26; (1988) 132 S.J. 851; [1988] 2 All E.R. 692; 1988 P.C.C. 236; [1988] 2 F.T.L.R. 107; (1988) 4 B.C.C. 415; [1988] B.C.L.C. 698; (1988) 138 New L.J. 119 .... 22–003, 22–020
London & Mashonaland Exploration Co. v. New Mashonaland Exploration Co. [1891] W.N. 165 26–018
London School of Electronics, *Re.* [1986] Ch. 211; [1985] 3 W.L.R. 474; (1985) 129 S.J. 573; 1985 P.C.C. 248 26–046
London United Investments plc, *Re.* [1992] Ch. 578; [1992] 2 W.L.R. 850; [1992] 2 All E.R. 842; (1992) 136 S.J. L.B. 32; [1992] B.C.C. 202; [1992] B.C.L.C. 285; (1992) 142 N.L.J. 87; [1992] *Gazette*, 26 February, 27; *The Times*, January 1, 1992; *The Independent*, January 9, 1992; *Financial Times*, January 17, 1992; *The Guardian*, February 5, 1992, C.A.; affirming [1991] B.C.C. 760; [1992] B.C.L.C.91 ... 26–074, 31–052
Lonrho v. Fayed [1992] 1 A.C. 448; [1991] 3 W.L.R. 188; [1991] 3 All E.R. 303; (1991) 135 S.L.L.B. 68; [1991] B.C.C. 641; [1991] B.C.L.C. 779; (1991) 141 N.L.J. 927; *The Guardian*, June 28, 1991; *The Times*, July 3, 1991; *The Independent*, July 3, 1991; *Financial Times*, July 3, 1991, H.L.; affirming [1990] 2 Q.B. 479; [1989] 3 W.L.R. 631; [1989] 2 All E.R. 65; 1989 P.C.C. 215; [1989] B.C.L.C. 485; (1989) 139 N.L.J. 539; C.A.; reversing [1990] 1 Q.B. 490; [1989] 2 W.L.R. 356; (1989) 133 S.J. 220; [1989] B.C.L.C. 75; 1989 P.C.C. 173; [1989] L.S.Gaz., March 8, 43 .... 28–015, 28–017

MC Bacon, *Re.* [1991] Ch. 127; [1990] B.C.C. 78; [1990] B.C.L.C. 324 .. 30–020
Macmillan v. Bishopsgate Investment Trust (3) [1996] 1 All E.R. 585 .. 27–042
Maidstone Building Provisions Ltd, *Re.* [1971] 1 W.L.R. 1085; 115 S.J. 464; [1971] 3 All E.R. 363 17–011
Manning v. Drexel Burnham Lambert Holdings Ltd [1994] O.P.L.R. 71; [1995] 1 W.L.R. 32 7–020
Marc Rich & Co. AG v. Bishop Rock Marine Co. (Nicholas H, The) [1995] 3 W.L.R. 227; [1995] 3 All E.R. 307; [1995] 2 Lloyd's Rep. 299; (1995) 145 N.L.J. Rep. 1033; (1995) 139 S.L.J.B. 165; *The Times*, July 7, 1995; *The Independent*, August 18, 1995, Lloyd's List, July 19, 1995 (I.D), H.L.; affirming [1994] 1 W.L.R. 1071; [1994] 3 All E.R. 686; [1994] 1 Lloyd's Rep. 492; *The Times*, February 23, 1994; *The Independent*, March 2, 1994, C.A.; reversing [1992] 2 Lloyd's Rep. 481; *Financial Times*, July 15, 1992; Lloyd's List, August 14, 1992, Q.B.D. 29–020

TABLE OF CASES

Marcel v. Commissioner of Police of the Metropolis: Anchor Brewhouse Developments v. Jaggard [1992] Ch. 225; [1992] 2 W.L.R. 50; [1992] 1 All E.R. 72; (1991) 135 S.J.L.B. 125; (1991) 141 N.L.J. 1224; (1992) 4 Admin.L.R. 309; *The Independent*, July 24, 1991; *The Times*, August 7, 1991; *The Guardian*, August 28, 1991, C.A.; reversing in part [1991] 2 W.L.R. 1118; [1991] 1 All E.R. 845; *The Times*, December 5, 1990 .... 25–017, 25–018
Melton Medes Ltd and another v. Securities and Investments Board [1995] Ch. 137; [1995] 2 W.L.R. 247; [1995] 3 All E.R. 880; *The Times*, July 27, 1994; *The Independent*, August 8, 1994 (C.S.), Ch.D. 4–068
Mercedes-Benz AG v. Herbert Heinz Horst Leiduck [1995] 3 W.L.R. 718; [1995] 3 W.L.R. 929; [1995] 2 Lloyd's Rep. 417; (1995) 145 N.L.J. Rep. 1329; (1995) 139 S.J.L.B. 195; (1995) 92 (28); L.S.Gaz. 28; *The Times*, August 11, 1993, C.A. 31–006
Metall und Rohstoff AG v. Donaldson Lufkin & Jenrette Inc. [1990] 1 Q.B. 391; [1989] 3 W.L.R. 563; (1989) 133 S.J. 1200; [1989] 3 All E.R. 14, C.A. 28–017, 28–018
Maiilhe v. France (No. 12661/87) (1993) 16 E.H.R.R. 332, E.C.H.R. 31–028
Miller v. Stapleton [1996] 2 All E.R. 449 9–008
Minories Finance Ltd v. Athur Young [1989] 2 All E.R. 105; 1988 Fin.L.R. 345 14–098
Mohamed Omar v. Chiiko Aikawa Omar, *The Times*, December 27, 1994 31–012
Morgan Crucible Co. v. Hill Samuel Bank [1991] Ch. 259; [1991] 2 W.L.R. 655; [1991] 1 All E.R. 142; (1990) 140 N.L.J. 1605; [1991] B.C.C. 82; [1991] B.C.L.C. 178; *The Independent*, October 25, 1990, C.A.; reversing [1990] 3 All E.R. 330; [1990] B.C.C. 686; [1991] B.C.L.C. 18; (1990) 140 N.L.J. 1271 .... 29–041, 29–042, 29–043
Morris v. Director of the Serious Fraud Office [1993] Ch. 372; [1993] 3 W.L.R. 1; [1993] 1 All E.R. 788; [1993] B.C.L.C. 580; [1992] B.C.C. 934; *The Independent*, September 11, 1992 .... 25–013, 25–016, 25–017
Moses v. Macferlan [1760] 2 Burr. 1005 28–020
Movitex Ltd v. Bulfield (1986) 2 B.C.C. 99 26–025
Murjani (a bankrupt), *Re.* [1996] 1 All E.R. 66 26–083
Murray Watson, *Re.*, April 6, 1977 (unreported) 17–008

NL Electrical, *Re.* [1994] 1 B.C.L.C. 22 21–037
NRG Victory Reinsurance Ltd, *Re.* [1995] 1 W.L.R. 239; [1995] 1 All E.R. 533; *The Times*, November 8, 1994, Ch.D. 10–010
Nanwa Gold Mines Ltd, *Re.* [1955] 3 All E.R. 219 27–011
Neptune (Vehicle Washing Equipment) Ltd, *Re.* [1995] T.L.R. 132 19–004
Nestlé v. National Westminster Bank (No. 2) [1993] 1 W.L.R. 1260; [1994] 1 All E.R. 118; [1992] N.P.C. 68; *The Times*, May 11, 1992, C.A. 27–029
New Generation Engineers Ltd, *Re.* [1993] B.C.L.C. 435 22–016
Nocton v. Ashburton [1914] A.C. 932 4–065
Norman v. Theodore Goddard (Quirk, Third Party) [1992] B.C.L.C. 1028; [1992] B.C.C. 14 26–020
North v. Marra Developments Ltd [1982] 56 A.L.J.R. 106 ..... 20–004, 20–049
Nurcombe v. Nurcombe [1985] 1 W.L.R. 370; (1984) 128 S.J. 766; [1985] 1 All E.R. 65; (1984) 81 L.S.Gaz. 2929; [1984] B.C.L.C. 557 26–039

O (disclosure order), *Re.* [1991] 1 All E.R. 330 23–036

TABLE OF CASES

PCW (Underwriting Agencies) Ltd v. Dixon (P.S.) [1983] 2 All E.R. 697;
    (1983) 133 New L.J. 204; [1983] 2 All E.R. 158; [1983] 2 Lloyd's
    Rep. 197, C.A. 31–009, 31–011
Paget, Re. [1927] 2 Ch. 85 31–051
Parlett v. Guppys (Bridport) Ltd, The Times, February 8, 1996 21–022
Parlides v. Jensen [1956] Ch. 565; [1956] 3 W.L.R. 224; 100 S.J. 452;
    [1956] 2 All E.R. 518 26–035
Percival v. Wright [1902] 2 Ch. 421 .... 20–009, 26–007
Peso Silver Mines v. Cropper [1996] 58 D.L.R. 281 (2d) 1; affirming (1965)
    56 D.L.R. (2d) 117; [1966] C.L.Y. 4399 26–017
Peters, Re. [1988] Q.B. 871; [1988] 3 W.L.R. 182; (1988) 132 S.J. 966;
    [1988] 3 All E.R. 46, C.A. 23–037
Plaut v. Steiner (1989) 5 B.C.C. 352 21–031
Polly Peck International plc (in administration) [1996] 2 All E.R. 433 .. 30–009
Popely v. Planarrive Ltd, March 28, 1996, unreported 20–050
Possfund Custodian Trustee Ltd v. Diamond [1996] 2 All E.R. 774 29–045
Practice Direction (Mareva Injunctions and Anton Piller Orders) [1994] 1
    W.L.R. 1233; [1994] 4 All E.R. 52; [1995] 1 F.C.R. 347; The Times,
    August 2, 1994; The Independent, August 11, 1994, Q.B.D. 31–026
Precision Dippings Ltd v. Precision Dippings Marketing & ors [1986] Ch.
    447; [1995] 3 W.L.R. 812; (1985) 129 S.J. 683; (1985) 1 B.C.C. 539;
    (1985) 82 L.S.Gaz. 3446; 1986 P.C.C. 105, C.A. 21–040
Price, Re. [1905] 2 Ch. 55 1–007
Produce Marketing Consortium Ltd (No. 2), Re. [1989] B.C.L.C. 520 .. 30–018
Purpoint, Re. [1991] B.C.C. 121; [1991] B.C.L.C. 491 30–019

R (restraint order), Re. [1990] 2 All E.R. 569 23–037
—— v. Allsop (1976) 64 Cr.App.R. 29 18–018
—— v. Anderson (William Ronald) [1986] 1 A.C. 27; [1985] 3 W.L.R. 268;
    (1985) 129 S.J. 522; [1985] 2 All E.R. 961; (1985) 81 Cr.App.R. 253;
    [1986] Crim.L.R. 651; (1985) 135 New L.J. 727; (1985) 82 L.S.Gaz
    3172, H.L.; affirming (1984) 128 S.J. 660; (1984) 80 Cr.App.R. 64;
    [1984] Crim.L.R. 550; (1984) 81 L.S.Gaz. 2141, C.A. 18–006, 21–043
—— v. Aspinall (1876) 2 Q.B.D. 731 18–004
—— v. Atakpu [1994] Q.B. 69; [1993] 3 W.L.R. 812; [1993] 4 All E.R.
    215; (1994) 98 Cr.App.R. 254; [1994] R.T.R. 23; [1994] Crim.L.R.
    693; (1993) 143 N.L.J. 652; The Times, March 22, 1993, C.A. 16–021
—— v. Austen (1985) 7 Cr.App.R.(S.) 214, C.A. 22–007
—— v. Ayres [1984] A.C. 447; [1984] 2 W.L.R. 257; (1985) 150 J.P. 183;
    (1984) 128 S.J. 151; [1984] 1 All E.R. 619; (1984) 78 Cr.App.R. 232;
    [1984] Crim.L.R. 353; (1984) 149 J.P.N. (1984) 81 L.S.Gaz. 732,
    H.L.; affirming (1984) 148 J.P. 458; (1984) 128 S.J. 63; (1984) 81
    L.S.Gaz. 354, C.A. 18–009
—— v. Bank of England, ex p. Mellstrom [1995] C.O.D. 161, Q.B.D. 14–054
—— v. Baxter [1972] Q.B. 1 [1971] 2 W.L.R. 1138; S.J. 246; [1971] 2 All
    E.R. 359; [1971] Crim.L.R. 281; sub nom. R. v. Baxter (Robert), 55
    Cr.App.R. 214, C.A. 16–081
—— v. Beck (Brian) [1985] 1 W.L.R. 22; (1985) 149 J.P. 276; (1984) 128
    S.J. 871; [1985] 1 All E.R. 571; (1984) 80 Cr.App.R. 355; (1985) 82
    L.S.Gaz. 762, C.A. 16–065
—— v. Benstead and Taylor (1982) 126 S.J. 308; (1982) 75 Cr.App.R. 276;
    [1982] Crim.L.R. 456, C.A. 16–064

TABLE OF CASES

R. v. Best, *The Times*, October 6, 1987, C.A. 16–045
—— v. Boal (Francis) [1992] Q.B. 591; [1992] 2 W.L.R. 890; [1992] 3 All E.R. 177; (1992) 136 S.J.L.R. 100; (1992) 156 J.P. 617; [1992] I.C.R. 495; [1992] I.R.L.R. 420; (1992) 95 Cr.App.R. 272; [1992] B.C.L.C. 872; (1992) 156 L.G.Rev. 763; [1992] *Gazette*, 3 June 26; *The Times*, March 16, 1992, C.A. 19–023
—— v. Bolton (Roger John Alexander) (1992) 94 Cr.App.R. 74; (1992) 156 J.P. 138; [1992] Crim.L.R. 57; (1991) 155 J.P.N. 620; *The Times*, July 3, 1991, C.A. 16–064
—— v. Central Criminal Court, *ex p.* Francis and Francis (a firm) [1989] A.C. 346; [1988] 3 W.L.R. 989; (1988) 132 S.J. 1592; (1989) 88 Cr.App.R. 213; [1989] Crim.L.R. 444; [1989] C.O.D. 231; (1988) 138 N.L.J. 316; [1989] L.S.Gaz. 39; (1994) 138 S.J.L.B. 58; *The Times*, February 1, 1994; *The Independent*, February 10, 1994, Q.B.D. 24–026
—— v. Chappell (1984) 128 S.J. 629; (1984) 80 Cr.App.R. 31; (1984) 6 Cr.App.R.(S.) 342; [1984] Crim.L.R. 574, C.A. 23–044
—— v. Chief Constable of Kent Constabulary, *ex p.* L (a minor), R. v. D.P.P., *ex p.* B [1993] 1 All E.R. 756; (1991) 93 Cr.App.R. 416; [1991] Crim.L.R. 841; [1991] C.O.D. 446; (1991) 155 J.P.N. 636; *The Times*, April 17, 1991; *The Daily Telegraph*, April 22, 1991; *The Independent*, April 30, 1991, D.C. 25–023
—— v. Clowes (No. 2) [1994] 2 All E.R. 316, C.A. 27–007
—— v. Cohen (1992) 142 N.L.J. 1267; *The Independent*, July 29, 1992; *The Guardian*, August 26, 1992, C.A. 18–011
—— v. Commissioner of Police of the Metropolis, *ex p.* Blackburn [1968] 2 Q.B. 118; [1968] 2 W.L.R. 893; *sub nom.* R. v. Commissioner of Metropolitan Police, *ex p.* Blackburn (1968) 112 S.J. 112; *sub nom.* R. v. Metropolitan Police Commissioner, *ex p.* Blackburn [1968] 1 All E.R. 763, C.A. 25–023
—— v. Corbett (1993) 14 Cr.App.R.(S.) 101; [1992] Crim.L.R. 833, C.A. 23–044
—— v. Corbin (1984) 6 Cr.App.R.(S.) 17; [1984] Crim.L.R. 303, D.C. ... 22–008
—— v. Cox and Railton (1884) 14 Q.B.D. 153 24–026
—— v. Crick, *The Times*, August 18, 1993, C.A. 16–028, 16–049, 16–064
—— v. C.P.S., *ex p.* Waterworth, December 1, 1995 (unreported) 25–025
—— v. Crutchley and Tonks (1994) 15 Cr.App.R.(S.) 627; [1994] Crim.L.R. 309; *The Times*, January 3, 1994, C.A. 22–042, 23–004
—— v. Dando (Trevor Lee) [1995] Crim.L.R. 750, C.A. 23–049
—— v. D.P.P., *ex p.* Chandhary, *sub nom.* R. v. D.P.P., *ex p.* C [1995] 1 Cr.App.R. 136; [1994] C.O.D. 375; (1995) 159 J.P. 227; (1995) 7 Admin.L.R. 385; (1995) 159 J.P.N. 214; *The Times*, March 7, 1994, Q.B.D. 25–025
—— v. Director of the Serious Fraud Office, *ex p.* Johnson (Malcolm Keith) [1993] C.O.D. 58 25–007
—— v. FIMBRA, *ex p.* Cochrane [1991] B.C.L.C. 106; [1990] C.O.D. 33; *The Times*, June 23, 1989, D.C. 4–038
—— v. General Council of the Bar, *ex p.* Percival [1991] 1 Q.B. 212; [1990] 3 W.L.R. 323; [1990] 3 All E.R. 137; (1990) L.S.Gaz., June 27, 44; (1990) 2 Admin.L.R. 711, D.C. 25–026
—— v. Georgiou (1988) 87 Cr.App.R. 207; (1988) 4 B.C.C. 322; [1988] Crim.L.R. 472, C.A. 22–009
—— v. Ghosh [1982] Q.B. 1053; [1982] 3 W.L.R. 110; (1982) 126 S.J. 429; [1982] 2 All E.R. 689; [1982] Crim.L.R. 608; (1982) 75 Cr.App.R. 154, C.A. 16–006

TABLE OF CASES

R. v. Gold; R. v. Schifreen [1988] A.C. 1063; [1988] 2 W.L.R. 984; (1988) 152 J.P. 445; (1988) 132 S.J. 624; [1988] 2 All E.R. 186; (1988) 87 Cr.App.R. 257; [1988] Crim.L.R. 437; (1988) 152 J.P.N. 478; (1988) 138 New L.J. 117; [1988] L.S.Gaz., May 18, 38 H.L.; affirming [1987] Q.B. 1116; [1987] 3 W.L.R. 803; (1987) 131 S.J. 1247; [1987] 3 All E.R. 618; (1988) 86 Cr.App.R. 52; [1987] Crim.L.R. 762; (1984) 84 L.S.Gaz. 2529, C.A. 16–073
—— v. Goleccha; R. v. Choraria [1989] 1 W.L.R. 1050; (1989) 133 S.J. 1001; [1989] 3 All E.R. 908; (1989) 90 Cr.App.R. 241, *The Times*, July 19, 1989, C.A. 16–061
—— v. Gomez, see D.P.P. v. Gomez [1993] A.C. 442; [1992] 3 W.L.R. 1067; [1993] 1 All E.R. 1; (1993) 96 Cr.App.R. 359; (1993) 137 S.J.(L.B.) 36; (1993) 157 J.P. 1; [1993] Crim.L.R. 304; (1993) 157 J.P.N. 15, H.L. 16–010, 16–012, 16–054
—— v. Goodman (Ivor Michael) [1993] 2 All E.R. 789; (1993) 97 Cr.App.R. 210; [1992] B.C.C. 625; [1994] 1 B.C.L.C. 349; (1993) 14 Cr.App.R.(S.) 147; [1992] Crim.L.R. 676, C.A. 22–010
—— v. Grantham [1984] Q.B. 675; [1984] 2 W.L.R. 815; (1984) 128 S.J. 331; [1984] 3 All E.R. 166; (1984) 79 Cr.App.R. 86; [1984] Crim.L.R. 492; (1984) 81 L.S.Gaz. 1437, C.A. 17–006, 17–015
—— v. Greenstein; R. v. Coreen [1975] 1 W.L.R. 1353; 119 S.J. 742; [1976] 1 All E.R. 1; *sub nom.* R. v. Greenstein (Allan): R. v. Green (Monty) (1975) 61 Cr.App.R. 296; [1975] Crim.L.R. 714, C.A. ... 16–046
—— v. Griffiths (1965) 49 Cr.App.R. 279 18–005
—— v. Grunwald [1963] 1 Q.B. 935 20–045
—— v. Halai [1983] Crim.L.R. 624, C.A. 16–068
—— v. Hallam; R. v. Blackburn [1995] Crim.L.R. 323; *The Times*, May 27, 1994; *The Independent*, June 13, 1994 (C.S.), C.A. 16–002, 16–014, 16–032
—— v. Hawkins, *The Times*, August 6, 1996 16–054
—— v. Holmes (David Leonard) [1991] B.C.C. 394; (1992) 13 Cr.App.R.(S.) 29; [1991] Crim.L.R. 790; *The Times*, April 29, 1991, C.A. 22–015
—— v. Hopkins; R. v. Collins (1957) 41 Cr.App.R. 231, C.C.A. 16–074
—— v. Inland Revenue Commissioners, *ex p.* Mead and Cook [1993] 1 All E.R. 772; [1993] C.O.D. 324; [1992] S.T.C. 482; [1992] C.O.D. 361; *The Guardian*, March 27, 1992; *The Independent*, April 7, 1992, D.C. 25–024
—— v. Inland Revenue Commissioner, *ex p.* Taylor (No. 2) [1990] 2 All E.R. 409; [1990] S.T.C. 379; 62 T.C. 578, C.A.; affirming [1989] 3 All E.R. 353; [1989] S.T.C. 600, D.C. 14–084
—— v. Inman [1967] 1 Q.B. 140; [1966] 3 W.L.R. 567; 130 J.P. 415; 110 S.J. 424; [1966] 3 All E.R. 414; 50 Cr.App.R. 247, C.C.A. 17–013
—— v. Insurance Ombudsman Bureau and Another, *ex p.* Aegon Life Assurance Ltd [1994] C.O.D. 426; *The Times*, January 7, 1994; *The Independent*, January 11, 1994, Q.B.D. 10–058
—— v. International Stock Exchange of the United Kingdom and the Republic of Ireland Ltd, *ex p.* Else (1982) Ltd [1993] Q.B. 534; [1993] 2 W.L.R. 70; [1993] 1 All E.R. 420; [1993] B.C.L.C. 834; [1993] B.C.C. 11; (1994) 6 Admin.L.R. 67; [1993] C.O.D. 236; *The Times*, November 2, 1992; *The Independent*, November 24, 1992; C.A.; reversing [1993] C.O.D. 141 .... 12–008, 12–037

Table of Cases

R. v. Investor Compensation Scheme, *ex p.* Bowden [1995] 3 W.L.R. 289; [1995] 3 All E.R. 605; [1995] 2 B.C.L.C. 342; (1995) 145 N.L.J. Rep. 1260; (1995) 139 S.J.L.B. 188; [1995] N.P.C. 126; *The Times,* July 18, 1995; *The Independent,* July 21, 1995, H.L.; reversing [1995] Q.B. 107; [1994] 3 W.L.R. 1045; [1995] 1 All E.R. 214; [1995] 1 B.C.L.C. 374; [1995] C.O.D. 12; *The Times,* June 30, 1994; *The Independent,* August 29, 1994 (C.S.), C.A.; reversing [1994] 1 W.L.R. 17; [1994] 1 All E.R. 525; [1994] 1 B.C.L.C. 494; [1993] C.O.D. 278; (1993) 90 (14) L.S.Gaz. 42; (1993) 143 N.L.J. Rep 1297; (1993) 137 S.J.L.B. 82; [1993] N.P.C. 27; *The Times,* February 22, 1993; *The Independent,* February 17, 1993, Q.B.D. 4–049
—— v. ——, *ex p.* Weyell; R. v. Same, *ex p.* Last [1994] Q.B. 749; [1994] 2 W.L.R. 678; [1994] 1 All E.R. 601; [1994] 1 B.C.L.C. 537; (1993) 137 S.J.L.B. 82; [1994] C.O.D. 87; (1993) 143 N.L.J. 1297; *The Times,* August 18, 1993; *The Independent,* July 22, 1993; *The Guardian,* July 26, 1993, D.C. 4–050
—— v. Jeraj [1994] Crim.L.R. 595, C.A. 16–074
—— v. Kassim [1992] 1 A.C. 9; [1991] 3 W.L.R. 254; [1991] 3 All E.R. 713; (1992) 156 J.P. 157; (1991) 93 Cr.App.R. 391; (1991) 141 N.L.J. 1072; (1991) 155 J.P.N. 720; *The Times,* July 19, 1991; *The Independent,* July 19, 1991; *The Guardian,* July 19, 1991; *Financial Times,* July 24, 1991, H.L.; reversing [1988] Crim.L.R. 372, C.A. 16–065
—— v. Kansal [1993] Q.B. 244; [1992] 3 W.L.R. 494; [1992] 3 All E.R. 844; (1992) 136 S.J.L.B. 146; [1992] B.C.C. 615; [1992] B.C.L.C. 1009; (1992) 142 N.L.J. 715; [1992] *Gazette,* July 15, 35; *The Independent,* May 14, 1992; *The Times,* May 15, 1992; *The Guardian,* June 3, 1992; *Financial Times,* June 5, 1992, C.A. 31–049
—— v. Kemp [1988] Q.B. 645; [1988] 2 W.L.R. 975; (1988) 152 J.P. 461; (1988) 132 S.J. 461; (1988) 87 Cr.App.R. 95; 1988 P.C.C. 405; [1988] B.C.L.C. 217; (1988) 4 B.C.C. 203; [1988] Crim.L.R. 376; (1988) 152 J.P.N. 538, C.A. 17–021
—— v. King; R. v. Webley; R. v. Neads; R. v. Cunningham [1992] 1 Q.B. 20; [1991] 3 W.L.R. 246; [1991] 3 W.L.R. 705; (1991) 93 Cr.App.R. 259; (1991) 135 S.J.L.B. 76; [1991] Crim.L.R. 906; (1991) 141 N.L.J. Rep. 1071; *The Times,* June 26, 1991, *The Guardian,* June 26, 1991 .... 16–028, 16–049, 16–064
—— v. Kohn (1979) 69 Cr.App.R. 395; [1979] Crim.L.R. 675, C.A. 16–018, 16–023, 16–024, 16–049
—— v. LAUTRO, *ex p.* Ross [1993] Q.B. 17; [1992] 3 W.L.R. 549; [1993] 1 All E.R. 545; [1993] B.C.L.C. 509; (1993) 5 Admin.L.R. 573; [1992] C.O.D. 455; *The Times,* June 17, 1992; *Financial Times,* June 25, 1992, C.A.; affirming [1992] 1 All E.R. 422; [1992] B.C.L.C. 34; [1991] C.O.D. 503; (1991) 141 N.L.J. 1001; *The Independent,* July 11, 1991; *Financial Times,* July 17, 1991; *The Times,* July 22, 1991, D.C. 4–039
—— v. ——, *ex p.* Tee; R. v. LAUTRO, *ex p.* Butlers (1995) 7 Admin.L.R. 289; *The Times,* May 30, 1994 4–040
—— v. Lampard [1968] 2 O.R. 20–050
—— v. Landy; R. v. White; R. v. Kaye [1981] 1 W.L.R. 355; (1981) 125 S.J. 80; [1981] 1 All E.R. 1172; (1981) 72 Cr.App.R. 237; [1981] Crim.L.R. 326, C.A. 18–011
—— v. Lloyd's of London, *ex p.* Briggs and others [1993] 1 Ll.R. 176; [1993] C.O.D. 66, D.C. 11–051

Table of Cases

R. v. Local Commissioner for Administration, *ex p.* Bradford Metropolitan City Council [1979] Q.B. 287; [1979] 2 W.L.R. 1; (1978) 122 S.J. 573; [1979] 2 All E.R. 881; (1978) L.G.R. 305; [1978] J.P.L. 767, C.A.; affirming [1978] J.P.L. 706 9–006
—— v. McHugh (Christopher John Patrick) (1993) 97 Cr.App.R. 335, C.A. 16–041
—— v. MacKinnon [1959] 1 Q.B. 150; [1958] 3 W.L.R. 688; 123 J.P. 43; 102 S.J. 861; [1958] 3 All E.R. 657; 43 Cr.App.R. 1 20–054
—— v. Mensah Lartey and Relery [1996] Crim.L.R. 203 16–064
—— v. Miles [1992] Crim.L.R. 657; [1992] T.L.R. 195 .... 17–010, 17–012
—— v. Millard (Ray) (1995) 15 Cr.App.R.(S.) 445; [1994] Crim.L.R. 146, C.A. 22–013
—— v. Monopolies and Mergers Commission, *ex p.* Argyll Group plc [1986] 1 W.L.R. 763; (1986) 130 S.J. 467; [1986] 2 All E.R. 257; (1986) 83 L.S.Gaz. 1225; C.A.; affirming *sub nom.* Argyll Group v. Distillers Co. [1986] 1 C.M.L.R. 764, Outer House of Ct. of Sessions 13–064
—— v. Morris (David); *sub nom.* Anderton v. Burnside [1984] A.C. 320; [1983] 3 W.L.R. 697; (1984) 148 J.P. 1; (1983) 127 S.J. 713; [1983] 3 All E.R. 288; (1984) 77 Cr.App.R. 309; [1983] Crim.L.R. 813, H.L.; affirming [1983] Q.B. 587; [1983] 2 W.L.R. 768; (1983) 127 S.J. 205; [1983] 2 All E.R. 448; (1983) 77 Cr.App.R. 164; [1983] Crim.L.R. 559, C.A. 16–082
—— v. Moses and Ansbro [1991] Crim.L.R. 617, C.A. 18–019
—— v. Naylor and Clowes, *The Independent*, August 10, 1993, C.A. 16–040, 16–049
—— v. PIA, *ex p.* Lucas Fettes and Partners (Financial Services) Ltd, July 10, 1995 (unreported) 5–001, 5–018
—— v. Panel on Take-overs, *ex p.* Datafin (Norton Opax Intervening) [1987] Q.B. 815; [1987] 2 W.L.R. 699; (1987) 131 S.J. 23; [1987] 1 All E.R. 564; [1987] P.C.C. 120; [1987] B.C.L.C. 104; [1987] 1 F.T.L.R. 181; (1987) 84 L.S.Gaz. 264; (1986) 136 New L.J. 1207, C.A. 1–014, 13–001, 13–015, 13–016
—— v. ——, *ex p.* Fayed [1992] B.C.C. 524; [1992] B.C.L.C.938; (1993) 5 Admin.L.R. 337; *Financial Times*, April 14, 1992; *The Times*, April 15, 1992, C.A. 13–018
—— v. ——, *ex p.* Guiness plc [1990] 1 Q.B. 146; [1989] 2 W.L.R. 863; (1989) 133 S.J. 660; [1989] 1 All E.R. 509; [1989] B.C.L.C. 255, C.A. 13–017
—— v. Phillipon (1989) 89 Cr.App.R. 290; [1989] Crim.L.R. 585, C.A. 17–021
—— v. Preddy [1996] 3 All E.R. 481   16–003, 16–047, 16–049, 16–052, 16–054, 16–064, 16–068
—— v. SFA, *ex p.* Panton, June 20, 1994 (unreported) 4–041
—— v. SIB, *ex p.* Independent Financial Advisors Association and LIBM Ltd, May 12, 1995 (unreported) 5–019
—— v. ——, *ex p.* Sun Alliance, August 31, 1995 (unreported) ... 4–045, 4–046
—— v. Saunders and others (No. 1), *The Independent*, May 17, 1991; *The Guardian*, May 17, 1991, C.A. 18–020, 21–043
—— v. Saunders [1996] Crim.L.R. 420 .... 26–082, 31–053
—— v. Scot-Simmonds [1994] Crim.L.R. 933, C.A. 16–057
—— v. Secretary of State for Trade and Industry, *ex p.* R. [1989] 1 W.L.R. 372; (1989) 133 S.J. 290; [1989] 1 All E.R. 647; [1989] B.C.L.C. 377; [1989] C.O.D. 370; [1989] F.C.R. 284; [1989] L.S.Gaz., May 3, 43, D.C. 2–029

TABLE OF CASES

R. v. Seillon [1982] Crim.L.R. 676, C.A. 17–018
—— v. Shortland (Dennis Reginald) [1995] Crim.L.R. 893; (1995) 92 (27) L.S.Gaz. 32; (1995) 159 J.P.N. 812; *The Times*, May 23, 1995; *The Independent*, June 19, 1995, (C.S.), C.A. 16–068
—— v. Sinclair (1968) 52 Cr.App.R. 618 18–014
—— v. Smith (1963) 36 DLR 2d 613; [1963] 1 C.C.C. 68 16–030
—— v.—— [1996] Crim.L.R. 329 .... 16–080, 17–019
—— v. Stinger (1991) 94 Cr.App.R. 13 16–020
—— v. Thompson (Michael) [1984] 1 W.L.R. 962; (1984) 128 S.J. 447; [1984] 3 All E.R. 565; (1984) 79 Cr.App.R. 191; [1984] Crim.L.R. 427; (1984) 81 L.S.Gaz. 1438, C.A. 16–024, 16–026, 16–049
—— v. Tillings and Tillings [1985] Crim.L.R. 393; (1985) 135 New L.J. 510 16–083
—— v. Utting [1987] 1 W.L.R. 1375; (1987) 131 S.J. 1154; (1988) 86 Cr.App.R. 164; [1987] Crim.L.R. 636; (1987) 84 L.S.Gaz. 2529 ... 16–074
—— v. Widdowson (1986) 130 S.J. 88; (1986) 82 Cr.App.R. 314; [1986] R.T.R. 124; [1986] Crim.L.R. 233; (1986) 83 L.S.Gaz. 288, C.A. ... 16–068
—— v. Wille (Bryan) (1988) 86 Cr.App.R. 296, C.A. 16–018, 16–049
—— v. Wilson, July 25, 1996 (unreported) 10–015
—— v. Young (Vincent John) (1990) 12 Cr.App.R.(S.) 279; [1990] Crim.L.R. 752, C.A. 22–006
R & H Electric v. Haden Bill Electrical [1995] 2 B.C.L.C. 280 26–047
Rank Film Distributors v. Video Information Centre [1982] A.C. 380; [1981] 2 W.L.R. 668; (1981) 125 S.J. 290; [1981] 2 All E.R. 76; [1981] Com.L.R. 90; [1981] F.S.R. 363; H.L.; affirming [1980] 3 W.L.R. 501; (1980) 124 S.J. 757; [1980] 2 All E.R. 273, C.A.; reversing [1980] 3 W.L.R. 487; (1979) 124 S.J. 48 .... 31–027, 31–032, 31–034, 31–041, 31–044, 31–050, 31–056
Regal (Hastings) Ltd v. Gulliver [1967] 2 A.C. 134; [1942] 1 All E.R. 378 26–016
Renworth Ltd v. Stephensen, December 21, 1995 (unreported) 31–048
Rio Tinto Zinc Corpn. v. Westinghouse Electric Corpn. [1978] A.C. 547; [1978] 2 W.L.R. 81; (1978) 122 S.J. 32; [1978] 1 All E.R. 434; [1978] 1 C.M.L.R. 100, H.L.; affirming [1977] 3 W.L.R. 492; 121 S.J. 663; [1977] 3 All E.R. 717; [1977] 2 C.M.L.R. 436, C.A.; reversing [1977] 3 W.L.R. 430; (1977) 121 S.J. 491; [1977] 3 All E.R. 703; [1977] 2 C.M.L.R. 420 31–031
Roscoe v. Winder [1915] 1 Ch. 62 27–032
Royal Brunei Airlines Sdn Bhd v. Tan (Philip Kok Ming) [1995] 2 A.C. 378; [1995] 3 W.L.R. 64; [1995] 3 All E.R. 97; [1995] B.C.C. 899; (1995) 145 N.L.J. Rep. 888; [1995] 139 S.J.L.B. 146; [1995] 92 (27) L.S.Gaz. 33; *The Times*, May 29, 1995; *The Independent*, June 22, 1995, C.A. 27–017, 27–024, 27–027
Royscot Trust Ltd v. Rogerson [1991] 2 Q.B. 297; [1991] 3 W.L.R. 57; [1991] 3 All E.R. 294; (1991) 135 S.J. 444; [1992] R.T.R. 99; (1992) 11 Tr.L.R. 23; [1991] C.C.L.R. 45; (1991) 141 N.L.J. 493; *The Times*, April 3, 1991; *The Times*, April 10, 1991; *The Daily Telegraph*, April 25, 1991, C.A. 28–011
Rozeik [1996] Crim.L.R. 271 16–044
Rumsey v. NE Railway [1863] 14 C.B. (NS) 641 28–026
Runciman v. Walter Runciman plc [1992] B.C.L.C. 1084; [1993] B.C.C. 223 19–004

TABLE OF CASES

SCF Finance Co. Ltd v. Masri (No. 2) [1987] Q.B. 1002; [1987] 2 W.L.R. 58; [1987] 1 All E.R. 175; [1986] 2 Lloyd's Rep. 366; [1986] F.L.R. 309; (1987) 131 S.J. 74; (1987) 84 L.S.Gaz. 492, C.A.; affirming [1986] 1 All E.R. 40; [1986] 1 Lloyd's Rep. 293; [1986] F.C.R. 95; (1985) New L.J. 914 .... 14–013, 14–014
S.H. & Co. (Realisations) 1990 Ltd, Re. [1993] B.C.L.C. 1309; [1993] B.C.C. 60 21–036
SIB v. FIMBRA [1992] Ch. 268; [1991] 4 All E.R. 398 4–048
—— v. Pantell SA and another [1989] 2 All E.R. 673; [1989] 3 W.L.R. 698 4–011
—— v. —— No. 2 [1993] Ch. 256; [1992] 1 All E.R. 134 4–009
—— v. Uberoi, Law Tel., September 26, 1995 4–013
Saloman v. Saloman [1987] A.C. 22 .... 30–010, 30–002
Sarflax, Re. [1979] 1 All E.R. 529 17–007
Saul O. Harrison & Sons plc, Re. [1995] 1 B.C.L.C. 14; [1994] B.C.C. 475, C.A. 26–044
Saunders v. Edwards [1987] 1 W.L.R. 1116; (1987) 131 S.J. 1039; [1987] 2 All E.R. 651; (1987) 84 L.S.Gaz. 2193; (1987) 137 New L.J. 389; (1987) 84 L.S.Gaz. 2535, C.A. 28–008
Savings and Investment Bank Ltd v. Gasco Investments (Netherlands) B.V. [1984] 1 W.L.R. 271; (1984) S.J. 115; [1984] 1 All E.R. 296; (1984) 81 L.S.Gaz. 657 26–075
Scher v. Policyholders Protection Board (Nos. 1 & 2) (Note) [1994] 2 W.L.R. 593; [1994] 2 All E.R. 37; [1993] 2 Lloyd's Rep. 533, H.L.; affirming 10–008
Scott v. Metropolitan Police Commissioner [1975] A.C. 819; [1974] 3 W.L.R. 741; [1974] 3 All E.R. 1032; 60 Cr.App.R. 124; *sub nom.* R. v. Scott, 118 S.J. 863; [1975] Crim.L.R. 94, H.L.; affirming *sub nom.* R. v Scott [1974] Q.B. 733; [1974] 2 W.L.R. 379; 118 S.J. 147; [1974] 2 All E.R. 204; [1974] Crim.L.R. 242, C.A. 18–012, 18–017
Scott v. Surman [1742] Willes 400 27–031
Secretary of State for Trade and Industry v. Ettinger [1993] B.C.C. 312; [1993] B.C.L.C. 896; *The Times,* February 18, 1993, C.A.; reversing in part [1992] B.C.C. 93; [1993] B.C.L.C. 1 ..... 22–001, 22–014, 22–016
Secretary of State for Trade and Industry v. Harry Laing June 20, 1996 (unreported) 22–021
Secretary of State for Trade and Industry v. Lewinsohn March 19, 1996 (unreported) 22–019
Secretary of State for Trade and Industry v. Rogers July 30, 1996 (unreported) 22–024
Securities and Investments Board v. Lloyd-Wright [1993] 4 All E.R. 210; [1994] 1 B.C.L.C. 147 4–012
Seifert v. Pensions Ombudsman and Lynch Ltd v. Farrand July 30, 1996 (unreported) 9–012
Selangor United Rubber Estates v. Craddock (No. 3) [1968] 1 W.L.R. 1555; 112 S.J. 744; [1968] 2 All E.R. 1073; [1968] 2 Lloyd's Rep. 21–021
Seven Oaks Stationery (Retail) Ltd, Re. [1991] Ch. 164; [1990] 3 W.L.R. 1165; [1991] 3 All E.R. 578; [1991] B.C.L.C. 325; [1990] B.C.C. 765; (1990) 134 S.J. 1367, C.A.; reversing [1990] B.C.L.C. 668 .... 22–012, 22–022, 22–026, 22–028
Sewator Hanseatische Wertwattungs Gesellschaft mbh, Re., July 24, 1996 (unreported) 28–029

xxxiv

TABLE OF CASES

Smith (Howard) v. Ampol Petroleum [1974] A.C. 821; [1974] 2 W.L.R. 689; 118 S.J. 330; [1974] 1 All E.R. 1126, P.C. 26–012
Smith v. Director of the Serious Fraud Office [1993] A.C. 1; [1992] 3 W.L.R. 66; [1992] 3 All E.R. 456; (1992) 136 S.J.L.B. 182; [1992] B.C.L.C. 879; [1992] Crim.L.R. 504; [1992] C.O.D. 270; (1992) 142 N.L.J. 985; [1992] Gazette, 15 July, 34; *The Independent*, June 12, 1992; *The Times*, June 16, 1992; *Financial Times*, June 17, 1992; *The Guardian*, July 1, 1992, H.L.; reversing [1992] 1 All E.R. 730; (1992) 135 S.J.L.B. 214; (1992) 95 Cr.App.R. 191; [1992] C.O.D. 188; [1992] Gazette, 11 March 33; *The Independent*, November 8, 1991; *The Guardian*, November 13, 1991; *The Times*, November 12, 1991, D.C. 25–005, 25–007
Smith & Fawcett Ltd, *Re.* [1942] Ch. 304 26–008
Sociedade Nacional de Combustiveis de Angola UEE v. Lundqvist [1991] 2 Q.B. 310; [1991] 2 W.L.R. 280; [1990] 3 All E.R. 283, C.A. 31–031, 31–036, 31–055, 31–058
Soden v. Burns and R. v. Secretary of State for Trade and Industry, *ex p.*, Soden *The Times*, July 5, 1996 26–084
South Australian Asset Management Corpn. v. York Montague Ltd [1996] 3 All E.R. 365 29–022
Space Investments Ltd v. Canadian Imperial Bank of Commerce Trust Co. (Bahamas) [1986] 1 W.L.R. 1072; [1986] 3 All E.R. 75; (1986) 130 S.J. 612; (1986) 83 L.S.Gaz. 2567, P.C. 27–036
Spokes v. Grosvenor House Hotel Company [1897] 2 Q.B. 124 26–037
Stafford v. Conti Commodity Services Ltd [1981] 1 All E.R. 691; [1981] 1 Lloyd's Rep. 466; [1981] Com.L.R. 10 29–030
Stanlake Holdings Ltd v. Tropical Capital Investment Ltd *FT Law Reports*, June 25, 1991 27–012
Steen v. Law [1964] A.C. 287; [1963] 3 W.L.R. 802; [1963] 3 All E.R. 770, P.C. 21–032
Swan, The; Bridges & Salman v. Swan, The (Owner); Marine Diesel Service (Grimsby) v. Same; [1968] 1 Lloyd's Rep. 5; *sub nom.* Bridges & Salman v. Swan, The (Owner) (1968) 118 New L.J. 182 30–014

Tai Hing Cotton Mill Ltd v. Lui Chong Hing Bank [1986] A.C. 80; [1985] 3 W.L.R. 317; (1985) 129 S.J. 503; [1985] 2 All E.R. 947; [1986] F.L.R. 14; [1985] 2 Lloyd's Rep. 313; (1985) 135 New L.J. 680; (1985) 82 L.S.Gaz. 2995, P.C. 16–027
Target Holdings Ltd v. Redferns (a firm) [1995] 3 W.L.R. 352; [1995] 3 All E.R. 785; (1995) 139 S.J.L.B. 195; [1995] N.P.C. 136; *The Times*, July 21, 1995; *The Independent*, July 21, 1995; *The Independent*, August 10, 1995, H.L.; reversing [1994] 1 W.L.R. 1089; [1994] 2 All E.R. 337; *The Times*, November 24, 1993; *The Independent*, December 3, 1993, C.A. 27–029
Tate Access Floors Inc v. Boswell [1991] Ch. 512; [1991] 2 W.L.R. 304; [1990] 3 All E.R. 303; (1990) 134 S.J. 1227; (1990) 140 N.L.J. 963 31–041
Taylor v. Pace Developments Ltd [1991] B.C.C. 406; *The Times*, May 1, 1991, C.A. 30–022
Taylor v. Plummer [1815] 3 M & S 562 27–031
Tee v. LAUTRO Ltd July 16, 1996 (unreported) 4–069

TABLE OF CASES

Ten Oever v. Stichting Bedrijfspensioenfonds voor het Glazenwassers -en Schoonmakbedrijf (C–109/91) [1993] I.R.L.R. 601; *Financial Times*, October 5, 1993; *The Times*, October 12, 1993, E.C.J. 8–029
Tesco Supermarkets v. Nattrass [1972] A.C. 153; [1971] 2 W.L.R. 1166; 115 S.J. 285; [1971] 2 All E.R. 127; 69 L.G.R. 403; 121 New L.J. 461, H.L.; reversing [1971] 1 Q.B. 133; [1970] 3 W.L.R. 572; 114 S.J. 664; [1970] 3 All E.R. 357; 68 L.G.R. 722, D.C. 19–022
Three Rivers District Council v. Bank of England *The Times*, April 22, 1996 .... 14–098, 14–100
Trevor v. Whitworth (1887) 12 App. Cases 409 21–004

United Norwest Co-operatives Ltd v. Johnstone, *The Times*, February 24, 1994; *The Independent*, March 1, 1994, C.A. 31–038
Universal City Studios Inc. v. Hubbard [1984] Ch. 225; [1984] 2 W.L.R. 492; (1984) 128 S.J. 247; [1984] 1 All E.R. 661; (1984) 81 L.S.Gaz. 1291, C.A. affirming [1983] Ch. 241; [1983] 2 W.L.R. 882; [1983] 2 All E.R. 596; [1983] Com. L.R. 162 .... 31–041, 31–050

Vaughan v. Matthews [1849] 13 Q.B. 187 28–022
Verity and Spindler v. Lloyds Bank plc [1995] N.P.C. 148; *The Independent*, September 19, 1995, Q.B.D. 29–032, 29–033

Wai Yu-Tsang v. The Queen [1992] 1 A.C. 269; [1991] 3 W.L.R. 1006; [1991] 4 All E.R. 664; (1991) 135 S.J.L.B. 164; (1992) 94 Cr.App.R. 265; [1992] Crim.L.R. 425; *The Times*, October 16, 1991, P.C. 18–018
Wallace Smith Trust Co. Ltd v. Deloitte July 10, 1996 (unreported) ... 25–019
Wallersteiner v. Moir (No. 1) [1974] 1 W.L.R. 991; 118 S.J. 464; [1974] 3 All E.R. 217, C.A. 21–021, 30–007
—— v. —— (No. 2) [1975] Q.B. 373; [1975] 2 W.L.R. 389; 119 S.J. 97; [1975] 1 All E.R. 849, C.A. 26–038
Waterhouse v. Wilson Barker [1924] 2 K.B. 759 31–043
Welham v. D.P.P. [1961] A.C. 103; [1960] 2 W.L.R. 669; 124 J.P. 280; 104 S.J. 308; [1960] 1 All E.R. 805; 44 Cr.App.R. 124, H.L. affirming *sub nom.* R. v. Welham [1960] 2 Q.B. 445; [1960] 2 W.L.R. 333; 124 J.P. 156; 104 S.J. 108; [1960] 1 All E.R. 260; 44 Cr.App.R. 79, C.A. ... 17–015, 18–016, 18–020
Westminster City Council v. Haywood and the Pensions Ombudsman [1996] 2 All E.R. 467 9–010
Whitcombe v. Jacob [1710] Salk 160 27–031
Wild v. The Pensions Ombudsman and Smith April 2, 1996 (unreported) 9–010
Williams C. Leitch Bros. Ltd, *Re.* [1932] 2 Ch. 71 17–014
William Makin & Son Ltd, *Re.* [1993] B.C.C. 453; [1993] O.P.L.R. 171   7–020
Williams v. Natural Life Health Foods Ltd, December 1, 1995 (unreported) 30–013
Witter Ltd v. TBP Industries [1996] 2 All E.R. 573 28–014
Woods v. Martins Bank [1959] 1 Q.B. 55; [1958] 1 W.L.R. 1018; 102 S.J. 655; [1958] 3 All E.R. 166; 102 S.J. 803; 5 Business L.R. 212; [1959] J.B.L. 51; [1959] C.L.J. 21; 227 L.T. 120 29–031
Wragge, *Re.* [1919] 2 Ch. 58 1–005

TABLE OF CASES

Wright v. Ginn [1994] O.P.L.R. 83 7–049

Yuen Kun Yeu v. Att.-Gen. of Hong Kong [1988] 1 A.C. 175; [1987]
3 W.L.R. 776; (1987) 131 S.J. 1185; [1987] 2 All E.R. 705; (1987)
84 L.S.Gaz. 2049; [1987] F.L.R. 291; (1987) 137 New L.J. 566;
P.C. 14–066, 14–098

Table of Statutes

All references are to paragraph numbers

1720	Bubble Act (6 Geo. I c.18) 12–003		1956	Copyright Act (4 & 5 Eliz. 2, c.74)—
1834	Friendly Societies Act 15–001			s. 21 31–032
1840	Loan Societies Act (3 & 4 Vict. c.110) 14–008		1958	Prevention of Fraud (Investments) Act (6 & 7 Eliz. 2, c.45) ... 2–005, 2–006
1845	Gaming Act (8 & 9 Vict. c.109) 2–017			s. 13 .... 20–003, 20–045
1874	Building Societies Act (37 & 38 Vict. c.42) 15–001, 15–002, 15–008			Variation of Trusts Act (6 & 7 Eliz. 2, c.53) 7–079 Insurance Companies Act (6 & 7 Eliz. 2, c.72) 10–001
1876	Bankers' Books Evidence Act (42 & 43 Vict. c.11) 31–043		1961	Trustee Investments Act (9 & 10 Eliz. 2, c.62) 6–011
1879	Bankers' Books Evidence Act (42 & 43 Vict. c.11) 31–010, 31–043			s. 6 7–041
1892	Gaming Act (55 & 56 Vict. c.9) 2–017		1962	Building Societies Act (10 & 11 Eliz. 2, c.37) 15–008
1896	Judicial Trustees Act (59 & 60 Vict. c.35) 7–002		1963	Protection of Depositors Act (c.16) 2–005
1913	Forgery Act (3 & 4 Geo. 5, c.27) 18–016		1967	Misrepresentation Act (c.7) 28–009, 28–011, 28–012, 28–013, 28–014
1925	Trustee Act (15 & 16 Geo. c.19)— s. 41 .... 7–002 s. 57 .... 7–079 Law of Property Act (15 & 16 Geo. 5, c.20) ... 1–020			s. 2(1) .... 28–010, 28–014 (2) .... 28–014 s. 3 .... 28–014 Companies Act (c.81) .. 10–001
1934	American Securities Exchange Act 20–004		1968	Theft Act (c.60) 16–001, 16–002, 16–003, 16–004, 16–006, 16–019, 16–081, 16–083, 28–019, 31–046, 31–047, 31–048, 31–049
1939	Prevention of Fraud (Investments) Act (2 & 3 Geo. 6, c.16) ... 2–004, 2–005, 20–054			s. 1 .... 1–015, 16–053 (1) 16–005
1947	Companies Act (10 & 11 Geo. 6, c.47) 2–005			s. 3 .... 16–009, 16–013
1948	Companies Act (11 & 12 Geo. 6, c.38) .... 2–005, 17–019 s. 54 .... 21–012, 21–014 s. 332 17–013			s. 4(1) .... 16–022, 16–052 s. 5 16–033, 16–034, 16–036, 16–041

xxxix

Table of Statutes

1968 Theft Act—*cont.*
    (1) 16–034, 16–039
    (2) 16–016, 16–034,
                    16–036
    (3) 16–034, 16–041
    (4) 16–034
    (5) 16–034
  s. 6 .... 16–042, 16–044
    (1) 16–042
    (2) 16–042
  s. 15 .... 16–006, 16–043,
           16–044, 16–045,
           16–047, 16–050,
           16–053
    (1) 16–043, 16–047,
           16–067
    (2) 16–043
    (4) 16–044
  s. 16 16–006
  s. 17 .... 16–006, 16–055,
           16–057, 16–058,
           16–071
    (1)(a) 16–056
      (b) 16–056
    (2) 16–056
  s. 20 16–062
    (1) 16–006, 16–062,
           16–065
    (2) 16–006, 16–062,
           16–065
    (3) 16–063
  s. 22 16–006
  s. 28 23–052
  s. 31 .... 31–048, 31–049,
           31–054, 31–058
    (1) 31–046, 31–047
  s. 34(2) 16–061
    (a) 16–059
  Civil Evidence Act
    (c.64)—
  s. 11(1) 31–061
    (2) 31–061
  s. 14(1) 31–033, 31–039
1970 Finance Act (c.24) 6–012
  Equal Pay Act (c.41) ... 8–024,
                      8–032
  s. 1 8–032
  s. 2 8–032
    (4) 8–032
    (5) 8–032
1972 Criminal Justice Act
    (c.71)—
  s. 6 23–052

1973 Matrimonial Causes Act
    (c.18) 8–020
  s. 23 8–018
  s. 24 8–018
    (1)(c) 8–017
  s. 24A 8–018
  ss. 25B–25D 8–018
  s. 25B(1) 8–020
    (2) 8–020
    (4) 8–020
    (5) 8–020
    (7) 8–021
  s. 25C 8–022
  s. 25D 8–022
    (4) 8–019
  Fair Trading Act (c.41) ......
                    13–064
  Pt. V 13–004
  s. 75 13–064
  Insurance Companies
    Amendment Act
    (c.58) 10–001
  Powers of Criminal
    Courts Act (c.62)—
  s. 31(1)–(3C) 23–021
    (2) 23–020
    (3A) 23–021
  s. 32(1) 23–021
    (2) 23–021
  s. 35 23–042
  s. 36 23–042
  s. 43 23–055
  s. 43A 23–055
1974 Insurance Companies Act
    (c.49) 10–001
1975 Sex Discrimination Act
    (c.65) 8–032
  Policyholders Protection
    Act (c.75)—
  s. 8(2) 10–008
1977 Torts (Interference with
    Goods) Act (c.32) .. 28–019
  s. 14 28–019
  Criminal Law Act (c.45) .....
                    32–011
  s. 1 18–001
    (1) 18–002
  Insurance Brokers
    (Registration) Act
    (c.46) 2–033, 11–014
  s. 8 10–056

TABLE OF STATUTES

1978	Interpretation Act (c.30) A4–047		1982	Insurance Companies Act (c.50) 7–045, 10–001, 10–004, 10–005, 10–010, 10–014, 10–015, 10–017, 10–020, 11–021, 26–060

1978 Interpretation Act (c.30) A4–047
Theft Act (c.81) 16–004, 16–006, 31–046, 31–047, 31–048
s. 1 .... 16–006, 16–070
  (1) 16–067
  (2) 16–067
s. 2 .... 16–006, 16–070
  (1) 16–069
    (a) 16–069
    (b) 16–069
    (c) 16–069
1979 Credit Unions Act (c.34) 14–008
Banking Act (c.37) ... 14–001, 14–002, 14–003, 14–014, 14–098
s. 23(2) 14–096
1980 Companies Act (c.22) .. 20–007
ss. 68–73 20–004
Insurance Companies Act (c.25) 10–001
Magistrates' Courts Act (c.43)—
Sched. 4 23–046
Limitation Act (c.58) .. 29–028
1981 Forgery and Counterfeiting Act (c.45) 16–004, 16–071, 16–073, 16–075, 16–079, 31–047
ss. 1–4 16–078
s. 1 .... 16–072, 16–073
s. 2 16–075
s. 3 16–076
s. 4 16–077
s. 5 .... 16–077, 16–078
  (5) 16–078
s. 8(1) 16–072, 16–073
    (d) 16–072
s. 9 16–074
s. 10 16–074
Supreme Court Act (c.54)—
s. 37 .... 31–008, 31–017
s. 51(1) 30–022
s. 72 31–050
Companies Act (c.62) 21–012, 21–014
1982 Civil Jurisdiction and Judgments Act (c.27) 31–006

1982 Insurance Companies Act (c.50) 7–045, 10–001, 10–004, 10–005, 10–010, 10–014, 10–015, 10–017, 10–020, 11–021, 26–060
Insurance Companies Act—
Pt. II 2–032, 10–023
Pt. I,
ss. 1–14 10–005
s. 1(1) 10–009
s. 2 .. 2–033, 10–013, 10–052, 22–009
  (1) 10–011, 10–014, 10–015
  (2) 10–011
s. 3 .. 10–011, 10–021, 14–008
  (1) 10–017
  (2) 10–017
s. 4 10–011, 10–017, 10–021, 14–008
s. 5 .... 10–017, 10–033
s. 6 10–019
s. 7 .. 10–019, 10–020, 10–033
s. 8 .. 10–019, 10–020, 10–033
s. 9 .. 10–019, 10–020, 10–033
s. 11(1) 10–020
  (2) 10–020
s. 13 10–020
s. 14 22–009
  (1) 10–012
  (2) 10–018
  (3) 10–012, 10–018
Pt. II,
ss. 15–71 10–006
s. 15 .... 2–032, 10–023
s. 16 10–021
  (1) 10–024
ss. 17–27 .... 10–006, 10–025
s. 17 10–025, 10–026, 10–028
s. 18 .... 10–026, 10–028
  (1) 10–025
  (2) 10–025
  (3) 10–025
s. 19 10–027
s. 20 .... 10–026, 10–028
s. 21 10–025, 10–026, 10–028
s. 22 10–042
s. 23 10–029
s. 28 .... 10–006, 10–030
s. 29 .... 10–006, 10–030
ss. 32–34 10–006
s. 32(1) 10–031

1982	Insurance Companies Act—*cont.*		1982	Insurance Companies Act—*cont.*	
	s. 33	10–032		Pt. IV,	
	ss. 37–48	10–006		ss. 82–89	10–007
	s. 37(1)	10–033		s. 96	10–008, 10–023
	(2)	10–033		s. 96(1)	10—008
	ss. 38–45	10–033, 10–036, 10–045		Sched. 1	10–009, 10–017, 10–022
	s. 38	10–035		Sched. 2	10–017
	(1)	10–037		Pt. I	10–010
	s. 39	10–039		Sched. 10	10–050
	(1)	10–037	1983	Mental Health Act (c.20)	6–026
	s. 40(1)	10–039			
	ss. 41–45	10–035	1984	Police and Criminal Evidence Act (c.60)—	
	s. 41	10–040		ss. 19–22	23–026
	s. 42	10–041		s. 78	26–082
	s. 43	10–042		s. 80	25–007
	s. 44(1)	10–043	1985	Companies Act (c.6)	4–036, 12–038, 12–098, 13–013, 19–005, 19–020, 19–025, 19–032, 25–012, 26–003, 26–029, 26–043, 26–060, 26–061, 26–074, 29–037, 30–002, 30–018, 31–052, 31–054, 31–058
	(2)	10–043			
	s. 45	10–045			
	s. 46	10–036			
	s. 47(1)	10–045			
	s. 49	10–016			
	ss. 60–64	10–006, 10–035, 10–046			
	Pt. III,				
	ss. 71–81	10–007		Pt. IV	19–017
	s. 71(1)(a)	10–030		s. 70	19–035
	(c)	10–027, 10–028, 10–041		s. 71	19–035
				s. 89	12–056
	(2)	10–027		(1)	12–054
	(3)(a)	10–026, 10–028, 10–032, 10–037, 10–038, 10–039, 10–040, 10–041, 10–043, 10–045		s. 95	12–054
				s. 97	12–062
				s. 98	12–062
				ss. 99–104	19–048
				s. 104	19–019
	(b)	10–038, 10–039, 10–040, 10–043, 10–045		s. 106	19–048
				s. 110(2)	19–019
				s. 143	12–098, 21–042
	(4)(a)	10–028, 10–041		(1)	21–003, 21–005, 21–009
	(b)	10–043		(2)	21–005, 21–007
	(6)	10–043		(3)	21–008
	s. 72	10–047		(a)	21–008
	s. 73	10–007, 10–053, 10–055		Chap. VI,	
	s. 74	10–007, 10–048		ss. 151–158	21–014
	ss. 75–77	10–007, 10–049		s. 151	12–098, 21–020, 21–022, 21–025, 21–026, 21–042, 21–043, 21–044
	s. 75	10–049			
	(4)	10–049			
	s. 76(1)	10–049			
	(2)	10–049		(1)	21–015, 21–016, 21–017, 21–026
	s. 81	10–049			

Table of Statutes

1985 Companies Act—*cont.*
    s. 151(2) 21–015, 21–016,
                      21–017, 21–026,
                      21–030
       (3) 21–016, 21–043
    s. 152(1)(a) 21–018
          (i) 21–018
          (ii) 21–018,
                  21–023
          (iii) 21–018
          (iv) 21–018
    s. 153 .... 21–034, 21–043
       (1) 21–026
       (2) 21–026, 21–034
       (3) 21–032
          (a) 21–032
          (b) 21–032
       (4) 21–032
          (a) 21–032
          (b) 21–032
          (c) 21–032
    s. 154 21–033
    ss. 155–158 21–034
    s. 155(2) 21–034
       (4) 21–035
       (5) 21–039
       (6) 21–035
    ss. 156–158 21–035
    s. 156(1) 21–036
       (4) 21–038
       (5) 21–037
       (6) 21–037
       (7) 21–038
    s. 157 21–034
       (2) 21–041
    ss. 159–181 21–008
    s. 160(4) 21–008
    s. 210 .... 19–021, 19–024
    s. 216(3) 19–021
    s. 221 ...... 19–026, 19–027,
                      19–031
       (5) 19–026
    s. 222 .... 19–027, 19–031
       (5) 19–027
    s. 242(1) 10–028
       (2) 10–028
       (4) 10–028
    s. 282(1) 26–003
    s. 303 26–053
    s. 309 26–009
    s. 310 .... 26–024, 26–025
       (3)(a) 26–024
    ss. 311–322 19–002

1985 Companies Act—*cont.*
    s. 317 .... 19–004, 26–014
       (1) 19–003
       (7) 19–003
    s. 323 .... 20–020, 26–079
       (1) 19–006, 19–008
       (5) 19–006
    s. 324 ...... 19–009, 19–010,
                19–011, 19–024,
                     26–079
       (7)(a) 19–009
         (b) 19–009
    s. 325 19–011
    s. 326(2)–(5) 19–011
    s. 327 19–007
    s. 328 19–010
       (6) 19–010
    s. 329 19–024
    ss. 330–347 19–012
    s. 330 ...... 19–013, 19–014,
                     19–016
       (2)(a) 19–013
         (b) 19–013
       (3)(a) 19–013
         (b) 19–013
         (c) 19–013
       (4)(a) 19–013
         (b) 19–013
       (5) 19–014
       (6) 19–013
       (7)(a) 19–013
         (b) 19–013
    ss. 332–338 19–016
    s. 332 19–016
    s. 333 19–016
    s. 334 19–016
    s. 335(1) 19–016
       (2) 19–016
    s. 336 19–016
    s. 337 19–016
    s. 338 19–016
    s. 346 19–015
    s. 363(1) 19–029
       (4) 19–029
    s. 384(1) 19–030
    s. 389A 19–021, 19–030,
                     32–008
       (2) 19–031
    s. 394(1) 19–021
    ss. 431–446 26–080
    s. 431 ...... 19–032, 26–070,
                26–071, 26–072,
                     26–075

1985 Companies Act—*cont.*
s. 432 ...... 19–032, 20–040,
26–071, 26–072,
26–075, 26–085,
31–052, 31–053
(1) 26–070
(2) 26–068
(2) 26–070, 26–074
s. 433 26–071
s. 434 .... 26–072, 26–073
s. 436 26–073
s. 437(1) 26–075
s. 438(1) 26–076
s. 441(1) 26–075
s. 442 ...... 19–032, 20–040,
26–077, 26–078,
31–053
(3c) 26–077
s. 444 .... 26–077, 26–078
(3) 19–032
s. 446 19–032
ss. 447–451 .. 19–021, 19–024
s. 447 ...... 10–034, 10–043,
26–064, 26–066
(5)(a)(ii) 26–066
(6) 19–032, 26–065
(7) 26–065
(9) 26–064
s. 448(1) 26–067
(2) 26–067
(7) 19–032
s. 449(2) 19–032
s. 450(1) 19–033, 19–034
(2) 19–033
s. 451 .... 19–032, 26–066
s. 454 26–078
s. 455 19–024
s. 458 ...... 17–003, 17–017,
17–019, 17–021,
19–034, 26–057
ss. 459–461 .. 26–029, 26–030,
26–041
s. 459 ...... 26–044, 26–045,
26–048, 26–049
(1) 26–041
s. 460 26–076
s. 461 ...... 26–030, 26–047,
26–048, 26–051
(1) 26–051
(2) 26–051
s. 727(1) 26–026
s. 732 19–024

1985 Companies Act—*cont.*
s. 733(2) 19–021
s. 734 19–021
s. 741(1) 26–003
(2) 21–006
s. 744 21–006
Sched. 13 26–079
Pt. IV 19–011
Sched. 24 19–020,
A6–001—A6–018
Company Securities
(Insider Dealing) Act
(c.8) 20–007, 20–010
Food and Environment
Protection Act (c.48) .....
25–018
Social Security Act (c.53) ....
7–071
1986 Drug Trafficking Offences
Act (c.32) 23–001
Insolvency Act (c.45) .. 4–036,
13–013, 30–015, 30–016,
31–052, 31–054, 31–058
s. 9 4–037
s. 122 26–029
(1)(g) .. 26–053, 26–055
s. 124(4)(b) 26–076
s. 125(2) 26–056
s. 213 .... 22–027, 26–057
s. 214 ...... 22–027, 26–020,
26–059
(4) 30–017
s. 236 ...... 25–013, 25–016,
26–085
(2) 25–014
s. 247(2) 6–026
s. 249 7–014
s. 290 31–051
s. 399 2–031
s. 435 7–014
Company Directors
Disqualification Act
(c.46) 6–022, 7–016,
22–003, 26–075
s. 1 22–001
s. 2 .... 22–005, 22–006
(1) 22–004, 22–010
(3) 22–011
s. 3 22–016
ss. 6–9 22–003
s. 6 22–017, 22–018, 22–019,
22–020, 22–023,
26–020

1986	Company Directors Disqualification Act—*cont.*		1986	Financial Services Act (c.60)	.... ii, 1–008, 1–012,
	(4)	22–022			1–014, 1–022, 1–026,
	s. 8	22–025, 22–026			2–001, 2–003, 2–005,
	s. 10	22–027, 22–028			2–007, 2–011, 2–012,
	s. 11	22–029, 22–030			2–013, 2–015, 2–017,
	s. 12(2)	22–030			2–029, 2–030, 2–033,
	s. 13	22–030			2–046, 3–001, 3–004,
	s. 18	22–031			3–015, 3–027, 3–055,
	Buildings Societies Act				3–056, 4–001, 4–002,
	(c.53)	1–012, 7–045,			4–011, 4–025, 4–027,
		14–008, 15–004, 15–005,			4–031, 4–036, 4–038,
		15–006, 15–008, 15–009,			4–042, 4–044, 4–048,
		15–014, 15–022, 15–032,			4–049, 4–050, 4–052,
		25–012			4–055, 4–058, 5–001,
	Pt. IV	15–022			5–004, 5–005, 5–006,
	s. 1	15–009			5–018, 7–037, 7–039,
	s. 5(1)	15–011, 15–024			7–043, 7–045, 10–004,
	s. 7	15–017			10–021, 10–022, 10–044,
	(3)	15–017			10–056, 10–058, 11–016,
	s. 9	15–013			11–021, 11–045, 12–006,
	s. 10	15–018			12–011, 12–018, 12–038,
	s. 16	15–019			12–061, 12–082, 12–089,
	s. 18	15–020			12–106, 13–003, 13–013,
	s. 21	15–021			14–107, 20–019, 24–031,
	s. 24	15–022			24–043, 25–012, 26–060,
	s. 25	15–022			27–005
	s. 26	15–022		Pt. I	2–032, 10–050
	s. 27	15–022		Chap. V	4–007, 4–008,
	s. 36	15–024			4–042, 12–076
	s. 37	15–024		Chap. VI	A3–017
	s. 38	15–025		Pt. III	3–002
	s. 40	15–025		Pt. IV	2–030, 2–044, 12–007,
	s. 42	15–026			12–012, 12–038,
	s. 43	15–026			12–039, 12–042,
	s. 45	15–014, 15–016			12–052, 12–078
	ss. 46–49	15–027		Pt. V	2–044, 12–079
	s. 50	15–028		Pt. VIII	2–034
	s. 51	15–028		Pt. IX	2–047
	s. 52	15–028		s. 1	4–048
	s. 53	15–028		(1)	2–017, 20–047
	s. 54	15–028		(2)	2–018
	ss. 55–57	15–029		(3)	2–028
	s. 71	15–015, 15–016		s. 3	1–015, 2–012, 3–002,
	s. 79(1)	15–016			4–005, 4–006, 4–007,
	s. 82	15–016			4–013, 5–003
	ss. 83–85	15–030		s. 4	2–012, 4–003
	Sched. 2	15–012		s. 5	4–005
	Sched. 3,			(1)(a)	4–005
	Pts. I–III	15–013		(b)	4–005
	Sched. 8	15–023		(3)(a)	4–005
				(b)	4–005

TABLE OF STATUTES

1986 Financial Services
Act—cont.
 (c) 4–005
s. 6 .... 4–006, 4–011
 (1) 4–006
 (2) 4–006, 4–009
 (3) 4–007
 (4) 4–007
s. 7(1) 3–005
 (9) 2–041
s. 8(1) 3–005
s. 10 3–005
s. 13(1) 3–024
 (2) 3–024
s. 15(1) 3–014
s. 16(2) 3–014
ss. 17–19 3–014
s. 19(1) 5–006
s. 22 .. 4–020, 10–021, 10–044
s. 24 4–020
s. 25 4–020
s. 26 3–003
s. 27(2) 3–003
 (5) 3–003
s. 28 4–031
 (3) 4–031
 (4) 4–031
s. 29(1) 4–032
 (2) 4–032
 (3) 4–032
 (4) 4–032
s. 30 4–033
s. 31 .... 3–015, 4–020
s. 32(1) 3–016
s. 33 3–015
s. 35 2–030
s. 36 2–030
s. 37 2–030
s. 38 2–030
s. 39 2–030
s. 40 2–030
s. 41 2–030
s. 42 .... 2–031, 11–016
s. 43 2–031
s. 44 2–031
s. 45 .... 2–031, 2–042
s. 46 2–030
s. 47 ... 2–038, 4–008, 4–013,
  19–035, 20–001,
  20–003, 20–042,
  20–060, 20–061,
  A4–040

1986 Financial Services
Act—cont.
s. 47(1) 20–042, 20–043,
  20–045, 20–058,
  20–059
 (a) 20–043
 (b) 20–043
 (2) 20–042, 20–048,
  20–050, 20–051,
  20–054, 20–055,
  20–056, 20–058,
  20–059
 (3) 20–056
 (4) 20–058
s. 47A 3–019, A3–012
 (3) A3–017
s.47B 3–019
s. 48 3–022, 20–031, A4–047
 (6) 12–023, A4–040
 (7) 12–023, 20–057
s. 49 3–022
s. 54 .... 4–046, 4–047
 (1) 4–044
 (3) 4–047
s. 55 .... 3–022, 3–035
ss. 56–58 2–038
s. 56 .... 3–022, 4–008
 (1) 2–045
 (2) 2–045
s. 57 ... 2–039, 2–040, 2–042,
  2–043, 2–044, 3–055,
  4–008, 12–038, 12–075,
  12–078, 12–094,
  12–095, 20–025
 (1) 3–056
 (2) 2–039, 3–056
 (3) 2–039
 (4) 2–039
 (5) 2–040
 (6) 2–040
 (10) 2–040
s. 58 ... 2–039, 2–042, 3–055,
  12–078, 12–094
 (3) 4–008
s. 59 .... 4–008, 4–034
s. 60 .... 4–020, 4–028
s. 61 .... 4–008, 4–020, 4–028
 (1) 4–009, A3–014
 (3) 4–008
s. 62 ... 4–020, 4–028, 4–042,
  4–043, 4–065, 20–060
s. 63 2–017
s. 63A 3–022, 3–035,
  A4–001, A4–047

Table of Statutes

1986	Financial Services Act—cont.		1986	Financial Services Act—cont.	
	(1)	3–022		(3)	10–055
	(2)	3–023		s. 138	2–033, 10–056
	(3)	3–024		s. 142	12–042
	s. 63B	3–023		(6)	12–012, 12–044
	s. 63C	3–025		s. 143(1)	12–045
	ss. 64–71	4–027, 4–029		(2)	12–045
	s. 64(4)(a)	4–027		s. 144	12–046
	s. 65	4–027		(1)	12–046
	s. 66	4–028		(2)	12–046, 12–063, 12–068
	s. 67	4–028		(3)	12–046
	s. 68	4–028		(4)	12–047
	s. 69	4–028		(5)	12–047
	s. 70	4–028		s. 145	12–050
	s. 71	4–028		s. 146	12–099
	s. 72	4–036		(1)	12–070, 12–073
	s. 75	2–034		(2)	12–071
	s. 76	2–035		(3)	12–071
	ss. 77–95	2–036		s. 147	12–073, 12–099
	s. 77	2–036		(2)	12–073
	(2)–(5)	2–036		s. 148(1)	12–072
	s. 78	2–036		(2)	12–072
	s. 79	2–037		s. 149	12–078
	s. 81	2–036, 2–037		s. 150	12–069, 12–099, 12–101, 12–102
	ss. 86–90	2–036		(4)	12–104
	s. 86(7)	A4–044		(5)	12–102
	ss. 91–95	2–037, 4–030		s. 151	12–100
	s. 102	3–002		s. 152	12–101
	s. 103	3–002		(2)	12–102
	s. 104	10–044		s. 154	2–044, 12–075, 12–076, 12–077
	(1)	4–020		(1)	12–076
	(1)	10–044		(3)	12–077
	(2)	4–021		(4)	12–077
	s. 105	2–029, 4–022, 4–024		(5)	12–077
	(2)	4–023		s. 154A	12–099
	(3)	4–024		s. 177	20–040
	(4)	4–024		(3)	4–026
	(5)	4–024		s. 177f	4–026
	(6)	4–024		s. 178	4–026
	(10)	4–024		(2)	4–026
	(11)	4–024		s. 179	4–068
	s. 106	4–022		(6)	4–068
	s. 107A	3–022		s. 180(1)(q)	4–068
	(2)	3–023		s. 183	14–048
	s. 129	2–032, 10–050		s. 187	4–069
	s. 130	2–033, 10–050, 10–051		(3)	4–068
	s. 131	2–033, 10–051		(4)	12–044, 12–052
	s. 132	2–033, 10–013, 10–052		s. 191	7–036
	(1)	10–013			
	s. 133	2–033, 10–053, 10–055			

Table of Statutes

1986	Financial Services Act—*cont.*		1987	Banking Act (c.22) 1–012, 7–045, 7–063, 14–002,
	s. 196 21–032			14–003, 14–004, 14–005,
	s. 207 6–002			14–014, 14–016, 14–017,
	ss. 434–436 26–081			14–018, 14–032, 14–039,
	s. 446 26–081			14–055, 14–061, 14–069,
	Sched. 1 ...... 2–015, 4–048,			14–070, 14–081, 14–084,
	A2–001—A2–056			14–085, 14–088, 14–095,
	Pt. I ... 1–008, 2–016, 20–047			15–006, 15–022
	para. 1 12–042			Pt. I 14–006
	para. 2 12–042			Pt. II 14–095
	para. 4 12–042			s. 1 14–006
	para. 5 12–042			(4) 14–006
	para. 9 2–017			s. 2 14–007
	Pt. II 2–018, 10–022			(5) 14–007
	paras. 12–15 5–003			s. 3 14–008, 14–014, 14–056,
	para. 12 2–017			14–057, 14–060,
	Pt. II,			14–078, 14–080,
	para. 12 .... 2–019, 2–023			14–083
	para. 13 .... 2–020, 2–026			(1) 14–008, 14–056,
	para. 14 2–020, 7–036, 7–039			14–059
	Pt. II,			(2) 14–008, 14–059
	para. 15 2–021			(3) 14–008
	para. 16 2–021			s. 4 14–008
	Pt. III 2–018, 2–022			s. 5(1) 14–009
	para. 17 2–023			s. 6(1) 14–011
	para. 18 2–024			(2) 14–012
	para. 19 2–025			(4) 14–012
	para. 20 2–026			ss. 8–10 14–018
	para. 21 2–026			s. 8(1) 14–019
	para. 22 2–026			(2) 14–020
	para. 23 2–026			(5) 14–020
	para. 24 2–026			s. 9(1) 14–021
	para. 25 2–026			(2) 14–021
	para. 25A 2–026			(4) 14–021
	para. 25B 2–026, 20–029			(5) 14–021
	Pt. IV 2–027			s. 10(1) 14–022
	Sched. 2 3–005			(2) 14–022
	para. 4 4–015			(4) 14–022
	para. 6 4–052			(5) 14–022
	Sched. 3 3–014			(6) 14–022
	Sched. 4 2–030			ss. 11–14 14–039
	para. 4 4–016			s. 11 14–039
	Sched. 5 2–031			s. 12 14–041
	Sched. 10 2–032			(1) 14–040
	para. 2(1) 10–021			(2) 14–040
	para. 4 .... A4–044			(4) 14–040
	Sched. 11,			(6) 14–041
	para. 13A A3–012			(7) 14–041
	para. 14 .... A4–044, A4–047			s. 13 14–042
	para. 22B A4–047			s. 15 14–043
	Sched. 11A 12–063			
	Sched. 17 19–035			

Table of Statutes

1987	Banking Act—cont.		1987	Banking Act—cont.	
	s. 16	14–018		(3)	14–078
	s. 17	14–018		(4)	14–078, 14–080
	s. 18	14–061, 14–062		(5)	14–078
	(1)(a)	14–061		(6)	14–078
	(b)	14–061		s. 43	14–079
	(2)	14–061		s. 44	14–083
	s. 19	14–091		s. 45(1)	14–089
	s. 21	14–048, 14–050, 14–052		(2)	14–089
	(1)	14–044		s. 46	14–090
	(a)	14–050		s. 47	14–085
	(b)	14–050		(1)	14–086
	(3)	14–044		(2)	14–087
	s. 22	14–046		(3)	14–087
	s. 23	14–048		s. 48	14–057
	s. 24	14–049		s. 49	14–057, 14–058
	s. 25(1)	14–050		s. 50(1)	14–095
	(2)	14–050		s. 58	14–096, 14–097
	(3)	14–052		(1)	14–097
	(a)–(c)	14–051		(2)	14–096
	(c)	14–052		s. 60	14–097
	s. 26	14–052		(1)	14–096
	s. 27	14–046, 14–091		ss. 82–84	14–084
	s. 28	14–092		s. 82	14–084
	s. 29(2)	14–093		s. 83	14–084
	(7)	14–093		s. 84	14–084
	s. 31(1)	14–094		s. 96(1)	14–060
	s. 35	14–078, 14–083		Sched. 1	14–007
	(1)	14–063, 14–064, 14–066		Sched. 2	14–008, 14–010
	(2)	14–064		Sched. 3	14–018, 14–021, 14–023, 14–039, 14–045
	(3)	14–066		(1)	14–024
	s. 39	14–070, 14–071, 14–072, 14–073, 14–076, 14–077, 14–088, 14–102		(2)	14–026
				(3)	14–027
	(1)(a)	14–070		para. 4	14–023
	(3)(a)	14–082		para. 4(1)	14–028
	(11)	14–071		para. (2)–(8)	14–028
	(12)	14–072		para. 4(9)	14–028
	(13)	14–072		Criminal Justice Act (c.38)	25–005
	s. 40	14–073		s. 1	25–013
	s. 41	14–074, 14–076, 14–077, 14–083, 14–088, 14–102		(1)	25–004
				s. 2	25–004, 25–007, 25–008, 25–010, 25–011, 25–012, 25–013, 25–019, 26–083
	(5)	14–074			
	(7)	14–075			
	(9)	14–075		(2)	25–005, 25–006, 25–011
	(a)–(d)	14–075			
	(10)	14–076		(3)	25–005, 25–006, 25–011, 25–013
	(11)	14–076			
	s. 42	14–078, 14–079, 14–080		(8)	25–011
	(1)	14–078		(9)	25–010

TABLE OF STATUTES

1987	Criminal Justice Act—*cont.*	1988	Criminal Justice Act—*cont.*
	(10) 25–010		(1) 24–010
	(13) 25–007		(3)(a) 24–007
	(14) 25–008, 25–011		(b) 24–010
	(15) 25–008		(4) 24–008, 24–011
	(16) 25–009		(c)(ii) 24–013
	(17) 25–009		(5) 24–012
	s. 3 .... 25–012, 25–013		s. 93B 24–014, 24–021
	(6) 25–012		s. 93C 24–019
	s. 12 18–009		s. 93D 24–022, 24–027,
	(1) 18–010		24–029
	(3) 18–010		(1)–(3) 24–028
1988	Income and Corporation Taxes Act (c.1)—		(1) 24–023
	s. 591(2)(g) 5–012		(a) 24–023
	s. 630 5–012		(b) 24–023
	Sched. 22 7–068		(2) 24–024
	Criminal Justice Act (c.33) 23–003, 23–004,		(a) 24–024
	23–019, 23–027, 23–033,		(b) 24–024
	23–036, 24–012, 24–013,		(3) 24–025
	24–019, 24–020, 24–027		(a) 24–025
	Pt. VI 23–001, 23–018		(b) 24–025
	s. 69 23–055		(4) 24–026
	s. 71 23–013		(5) 24–026
	(1) 23–006, 23–007		(6) 24–028
	(7) 23–051		(10) 24–027
	s. 72AA 23–013, 23–014,		s. 93H 23–024, 23–025
	23–015		s. 93J(1) 23–027, 23–028,
	(5) 23–016		23–029, 23–030
	s. 73 23–018		(3) 23–028
	s. 73A 23–017		(5) 23–029
	(2) 23–010, 23–011		(7) 23–030, 23–031
	(5) 23–010		(9) 23–031, 23–032
	s. 74A 23–019		s. 104 23–042
	s. 74B 23–019		Sched. 4 23–008
	s. 74C 23–019		Sched. 15 23–055
	s. 75 23–021	1989	Prevention of Terrorism (Temporary Provisions) Act (c.4) .. 23–001, 23–014
	s. 75A 23–022		
	s. 76(1) 23–027		
	(2) 23–027		Pt. III 23–008
	s. 77 .... 23–033, 23–035		Companies Act (c.40) .. 3–019, 3–022
	s. 78 .... 23–033, 23–040		
	s. 80 23–023		
	s. 81 23–023		Pt. III 26–060
	(7) 23–051		s. 63 26–064
	s. 89 23–037		s. 132 21–032
	Pt. VI, ss 93A–G 24–003		Sched. 18, para. 33 21–032
	s. 93A 24–004, 24–009, 24–016, 24–017, 24–018, 24–021	1990	Computer Misuse Act (c.18) 16–073

1

Table of Statutes

1993	Criminal Justice Act (c.36) 18–021, 20–007, 20–008, 23–003, 24–003	1993	Criminal Justice Act—*cont.*
	Pt. I 16–021, 16–080, 18–021		(2) 20–013
	Pt. III 24–002		(a) 20–013
	Pt. V 20–007		(i) 20–013
	ss. 1–6 16–079		(ii) 20–013
	s. 1(3) 18–021		(b) 20–013
	s. 3(1) 16–079		s. 58(2) 20–017
	s. 5 18–021		(a) 20–017
	(3) 18–021		(b) 20–017
	s. 6 18–021		(c) 20–017
	ss. 29–33 24–003		(i) 20–017
	s. 29 24–004		(ii) 20–017
	s. 35 24–003		(d) 20–017
	s. 52 .... 20–010, 20–011, 20–012, 20–013		(3) 20–017, 20–018
			(a) 20–017
	(1) 20–011, 20–034		(b) 20–017
	(2) 20–011, 20–034		(c) 20–017
	(a) 20–011		(d) 20–017
	(b) 20–011		(e) 20–017
	(3) 20–011		s. 59 20–024
	(4) 20–011		(1) 20–024
	s. 53 20–026, 20–027, 20–028		(a) 20–024
	(1) 20–028		(b) 20–024
	(a) 20–028		(2) 20–024
	(b) 20–028		(a) 20–024
	(c) 20–028		(b) 20–024
	(2) 20–028		s. 61(1) 20–032
	(a) 20–028		(2) 20–033
	(b) 20–028		s. 62 20–034
	(c) 20–028		Sched. 1 20–029
	(3) 20–028		Sched. 2 20–019
	(a) 20–028		Pensions Schemes Act (c.48) 6–009, 6–034, 7–039, 8–002, 8–006, 9–006
	(b) 20–028		
	s. 55 20–022		
	(1) 20–022		Pt. IV,
	(a) 20–022		Chap. IV 7–071, 7–073
	(b) 20–022		s. 1 .... 6–002, 8–019, 8–043, 8–045
	s. 56 .... 20–015, 20–016, 20–017, 20–036		
			s. 7(2A) 8–015
	(1) 20–015		(2B) 8–015
	(a) 20–015		s. 9(2B) 8–007
	(b) 20–015		(3) 8–010
	(c) 20–015		(5)(a) 7–048
	(d) 20–015		ss. 12A–12C 8–006
	(2) 20–015		ss. 12A–12D 8–008
	(3) 20–015		s. 12A 8–007, 8–009
	s. 57 .... 20–013, 20–014		ss. 13–24 8–006
	(1) 20–013		s. 33A 7–048
	(a) 20–013		s. 34(a)(ii) 8–015
	(b) 20–013		ss. 93–95 7–072
			s. 93 .... 7–073, 7–075

Table of Statutes

1993	Pensions Schemes Act—*cont.*		1995	Pensions Act—*cont.*	
	s. 93A	7–075		(2)	6–020
	s. 94(1)	7–074		(3)	6–021
	ss. 97–99	7–072		(4)	6–021
	s. 99	7–077		s. 4	6–022, 6–024
	s. 113	7–078		(5)	6–022
	s. 118	8–030		s. 5	6–023
	s. 124	8–042		s. 6(1)	6–024
	(3)	8–042		(3)	6–024
	(3A)	8–042		(4)	6–024
	ss. 136–140	7–085		s. 7	6–028, 7–007, 7–015
	s. 136	7–079		(1)	7–015
	ss. 145–152	9–006		(3)	7–015
	s. 146	9–007		(5)	7–015
	s. 151	6–039		s. 8	7–019
	s. 155	7–078		(1)	7–015
	s. 168(4)	6–038		(3)	7–015
	s. 175	6–019		(4)	7–015
	s. 181(1)	8–038		s. 10	6–029, 6–034, 6–038,
1994	Criminal Justice Act (c.33)—				7–011, 7–018, 7–031, 7–032, 7–033, 7–040,
	s. 35	31–057, 31–58			7–041, 7–043, 7–044,
1995	Pensions Act (c.26)	2–001,			7–046, 7–051, 7–055,
		5–001, 5–006, 6–001,			7–057, 7–063, 7–064,
		6–006, 6–008, 6–009,			7–069, 7–075, 8–041,
		6–014, 6–015, 6–025,			9–002
		6–034, 6–040, 6–041,		s. 11	6–030
		6–042, 6–043, 6–045,		s. 12	6–030
		7–001, 7–004, 7–005,		s. 13	6–031
		7–009, 7–018, 7–023,		s. 14	6–032, 7–070
		7–024, 7–034, 7–035,		(1)	7–052
		7–037, 7–042, 7–045,		s. 15(1)	7–087
		7–049, 7–053, 7–065,		ss. 16–20	7–008
		7–072, 7–079, 7–083,		ss. 16–21	7–005
		7–087, 8–001, 8–002,		s. 16(1)	7–084
		8–017, 8–018, 8–024,		(3)(b)	7–006, 7–019
		8–040, 8–044, 8–047,		(5)	7–006
		9–005, 9–007, 9–013		(6)	7–006
	Pt. I	6–015, 7–021		(7)	7–007, 7–015
	Pt. II	6–015		(8)	7–006
	Pt. III	6–015		s. 17	7–008, 7–011
	Pt. IV	6–015		(2)	7–084
	s. 1	6–017		s. 18	7–009, 7–014
	s. 3	6–020, 6–022, 6–023,		s. 19	7–009
		6–024, 6–026, 6–034,		s. 20(5)	7–006
		6–038, 7–011, 7–013,		s. 21	7–011
		7–015, 7–018, 7–031,		(4)	7–008
		7–032, 7–033, 7–040,		s. 22	7–019
		7–041, 7–043, 7–044,		s. 25(2)(a)	7–019
		7–051, 7–055, 7–057,		s. 27	7–013, 7–014, 7–043
		7–063, 7–069, 8–035,		(1)	7–012, 7–056
		8–041		(2)	7–012

Table of Statutes

1995	Pensions Act—cont.		1995	Pensions Act—cont.	
	(4)	7–013		(8)	7–041
	s. 28(1)	7–013		s. 37	6–032, 7–068, 7–070
	(3)	7–013		(1)(a)	7–069
	(4)	7–013		(2)	7–068, 7–084
	s. 29	6–022, 6–025, 7–015, 7–016, 7–017		(4)	7–068
				(a)	7–068
	(1)	6–025, 6–027, 7–016		(b)	7–068
	(a)	7–016		(c)	7–068
	(b)	7–016		(8)	7–069
	(c)	7–016		(9)	7–069
	(d)	7–016		s. 38	8–040
	(e)	7–016		s. 39	7–020
	(f)	7–016		s. 40	6–032, 7–052, 8–007
	(3)	6–025, 6–026, 6–027, 6–038		(1)	7–049, 7–051
				(2)	7–050
	(4)	6–025, 6–026, 6–027, 6–038		s. 41	7–058, 7–078, 8–047
				s. 42(1)	7–062
	(5)	6–026, 7–017		s. 43	7–062
	s. 30(1)	7–016		s. 44	7–062
	(7)	6–027		s. 45	7–062
	s. 31(1)	7–057		s. 46	7–034, 8–041
	(b)	6–029		s. 47	7–027, 7–043, 7–059, 8–047
	(2)	7–057			
	(3)	7–057		(1)	7–043
	(4)	7–057		(2)	7–043
	(5)	7–057		(3)	7–044
	s. 32	7–015, 7–018		(9)	7–043
	(2)(a)	7–018		(10)	7–043
	(b)	7–018		(11)	7–043
	(5)	7–018		s. 48	7–045, 7–046, 7–059, 8–047
	s. 34	7–036, 7–037, 7–039			
	(1)	7–037		(1)	7–045, 7–046
	(2)(a)	7–039		(2)	7–046
	(b)	7–039		(3)	7–046
	(4)	7–039		(4)	7–047
	(5)	7–039		(5)	7–047
	(a)	7–039		(7)	7–046
	(b)	7–039		(8)	7–046
	(7)	7–039		(12)	7–046
	s. 35	7–040		s. 49	7–063
	(1)	7–040		(1)	7–063
	(2)	7–040		(2)	7–055
	(3)	7–040		(3)	7–055
	(4)	7–040		(4)	7–055
	(5)(a)	7–040		(5)	7–064, 7–087
	(b)	7–040		(6)	7–055, 7–063
	s. 36	7–039, 7–040, 7–041		(7)	7–055, 7–064
	(2)	7–041		(8)	7–064
	(3)	7–041		s. 50	9–002
	(6)	7–041		(2)	9–002
	(7)	7–041		(6)	9–002
				(7)	9–002

1995	Pensions Act—*cont.*		1995	Pensions Act—*cont.*	
	ss. 56–61	7–023, 7–027		ss. 69–72	7–079
	s. 56	7–025, 7–040		s. 72	7–086
	(1)	7–025		s. 76	6–032, 7–066
	(2)	7–025		(2)	7–084
	(3)	7–027		s. 77	6–032, 7–066
	ss. 57–60	7–026		(2)	7–088
	s. 57	7–058		(4)	7–088
	(1)	7–028		(5)	7–088
	(a)	7–026, 7–028		ss. 78–86	9–013
	(b)	7–026, 7–028		s. 78	9–013
	(2)	7–029		s. 80	9–017
	(4)	7–029		s. 81(1)	9–014
	s. 58	7–029, 7–034, 7–058, 8–041		(c)	9–015
	(1)	7–031		s. 82(4)	9–015
	(3)	7–031		s. 83	7–084, 9–016
	(c)	7–026		s. 84	7–084, 9–016
	(4)	7–031		s. 85	9–017
	(6)	7–029		(1)	9–017
	(8)	7–031		ss. 87–90	7–034, 8–047
	s. 59	8–041		s. 87	7–034, 8–041
	(1)	7–032, 7–078		(5)	8–041
	(3)	7–029, 7–032, 7–058, 7–078		(5)	8–041
				s. 88(1)	7–078
	(4)	7–032, 7–078		(4)	7–078
	s. 60	7–029		s. 89	8–040
	(1)	7–033		(1)(a)	7–025
	(2)	7–033		s. 90	8–042
	(3)	7–033		s. 91	7–084, 7–088
	(4)	7–033, 7–078		s. 92	7–084, 7–088
	(8)	7–033, 7–078		s. 96	6–038
	ss. 62–65	8–035		(2)	6–038
	ss. 62–66	8–025, 8–044, 8–047		(3)(a)	6–038
				(b)	6–038
	s. 62	8–030, 8–032		(4)	6–038
	(1)	8–024		s. 97	6–039
	(2)	8–031		(1)	6–039
	s. 63	8–032		(2)	6–039
	(4)	8–032		(3)	6–039
	s. 64	8–034		ss. 98–103	6–033
	s. 65	8–031		s. 98	6–034, 6–035, 7–078
	s. 66	8–032		(1)	6–033
	ss. 67–70	7–086		(3)	6–033
	ss. 67–72	7–079		s. 99	6–034, 6–035
	s. 67	7–079, 7–082		(5)	6–035
	(2)	7–080		(6)	6–035
	(3)	7–080, 7–081		s. 101(1)	6–035
	(4)(a)	7–082		(2)	6–035
	s. 68	7–079, 7–084		(3)	6–035
	(2)	7–084		(5)	6–035
	ss. 69–71	7–085		(6)	6–035
				(7)	6–035

Table of Statutes

1995	Pensions Act—*cont.*		1995	Pensions Act—*cont.*	
	s. 102	6–033		s. 152	7–073
	s. 103(1)	6–036		s. 153	7–075
	(2)	6–036		s. 154	7–074
	s. 104	6–037		s. 155	6–038
	(1)	7–078		ss. 156–160	9–007
	(3)	7–078		s. 157	9–007
	ss. 106–108	6–037		s. 165	6–019
	s. 106	6–037		ss. 166–167	8–047
	s. 107	6–037		s. 166	8–018, 8–023
	s. 108	6–037		s. 167	8–023
	s. 110	7–078, 9–019		Sched. 1	6–017, 6–018
	s. 111	7–078		Sched. 2	9–013
	(1)	9–019		Sched. 4	8–016, 8–025
	(2)	9–019		Pt. I	8–036
	(4)	7–078, 9–019		Pt. II	8–036
	(5)	7–078, 9–019		Pt. III	8–036
	(6)	9–019		Sched. 5,	
	s. 112	9–019		para. 37	8–015
	s. 117	7–021		Sched. 6	7–072
	s. 123	7–014		para. 6	7–077
	s. 124	8–044		Proceeds of Crime Act	
	(2)	7–083		(c.11)	23–002, 23–003, 23–007, 23–021, 23–050
	s. 125(1)	8–039		s. 1	23–006
	ss. 126–134	8–016		s. 2	23–013, 23–014, 23–015
	s. 126	8–025, 8–036		s. 3	23–017
	s. 135	8–002		s. 4	23–010, 23–018
	(5)	8–007		s. 5	23–019
	s. 136	8–006, 8–015		s. 6	23–019
	(3)	8–007		s. 7	23–019
	(5)	8–008		s. 9	23–022
	s. 147	7–048		s. 11	23–024
	s. 150	6–017		s. 13(1)	23–027
	ss. 152–154	7–072			

Table of Statutory Instruments

All references are to paragraph numbers

1976 Occupational Pension Schemes (Equal Access to Membership) Amendment Regulations (S.I. 1976 No. 142) 8–030
1980 Insurance Companies (Accounts and Statements) Regulations (S.I. 1980 No. 6)
    regs. 5–8 10–025
    regs. 9–12 10–025
    reg. 15 10–025
    Sched. I 10–025
1981 Insurance Companies Regulations (S.I. 1981 No. 1654) 10–007
    regs. 3–13 10–031
    reg. 9 10–032
    reg. 31 10–046
    reg. 65 10–047
    reg. 66 10–047
    regs. 67–69 10–048
    reg. 70 10–049
    reg. 71 10–049
    Sched. 1 10–031
    Sched. 3 10–032
    Sched. 6 10–046
    Sched. 10 10–049
1982 Insurance Companies (Accounts and Statements) (Amendment) Regulations (S.I. 1982 No. 305) 10–025
1985 Companies (Forms) Regulations (S.I. 1985 No. 854)
    reg. 4(1) 21–036
    Sched. 3 21–036
    Sched. 4, Pt. II 21–036
1986 Insolvency Rules (S.I. 1986 No. 1925)
    r. 6.175(5) 31–051
    r. 9.4(3) 31–051
Companies (Unfar Prejudice Application) Proceedings Rules (S.I. 1986 No. 2000) 26–042
1987 Pension Scheme Surpluses (Valuation) Regulations (S.I. 1987 No. 412) 7–067
Financial Services Act 1986 (Delegation) Order (S.I. 1987 No. 942) 2–013
Banking Appeal Tribunal Regulations (S.I. 1987 No. 1299)
    para. 4 14–091
1988 Financial Services Act 1986 (Stabilisation) Order (S.I. 1988 No. 717) 20–057
1991 Financial Services (Client Money) Regulations 3–031, 3–033, 3–035, 3–036, 3–037
    reg. 2.12 3–032
    regs. 4.01–4.02 3–032
    regs. 4.03–4.08 3–032
    reg. 4.11 3–032
    reg. 4.12 3–032
Financial Services (Client Money) (Supplementary) Regulations 3–033, 3–035, 3–036, 3–037
    reg. 2.01 3–033
    reg. 3.01 3–034

Table of Statutory Instruments

1991 Official Listing of Securities (Change of Competent Authority) Regulations (S.I. 1991 No. 2000) 12–043
1992 Occupational Pension Schemes (Investment of Scheme's Resources) Regulations (S.I. 1992 No. 246) 7–049
Transfer of Functions (Financial Services) Order (S.I. 1992 No. 1315)
art. 2(1)(b) 2–013
Banking Co-ordination (Second Council Directive) Regulations S.I. 1992 No. 3218) 12–018, 12–060
1993 Money Laundering Regulations (S.I. 1993 No. 1933) 24–003, 24–030, 24–031
reg. 2 24–034
reg. 4 24–031
reg. 5 .... 24–032, 24–033, 24–035, 24–037
(1) 24–038
reg. 6 24–033
regs. 7–11 24–034
reg. 7 24–035
reg. 8 24–036
reg. 9 24–037
reg. 10 24–038
reg. 11 24–039
reg. 12 ...... 24–040, 24–041
reg. 13 ...... 24–040, 24–041
reg. 14 ...... 24–040, 24–042
reg. 15 24–043
reg. 16 24–044

1994 Financial Services (Compensation of Investors) Rules .. 4–044, 4–045
1995 Occupational Pension Schemes (Equal Access to Membership) Amendment Regulations (S.I. 1995 No. 1215) 8–030
Public Offers of Securities Regulations (S.I. 1995 No. 1537) ......
12–012, 12–038, 12–063, 12–079, 12–083, 12–089
reg. 4 12–089
(1) 12–089
(2) 12–089
reg. 5 12–092
reg. 6 12–093
reg. 7 .... 12–094, 12–097
reg. 8 .... 12–065, 12–067, 12–090
(3) 12–065
reg. 9 .... 12–066, 12–067, 12–090
reg. 10 ...... 12–067, 12–091
reg. 12 12–095
reg. 14 12–103
reg. 15 12–103
reg. 16(1) 12–089
(2) 12–089
(4) 12–089
reg. 20 12–096
Sched. 1 12–065
Sched. 1 12–090
Sched. 4 12–096

lviii

Table of Rules of Supreme Court

All references are to paragraph numbers

Ord. 14 ...... 4–013, 31–060, 31–062, 31–063
Ord. 29,
  r. 1A 31–023
Ord. 85,
  reg. 2 7–002
Ord. 115,
  reg. 4 23–035

Table of Treaties and Conventions

All references are to paragraph numbers

1953 European Convention for the Protection of Human Rights and Funadamental Freedoms 31–028
    Art. 6(1) 31–039, 31–053, 31–054, 31–057

1957 E.C. Treaty (Treaty of Rome) 2–008
    Art. 59 2–010
    Art. 86 13–004
    Art. 119 ...... 8–025, 8–026, 8–027, 8–028, 8–029

Table of E.C. Directives

All references are to paragraph numbers
Directives are arranged in Chronological order

E.C. Directive 73/239 10–001
Second EEC Directive (77/91) [1977] O.J. L26/1 21–044
Admissions Directive (79/279); [1979] O.J. L66/21 12–007
    Art. 15 .... 12–088, 12–037
Sixth Council Directive on Company Law Harmonisation (80/390); [1980] O.J. L1001/1 .... 12–007, 12–063
Interim Reports Directive (82/121) [1982] O.J. L48/26 12–007
Equal Treatment Directive (86/378) 8–025
E.C. Prospectus Directive 89/298; [1989] O.J. L124/8 ..... 12–079, 20–006, 20–007, 20–016, 20–018
    Art. 1 20–076
Second Banking Co-ordination Directive (89/646) [1989] O.J. L386/1 14–053
E.C. Money Laundering Directive (91/308) [1991] O.J. L166 .... 24–002, 24–008
Capital Adequacy Directive (CAD) 93/6/EEC .. 2–009, 3–017
Investment Services Directive (ISD) 93/22/EEC .. 2–009, 3–017

Part 1

Introduction

Chapter 1

Investor Protection in Context

Before embarking upon a study of the way in which the interests of an investor are protected by the law, it is necessary to ask one or two preliminary questions. Who is an investor, and what is an investment? Like so many questions in the discipline of law, the questions are easier to ask than answer. In this chapter the different attempts to reach a comprehensive definition of these terms are explored. As a working definition, this book proceeds upon the basis that an investor is a person who uses money for the purchase of some species of property from which interest or profit is expected. In the second part of this chapter, consideration is given to the way in which investor interests have come to be recognised in law. 1–001

1–002

Definition of an Investor

Definitions in the Courts

In *Inland Revenue Commissioners v. Rolls Royce Ltd* [1944] 2 All E.R. 340, Macnaghten J. offered a general definition in the following terms: 1–003

> "The word 'investment', though it primarily means the act of investing, is in common use as meaning that which is thereby acquired; and the meaning of the verb 'to invest' is to lay out money in the acquisition of some species of property."

That said, the courts have been reluctant to qualify the definition of an investment by reference to the nature of property which is acquired. For as Lord Greene MR noted two years later in *Inland Revenue Commissioners v. Desoutter Brothers* [1946] 1 All E.R. 58: 1–004

> "the question whether or not a particular piece of income received from an investment must, in my view, be decided on the facts of the case . . . [Investment] is not a word of art but has to be interpreted in a popular sense".

There are two problems with a qualified definition of an investment. First, there are too many different species of property in English law. Any attempt to define the meaning of an investment by reference to the 1–005 nature of the property acquired would be unworkable. Secondly, the purpose for which property is acquired may be quite different. One man's investment may be another man's indulgence. One man may purchase diamonds to leave in his Bank Security Box for the benefit of his grandchildren in 50 years time. Another man might purchase the same diamonds to use in his wife's eternity ring, with no intention of investment in mind. Also, the prevailing state of the economy can affect the motive with which a particular type of property is acquired. When considering the scope of an investment clause in a deed of trust, Lawrence J. in *Re Wragge* [1919] 2 Ch. 58 noted that "the expression 'investing in house property' is one which every lawyer must frequently have heard, and who could doubt that in such a case the house property purchased is properly described as 'an investment' ". There are few lawyers today who would not entertain such doubts!

Tax legislation

1–006   There have been many cases in which the meaning of "investment income" has been discussed within the context of the tax legislation, but following the abolition of the surcharge on investment income as from 1984/1985, the distinction between earned and investment income is relevant only in relatively few situations. The juristic task of attempting to find a definition of an investment is not advanced by a consideration of the old cases on this point.

Construction of Deeds of Trust

1–007   The law reports contain a number of reported cases in which the courts have considered the meaning of an investment within the confines of an investment clause in a deed of trust. Each case turns on the particular language which was used by the trust draftsman, and the unhelpful nature of these cases can be demonstrated by a consideration of the decision in *Re Price* [1905] 2 Ch. 55, where Farwell J. held that the phrase "pecuniary investments" did not include money placed on deposit at a bank. According to the judge:

> "the money that is deposited with a man's banker is money that awaits investment—it is not, in fact, already invested. Whether or not it produces interest by being put on deposit account is immaterial".

The financial world has advanced significantly since this case was decided.

The Financial Services Act 1986

1–008   A glimpse at Schedule 1, Part 1 to the Financial Services Act 1986 reveals the variety of investments which were identified by Parliament as constituting investments for the purposes of that legislation. The provisions of the Financial Services Act 1986 are considered in Part 2 of this book at some length. Suffice it to note here that instead of defining the scope of investment generically, Parliament chose to list 11 different species of investment in the Schedule.

The Dictionary Definition

The word "invest" derives from the Latin verb *"investire"*, which **1–009** means to clothe or adorn, in the sense that powers may be invested in a body, or a person may be invested with the insignia of office. A secondary meaning which developed in the use of the English language bore a financial connotation, and the Oxford Shorter English Dictionary notes that by 1613 the verb "to invest" was used to indicate the employment of money from which interest or profit is expected. This secondary meaning presents an appropriate working definition for the purposes of this book. The obtaining of interest or profit is the defining characteristic of an investor.

Recognition of Investor Interests

Sources of Law

Having identified a working definition of an investor, the next **1–010** question to consider is this: are the interests of investors recognised in English law? The answer, again, is not susceptible to a simple statement. Essentially, English law recognises investor interests in four principal ways.

Civil Law

The interests of an investor are recognised in the application of civil **1–011** law which governs the particular arrangement into which the investor has entered. So, for example, if an investor has purchased shares in a company, his rights and obligations will be governed by principles of company law. If the investment involves the deposit of funds in a bank account, the rights and obligations of the parties will be determined by the law of contract. If an investor has purchased property, his landowning interests will be determined by the law of property, etc.

Statutory Systems of Regulation

In some cases the interests of an investor are recognised in specific **1–012** Acts of Parliament which have been passed to regulate the provision of investment services in different areas. The Financial Services Act 1986 is a primary example, since this Act was passed to regulate the conduct

CHAPTER 1: INVESTOR PROTECTION IN CONTEXT

of investment business. There are a number of Acts of Parliament which regulate other spheres of commercial activity and impinge on the interests of an investor who has used his money to purchase some species of property from which interest or profit is expected. Examples of this type of legislation are the Banking Act 1987 and the Buildings Societies Act 1986.

1–013   It is important to stress that, in contrast to the first way in which investor interests may be protected, Acts of Parliament tend to be directed at the regulation of investment dealings and not the rights and obligations of the particular investment arrangement which continue to be determined by the incidence of the general law.

Non-statutory Systems of Regulation

1–014   Investor interests may be recognised under systems of self-regulation. The Panel on Take-overs and Mergers is a classic example of a truly self-regulatory system, because unlike the bodies set up under the auspices of the Financial Services Act 1986 which embody a large element of self-regulation, the powers of the Panel are derived exclusively from the voluntary arrangement made between the people who agreed to be bound by a code of conduct of their own devising—*R. v. Panel on Take-overs and Mergers, ex p. Datafin* [1987] 1 All E.R. 564.

Criminal Law

1–015   English law also recognises investor interests through the mechanism of the criminal law. In addition to the creation of various criminal offences to support prohibitions which have been included in Acts of Parliament passed to regulate commercial dealings in a particular area, for example section 3 of the Financial Services Act 1986 which makes it a criminal offence for an unauthorised person to conduct investment business, the criminal law can operate more generally to protect the interests of an investor. Unauthorised movement of funds from a company's bank account may, if undertaken dishonestly, amount to an offence of theft contrary to section 1 of the Theft Act 1968. Also, on occasions Parliament has created criminal offences directed at the protection of investors' interests which stand independently from any regulatory system. The legislation which criminalises insider dealing comes to mind. Additionally, there are an array of criminal offences not drafted specifically with the investor in mind which may be utilised in cases in the investment context, where the unfortunate investor stands as a victim of a fraud.

1–016   The problems encountered in the prosecution of investor fraud cases often reflects the practical problems of prosecuting serious fraud as much as some deficiency in the criminal law. For instance, it is not uncommon for prosecutors to meet investor witnesses who, having lost money in some investment swindle, are reluctant to testify against the perpetrators because the invested funds had been concealed from the attentions of the Inland Revenue in the first place!

1-017 It follows, therefore, that English law does recognise investor interests. There are legal provisions directed at the protection of these interests, but for a variety of different reasons these provisions are diverse and can be found only on a consideration of disparate areas of substantive law and in an eclectic collection of Acts of Parliament passed since the Second World War. There is no generic, coherent code of investor protection law. The relevant law has developed slowly, without the benefit of any grand overview, and above all, the development has been responsive to advances made in the investment sector.

Re-active Recognition of Investor Interests

1-018 By definition the legal system is re-active and not pro-active, and traditionally there is lengthy delay before the legal system responds to changes and innovations in commercial activity. This is certainly true in the field of investor protection. A consideration of legal developments in the field of property investment well demonstrates the point.

1-019 In the eighteenth and nineteenth centuries an investor who purchased property invariably would have done so without assistance from any third party. Investor protection was rooted in the rights and incidents of property ownership. As Milsom noted in *The Historical Foundations of the Common Law* (1969), from the earliest settlements until the industrial revolution the economic basis of society was agrarian. Land was wealth, livelihood, family provision, and the principal subject matter of the law. "Lordship was property, the object of legal protection from above, just as it was the source of legal protection for rights below" (p. 88).

1-020 Complications started to occur when other investors sought to join an investment proposition. Lordship, to use Milsom's word (derived from the Latin *dominium*), was difficult to divide. Where property was purchased in the name of more than one person, under the provisions of the Law of Property Act 1925 the law deemed that the owners held the property as joint tenants in law. Severance of joint tenancies into tenancies in common, whereby the equitable interests of each owner could be identified, was a cumbersome procedure, and there were obvious problems where one or more of the co-owners wished to realise his investment in the property. The concept of joint ownership in law was not easily adapted to multiple ownership of property in the investment sector. In recent times, following the heady days of property market boom in the 1970s and 1980s, the value of "blue-chip" property increased beyond the reach of the non-institutional investor. Even large pension funds thought twice before committing substantial funds to the purchase of a large single building in the City of London.

1-021 It was against this background that the financial services sector sought to create mechanisms which would enable investors to acquire a part interest in a single property, and to be able to trade the part interest separately on a secondary property market. Various complicated mechanisms were devised, such as the Single Asset Property Company ("SAPCOs"), Single Property Ownership Trust ("SPOTs"), and Property Income Certificates ("PINCs"). For a number of reasons PINCs appeared to be the most attractive vehicle for investors. The scheme involved the establishment of a specially formed vehicle company, the granting of a headlease and an underlease, and the issue of certificates which would be similar to bonds. Under the proposed scheme the investor would be afforded two principal rights—the right to receive income and rents from an intermediary, and the right to receive shares in a vehicle company.

1–022 In the event, due to the recession in investment property values, the scheme did not catch the imagination of the investing public. In legal terms, this was probably just as well. Whilst the Financial Services Act 1986 and delegated legislation made under that Act permitted this sort of investment mechanism to be regulated as a collective investment scheme in certain cases, there was some doubt as to the precise status of the scheme. To take just one issue, the Financial Services Act does not apply where the participant carries on a non-investment business and enters into the arrangement for commercial purposes relating to that business. In what circumstances would a participant who is entering a property transaction for the first time or is merely a landowner be deemed to be carrying on non-investment business? This sort of question, together with clarification of the rights and obligations of the investor, would fall to be determined by the courts with reference to the provisions of the Financial Services Act 1986 and the application of existing principles of company law, land law and the law of contract, to which this investment device would have been completely unknown.

1–023 Thus, the courts must respond to developments in the financial services sector but inevitably protection of investor's interests falls to be considered *ex post facto*, in this discursive and piecemeal way.

The European Influence

1–024 The influence of the European Community should not be overlooked as a catalyst in the development of the law in this area. The emphasis of the Community has focused on the need for harmonisation, but not by the imposition of a single set of rules which would be directly applicable throughout the Community. Rather, the Community has endeavoured to promote harmonisation by mutual recognition of domestic systems of regulation, particularly with regard to company law, banking and investment services. Reference to the role and influence of the European Community will be made at various stages in this book.

Striking a Balance

1–025 Protection of investors' interests has to be balanced against the needs and demands of the financial markets. The market place is essentially pragmatic, and whilst the protection of investors' interests are paramount, the realities of commercial life must not be eclipsed. As Professor Gower wrote in his *Discussion Document on Investor Protection:*

"it would be lamentable if our regulations were so strict in comparison with those of other countries that London ceases to be the world's centre for financial services as it still is. If the constraints imposed here are unduly severe, market makers will move elsewhere" (at para 7.01).

Concern for the protection of investors' interests has to be balanced against the need to maintain international competitiveness. There was considerable turbulence generated by the voluminous rule books which were created by the self regulatory organisations (SROs) recognised under the Financial Services Act 1986, as investment businesses contended that the extent of regulation was overburdensome. The Securities and Investments Board subsequently promulgated a series of principles (known as the Ten Commandments) and 40 core rules in an effort to simplify the regulatory requirements and focus on the critical areas of attention. **1–026**

Part 2

The Financial Services Act 1986

Chapter 2

An Overview

In the mid-1980s the Financial Services Act 1986 became the focal point of investor protection legislation in the United Kingdom. Although other statutes had been passed by Parliament to regulate certain fields of commercial activity, consideration of the 1986 Act is central to an understanding of United Kingdom investment regulation. For this reason the application of the Financial Services Act 1986 is considered in some detail in the first four chapters of this book. An overview of the Act is set out in this chapter. The following chapter, Chapter 3, contains an examination of the way in which the Act operates in practice, and in the last chapter on the Act, Chapter 4, enforcement and sanctions are considered. Regulation of the sale and administration of personal pensions has particular significance in the investment context since, apart from the purchase of a house, this will almost certainly represent the largest investment which an average investor will make during the course of his life. Regulation of personal, non-occupational, pensions within the framework of the Financial Services Act 1986 is considered in Chapter 5, and in the next chapter, Chapter 6, regulation of occupational pensions under the Pensions Act 1995 is examined. 2–001

Background

The first attempt at regulation in the City was in 1697 when an Act was passed requiring those who worked in the City of London, who were engaged in dealings in Government securities and the shares or stock of companies, to be licensed annually by the Court of the Alderman of the City. The licensed brokers were required to take an oath to transact business honestly and without fraud. However this effort at regulation lapsed early in the eighteenth century. 2–002

Further efforts towards market regulation were not attempted until the middle of the nineteenth century with the passage of a series of Company's Acts concerning the setting up and running of limited companies. The pace of company legislation increased as time went on and this was the main source of what little regulation of the investments markets there was before the enactment of the Financial Services Act. 2–003

Prevention of Fraud (Investments) Act

The only exception to this general laissez-faire approach to regulation was the Prevention of Fraud (Investments) Act 1939 which was the first major piece of legislation in the United Kingdom concerned specifically 2–004 with the protection of the interests of the individual investor. The 1939 Act was concerned with regulating unit trusts and introducing a system of licensing and regulating individuals, firms and companies carrying on the business of dealing in securities. Unlicensed dealing became a criminal offence under the 1939 Act as did distributing circulars containing information or invitations calculated to induce investment through a unit trust. Under the Act the Board of Trade (later the Department of Trade and Industry) issued Conduct of Business Rules for licensed dealers in securities. These rules were periodically updated, the last time being in 1983, but they were of limited application.

2–005 The Prevention of Fraud (Investments) Act 1958 was a consolidating Act which amended the 1939 Act and included various provisions of the Companies Acts 1947 and 1948. Under this Act the Board of Trade was given the power to appoint inspectors to investigate the administration of unit trusts. The 1958 Act remained in force (as amended by the Protection of Depositors Act 1963) until the Financial Services Act 1986 came into force on April 29, 1988. However, the Prevention of Fraud (Investments) Acts were of very limited scope in practice, regulating only a fraction of investment business, by imposing criminal sanctions on those who, as principals or agents, dealt in securities without being duly licensed. The limitations of the Act were clearly demonstrated in the case of *Hughes and others v. Asset Manager plc* [1995] 3 All E.R. 669. The appellants had brought an action for summary judgment to recover losses of nearly £1 million arising out of the purchase of shares through various investment management agreements by Asset Manager plc. The appellants argued that the agreements were a nullity because, although the respondent company had been licensed under the Prevention of Fraud (Investments) Act 1958, the individual who had signed the agreements on behalf of the respondent had not. The Court of Appeal held that the purpose of the Act was to protect the investing public by imposing criminal sanctions on those who dealt in securities without being licensed and that there was nothing in the Act which rendered deals done by the unlicensed ineffective or a nullity.

2–006 In the last decade, the City's financial markets and the investment industry has undergone a period of rapid and far-reaching change triggered by "Big Bang" on October 27, 1986 and by the increasing internationalisation of the financial markets. In the 1980s there was a growing appreciation of the need for comprehensive regulation of investment business following a number of financial scandals. Professor L. C. B. Gower was commissioned by the Government to undertake a review intended to consider and advise upon what statutory protection was required by both private and business investors, and on the need for statutory control of dealers in securities, investment consultants and investment managers. In January 1984, Professor Gower's report the *Review of Investor Protection: Report, Part 1* (Cmnd. 9125) was published. The report recommended that the Prevention of Fraud (Investments) Act be replaced by a new Investor Protection Act providing a system of statute backed self regulation subject to the supervision of a government agency.

In response to Professor Gower's recommendations the government 2–007
published a white paper—*Financial Services in the United Kingdom: A new framework for investor protection* (Cmnd. 9432) which set out the Government's proposals for legislation on financial services in the United Kingdom. This eventually took shape as the Financial Services Act 1986.

Europe

In his report, Professor Gower was conscious of the need to balance 2–008 regulation of the domestic financial services market and the need to protect United Kingdom investors from concerns based in foreign jurisdictions without the same degree of regulation, with the United Kingdom's obligations under the Treaty of Rome to allow freedom of establishment and the supply of services by concerns based in other Member States. Professor Gower recommended that legislation should empower the Secretary of State to recognise that firms established in countries which have comparable controls should be treated as complying with the United Kingdom investment law.

It has long been the intention of the European Union that there 2–009 should be harmonisation of the regulation of financial services across Europe, to be achieved by the implementation in domestic law of European Union Directives. A major step towards this has been the European Union Directive on investment services in the securities field (ISD) 93/22/EEC which was due to implemented on January 1, 1996. Also intended to be implemented on January 1, 1996 was the European Union Directive on capital adequacy requirements for investment firms and credit institutions (CAD) 93/6/EEC.

The principle of freedom of establishment in the context of the 2–010 financial services markets was considered by the European Court in *Alpine Investments BV v. Minister van Financien* [1995] All E.R. (E.C.) 543. The European Court was asked to decide whether Netherlands law regulating financial services, which restricted the cold calling of customers both in Holland and other European Union Member States constituted a restriction of the freedom to provide services within the meaning of Article 59 of the EEC Treaty. The European Court held that investor confidence and the maintenance of the good reputation of the national financial sector could constitute an imperative reason of public interest capable of justifying restrictions on the freedom to provide financial services. In particular, the court held that the smooth operation of financial markets was largely contingent on the confidence they inspired in investors. That confidence depended in particular on the existence of professional regulation serving to ensure the competence and trustworthiness of the financial intermediaries on whom investors were particularly reliant.

CHAPTER 2: AN OVERVIEW

Framework

2–011 The Financial Services Act 1986 came into force on April 29, 1988 and brought about a major restructuring of the way in which investment services are regulated. It introduced a framework for the conduct of investment business through a system of self regulation. Since the regulatory system was put in place it has been the subject of frequent and continuing amendment.

2–012 The Financial Services Act regime covers all those "carrying on investment business in the United Kingdom" and also extends to certain managers of occupational pension schemes. Any person carrying on investment business (or purporting so to do) must be either authorised or exempted from authorisation—see section 3. The Financial Services Act, s.4, makes it a criminal offence to carry on an investment business without being authorised.

2–013 When the Act first came into force the Secretary of State for Trade and Industry had overall supervision of the regulatory scheme. These powers have been transferred to the Treasury (see—Transfer of Functions (Financial Services) Order 1992 (S.I. 1992 No. 1315), Art. 2(1)(b)). In practice, the majority of the functions of the Secretary of State had been delegated to the Securities and Investments Board (the "SIB")—see the Financial Services Act 1986 (Delegation) Order 1987 (S.I. 1987 No. 942). The SIB co-ordinates and monitors the regulatory system as a whole. It is empowered to prosecute unauthorised investment business. It recognises and oversees the Self Regulatory Organisations, membership of which confers authorisation to conduct investment business under the Financial Services Act 1986. An alternative route to authorisation is membership of one of the Recognised Professional Bodies. A list of these bodies is set out in Appendix 1.

2–014 The SIB is funded by fees levied on the financial services industry. There are three aspects to the SIBs role, first, recognising and supervising the SROs, secondly, direct intervention in serious cases and thirdly, ensuring that there are satisfactory rules with which their members must comply.

Key Statutory Concepts Within the Financial Services Act

2–015 The regulatory system introduced by the Financial Services Act is based on certain key concepts which are defined by the Act in Schedule I which is reproduced in its entirety in Appendix 2. In the following paragraphs we offer a summary of its main provisions.

Investments

2–016 An investment is defined as any asset, right or interest falling within Part 1 of Schedule 1. It includes shares and stocks in the share capital of a company, debentures, government and public securities, instruments entitling the holder to shares or securities, *i.e.* warrants, certificates representing securities, units in collective investment schemes including unit trusts, options, futures, contracts for differences, long-term insurance contracts, and rights and interests in investments other than occupational pension schemes.

The definition of an investment offered by the Act is not exhaustive and much will depend on the particular circumstances of the case as to whether any given transaction will amount to an investment within the Act. An example of a situation where the courts have construed a transaction as an investment where the transaction in question would on the face of it appear to be anything but an investment is the case of *City Index v. Leslie* [1991] 3 W.L.R. 207; [1991] 3 All E.R. 180. This was the first case involving the interpretation of the term "investment" under the Financial Services Act 1986. City Index Ltd was a member of the Association of Futures Brokers and Dealers and a licensed bookmaker. The business of City Index was index betting. Mr Leslie placed a number of bets with City Index running up a debt of £43,080 of which he was unable to pay £34,580. City Index sued him for this amount. It was argued in Mr Leslie's defence that the sum was not recoverable by virtue of the Gaming Acts 1845 and 1892. City Index argued that the Gaming Acts did not apply in this case by virtue of section 63 of the Financial Services Act 1986, because the transactions fell within the meaning of buying and selling investments in paragraph 12 of Schedule 1. It was argued that this transaction was an investment in that it was either "a contract for differences" or "any other contract" within the meaning of section 1(1) of the Financial Services Act 1986 and Schedule 1, paragraph 9. The Court of Appeal held that the transactions were indeed investments within the meaning of paragraph 9 of Schedule 1. Lord Donaldson held that they fell within the meaning of "any other contract the purpose or pretended purpose of which is to secure a profit or avoid a loss". Whereas Lord Justice McCowan and Lord Justice Legatt held that the transactions were "contracts for differences". 2–017

Investment business

The Financial Services Act 1986, s.1(2) defines "investment business" as the business of engaging in one or more of the activities which fall within Part II of Schedule 1 and which are not excluded by Part III. 2–018

Paragraph 12 of Part II states that investment business includes dealing in investments by buying, selling, subscribing for or underwriting investments or offering or agreeing to do so, either as principal or agent. 2–019

Under paragraph 13, investment business also includes arranging deals in investments with a view to another person buying, selling, subscribing for or underwriting investments. Paragraph 13 covers arrangements in relation to particular investments and also persons who participate in the arrangements dealing in investments (*i.e.* not a particular investment) such as computerised deal-matching services. Whether this paragraph includes a person who merely introduces a potential investor to an 2–020

CHAPTER 2: AN OVERVIEW

investment business is likely to depend on the particular facts of each case.

Paragraph 14 includes managing or agreeing to manage, assets belonging to another person if those assets consist of or include investments but does not include managing another person's cash.

2-021 Paragraph 15 includes advising on investments by giving or agreeing to give, to persons in their capacity as investors or potential investors advice on the merits of their purchasing, selling, subscribing for or underwriting an investment or exercising any right conferred by an investment to acquire, dispose of, underwrite or convert an investment. Merely giving advice about where to obtain investment advice would not fall within this paragraph.

In addition, establishing collective investment schemes including unit trusts are included by paragraph 16 as investment activities.

Excluded Activities

2-022 Part III sets out activities which are excluded from being investment business these include:

2-023 Dealings as a principal—paragraph 17 contains two exclusions for own account dealings, the purpose of the paragraph is, essentially, to take out of "investment business" activities which would otherwise fall with paragraph 12 as being investment business, but which are done by the person concerned for his own account rather than for clients and customers.

2-024 Paragraph 18 creates a series of exclusions for transactions between bodies corporate within the same group or where the participators are involved in, or propose to become involved in, a joint venture.

2-025 Paragraph 19 provides an exclusion where the main purpose of the supplier is the sale of goods or supply of services and is not to engage in activities which would fall within the definition of activities constituting investment business. The exclusion covers various activities concerned with financing the sale of goods or services.

2-026 Other exclusions are supplied in respect of employee's share schemes, (para. 20), the sale of bodies corporate (para. 21), the activities of trustees and personal representatives (para. 22), dealings in the course of non-investment business which is designed to exclude certain corporate treasury functions of non-investment businesses (para. 23), advice given in the course of a profession or non-investment business where the advice given is a necessary part of other advice or services given in the course of that profession or business (para. 24), advice given in a newspaper, journal, magazine or other periodical publication (para. 25), advice given in television, sound or teletext services (para. 25A), and activities which amount to arranging deals in investments under paragraph 13, where the activity is engaged in for the purposes of carrying out the functions of a body which is approved as an International Securities Self-Regulating Organisation (para. 25B).

2-027 Part IV of Schedule 1 provides additional exclusions for persons without a permanent place of business in the United Kingdom. These exclusions do not affect the meaning of investment business but are merely exclusions from the requirement for authorisation or exemption for "overseas persons" who do not carry on investment business from a permanent place of business in the United Kingdom. The exclusion applies to transactions carried out with or through an authorised or exempted person. In addition, an overseas person does not need authorisation for certain unsolicited or legitimately solicited transactions with or for other persons.

Carrying on Investment Business

Section 1 (3) states that a person carries on an investment business in the United Kingdom if he: **2–028**

"(a) carries on investment business from a permanent place of business maintained by him in the United Kingdom; or
(b) engages in the United Kingdom in one or more of the activities which fall within the paragraphs of Part II of Schedule 1 and are not excluded by Parts III or IV of Schedule 1 and his doing so constitutes the carrying on by him of a business in the United Kingdom."

The scope of what amounted to investment business was considered in the case of *R. v. Secretary of State for Trade and Industry, ex p. R.* [1989] 1 W.L.R. 372. In that case the question of whether definitions under the Financial Services Act 1986 could apply to activities which took place before the Act came into force was considered. Under section 105 of the Financial Services Act 1986 the Secretary of State has the power to require any person to produce specified documents which relate to any matter relevant to an investigation being carried out into the affairs of a person carrying on any investment business. Such a request was made of the applicant for specified documents which related to business activities of the applicant before the section 105 came into force on December 18, 1986. The applicant resisted the request arguing that activities which took place prior to December 18, 1986 could not amount to investment business within the meaning of the Financial Services Act 1986 and also, that the Act could not be retrospective in its application. It was held that the Act did not cover pre-December 1986 business and could not be applied retrospectively to transactions which were over and done with before the Act came into force. **2–029**

Exemptions

Anyone carrying on (or purporting to carry on) an investment business must be authorised to do so under the Act unless that person is exempt. Part IV of the Act lists those persons who are exempt from the requirement to be authorised under the Act. The Secretary of State has the power to extend or restrict the list of exemptions (s.46). **2–030**
Persons exempted include:

— the Bank of England (s.35).

CHAPTER 2: AN OVERVIEW

— recognised investment exchanges (ss.36, 37 and 41). The United Kingdom investment exchanges are listed in Appendix 1. Schedule 4 to the Act sets out the requirements for the recognition of investment exchanges, including proper financial resources, that the rules and practices of the exchange ensure that business is conducted in an orderly manner and so as to afford proper protection to investors, the exchange must have proper monitoring and enforcement provisions, it must have a proper procedure for the investigation of complaints and must be willing to promote and maintain high standards of integrity and fair dealing in the carrying on of investment business and be prepared to co-operate with other bodies responsible for the supervision or regulation of investment business or other financial services.

— clearing houses (ss.38, 39 and 41).

— overseas investment exchanges and clearing houses that satisfy the requirements of section 40.

2–031 — Lloyd's and persons permitted by the Council of Lloyd's to act as underwriting agents are exempted persons in respect of investment business carry out in connection with the insurance business (s.42).

— listed money market institutions (s.43 and Sched. 5) *i.e.* one listed by the Bank of England as a "listed institution".

— appointed representatives (s.44)—are those employed by an authorised person (principal) under a contract of service which requires or permits him to carry on investment business for which his principal has accepted responsibility in writing. Essentially an appointed representative is brought within the scope of his principal's authorisation.

— section 45 contains a list of various other persons who are exempt from requiring authorisation including various court officials, the Central Board of Finance of the Church of England, an official receiver appointed under section 399 of the Insolvency Act 1986 and a trustee in bankruptcy or liquidator of an authorised person.

Life Insurance

2–032 The investment business provisions of Part I of the Act are adapted for regulated insurance companies by virtue of section 129 and Schedule 10 to the Act. A regulated insurance company is one to which Part II of the Insurance Companies Act 1982 applies and is broadly defined as "all insurance companies, whether established within or outside the United Kingdom, which carry on insurance business within the United Kingdom" (section 15 of the Insurance Companies Act 1982). Certain members of Lloyd's and registered friendly societies are exceptions to this. This is considered in further detail in Chapter 10.

Section 130 sets out certain restrictions on the promotion of contracts 2–033
of insurance, section 131 concerns contracts made after contravention of
section 130 and section 132 is concerned with insurance contracts
effected in contravention of section 2 of the Insurance Companies Act
1982. Section 133 concerns the making of misleading statements as to
insurance contracts, section 138 concerns the interaction between
authorisation under the Financial Services Act 1986 and applications for
registration or enrolment under section 8 of the Insurance (Registration)
Act 1977.

Collective Investment Schemes

Collective investment schemes are covered by Part VIII of the 2–034
Financial Services Act 1986. Collective investment schemes are defined
by section 75 as:

"any arrangements with respect to property of any description
including money, the purpose of which is to enable persons taking
part in the arrangements to participate in or receive profits or income
arising from the acquisition, holding, management or disposal of the
property or sums paid out of such profits or income."

The participants in the scheme must not have day-to-day control over 2–035
the management of the property and the arrangements must have either
or both of the following characteristics; the contributions of the participants and the profits or income are pooled; and/or the property in
question is managed as a whole by or on behalf of the operator of the
scheme. The promotion of collective investment schemes is covered by
section 76.

Unit Trusts and Investment Trusts

Sections 77 to 95 of the Financial Services Act 1986 contain the 2–036
provisions relating to unit trust schemes. A unit trust scheme must be
authorised. Section 77 concerns applications for authorisation which
must be made by the manager or trustee or the proposed manager or
trustee of the scheme who must be different persons. The procedure for
application is set out in sections 77(2) to (5). The SIB may then make an
order declaring a unit trust scheme to be an authorised unit trust
scheme (s.78). For a scheme to be authorised it must comply with the
requirements of constitution and management regulations made under
section 81, a copy of the trust deed must be furnished together with a
certificate that the scheme complies with the constitution and management relating to its contents. Further, the manager and trustee must
each be a United Kingdom or European Union Member State registered
body corporate, with its affairs administered in the United Kingdom. If
it is an European Union company, it must not come within the
requirements for automatic recognition as an European Union scheme.

CHAPTER 2: AN OVERVIEW

(The recognition of overseas schemes is covered in ss.86 to 90.) The manager and trustee must each be authorised persons, the name of the scheme must not be misleading or undesirable and the purpose of the scheme must have a reasonable prospect of being successfully carried into effect. The participants in the scheme must be entitled to have their units redeemed at a price related to the net value of the property to which the units relate or be able to sell units on an investment exchange at a price not significantly different from that price.

2–037 Authorisation of a scheme may be revoked if the requirements for authorisation are no-longer being met, or where continuation of the scheme is undesirable for the participants, or where the manager or trustee has committed regulatory infringements—see section 79. The SIB is empowered to make regulations as to the constitution and management of authorised unit trust schemes—see section 81. The powers of intervention and investigation in unit trust schemes are more limited than those for other companies and are contained in sections 91 to 95.

Promotion and Advertising Restrictions

2–038 Parliament supported the machinery for the regulation of investment business by introducing a number of restrictions on the promotion and advertising of financial services. These provisions are contained in sections 56 to 58 of the Financial Services Act 1986. Additionally, a criminal offence of making misleading statements is contained in section 47 of the Act. Reference should be made to Chapter 24 (market manipulation) for consideration of this provision.

Advertising

2–039 The restrictions on advertising are contained in section 57 of the Financial Services Act 1986 and provide that no person other than an authorised person shall issue or cause to be issued an investment advertisement in the United Kingdom unless its contents have been approved by an authorised person. "An investment advertisement" is an advertisement inviting persons to enter into an investment agreement or to exercise any rights conferred by an investment (s.57(2)). Contravention of section 57 is an offence triable either way and punishable by a maximum of two years' imprisonment and/or an unlimited fine if convicted in the Crown Court and six months' imprisonment and/or a fine not exceeding £5,000 if convicted in the magistrates' court (s.57(3)). It is a defence if a person in the ordinary course of business other than investment business issues an advertisement to the order of another person if he proves that he believed on reasonable grounds that the person to whose order the advertisement was issued was an authorised person, that the contents of the advertisement were approved by an authorised person or that the advertisement was permitted under section 58 (s.57(4)).

2-040 If an advertisement in contravention of section 57 is issued, the person issuing or causing the advertisement to be issued cannot enforce an agreement to which the advertisement related and the other party is entitled to recover any money or property transferred by him under the agreement (s.57(5) and (6)). If the property has passed to a third party, it is the value of the property at the time of the transfer that is recoverable (s.57(10)).

2-041 A court may allow an agreement entered into to be enforced where it is satisfied that the person against whom enforcement is sought was not influenced to any material extent by the advertisement or that the advertisement was not misleading as to the nature of the investment, the terms of the agreement or the consequences of exercising investment rights (s.57(9)).

2-042 Section 58 sets out a number of exceptions from restrictions on advertising: section 57 does not apply to any advertisement issued by government, a local authority, the Bank of England or any other central bank or any international organisation the members of which include the United Kingdom or another Member State of the European Union. The restrictions do not apply to advertisements issued by exempted persons in respect of matters for which he is exempt. These include recognised investment exchanges, clearing houses, Lloyd's, listed money market institutions, appointed representatives and those falling within the miscellaneous exemptions of section 45.

2-043 Section 57 restrictions do not apply to advertisements issued by a national of an European Union Member State in respect of investment business lawfully carried on by him in a Member State, which complies with advertising requirements in that State.

2-044 Restrictions do not apply to any advertisement that falls within section 154 or consists of any part of listing particulars, supplementary listing particulars or other document required or permitted to be published under Part IV of the Financial Services Act 1986 or by an approved exchange under Part V of the Financial Services Act 1986. Section 57 does not apply to an advertisement inviting persons to subscribe in cash for any investments to which Part V of Financial Services Act 1986 applies if the advertisement is issued or caused to be issued by the person by whom the investments are to be issued and the advertisement consists of a prospectus.

The Personal Investment Authority Ombudsman received one complaint in 1994/1995 concerning the breach of advertising rules out of a total of 1,500 complaints received.

Unsolicited Calls

2-045 Section 56(1) of the Financial Services Act 1986 restricts the practice of "cold calling". It is not an offence to make an unsolicited call but any investment agreement entered into by a person cold called is not enforceable against that person and that person is entitled to recover any money or property paid or transferred by him under the agreement together with any compensation for and loss sustained by him as a result of having parted with it (s.56(2)). An agreement made as a result of cold calling may be enforced if a court is satisfied that:

(i) the person to whom the call was made was not influenced to any material extent by the call; or
(ii) the person entered into the agreement following discussions over a period and was aware of the nature of the agreement and any risks involved in entering into it; or
(iii) the call was not made by the person seeking to enforce the agreement or on his behalf by an appointed representative whose principal he was.

Jurisdiction

2–046   A regulatory system, however effective, will be undermined by foreign concerns established in countries lacking comparable regulatory systems which operate in this country but whose activities are effectively outside the United Kingdom jurisdiction. Professor Gower in his 1984 Report identified this as the "off-shore problem" (at para. 1.19). Where the foreign company is based in a jurisdiction which has comparable regulatory provisions there may be little problem in practice. However, no domestic regulatory system can be effective against firms based in jurisdictions where the standards of regulation fall short of those of the United Kingdom and Europe. In the Barlow Clowes case which pre-dated the Financial Services Act 1986, the portfolios were moved from Gibraltar which had a comparable system of regulation to Switzerland which did not. Notwithstanding that the Financial Services Act 1986 is now in force, such a manoeuvre would still leave investors in the United Kingdom in a similar position as regards regulation and compensation.

2–047   Part IX of the Financial Services Act contains provisions intended to give the United Kingdom leverage in seeking access for financial services firms to foreign markets. Under Part IX there is power to disqualify or restrict a foreign connected firm from carrying out investment or insurance business in the United Kingdom if United Kingdom firms do not enjoy access to the foreign market equivalent to that which foreign firms enjoy here. The Government has been reluctant to exercise these powers.

2–048   Under the Investment Services Directive (ISD), the SFA becomes responsible for supervision of some aspects of the investment business undertaken by its members throughout the European Economic Area. Foreign establishments of authorised firms have not previously been routinely monitored by United Kingdom SROs.

Chapter 3

Implementation

In this chapter the practical application of the Financial Services Act 3-001
1986 is considered. As well as examining the provisions concerning authorisation, the main features of the regulatory regime are highlighted. There are certain rules which spell out the requirements which must be satisfied whenever an investment is made within the scope of the Financial Services Act 1986. These rules are designed to promote the interests of investor protection and regulation, and accordingly their consideration is central to an understanding of the way in which the financial services legislation operates in practice.

As we have already seen, any person who carries on or purports to 3-002
carry on investment business in the United Kingdom must be either authorised or exempted—section 3 of the Financial Services Act 1986. Persons may be authorised to carry on investment business directly by the Securities Investment Board (the "SIB") or more commonly, by virtue of membership of a recognised Self Regulatory Organisation (an "SRO") or of a Recognised Professional Body (an "RPB"). Part III of the Financial Services Act 1986 sets out the provisions relating to authorisation. The SIB has a Central Register which is a computerised database holding details of all those who are authorised to carry on investment business whether by the SIB or an SRO. Currently on the register, there are about 50,000 authorised investment firms. There is a requirement imposed on the SIB to maintain the register pursuant to section 102 of the Act and to allow inspection of the register under section 103.

Direct Authorisation

Applications for direct authorisation by SIB may be made by an 3-003
individual, a body corporate, a partnership or an unincorporated association. An application must contain information as to the investment business which the applicant proposes to carry on and the services which he will hold himself out as able to provide in the carrying on of that business (s.26). The application will be granted if, on the basis of the available information, the applicant appears to be a fit and proper person to carry on investment business (s.27(2)). If an applicant is authorised to carry on investment business in another European Union Member State, then regard must be had to that authorisation (s.27(5)). However, as a matter of policy the SIB is actively seeking to draw away from direct regulation.

CHAPTER 3: IMPLEMENTATION

3-004 Authorisation may be withdrawn or suspended if it appears that the holder of the authorisation is not a fit and proper person to carry on the investment business and/or the authorised person has not complied with any provision of the Act or any of the requirements of any rules or regulations made under the Act or in purported compliance with any such provision has furnished information which is false, misleading or inaccurate or has contravened any prohibition or requirement imposed under the Act.

Authorisation by an SRO

3-005 Membership of an SRO will confer authorisation to carry on investment business (s.7(1)).

An SRO is defined by section 8(1) of the Financial Services Act 1986 as a body which "regulates the carrying on of investment business of any kind by enforcing rules which are binding on persons carrying on business of that kind either because they are members of that body or because they are otherwise subject to its control." An SRO must be recognised by the SIB, it must fulfil statutory requirements for recognition set out in section 10 and Schedule 2 to the Financial Services Act 1986. The SRO must be under the control of a governing body responsible for enforcing the rules of the organisation. The rules and practices of the SRO must be such as to secure that its members are "fit and proper" persons to carry on investment business of the kind with which the SRO is concerned. The SRO's rules for the admission, expulsion and disciplining of its members must be sufficient. As must its rules to safeguard investors including its powers to order compliance and its rules designed to ensure that there are adequate arrangements for monitoring and enforcement of the rules, the investigation of complaints and the promotion and maintenance of standards.

3-006 In recent years there has been an attempt to simplify the whole system of regulation, by way of moves towards single rule books and a reduction in the numbers of SROs. As from October 1996 (following the completion of a transitional period) there will be three SROs under the control of the SIB. These are the Securities and Futures Authority (SFA), the Personal Investment Authority (PIA) and the Investment Management Regulatory Organisation (IMRO). The SROs are funded by the firms they supervise.

The Securities and Futures Authority

3-007 The SFA mission statement:

"To achieve a high standard of protection for investors and other market users, to be responsive and adaptive to firms' needs, to

AUTHORISATION BY AN SRO

anticipate investor needs and firms' problems, to operate by consensus and persuasion where possible, to work together, with the SIB and others to further good regulation and be perceived as professional and cost effective."

The SFA regulates a wide range of financial services including firms which deal in securities, futures, options, other derivatives and corporate finance work. By the end of 1994/1995, the SFA authorised a total of 1,336 firms and some 40,237 individual registrants. About half of the SFA's membership are United Kingdom firms the remainder are incorporated overseas notably in North America, Japan and Western Europe with branches in the United Kingdom. Individual applicants are required to pass an examination before membership is granted unless they are exempt by virtue of relevant professional experience (typically this applies to persons coming to London from overseas). 3-008

The Personal Investment Authority (PIA)

The PIA Mission Statement: 3-009

"To protect investors by the regulation and supervision of the retail investment sector, enabling investors to make properly informed decisions in an open, competitive and innovative market place."

The PIA is the main regulator of retail financial services business. The regulatory focus of the PIA is investment business carried out for private investors (except private clients of stockbrokers). It replaces the Financial Intermediaries, Managers and Brokers Regulatory Association (FIMBRA) and the Life Assurance and Unit Trust Regulatory Organisation (LAUTRO). 3-010

The types of investment business conducted by members of the PIA include: 3-011

Life insurance (including endowment policies);
Personal Pensions;
Unit Trusts;
Personal Equity Plans (PEPS);
Guaranteed Income Bonds;
Investment Trust Savings Schemes;
Offshore Funds (*e.g.* Gilt Funds and Bond Funds);
Advice on and arranging deals in shares;
Management of a Portfolio of investments;
Broker Funds;
Advice on Enterprise Investment Schemes;
Advice on arranging deals and trading options.

The Investment Management Regulatory Organisation

The IMRO Mission statement: 3-012

CHAPTER 3: IMPLEMENTATION

"To protect investors by setting and promoting standards of integrity, competence and solvency for those IMRO regulates; and to monitor and enforce those standards effectively and efficiently."

3–013 IMRO regulates firms whose main investment business is the managing of investments, the management of occupational pension schemes (OPS) assets as an OPS member of IMRO, acting as manager or trustee of authorised unit trust schemes, managing or operating other collective investment schemes and investment advice to non-private investors.

Recognised Professional Bodies

3–014 RPBs regulate those involved in professions such as solicitors, accountants and actuaries who are involved in carrying on investment business. A member of an RPB becomes an authorised person for the purposes of carrying on investment business if he holds a certificate issued by an RPB—see section 15(1) of the Financial Services Act 1986. The certificate may be issued to an individual, a body corporate, a partnership or an unincorporated association. A member of an RPB is any person who is entitled to practice the profession in question and in so doing is subject to the rules of a professional body (s.16(2)). The RPB must be recognised by the SIB before its members can enjoy authorisation under the Financial Services Act 1986 (ss.17-19 and Sched. 3). A list of RPBs is set out in Appendix 1.

Europe

3–015 The Act provides automatic authorisation for "Europersons" carrying on investment business in the United Kingdom on a services basis *i.e.* without a permanent place of business in the United Kingdom, from another European Union Member State. A "Europerson" is a person authorised under an equivalent harmonised regime in another European Union Member State (s.31). Authorisation may be terminated or suspended for contraventions of the Financial Services Act 1986 or any rules or regulations made under it or for furnishing the SIB with false, inaccurate or misleading information (s.33).

3–016 It is a criminal offence for a "Europerson" to carry on investment business in the United Kingdom unless he has given notice seven days prior to starting to operate in the United Kingdom of his intention to do so (s.32(1)). Contravention is triable either way and is punishable by a fine.

3–017 A major step towards harmonisation of financial services regulation in the European Union has been achieved by the issue of two European Union Directives on investment services in the securities field ("ISD")

93/22/EEC and the Directive on capital adequacy requirements for investment firms and credit institutions ("CAD") 93/6/EEC which came into force on January 1, 1996. However, a number of Member States have experienced difficulties in achieving this deadline. The scope of the ISD is based on the general principle of freedom of establishment which is intended to ensure that investment firms are free to set up and transact business throughout the European Union when they satisfy certain minimum conditions. Once implemented by all Member States, the ISD will confer on United Kingdom authorised firms a business "passport" into all other European Union states enabling them to transact investment business either by establishing branches in the host country or by cross-border operations. The regulation of the conduct of business will remain the responsibility of the host country supervisor but prudential supervision will rest with the home state.

The Three Tiers

In practice the regulation of investment business is governed by the "three tiers" of regulation: the SIB statement of principles, the SIB core rules and the SRO rule books. Taken together these are intended to provide "an adequate level of protection for investors", *i.e.* the adequacy test. Three factors must be considered in assessing adequacy, these are: first, the nature of the investment business carried on by members of the SRO, secondly, the kinds of investor involved (whether private or professional), and thirdly, the effectiveness of the SROs enforcement procedures. **3–018**

First Tier—SIB "Statement of Principles"

By the summer of 1988 it had become apparent that the rule books of the SIB and the SROs were so complex that those involved in the industry were having difficulty recognising the basic principles underlying the scheme of regulation. In an effort to remedy this the SIB issued 10 core principles which soon gained the name "the 10 commandments." Under section 47A of the Financial Services Act 1986, added by the Companies Act 1989, the SIB is empowered to issue "statements of principle" as to the conduct and financial standing of those authorised to carry on investment business. Section 47B of the Financial Services Act 1986 allows for the modification or waiver of any of the principles in certain circumstances. **3–019**

The statements of principle may include adherence to the code or standards issued by another person and failure to comply with such may also give rise to disciplinary action. From January 19, 1995 the SIB has required adherence to the provisions of the Takeover Code—see the Financial Services (Statement of Principles) (Endorsement of Codes and Standards) Instrument 1995. **3–020**

Chapter 3: Implementation

The SIB Statement of Principles and the requirement to adhere to the Takeover Code are reproduced in Appendix 3.

3–021 Failure to comply with a statement of principle is a ground for taking disciplinary action but does not give rise to any right of action by investors or other persons affected nor does it affect the validity of the transaction. Disciplinary action may include the withdrawal, suspension or termination of authorisation, an order of disqualification, the making of a public statement, or the application for an injunction.

Second Tier—SIB Core Rules

3–022 Sections 63A and 107A of the Financial Services Act 1986 (both inserted by the Companies Act 1989) enable the SIB to render certain "core rules" applicable to SRO members directly. The core rules apply to investment businesses whether they are directly authorised by the SIB or authorised by an SRO. Under section 63A(1) the core rules may concern only the conduct of business rules (s.48), the financial resources rules (s.49), the clients money regulations (s.55), the unsolicited calls regulations (s.56) and the auditors rules (s.107A).

3–023 The objective underlying the introduction of core rules is to encourage a uniform, across the board approach and to achieve consistency of standards between regulators. However, the SIB has the power to decide whether the core rules have a general effect or whether they may be adapted subject to the rules of an individual SRO (ss.63A(2) and 107A(2)). Under section 63B, an SRO has the power to modify or waive core rules for particular members, on the application of the member, where it appears that compliance with the core rule would be unduly burdensome on the member and modification or waiver of the rule would not result in any undue risk to investors.

The core rules, known formally as the Core Conduct of Business Rules, and the SIB Financial Supervision Rules, are reproduced in Appendix 4.

3–024 A member of an SRO who contravenes one of the core rules is treated as if he has contravened one of the rules of the SRO (s.63A(3)). It follows that breaches of the core rules will be dealt with under the disciplinary procedures of the individual SRO.

As a result of the introduction of the core rules, the SIB's powers of direct intervention to change an SRO rule book were curtailed (s.13(1) was repealed), but the SIB is left with the power under section 13(2) to intervene to alter the rules of an SRO concerning the scope of the investment business which it authorises.

It should be noted that members of RPBs are not covered by the core rules.

Codes of Practice

3–025 Section 63C enables the SIB to issue "codes of practice" to amplify the statements of principle and/or its rules and regulations. The status of such a code of practice is such that a failure to comply with the code may be evidence of failure to comply with the underlying principle. To date, the SIB has not issued such a code of practice.

Third Tier—SRO Rule Books

The relationship between an SRO and its members is a contractual one in which the members are bound to comply with the rules issued by the SRO in question. In April 1996 the PIA announced plans to require its members to sign individual contracts under which they will become personally liable for payment of fines. It is estimated that this will affect approximately 120,000 members. **3–026**

The SRO rules are critical in terms of investor protection and regulation because they spell out the requirements which must apply whenever an investment is made with an authorised person within the scope of the Financial Services Act 1986. For this reason attention is focused on certain of the core rules which are directed at the prevention of fraud and the protection of investors' interests and investors' funds. The relevant core rules in this context are the rules governing: **3–027**

— separation of client accounts and dealings with clients money;
— the suitability of investments;
— the understanding of risk;
— the customer agreement;
— advertising standards;
— financial resources and solvency.

Inevitably, because of the extensive nature of each of the SRO rule books, the examination of these core rules has been selective and is by no means exhaustive. Reference must be made to the individual SRO rule book whenever a particular problem arises. Although the overall regulatory scheme appears to be settled for the time being, the SRO rule books are subject to regular amendment. **3–028**

Separation of Client Accounts and Dealings with Client Moneys

General

In any industry where professionals deal with client's money it is essential for investor confidence and the proper operation of the industry that there should be a framework in place to prevent any **3–029**

Chapter 3: Implementation

untoward use of client's money when it is in the hands of the profession. Where a professional takes a client's money for onward transmission good practice suggests that the client's money should be kept separate from that of the business in a designated client account. In the financial services industry where a large proportion of professionals involved act as intermediaries it is essential that there are definite rules governing dealings with client moneys and the separation of client's accounts.

3-030 The SIB Statement of Principle No. 7 concerns customer assets and states:

> "Where a firm has control of or is otherwise responsible for assets belonging to a customer which it is required to safeguard, it should arrange proper protection for them, by way of segregation and identification of those assets or otherwise, in accordance with the responsibility it has accepted."

3-031 Rules governing dealings with client moneys and the separation of client accounts are contained in the Financial Services (Client Money) Regulations 1991 which apply directly to members of SROs, to persons directly authorised by the SIB and to members of the Institute of Actuaries. They do not apply to members of other RPBs or exempted persons, approved banks, insurers and friendly societies, trustees and oil market participants. The Financial Services (Client Money) Regulations 1991 apply to money held by a firm which is client money until the time when the fiduciary duty imposed by the regulations is discharged.

3-032 The regulations require that a firm must:

    (a) keep client money separate from its own money (reg. 2.12);
    (b) hold client money as a fiduciary for the client in accordance with the purpose, trust or agency arrangement established;
    (c) pay interest on client money to the client (regs 4.01-4.02);
    (d) account for the money properly (regs 4.03 to 4.08);
    (e) follow the requirements relating to audit (reg. 4.11 and 4.12).

3-033 The Financial Services (Client Money) Regulations 1991 were supplemented by the Financial Services (Client Money) (Supplementary) Regulations 1991 which apply directly to authorised persons who are members of FIMBRA, LAUTRO, directly authorised by SIB or a member of the PIA. Under these regulations a firm must open a settlement bank account where it must hold clients money which is client settlement money (reg. 2.01). These regulations deal with the client money received by firms for the settlement of shares, debentures, government and public securities, certain warrants and units in collective investment schemes.

3-034 A firm must open a margined transaction bank account to deal with money received by the firm from clients in respect of futures, options and contracts for differences under the terms of which the clients may be liable to pay further amounts of cash or collateral over and above the amount initially received by the firm (reg. 3.01).

IMRO

As designated regulations, the Financial Services (Client Money) **3–035**
Regulations 1991 have a direct statutory effect on IMRO members by
virtue of sections 55 and 63A of the Financial Services Act 1986. A
member of IMRO has a duty to comply with the regulations under the
IMRO rules—Chapter II, 5.2(1). The Financial Services (Client Money)
(Supplementary) Regulations 1991 are not designated regulations and
do not have direct statutory effect but IMRO has incorporated them into
its rules and any breach of the regulations shall be treated as a breach of
the rules—see IMRO rules, Chapter II, rule 5.2(2).

SFA

Firms regulated by the SFA are subject to the Financial Services **3–036**
(Client Money) Regulations 1991 and the Financial Services (Client
Money) (Supplementary) Regulations 1991. Chapter 4 of the SFA rules
contains the provisions in respect of safeguarding customers' investments and assets.

PIA

Firms regulated by the PIA are subject to the Financial Services **3–037**
(Client Money) Regulations 1991 and The Financial Services (Client
Money) (Supplementary) Regulations 1991 which are reproduced in
Appendix 2 to the PIA rules.

Suitability of Investment

General

The unsuitability of a particular investment for an individual investor **3–038**
has been at the heart of many past financial scandals. Breach of the
suitability and best advice rules form the basis of the majority of
complaints made to the PIA Ombudsman. In the PIA Ombudsman
Annual report for 1994/1995, 229 of the cases received were about the
suitability/breach of best advice rules out of a total of 330 cases received.
Of complaints referred to IMRO in the year to March 31, 1995 the
largest single category of complaints related to product suitability—260
complaints out of a total of 887 complaints (see IMRO Annual Report
and accounts 1994/1995). Safeguards are necessary to prevent the
unscrupulous investment advisor from recommending investments
which although unsuitable for the investor carry a greater level of
commission or some other advantage for the adviser. SIB Core Rule 16

requires that a firm must take reasonable steps to ensure that it does not in the course of regulated business or associated business make any recommendation about an investment unless the recommendation or transaction is suitable for the investor having regard to the facts disclosed by the customer and other relevant facts about the customer of which the firm is, or reasonably should be, aware. In practice a notice of risk is likely to be a standard term of any customer agreement.

IMRO

3–039　Chapter II, rule 3.1 incorporates SIB core rule 16 and also requires that IMRO members should find out such facts about a private customer's personal and financial circumstances as are relevant to ensure the suitability of investment recommendations. A firm must also review the facts about a customer's personal and financial circumstances, including any change, on which the suitability of investments are based, at least once a year.

SFA

3–040　Rule 5.31 incorporates the SIB core rule 16 on suitability and further requires that a firm which acts as an investment manager for a private customer or as a discretionary investment manager for a non-private customer must ensure that the customer's investments remain suitable.

PIA

3–041　The PIA has not yet made any rules of its own concerning the suitability of investments instead it has adopted the existing rules of IMRO (rule 3.1), FIMBRA (rule 29.5) and LAUTRO (rule 3.15).

FIMBRA rule 29.5 requires that a member recommends a specific investment or investment agreement to a client only if there are good grounds for believing it to be suitable for that client in the light of information provided by the client and any other relevant facts about the client which the member is or should be aware of. A member may only arrange an unsuitable transaction if it is an execution only transaction and where the advisor has advised the client, in writing, that the transaction is not suitable for him and despite such advice the client has instructed the member to proceed with the transaction.

3–042　LAUTRO rule 3.15 requires that a member gives written reasons for making a particular recommendation. The recommendation must be of an investment which is suitable for the client. Such a written recommendation must be signed by a representative of the member and must make it clear why the recommendation has been made having regard to the investor's financial and other circumstance of which the member is aware. Rule 3.15 applies to regular life policies, single premium life policies where all or part of the premium paid is derived from the transfer value from an occupational pension scheme, an annuity or a collective investment scheme where all or part of the sum invested is derived from the transfer value from an occupational pension scheme. The rule does not apply where an investor refuses to act upon a recommendation or where the client is a professional investor.

Understanding of Risk

General

3–043 Not only is it important that investors are sold investments which are suitable to their needs but they must also be made aware of any risks involved in making an investment. This is reflected in the wording of SIB core rule 10 which states that:

"a firm must not recommend a transaction to a private customer, or act as a discretionary manager for him, unless it has taken reasonable steps to enable him to understand the nature of the risks involved".

In practice most standard customer agreements are likely to carry a risk warning in any event.

IMRO

3–044 IMRO has incorporated SIB core rule 10 in Chapter II, rule 3.2(1). In addition, a member must give the customer risk warnings referred to in IMRO rules, Appendix 1.1: the Advertising Code in paragraphs 23 to 29 and in Appendix 2.4 which sets out the contents required in a full customer agreement in paragraphs 15, 18-2, 23, 25, 27, 30.

SFA

3–045 The SFA has incorporated SIB core rule 10 in its own rule 5.30(1). In addition, where the investor is a private customer and the intended transaction is in respect of warrants or derivatives, under rule 5.30(2) an SFA member must send an investor the Warrants and Derivatives Risk Warning Notices which are set out in Appendices 14 and 15. Certain exceptions to this requirement are set out in rule 5.30(3) and (4). Further, a firm must not recommend to a private customer a transaction in an investment which is not a readily realisable investment unless it warns him of the difficulties in establishing a proper market price and discloses any position held by the firm or and associate in the investment or a related business (see rule 5.30(5)).

PIA

3–046 The PIA has adopted the FIMBRA and LAUTRO rules concerning risk warnings. Under the FIMBRA rules, the member must provide a client with an explanation of the nature of the risks involved in the transaction in terms that the client is likely to understand. Appendix 6 of the FIMBRA rules contains a number of standard form written risk warnings for various types of investment (see rule 29.5.3).

3–047 Under the LAUTRO rules an investor must be sent a document containing the "Key Features" of the investment in accordance with LAUTRO rule 5.8 and Part 1 of Schedule 6. Included in the "Key Features" must be a heading "Risk Factors" under which must appear a brief description of the factors which may have an adverse effect on performance or which are otherwise material to the decision to invest. Certain additional warnings are set out in Part III of Schedule 6 which should be included where appropriate.

The Customer Agreement

General

3–048 The customer agreement sets out the terms on which the investor and the regulated person enter into investment business. The SIB core rule 14 provides that:

> "where a firm provides investment services to a private customer (other than an indirect customer) on written contractual terms, the agreement must set out in adequate detail the basis on which those services are provided."

In most circumstances, the expectation should be that the customer agreement will be a two-way agreement. All the SRO rules contain the requirement for proper customer agreements and set out examples of standard form customer agreements.

3–049 A customer agreement will typically contain details of the firm's membership of an SRO, the nature of the services provided by the firm, the basis on which remuneration between the customer and the firm is to be calculated and paid, the arrangements for accounting to the customer for any transaction on his behalf, how the agreement may be terminated and the consequences of termination, details of the complaints procedure and the customer's rights to compensation. A customer agreement will also contain various matters particular to the type of investment business which is being entered into.

IMRO

3–050 The content required in customer documents is set out in IMRO Chapter II, rule 2.4 and various appendices. In respect of private clients, IMRO rule 2.4(1) says that the agreement must set out in adequate detail

The Customer Agreement

the basis on which services are provided. An example of a full customer agreement for private clients is set out at Appendix 2.4(1)(a). For non-private clients, IMRO rule 2.4(2) requires that the documents provided should have regard to the standards set by IMRO for the contents of the documents. The format and presentation of customer documents must be in accordance with rule 2.4(3). Where the investment under consideration is a PEP or BES the customer agreement must contain provision for a cooling off period—rule 2.4(5).

IMRO rule 2.2(3) adopts the SIB core rule 14(2) relating to the requirement for two way customer agreements where a firm provides to a private customer investment services involving contingent liability or the discretionary management of the customer's assets. **3–051**

SFA

The SFA rules concerning customer agreements are found in Chapter 5, rules 5.23–5.28. The SFA rules adopt the SIB core rule 14 on customer agreements in SFA rule 5.23(1) and (2). The SFA rules require that two-way customer agreements must set out in adequate detail the basis on which the services are to be provided and the discretion to be exercised by the firm. Tables 5.23(4)(a) and (b) set out the required contents of two-way customer agreements. **3–052**

PIA

The rules governing customer agreements have been adopted by the PIA from the FIMBRA and LAUTRO rules. Part 15 of the FIMBRA rules sets out the standard form expected in respect of terms of business letters. The contents of a terms of business letter is set out in rule 15.2 and Table 15. The exact contents may vary depending on the category of membership of a firm. **3–053**

LAUTRO rule 5.8 sets out the key features and important information which must be included in what is called a "Key features document" which must be supplied to the investor. Schedule 6 sets out the requirements of the key features document. This document must contain details of the key features of the policy, a description of the nature of the contract including its aims, the customer's commitment and the risk factors involved and an example of how the principle terms of the contract would apply to the investor. The document must also include a description of the policy set out in the form of questions and answers and any other information necessary to enable the investor to understand the proposed investment including details of commission/remuneration and any deductions that would be made under the policy. **3–054**

CHAPTER 3: IMPLEMENTATION

Advertising Standards

General

3–055 Proper advertising standards form the front line of the regulatory system. Potential investors who are sucked into schemes offering extravagant claims in unregulated adverts will almost inevitably be disappointed. Advertising standards form an integral part of the Financial Services Act 1986 in sections 57 and 58 (see Chapter 2). The basic advertising standards expected are set out in the SIB core rule which concerns the issue and approval of advertisements. Broadly where a firm issues or approves an investment advertisement, it must apply appropriate expertise and be able to show that it believes on reasonable grounds that the advertisement is fair and not misleading.

3–056 The Financial Services Act 1986 requires that investment advertisements may only be issued by authorised persons or if its contents have been approved by an authorised person—see section 57(1). An investment advertisement is defined by section 57(2) of the Financial Services Act 1986 and is an advertisement which invites anyone to enter, or offers to enter into, an investment agreement, or to exercise any rights conferred by an investment to acquire, dispose of, underwrite or convert an investment or contains information calculated to lead, directly or indirectly to anyone doing so. An advertisement includes mailshots, circulars, catalogues, price lists, notices and signs. It may be printed, broadcast on radio or television or communicated by other means. In addition to the requirements set out in the SRO rule books, an advertisement must also comply with the British Code of Advertising Practice, the ITC Code or the Radio Authority Code where appropriate.

IMRO

3–057 IMRO has adopted the SIB core rules 5, 6 and 40.2(a) in respect of advertising in Chapter II, rule 1. The standards which a member of IMRO should consider when judging whether information contained in an advertisement is adequate and fair are contained in Appendix 1.1(1) of the The Advertising Code.

SFA

3–058 The SFA rules on advertising and marketing are contained in Chapter 5, rules 5.9–5.16. The SFA has adopted the SIB core rules on advertising and marketing. The SFA rules set out the requirements with which an advertisement must comply to be viewed as adequate and fair.

PIA

3–059 The rules governing advertising and promotion of business have been adopted by the PIA from FIMBRA and LAUTRO. The FIMBRA rules are contained in Part 18 of the FIMBRA rules. Rules 18.1 and 18.2 relate to all types of advertisement, whilst rules 18.3 to 18.15, the tables in Part 18 and Appendix 2B relate only to investment advertisements. The LAUTRO rules governing advertisements are contained in Part VI of the LAUTRO rules.

Financial Resources and Solvency

General

3–060 The purpose of financial resources and solvency rules is to minimise the risk to investors that would result from the failure of an investment firm. The requirement for adequate financial resources is set out in the SIB Statement of Principle number 8 which states: "A firm should ensure that it maintains adequate financial resources to meet its investment business commitments and to withstand the risks to which its business is subject."

3–061 This is reiterated in the SIB Financial Supervision Core Rule A which states that: "A firm must at all times have available the amount and type of financial resources required by the rules of its regulator."

3–062 Whilst the basic need for adequacy of financial resources is obvious, the third tier rules relating to financial adequacy are, inevitably, detailed and complex to deal with the wide diversity of firms and investment types that exist in the markets. The rules are designed to ensure that firms have sufficient capital to settle actual liabilities and potential future losses such as those arising from a general decline in the markets affecting income, adverse movements in the price of marketable securities, losses arising from the firms' customers or counterparties defaulting on settlement of a transaction and adverse currency exchange movements.

3–063 Regulated firms must maintain sufficient assets in liquid form to cover the various risks which may arise. These assets are the firm's "financial resources" or "qualifying capital." The calculation of financial resources depends on the rules of the regulating SRO. Risks will vary depending on the type of firm and the type of business undertaken and this is recognised by imposing differing financial resources requirements on differing categories of firms.

3–064 The monitoring of financial resources is fundamental to the proper regulation of the financial services industry and all regulated firms are required to calculate and report their financial resources to their regulator on a regular basis. Broadly, the calculation of the adequacy of a firm's financial resources depends on three things: first, the category of membership of the firm, *i.e.* whether it is a low, medium or high risk; secondly, the financial requirement itself based on set calculations (the requirement will reflect the category of the member); and thirdly, the requirement to make regular financial returns to the SRO to demonstrate that the financial adequacy requirement is continuously met. The

European Union Capital Adequacy Directive establishes minimum capital requirements which depend on the type of business undertaken by the investment firm.

3–065 The rules governing financial adequacy form a substantial part of the rules of each of the SRO's and each SRO sets out in considerable detail examples of the calculations necessary for the computation of the financial requirements.

IMRO

3–066 The financial resources rules are contained in Chapter V of its Rules. All members of IMRO are subject to its capital adequacy rules unless they fall into one of the following types:

occupational pension schemes;
life offices;
local authorities;
committees of management of exempt unauthorised unit trust schemes;
investment advisory panels;
individuals whose sole investment business is giving investment advice to institutional or corporate investors;
members subject to lead regulator arrangements.

3–067 The application of the IMRO capital adequacy rules to its members depends on the category of the member. The categories are:

(a) trustees of authorised unit trust schemes;

(b) advisory firms;

(c) venture capital firms;

(d) managers of authorised unit trust schemes;

(e) other investment managers who do not hold customers money or assets and do not procure the appointment as custodian or one of their Associates (unless it is an approved bank);

(f) other investment managers who do not hold customers' money or assets or procure the appointment of a non-bank associate as custodian.

3–068 Firms in categories (a) to (c) are subject to a "gross capital" requirement and firms in categories (d) to (f) are subject to a "liquid capital" requirement—see IMRO rule 2.

3–069 The starting point for the calculation of gross capital is total net assets to which adjustments are made for the following: intangible fixed assets, qualifying subordinated loans limited to four times the firm's capital reserves less tangible assets, deficiencies of shareholders funds in subsidiary companies, other assets or liabilities specified by IMRO in writing. The gross capital requirement is £4 million for trustees of authorised unit trust schemes and £5,000 for others.

Liquid capital is calculated by taking gross capital and making **3–070** adjustments for tangible fixed assets, fixed asset investments, investments in subsidiaries, physical stocks, trade debtors, unsecured non-trade debtors, pre-payments, accrued income, a percentage of qualifying deposits not encashable within 90 days. The liquid capital requirement is £5,000 plus a specified fraction of Annual Audited Expenditure. For firms in categories (d) to (e) this is 6/52 and for firms in category (f) this is 13/52.

IMRO rules are much less detailed than the other rules books concerning the risks associated with counterparty or customer defaults.

Financial returns required by an IMRO member depend on the **3–071** member's category. All those subject to capital adequacy rules are required to submit Annual Financial Returns within four months of the year end containing a profit and loss account, a statement of financial resources, a calculation of the firms expenditure based requirement, information about funds under management, the holding of client money and assets and own account trading and an independent audit report. Members subject to a liquid capital requirement must also submit quarterly financial statements within one month of the end of the quarter. No IMRO member is required to make monthly financial returns.

SFA

The financial rules are set out in Chapter 3 of the SFA rules. Again **3–072** the category of a member has an effect on the application of financial rules. The types of SFA members are set out in Chapter 9 of the SFA rules and are:

> broad scope firms;
> arrangers;
> corporate finance advisory firms;
> venture capital firms;
> advisers;
> local/traded options market makers.

The majority of SFA members are broad scope firms to which all **3–073** financial resources rules apply. SFA rule 3.61 requires all firms to maintain at all times financial resources in excess of its financial requirements. A firm must calculate its "Financial Resources Requirement" in accordance with rules 3.70 to 3.182 and table 3.61.

The financial reporting requirements for SFA members are set out in **3–074** rules 3.20 to 3.21 of the SFA rules. Different reporting forms and reporting dates are required by the SFA depending on the category of the member firm. These may include:

audited annual financial statements;
annual reporting statement;
auditor's report;
internal control letter;
quarterly reporting statement;
position risk reporting statement;
counterparty risk reporting statement;
monthly reporting statement;
solvency statement and auditor's report;
subsidiary accounts;
annual reconciliation.

PIA

3–075 The PIA financial resources requirement is set out in rule 1.3.2. Members of the PIA are divided into categories, in which category 1 firms are higher risk, category 2 firms which may hold client assets and money are medium risk and category 3 firms which are likely to make up the bulk of membership are intermediaries which do not hold client money or assets and are thus low risk firms.

Category 1 members must comply with the liquid capital requirement. Category 2 members with 1-25 investment staff must comply with the lower adjusted capital requirement. Category 2 members with 26 or more investment staff must comply with the medium adjusted capital requirement. Category 2 members with a network must comply with the higher adjusted capital requirement.

3–076 Category 3 members with 1-25 investment staff must comply with the minimum capital requirement. Category 3 members with 26 or more investment staff must comply with the lower adjusted capital requirement. Category 3 members with a network must comply with the higher adjusted capital requirement.

Liquid capital is calculated by deducting liabilities, with relevant adjustments, from assets—see FIMBRA rule 20.3.

The starting point for calculating the adjusted capital requirement is the member's net assets with adjustment made for the value of tangible fixed assets, pre-payments, accrued income, shares in connected companies, cash deposits, third party debtors and long term liabilities—see FIMBRA rule 21.4. A PIA member must include in his financial returns, which may be required monthly, quarterly or annually, sufficient information to demonstrate the members' compliance with the financial resources requirement.

Chapter 4

Enforcement and Sanctions

Parliament had envisaged that the enforcement of the Financial Services Act 1986 would be undertaken on a number of levels. At the first level, Parliament created a criminal offence of unauthorised trading. This sanction is buttressed by the consequences which flow in civil law where unauthorised trading has taken place. At the second level, Parliament empowered the enforcement authorities to intervene in cases where investment funds are put at risk by applying to the courts for various restraint of assets orders. At the third level, the Financial Services Act 1986 created machinery under which authorised persons can be monitored, inspected and disciplined for any breach of rules which may have occurred. Each level of enforcement is considered in turn. In the fourth section of this chapter, the compensation and complaints procedures are considered. 4–001

1. Unauthorised Trading

The requirement that investment business is only carried on by those who are authorised lies at the heart of the system of regulation established by the Financial Services Act 1986. Unauthorised trading may result in the imposition of both criminal and civil sanctions. 4–002

Criminal Sanction

It is a criminal offence to carry on or to purport to carry on investment business when not authorised to do so or when not being exempted from authorisation. The penalty for contravention being a maximum of two years' imprisonment and/or an unlimited fine if convicted on indictment or six months' imprisonment and/or a fine of the statutory maximum if convicted summarily—see section 4 of the Financial Services Act 1986. It is a defence to show on the balance of probabilities that the defendant took all reasonable precautions and that he exercised all due diligence to avoid commission of the offence. 4–003

The first successful prosecution for unauthorised trading was brought against John and Sara Saville in November 1990 following an investigation by the SIB which passed information to the police. John Saville was 4–004

CHAPTER 4: ENFORCEMENT AND SANCTIONS

charged with theft, perjury and carrying on an illegal investment business for which he was sentenced to a total of four years' imprisonment. Sara Saville admitted perjury, procuring the execution of cheques by deception and carrying on an illegal investment business for which she was sentenced to a total of 18 months' imprisonment.

Civil Sanction

4–005 Section 5 of the Financial Services Act 1986 renders agreements made by or through unauthorised persons unenforceable. Any agreement which is entered into by an unauthorised person in the course of carrying on investment business in contravention of section 3 is unenforceable against the other party. The other party is entitled to recover any money or other property paid or transferred by him under the agreement, together with compensation for any loss sustained by him as a result of having parted with it (s.5(1)(a)). The agreement is rendered unenforceable, but it is not rendered void by virtue of section 5(1)(a) and a court may allow such an agreement to be enforced or money or property transferred under it to be retained if the unauthorised person reasonably believed that his entering into the agreement did not constitute a contravention of section 3 or where the court finds that it is just and equitable for the agreement to be enforced (ss.5(3)(a) and 5(3)(c)). An agreement may also be rendered unenforceable as a consequence of anything said or done by an authorised or exempted person in the course of carrying on investment business in contravention of section 3. Again this may result in the other party being entitled to recover any money or other property paid or transferred by him under the agreement, together with compensation for any loss sustained by him as a result of having parted with it. The agreement is rendered unenforceable, but it is not rendered void by virtue of section 5(1)(b) and a court may allow such an agreement to be enforced or money or property transferred under it to be retained if the authorised or exempted person did not know that the agreement entered into was in contravention of section 3 or where the court finds that it is just and equitable for the agreement to be enforced (s.5(3)(b) and (c)).

2. Injunctions and Restitution Orders

4–006 Section 6 of the Financial Services Act 1986 contains provisions for the grant of injunctions and restitution orders in support of the restriction on carrying on investment business without authorisation. An injunction may be granted where there is a reasonable likelihood that a person will contravene section 3 of the Financial Services Act

INJUNCTIONS AND RESTITUTION ORDERS

1986 or where the contravention has already happened, that the contravention will continue or be repeated (s.6(1)). The court may order the person who has entered into the transaction in contravention of section 3 and any other person who appears to the court to have been knowingly concerned in the contravention, such as a company director, to take such steps as directed by the court to restore the parties to the position as it was pre the transaction (s.6(2)). The advantage of an injunction over simply relying on the criminal sanction is that an injunction may restrain behaviour before it has happened whereas the criminal sanction only comes into play once the damage has been done.

When a court is satisfied that there has been a contravention of section 3 of the Financial Services Act 1986 and that profits have accrued as a result and that one or more investors has suffered loss or been otherwise adversely affected by contravention of the rules relating to the conduct of investment business contained in Chapter V of the Financial Services Act 1986 or by contravention of the rules concerning unsolicited calls and advertising, the court may order payment into court by the person in contravention of section 3 of any profits appearing to the court to have accrued, an amount to cover any loss or other adverse effect or both (s.6(3) and (4)). The power to order restitution attaches only where a transaction has been entered into by an investor. It does not appear to extend to a situation where the investor has simply been given advice. **4–007**

The SIB may apply to the court under section 61 of the Financial Services Act 1986 for the grant of an injunction (an interdict in Scotland) prohibiting the contravention, or where the contravention has occurred it may order the person or any other person who appears to the court to have been knowingly concerned in the contravention to take such steps as may be directed to remedy it. Injunctions may be granted where the court is satisfied that there is a reasonable likelihood that any person will contravene any rules or regulations made under Chapter V Financial Services Act 1986. These are the rules and regulations concerning the conduct of investment business, (ss.47, 56, 57 or 59), any requirements imposed by an order under section 58(3), or the rules of a recognised SRO, RPB, investment exchange, or clearing house to which the person is subject. Applications for injunctions under section 61 may only be made where the SIB is satisfied that the SRO is unable or unwilling to take appropriate steps to restrain or remedy the contravention. **4–008**

Under section 61(3) a restitution order may be made on the application of the SIB where the same criteria apply.

The scope of the phrase "knowingly concerned" in this context was considered in the case of *SIB v. Pantell SA and another No. 2* [1993] Ch. 256; [1992] 1 All E.R. 134. The SIB brought an action against solicitors who had acted for Pantell SA and Swiss Atlantic in the United Kingdom and who had been knowingly concerned in the unauthorised trading of the two foreign companies within the meaning of sections 6(2) and 61(1) of the Financial Services Act 1986. The solicitors contended that a **4–009**

45

restitutionary order could only be made against a party to the transaction who has or had something to restore. If the powers extended beyond such parties they would amount to compensatory powers rather than restitutionary ones. This argument was rejected by the Court of Appeal. The statutory language warranted no distinction between the type of order that may be made against the contravener and one "knowingly concerned" in the contravention. Simply because the person knowingly concerned has not himself received anything does not restrict the power of the court to make an order under section 6(2). Steyn L.J. suggested in his judgment that the term "knowingly concerned", although not statutorily defined, must require proof of actual involvement in the transaction. Mere passive knowledge would be insufficient.

Mareva Injunctions

4–010 In cases where there is a risk that an authorised person might dissipate or remove investors' funds from the jurisdiction, the SIB may apply for a restraint of assets order under the Mareva jurisdiction. This is considered in more detail in Chapter 31. Suffice it here to consider the two cases where the SIB succeeded in obtaining an order under this jurisdiction.

4–011 In *SIB v. Pantell SA and another* [1989] 2 All E.R. 673; [1989] 3 W.L.R. 698, the SIB applied for a Mareva injunction restraining the assets of Pantell SA in the United Kingdom pending the final determination of an application for a restitution order under section 6 of the Financial Services Act 1986. Pantell SA was a Swiss company which was not authorised or exempt within the Financial Services Act 1986. Pantell had sent advertisements from overseas to people in the United Kingdom offering them investment advice and services. The SIB was made aware that Pantell SA had been closed down by the public prosecutor in Lugano, and that there were criminal proceedings being brought against its managers. Issues arose concerning whether Pantell was carrying on investment business in the United Kingdom and whether the SIB had any cause of action against the company as the SIB itself had no beneficial interest in the assets of Pantell in the United Kingdom. It was held that the activities of the company by sending advice and taking investor's monies in the United Kingdom amounted to carrying on investment business in the United Kingdom so that the provisions of section 6 applied. Secondly, the court held that the statutory right of action for the benefit of investors conferred on the SIB by section 6 was a right of action as any normal right of action in common law and it followed that the SIB was entitled to apply for a Mareva injunction on behalf of the investors adversely affected by breaches of the Act.

4–012 It has been established that the SIB does not need to give a cross-undertaking in damages when a Mareva injunction is sought. In *Securities and Investments Board v. Lloyd-Wright* [1993] 4 All E.R. 210, the SIB sought injunctions restraining the continuation of the carrying on of investment business in the United Kingdom and worldwide Mareva injunctions against Mr Lloyd-Wright and his company. The issue in the case was whether there should be cross-undertakings in damages given by the SIB. It was held that the circumstances were such that the SIB had a strictly law enforcement function and cross-undertakings for damages would not be appropriate.

In clear cases, the procedure for summary judgment under Order 14 of the Rules of the Supreme Court can be utilised in the SIB's favour. In *SIB v. Uberoi*, Law Tel, September 26, 1995, the SIB applied for summary judgment under Order 14 against the defendants for carrying on investment business in the United Kingdom in contravention of section 3 of the Financial Services Act 1986 and against one defendant for making false or deceptive statements in contravention of section 47 of the Financial Services Act 1986. The defendants had invested monies collected from a number of families into various of the major privatisations (*e.g.* National Power, Powergen). Millett J. held that Mareva injunctions outstanding against the defendants would only be discharged when they had paid into court money to cover investors' losses plus interest, the legal costs of the SIB and the costs of the investigation. 4–013

A deliberate breach of a court order obtained by the SIB will be treated as a contempt of court. In the unreported case of *Fallon v. Securities and Investments Board*, May 5, 1994, the Court of Appeal upheld the committal to prison for nine months of Mr Fallon for contempt of court for breach of a court order restraining him from carrying on investment business. 4–014

3. Monitoring, Inspection and Discipline

One of the most important aspects of any regulatory system is the ability to enforce it. In practice the job of monitoring compliance falls on the SROs. Under Schedule 2, paragraph 4 of the Financial Services Act 1986, SROs have obligations to monitor and enforce compliance with the provisions of the Act: 4–015

"(1) The organisation must have adequate arrangements and resources for the effective monitoring and enforcement of compliance with its rules and with any [statements of principle, rules, regulations or codes of practice] to which its members are subject under Chapter V of Part I of this Act in respect of investment business of a kind regulated by the organisation."

An RPB must also have adequate arrangements and resources for the effective monitoring of the continued compliance by its members including arrangements for the withdrawal or suspension of certification in the event of breaches of its rules. This requirement is imposed by Schedule 4, paragraph 4. 4–016

Inspections

4-017 The surveillance/monitoring department of each SRO has the function of monitoring the SROs members' compliance with the SRO rule book. For example, PIA rule 7.3 states that the PIA aims to monitor (1) members' compliance with the rule book and (2) members' conduct, to determine whether they continue to be fit and proper. In particular, the SRO will be looking for adherence to its rules, proper documentation and record keeping and an adequate internal compliance system.

4-018 The SRO monitors adherence to its rules by making periodic inspection visits to its members. In the course of an inspection visit, the inspection team would expect to be allowed access to all the members' files (unless subject to legal professional privilege). Following the visit, a report is prepared and sent to the member which will contain any areas of concern and/or criticisms of the members' compliance procedures. The member is expected to act upon the areas highlighted in the report, it may make representations to the SRO about the report but if no remedial action is taken, the member may be faced with further investigation, disciplinary proceedings and, in the most serious of cases, with direct intervention by the SRO. There are equivalent inspection procedures for SFA and IMRO members.

4-019 Inspection visits may be either routine or made in response to a particular problem that has arisen. The SFA has reported a trend away from routine visits and a move towards targeted visits since 1993. For example in 1994 the SFA made a total of 1,731 inspection visits to member firms of which 55 per cent were non-routine.

Information and Investigations

Information

4-020 The SIB may require a person who is authorised to carry out investment business being an authorised insurer (s.22), an operator or trustee of a recognised scheme (s.24), directly authorised by the SIB (s.25) and those authorised in another Member State of the European Union (s.31) to furnish it with such information as it may reasonably require for the exercise of its functions by giving a notice in writing (s.104(1)). Failure to comply with such a requirement by an authorised person may be dealt with by the making of a public statement as to conduct (s.60), by way of injunction or restitution order (s.61) or by an action for damages (s.62).

4-021 The SIB may also require an SRO, an RPB, a recognised investment exchange or a recognised clearing house to furnish it with such information as it may reasonably require for the exercise of its functions by giving a notice in writing (s.104(2)).

Investigations

4-022 The SIB has wide investigatory powers under sections 105 and 106 of the Financial Services Act 1986 which may be exercised where it appears that there is good reason to do so for the purpose of investigating the

Monitoring, Inspection and Discipline

affairs or any aspect of the affairs of any person so far as it is relevant to the carrying on of any investment business.

Powers of investigation do not extend to exempted persons unless he is an appointed representative or the investigation is in respect of investment business in respect of which he is not an exempted person. Nor do powers extend to investigate members of SROs or RPBs unless the SRO or RPB has requested the SIB to investigate or if it appears to the SIB that the SRO or RPB is unable or unwilling to investigate the person in a satisfactory manner (s.105(2)).   4–023

The SIB can require persons to answer questions, provide information and to provide documents and an explanation of those documents to inspectors (ss.105(3) and (4)). A person making any statement in compliance with section 105 may have that statement used in evidence against him (s.105(5)). Legal professional privilege amounts to a good reason for not disclosing information under this section (s.105(6)). Failure to provide information or documents without reasonable excuse amounts to a summary only criminal offence for which the maximum penalty is imprisonment of six months and/or a fine of the statutory maximum (s.105(10)). A person convicted of a criminal offence under this section may also be ordered to pay for the costs of the investigation (s.105(11)).   4–024

Liability of Informant

In *Re a Company's Application, The Times*, February 13, 1989, it was held that it would be contrary to public policy for a former employee of a financial services company to be prevented by injunction from reporting breaches of the Financial Services Act 1986 to an SRO or the Inland Revenue. However, if the reports turned out not to have been founded on any reasonable basis, the employee might be liable in defamation or malicious falsehood for the damage caused. Interesting issues concerning the application of a defence of qualified privilege would arise in these circumstances.   4–025

Obtaining Identity of Informant from a Journalist

In *Re an inquiry under the Company Security (Insider Dealing) Act* [1988] 1 All E.R. 203, a journalist had accurately forecast the result of inquires by the Monopolies and Mergers Commission and the Office of Fair Trading into two take-over bids. It was obvious that the journalist had received official information which had been leaked to him. Inspectors were appointed to investigate suspected leaks of price-sensitive information about take-over bids from government departments pursuant to section 177f of the Financial Services Act 1986 concerning investigations into insider dealing. The Inspectors requested the journalist to reveal the source of his information under section 177(3) of the Financial Services Act 1986 but the journalist refused. The matter was certified by the inspectors for an inquiry by the court into his refusal   4–026 under section 178. Under section 178(2) a court has power to punish a refusal made without reasonable excuse as a contempt of court. The journalist argued that he had a reasonable excuse to protect his source. On appeal, the House of Lords held that this excuse was not reasonable and the journalist would be in contempt of court for refusing to reveal his source if it could be established that disclosure was necessary for the prevention of crime generally.

Intervention Powers

4-027   Sections 64 to 71 of the Financial Services Act 1986 set out the scope of the intervention powers. The SIB has powers in relation to any authorised person and any appointed representative of his, if it appears to the SIB that the exercise of the powers is desirable for the protection of investors, that the authorised person is not fit to carry on investment business of a particular kind or that the authorised person has contravened any provision of Financial Services Act 1986 or any rules or regulations made under it or he has furnished the SIB with false, inaccurate or misleading information. The powers are not exercisable against persons who are authorised by virtue of membership of an RPB (s.64(4)(a)), or an appointed representative whose principle is authorised by an RPB unless the RPB itself requests such intervention. Section 65 provides that the SIB may prohibit an authorised person from entering into particular kinds of transactions, soliciting business from persons of a particular kind, or from carrying on business in a specified manner.

4-028   Under section 66 the SIB may prohibit an authorised person from disposing or otherwise dealing with any assets, or any specified assets generally or in a particular way. This prohibition may relate to assets outside the United Kingdom. By section 67, the SIB may require that any assets belonging to an authorised person or being held by him for investors should be transferred to be held by a trustee approved by the SIB. Section 68 permits the SIB to require an authorised person to maintain in the United Kingdom assets of such value as appears desirable to enable the authorised person to meet his liabilities in respect of investment business carried on by him in United Kingdom. Section 69 contains power for the SIB of its own motion or on the application of the person against whom the prohibition has been imposed to vary or rescind any prohibition or requirement. This power is exercisable by written notice (s.70). Breach of a prohibition or requirement may result in any of the sanctions available under sections 60, 61 and 62 (s.71).

4-029   The SRO rule books must provide the SROs with powers in relation to their members which are comparable to those conferred on the SIB by sections 64 to 71. However, there is no corresponding rule requiring the rules of the RPBs to do the same.

4-030   The powers of intervention in respect of collective investment schemes are less far reaching than those applicable to other authorised persons. These powers are contained in sections 91 to 95 of the Financial Services Act 1986.

Withdrawal of Authorisation

Under section 28 of the Financial Services Act 1986 authorisation may **4–031** be withdrawn or suspended if it appears to the SIB that the holder of the authorisation is not a fit and proper person to carry on an investment business; or that the holder of authorisation has contravened any provision of the Act or any rules or regulations made under the Act; or where in purported compliance with the Act or rules or regulations made under the Act, he has furnished information to the SIB which is false, inaccurate or misleading. This is the ultimate sanction that can be imposed on an authorised person who declines to comply with the rules. Where an authorised person is a member of an SRO or an RPB, authorisation may be withdrawn for any contravention of the rules and regulations of the SRO (s.28(3)). Where an authorised person has his authorisation suspended, suspension must be for a specified period (s.28(4)).

Before authorisation can be withdrawn or suspended there must be **4–032** notice given in writing to the authorised person stating the intention to withdraw or suspend authorisation and the reasons for the proposed action. The notice must state the date on which withdrawal or suspension is to take effect (ss.29(1) and (2)). Where the reasons in the notice refer to identified persons other than the holder of the authorisation and are prejudicial to that other person, that other person must also be served with a copy of the notice unless it would be impracticable to do so (s.29(3)). The notice must give particulars of the right to have the case referred to a tribunal (s.29(4)).

Authorisation may also be withdrawn at the request of the authorised **4–033** person himself. However, the SIB may refuse to withdraw authorisation if it would not be in the public interest to do so. Such a situation may arise where the person is about to be or is being investigated or where it would be desirable that some prohibition or restriction should be imposed on the authorised person (s.30).

Discipline

The powers of a Tribunal to compel compliance with the rules are **4–034** wide-ranging. By way of example, the SFA may require firms to rectify any financial deficiencies, non-compliance or bad practice by the issuing of formal warnings or directions, or a formal discipline or intervention order. A firm may also be required to make good any losses suffered by clients as a result of non-compliance. In 1994 there were 36 cases where individuals or firms were brought before the SFA Disciplinary Tribunal. Of the cases heard in 1994, 14 individuals were expelled from the SFA's register. In one case an individual was banned from working in all areas of the financial services industry under section 59 of the Financial Services Act 1986.

Although at one time findings of the SRO disciplinary tribunals were **4–035** not made public, it is now the general rule that disciplinary findings will be made known to the public through the issue of a press release. Unless there is a compelling reason for secrecy, the courts will not intervene to prevent publication of a disciplinary finding. For example, in November 1994 the SIB obtained injunctions against two people, Messrs West and Bingham, arising from their conduct of investment business without authorisation and for making misleading statements or concealing material facts. In respect of this behaviour, the SIB made disqualification orders. Mr West applied for an injunction to prevent the SIB from publishing the Tribunal's report but this was refused by Hidden J. on February 4, 1995. Both Mr West and Mr Bingham's names appear on the SIBs register of disqualified persons.

Winding up and Administration Orders

4–036 The SIB has power, under section 72 of the Financial Services Act 1986, to present a petition for the winding up by order of the court of an authorised person or an appointed representative. This applies in the case of both an individual and a company. There are strict requirements which have to be established before this power can be exercised. Broadly, in the case of a company the SIB has to show that a company is registered under the Companies Act 1985, or is a foreign company with a United Kingdom operation. If an individual, the person must be to subject to the jurisdiction of the court under the Insolvency Act 1986. If the person or company is a member of an SRO or RPB, the SIB may present the winding-up petition only with the regulatory organisation's consent. The grounds for the winding up may be either that the person or firm is unable to pay its debts or that it is just and equitable that the company or partnership should be wound up. The Financial Services Act 1986 does not confer any power on an SRO or RPB to petition for winding-up.

4–037 An administration order may be applied for under section 9 of the Insolvency Act 1986 in respect of an authorised person by the SRO by whom he is authorised, or of an appointed representative by the SIB.

Intervention by the Courts

4–038 On some occasions persons authorised under the Financial Services Act 1986 have sought the intervention of the court to restrain the SIB and SROs from taking enforcement action in pursuance of their powers under the Financial Services Act 1986. However, the courts have been reluctant to allow the legal process to be used to frustrate the SIB and SROs in performance of their compliance duties. The reluctance of the courts to intervene is neatly demonstrated by the case of *R. v. FIMBRA, ex p. Cochrane* [1991] B.C.L.C. 106 where Mr Cochrane sought judicial review of the decision of the appeal tribunal of FIMBRA to uphold the decision of the council of FIMBRA to terminate the membership of Mr Cochrane's firm, Family Investment Services. Mr Cochrane admitted breaches of various FIMBRA rules but contended that these had come about because he had had insufficient time to comply with the FIMBRA requirements whilst he was actively involved in the campaign for election to the council of FIMBRA. The council of FIMBRA terminated Mr Cochrane's company's membership because it felt that he was a danger to the public and unwilling or unable to comply with the FIMBRA rules both at the present time and in the future. Mr Cochrane alleged that his campaign activities had been a nuisance to the Council and it was for this reason that his company's membership was terminated. On the application for judicial review it was held that the decision of the appeals tribunal was independent of that of the council and that the concern that Mr Cochrane might again put his campaigning activities before his obligation to comply with FIMBRA rules was not an irrational fear. Perversity, irrationality, or bad faith had to be established by an aggrieved litigant before the court would interfere.

The courts have recognised that the protection of investors can require urgent action. An SRO was therefore, entitled to issue an intervention notice with immediate effect without giving those who would be adversely affected a proper opportunity to make representations to show that the giving of the proposed notice was not justified— *R. v. LAUTRO, ex p. Ross* [1993] Q.B. 17. Following an investigation into Winchester Group plc, LAUTRO served a notice ordering Norwich Union Life Assurance Society to stop taking business from Winchester Group plc with whom it had an agency agreement. Mr Ross was the sole director of Winchester Group plc following the resignation of the three previous directors following allegations of fraud. The order had the effect of forcing Winchester to cease trading. Mr Ross applied for judicial review of LAUTRO's decision on the basis that LAUTRO had acted unreasonably in failing to give Winchester Group plc an opportunity to answer the serious allegations made against it *before* making the order to stop Norwich Union from taking business from Winchester Group plc and making the order public. The Court of Appeal held that as Winchester Group plc was not a member of LAUTRO it had no right of appeal to LAUTRO under the LAUTRO rules. LAUTRO had a duty to act fairly to its members and in appropriate circumstances towards those appointed representatives on whom under its rules an intervention notice could be served. LAUTRO had to take into account and balance the fairness of allowing those affected by an intervention notice to make representations to it with the interests of investors. Since an SRO such as LAUTRO might have to act with urgency in intervening in the business of a member in order to protect investors and it would be incompatible with that object to require the organisation to hear representations from a member or other person affected by its decision *before* it acted, fairness did not require that an affected person be given an opportunity to make representations *before* the intervention notice was served. **4–039**

In *Ross* the court expressed the view that in so far as LAUTRO's rules did not allow for representations to be made by Winchester *after* the notice was served, these rules were unfair. An affected person should be **4–040** afforded an opportunity *after* exercise of intervention powers to make representations and to make immediate application to set aside the enforcement decision. This point was confirmed by the Court of Appeal in the associated case of *R. v. LAUTRO, ex p. Tee* (1995) 7 Admin. L.R. 289. The court noted that the situation would not recur as LAUTRO had changed its rules after the *Ross* case.

4–041   Just as the courts are reluctant to intervene to frustrate the SIB and SROs in the exercise of their compliance duties, the courts have also demonstrated a reluctance to become involved in attempts to compel investigation at the instigation of an aggrieved investor. In *R. v. SFA, ex p. Panton*, June 20, 1994, unreported, Mr Panton sought mandamus to force the SFA to exercise its powers of investigation and enforcement. Mr Panton had sold shares in a company, Telecomputing plc, in a transaction undertaken by a merchant bank. Although the sale eventually went ahead, a dispute arose as to the agreed completion date for the sale and Mr Panton became dissatisfied with the manner in which the merchant bank had conducted the transaction. As a result, he complained to the SFA who embarked upon an investigation and a long correspondence with Mr Panton, but the SFA did not go as far as instituting any form of proceedings against the merchant bank. Mr Panton sought judicial review of the decision of the SFA not to pursue the investigation further or to embark on proceedings under their powers of enforcement. The Court of Appeal rejected Mr Panton's application. Sir Thomas Bingham M.R. said:

> "These bodies [SROs] are amenable to judicial review but are, in anything other than very clear circumstances, to be left to get on with it. It is for them to decide on the facts whether it is, or is not, appropriate to proceed against a member as not being a fit and proper person and it is essentially a matter for judgment as to the extent to which a complaint is investigated."

4. Compensation and Complaints

Action for Damages

4–042   Section 62 of the Financial Services Act 1986 allows a private investor to seek compensation in the courts where he has suffered loss as a result of contravention of any rules or regulations made under Chapter V of the Financial Services Act 1986 or of certain other specified sections of the Financial Services Act 1986. This remedy is available in addition to the individual complaints procedures of the SROs. The investor may bring an action to recover damages from the persons responsible including members of SROs and RPBs. The action is subject to the usual defences, limitation period, etc., which apply to actions for breach of statutory duty.

The potential for civil actions to recover lost investments under **4–043**
section 62 of the Financial Services Act 1986 has yet to be realised. Aggrieved investors should focus on the possibilities of a civil action under this section whenever investment losses have been sustained in a financial services context. The scope of the section is extremely wide in the sense that a civil action may be brought by an aggrieved investor whenever he can establish that he has suffered loss as a result of an authorised person's breach of the core rules or any rule included in an SRO rule book. A glut of legal actions is expected following the turmoil which followed the recent losses sustained by Sumitomo Corporation in the copper market. Investors lost large amounts of money after a fall in copper prices triggered by the discovery of unauthorised dealings. The scope of potential liability under section 62 is demonstrated by the fact that the section is sufficiently wide to permit corporations to sue each other for dealing when in possession of unpublished price sensitive information in breach of the various regulatory requirements.

Investors' Compensation Scheme

The Financial Services Act 1986 empowered the SIB to set up a **4–044**
compensation scheme for investors where investment business has been carried out by authorised persons or firms which are unable or likely to be unable to satisfy claims in respect of civil liability incurred by them in connection with the carrying on of investment business (s.54(1)). The SIB established the Investors Compensation Scheme (ICS) on August 28, 1988 which now operates under the Financial Services (Compensation of Investors) Rules 1994 (release 146). By August 1995, the ICS had helped customers of 192 failed investment firms and paid out more than £85 million to over 8,000 investors.

Funding of ICS

Initially the scheme was funded by a levy on each authorised person **4–045**
or firm in a complicated system of cross contribution. In practice, however, raising funds in this way had the effect of undermining the way in which the SROs themselves were funded. In 1991, because of the amounts levied to meet the demand for compensation, there was a real risk that FIMBRA would go bankrupt. In 1994 there was a review of the way in which the funding for compensation was raised and it is now the position that the costs of the ICS are funded by the SROs themselves, each of which must provide up to a maximum of £100 million to the scheme each year. In practice, the SROs pass the costs of funding the ICS on to their members. (Financial Services (Compensation of Investors) Rules 1994 Annex 2). In the year 1994/1995, the total levy announced by the ICS was £16,629,487 (£15,858,756 from the PIA, £663,867 from the SFA and £106,864 from IMRO). However, in 1994/5, because of the pending case of *R. v. SIB, ex p. Sun Alliance,* the

contributions to the ICS by the PIA were held in abeyance and the Treasury had to guarantee £17 million to the ICS to enable claims to be processed without interruption.

4–046 The history of the compensation scheme has been marred by some resistance from the financial services industry which has led to litigation in the courts. In *R. v. SIB, ex p. Sun Life Assurance*, August 31, 1995, unreported, the court considered the legality of provisions for funding the ICS and the proper interpretation of section 54 of Financial Services Act 1986. Sun Life challenged the legality of provisions whereby the ICS allocated to members of an SRO liability to contribute to the cost of making good the defaults of non-members. This situation arose in the context of the re-organisation of the SROs which has been a rolling process of de-recognition of FIMBRA and LAUTRO and the eventual absorption of their members into one of the three continuing SROs. In practice the vast majority of former FIMBRA and LAUTRO members have become members of the PIA. Sun Life argued that the ICS rules which made the PIA responsible for administering FIMBRA and LAUTRO compensation and for assessing how much ex-members of these groups were to pay towards these compensation costs amounted to an unlawful delegation of authority to the PIA in breach of section 54 of the Financial Services Act 1986. It was argued that funding the ICS was restricted to past, present or future members of the particular SRO whose member was liable. The arguments advanced by the parties in this case turned on the proper construction of section 54 of the Financial Services Act 1986 and at one point in his judgment Sedley J. commented that:

"[Counsel's] ingenious argument [concerning the interpretation of section 54 Financial Services Act 1986] assumes a capacity for syntactical sadism in the drafter and for literary clairvoyance in the reader which I do not believe exists."

4–047 Although Sedley J. accepted in his judgment that the drafting of section 54(3) left something to be desired, he held that a proper construction of section 54 did not fetter the mode of distribution of the burden of claims among different groups of authorised persons and that, accordingly, the PIA did have an obligation to meet compensation claims made in respect of liabilities incurred by the former members of FIMBRA and LAUTRO.

Scope of the Investors' Compensation Scheme

4–048 The extent of the liabilities covered by the ICS was considered in *SIB v. FIMBRA* [1991] 4 All E.R. 398; [1992] Ch. 268, where it was held that the ICS was restricted to liabilities incurred on or after December 18, 1986 when the provisions of section 1 and Schedule 1 to the Financial Services Act 1986 which gave meaning to the words "investment business" were brought into effect. Compensation is only payable in cases where the liability has been incurred by an authorised person. Clearly no-one could have been authorised prior to the coming into effect of the Financial Services Act 1986, therefore advice given before this date does not attract the protect of the ICS. It was not essential that the scheme had come into operation or that the person carrying on the investment business giving rise to the liability had been authorised at the time that liability occurred.

The scope of the ICS was again considered in *R. v Investor Compensation Scheme, ex p. Bowden* [1995] 3 W.L.R. 289, which concerned investors who had been advised to enter into home income plans by nine authorised brokers. The home income plans turned out to be disastrous and the conduct of the brokers contravened rules made under the Financial Services Act 1986. The brokers themselves went into liquidation. The investors sought relief from the Investors Compensation Scheme. The ICS accepted that the investors were entitled to compensation but decided that it was not bound to compensate them in respect of monies received and expended by them in reliance on the brokers advice and limited compensation to £500 for professional fees incurred in connection with mitigation of their loss. The Divisional Court rejected the investors' application for judicial review of the ICS decision. The investors appealed successfully to the Court of Appeal. However, the House of Lords reversing the decision of the Court of Appeal, held that under the rules of the ICS, the decision to limit the amount of compensation payable was reasonable within the rules of the ICS. 4–049

Mann J. at first instance in *ex p. Bowden* [1994] 1 W.L.R. 17, considered the question of whether an application for compensation to the ICS could be made or continued by a personal representative of a deceased eligible investor and found that such an application could be made. Mann J's decision was considered in *R. v. Investor Compensation Scheme Ltd, ex p. Weyell* [1994] 1 All E.R. 601, which was decided before the judgment of the Court of Appeal in *ex p. Bowden*. The issue in *ex p. Weyell* was whether a personal representative of an eligible investor could make a claim for compensation if the investor had died before the participant firm went into default. The ICS had sought to limit claims to compensation by arguing that the right to claim compensation only arose when the participant firm went into default and so if the investor died prior to default being declared, the personal representative could not pursue a claim on his behalf. This argument was rejected by the Court. *Ex p. Weyell* was a case concerning home investment schemes where the brokers authorised under the Financial Services Act 1986 had become worthless and where the investors were elderly couples who had been persuaded to mortgage their homes and invest in income bonds. The scheme went wrong because of falling property values and increased interest rates. The second issue in the case was whether the investors were entitled to compensation under the ICS as the initial advice had been received before the ICS had come into operation. It was held that 4–050 the brokers had a continuing obligation to manage the investments after the time that the ICS came into operation and that this amounted to conducting investment business so that compensation was indeed payable.

4–051 These cases demonstrate that the courts are prepared to implement the legislation in favour of aggrieved investors, provided that the investors can bring themselves within the scope of the scheme.

Complaints

4–052 The Financial Services Act 1986 requires that an SRO has in place effective arrangements for the investigation of complaints against itself or its members (Financial Services Act 1986, Sched. 2, para. 6).

4–053 An RPB must also have effective arrangements for the investigation of complaints relating to (a) the carrying on by persons certified by the RPB of investment business in respect of which they are subject to its rules and (b) its regulation of investment business.

The PIA Complaints Procedure and the PIA Ombudsman Bureau

4–054 The PIA Ombudsman Bureau was established in July 1994 to coincide with the establishment of the PIA itself. The Bureau operates as the external, independent complaints handling agency dealing with complaints against PIA members. It is intended to be impartial as between investor and the industry, with the Ombudsman acting: "as councillor, conciliator or adjudicator" in connection with complaints against members of the PIA.

4–055 The complaints procedure to be followed by members of the PIA is set out in the PIA Rule Book, Chapter 8. To constitute a complaint that comes within the rules the complainant must, or might, be seeking a remedy from the member in respect of loss, damage or inconvenience. A complaint must allege a breach of PIA rules or guidance, or a failure to comply with any obligation arising under or by virtue of the Financial Services Act 1986, or negligence, or the breach of a term of any customer agreement, or the breach of any enactment or other rule of law which may be applicable to the relevant business of a member, or misrepresentation, bad faith or other malpractice. The Ombudsman may only consider a complaint once he is satisfied that the PIA member has failed to respond adequately to the complainant.

4–056 As regards time limits for complaints, the Ombudsman may only consider a complaint where the act or omission giving rise to the complaint took place on or after April 29, 1988 or first occurred on or after the date when the PIA member became an authorised person, whichever is the later. The Ombudsman has the power only to consider complaints where he is satisfied that the PIA member first received notice of the complaint from the complainant on or after July 18, 1994 or after the date of the members admission to the PIA whichever is the later.

The Ombudsman's Bureau is funded from two sources; the fixed costs 4–057
and 30 per cent of the variable costs are met by the whole of the PIA
membership as part of the Membership fee. The remainder is funded by
the income from Case Fees which are charged in respect of every case
handled by the Bureau (*i.e.* once a complaint has been screened and
transferred to a specialist Case Officer). The case fee is currently fixed at
£375, it is levied irrespective of the outcome of the case and is payable by
the member against whom the complaint has been made.

The jurisdiction of the PIA Ombudsman Bureau is limited to matters 4–058
falling within its terms of reference. It has a mandatory jurisdiction
which covers complaints against PIA members or their representatives
which relate to investment business and any other business which is
regulated by the Financial Services Act 1986. The maximum compensation that the Ombudsman can award is £50,000 or £20,000 per annum in
respect of a Permanent Health Insurance policy. The award can include
up to £750 for distress and inconvenience. The voluntary jurisdiction
extends to firms which elect that it applies and will include jurisdiction
over complaints concerning the administration of policies, term
assurance and permanent health insurance policies not within the
mandatory jurisdiction and events occurring before April 29, 1988.
Under the voluntary jurisdiction, the maximum compensation is
£100,000 (or £20,000 per annum in respect of a Permanent Health
Insurance policy) with no limit on the figure which can be included for
distress and inconvenience. The Ombudsman may also make non-legally
binding recommendations to PIA members in the same way as the
Insurance Ombudsman.

Some 1,500 initial complaints were received by the PIA Ombudsman 4–059
in the first eight-and-half months of operation. The vast majority of
these being for breach of best advice/suitability rules (801), pension
transfers (218) and misrepresentation as to nature of investment (187).
The number of initial complaints was expected to increase substantially
in 1995/1996 because of the problems with pension transfers and
optouts.

IMRO Complaints Unit

Before May 1995 complaints to IMRO were considered by the IMRO 4–060
Complaints Unit which aimed to achieve a conciliated settlement.
Where no conciliation could be reached, the complainant could take his
case to the Investment Ombudsman who is independent of IMRO. Since
May 1, 1995, all new complaints by investors seeking redress from
IMRO registered firms will be handled by the Investment Ombudsman.

In the year 1994/1995, a total of 887 complaints were referred to
IMRO.

The SFA Complaints Bureau

As with complaints to the PIA Ombudsman, the first step for any 4–061
complainant is to complain to the firm itself, usually through its
compliance officer. If the matter cannot be resolved in this way, the

CHAPTER 4: ENFORCEMENT AND SANCTIONS

complainant should contact the Complaints Bureau of the SFA which considers complaints relating to SFA authorised business, which is not already the subject of litigation or arbitration and the subject matter of which occurred on or after April 29, 1988. The service is free to complainants. The Complaints Bureau may refer the matter back to the firm for settlement, it may attempt to conciliate between the complainant and the firm, or it may send the matter for further consideration by SFA enforcement inspectors with the possibility of disciplinary action being taken. If the SFA Complaints Bureau cannot resolve the complaint, the complainant has the right to have it referred to the Consumer Arbitration Scheme, and if still not satisfied, there is an appeal procedure before a Board of Appeal. In 1994/1995 there were 25 references to the Panel of Arbitrators under the Consumer Arbitration Scheme under which jurisdiction is limited to £50,000. There is also a Full Arbitration Scheme which is available by mutual agreement between the complainant and the firm. In 1994/1995 there were no references under the Full Arbitration Scheme where jurisdiction is unlimited. If the complaint is referred for arbitration the complainant may not pursue the matter in the courts.

4–062   The work of the SFA Complaints Bureau is independently reviewed by the Complaints Commissioner. In 1994/1995 the SFA Complaints Bureau received a total of 393 complaints against 104 firms compared with an estimated seven million transactions conducted annually by authorised firms.

4–063   The largest fine imposed to date on a member by the SFA is £247,000 on Morgan Stanley in addition to which the firm made a substantial payment to cover the costs of investigation and offered compensation of about $30 million to five private clients who suffered losses incurred in currency transactions which had not been requested by the clients. The impropriety came to light following an internal investigation by Morgan Stanley who reported its findings to the SFA.

City Disputes Panel

4–064   The City Disputes Panel was established in 1994 to provide a quick, flexible and cheaper alternative to litigation in the courts. The Panel is sponsored by the Corporation of London, the Bank of England, the SIB, Lloyds and the Faculty of Advocates.

Common Law—Lack of Remedies

4–065   Common law actions in tort for breach of a statutory obligation will not be possible where the subject-matter is covered by an action within section 62 of the 1986 Act. It is well established by the courts that the statutory action will pre-empt and exclude any action being brought at common law—see *Nocton v. Ashburton* [1914] A.C. 932. Any actions in common law for breaches which are not covered by section 62 are also unlikely to be successful because of the judicial reluctance to interpret statutes as conferring rights to sue for damages on persons who suffer loss as a result of breaches of the requirements of the statute unless it is the clear intention of Parliament to confer such rights. Arguably, the inclusion of section 62 in the Financial Services Act 1986 conferring limited statutory rights to bring an action for damages demonstrates that Parliament intended that the right to sue should be limited to those areas covered by section 62. Since the scope of potential liability under section 62 is potentially very wide, this limitation should not cause any injustice in practice.

4–066 The potential liability in negligence of regulatory agencies was considered in the Hong Kong case of *Yuen Kun-Yeu v. Att.-Gen. of Hong Kong* [1987] 2 All E.R. 705, P.C. The question before the court was whether a regulator owed to members of the public, who might become investors, a duty in the discharge of its supervisory powers to exercise reasonable care to see that such members of the public did not suffer loss through the affairs of regulated companies which were conducted fraudulently or in an improvident fashion. The Privy Council held that as the regulator had no power to control the day-to-day activities of companies which caused loss or damage and only had the discretionary power to withdraw registration even though the regulator had reason to suspect that the company was being carried on fraudulently and improvidently this did not create a special relationship between the regulator and the company or between the regulator and members of the public who might in future become exposed to the risk of financial loss through investing through the company.

4–067 The case arose in the following circumstances. A number of investors deposited money with a company registered by the Commissioner of Deposit-Taking Companies. The investors lost money because of the fraudulent way in which the company was run. The investors brought an action against the Attorney General of Hong Kong who acted for the Commissioner alleging that the Commissioner owed them a duty of care not to register companies which were not properly run, or to allow companies to continue to be registered when they were not properly run. The Privy Council held that in order to establish a duty of care, it was necessary to establish the foreseeability of harm and a close and direct relationship of proximity between the parties. The critical question in this case was whether such a close and direct relationship existed between the Commissioner and the investors. There was no special relationship between the Commissioner and the investors because the commissioner had no control over the day-to-day management of deposit-taking companies and had to consider the position of existing depositors when considering whether to de-register a company.

4–068 Similarly, a Court is not likely to hold a regulatory authority liable in damages for breach of a statutory duty. In *Melton Medes Ltd and another v. Securities and Investments Board* [1995] 3 All E.R. 880; [1995] Ch. 137, the plaintiffs were trustees of employee's pension funds for two other companies. A number of beneficiaries of the pension funds initiated proceedings against the plaintiffs seeking compensation for losses allegedly incurred in making a £5 million loan from the pension funds to the trustees. The SIB initiated an investigation into the trustees' management of the funds during which it obtained information from the company's auditors and disclosed this information to the auditors under section 180(1)(q) of the Financial Services Act 1986. The SIB suggested that the auditors make this information available to the beneficiaries who could ask the auditors if they should continue to rely upon the auditors certificate. As a result, negotiations between the plaintiffs and the beneficiaries broke down. The plaintiffs brought proceedings against the SIB alleging that the SIB had disclosed restricted information without the plaintiff's consent in contravention of section 179 but for which disclosure, the plaintiffs and the beneficiaries might have reached a settlement. The plaintiffs sought damages pursuant to section 187(3) alleging that the SIB had acted in bad faith. The SIB contended that disclosure of restricted information was not actionable under section 179. Accepting the SIB's contentions, the court held that the only sanction for breach of section 179 was a criminal one under section 179(6). The allegations that the SIB had acted in bad faith were groundless because the motives of the SIB in disclosing information had been to assist the beneficiaries which accorded with the aims of the 1986 Act.

4–069 A different avenue of attack was employed in *Tee v. LAUTRO Ltd*, July 16, 1996, unreported, where a plaintiff brought proceedings against LAUTRO for negligence and misfeasance in a public office on the grounds that it had wrongfully taken enforcement proceedings against a company in which the plaintiff held 51 per cent of the shares. LAUTRO relied on section 187 of the Financial Services Act 1986 which required that bad faith be proved in such a case where damages were sought from an SRO. The plaintiff's claim was struck out. So far as the claim in negligence was concerned there was no duty of care owed by LAUTRO to the plaintiff. A public law duty and a private law duty were based on very different principles. So far as misfeasance was concerned, it was necessary to prove malice as opposed to mere recklessness to succeed in an allegation of misfeasance in public office.

This decision is consistent with the reluctance of the court to fetter the discretion exercised by the regulatory authorities in enforcing compliance with the supervisory regime.

Chapter 5

Personal Pensions

Pensions are often the second largest personal investment after the family house. As Buxton J. said (at p.5D) in *R. v. PIA, ex p. Lucas Fettes and Partners (Financial Services) Ltd*, July 10, 1995, unreported "proper pension provision, or proper provision for old age is something that every citizen now rightly expects." The effective regulation of personal pensions is therefore, of very major concern to large numbers of investors. The legislation has drawn a distinction between non-occupational pensions which are regulated by the Financial Services Act 1986 and occupational pension schemes which are regulated by the Pensions Act 1995. The latter are the subject of Chapter 6. The operation of the Financial Services Act 1986 has been considered at length in the preceding chapters. In addition to the general application of the Act there are certain specific provisions which apply to the sale and administration of non-occupational pensions and these are considered in this chapter. 5–001

It is estimated that over five million personal pensions have been sold since April 1988 when it became possible to transfer or opt-out of an employer's occupational pension scheme for the first time. The quality of the advice received by large numbers of those who took the decision to transfer or opt-out of an occupational pension scheme has become a subject of major public concern. The response of the regulatory authorities has been criticised and developments concerning an SIB pensions review are discussed in the last part of this chapter. 5–002

Authorisation

Those involved in the personal pensions industry, offering pensions advice and managing pension funds are required to be authorised under section 3 of the Financial Services Act 1986 and Schedule 1, paragraphs 12–15 which set out the activities which constitute investment business (including dealing in investments, arranging deals in investments, managing investments and giving investment advice). Those involved in the personal pensions industry are regulated by the PIA. 5–003

Investment Advice and Business

For pensions advice to be investment advice within the Financial Services Act 1986, the advice must satisfy the following tests: 5–004

63

Chapter 5: Personal Pensions

    (a) the advice must relate to an investment;
    (b) the advice must relate to an investment rather than to a class of investments;
    (c) the advice must be on the merits of buying, selling etc, the investment;
    (d) the advice must be given to persons in their capacity as investors or potential investors;
    (e) the advice must not otherwise be exempted under the Act.

These requirements are set out in paragraph 5 of the SIB guidance note which was issued in March 1988, *Pensions Advice and Management: The Financial Services Act 1986*.

5–005   A pension scheme member's rights under a personal pension scheme are an investment under the Financial Services Act 1986 if the underlying assets include investments but not otherwise. This will include schemes based on life policies or unit trust contracts but not those based on bank or building society deposit accounts (unless these are structured as collective investment schemes).

5–006   Although the regulation of occupational pensions falls outside the scope of the Financial Services Act 1986, a person who is involved in the management of investments held under an occupational pension scheme (regulated under the Pensions Act 1995) will be deemed to be carrying on an investment business within the meaning of the 1986 Act (s.191(1)).

The Rules

5–007   Regulation of non-occupational personal pensions is carried out by the PIA (having taken over from FIMBRA and LAUTRO). The PIA has adopted the rules of FIMBRA in respect of the regulation of personal pensions.

5–008   Between 1988 to 1994, a large number of people decided to change their pension arrangements by transferring or opting-out of occupational pension schemes in favour of personal pension schemes. The quality of the advice on which many of these decisions was based has been and continues to be the source of great concern. In response to this public concern the SIB issued guidelines addressed to the relevant SROs (now the PIA having taken over the role from FIMBRA and LAUTRO). The PIA issued a Statement of Policy in February 1995 which required PIA members to embark on a review of their past pensions business in accordance with the SIB's Guidelines.

5–009   A pension transfer is defined as:

"a transaction resulting from a decision made with or without advice from a Member, by a client who is an individual to:
    (a) transfer deferred benefits from a final salary occupational pension scheme; or
    (b) transfer deferred benefits from a money-purchase occupational pension scheme,

in favour of an individual pension contract or contracts" (PIA adopted FIMBRA Rule 12.1.1).

5–010
A pension opt-out is defined as

"a transaction resulting from a decision, made with or without advice from a member, by a client who is an individual, to opt-out of or decline to join a final salary or money-purchase occupational pension scheme of which he is a current member, or which he is, or at the end of a waiting period will become eligible to join, in favour of an individual pension contract or contracts." (The PIA has adopted FIMBRA Rule 12.1.2.)

5–011
An opt-out is presumed to be adverse to the interests of the individual concerned unless the contrary can be affirmatively shown.

5–012
An individual pension contract is defined as meaning:

"a pension policy or pension contract under which contributions are paid to:
(a) a personal pension scheme approved under section 630 of the Income and Corporation Taxes Act 1988, whose sole purpose is the provision of annuities or lump sums under arrangements made by individuals in accordance with the scheme;
(b) a retirement benefits schemes approved under section 591(2)(g) of the Income and Corporation Taxes Act 1988, for the provision of relevant benefits by means of an annuity contract made with an insurance company of the employee's choice." (PIA adopted FIMBRA Rule 12.5.)

5–013
The PIA has adopted the relevant FIMBRA rules which set out the standard terms and conditions for opt-out (rules 12.2–12.2.7) and for pension transfers (rules 12.3–12.3.9).

The SIB Pension Review

5–014
As noted, it is estimated that over five million personal pensions have been sold since April 1988 when it became possible to transfer or opt-out of an employer's occupational pension scheme for the first time. The quality of the advice received by large numbers of those who took the decision to transfer or opt-out of an occupational pension scheme has become a subject of major public concern. In October 1994, the SIB initiated a review of the way in which personal pension policies had been sold between April 1988 and 1994. The object of the review was to identify investors who had been wrongly sold personal pensions and to provide a mechanism of redress.

5–015
The scale of the problem is quite daunting. The PIA Ombudsman estimated in his 1994/1995 Annual Report that some 350,000 cases would have to be reviewed (see p. 26 at para. 6(a)). Other estimates have

CHAPTER 5: PERSONAL PENSIONS

put the figure at nearer 1.5 million people who may have been wrongly advised to transfer out of occupational pension schemes since 1988. The cost of putting right the blunders has been estimated as running to £2 billion.

5–016   The review covered: (a) pension transfers where a person takes money out of an ex-employer's pension scheme and puts it into a person pension plan; (b) a buy-out contract where a person changes jobs; (c) pension opt-outs where people who were members of an employer's pension scheme but who have left the scheme whilst still working for the same employer and have taken out a personal pension instead; and (d) non-joiners who could have joined an employer's pension scheme but decided to take out a personal pension scheme instead. The review was not concerned with people whose employer did not have a pension scheme or with arrangements made by or on behalf of self-employed people.

5–017   In January 1996 the SIB issued a progress report on the review (*Redress for the mis-selling of personal pensions—a progress review* issued on January 16, 1996). The review was intended to target specified priority groups. Broadly, the priority groups comprised of the cases of older pension scheme members. Scheme holders qualify for redress if the firm that advised on the pensions scheme gave advice which broke the rules in force at the time and the scheme holder suffered financial loss or expects to suffer financial loss in the future. The SIB and the SROs have issued rules and/or guidelines on how firms should implement review and redress programmes. It is expected that complaints about the mis-selling of pensions will form a major part of the work load of the PIA and the PIA Ombudsman for the next few years.

5–018   Both the SIB Guidelines and the PIA's Statement of Policy were the subject of judicial review proceedings in 1995. In *R. v. PIA, ex p. Lucas Fettes and Partners (Financial Services Ltd)*, July 10, 1995, unreported, a court was asked to consider the legality of the PIA's Statement of Policy. The case was brought by Lucas Fettes and Partners (Financial Services) Ltd, which operated as an investment business giving advice about pension investments which required it to be authorised under the Financial Services Act 1986. Lucas Fettes asked the court to declare as unlawful the PIA Statement of Policy which required every PIA member who sold pension policies between 1988 and 1994 to embark on a review of every such transaction over that period by contacting relevant customers and assessing, at the member's expense, the legality of each transaction. Lucas Fettes' objection was founded on the cost of undertaking such a review and on the potential damage that such an investigation might inflict on their relationships with their clients. Lucas Fettes said that the blanket nature of the investigation was unfair. Buxton J. upheld the legality of the PIA's policy, rejecting the application on the grounds that Parliament had conferred wide powers on the SIB, and by delegation to the PIA, to undertake an extensive review where this was justified in the public interest:

"It seems to me that the regulatory system that has been imposed by the Financial Services Act does deliberately . . . give the PIA a wide discretion in deciding what it needs to do adequately in the interests of the industry. That is important not merely for the industry itself but also of course for the people who have dealt with it. In formulating the Financial Services Act in the way that it has, and dedicating this very important part of an individual's life to a system of self-regulation, Parliament must be taken to have accepted that the regulators would have very wide powers to take such steps as they thought necessary."

In reaching this conclusion Buxton J. was guided by the earlier decision of the Court of Appeal in *R. v. SIB, ex p. Independent Financial Advisors Association and LIBM Ltd*, May 12, 1995, unreported, where the SIB Guidelines had themselves been subjected to attack. In the course of his judgment Staughton L.J. noted that the problem which the SIB sought to confront was grave and of acute public concern: 5–019

"At stake was the reputation, which in this context means nothing less than the credibility, of the industry and, of even greater concern the reduction in the pension entitlements of perhaps thousands of investors."

Unfortunately, the pursuit of these two cases impeded the progress of the PIA review and delayed the consideration of complaints by the PIA Ombudsman. In a civil action for damages brought by a number of investors for breach of contract and negligence in the selling of personal pension plans, the defendants (the Prudential, Gan Life, Hill Samuel, TSB and Irish Life) argued that aggrieved investors should not be allowed to pursue their claims because the matter was the subject of review by the PIA. The insurance companies asserted that the applications should be stayed pending the conclusion of the PIA review. The Judge, Judge Raymond Jack Q.C. sitting in the Bristol Mercantile Court on the January 8, 1996, unreported, held that the actions should not be stayed. 5–020

Pensions Ombudsman

In respect of the investigation of complaints concerning personal pensions there is an overlap in jurisdiction between the Pensions Ombudsman, the PIA Ombudsman and the Insurance Ombudsman. In practice this has been resolved by an agreement between the Pensions Ombudsman and the PIA Ombudsman. In a memorandum of understanding between them (issued March 31, 1995), it was agreed that the PIA Ombudsman would have jurisdiction to investigate the vast majority of complaints and disputes in respect of personal pensions. The Insurance Ombudsman will deal with all complaints or disputes concerning companies in the membership of the Insurance Bureau. The Pensions Ombudsman will only investigate a dispute concerning a 0–021

CHAPTER 5: PERSONAL PENSIONS

personal pension if it has slipped through the net of the other Ombudsman. In 1994/1995 the Pensions Ombudsman only investigated five personal pensions cases whereas, the PIA Ombudsman in the same period received some 336 complaints in respect of pension transfer or opt-outs. Complaints concerning personal pensions are expected to continue to form a large proportion of the workload of the PIA Ombudsman for some time to come.

Part 3

Pensions Act 1995

Chapter 6

Overview

Background

The Pensions Act 1995 was introduced largely in response to public concerns about the safety of occupational pension schemes following the Maxwell affair. The Government also saw it as an opportunity to widen the choice of available pension schemes and to provide more flexibility in the way in which funds can be converted into retirement income. The objective of this section is to set out the regulatory regime which governs the administration and management of occupational pensions. In this chapter the scheme of the Act is considered. The Act seeks to achieve its objective by imposing extensive duties and conferring extensive powers on trustees and employers, and these are examined in Chapter 7. Ancillary provisions are considered in Chapter 8. Mechanisms for dispute resolution and compensation are covered in Chapter 9. **6–001**

An "occupational pension scheme" is defined by section 1 of the Pension Schemes Act 1993 (and by section 207 of the Financial Services Act 1986 in identical terms) as: **6–002**

> "any scheme or arrangement which is comprised in one or more instruments or agreements and which has, or is capable of having, effect in relation to one or more descriptions or categories of employment so as to provide benefits, in the form of pensions or otherwise, payable on termination of service, or on death or retirement, to or in respect of earners with qualifying service in an employment of any such description or category."

The regulation of occupational pensions is of very real importance to a very large number of people, indeed for many people, a pension scheme will be their second largest single asset after the family home. It is estimated that over 20 million people have rights to a pension from an occupational pension scheme and accrued rights in occupational pensions are worth about £600 billion. The last two decades have seen a major shift in the way in which pensions are provided and administered. In the past, many if not most people have relied on the State to provide for them in their retirement but as Phillip Thorpe, the chief executive of IMRO, observed in April 1996: **6–003**

> "Whichever government is in power it is an inescapable fact that people are having to make more and more provision for themselves

rather than rely on the State. This applies to pensions and retirement as much as long-term care and critical illness policies" (*The Times*, April 20, 1996).

6–004 For those in employment there have traditionally been two ways of getting pension cover; the first is to rely on the State scheme made up of a basic State pension which may be topped up by SERPS (the state earnings related pension scheme introduced in 1978) which is dependent on how much a person earns. However, many people have contracted out of SERPS in favour of occupational pension schemes run by their employers which usually provide better benefits. Occupational pension schemes have traditionally been tied to the employer and could not be transferred when an employee changed jobs. In an attempt to meet this problem, in the last 10 years, large numbers of people (estimated at some five million) were advised to take advantage of the right to transfer out of an employer's occupational pension scheme into a personal pension scheme. As we have seen in the last chapter, the quality of advice which many of these people received has fallen woefully below the proper standard and for many, redress is still awaited.

6–005 Confidence in the management and regulation of occupational pension schemes was severely rocked by the disappearance of more that £400 million from the Maxwell pension funds. The public outcry that followed the revelations of the Maxwell pension fund losses lead to calls for tighter controls on fund assets and for a "code of conduct" for pension fund trustees.

6–006 The existing law was also extremely complex and lacked both structure and organisation. It left wide powers and discretions in the hands of employers and trustees which were open to abuse by the unscrupulous and provided little protection for the interests of scheme members. Under the law before the 1995 Act there was no independent regulator and no compensation scheme to which an aggrieved pensioner could turn.

The Goode Report

6–007 The Government recognised the general level of disquiet and concern about occupational pension schemes and as a result the Goode Committee, under the Chairmanship of Professor Goode, was appointed in July 1992 to conduct a comprehensive review of the law relating to occupational pensions. The Committee made a number of key recommendations (see paras 1.1.13–1.1.15 of *Pension Law Reform* 1993 Cm. 2342):

— trust law should continue to provide the foundation for occupational pension schemes but that this should be supplemented by a Pensions Act administered by a Pensions Regulator;

OVERVIEW

— the freedom of trusts should be limited to ensure the reality of the pension promise and protect the rights accrued;

— there should be greater provision of information to scheme members;

— the security of members entitlements should be strengthened by a minimum solvency requirement, monitored by a Pensions Regulator and by scheme auditors and actuaries;

— there should be restrictions on the withdrawal of surpluses by employers;

— a compensation scheme should be introduced;

— there should be a general reduction in the administrative burdens imposed on employers and scheme administrators through the simplification of the law by the replacement of detailed investment rules with a general prudent person standard and statutory investment criteria.

In response to the recommendations of Professor Goode, the Government commissioned a White Paper (see *Security, Equality, Choice: The Future for Pensions* 1994 Cm. 2594) and this resulted in the Pensions Act 1995. The Government adopted many but by no means all of the Professor Goode's recommendations and other recommendations have been watered down in the legislation, most notably the solvency requirement has become a minimum funding requirement. **6–008**

The Pensions Act 1995 introduces a major overhaul of the way in which occupational pensions are regulated and administered. Most provisions of the Act are expected to come into force on April 6, 1997. In addition, the regulation of occupational pensions continues to be governed by the Pensions Schemes Act 1993 (supplemented and amended by the 1995 Act) which came into force on February 7, 1994 replacing and consolidating the previous social security legislation relating to pension schemes. In particular the Act consolidated all of the detailed requirements of the Occupational Pensions Board for the certification of contracted-out pension schemes. **6–009**

Pension funds have always been run as trusts by trustees and this continues to be the case. The pensions legislation imposes certain specific requirements on the administration of pension trusts but the guiding principles of trust law are still very much the foundation of pensions law. **6–010**

In many ways there has been a somewhat anachronistic application of the law of trusts in respect of pension schemes. The investment powers of pension fund trustees have been constricted by the law of trusts, the terms of the Trustee Investments Act 1961 and the language of the particular trust instrument in question. Many problems have been encountered over the years, including having to decide whether the employer was a beneficiary under the trust and in choosing what standards of control to apply. **6–011**

CHAPTER 6: OVERVIEW

6–012   The problem of whether the employer has rights as a beneficiary arises in relation to pre-1971 schemes which often made no provision for the employer to benefit under any circumstances or any provision for residual surpluses. After the Finance Act 1970, it became a requirement that new schemes include a clause stipulating that a surplus on winding up should be returned to the employer. Arguably, under such schemes the employer became a beneficiary only under the doctrine of resulting trusts but in the 1970s the courts became more reluctant to find that such a resulting trust existed but more recently the courts have been willing to find that a resulting trust exists. The case law showed an increasing willingness by the courts to treat employers favourably under schemes in which there was no duty to consider them.

The Scheme of the Pensions Act 1995—OPRA

6–013   Four fundamental principles underlie the legislation. These are first, to restore public confidence by improving the security of occupational pension schemes. Secondly, to introduce equal pensions rights for men and women following a number of European Court rulings. Thirdly, to secure fair and sustainable state pensions in the next century and fourthly, to make personal pensions attractive across a broader age range.

6–014   In introducing the second reading of the Pensions Bill to the House of Lords on January 24, 1995, Lord Mackay of Adebrecknish outlined the scheme of the Act:

> "We now intend to provide a clear framework of statutory obligations on employers, trustees, scheme professionals and others connected with pension schemes. The measures in the Bill will re-inforce trust law as the basis for pension law; bring the management of all schemes up to the level of best practice; give scheme members more influence in the running of their schemes by giving them the right to select at least one-third of the trustees; underline the fact that trustees are responsible for running schemes properly, and give them the tools they need in order to do so; introduce a statutory solvency requirement to maintain the adequacy of pension fund assets; establish an occupational pensions regulator with robust and wide ranging powers; and set up a compensation scheme" (*Hansard*, H.L. Vol. 560, col. 975).

6–015   The Act is divided into four parts: Part I is concerned with the provisions which amend and control certain aspects of occupational pensions schemes including the introduction of the Occupational Pensions Regulatory Authority. Part II concerns the progressive equalisation of state pensions at the age of 65 for both sexes. Part III provides for the certification of schemes and introduces considerable changes in the provisions for contracting out of the State scheme. Part IV contains miscellaneous provisions which include measures intended to extend the scope the powers of the Pensions Ombudsman.

The Occupational Pensions Regulatory Authority

6–016 The Goode Committee recommended that a statutory regulator should be established to oversee pensions regulation. This was accepted in principle in the White Paper although the scheme preferred by the Government limits the regulator to a responsive role, the regulator becoming involved only where schemes in difficulty were brought to its attention rather than having a regulator who monitored all pensions schemes which was perceived as being an impossible task given the numbers of schemes in existence.

6–017 Section 1 of the Pensions Act (together with Schedule 1) establishes the Occupational Pensions Regulatory Authority ("OPRA"). The Occupational Pensions Board is abolished (by section 150) and its functions will be taken over by OPRA from April 1997.

6–018 OPRA must consist of at least seven members to be appointed by the Secretary of State, members must include representatives of employers, employees, and members with knowledge and experience of the life assurance business, the management or administration of occupational pension schemes and two members with knowledge of occupational pension schemes.

Under Schedule 1, the Secretary of State has the power to make regulations as to the procedure to be followed by OPRA in the exercise of its functions and the manner in which those functions are to be performed.

6–019 OPRA is under an obligation to prepare an annual report for the Secretary of State and is funded from levies on occupational pensions schemes according to their total membership. Section 165 of the Pensions Act 1995 substitutes a new section 175 into the Pension Schemes Act 1993 which allows for the making of regulations to cover the imposition of a levy on pension schemes to cover the cost of setting up and operating OPRA. It is expected that regulations will also be made which allow for a levy to be made to cover the cost of the Compensation Board.

Supervision by OPRA

Prohibition Orders

6–020 Section 3 gives OPRA the power to prohibit a person from being a trustee of specified trust schemes in certain circumstances which are set out in section 3(2). This power only applies to occupational pension schemes set up under a trust.

6–021　The circumstances in which OPRA may prohibit a person from being a trustee include; where OPRA is satisfied that whilst a trustee, the person has been in serious or persistent breach of his duties under the Act (with certain exceptions relating to the indexation of pensions, the equal treatment requirement and the gathering of information by the Compensation Board) or that the person is a company and any director of the company is prohibited from being a trustee of the scheme, or that the person is a Scottish partnership the partners of which are prohibited from being a trustee of the scheme, or the person is a director of a company prohibited from being a trustee by virtue of having been in serious or persistent breach of its duties and those breaches have occurred with the connivance or are attributable to the neglect of that director. The effect of prohibiting a person from being a trustee has the effect of removing him (s.3(3)). A person who is the subject of a prohibition order has the right to apply to OPRA to have the order revoked (s.3(4)).

Suspension Orders

6–022　These are designed to allow for the interests of beneficiaries to be protected as soon as the regulator has a suspicion of any wrongdoing. A suspension order is intended to protect the trust and not to imply any wrongdoing, it allows the regulator to investigate whether it should use its powers under section 3 or whether section 29 (the automatic disqualification of trustees) arises. Section 4 provides for the interim suspension of trustees pending consideration of their actions or omissions or pending proceedings for making a prohibition order under section 3, or for criminal proceedings involving dishonesty, or where a bankruptcy petition has been presented to the court against him, or where an application has been made for his disqualification as a director under the Company Directors Disqualification Act 1986. An initial suspension order may be made for a maximum of 12 months pending consideration of the making of a suspension order or until the outcome of any other proceedings. Orders for suspension may apply to specific trust schemes or to all trust schemes with which the trustee is involved. A person who is the subject of a suspension order has the right to apply to OPRA to have the order revoked (s.4(5)).

6–023　Section 5 concerns the notices required to be served on a trustee prior to his removal as a trustee under section 3. Usually a trustee must be given one month's notice of the proposed prohibition.

6–024　A person who purports to act as a trustee of a trust scheme whilst prohibited from being a trustee under section 3 or suspended under section 4 commits a criminal offence which is triable in both the Crown Court and the magistrates' court and which is punishable by a fine (unlimited in the Crown Court and up to a maximum of £5,000 in the magistrates' court) (s.6(1)). Sections 6(3) and (4) preserve the validity of the acts done by a person who is prohibited or suspended from being a trustee.

Disqualification

For the first time in relation to occupational pension schemes the Pensions Act contains provisions which allow for the disqualification of trustees from acting as trustees of any occupational pension scheme established under a trust. Section 29 operates in two ways, first it allows for disqualification by the regulator (ss.29(3)(4)) and secondly it allows for automatic disqualification (s.29(1)). **6–025**

Section 29(3) allows that where a person is prohibited from being a trustee of a trust scheme under section 3 or has been removed as a trustee of a trust scheme by a court order on the basis of misconduct or mismanagement of the scheme, OPRA may disqualify him from being the trustee of any trust scheme if, in its opinion, it would not be desirable for him to continue as a trustee. Section 29(4) gives OPRA the power to disqualify a person from being a trustee of any trust scheme where in its opinion he is incapable of acting because of a mental disorder (Mental Health Act 1983), or where the trustee is a company which has gone into liquidation (within section 247(2) of the Insolvency Act 1986). **6–026**

A person who is the subject of a disqualification order (other than automatic disqualification) has the right to apply to OPRA to have the order revoked (s.29(5)).

Register of Disqualification

OPRA is required to set up a register of persons against whom a disqualification order has been made under section 29(3) or (4) but this does not include those automatically disqualified under section 29(1) and (s.30(7)). **6–027**

Appointment of Trustees

Section 7 of the Act gives OPRA the power to appoint trustees in certain circumstances. This power is discussed in the next chapter. **6–028**

Civil penalties

Fines

Section 10 provides OPRA with the power to impose civil penalties in respect of certain acts or omissions of trustees. The penalties being a fine of up to £5,000 for an individual and up to £50,000 for any other person. A penalty may not be re-imbursed out of the trust assets to any trustee upon whom it is levied (s.31(1)(b)). The procedure for imposing a civil penalty under section 10 is expected to be contained in regulations. **6–029**

Power to Wind-up

OPRA also has powers under sections 11 and 12 to wind-up schemes including public service schemes. **6–030**

Injunctions

6–031   OPRA is empowered to seek an injunction from the High Court (the Court of Session in Scotland) to prevent, or to prevent the repeat of the misuse or misapplication of any of the assets of a scheme (s.13).

Restitution

6–032   Under section 14 OPRA may also apply to the High Court (the Court of Session in Scotland) for an order for restitution where there has been any contravention of the provisions of section 37 (payment of surplus to an employer from the assets of an ongoing scheme), section 40 (controlling the extent of employer related investments), section 76 (relevant to the power to distribute the surplus on the winding up of a scheme) or section 77 (relates to schemes with imperfect winding up provisions).

Information and Inspection

6–033   The powers of OPRA to gather information in pursuance of its duties in respect of occupational pension schemes are contained in sections 98–103 of the Act. A trustee, manager, professional advisor or employer and any other person appearing to OPRA to be a person holding information relevant to the discharge of OPRA's functions must produce to OPRA any document relevant to the discharge of those functions if required by notice in writing to do so (s.98(1)). "Document" includes information recorded in any form including information held on computer (s.98(3)). Legal professional privilege and the protection against self-incrimination are preserved by section 102.

6–034   Section 99 gives inspectors appointed by OPRA the power to enter premises to make such enquiries as are necessary and to require the production of relevant documents for inspection where the inspector has reasonable grounds to believe that members of the scheme are employed on those premises, documents relevant to the administration of the scheme are being kept on the premises or the administration of the scheme or work connected with the scheme is being carried out on those premises. A magistrate may issue a warrant where there are reasonable grounds for believing that there are relevant documents on the premises which have not been produced in accordance with section 98 or that such documents are on the premises and there is a risk that they would not be produced and would be removed from the premises, hidden, tampered with or destroyed or that an offence under the Act or the Pension Schemes Act 1993 has been committed, that a person will do any act which constitutes a misuse or misappropriation of the assets of an occupational pension scheme or that a person is liable to pay a penalty under section 10 of the Act or a person liable to be prohibited under section 3.

6–035   Non-compliance with a requirement to produce documents under section 98 is an offence, as it is for a person who without reasonable excuse delays or obstructs an inspector exercising his powers under

The Scheme of the Pensions Act 1995

section 99. Both offences are triable summarily and may be punished by a fine of the statutory maximum (ss.101 (1), (2) and (3)). Knowingly or recklessly providing OPRA with information that is false or misleading in a material particular is also an offence if the information is provided in purported compliance with a requirement under section 99 or is provided in circumstances where the person providing it intends or could reasonably be expected to know that it would be used by OPRA for the purpose of discharging its functions. It is also an offence to alter, suppress, conceal or destroy any document which a person is liable to produce to OPRA under sections 98 or 99. A person guilty of an offence under sections 99(5) or (6) is liable on conviction in the magistrates' court to a fine not exceeding £5,000 or on conviction the Crown Court to imprisonment (maximum of two years) and/or a fine (s.101(5), (6) and (7)).

OPRA may publish a report of an investigation where they consider it appropriate to do so (s.103(1)). OPRA is absolutely privileged for the purposes of the law of defamation (s.103(2)). 6–036

Information obtained by OPRA in the exercise of its functions which relates to the business or other affairs of any person except information which is publicly available or which forms part of a general summary is "restricted information". The disclosure of restricted information is prohibited save with the consent of the person to whom it relates. Disclosure of restricted information is an offence punishable by a fine in the magistrates' court or by imprisonment and/or a fine if convicted in the Crown Court (s.104). Sections 106 to 108 provide exceptions to the general prohibition on the disclosure of information where the disclosure is for the purpose of facilitating the discharge of OPRA's functions (s.106), to facilitate the discharge of the functions of other supervisory bodies including the Secretary of State, the Treasury, the Bank of England and the Pensions Ombudsman (s.107) and for certain other reasons which are in the interests of the members of an occupational pension scheme or in the public interest (s.108). 6–037

Questioning the Decisions of the Regulator

Section 96 gives OPRA the power to review its own decisions. It may review decisions on its own volition or the review may be as a result of an application by a person against whom a section 3 order has been made, or by an applicant against whom there has been an order to pay a penalty under section 10 of the Pensions Act or section 168(4) of the Pensions Schemes Act 1993 (as substituted by Pensions Act 1995, s.155) or by an applicant against whom an order disqualifying him from being a trustee of a scheme under sections 29(3) or (4) has been made (s.96(2)). OPRA may also review a decision at any time on the application of an interested person where there has been a change in circumstances since the determination was made or where the determination was made in ignorance of or based on a mistake as to a material fact or was erroneous in point of law (s.96(3)(a)). The decision may be reviewed within six 6–038 months (or a longer period within the discretion of OPRA) on any ground (s.96(3)(b)). OPRA may revoke a determination, substitute a new determination or deal generally with matters arising on the review as if they had arisen on the original determination (s.96(4)).

Appeals

6–039 Section 97 concerns references and appeals from decisions of OPRA. Any question of law or any matter arising out of a review of a decision may be referred to the High Court (the Court of Session in Scotland) by OPRA by way of a notice in writing (s.97(1)and (2)). In contrast, an aggrieved person may only appeal to the Court on a question of law where OPRA has not itself referred the matter to the High Court (or Court of Session) (s.97(3)) and also see Pensions Schemes Act 1993, s.151).

Conclusion

6–040 It remains to be seen once its provisions have come into force in April 1997 just how effective the legislation is in practice. However, there are a number of reservations which may be voiced concerning the efficacy of the regulatory regime. These should be borne in mind when considering the detailed provisions of the Act which are summarised in subsequent chapters.

6–041 To begin with, of course, the introduction of an independent Pensions Regulator is to be welcomed. In the past it has been a very real problem that there has been no independent body overseeing the pensions industry. The powers which the 1995 Act has given to the Regulator are largely responsive in nature. Professor Goode envisaged a regulator with a more pro-active role but it is perhaps understandable given the scope of the pensions industry why this did not prove attractive to the Government. The Pensions Regulator will obviously supplement the work already done by the Pensions Ombudsman and by OPAS which, although voluntary, has a very useful part to play in the resolution of disputes. Perhaps one of the most significant roles that the Regulator will play will be as the recipient of information from scheme auditors and actuaries under the "whistle blowing" provisions of the Act, although again those in the industry have expressed some reservations over the weight of the burden that these provisions impose on the professional involved. Again only time will tell how effective the provisions work in practice.

6–042 The Act places a much greater emphasis than hitherto on the protection of the rights of the member of a scheme by introducing provisions designed to limit the freedom of trusts and particularly the influence of employers over trustees. The introduction of member

Conclusion

nominated trustees (see Chapter 7) is intended to ensure that members interest are properly represented. Two potential problems may arise, the first is that member nominated trustees will have to take care in practice that they do not find themselves with a conflict of interests between their obligations as trustees to the trust and the interests of the scheme members. Secondly, it has been suggested that in some of the better run existing schemes the new provisions imposing a minimum number of member nominated trustees may actually have the effect of reducing the numbers of member nominated trustees.

The recommendation of the Goode Committee that the security of members entitlements should be strengthened by the introduction of a minimum solvency requirement has been watered down to a minimum funding requirement by the 1995 Act. This is discussed in Chapter 7. The minimum funding requirement introduced by the Act falls short of a minimum solvency requirement and those in the accountancy and actuarial professions have expressed reservations as to whether the test to be applied will offer proper safeguards for member's future rights. **6–043**

As regards the introduction of the compensation scheme (see Chapter 9), the limitations on the scope of the scheme which comes into effect only on the insolvency of the employer and in very limited circumstances raises questions as to just who this scheme will cover in reality. If the compensation provisions had been in force at the time of the Maxwell débâcle, the Mirror Group pensioners would not have been covered by the scheme as the Mirror Group continued to trade. **6–044**

The 1995 Act introduces a large number of criminal offences for non-compliance with its provisions but as we shall see in later chapters, very few regulatory offences are prosecuted in practice. **6–045**

Chapter 7

Duties and Powers

7–001 In this chapter the extensive duties and powers imposed and conferred by the Pensions Act 1995 on trustees and employers are considered.

Trustee Appointment and Removal

7–002 The eligibility and appointment of trustees is a matter for the terms of a trust. As a matter of general law, any person (including a body corporate) who can hold or dispose of any legal or equitable interest in property may be a trustee. The appointment and removal of trustees is subject to the supervision of the courts which may appoint a new trustee (Trustee Act 1925, s.41), remove trustees (*Re Chetwynd's Settlement* [1902] 1 Ch. 692), appoint a judicial trustee (Judicial Trustees Act 1896), give directions to trustees (Ord. 85, r.2 of the Rules of the Supreme Court) and generally administer the trust (*Re Blake* (1885) 29 Ch.D. 913). A discussion of the general powers of appointment and removal of trustees is to be found in any of the standard text books on equity and trusts and is beyond the scope of this work.

7–003 The Goode Committee made a number of recommendations in relation to the appointment of trustees of occupational pension schemes which included the recommendation that employers should not have the sole power to appoint trustees and that there should be implemented a system of statutory disqualification of trustees whereby trustees would automatically be disqualified if they fell within certain statutory criteria or where they had a conflicting role within the scheme.

7–004 The Pensions Act limits the freedom of pension schemes to fix their own structures for choosing trustees in four ways: first, by imposing requirements in relation to member nominated trustees. Secondly, by imposing limitations on links with the scheme auditor or scheme actuary. Thirdly, by giving OPRA powers to appoint, suspend, prohibit or disqualify trustees and fourthly, by way of automatic disqualification provisions.

Member Nominated Trustees

7–005 Prior to the Pensions Act there have been very few special requirements as to the identity, appointment or removal of trustees of pension schemes, but employers have found the right to nominate the trustees of a scheme a valuable power because where the trustees act through the use of powers or discretion it is helpful to the employer if the trustee is sympathetic to the employer's wishes. Traditionally, the courts have accepted that the implementation of powers or discretion may take many legitimate forms and interference with the decisions of trustees exercising their powers or discretion has been very limited in practice. Sections 16 to 21 are intended to ensure that the views of the general membership of pension schemes will be heard through member nominated trustees. It is expected that these powers will be supplemented in due course by regulations to be issued by the Department of Social Security.

7–006   Under the new provisions, one third of the total number of trustees must be nominated by members. In schemes of more than 100 members there must be at least two member nominated trustees (where membership is less than 100, there must be at least one) (s.16 (6)), who are appointed for a minimum of three years but for not more than six years (s.16(5)), although at the conclusion of his period of appointment, a member nominated trustee may be re-selected. An employer has the right to veto a candidate for selection (s.20(5)). A member nominated trustee automatically ceases to be a trustee if he ceases to be a member of the scheme (s.16(8)) but he continues to be a member if he becomes a deferred pensioner. A member nominated trustee may only be removed with the consent of all the other trustees (s.16(3)(b)). The rules governing implementation may be designed by the trustees to meet the needs of the trust, however, if the trustees fail to design such rules, a set of prescribed rules will apply. It is expected that the Department of Social Security will issue regulations governing procedure in due course.

7–007   Member nominated trustees will perform the same functions as other trustees (s.16(7)), except that OPRA has the power under section 7 to confer specific functions on member nominated trustees.

7–008   The requirement to appoint member nominated trustees does not apply where alternative proposals for the nomination of trustees by the members have been put forward in an employer opt-out scheme within the provisions of section 17. The opt-out allows for greater flexibility which is limited by the need to seek membership approval of alternative proposals. Any limitations on the role of the member nominated trustee by the employer can only be achieved through the alternative route under section 17 and with member approval. Again, it is expected that the procedure will be set out in regulations to be made by the Department of Social Security in due course.

Compliance with the provisions of sections 16 to 20 may be subject to time limits imposed by regulations created under section 21(4).

7–009   Sections 18 and 19 concern corporate trustees who are often special purpose companies acting as the sole trustee of a scheme which are connected to the sponsoring employer. Sections 18 and 19 allow that the approach where there is a corporate trustee will be broadly similar to when the trustees are individuals. The term "connected" in section 18 is not defined in the Act, a wholly owned subsidiary would certainly be "connected" but it remains to be seen whether the term "connected" will extend to situations where the employer holds only a minority shareholding in the trustee company.

It has been suggested that in practice the imposition of member nominated trustees may give rise to a number of problems including the possibility that a member nominated trustee may feel that he represents the interests of the class of members who nominated him rather than acting in the interests of all the beneficiaries which may give rise to a conflict of duties in practice. 7–010

Where trustees have failed to take all reasonable steps to ensure compliance with the obligation to put in place arrangements or to take reasonable steps to do so, OPRA has the power to make an order under section 3 prohibiting them from being trustees of the scheme and/or to require them to pay a fine under section 10. Where the employer has followed the opt out route under section 17, OPRA may impose a fine under section 10 (s.21). 7–011

Auditors and actuaries as trustees

A trustee of a trust scheme and any person who is connected with or an associate of such a trustee is ineligible to act as an auditor or actuary of the scheme (s.27(1)). However, a director, partner or employee of a firm of actuaries is not ineligible simply because another director of the firm is a trustee (s.27(2)). It is anticipated that regulations made by the Department of Social Security in due course will exempt certain specified classes of trustees and connected or associated persons to allow them act as actuary or auditor to the pension scheme. (See the Department of Social Security consultation paper—August 18, 1995.) 7–012

A person who is ineligible from acting as a trustee is prohibited from so acting (s.27(4)). Contravention of the prohibition is a criminal offence the punishment for which is imprisonment of up to two years and/or a fine if convicted in the Crown Court and a fine of up to £5,000 if convicted in the magistrates' court (s.28(1)). However, acts done as an auditor or actuary by a person who is ineligible are not invalid because of that fact (s.28(3)). Acting whilst ineligible to do so under section 27 renders that person liable to removal as a trustee under section 3 (s.28(4)). 7–013

For the purposes of section 27, the terms "connected" and "associated" are defined by section 123 as being the same as in sections 249 and 435 of the Insolvency Act 1986. Section 123 does not apply for the purposes of section 18 of the Act. 7–014

Trustee Appointment by OPRA

The powers conferred on OPRA allowing it to appoint trustees are intended to be used to protect scheme members from incompetent and dishonest trustees. OPRA is given power under section 7 of the Pensions Act to appoint pension scheme trustees in specified circumstances. 7–015

Chapter 7: Duties and Powers

OPRA may replace a trustee it has removed under its section 3 powers or where the trustee ceases to act by reason of his disqualification under section 29 (s.7(1)). OPRA may also appoint new trustees to the scheme where it is necessary (*i.e.* more than merely desirable) to ensure that the trustee board has the necessary expertise for the administration of the scheme, that the number of trustees is sufficient for the proper administration of the scheme or that the assets of the scheme are properly used and applied (s.7(3)). Section 7(5) allows OPRA to specify the number of trustees in the scheme, it may require that the trustees' fees be paid out of the scheme, and to provide for the appointment and removal of the trustee appointed. The employer may also be made liable for the payment of the appointed trustees fees (s.8(1)). The powers and duties of an appointed trustee will be the same as those of any other trustees unless OPRA exercises its power to restrict the powers and duties of the appointed trustee (s.8(3) and s.8(4) overriding s.16(7) and s.32).

Automatic Disqualification

7–016　A trustee is automatically disqualified from being a trustee of any trust scheme under section 29(1) if he has been convicted of an offence of dishonesty or deception (s.29(1)(a)), if he is an undischarged bankrupt (s.29(1)(b)), or where the trustee is a company (or partnership in Scotland) and any director (partner) is disqualified under section 29, (s.29(1)(c) and (d)), where the trustee has made a composition with creditors and not been discharged (s.29(1)(e)), or where the trustee has been disqualified under the Company Directors Disqualification Act 1986 (s.29(1)(f)).

The effect of the disqualification is that the trustee automatically ceases to be a trustee. The trustee will not have to take any steps to resign his position (s.30(1)).

7–017　A person who purports to act as a trustee of a trust scheme whilst he is disqualified under section 29 commits an offence which is punishable on conviction in indictment to imprisonment for two years and/or a fine and if convicted in the magistrates' court to a fine of up to the statutory maximum.

A person automatically disqualified may apply for a notice in writing waiving his disqualification (s.29(5)).

Decisions by Majority

7–018　Trusts law has traditionally required unanimity in the decision-making process from trustees unless the trust instrument has specifically allowed them to act by majority. The Pensions Act 1995 has effectively reversed this by allowing decisions of trustees to be made by majority unless the trust instrument requires unanimity or a "super majority", *i.e.* a two thirds majority for certain decisions. A majority usually means a majority of all the trustees not simply a majority of those present at a meeting although section 32(2)(a) allows the trustees to determine the quorum requirements for their meetings (s.32). Notice must be given to all trustees of meetings at which decisions may be taken (s.32(2)(b)), a failure to ensure that notice requirements have been met by any trustee may lead to the impositions of section 3 or section 10 sanctions (s.32(5)).

The majority rule will not apply where OPRA has ordered that a trustee appointed under section 8 may exercise powers to the exclusion of other trustees, or for a decision to remove a member nominated trustee under section 16(3)(b), or where an independent trustee has been appointed because of employer insolvency under section 22 (and s.25(2)(a)). 7–019

Trustee Conflicts of Interest and Duty

It is a general rule of equity that "a trustee must not place himself in a position where his duty and his interest may conflict": *per* Lord Upjohn in *Boardman v. Phipps* [1967] 2 A.C. 46 at 123. However, in practice this has meant that a trustee who is also a beneficiary may not be able to exercise a power in a way that would incidentally benefit himself without applying to the court for authorisation. (See *Re William Makin & Son Ltd* [1993] O.P.L.R. 171 and *Manning v. Drexel Burnham Lambert Holdings Limited* [1994] O.P.L.R. 71; [1995] 1 W.L.R. 32.) Section 39 is intended to solve the difficulties raised as a matter of general trust law in the *Drexel* case by removing the strict conflict rule. Section 39 provides that: 7–020

"No rule of law that a trustee may not exercise the powers vested in him so as to give rise to a conflict between his personal interest and his duties to the beneficiaries shall apply to a trustee of a trust scheme, who is also a member of the scheme, exercising the powers vested in him in any manner, merely because their exercise in that manner benefits, or may benefit, him as a member of the scheme."

The provisions of Part I of the Pensions Act and the regulations made under it are intended to be overriding where they conflict with the provisions of a pension scheme (s.117). 7–021

The Minimum Funding Requirement and the Collection of Contributions

The continued funding of a pension scheme's accrued liabilities is fundamental to the promise to pay a pension. In the past many schemes have made no provision to cover the costs of benefits until they become payable; such schemes obviously depend on the employer continuing to 7–022 be in existence and in a position to meet the costs of the benefits payable under the scheme at the time they fall due. Many public service schemes operate in this way by placing the burden of meeting the costs of future benefits on future tax payers and indeed will continue to operate in this way as they are exempted from the requirements of a minimum funding requirement. However, there is the obvious danger that in the event of an employer's insolvency, a scheme which is not properly funded or which has made no advance funding provisions will not be in a position to meet its liabilities and the pensioners will suffer as a consequence.

7–023 Prior to the 1995 Act, there has been no legal requirement to fund a scheme in advance. The 1995 Act introduces a minimum funding requirement in respect of occupational pension schemes. The provisions are contained in sections 56–61 and are expected to come into force over a five year transitional period from April 5, 1997. Schemes will be required to have their first minimum funding valuation within three years of their previous funding valuation, which in practice, means by the year 2000.

7–024 The purpose of a minimum funding requirement is to ensure that in the event of the employer's insolvency the assets of the scheme would still be able to meet its liabilities. The Goode Committee envisaged that this should be accomplished by introducing a minimum solvency requirement, however, the minimum funding requirement introduced by the Act falls short of such a solvency test. This has inevitably lead to debate and concern within the industry that in practice the level of minimum funding required to meet the requirement of the Act and the anticipated regulations will in practice fall short of providing full protection for future beneficiaries under a pension scheme.

The Minimum Funding Requirement

7–025 Section 56 of the Pensions Act requires that in order to satisfy a minimum funding requirement, the value of the assets of a scheme must not be less than the amount of the liabilities of the scheme (s.56(1)). The requirement is applicable to all on-going occupational schemes other than money purchase schemes and schemes specifically excepted by the regulations (s.56(2)). Some money purchase schemes may be brought within the minimum funding requirement by virtue of section 89(1)(a). Schemes which are likely to be exempted by the regulations include public service schemes, schemes with a government guarantee, local authority schemes and unapproved top-up pension schemes set up to provide benefits in excess of the normal Inland Revenue limits.

7–026 Sections 57–60 lay the statutory ground work for the operation and implementation of the minimum funding requirement. The detail necessary for its operation is expected to be contained in regulations. The minimum funding requirement is based on full actuarial valuations undertaken at least every three years where the minimum funding level will be certified by an actuary (s.57(1)(a)), the agreement of a contribution schedule after each valuation (s.58(3)(c)) and annual reviews by the scheme actuary of the contribution schedule (s.57(1)(b)).

The Minimum Funding Requirements

Valuation and Certification of Assets and Liabilities

For the purposes of sections 56–61, the liabilities and assets to be taken into account, and their amount or value are to be determined, calculated and verified by a prescribed person in a prescribed manner where the person and manner are to be determined by regulations (s.56(3)). In practice the valuations will be carried out by the scheme actuary (appointed under s.47) who will be assisted by a guidance note to be issued by the Institute of Actuaries and Faculty of Actuaries. 7–027

Section 57(1) requires the trustees or managers of an occupational pension scheme to obtain from an actuary an actuarial valuation and a certificate of his opinion as to whether the contributions payable to the scheme are adequate for the purpose of securing the minimum funding requirement and indicating any changes since his last valuation at certain prescribed intervals. The prescribed intervals are to be determined by the regulations to be issued in due course (s.57(1)(a) and(b)). 7–028

If the actuary is of the opinion that contributions are inadequate to secure the minimum funding requirement throughout the period or within prescribed circumstances, a further actuarial valuation must be obtained within six months or a prescribed time-limit (ss.57(2)) and 57(4)). Before a further valuation can be obtained, the trustees and the employer must agree a rate of contributions under section 58 such that it can be certified by the actuary (s.58(6)). The actuary must be satisfied that the rate of contributions will allow the scheme to meet the minimum funding requirement throughout the period or at least by the end of the period. If the minimum funding requirement is not met by the end of the period, the trustees must make a report to OPRA (s.59(3)). If the scheme is seriously under-funded, *i.e.* less than 90 per cent funded, the provisions of section 60 apply. 7–029

There is considerable concern within the industry as to the standards to be applied to the valuations required for calculation of whether the minimum funding requirement is being met. The indications to date are that the regulations will set a standard for the calculation of the minimum funding requirement which is likely to be to a lower standard than the standard that would be necessary to purchase annuity policies to satisfy the schemes liabilities. 7–030

Schedule of Contributions

The trustees or managers of an occupational pension scheme must ensure that a schedule of contributions is prepared and that it is kept updated for each prescribed period (expected to be a five year period). The schedule must show the rates of contributions payable to the scheme by the employer and by active members of the scheme and the dates on which such contributions are to be paid (s.58(1) and (3)). The rates of contribution shown in the schedule must be agreed between the trustees and the employer or in the event that they cannot agree, the 7–031 rates of contributions must be determined by the trustees (s.58(4)). A failure by the trustees to decide the rate of contributions may lead to the imposition of sanction under section 3 and section 10 (s.58(8)).

Reporting to OPRA

7–032 The trustees or managers of a scheme must notify OPRA if the contributions required from the employer or from the active members have not been made in accordance with the schedule of contributions (s.59(1)). A report must also be made to OPRA if it appears to the trustees or managers of a scheme that the minimum funding requirement is not met (s.59(3)). The failure to take all steps to comply with these requirements may lead to the imposition of sanctions under section 3 and section 10 (s.59(4)).

Serious under-provision

7–033 Where a scheme does not meet the minimum funding requirement *i.e.* where the scheme is less than 90 per cent funded on the minimum funding requirement basis, the employer must, by making a payment to the trustees or managers or by some other prescribed method, secure an increase in the value of the scheme assets which together with the contributions will cover the shortfall (s.60(1) and (2)). This must be accomplished within a set time (s.60(3)). A failure to make up the shortfall by the employer must be reported in writing within 14 days of the end of the time-limit by the trustees or managers of the scheme to OPRA and to the members of the scheme (s.60(4)). A failure to notify may lead to the imposition of section 3 and section 10 sanctions (s.60(8)).

Money Purchase Schemes

7–034 Corresponding provisions in relation to schedules of contributions for money purchase schemes are to be found in sections 87–90. In particular, section 87 prescribes that a schedule of contributions should be kept for money purchase schemes and corresponds to section 58 from which money purchase scheme are exempted by virtue of section 46. Money purchase schemes are discussed in Chapter 8.

In the event that assets have been lost the compensation scheme set up under the Act may take effect if its conditions are satisfied. The compensation scheme is discussed in Chapter 9.

Investment

7–035 Proper investment is obviously of fundamental importance to the security of pension rights. The powers and duties imposed on trustees in relation to investment should make little difference to properly run occupational pension schemes. The main impact of the Pensions Act 1995, is the imposition of sanctions on trustees for failures to comply with the Act.

Investment Powers: Trustees' Duty of Care

7–036 A trust instrument cannot restrict the liability for breach of any obligation imposed by law to take care or exercise skill in the performance of any investment functions which is owed by trustees or by a person to whom the function has been delegated. This is of particular importance in restricting the previous freedom of trust law which meant that trust instruments could often be over generous in its treatment of trustees and employers to the detriment of the beneficiaries. Unless the trustees are themselves authorised or exempted they are bound to delegate day-to-day investment decisions with regard to the pension scheme to a person authorised or exempted for the purposes of section 191 of the Financial Services Act, Schedule 1, paragraph 14, or to persons who do not require authorisation. The powers of the trustee to delegate management of the scheme are contained in section 34.

Powers of Investment and Delegation

7–037 Section 34 of the Pensions Act is intended to provide flexible guidelines for investment by trustees of occupational pension schemes. Under the Act, trustees have the power to make any investment as if they were absolutely entitled to the assets of the scheme subject only to any restriction imposed by the trust instrument (s.34(1)). What amounts to an investment under this section is not defined either by the Pensions Act or by reference to the Financial Services Act unlike elsewhere in the Act.

Duty to Act Prudently

7–038 A trustee must act prudently in his choice of investment notwithstanding that he is entitled to act as if "absolutely entitled to the assets."(See *Learoyd v. Whiteley* (1887) 12 App. Cas. 727; *Bartlett v. Barclays Bank Trust Co Ltd (No. 1)* [1980] 1 Ch. 515.)

Delegation

7–039 The trustees may delegate their power to make investments to two or more trustees who may exercise the discretion as to investments or to an unauthorised fund manager in relation to investment business outside the definition of investments by the Financial Services Act (s.34(5)(a) and (b)) or to a fund manager falling within section 191(2) of the

Financial Services Act. (s.34(2)(a)). The trustees may not delegate the power to make investment to any other person except under section 25 of the Trustee Act 1925 (s.34(2)(b)). The fund manager chosen by trustees must fall within section 191(2) of the Financial Services Act (and Schedule 1, paragraph 14 of the Financial Services Act). The trustees have only limited vicarious liability in respect of the acts or defaults of a fund manager as long as they have taken reasonable steps to satisfy themselves that the fund manager has the knowledge and experience for managing the scheme's investments and that he is carrying out the work competently and in accordance with section 36 (s.34(4)). In contrast, where the trustees have nominated two or more of their number under section 34(5) they remain fully vicariously liable for their acts or defaults. The provisions of section 34 override any restriction inconsistent with it by any other enactment apart from the Pensions Schemes Act 1993 (s.34(7)).

Investment Principles

7–040   Investment principles are set out in section 35. Trustees are required to have prepared and to keep updated a written statement of the principles governing decisions about investments for the purposes of the scheme (s.35(1)). The written statement must cover the trustees' policy for securing compliance with sections 36 and 56, the policy about the kinds of investment to be held, the balance between investments, the realisation of investments and any other matters prescribed (s.35(2)) and (3). The trustees must seek proper investment advice in writing from a suitably qualified person, *i.e.* someone who is knowledgeable with regard to the investment of pension schemes (s.35(5)(a)) and they must consult the employer (s.35(5)(b)). Consultation of the employer is especially important in respect of money purchase schemes, where the performance of the investments will affect the employer's contributions to the scheme. However, to prevent the employer from exercising control over the investments of a scheme, no restriction in which the consent of the employer is required may be imposed (s.35(4)). Failure to obtain written investment advice renders the trustees liable to the penalties available under sections 3 and/or 10.

Choosing Investments

7–041   The principles which govern the choice of investments are set out in section 36 and are broadly the same as the requirements applying to trust schemes under the provisions of section 6 of the Trustee Investments Act 1961. Trustees or fund managers must have regard to the need for diversification and the suitability of the chosen investments (s.36(2)). The trustees must obtain proper advice in writing before making an investment (ss.36(3), (6) and (7)). Failure to obtain proper advice renders the trustees liable to the penalties available under sections 3 and/or 10 (s.36(8)). The choice of investments must also take into account the provisions relating to the minimum funding requirements.

Professional Advisers

The proper operation and smooth running of an occupational pension scheme can be greatly assisted by the appointment of appropriate professional advisers. The 1995 Act introduces measures requiring the appointment of a number of professional advisers in respect of occupational pension schemes and introduces measures which are intended to clarify who the professional adviser is to be appointed by and be responsible to. In the past it has often been the position that advisers have been appointed or recommended by the employer which has the obvious disadvantage of leading to a certain blurring in the line of command and the possibility of a lack of impartiality as between the adviser and the trust. 7–042

The advisers required under the act are a scheme auditor and a scheme actuary (who must be a named person) (s.47(1)) and a fund manager where the assets of an occupational pension scheme include investments within the meaning of the Financial Services Act (s.47(2)). Trustees are prohibited from being a scheme auditor or actuary under section 27. A failure to appoint the necessary professional advisers may render the trustees liable to the penalties available under section 3 and/or 10. The scope of section 47 is likely to be further defined through regulations and any failure to comply with these by the trustees, managers may render them liable to penalties under section 3 and/or 10 and may render an employer who has failed to comply liable to penalties under section 10 (ss.47(9),(10) and (11)). 7–043

Legal advisers have in the past often been appointed by employers. This has often meant in practice that the legal advice given to trustees has been less than impartial. However, section 47(3) renders the trustees of a scheme liable to the penalties available under section 3 and/or 10 of the Act if they place any reliance on the skill or judgment of a legal adviser or a fund manager who has not been appointed by the trustees or managers of the scheme. 7–044

"Blowing the Whistle"

Section 48 places duties on the auditor and the actuary appointed to a scheme to "blow the whistle" in circumstances set out in section 48(1). Professional advisers are often in a good position to monitor any irregularities or wrong doing which may affect the members interests at an early stage. As we see elsewhere in this book, professional advisers and particularly auditors, already have a statutory monitoring role in various areas of financial regulation, namely: under the Financial Services Act 1986, the Banking Act 1987, the Building Societies Act 7–045

CHAPTER 7: DUTIES AND POWERS

1986 and the Insurance Companies Act 1982. Before the establishment of OPRA under the 1995 Act, where professional advisers had suspicions of any kind there was no obvious body to whom they could report their concerns. However, the introduction of the "whistle blowing" obligation on auditors and actuaries has been met by some concern from the industry because of the burden which these requirements impose on the auditor and/or the actuary which will in practice effectively require the auditor and/or the actuary to have a detailed knowledge of the complicated and ever developing area of trust law which applies to pension schemes.

7–046 The auditor or actuary must "blow the whistle" by giving OPRA a written report if he has reasonable cause to believe that any duty relevant to the administration of the scheme imposed by law on the trustees, managers, the employer, any professional adviser or any prescribed person acting in connection with the scheme has not been or is not being complied with and the failure to comply is likely to be of material significance in the exercise of the functions of OPRA or for any other reason which may be prescribed by regulations although it is anticipated that in practice reliance may be placed on guidance notes issued by the appropriate professional bodies (ss.48(1) and (2)). Section 48(3) exempts the auditor and the actuary from being in breach of any duty of confidentiality or other duty by reason making such a report. A failure to make such a report renders the auditor or actuary liable to the penalties available under section 10 (s.48(7)) and OPRA may disqualify him from being the auditor or actuary of any occupational pension scheme (s.48(8)). A person who purports to act as an auditor or actuary of an occupational pension scheme whilst disqualified under section 48, commits an offence which is punishable by imprisonment and/or a fine if convicted in the Crown Court and with a fine up to the statutory maximum if convicted in the magistrates' court (s.48(12)). As yet it is unclear whether a failure to "blow the whistle" under section 48 by the scheme auditor or actuary would give rise to a civil claim by a person suffering loss.

7–047 Professional advisers other than auditors and actuaries have the power but not the duty to make a report (s.48(4)), but they enjoy a more limited cover against breach of confidentiality than that covering auditors and actuaries especially in connection to matters covered by legally professional privilege (s.48(5)).

"Whistle Blowing" and Personal (non-occupational) Pensions

7–048 Section 147 of the 1995 Act inserts a new section 33A into the Pension Schemes Act 1993 introducing a reduced concept of "blowing the whistle" by the auditors and actuaries of a personal (non-occupational) pension scheme. The auditor or actuary is under an obligation to make an immediate written report to the Secretary of State if he has reasonable cause to believe that section 9(5)(a) (the requirements to be fulfilled by a personal pension scheme for certification as an appropriate scheme for the purposes of contracting out) of the Pensions Schemes Act 1993 has not been satisfied and the failure to satisfy this requirement is likely to be of material significance to the Secretary of State's functions in relation to the pension scheme.

Self-investment

Section 40(1) imposes broad restrictions on employer-related investments. The detailed provisions relating to self-investment are anticipated to be contained in regulations. The trustee or managers of an occupational pension scheme must ensure that the scheme complies with any prescribed restrictions with respect to the proportion of its resources that may at any time be invested in employer related investments. At present, the restriction is limited to 5 per cent of the scheme's resources by market value contained in the Occupational Pension Schemes (Investment of Scheme's Resources) Regulations 1992 (S.I. 1992 No. 246) which are expected to be replaced by new regulations once the 1995 Act comes into force. The scope of the Occupational Pension Schemes (Investment of Scheme's Resources) Regulations 1992 was considered in *Wright v. Ginn* [1994] O.P.L.R. 83. Millett J. held that when the limits prescribed by the regulations are reached and the investment becomes unauthorised it can continue to be held provided the trustees can justify continuing to hold the investment. But, if they cannot justify holding the investment, they might be liable for a breach of trust. 7–049

Employer related investments means shares or other securities issued by the employer or a person connected or associated with the employer, land which is occupied by the employer or connected or associated persons or is subject to a lease in favour of the employer or connected or associated persons, property other than land which is used for the purposes of carrying on the employer's business or that of connected or associated persons, loans to the employer or connected or associated persons and any other prescribed investments (s.40(2)). 7–050

A failure to comply with the restrictions imposed by section 40(1) may render a trustee who has failed to take all reasonable steps to ensure compliance liable to penalties under sections 3 and/or 10. If the resources of an occupational pension scheme are invested in contravention of section 40(1), any trustee or manager who agreed to the making of the investment is guilty of an offence punishable by imprisonment and/or a fine if convicted in the Crown Court or by a fine of up to the statutory maximum if convicted in the magistrates' court. 7–051

In addition, if a court is satisfied on the application of OPRA that the trustees or managers of an occupational pension scheme have acted in contravention of section 40 the court may order the employer and any other person who appears to have been knowingly concerned in the contravention to take such steps as the court may direct for restoring the parties to the position in which they were before the act or omission occurred (s.14(1)). 7–052

CHAPTER 7: DUTIES AND POWERS

Administration

7–053   The administration of a pension scheme remains largely a matter for the trustees acting under the trust deed. However, the 1995 Act has introduced a number of measures which will affect the way in which the trustees of a scheme carry out the administration of the scheme, many of these measures have been introduced in response to the feeling that many of the consequences of the Maxwell disaster could have been avoided if adequate procedures had been in place. The measures introduced include:

Separate Bank Accounts

7–054   These measures are designed to ensure that trust receipts are held in separate bank accounts.

Records

7–055   Section 49(2) allows for the making of regulations which may require trustees to keep records of their meetings and books and records in relation to certain prescribed transactions. Section 49(3) allows for similar regulations to cover the keeping of records by employers and other prescribed persons. The regulations will set out the form in which records are to be kept and the period for which they are to be retained (s.49(4)). A failure to comply with the requirement to keep and maintain records in accordance with the regulations may render a trustee liable to penalties under section 3 and/or section 10 of the Act and may render an employer or any other prescribed person liable to penalties under section 10 (ss.49(6) and (7)).

Ineligibility of Trustees to Act as Scheme Auditors or Accountants

7–056   Under section 27(1) the trustees of a trust scheme and any person who is connected with or an associate of such a trustee is ineligible to act as an auditor or actuary of the scheme. Ineligibility is discussed earlier in this chapter.

Indemnity

7–057   Trustees must not be indemnified for fines or civil penalties this includes providing for the payment of premiums in respect of insurance policies to cover the imposition of such a fine or civil penalty (ss.31(1) and (2)). If a trustee is re-imbursed from the assets of a trust scheme in respect of a fine or civil penalty, any trustee who has not taken all reasonable steps to ensure compliance with the prohibition may be liable to penalties under section 3 and/or section 10 (s.31(3)). The trustee who has been re-imbursed commits an offence if he knows or has reasonable grounds for believing that he has been re-imbursed out of the assets of the scheme and he has not taken all reasonable steps to secure that he is not so re-imbursed (s.31(4)). The penalty on conviction in the Crown Court is imprisonment for up to two years and/or a fine and if convicted in the magistrates' court a fine of up to the statutory maximum (s.31(5)).

Disclosure

Regulations made under section 41 may require the trustees or managers of an occupational pension scheme to obtain copies of certain prescribed documents and make these available to members and prospective members of the scheme, the spouses of members and prospective members, other persons within the application of the scheme and qualifying or prospectively qualifying for its benefits and independent trades unions recognised for the purposes of collective bargaining in relation to members and prospective members. The documents which must be made available include audited accounts, the auditor's statement about contributions under the scheme, a valuation of the assets and liabilities of the scheme drawn up by an actuary, any valuation or certificate prepared by the actuary of the scheme under section 57 (valuation and certification of assets and liabilities) or section 58 (schedules of contributions) and any report prepared by the trustees or managers under section 59(3) (the minimum funding requirement). 7–058

Professional Advisers

The trustees of a scheme are required to appoint certain professional advisers and to delegate certain functions to them by virtue of sections 47 and 48. These have been discussed earlier in this chapter. 7–059

Dispute Resolution

The various ways in which disputes may be resolved are discussed in Chapter 9. 7–060

Payment of Trustees Expenses

Payment of trustees expenses by the employer are discussed elsewhere in this chapter. 7–061

Protection for Employee Trustees

The Act contains a number of provisions designed to protect employee trustees. An employer is required to permit an employee trustee to take time off during working hours to perform his duties as 7–062 trustee and to receive training (s.42(1)). An employee is entitled to payment for time off to perform his duties as a trustee or for training (s.43). A failure by the employer to meet these requirements may form the basis of a complaint to an industrial tribunal (ss.44 and 45). An employee trustee also has the right not to suffer detriment in his employment or be unfairly dismissed because of his position as an employee trustee and he may complain to an industrial tribunal of such behaviour. The purpose of these provisions is to protect the employee trustee who may, because of the nature of his duties as a trustee have to act in a way which might be detrimental to the interests of the employer but in the interests of the pensioners. Guidance in this area is likely to come from the Codes of Conduct for trustees and employers being drawn up by the pensions industry.

Receipts by Trustees: Separate Bank Accounts

7–063   Trustees of any trust scheme must keep any money received by them in a separate account kept by them at an institution authorised under the Banking Act 1987 (s.49(1)). Section 49 applies only to trust schemes and is intended to reduce the risk of the confusion of scheme assets with those of the employer by providing for and safeguarding the benefits payable in a case where the employer pays benefits on behalf of the scheme. A failure to comply with this requirement renders the trustees liable to the imposition of penalties under section 3 and/or section 10 where the trustee has failed to take all reasonable steps to secure compliance (s.49(6)).

7–064   The employer is also under a duty, where payments of benefits to members of a trust scheme are made by the employer, to pay into a separate bank account any payments of benefits which have not been made to the members within a prescribed period (s.49(5)). A failure to do so renders the employer liable to the imposition of section 10 penalties (s.49(7)). The employer may be guilty of an offence where, if on deducting contributions from a member's earnings, the amount deducted is not paid to the trustees or managers of the scheme within the prescribed time (expected to be within 14 days of the end of the tax month in which the deductions were made) and without a reasonable excuse. The penalty is one of up to two years' imprisonment and/or a fine if convicted in the Crown Court or a fine of up to the statutory maximum if convicted in the magistrates' court (s.49(8)).

Ongoing Surplus

7–065   Surpluses became an issue in the 1980s because of the growth in the equities markets and the reduction in the size of the workforce which resulted in schemes building up surpluses which employers tried to utilise. Many of the Goode Committee proposals in respect of the repayment of surpluses have not found their way into the final Act. Critics of the Act say that the provisions contained in the Act do not go far enough to implement the original intention of "strengthening the security of the fund."

The payment of a surplus to an employer may arise in the context of an ongoing scheme or in the context of a winding-up. A surplus arises in an ongoing scheme where an actuarial valuation shows that scheme assets exceed scheme liabilities at the date of valuation. A surplus on winding-up arises where there are assets remaining after paying for all the benefits due under the scheme and for the costs of winding up. The distribution of assets on winding up is covered by sections 76 and 77 of the 1995 Act. Section 76 of the 1995 Act is confined to a case where there is power conferred on an employer or the trustees to distribute assets to a person on the winding up of a scheme. Section 77 is intended to fill the gap where there is no power in the trust deed to return surplus assets to an employer on winding up. Where the trust deed has made express provision for the distribution of any surplus, *e.g.* by distribution to members, these arrangements will not be affected by the provisions of section 77. **7–066**

Payment of Surplus to Employer

The increase in surpluses in the 1980s led to the introduction of a number of measures to try to reduce the levels of surpluses (see the Pension Scheme Surpluses (Valuation) Regulations 1987 (S.I. 1987 No 412)). A reduction could be achieved in a number of ways. These included the repaying of some of the surplus, the reduction of the level of contributions (often by declaring a contributions holiday) or by the improvement of benefits. **7–067**

Section 37 covers the payment of surplus funds to an employer from an ongoing Inland Revenue approved pension scheme (*i.e.* one to which Schedule 22 to the Income and Corporation Taxes Act 1988 applies—self-administered schemes and insured schemes) where the trust deed confers the power on any person to make refunds to the employer. However, the effect of section 37(2) is to override the rules of a scheme so that the power to make repayments to an employer are only exercisable by the trustees of the scheme when certain conditions are met which are listed in section 37(4). The power must be exercised in pursuance of proposals made by the administrator of the scheme which must accord with the Inland Revenue's approved methods for a reduction or elimination of surplus (s.37(4)(a)). The trustees must be satisfied that it is in the best interests of the members that the power is exercised (s.37(4)(b)). Where the power is conferred on the employer by the trust deed, the employer must have asked for or consented to the power to being exercised (s.37(4)(c)). **7–068**

The trustees are liable if they purport to make a payment under section 37(1)(a) but have failed to take reasonable steps to ensure compliance with the requirements of this section they may be liable to **7–069** penalties under section 3 or section 10 (s.37(8)). Any other person who purports to exercise the power to make a repayment under section 37(1)(a) may be liable to a penalty under section 10 (s.37(9)).

7–070   OPRA may also become involved where a scheme member or an auditor or actuary exercising their "whistle blowing" function, has complained that the trustees have failed to comply with the requirements of section 37. OPRA has power under section 14 to apply to the court for restitution of the payment if it has been made in contravention of section 37.

Transfer Values

7–071   Under the Social Security Act 1985 a member who left a scheme on or after January 1, 1986 acquired the right to require the trustees of the scheme to transfer the cash equivalent of his accrued benefit to the scheme of his new employer or to a personal pension scheme (from July 1, 1988). Chapter IV of Part IV of the Pensions Schemes Act 1993 contains the current law in relation to transfers to and from occupational pension schemes. Problems with transfers have been common and transfers out of occupational pension schemes into personal pension schemes and the quality of the advice which many transferees received has been the subject matter of an SIB inquiry which is discussed elsewhere.

7–072   The amendments introduced by the 1995 Act are designed to cover the situation of those who left an occupational pension scheme before January 1, 1986 whose situation has continued to be governed by the terms of the trust deed. This situation has been altered by the introduction of the provisions contained in sections 152–154 and Schedule 6 to the Pensions Act 1995 which act by amending sections 93–95 and 97–99 of the Pensions Scheme Act 1993.

Extensions of Scope of the Right to a Cash Equivalent

7–073   Section 152 of the Pensions Act extends the rights to cash equivalents which exist under Chapter IV of the Pensions Schemes Act 1993 by amending section 93 of that Act. The scope of the right to a cash equivalent is extended by giving the right to a cash equivalent to members who left pensionable service under an occupational pension scheme before January 1, 1986.

7–074   Section 154 amends section 94(1) of the Pensions Schemes Act and gives the members rights to a cash equivalent of the amount contained in the statement of entitlement if an application is made within three months of it being supplied.

Statement of Entitlement

7–075   Section 153 amends section 93 of the Pensions Schemes Act 1993 by inserting a new section 93A under which a member is entitled on application to a statement of entitlement showing him the amount of his cash equivalent. Regulations will control the date at which a statement has to be made and other matters concerning the application including the frequency with which applications can be made. Failure to provide a statement may incur a penalty under section 10.

The draft transfer value regulations require that from April 1997, schemes must supply a transfer value within eight days of its effective date of calculation ("the guarantee date"). The guarantee date must normally be no later than three months after the date of application for a transfer value calculation. **7–076**

Payment of Transfer Values

Section 99 of the Pension Schemes Act 1993 requires the trustees of an occupational pensions scheme to pay a transfer value within 12 months of the date on which they receive the application. The amendment introduced by paragraph 6 of Schedule 6 effectively reduces this time scale to six months of receipt of the application or the guarantee date. **7–077**

Communication

The trustees of an occupational pension scheme have an number of obligations in respect of communication with OPRA and with scheme members. These obligations are covered elsewhere in this chapter. These include the disclosure to members of audited accounts, contributions statements and actuarial valuation reports under section 41; the obligation to make a report to OPRA if the minimum funding requirement is not met under sections 59(3) and (4): the obligation to notify OPRA and scheme members within a certain time if contributions are not paid in accordance with he contributions schedule (ss.59(1) and (4), and 88(1)(4)); the obligation to notify OPRA within 14 days of any serious under provision in relation to the minimum funding requirement (ss.60(4) and (8)); the obligation to produce documents required by OPRA (s.98) and to the Compensation Board (s.110 and sections 111(4) and (5)); the obligations to provide information to OPRA and the Compensation Board under sections 98, 110 and 111 also apply to the employer; the obligation not to disclose restricted information (ss.104 (1) and (3)). This obligation also applies to the employer; the obligation to comply with the information provisions of the Pension Scheme Act 1993, ss.113 and 155. **7–078**

The Modification of Schemes: Amendment

Occupational pension schemes must be able to change with changing commercial circumstances. Before the 1995 Act, change required a specific power to amend in the trust deed (in practice such a power is **7–079**

CHAPTER 7: DUTIES AND POWERS

usually drawn in the widest terms) or required there to be an application for a court order (under s.57 of the Trustee Act 1925 and the Variation of Trusts Act 1958) or to the Occupational Pensions Board (s.136 of the Pension Schemes Act 1993). The Goode Committee was concerned that the existing law on amendment of pensions schemes allowed the employers too much discretion and did not adequately protect members interests. The 1995 Act seeks to remedy this through sections 67 to 72 which will be supplemented by regulations and which are designed to prevent amendments which reduce a member's accrued rights (s.67), and which will allow the trustees to amend a scheme by resolution in certain circumstances (s.68), and will allow OPRA to grant modification orders in respect of a scheme (ss.69 to 72).

Restriction on the Power of Amendment

7–080   Section 67(2) provides that the power of amendment cannot be exercised on any occasion in a manner which would or might affect any entitlement or accrued right, of any member of the scheme acquired before the power is exercised unless the requirements of subsection 3 are satisfied.

7–081   Section 67(3) requires that the trustees have satisfied themselves that the certification requirements or the requirements for consent in respect of that member have been met. If the power is to be exercised by someone other than the trustee that the trustees must have approved the exercise of that power.

7–082   The certification requirement means prescribed requirements for the purpose of securing that no power to which section 67 applies would in the opinion of the actuary adversely affect entitlement or accrued rights of any member of the scheme (s.67(4)(a)). The consent requirements means prescribed requirements for the purpose of obtaining the consent of members of a scheme to the exercise of a power to which section 67 applies. Both requirements are expected to be the subject of regulations.

7–083   "Entitlement" is not defined in the Act and its meaning will no doubt be the subject of consideration by the courts at some stage. However, it may well indicate the position under a scheme where rights under it have crystallised, *i.e.* where the pension has become payable leaving the term. "Accrued rights" are defined by section 124(2) as "the rights which have accrued to or in respect of him (the member) at that time to future benefits under the scheme".

Power of Trustees to Modify Schemes by Resolution

7–084   Section 68 allows the trustees of a scheme to modify the scheme by resolution for the specific purposes set out in section 68(2). These are: to extend the class of persons who may receive benefits under the scheme in respect of the death of a member of the scheme; to enable the scheme to conform with such arrangements as are required by sections 16(1) and

17(2) (the appointment of member nominated trustees); to enable the scheme to comply with such terms and conditions as may be imposed by the Compensation Board in relation to payments under sections 83 or 84 (the payment of compensation); to enable the scheme to conform with section 37(2) (the exercise of power to refund surplus only by trustees), section 76(2) (restrictions on distribution of surplus on a winding-up), sections 91 or 92 (inalienability of occupational pensions and restrictions on forfeiture) and (e) prescribed purposes.

Modification Orders

Sections 69 to 71 replace the alteration powers of the Occupational Pensions Board contained in section 136 to 140 of Pension Schemes Act 1993 and allow OPRA on the application of a competent person to modify schemes except public service schemes for certain purposes. 7–085

Modification of Public Service Pension Schemes

Modification of such schemes is covered by section 72 which gives similar powers as those that are available to other occupational pension schemes under sections 67 to 70 to Public Service pension schemes. 7–086

Benefits

As set out in Chapter 8, the 1995 Act introduces provisions aimed at equalising the benefits payable to men and women members of pensions schemes. 7–087

Where there is a delay in paying benefits to a member of a scheme, the employer is obliged to keep the money due to be paid in a separate bank account (s.49(5)). If the employer fails to do so, OPRA may direct the trustees of the scheme to make arrangements for the payment of the benefit to made to the members (s.15(1)).

Augmentation on Wind-up

If a surplus is unavailable for return to an employer it may be used to increase pension benefits by an appropriate percentage and to augment benefits up to prescribed limits (ss.77(2), (4) and (5)). 7–088

Alienability and forfeiture are covered in sections 91 and 92 of the 1995 Act.

Chapter 8

Ancillary Provisions

8–001 In this chapter various ancillary provisions introduced by the Pensions Act 1995 are considered.

Contracting out of the Act: State Pensions

8–002 The Pensions Act 1995 introduces by way of amendment to the Pension Schemes Act 1993, new provisions on contracting out which break the link between the State Earnings Related Pension Scheme (SERPS) and contracted out pension schemes. The new system comes into effect on the Principal Appointed Day (PAD) expected to be April 6, 1997 (s.135 of the Pensions Act 1995). The five main changes are introduced by the Act are first, that the link between contracted out schemes and SERPS is to be broken. This is intended to reduce the complexity of contracting out but in practice it is feared that the simplification will take decades to take effect and that the administrative burden may actually be increased. Secondly, the option to buy back guaranteed minimum pensions (GMPs) into SERPS will disappear except when an insolvent scheme is wound up. Thirdly, schemes will have to pass a quality test. Fourthly, National Insurance rebates paid to schemes contracted out on a protected rights basis and also to personal pensions will increase with age and fifthly, it will be possible to mix salary-related and protected rights contracting out within one scheme for the first time.

8–003 The state pension is made up of two main parts which are the basic state retirement pensions and an additional pension known as a State Earnings Related Pension Scheme (SERPS). The basic retirement pension is based on National Insurance contributions whereas SERPS is based on how much has been earned and paid in National Insurance contributions since April 1978. By opting to leave SERPS and joining a contracted-out occupational pension scheme both the employer and the employee will pay a lower rate of National Insurance contributions (known as the contracted-out rebate).

Contracted Out Salary Related Schemes (COSRS)

8–004 It has always been possible for an employer to contract out their employees from SERPS by the employer undertaking to provide an equivalent pension which is known as the guaranteed minimum pension

(GMP) in return for a reduction in the national insurance contributions paid by both employer and employee. GMPs are calculated in more or less the same way as the SERPS benefits they replace and are index linked. However, the test which is applied in respect of GMPs in practice was criticised by the Goode Committee for being complicated and for placing a considerable administrative burden on defined benefit schemes.

8–005 In 1988, the contracting out arrangements were extended to cover defined contribution schemes including personal pensions. Under these the employer undertakes to pay contributions equal to the contracted out rebate into the scheme. These are known as contracted out money purchase schemes (COMPS). Contracted out personal pensions are known as appropriate personal pensions (APPs) where if the employee has a personal pension plan that is contracted out of SERPS (an Appropriate Personal Pension) both the employer and the employee continue to pay full National Insurance contributions and the DSS pays the rebate directly into the personal pension plan.

New Contracting Out Requirements

8–006 Section 136 of the Pensions Act 1995 inserts a number of new provisions into the Pension Schemes Act 1993 which provides for new certificates and for new criteria to be fulfilled for the purpose of obtaining certificates in respect of schemes contracting out under the Act. To be contracted out after the Principle Appointed Day a scheme must comply with the present requirements for contracting out set out in sections 13 to 24 of Pension Schemes Act 1993 in respect of any period before the Principle Appointed Day. In respect of any period after the Principle Appointed Day, the scheme must comply with the requirements of sections 12A to 12C and with the requirements regarding employer related investments.

8–007 Schemes contracting out on a defined benefit (salary related) basis are no longer required to provide GMPs but must meet alternative requirements contained in section 9(2B) of the Pensions Schemes Act 1993 (inserted by section 136(3) of the 1995 Act). The new requirements are that the scheme must comply with section 12A of the Pension Schemes Act (inserted by section 135(5) of the 1995 Act) introducing a new scheme-based quality test; the restrictions imposed on employer related investment by section 40 of the 1995 Act apply and the scheme must comply with these restrictions; the scheme must satisfy any other prescribed requirements including the minimum funding requirement and the scheme must not fall within a prescribed class or description.

The Scheme-based Contracting Out Test

8–008 COSRS will have to meet a statutory standard of overall scheme quality in respect of pensionable service after the Principle Appointed Day. The scheme must provide pensions which are broadly equivalent or better than those which would be provided under a reference scheme defined in section 136(5) of the Pensions Act 1995 (inserting sections 12A to 12D into the Pension Schemes Act 1993) as an occupational pension scheme which provides a normal pension age of 65 for men and women; an annual accrual rate of 1/80th of qualifying earnings averaged over the previous three complete tax years up to a maximum of 40 years service; a spouse's pension of 50 per cent of the member's pension or accrued pension to normal pension age if the member dies before normal pension age; and increases to pension of five per cent per annum or at the rate of the Retail Price Index whichever is the lower.

The scheme's actuary must certify that the scheme meets the test. Section 12A of the Pension Schemes Act and the DSS Contributions Agency will rely on the actuary's certificate. **8–009**

The role of the Occupational Pensions Board in respect of the issue, variation and withdrawal of employers certificates will be taken over by the Contracted out Employment Group within the DSS Contributions Agency.

Contracting out for COMPS and APPs

These will continue to be contracted out on the basis that the contributions made to the scheme in respect of employees are not less than the amount of the contracted-out rebate applicable. The scheme must also satisfy the requirements of section 9(3) of the Pension Schemes Act 1993. **8–010**

Treatment of accrued GMPs for service before the Principal Appointed Day: the Act introduces a number of changes in the treatment of GMPs after the Principle Appointed Day. The two main changes concern the revaluation of GMPs in deferment and the indexation of GMPs in payment for female members following the equalisation of State pension age. **8–011**

Revaluation of GMPs in Deferment

A member's GMP element is revalued according to one of three methods adopted at the time the member leaves pensionable service until the member reached 65 or 60 for women or until the member dies if sooner. The three permitted methods of revaluation are by the revaluation of earnings factor, by a prescribed fixed rate valuation which varies according to the date when service terminated or by the limited rate valuation which is a limited rate of earnings growth up to a maximum or five per cent p.a. compound. **8–012**

It is expected that after the Principal Appointed Day, even though GMPs will not continue to accrue, the member will not cease to be in contracted-out employment triggering revaluation until they actually cease to be in contracted-out employment under the scheme and the GMPs will continue to be increased in line with the revaluation of earnings factor. **8–013**

Chapter 8: Ancillary Provisions

The indexation of GMPs will continue with schemes being liable for increases of up to three per cent and SERPS topping up any extra.

New Contracting Out Procedure: How the Test will Work in Practice

8–014 The DSS Contributions Agency will issue a contracting-out certificate to the employer on receipt of a completed election package. The election package is expected to include an election form signed by the employer and containing information about the employer and the scheme and confirming that there has been consultation with trade union where appropriate; and that the scheme does not have an overseas element; is not a funded or unfunded unapproved benefit scheme; the scheme complies with regulations covering employer related investment; the scheme is not under investigation by OPRA; that the new quality test is satisfied; a schedule of contributions is included; and the date from which the certificate is to be effective.

8–015 Certificates must be renewed every three years—see section 34(a)(ii) of the Pension Schemes Act 1993 as amended by paragraph 37 of Schedule 5 of the 1995 Act.

Transitional provisions are contained in sections 7(2A) and 7(2B) of the Pension Schemes Act inserted by section 136 of the 1995 Act. These provide for the transition from the current contracting out certificates to the new contracting out arrangements. The transitional period is expected to be for 10 years from the Principal Appointed Day.

State Schemes

8–016 The Goode Committee was not concerned with State pensions except in as much as they relate to occupational pension schemes. Sections 126 to 134 and Schedule 4 to the Pensions Act 1995, introduce a number of provisions relating to State pensions designed to eradicate the inequalities in pension and other employment benefit provision as between men and women including the equalisation of pensionable age which is discussed below.

Divorce

8–017 Of the numbers of people who divorce, about half of those in employment are also members of an occupational pension scheme. What happens to pension rights in the event of divorce is therefore something of very great importance to large numbers of people. Prior to the passage of the Pensions Act 1995, the courts had a duty to take pension assets into account in divorce settlements but their power to intervene in pension schemes has been held to be extremely limited. In the case of *Brooks v. Brooks* [1995] 3 All E.R. 257 the court held that there was a power to intervene in some types of pension scheme but the power is applicable to very limited types of scheme. In this particular case, the decision turned on the proper construction of the term "any ante-nuptial or post-nuptial settlement" in section 24(1)(c) of the Matrimonial Causes Act 1973 and whether it gave the court jurisdiction on the dissolution of a marriage to vary all property comprised in a settlement made on the parties to the marriage. The court found that as long as a pension fund constituted a settlement made by the husband then the Court had the power to vary it and that a sole member scheme entered into by a husband with the intention of providing financial support for himself and his wife on retirement was a disposition which fell within the meaning of a marriage settlement for the purposes of the Act and could thus be varied by the ourt.

The powers of the courts to make orders for maintenance and adjustment of property rights on divorce are contained in sections 23, 24 and 24A of the Matrimonial Causes Act 1973. The Pensions Act introduces legislation for the first time to address what will happen to pension rights in the event of divorce. Section 166 of the Pensions Act introduces sections 25B to 25D to be inserted into the Matrimonial Causes Act 1973 which provides for benefits which either spouse has or is likely to have under a pension scheme to be taken into account by the court which is also to take into account any benefits which a party to the marriage is likely to lose under a scheme. The new provisions are likely to apply only to new settlements effected after April 6, 1996 and then only to payments due on or after April 6, 1997. The effectiveness of the new legislative provisions remains to be seen in practice, but the new provisions would appear to be a move away from the "clean break" settlement favoured by the courts where the circumstances of a divorce allow. **8–018**

A pension scheme is defined in section 25D(4) as meaning an occupational or personal pension scheme broadly applying the definitions contained in section 1 of the Pension Schemes Act 1993. **8–019**

Under the amended Matrimonial Causes Act the court must have regard to any benefits under a pension scheme which a party to the marriage has or is likely to have in the foreseeable future and to any benefits under a pension scheme which any party to the marriage is likely to lose the chance of acquiring by reason of the dissolution of the marriage (s.25B(1) of the Matrimonial Causes Act). Section 25B(2) of the Matrimonial Causes Act requires the court to consider whether to make an order in respect of the pension benefits. An order may be made under section 25B(4) of the Matrimonial Causes Act directly against the trustees or managers of the scheme and may require that where any payment is due at any time under the scheme to one party to a marriage is shall be paid to the other party. Section 25B(5)of the Matrimonial Causes Act limits the amount which the trustees or managers of a scheme can be ordered to pay to 100 per cent of the scheme member's pension. **8–020**

CHAPTER 8: ANCILLARY PROVISIONS

8–021   Section 25B(7) of the Matrimonial Causes Act provides that a scheme member may be ordered to commute the whole or any part of his pension to a lump sum, if he has the right to do so, which may then be offset against other assets so enabling a clean break settlement.

Lump Sums on Death

8–022   Section 25C of the Matrimonial Causes Act empowers the court to order trustees or managers of a scheme who have a discretion in respect of a lump sum to exercise it in favour of the receiving party.
   Section 25D of the Matrimonial Causes Act deals with other miscellaneous matters including in the event of the transfer of pension rights to a new scheme that the liability under the court order shall also transfer to the new scheme.

Pensions on Divorce in Scotland

8–023   Section 167 provides similar provisions to those contained in section 166 in respect of pensions on divorce in Scotland.

Equal Treatment

8–024   The equal treatment rule relates to the terms on which persons become members of a scheme and the way in which members are treated (s.62(1)). The provisions of the 1995 Act in respect of equal treatment are modelled on the Equal Pay Act 1970 which was intended to ensure that the terms of all contracts of employment were not more favourable towards one sex rather than the other. At the time it was passed the Equal Pay Act did not include pension arrangements within its scope because it was anticipated at the time that specific legislation would be introduced within the life of the next Parliament covering equal pension rights. In fact, it has taken another 25 years and a number of European Court judgments for such provisions to be introduced.

8–025   The equal treatment rule is designed to make occupational pensions equal for men and women in respect of pensionable service after May 17, 1990. Sections 62 to 66 are designed to put into operation the requirements of Article 119 of the Treaty of Rome and the Equal Treatment Directive (Directive 86/378) as they apply to occupational pension schemes. Section 126 and Schedule 4 deal with the raising over time of the State pension age for women to 65 together with various other provisions designed to equalise the treatment of men and women.

The Scope of Article 119

8–026   Article 119 of the EEC Treaty provides that:

"Each Member State shall ... maintain the application of the principle that men and women should receive equal pay for equal work. For the purposes of this article 'pay' means the ordinary basic or minimum wage or salary and any other consideration, whether in cash or kind, which the worker receives, directly or indirectly in respect of his employment from his employer..."

The scope of Article 119 was considered by the European Court of Justice in *Barber v. Guardian Royal Exchange Assurance Group* [1990] 2 All E.R. 660; judgment given on May 17, 1990. The European Court held that since a pension paid to an employee under a contracted-out private occupational pension scheme amounted to consideration paid in respect of employment it fell within the scope of "pay" under Article 119 and so a pension scheme which had differential age qualifications offended against the principle of equal pay set out in Article 119. However, the effect of the judgment was limited to service after May 17, 1990. 8–027

The scope of Article 119 was further considered by the European Court in a number of case. In *Coloroll Pension Trustees v. Russell* [1994] I.R.L.R. 586, which arose out of the financial collapse of the Coloroll Group and the appointment of receivers. Coloroll Pension Trustees Ltd became the trustees of eight separate pension schemes with the task of winding them up and disposing of their assets. All of the schemes made different provisions for men and women which in some cases had the effect of meaning that different pensions were payable to men and women who had exactly the same length of service. The case was brought because of concerns that Article 119 might override the provisions of the trust deeds and that until the matter was clarified by the European Court it was not possible to say with certainty how the funds should be distributed. The question to be decided by the European Court was whether the effect of Article 119 could be relied upon by both employees and their dependants as against the employer and the trustees of a scheme. The European Court held that Article 119 could be relied upon by both an employee and by his dependants because the right to payment of a survivor's pension derives from the survivor's spouse's membership of the occupational pension scheme. Article 119 could be relied upon as against the trustees of an occupational pension scheme and neither the employers nor the trustees could rely upon the rules of their particular pensions scheme to evade their obligations under Article 119. The temporal limitations of the Barber judgment (*i.e.* that the judgment only effected service after May 17, 1990) applied to survivor's pensions as well as to employees and concerned non-contracted out as well as contracted out occupational pension schemes. The actuarial factors which differ according to sex and which result in an inequality of employers contributions to a defined benefit occupational pension scheme did not offend Article 119. Neither did voluntary contributions by an employee fall within the scope of Article 119. Article 119 continued to apply even where an employee 8–028 changed jobs and transferred to a new pension scheme. Finally, Article 119 was not applicable to pension schemes which at all times had members of only one sex.

8–029   In *Ten Oever v. Stichting Bedrijfspensioenfonds voor het Glazenwassers-en Schoonmakbedrijf* [1993] I.R.L.R. 601, the European Court held that a survivor's pension fell within the scope of Article 119 even though is was not paid to the employee but to his survivor it is an advantage deriving from the employee's membership of the scheme and arose by reason of the employment relationship between the employer and the employee. However, the Barber judgment meant that equality of treatment could only be claimed in relation to benefits payable in respect of periods of employment after May 17, 1990. Mr Ten Oever's wife had been a member of an occupational pension scheme in the Netherlands which did not provide for a survivor's pension for widowers. Mr Ten Oever's action was based on the argument that pension rights were pay which fell within Article 119 (the Barber judgment) and that it was wrong to discriminate against him because he was a widower rather than a widow.

8–030   The equal treatment rule contained in section 62 of the Pensions Act 1995 is intended to replace the measures brought in under the Occupational Pension Schemes (Equal Access to Membership) Amendment Regulations 1995 (S.I. 1995 No. 1215) which came into force on May 31, 1995 by amending the 1976 regulations of the same name and by modifying section 118 of the Pension Schemes Act 1993 in such a way that the membership of an occupational pension scheme had to be open to both men and women on equal terms as to age and length of service.

8–031   Trust deeds which do not contain an equal treatment rule are to be treated as if they do have such a rule (s.62(2)). Section 65 enables but does not require trustees to amend trust deeds without an equal treatment provision so that such a provision is included.

8–032   Section 63(4) says that the provisions of section 62 are to be construed in the same way as those of section 1 of the Equal Pay Act 1970 and that section 2 of that Act in governing disputes and enforcement shall have effect over section 62 of the Pensions Act 1995 with some amendments. This means that claims for breach of section 62 can be referred to an Industrial Tribunal within the time-limits imposed by section 2(4) and (5) of the Equal Pay Act 1970 as amended by section 63 of the Pensions Act 1995. It remains to be seen whether these time-limits apply to complaints made to the Pensions Ombudsman. Section 66 amends the Equal Pay Act 1970 and the Sex Discrimination Act 1975 to allow enforcement of the equal treatment rule against an employer and in relation to the terms of employment relating to a member of a scheme.

8–033   In practice, the equal treatment rule applies where a woman is employed on like work with a man in the same employment or the woman is employed on work rated as equivalent with that of a man in the same employment or a woman is employed on work which in terms of the demands made on her is of equal value to that of a man in the same employment.

Section 64 provides certain exceptions to the equal treatment rule **8–034** which will not operate in relation to any differences as between a woman and a man in the operation of the terms relating to access and the treatment of members if the trustees or the managers of the scheme prove that the difference is due to a material factor which is not the difference in sex but is a material difference between the woman's case and the man's case. The variations are expected to be set out in regulations and are anticipated to include variations in the amounts of pension payable to a man and a woman. However, these variations will only apply where the differences are attributable to the differences in State pension they are entitled to receive, and the application of different actuarial factors as between the sexes which apply when calculating the employer's contributions to the scheme and in relation to calculating benefits from a scheme (see *Coloroll*).

Sections 62 to 65 of the Pensions Act are expressly excluded from the **8–035** supervisory scope of OPRA. A trustee who is in breach of the requirements under these sections cannot be prohibited from being a trustee under section 3 of the Act. In contrast the Pensions Ombudsman does have power to adjudicate in questions of equal treatment.

State Pensions: The Equalisation of Pensionable Age

Section 126 and Schedule 4, Part I are intended to equalise the **8–036** pensionable age for men and women progressively over a 10 year period starting on April 6, 2010. A woman born before April 6, 1950 will reach pensionable age when she reaches 60 and a woman born after April 6, 1955 will reach pensionable age when she is 65. Those born in the intervening five years will reach pensionable age according to a sliding scale.

Schedule 4, Parts II and III provide for the equality in benefits for men and women in relation to certain pensions and other benefits.

Money Purchase Schemes

A money purchase scheme is different from a final salary benefit **8–037** scheme in that a final salary benefit scheme promises a pension benefit based on a proportion of the termination salary of the employee concerned. In a money purchase scheme the benefit depends directly on the amount of contributions made adjusted by the investment return.

Section 181(1) of the Pension Schemes Act 1993 defines a money **8–038** purchase scheme as "a pension scheme under which all the benefits that may be provided are money purchase benefits." Money purchase benefits are defined as "benefits the rate or amount of which is calculated by reference to a payment or payments made by the member or by any other person in respect of the member and which are not average salary benefits."

8–039   Salary related schemes are defined by section 125(1) of the Pensions Act 1995 as being salary related if "the scheme is not a money purchase scheme and the scheme does not fall within a prescribed class of description." It is possible that in due course regulations may exclude a scheme from the definition of being salary related.

8–040   Money purchase schemes are treated differently from final salary pension schemes in the Pensions Act 1995. The main areas of difference are in respect of the minimum funding requirement which does not apply to money purchase schemes although there is a power to extend it to cover them (see s.89). The provisions concerned with refunds of surpluses to the employer do not apply to money purchase schemes. The power given to trustees to defer the winding up of a scheme under section 38 does not extend to money purchase schemes.

Schedule of Payments to Money Purchase Schemes

8–041   The minimum funding requirement does not apply to money purchase schemes and thus there is no need to set a minimum rate of contribution as the benefit is necessarily defined by the rate of contribution made. The requirements for a schedule of contributions contained in sections 58 and 59 do not apply to money purchase schemes (s.46). In practice the rates of contributions in money purchase schemes will be agreed between the employer and the member, but section 87 still imposes an obligation on the trustees or managers of money purchase schemes to have "prepared, maintained and from time to time revised" a payment schedule showing: the rates of contribution payable towards the schemes by both the employer and the members; any other amounts payable towards the scheme as may be set out by regulations; and the due dates for the payments of the contributions. A failure to take all reasonable steps to ensure compliance with these requirements may render the trustees liable to penalties under section 3 and section 10 and a manager may be liable under section 10 (s.87(5)).

Contributions on Insolvency

8–042   Section 90 (which came into force on October 2, 1995) amends section 124 of the Pension Schemes Act 1993 by inserting a new section, section 124(3A). Section 124 deals with the ability of trustees of pension schemes to claim from the National Insurance Fund payment of unpaid contributions to schemes on employer insolvency. Section 124(3) limits the amount of such claims by providing that the sum payable shall not exceed such sum as is necessary to enable the scheme to meet its liabilities in respect of employees of the employer. Since the liabilities of a money purchase scheme are usually measured by the amount of money in the scheme or in each member's "pot" unless excluded the subsection would have the result set out above.

Overseas Schemes

An overseas scheme is a scheme which has one or more overseas **8–043** element, *i.e.* the scheme may be established overseas, have overseas trusts which are administered overseas, have overseas individuals as members of the scheme or have overseas companies participating in the scheme. Overseas schemes may be based wholly or partly overseas, they may have some United Kingdom employees or be wholly or in part for overseas employees but be based in the United Kingdom. Many overseas schemes will fall within the definition of an occupational pension scheme set out in section 1 of the Pension Schemes Act. Some existing pensions legislation makes provision for overseas schemes either by excluding overseas schemes or by applying the legislation in a modified form. Where there has been no express provision, the courts are unlikely to interpret the legislation as applying outside the United Kingdom. So United Kingdom pensions legislation will not generally apply to schemes which have no United Kingdom connection.

Public Service Schemes

Apart from the equal treatment provisions introduced by sections 62 **8–044** to 66 of the Pensions Act 1995, Public Service Schemes are largely unaffected by the obligations imposed by the 1995 Act. Public Service Schemes are occupational pension schemes but as they are not established under a trust they are not a trust scheme within the definition in section 124 of the Pensions Act 1995.

The term "Public Service Scheme" is defined in section 1 of the **8–045** Pension Schemes Act 1993 as:

"an occupational pension scheme established by or under an enactment or the Royal prerogative or a Royal charter being a scheme:

(a) all the particulars of which are set out in, or in a legislative instrument made under, an enactment, Royal warrant or charter, or

(b) which cannot come into force, or be amended, without the scheme or amendment being approved by a Minister of the Crown or government department,

and includes any occupational pension scheme established, with the concurrence of the Treasury, by or with the approval of any Minister of the Crown and any occupational pension scheme prescribed by regulations made by the Secretary of State and the Treasury jointly as being a scheme which ought in their opinion to be treated as a public service pension scheme for the purposes of this Act."

Public Service Schemes apply to the armed forces, police and fire **8–046** service who are all within a "fast accrual" scheme because of their early retirement age, and the Principal Civil Service Scheme, the National

CHAPTER 8: ANCILLARY PROVISIONS

Health Service, teachers and local government schemes where there is a normal retirement age and thus normal accrual. Public Service Schemes provide a core range of benefits and are index linked and account for about 40 per cent of all members of occupational pensions.

8–047 There is no requirement under the 1995 Act for Public Service Schemes to appoint member nominated trustees, to meet the minimum funding requirement or to take part in the compensation fund this is largely because public service schemes are "pay as you go" schemes with no advance funding. (The only exception being the local government scheme.) The application of other provisions of the 1995 Act to public service schemes are also obviously inappropriate such as the provisions relating to the repayment of surpluses to employers, the modification of schemes, the winding-up of schemes, etc. The provisions of sections 62 to 66 of the 1995 Act which apply to the equality of treatment as between men and women do apply to Public Service Schemes. Other provisions of the 1995 Act which apply to Public Service Schemes include those in relation to the provision of documents to members (s.41), the appointment of independent advisers and whistle blowing (ss.47 and 48), payment schedules in relation to money purchase scheme (ss.87–90) and pensions on divorce (ss.166–167).

8–048 Disputes arising in relation to Public Service Schemes are settled by way of appeal to the appropriate Secretary of State. The Pensions Ombudsman has no jurisdiction over disputes arising in relation to Public Service Schemes apart from National Health Service Schemes.

Chapter 9

Disputes and Compensation

9–001 Dispute resolution and compensation in the context of occupational pensions are discussed in this chapter.

Dispute resolution

9–002 Section 50 of the Pensions Act 1995 imposes a statutory requirement on trustees and managers of occupational pension schemes to establish and operate procedures for the resolution of disagreements. The procedure must specify a named person who will give a decision on disagreements between prescribed persons and secondly, provide for the trustees or managers to reconsider the decision of the named person if requested to do so by the complainant (s.50(2)). Prescribed persons are likely to be the trustees or managers of the scheme and actual or potential beneficiaries under the scheme. It is expected that the procedure for making and determining applications will be contained in regulations. The regulations may also exclude some disputes from the internal dispute resolution procedure (s.50(7)). Excluded disputes may well include matters which are beyond the control of the trustees or managers, matters which have already been the subject of the internal procedure and disagreements already under investigation by the Pensions Ombudsman. Non-compliance by the trustees or managers of a scheme with the requirement to set up an internal disputes resolution mechanism may be punished by a penalty under section 10 (s.50(6)).

9–003 If disagreements are not settled by way of the internal dispute resolutions scheme then they may be referred to the Occupational Pensions Arbitration Service (OPAS) and ultimately to the Pensions Ombudsman.

Occupational Pensions Advisory Service (OPAS)

9–004 OPAS is a free service available to members of the public who have a problem concerning either a personal or a company pension. OPAS does not have any statutory powers and operates utilising the good will of scheme authorities and voluntary advisers all of whom are experienced

CHAPTER 9: DISPUTES AND COMPENSATION

pension professionals. Unresolved complaints are passed on to the Pensions Ombudsman, the Insurance Ombudsman, the PIA or to another appropriate regulatory authority. In 1994/1995 only 82 cases were passed on to the Pensions Ombudsman. This increased significantly in 1995/1996 when 309 cases were referred.

9–005   In 1994/1995 OPAS received some 32,000 queries of which some 2,400 developed into serious investigations. Enquiries mainly concerned problems with winding-up, mergers and the use of surplus funds (25 per cent of enquiries), clarification of benefit entitlement and membership conditions (24 per cent), leaving service benefits including transferability (18 per cent), ill health and early retirement (8 per cent) including the problem of materially incorrect estimates being given which influenced the decision to retire. Some 50 per cent of complaints received by OPAS in 1994/1995 concerned the insured sector, this was because most schemes in this sector are run by small companies acting as sole trustee but having a limited knowledge of their responsibilities. Obviously these figures relate to the situation before the Pensions Act 1995 came into operation, but OPAS anticipates that its case load is likely to grow rather than diminish following the passage of the Act.

The Pensions Ombudsman

9–006   The function and powers of the Pensions Ombudsman are to be found in the Pension Schemes Act 1993 (ss.145–152). His function under this Act has been to investigate and decide upon complaints and disputes of maladministration concerning pension schemes and issues of fact or law arising in relation to pension schemes. Lord Denning considered the meaning of maladministration in *R. v. Local Commissioner for Administration, ex p. Bradford Metropolitan City Council* [1979] 2 All E.R. 881 at 898C-D, and adopted as a guide the following list of matters which might amount to maladministration: "bias, neglect, inattention, delay, incompetence, ineptitude, perversity, turpitude, arbitrariness and so on", (often referred to as the "Crossman catalogue").

9–007   In practice, the Pensions Ombudsman has investigated complaints and disputes in connection with occupational pension schemes. The Pensions Act 1995, ss.156 to 160 have amended the powers of the Pensions Ombudsman as set out in section 146 of the Pensions Schemes Act 1993. The Pensions Ombudsman will continue to investigate complaints arising out of the maladministration of a scheme but, under the Pensions Act 1995, those who may be complainants has been widened to include actual and potential beneficiaries of a scheme rather than simply the members of a scheme and the scope of complaints has been extended to cover complaints made by one trustee against another, by the trustees of one scheme against the trustees of another scheme and by employers against trustees (Pensions Act 1995 s.157, amending Pensions Schemes Act 1993, s.146). The ambit of complaints may be widened further by the introduction of regulations.

The Jurisdiction of the Pensions Ombudsman

It is now established that insurance companies running occupational **9–008** pension schemes for employers and trustees are subject to investigation by the Pensions Ombudsman. This was established in the case of *Century Life plc v. The Pensions Ombudsman* [1995] P.L.R. 135, which concerned Century Life, an insurer, which had the task of sorting out the administration of pension policies issued by another insurer. A number of complaints were made to the Pensions Ombudsman about certain pension schemes administered by the insurance company acting as a manager and the question arose as to whether the Ombudsman had jurisdiction to hear the complaints. The issue turned on what construction should be placed on the word "manager" and it was held that as it was not defined in the legislation, it should be given its ordinary English meaning so that where an insurance company carried out the day-to-day running of a pension scheme it would be ridiculous to suggest that the insurance company was doing anything other than managing the scheme and therefore the Pensions Ombudsman had jurisdiction over an insurer even where there were separate trustees. The pensions Ombudsman does not have power to direct compensation for distress and inconvenience for maladministration such as rudeness, incompetence and the insensitive handling of claims—*Miller v. Stapleton* [1996] 2 All E.R. 449.

Personal Pensions

In respect of the investigation of complaints concerning personal **9–009** pensions there is a potential overlap in jurisdiction between the Pensions Ombudsman, the PIA Ombudsman and the Insurance Ombudsman. In practice this was resolved by an agreement between the Pensions Ombudsman and the Insurance Ombudsman under which the Insurance Ombudsman would deal with all complaints of disputes concerning companies in the membership of the Insurance Bureau. The role of the Insurance Ombudsman in respect of personal pensions has been largely taken over by the PIA Ombudsman and the overlap between the jurisdictions of the Pensions Ombudsman and the PIA Ombudsman has been resolved by the issuing of a Memorandum of understanding between the two Ombudsman (issued March 31, 1995) which gives the PIA Ombudsman the jurisdiction to investigate the vast majority of complaints and disputes in respect of personal pensions. The Pensions Ombudsman will only investigate a dispute concerning a personal pension if it has slipped through the net of the other Ombudsman.

Judicial Review of the Pensions Ombudsman

Decisions of the Pensions Ombudsman, like those of the other **9–010** regulatory Ombudsman, are subject to judicial review. Recent cases where decisions of the Pensions Ombudsman have been reviewed by the courts include the case of *Westminster City Council v. Haywood and the Pensions Ombudsman* [1996] 2 All E.R. 467, where the court reviewed a determination and direction of the Pensions Ombudsman concerning the case of an employee of Westminster Council who had taken voluntary retirement at the age of 50 whose monthly payments had been reduced by the Council. In *Wild v. The Pensions Ombudsman and Smith*, April 2, 1996, unreported, the court reviewed whether the Ombudsman had the power to substitute his own view for that of the trustees of a scheme. In both cases the applicants for judicial review were successful.

9–011   A recent decision has illustrated the reluctance of the Court to restrict the scope of the Pensions Ombudsman's powers. In *Hillsdown Holdings plc v. The Pensions Ombudsman*, July 12, 1996, unreported, trustees of a pension fund had used their powers in the trust scheme to transfer the scheme's liabilities and assets to another pension scheme in order to overcome a restriction which precluded the trustees from paying a surplus on the fund to the employer company. The Pensions Ombudsman directed the employer company to repay the surplus to the second pension scheme. The company challenged this decision but the court held that since the employer company was obliged to repay the surplus as a matter of law (being a constructive trustee of the surplus), the employer company had improperly played an active part in influencing the trustees in the exercise of their powers. In these circumstances the Pensions Ombudsman had jurisdiction to direct steps to be taken with a view to remedying the consequences of maladministration to someone other than the complainant before him.

9–012   In reaching his decision, it is essential that the Pensions Ombudsman follows the minimum requirements of fairness as required by natural justice. The High Court will quash his determination if he fails to do so. In *Seifert v. Pensions Ombudsman* and *Lynch Ltd v. Farrand*, July 30, 1996, unreported, the Pensions Ombudsman failed to disclose to the trustees a letter from the complainant responding to answers which the trustees had sent to the Ombudsman. This failure rendered the Ombudsman's decision "fundamentally flawed." As Lightman J. acknowledged, a determination by the Ombudsman could damage or destroy reputations, as well as impose financial penalties. Accordingly, it was mandatory for the Ombudsman to comply with the principles of natural justice, which required him to make clear to the trustees the specific allegations made in the complaint. It was highly desirable that the Ombudsman, rather than merely transmitting copies of his correspondence with the complainant, should express in his own words in plain and simple language what he perceived to be the substance of the allegation. This would limit the risk of misunderstanding. All evidence and representations received by the Ombudsman must be disclosed. Whilst the procedure before the Ombudsman was intended to be quick, inexpensive and formal, these were the minimum requirements for fairness.

The Pensions Compensation Board

9–013 The need for some way of providing pension scheme members with compensation was brought to the forefront of public awareness by the Maxwell scandal which highlighted the vulnerability of pension schemes and undermined public confidence in the pensions industry. The Goode Committee recommended that "a compensation scheme should be established to protect members of occupational pension schemes against the defaults of those dealing with the pension fund assets." Such a scheme has been introduced by the Pensions Act (ss.78–86 and Sched. 2). The provisions of the Act are expected to be substantially supplemented by regulations. The scheme is to be administered by the Pensions Compensation Board (established by s.78). Although not specifically provided for by the Act, it is understood that the Pensions Ombudsman will be appointed by the Secretary of State as Chairman of the Compensation Board so linking the compensation scheme and the ombudsman scheme in practice.

9–014 The scheme does not provide a complete guarantee against all loss but is intended to be a scheme of last resort which applies only in limited circumstances. Under the scheme it is intended that compensation will be payable where certain requirements are met. The requirements are that:

— the scheme is a trust scheme;

— the employer is insolvent;

— that the value of the assets of the scheme has been reduced by an act or omission which there are reasonable grounds to believe constitutes a prescribed offence (a prescribed offence is expected to be defined by regulations but it is expected that a prescribed offence will be restricted to situations of fraud, theft or dishonest appropriation and will not include incompetent administration or breach of trust);

— in relation to a salary related schemes, the liabilities exceed the assets at the date of application by more than 10 per cent; and

— it is reasonable for the members to be assisted by the payment of compensation (s.81(1)).

9–015 Applications for compensation must be made within 12 months of the insolvency date or within 12 months from when the auditor or actuary of the scheme or the trustees of the scheme knew or ought reasonably to have known that a reduction of value falling within section 81(1)(c) had occurred (s.82(4)). The provisions of the scheme will apply to reductions in scheme's assets which take place after the Compensation Board comes into force (it is anticipated that it will come into force on April 6, 1997).

CHAPTER 9: DISPUTES AND COMPENSATION

9–016 The amount of compensation is to be determined in accordance with regulations to be made, but is to be restricted to 90 per cent of the shortfall and in the case of a salary related scheme, broadly to such sum as will cause the assets of the schemes to provide for 90 per cent of its liabilities (s.83). Section 84 makes general provision for interim payments of compensation to be made.

9–017 Decisions of the Board are reviewable by the Board on the application of any interested person within three months of the determination (or such longer period as the Board shall determine in any particular case) (s.80).

The Compensation scheme will be funded from levies upon occupational pension schemes. The Secretary of State has the power under section 85, after consultation with the Board, to order the distribution of surplus funds held by the Board amongst occupational pension schemes (s.85(1)).

9–018 In practice, the scope of the compensation scheme is very severely limited by the pre-condition that the employer must be insolvent before the compensation scheme can take effect. In the Maxwell case, the Mirror Group continued trading and never became insolvent, thus the compensation scheme even if it had been in place at the time of the pension fund losses would not have protected the Mirror Group pensioners. Indeed there must be many examples where the members of a pension scheme have been the victims of "the defaults of those dealing with the pension fund assets" by way of fraud or dishonesty but where the employer does not become insolvent. It remains to be seen, therefore, whether the compensation scheme will serve as much of a practical remedy for defrauded pensioners.

9–019 The Compensation Board has the power to gather information in order that it may carry out its functions by giving a notice in writing to a trustee, professional adviser or employer and from any other person appearing to the Board to be a person who holds or is likely to hold information relevant to the discharge of the Board's functions (s.110). Failure to comply with such a notice without reasonable excuse is an offence punishable on summary conviction to a fine of the statutory maximum (ss.111(1) and (2)). It is an offence for any person to knowingly or recklessly provide the Board with information which is false or misleading in a material particular where the person providing the information knows or could reasonably be expected to know that the Board required the information for the discharge of its duties (s.111(4)). It is also an offence to intentionally and without reasonable excuse alter, suppress, conceal or destroy any document which is required to be produced to the Board under section 110 (s.111(5)). The penalty for contravention of section 111(4) or (5) is imprisonment of up to two years and/or a fine if convicted in the Crown Court or a fine of up to the statutory maximum if convicted in the magistrates' court (s.111(6)).

Legal professional privilege and the privilege against self-incrimination are preserved by section 112.

Industrial Tribunals

Industrial tribunals have jurisdiction which covers statutory employment disputes which may and often do include issues relating to pensions entitlements. The ambit of this jurisdiction is beyond the scope of this book. **9–020**

Part 4

Statutory and Non-statutory Systems for the Regulation of Investment

Chapter 10

The Insurance Companies Act 1982

The Insurance Companies Act 1982 was a consolidation of the 1974, 1980 and 1981 Insurance Companies Acts. The 1974 Act was a consolidating measure designed to bring together legislation from the Insurance Companies Act 1958 and Part II of the Companies Act 1967 and the Insurance Companies Amendment Act 1973. The enactment of further legislation in the 1970s and early 1980s was as a result of the issuing of a number of E.C. Directives requiring Member States to bring their legislation into line in respect of the regulation of insurance companies. This included the introduction of a solvency margin to be calculated uniformly throughout the EEC—see E.C. Directive 73/239. 10–001

The regulation of insurance companies is a matter of very real importance to large numbers of investors. In the same way as pensions, insurance policies designed to provide annuities and life assurance form a major plank of many small investors total provision for old age and death. 10–002

Policies of insurance are essentially contracts like any other, whereby one person (the "Insurer") undertakes in return for a consideration (the "Premium") to pay another person (the "Assured") a sum of money on the happening of a specified event which is of a character adverse to the assured and which must have an element of uncertainty about it, *i.e.* as to timing (life assurance) or as to the event happening at all. 10–003

In this chapter we examine the main provisions of the Insurance Companies Act 1982. In many respects this Act was a precursor of the Financial Services Act 1986, relying as it does on a system of authorisation, supervision and regulation, laying down rules for the filing of accounts and introducing a solvency requirement. In addition the Insurance Companies Act has been supplemented by the provisions of the Financial Services Act 1986 and these are also summarised in this chapter. 10–004

The Scheme of the Insurance Companies Act 1982

Part I (ss.1–14) of the Act sets out the basic premise that only those authorised by the Secretary of State or those exempted by the Act may carry on insurance business in the United Kingdom. 10–005

10–006 Part II (ss.15–71) establishes the system of supervision and regulation applicable to insurance companies including the filing of accounts and returns with the Secretary of State (ss.17–27), the principle that life business and general business are to be separately accounted for (ss.28 and 29), the solvency requirement (ss.32–34), and the powers of intervention conferred on the Secretary of State (ss.37–48 and 60–64).

10–007 Part III (ss.71–81) contains a number of miscellaneous provisions concerning the conduct of insurance business including the requirement for disclosure by intermediaries who are connected with insurers (s.74) and the system whereby proposers for life assurance are allowed a "cooling off" period (ss.75–77). Section 73 makes it an offence to make false or misleading statements for the purpose of inducing a person to enter into an insurance contract.

Part IV (ss.82–89) concerns Lloyd's. The position concerning Lloyd's is considered in Chapter 11.

The Act also allows for the making of regulations by the Secretary of State. The Insurance Companies Regulations 1981, S.I. 1981 No. 1654, as amended, are the relevant regulations currently in force.

Policyholder

10–008 The meaning of "policyholder" was considered in the case of *Scher v. Policyholders Protection Board* [1994] 2 W.L.R. 593. A person is a policyholder within the meaning of section 96 of the Insurance Companies Act 1982 even if he is not the legal holder of the policy if a sum is due to him under the policy. However, where a person who is not a policyholder within the meaning of section 96(1) at the beginning of a liquidation and he becomes a policyholder subsequent to that date, he does not qualify as a policyholder entitled to claim under section 8(2) of the Policyholders Protection Act 1975.

The Classification of Insurance Business

10–009 Insurance business is divided into long-term business and general business. What constitutes long-term business is set out in Schedule 1 to the Act and includes life assurance, annuities and permanent health insurance (s.1(1) and Sched. 1).

10–010 Whether reinsurance fell within the scope of long term business was considered in the case of *In Re NRG Victory Reinsurance Ltd* [1995] 1 W.L.R. 239, where Lindsay J. held that reinsurance was insurance business within the meaning of the Insurance Companies Act 1982 and "long term reinsurance business" was accordingly "long term business".

What constitutes general business is set out in Part 1 Schedule 2 to the Act and includes insurance to cover accident, sickness, vehicles (including motor vehicles, ships, aircraft and railway rolling-stock), goods in transit, fire and natural forces, damage to property and credit.

The Scheme of the Insurance Companies Act 1982

Authorisation

A person carrying on any insurance business in the United Kingdom **10–011** must be authorised under sections 3 or 4 of the Act (s.2(1)). The exceptions to this are members of Lloyd's, friendly societies and trade unions or employer's associations in respect of provision for member's benefits or strike benefits (s.2(2)).

Carrying on insurance business requires that a person or company enters into contracts of insurance and carries them out by paying claims.

A person who carries on insurance business without being authorised **10–012** or exempted commits an offence under section 14(1) of the Act which is punishable by imprisonment of up to two years and/or a fine if convicted in the Crown Court and to a fine if convicted in the magistrates' court (s.14(3)).

Section 132 of the Financial Services Act 1986 is concerned with **10–013** insurance contracts effected in contravention of section 2 of the Insurance Companies Act 1982. A contract entered into by a person in the course of carrying insurance business in contravention of section 2 of the Insurance Companies Act 1982, is unenforceable against the other party and the other is entitled to recover any money or other property paid or transferred by him under the contract together with compensation for any loss sustained by him as a result of having parted with it (s.132(1) of the Financial Services Act 1986).

The meaning of "carrying on insurance business" has been considered **10–014** by the courts in a number of recent cases. It was held in *Re Great Western Assurance Co*, July 31, 1996, unreported, that section 2(1) was to be given a narrow construction, since breach thereof carried with it the possibility of penal sanctions. The court said that it is only business which provides the insurance cover which is required to be authorised. In that case there were two off-shore insurers, two off-shore agents and two brokers operating in the United Kingdom. The role of the United Kingdom brokers was to act as intermediaries between the off-shore agents and the off-shore insurers, and as brokers for members of the public in the United Kingdom, but they did not make any underwriting decisions, nor did they negotiate any terms of insurance policies. It was in these circumstances that the Court of Appeal concluded that the United Kingdom brokers did not need to be authorised. The fact that the off-shore agents were carrying on business of insurance in the United Kingdom did not mean that the United Kingdom brokers who performed the activities which amounted to the business were carrying on that business themselves. The Act does not prohibit the placing of United Kingdom risk with unauthorised insurers but prohibits the effecting and carrying out of insurance business in the United Kingdom by unauthorised insurers. This is not to say, however, that in all cases where a contract of insurance is made outside the United Kingdom it necessarily follows that there cannot be the carrying on of an insurance business within the United Kingdom. The Court of Appeal made it clear that insurance business under the Insurance Companies Act 1982 is not confined to the provision of cover under contracts of insurance but extends to the "effecting and carrying out" of those contracts. Each case must turn on its own particular facts. What is required is some continuity or regularity of provision within the United Kingdom of activities which are an integral part of the way in which the insurer conducts its affairs. In this case there could be little doubt that the offshore insurers were carrying on insurance business in the United Kingdom, notwithstanding that their activities were performed by United Kingdom brokers.

10–015 Not surprisingly, perhaps, the matter has also come before the courts in the criminal context. In *R. v. Wilson, The Times,* August 14, 1996, the appellant issued a document in which he sought insurance business and held himself out as having authority both to make insurance contracts and to receive premiums on behalf of an insurer. Not being authorised, the appellant was prosecuted for acting in breach of section 2(1). The Court of Appeal rejected his appeal on the basis that he had not carried out insurance business. In the context of the Act, "carrying on business" includes the soliciting of such business.

10–016 It is axiomatic that the business carried out must involve a policy of insurance—see *Fuji Finance Inc v. Aetna Life Insurance Ltd* [1995] Ch. 122—and that the business must be carried out within the jurisdiction. In *Re Eagle Star Insurance Co Ltd and Eagle Star Life Assurance Co Ltd, The Times,* December 7, 1990, the court held that it had no power to sanction a scheme under section 49 of the Insurance Companies Act 1982 for the transfer of long-term insurance business wherever carried out but it could sanction that part of the scheme that was confined to insurance business conducted in the United Kingdom.

Authorisation by the Secretary of State

10–017 Under the Act the Secretary of State may authorise a body to carry on any class of insurance business specified in Schedules 1 and 2 to the Act in the United Kingdom (s.3(1)). Authorisation may be restricted to industrial assurance business or to reinsurance business (s.3(2)). Section 4 of the Act allowed for the authorisations granted under the earlier legislation to continue in operation.

Applicants for authorisation must submit to the Secretary of State proposals as to the manner in which they propose to carry on business (s.5). Decisions of the Secretary of State on whether or not to grant authorisation are subject to judicial review.

10–018 It is an offence for a person to obtain authorisation by furnishing information which he knows to be false in a material particular or to recklessly furnish information which is false in a material particular (s.14(2)). This offence is punishable by imprisonment of up to two years and/or a fine if convicted in the Crown Court and to a fine if convicted in the magistrates' court (s.14(3)).

10–019 Authorisation will not be granted to new composite insurers, *i.e.* those carrying on both life and non-life insurance although those already in business prior to the 1982 Act were permitted to continue (s.6).

The Scheme of the Insurance Companies Act 1982

The Act makes separate provision for the authorisation of United Kingdom companies (s.7) and for applicants from other E.C. Member States (s.8) and for applicants from outside the EEC (s.9).

Withdrawal of Authorisation

10–020 The Secretary of State may withdraw authorisation at the request of the company or where it appears that the company has failed to satisfy an obligation under the Act, where authorisation is prohibited by virtue of sections 7, 8 or 9 of the Act or where a company based in an E.C. Member State has ceased to be authorised in its Member State (ss.11(1) and (2)). The withdrawal of authorisation may be total or may be in respect of a particular class of business. The withdrawal of authorisation prohibits companies from entering into new contracts but allows them to continue to carry out existing contracts by continuing to pay claims etc. Once all its business has been run off and the company ceases to carry on any insurance business in the United Kingdom, authorisation can be finally withdrawn under section 13.

Automatic Authorisation under the Financial Services Act 1986

10–021 Section 22 of the Financial Services Act 1986 provides that a body which is authorised under sections 3 or 4 of the Insurance Companies Act 1982 to carry out insurance business which is investment business in the United Kingdom is also an authorised person for the purposes of the Financial Services Act 1986. This authorisation covers any insurance business which is investment business and any other business which that body may carry out without contravening section 16 of the Insurance Companies Act 1982 which restricts an insurance company to carrying on insurance business. An insurance company which falls within the scope of section 22 of the Financial Services Act 1986 can only be authorised by section 22. It cannot be authorised by any other method, *e.g.*, by membership of an SRO (see the Financial Services Act 1986, Sched. 10, para. 2(1)).

10–022 Whether a policy of insurance constitutes an investment for the purposes of the Financial Services Act 1986 is determined by Schedule 1, Part II and includes most but not all long-term business within Schedule 1 to the Insurance Companies Act 1982. General insurance business does not fall within the Financial Services Act 1986 although there have recently been moves to include general insurance policies where the benefit to be paid is index linked within the scope of the Financial Services Act 1986.

Supervision and Regulation of Insurance Companies

Regulated Insurance Companies

10–023 A regulated insurance company is one to which Part II of the Insurance Companies Act 1982 applies and is defined as "all insurance companies, whether established within or outside the United Kingdom, which carry on insurance business within the United Kingdom" (s.15 and s.96). Members of Lloyd's and registered friendly societies are exempted.

10–024 By section 16(1), a regulated insurance company is restricted to the carrying on of activities in the United Kingdom or elsewhere for the purposes of insurance business. This restriction is a fundamental feature of the regulatory regime and was imposed in response to the E.C. Directives. The phrase "insurance business" is not easy to define since policies of insurance are sufficiently flexible, if appropriately worded, to be used as vehicles for investment. In *Fuji Finance Inc. v. Aetna Life Insurance Company Limited* [1994] 4 All E.R. 1025, an issue arose over whether a policy issued in October 1986 was a policy of insurance. The facts of the case were as follows: Fuji Finance Inc. was a Panamanian finance company in which Mr Tait was a prime mover. In October 1986 Fuji took out a policy of "life assurance" with Tyndall Assurance Ltd (later taken over by Aetna Life Insurance) for Mr Tait. Under the policy, Mr Tait was due to receive a benefit on death calculated on the value of investments in various unit trust schemes. The policy allowed for the surrender of the policy at a time before death, on which surrender Mr Tait was entitled to receive the same benefit as his estate would have received on death. There was also a switching option which meant that in the six years that the policy was in operation, Mr Tait contrived to increase the value of the policy from £50,000 to over £1 million. The court concluded that this policy could not be described as an insurance policy because Mr Tait would receive exactly the same benefit whether he surrendered the policy or whether he died. Only where the principal object was to insure could a contract be called a contract of insurance.

Accounts and Statements

10–025 Sections 17 to 27 cover the preparation and filing of accounts and returns with the Secretary of State. Insurance companies are required to prepare audited annual accounts in accordance with regulations (ss.17 and 21 and the Insurance Companies (Accounts and Statements) Regulations 1980 (S.I. 1980 No. 6 as amended by S.I. 1982 No. 305), regs. 5–8 and Sched. 1). Companies carrying on long-term business are also required to undergo annual actuarial investigation including a valuation of the liabilities of the company attributable to its long-term business (s.18(1) and (2)). Every five years, a company carrying out long term business must prepare a statement of its long-term business at the date to which the accounts of the company are made (s.18(3)). Particular classes of insurance companies are required to prepare an annual statement of business (s.20 and the Insurance Companies (Accounts and Statements) Regulations, 1980 (S.I. 1980 No. 60), regs. 9–12 prescribe the classes of business covering general business and reg. 15 provides for long-term business).

10–026 Non-compliance with the requirements of sections 17, 18, 20 and 21 constitutes an offence under section 71(3)(a) punishable on summary conviction by the imposition of a fine of the statutory maximum.

Every regulated insurance company carrying on long-term business must appoint an actuary as actuary to the company, notice of whose name and qualifications must be given to the Secretary of State (s.19). If the notice to the Secretary of State contains false information it is an offence under section 71(1)(c) punishable on conviction in the Crown Court by imprisonment of up to two years and or a fine or by a fine if convicted in the magistrates' court (s.71(2)). **10–027**

Accounts, balance sheets, abstracts or statements required by sections 17, 18 and 20 and any auditor's report prepared under section 21 must be deposited with the Secretary of State within six months of the close of the accounting period. Non-compliance with these requirements may give rise to the commission of offences under section 71(1)(c), section 71(3)(a) and section 71(4)(a). **10–028**

Shareholders and policy holders are also entitled to receive copies of deposited documents (s.23). **10–029**

Separate Accounting for Life Business and General Business

Section 28 lays down the general principle that assets relating to long-term business must constitute a fund separate from those relating to general business. Non-compliance with this section is an offence under section 71(1)(a). Section 29 is designed to ensure that the assets comprising the separate long-term business fund are used exclusively to meet the liabilities on the company's long-term business. Again, non-compliance with this section is an offence under section 71(1)(a). **10–030**

The Solvency Requirement

The E.C. Directives in 1973 and 1979 required that insurance companies maintain a minimum solvency requirement. Every regulated insurance company whose head office is in the United Kingdom or which carries on reinsurance business in the United Kingdom must maintain a margin of solvency of such amount as is prescribed by regulation (s.32(1)). Solvency margins are calculated depending on the type of business conducted by the company—see the Insurance Companies Regulations 1981, regs 3-13 and Schedule 1. **10–031**

If the margin of solvency is not met the Secretary of State may require the company to submit to him a short-term financial scheme which may propose amendments to the scheme—see section 33 and the Insurance Companies Regulations 1981, reg. 9 and Schedule 3. **10–032**

A failure to comply with the minimum solvency requirement may also be an offence under section 71(3)(a).

Powers of Intervention by the Secretary of State

The Secretary of State has a wide discretion to exercise his various powers of intervention conferred upon him by sections 38 to 45 in relation to any regulated insurance company. He may exercise his **10–033** powers if he considers that to do so is desirable for the protection of policy holders or potential policy holders against the risk that the company may be unable to meet its liabilities or to fulfil the reasonable expectations of long-term policy holders or potential policy holders:

— where the company (or its subsidiary or subordinate) has failed to satisfy an obligation under the Act;
— where the company has furnished misleading or inaccurate information to the Secretary of State;
— where he is not satisfied that adequate arrangements are in force for the reinsurance of risks against which persons are insured by the company;
— that a ground for prohibiting authorisation under sections 7, 8 or 9 exists;
— where there has been a substantial departure from any proposal or forecast submitted to him under section 5;
— where the company has ceased to be authorised by its home Member State (s.37(1), (2)).

10–034   The powers of investigation are usually carried out in practice by DTI inspectors although other suitable persons may be appointed. As with section 447 of the Companies Act 1985 these investigations are not announced and no report is published.

10–035   The Secretary of State may also exercise his powers under sections 38 and 41 to 45 in respect of notices given under sections 60 to 64. Notice of new appointments of directors, mangers and main agents or insurance companies must be given to the Secretary of State.

10–036   The Secretary of State must serve written notice that he is considering exercising any of his powers under sections 38 to 45 prior to exercising them. The person on whom such a notice is served has a right to make written representations to the Secretary of State within one month of the date of service of the notice which must be taken into account by the Secretary of State before he exercises any of his powers (s.46).

Requirement about investments

10–037   The Secretary of State may require a company not to make investments of a specified class or description or to realise within a specified period, the whole or specified portions of investments of a specified class or description held by the company (s.38(1)). Non-compliance is an offence under section 71(3)(a).

Maintenance of Assets in the United Kingdom

10–038   The Secretary of State may require that a company maintains assets in the United Kingdom of a value equal to the whole or a specified proportion of the amount of its domestic liabilities (s.39(1)). Non-compliance is an offence under section 71(3)(a) or (b).

Custody of Assets

Where a requirement has been imposed under section 39, the Secretary of State may impose an additional requirement that the assets should be held by a person approved by him as a trustee for the company (s.40(1)). Non-compliance is an offence under section 71(3)(a) or (b). — **10–039**

Limitation of Premium Income

The Secretary of State may require a company to take steps to limit the amount of premiums it receives for a specified period or in respect of specified business (s.41). Non-compliance is an offence under section 71(3)(a) or (b). — **10–040**

Actuarial Investigations

An actual investigation may be required for a company that carries out long-term business (s.42). Non-compliance with the requirements of this section may amount to offences under section 71(1)(c), (3)(a) or (4)(a). — **10–041**

Acceleration of Information Required by Accounting Provisions

The Secretary of State may require any documents which should be deposited with him under section 22 to be deposited on a specified date before the end of the usual period (s.43). — **10–042**

Power to Obtain Information and Require the Production of Documents

The Secretary of State may require a company to furnish him with information about specified matters at specified times or intervals or to produce to him such books or papers as may be specified. These powers are very similar to those available to the Secretary of State under section 447 of the Companies Act (s.44(1) and (2)). Non-compliance may be an offence under sections 71(3)(a) or (b) or (4)(b) and for a possible defence—see section 71(6). — **10–043**

The SIB has power under section 104(1) of the Financial Services Act 1986 to require, on the giving of written notice, such information as it may reasonably require for the exercise of its functions under the Financial Services Act 1986. This power applies to those authorised under the Financial Services Act 1986 including those who are automatically authorised—see section 22 of the Financial Services Act 1986. The exercise of the SIBs powers under section 104 are subject to judicial review. — **10–044**

Residual power to impose requirements for the protection of policyholders

The Secretary of State may require a company to take such action as appears to him appropriate for the purpose of protecting policyholders of the company against the risk that the company may be unable to meet — **10–045** its liabilities or the reasonable expectations of policyholder or potential policyholders (s.45). Non-compliance is an offence under section 71(3)(a) or (b). The Secretary of State may rescind or vary any requirement imposed under sections 38 to 45 (s.47(1)).

Changes of Director, Controller or Managers

10–046 Sections 60 to 64 of the Insurance Companies Act 1982 impose requirements on insurance companies to notify the Secretary of State of the appointment of directors, controllers and managers. The provisions are designed to ensure that the personnel holding key positions in insurance companies come under the scrutiny of the Secretary of State and are fit to hold their positions—see the Insurance Companies Regulations 1981, reg. 31 and Schedule 6.

The Conduct of Insurance Business

Advertisements

10–047 Section 72 of the Act allows for the making of regulations designed to regulate insurance advertisements—see the Insurance Companies Regulations 1981, regs 65 and 66.

Intermediaries in Insurance Transactions

10–048 Section 74 requires disclosure of intermediaries who are connected with insurers—see section 74 and the Insurance Companies Regulations 1981, regs 67 to 69. The requirement to disclose intermediaries fixes on the intermediary and not the insurer under section 74. The point was raised at first instance in *Re Great Western Assurance Co* [1995] 2 B.C.L.C. 539 when Parker J. held that the section and the regulations did not apply to an insurance company dealing with an intermediary. However, where the section and regulations do apply, the court noted that disclosure must be made to both the insured and professionals with whom the intermediaries dealt. The Court of Appeal determined an appeal in the case on other grounds on July 31, 1996, unreported.

The "Cooling Off Period"

10–049 Sections 75 to 77 make provision for allowing the insured under a life policy a "cooling-off" period in which he may withdraw from the transaction. The insurer is obliged under section 75 to give a statutory notice which draws the attention of the assured to the need to consider the contract carefully and his right to withdraw from the contract. The right to withdraw may be exercised within 10 days of receipt of the statutory notice under section 76(1) or at any time in a case where the notice has not been sent (s.76(2)). Exemptions from these requirements are contained in regulations 70, 71 and Schedule 10. Contravention of the obligation to send a statutory notice under section 75 is an offence (s.75(4)) punishable by two years' imprisonment and/or a fine if convicted in the Crown Court or a fine if convicted in the magistrates' court (s.81).

The Overlap Between the Financial Services Act 1986 and Life Insurance

Regulated Insurance Companies

10–050 The investment business provisions of Part I of the Financial Services Act are adapted for regulated insurance companies by virtue of section 129 of the Financial Services Act 1986 and Schedule 10 to the Act.

Section 130 of the Financial Services Act 1986 sets out certain restrictions on the promotion and advertisement of contracts of insurance.

10–051 Section 131 of the Financial Services Act 1986 concerns contracts made after contravention of the provisions concerning the promotion and advertisement of contracts of insurance contained in section 130. Under section 131 where there has been a contravention of section 130, the insurance company will not be entitled to enforce any contract of insurance with which the advertisement, advice or procurement was concerned and which was entered into after the contravention but the other party to the contract is entitled to recover any money or other property paid or transferred by him under the contract together with compensation for any loss sustained by him as a result of having parted with it.

10–052 Section 132 of the Financial Services Act 1986 is concerned with insurance contracts effected in contravention of section 2 of the Insurance Companies Act 1982. A contract entered into by a person in the course of carrying insurance business in contravention of section 2 of the Insurance Companies Act 1982, is unenforceable against the other party and the other is entitled to recover any money or other property paid or transferred by him under the contract together with compensation for any loss sustained by him as a result of having parted with it.

Misleading Statements as to Insurance Contracts

10–053 Section 133 of the Financial Services Act 1986 replaces section 73 of the Insurance Companies Act 1982 making it an offence to induce another to enter into an insurance contract by reason of false or misleading statements. Section 133 makes it an offence for a person to make a statement, promise or forecast which he knows to be misleading, false or deceptive or to dishonestly conceal any material facts; or to recklessly make (dishonestly or otherwise) a statement, promise or forecast which is misleading, false or deceptive. The person is guilty of an offence under this section if he makes the statement, promise or forecast or conceals the facts for the purpose of inducing, or if he is reckless as to whether it may induce another person to enter into or to offer to enter into or to refrain from entering or offering to enter into, a contract of insurance with an insurance company or to refrain from exercising any rights conferred by such a contract.

10–054 The statement, promise or forecast must be made in or from the United Kingdom or the facts must be concealed in or from the United Kingdom. The person on whom the inducement is meant to have effect must be in the United Kingdom and the contract or rights in question must be exercisable in the United Kingdom.

10–055 The punishment for an offence under section 133 is imprisonment of up to seven years and/or a fine if convicted in the Crown Court or up to six months' imprisonment and or a fine of up to the statutory maximum if convicted in the magistrates' court (s.133(3)). The maximum penalty of seven years' imprisonment is a substantial increase on the maximum available under the section 73 of the Insurance Companies Act 1982 offence which was limited to two years' imprisonment if convicted in the Crown Court and perhaps indicates a shift in opinion as to how seriously offences of this kind should be treated.

10–056 Section 138 of the Financial Services Act 1986 concerns the interaction between authorisation under the Financial Services Act 1986 and applications for registration or enrolment under section 8 of the Insurance (Registration) Act 1977.

Insurance Ombudsman Bureau

10–057 The Insurance Ombudsman Bureau (IOB) is an independent body which has the power to make awards of up to £100,000. The scheme was set up in 1981 by a group of insurance companies and its powers are conferred by contract over member companies. The Ombudsman can only consider complaints if the company with which the complainant is insured is a member of the scheme and in circumstances where the complainant and the insurer have failed to reach an agreement and the complaint is made within six months of the final decision of the company's management. Membership of the scheme now covers approximately two-thirds of the United Kingdom market for individual policies.

10–058 The decisions of the IOB are not subject to judicial review because the relationship between the IOB and the insurance companies is purely contractual with no basis in legislation—see *R. v. Insurance Ombudsman*

Bureau and Another, ex p. Aegon Life Assurance Ltd, The Times, January 7, 1994. The IOB was a free-standing independent body whose jurisdiction was dependent on the contractual consent of its members and, in the view of the court, it conspicuously lacked any trace of governmental underpinning. The court considered whether the position of the IOB had been altered by the enactment of the Financial Services Act 1986, particularly as many insurance companies had become regulated by an SRO. The court concluded that this made no difference and the IOB continued to remain outside the ambit of judicial review.

Chapter 11

Lloyd's of London

11–001 Lloyd's is not an insurance company but is a formally constituted society of underwriters which comprise traditional "Names"—private individuals who trade with unlimited liability—and corporate members who trade with limited liability. The capital they provide supports 170 syndicates which vary in size. Syndicates are managed by an underwriting agent who appoints a professional underwriter for each main class of business the syndicate deals with.

11–002 As Lord Cromer set out in the Cromer Report, a Lloyd's working party report in December 1969:

"The Name does not invest in Lloyd's, as does a shareholder in a company, but he does put his capital at risk in the anticipation of profit being earned thereon by the skill of the underwriter. Against these considerations, the Name is liable, without any control over the conduct of the business and can only withdraw from participation (profitable or unprofitable) after a protracted period."

11–003 Since a Name puts his capital at risk in anticipation of the making of profit, though not in a technical sense, he is to be regarded for all practical purposes as an investor of funds whose interests need to be protected and regulated, just as if he were making an investment in a more conventional way.

11–004 Lloyd's is currently facing a crisis unparalleled in its 300 year history which has been brought about by huge losses incurred in the 1980s which has left thousands of Names facing bankruptcy and ruin. The Lloyd's crisis has attracted a great deal of publicity, often unsympathetic in its treatment of the Names. The way in which Lloyd's regulates itself is the subject of this chapter, with particular attention being paid to the proposals which have been put forward by Lloyd's in its 1996 Plan for Reconstruction and Renewal.

11–005 Lloyd's is regulated by the Lloyd's Acts 1871 to 1982 which are private Acts of Parliament and by numerous byelaws. It is beyond the scope of this book to do any more than offer a brief summary of these Acts and byelaws. They can be found in "Lloyd's Acts, byelaws and Regulations" published by Lloyd's of London Press Ltd.

CHAPTER 11: LLOYD'S OF LONDON

History

11-006 Lloyd's of London began its long and eventful history in the coffee house of Edward Lloyd in Tower Street in the City of London. Lloyd's coffee house was well established by the end of the 1680s as a place where those willing to issue insurance gathered and it soon became the centre for marine underwriting in London. It was also a centre where information about shipping could be exchanged, Edward Lloyd founded a short-lived newspaper, "Lloyd's News" which contained shipping information. This was the forerunner of "Lloyd's List" which was first published in 1734 and continues today.

11-007 Following the collapse of the South Sea Company in 1720, Parliament restricted the issuing of marine insurance to two charter companies, The Royal Exchange and London Assurance but did not restrict individuals from issuing marine insurance. These "merchant underwriters" were to be found at Lloyd's coffee house and it is from their activities that today's Lloyd's has developed. By 1771, a group of 79 merchants and brokers paid £100 each to set up a formal organisation. The Napoleonic Wars were a time of expansion for Lloyd's when there huge profits to be made. By 1814 Lloyd's had grown to some 2,150 underwriters. In 1811, Lloyd's' first formal constitution in the form of a Trust Deed was introduced which established the authority of the Lloyd's Committee.

11-008 In 1871 Lloyd's was incorporated as a society of private underwriters by Act of Parliament. But, true to its early roots, Lloyd's has always been a collection of individuals rather than a single entity. The workings of Lloyd's have always been based on trust, its motto is *Fidentia* meaning confidence and its traditional trading standard has been *Uberrima Fides* meaning utmost good faith. Until the crisis of the 1980s, Lloyd's has had a virtually unassailable reputation for probity and profitability. In the twentieth century, prior to the 1980s, the only known recorded years of loss were three years in the 1960s following Hurricane Betsy in September 1965. This sound reputation has been tarnished by recent events.

The Structure of Lloyd's

11-009 Lloyd's is regulated by the Lloyd's Acts 1871 to 1982 and by numerous byelaws. The Corporation of Lloyd's is a collection of individuals who trade under the Lloyd's banner and are subject to its rules. Lloyd's does not carry any responsibility for individual underwriters but provides a market place for them to work. Lloyd's writes worldwide business and is licensed in many countries as a direct insurer. The market has four main divisions: non-marine, marine, motor and aviation.

The Membership of Lloyd's

11–010 Underwriters undertake liability on contracts of insurance and associate together to form syndicates, in which one of the members is given the authority to underwrite policies in the names of the other members of the syndicate (the "Names"). The management of underwriting syndicates is undertaken by a managing agency which charges Names an annual fee of between £150 and £300 for participation in a syndicate.

11–011 Names provide the risk capital. There are two types of Name, the working Name and the external Name. Working Names are professionals who work in the market as underwriters, brokers and agents. External Names are passive investors with no control over the underwriter who writes insurance business. Unlike every other type of investor, Names take on unlimited liability, typically a Name will spread his risk by joining several syndicates. Names are required to show a minimum amount of capital (now £250,000) often in the form of bank guarantee on his home, and to deposit a proportion of his "shown" capital with Lloyd's for safekeeping in a form of liquid assets, *e.g.* shares. Names are placed on syndicates by members' agents who supervise the Names' affairs and act as the link between the Name and the underwriter. A good managing agent will make the difference between a Name making a profit or a loss but it was not until 1988 that members' agents were required to publish annual information about their results.

Names may take out stop-loss policies but these have proved to be somewhat limited in their effectiveness when faced with the enormous losses incurred by some syndicates in the 1980s.

11–012 Lloyd's keeps a register revised annually on July 1, of both the working and non-working Names of the Society—Schedule 1 to Lloyd's Act 1982 and Byelaw 122: The Register of Members Byelaw No. 22 of 1983.

11–013 The practice of Lloyd's is that underwriters do not do business directly with the public, but deal with brokers who act as intermediaries between underwriters and those wishing to effect insurance with them. The relationship between the underwriter and the broker is that of principals, although once the contract has been made, privity of contract is established between the underwriter and the assured. The underwriter looks to the broker for his premium who in turn looks to the assured, and it is usually through the broker that the underwriter receives notice of a claim.

11–014 Brokers are required to comply with minimum professional standards and to have professional liability insurance under the Insurance Brokers (Registration) Act 1977. Lloyd's brokers are entitled to be registered under the 1977 Act as of right.

11–015 Lloyd's requires that members satisfy the test of whether they are fit and proper to conduct business at Lloyd's. Authorisation is required by underwriting agents, run-off companies (see later), Lloyd's advisers and Lloyd's brokers. Individual members who underwrite as principals are admitted only if they can demonstrate that they have the financial resources required to support their underwriting and that they fully understand the risks involved with Lloyd's.

Lloyd's and the Financial Services Act 1986

11–016 By virtue of section 42 of the Financial Services Act 1986 the Society of Lloyd's and underwriters who come under the control of the Council of Lloyd's are exempted persons in respect of investment business. The question of whether Lloyd's Names required authorisation under the Financial Services Act 1986 was considered and rejected by the SIB in 1989 (see the SIB Guidance Release 2/89 Lloyd's Names).

The Regulation of Lloyd's

11–017 Lloyd's is regulated by the Lloyd's Acts 1871 to 1982 and by a host of byelaws. Today the regulation of Lloyd's is governed by the Council of Lloyd's which was established by the 1982 Act. Before this, the power to make byelaws had been vested in the members of Lloyd's acting in general meeting. By 1982 this method had clearly become impractical and the 1982 Act established a Council of Lloyd's to undertake the management and regulation of the Society of Lloyd's with the power to make byelaws making provision for the regulation of admission, suspension and disciplining of members of the Society, Lloyd's brokers, underwriting agents, etc.

The Council of Lloyd's

11–018 The Council of Lloyd's is established by section 3 of the Lloyd's Act 1982. Members of the Council include working members and external members (elected by working and external members), members nominated by the Bank of England and a chief executive officer. Under section 4, the Council is required to elect from the working members of the council a Chairman of Lloyd's and Deputy Chairmen. The powers of the Council are set out in section 6 of the Lloyd's Act 1982 which provides that:

> "the Council shall have the management and superintendence of the affairs of the Society and the power to regulate and direct the business of insurance at Lloyd's."

11–019 Schedule 2 sets out the purposes for which byelaws may be made and it is through the byelaws that Lloyd's is regulated. As at February 7, 1996 there were some 313 Lloyd's byelaws. The balance of working and external members of the Council is now such that external members are in the majority. The Council comprises a balance of working members, external members (elected by working and external Names) and members nominated by the Bank of England as well as the chief executive officer.

The Lloyd's Acts 1871 to 1982 require the Council to prepare accounts giving a view of the state of affairs of the Corporation and or the surplus or deficit for each financial year.

Lloyd's Regulatory Board

11–020 The Regulatory Board was created by the Council of Lloyd's in 1993 to act as an independent-minded and objective source of authority for Lloyd's regulation. It is responsible for supervisory and regulatory matters and is the body through which the Council exercises most of its regulatory responsibilities and powers. The Board comprises five nominated members (four working members) including its Chairman, five external members representing non-working Names and a director of regulatory services.

11–021 The Board is responsible for ensuring that those trading in the market are regulated in a similar way to other "authorised" businesses in the rest of the financial sector. This is intended to be achieved by way of compliance with detailed rules and regulations intended to ensure the fair and transparent operation of the market. The goal of regulation at Lloyd's is to balance regulation so that policyholders have confidence that their valid claims will be met and by ensuring the fair treatment of the members of Lloyd's by their underwriting agents and by ensuring that there is a high standard of professionalism throughout the market. As members of Lloyd's have statutory exemptions from parts of the Financial Services Act 1986 and the Insurance Companies Act 1982, the Regulatory Board aims to provide comparable protections to policy holders and members.

11–022 In addition, the Department of Trade and Industry acts as an external regulator which monitors Lloyd's global solvency and agrees standards for valuation of liabilities. Solvency is assessed in terms of technical reserve assets and liabilities and individually in terms of each members' surplus of deficit on capital account. Technical reserves are the reserves available to meet unpaid claims liabilities. Syndicates are required to have sufficient reserves each year to meet the highest of known claims including an allowance for incurred but not reported claims and minimum percentages of premium for each under writing year for which there are still outstanding claims.

11–023 Many of the investigations into the various scandals which hit Lloyd's in the 1980s were conducted by the Department of Trade and Industry—namely: the Department of Trade and Industry Report into Alexander Howden 1990, the Department of Trade and Industry Report into Minet Holdings and WMD underwriting agencies 1990, and the Department of Trade and Industry inquiry into Unimar 1986.

11-024   The Regulatory Board's responsibilities are:

— to ensure that all those who work in the market are appropriately qualified and that all businesses in the market are properly reserved and managed; this is to be achieved by authorising only those individuals and entities that are fit and proper and meet standards of sound and prudent management and meet high standards of market behaviour and practice;

— to ensure sufficient resources in the market to support the underwriting;

— to safeguard policyholders' rights and to look after the best interests of all categories of members;

— to work for transparency in the market, and to ensure all relevant information including accounts is properly disseminated;

— to provide the necessary written rules and guidelines to enable all the principles of fair and proper commercial conduct to be observed.

Other Lloyd's Boards

11-025   The Lloyd's Market Board is responsible for all other market services. There are six market associations representing marine, non-marine and aviation underwriters, underwriting agents and brokers.

Lloyd's members are served by the Association of Lloyd's Members.

11-026   The Central Fund is held and administered by the Council of Lloyd's. It is primarily a fund available for the protection of policyholders. Members contribute to the Fund annually on a percentage basis of their allocated premium limit. The Fund may be used to cover underwriting deficiencies of Names as at the preceding December 31, to enable them to pass the Solvency Test and meet the requirements of the Department of Trade and Industry. Assets are also available to discharge the underwriting liabilities of Names should they become due in the event of default (see The Central Fund Byelaw No. 4 of 1986).

The Disciplinary Committee and the Appeal Tribunal

11-027   The Council of Lloyd's is required under section 7 of the Lloyd's Act 1982 to provide for a Disciplinary Committee and to establish an Appeals Tribunal. The Disciplinary Committee is now set up under the Disciplinary Committees Byelaw (No. 10 of 1993) which also created a new summary disciplinary procedure to be administered by Summary Disciplinary Committees. The Appeals Tribunal is established under the Appeal Tribunal Byelaw (No. 18 of 1995).

Other Lloyd's Boards

11-028 In 1994, 14 inquiries into alleged cases of misconduct and breaches of the byelaws were underway of which four were concluded in the year. There were also five disciplinary cases involving 14 defendants of which two were concluded resulting in findings of guilt and the imposition of penalties. Reports on disciplinary proceedings are published.

11-029 Members of Lloyd's may be disciplined for acts of misconduct which fall within the Misconduct, Penalties and Sanctions Byelaw (No. 9 of 1993). Misconduct broadly includes any contravention or failure to observe any provision of the Lloyd's Acts 1871 to 1982, a contravention or failure to observe any verdict, order, award, penalty or sanction imposed under the Lloyd's Acts 1871 to 1982, a contravention or failure to observe any regulation made under the Lloyd's Acts 1871 to 1982, conduct detrimental to the interest of Lloyd's policyholders or others doing business at Lloyd's, the conduct of insurance business in a discreditable manner or with a lack of good faith or for the conduct of one who conducts himself in any manner which is dishonourable or disgraceful or improper.

11-030 Sanctions include exclusion or suspension from membership of Lloyd's, a requirement to cease underwriting which may be either permanent or temporary, revocation or suspension of the permission to act as a Lloyd's adviser, revocation of permission to act as a broker of insurance business, revocation or suspension of permission to act as a members' agent or managing agent, suspension of rights of admission to the Room and revocation either permanent or temporary of the right to transact the business of insurance at Lloyd's, a fine, the posting of notice of censure in the Room or a reprimand.

11-031 Summary offences are punishable by the imposition of a fine up to a maximum of £5,000 for each offence, or a fine of up to £1,000 per day for each day that the offence continues or a reprimand. (Misconduct—penalties and sanctions, Byelaw No. 9 of 1993).

11-032 The Misconduct (Reporting) Byelaw imposes a duty on members of Lloyd's, underwriters, brokers, their agents and employees to report instances of misconduct (where the misconduct is more than a minor nature) to the Director of Regulatory Services. The duty to report applies to a person who knows of any actual or proposed misconduct or believes or has reason to believe that such misconduct is likely to occur or is likely to have occurred. (Misconduct (Reporting) Byelaw No. 11 of 1989).

The Regulatory Board has instituted a system of on-site investigative reviews which is combined with office based analysis of regular returns.

Lloyd's Members Ombudsman

11-033 The role of the Lloyd's members' Ombudsman is to investigate complaints by members of the Society or resigned members with open years of account who believe that they have suffered injustice in consequence of maladministration in relation to action taken by the Society. The jurisdiction of the Ombudsman does not extend to complaints made by Names against underwriting agents—see The Members' Ombudsman Byelaw No. 13 of 1987, Members Ombudsman (Amendment No. 1) Byelaw No. 3 of 1989, and Members Ombudsman (Amendment No. 2) Byelaw No. 3 of 1994.

Lloyd's Regulatory Plan 1996

11–034   The problems faced by Lloyd's in the 1980s demonstrated the shortcomings in the regulatory system then in place. The Society of Lloyd's has been forced to reconsider the efficacy of its internal regulation so as to encourage new Names (*e.g.:* new investors) to come forward.

The Losses of the 1980s

11–035   Underlying the problems faced by Lloyd's are the enormous losses incurred on its 1987 to 1992 underwriting years. These losses arose out of a series of disasters in both the marine and non-marine insurance and reinsurance markets between 1987 and 1993 which included the Piper Alpha disaster, Hurricanes Gilbert (1988), Hugo (1989), Andrew (1992) and Iniki (1992), a number of storms in Europe and the U.S., the Los Angeles riots in 1992 and various typhoons and earthquakes around the world. From 16 major catastrophes between 1987 and 1992 it is estimated that the insurance loss was something approaching U.S. $45,389 million. In addition to losses arising from these natural disasters were the problems arising out of "long-tail" U.S. liability, in which insured risks take a long time for the claims to emerge and even longer to settle. Long-tail liability has typically been linked to claims arising in connection with asbestosis and other latent diseases, *e.g.* claims arising from the use of Agent Orange by the U.S. army in the Vietnam War and the remedial action required to combat pollution and health hazards. Whilst accurate assessments of the cost of these long-tail risks to insurers are impossible, it has been estimated that the losses to insurers arising out of asbestosis claims alone will be between U.S. $50-100 billion.

11–036   The losses arising out of these natural disasters and the long-tail liability have been compounded by incompetence and, in some cases, malpractice on the part of some underwriters which has come to light in a series of scandals involving underwriters in the 1980s.

11–037   In a market place concerned with risk, the question has to be asked why was something not done to prevent such a state of affairs arising. The management and regulation of Lloyd's has traditionally relied upon Lloyd's being essentially a "club" and the governing Committee has always been enormously secretive. For example, in the wake of Hurricane Betsy in 1965 and three years of losses, Lord Cromer was

Lloyd's Regulatory Plan 1996

appointed by the Committee of Lloyd's to chair a committee to examine whether the existing capital structure of Lloyd's was adequate for the needs of the market. The Committee made a number of criticisms and recommendations but its report was circulated in confidence only to the professionals in the market. Not even the external Names whose interests the committee was seeking to safeguard were permitted to see the report.

One of the few recommendations of the Cromer Committee that was implemented was a relaxation in the qualifying requirement for becoming a Name. This lead to a rapid expansion in Lloyd's membership in the 1970s and 1980s. Membership grew from 8,565 in 1976 to 19,137 by 1981 and to 33,532 by 1987 (a rise of some 436 per cent between 1976 and 1987). The rise in the numbers of members was accompanied by a number of good years between 1977 to 1987 when Lloyd's made a pre-tax profit to Names of £3,084 million. At this time, few took seriously the formal warning given to new names that they could lose everything "down to their last shirt button" and the large profits being made often masked the levels of incompetence and malpractice amongst underwriters. **11–038**

The Fisher Report

In 1979, Sir Henry Fisher was appointed to chair an inquiry into self-regulation at Lloyd's. There was never any question at this time that anything other than a system of self-regulation should persist. Sir Henry Fisher's recommendations lead to the Lloyd's Act 1982, the principal plank of which is that the old Lloyd's Committee should be replaced by a broadly based Council in which working members would be balanced by external Names. The Council would have powers of inquiry and discipline over brokers, agents and underwriters. The Fisher Committee also recommended that brokers should no-longer be allowed to own managing agencies because of the obvious conflict of interests that such ownership engendered. This recommendation found its way into the 1982 Lloyd's Act in sections 10 to 12 (*Self-Regulation at Lloyd's*—Report of the Fisher Working Party, May 1980.) **11–039**

The Neill Report

Following a number of scandals in the 1980s, including the disciplining of Sir Peter Green, a Former Chairman of Lloyd's (disciplined by a Lloyd's Tribunal for discreditable conduct. He was fined a total of £50,000 and a notice of censure was posted in the underwriting room.) Sir Patrick Neill Q.C. was appointed to look into regulation at Lloyd's. His report was published in February 1987 and drew attention to the conflicts of interest that continued to exist at Lloyd's. An example of this was the existence of "baby syndicates" in which market insiders creamed off profits from the main syndicates. Sir Patrick Neill recommended that the composition of the Lloyd's Council should be changed **11–040**

CHAPTER 11: LLOYD'S OF LONDON

to increase the number of independent members so that working members were no-longer in the majority. (Regulatory Arrangements at Lloyd's—Sir Patrick Neill Q.C., January 1987).

Pressure for Reform

11–041   Not surprisingly in the wake of the disastrous results of the late 1980s, individual membership of Lloyd's has fallen substantially from 32,433 in 1988 to 14,804 in 1995. This has dramatically reduced the "capacity" provided by individual members which has fallen from £11.02 billion in 1988 to £7.84 billion in 1995. Interestingly of those individual members remaining, the average capacity of each individual member has increased from £304,000 in 1988 to £529,000 in 1995. 1994 saw the introduction of corporate members with limited liability to Lloyd's for the first time and various significant changes for individual names.

11–042   For the 1985 to 1991 underwriting years Lloyd's made an underwriting loss of £4,851 million on £17,844 million non-marine net premiums and an underwriting loss of £3,887 million on £12,037 million marine and aviation net premiums. These figures are before investment income of £3,655 million and after syndicate expenses. The overall pre-tax result for the period was a loss of £4,182 million. Lloyd's losses for 1985 to 1991 are largely from U.S. long-liability and marine LMX spiral. In April 1993, Lloyd's issued a business plan setting out its programme designed to restore profitability and solve the problems it faced.

11–043   In May 1995, Lloyd's announced its plans for reconstruction and renewal these are intended to resolve the problems of the past and to build a strong market for the future. This has led to the publication of the Lloyd's Regulatory Plan 1996.

The Lloyd's Regulatory Plan 1996

11–044   The main planks of the plan are intended to end the uncertainties of open years and old liabilities, to help members to trade on and create new sources of capital, to improve efficiency, to improve levels of competence and professionalism and to exploit fresh market opportunities. It is the stated goal of the Regulatory Board in issuing the 1996 Regulatory plan that:

> "Policyholder security is, and must continue to be, the Council's paramount responsibility but it is also concerned to ensure that the appropriate protections are in place for those who commit their capital to the market" (para. 4.2 Lloyd's Regulatory Plan 1996).

11–045   Chapter 2 of the Lloyd's Regulatory Plan 1996 sets out the following policy priorities for 1996:

> — registration of individuals: new powers are intended to register individual officers and executives of regulated entities;

— core principles: the overall standards of conduct expected of underwriting agents have been distilled in a statement of core principles of behaviour. These are intended to be consistent with the principles of behaviour expected of businesses regulated under the Financial Services Act 1986;

— criteria of sound and prudent management: prudential supervision of those operating in the market is to be developed through the introduction of sound and prudent management as used in other insurance and regulatory regimes. It is expected that Guidance notes will be prepared;

— risk based capital: a consultative document was issued in August 1995 on a scheme designed to show what levels of funds at Lloyd's should reasonably be expected to meet a members liabilities the quantum of those funds being calculated by reference to the volatility of each type of business in the capital providers portfolio;

— realistic disaster scenarios: guidance was issued in May 1995 on the way in which agents should reveal to capital providers the nature and extent of risks which they propose to underwrite;

— annual accounting: An undertaking was given in the reconstruction and renewal document that Lloyd's will move to annual accounting. Proposals as to how this is to be achieved are under consideration and consultation these are not expected until 1997 at the earliest;

— role of auditors: consideration is being given to whether auditors should be given a "whistle blowing" role under which they would be required to report to the regulators in situations when there appears to be prejudice to the interests of policyholders or members interests;

— errors and omissions insurance for underwriting agents: a range of proposals is under consideration.

Equitas

Equitas has been set up as a limited liability reinsurance run-off **11–046** company subject to regulation by the Department of Trade and Industry to reinsure syndicate liabilities pre-dating 1986. It was intended that by Spring 1996 Lloyds would have re-insured all 1992 and prior liabilities from both closed and open syndicates into Equitas.

This has been set up in response to the problems by the Lloyd's **11–047** practice of "open years." Lloyd's syndicates normally close each underwriting year at the end of the third calendar year (fourth for personal stop loss syndicates) with outstanding liabilities reinsured to its next open underwriting year (reinsurance to close, "RITC"). RITC transfers liability for all claims arising from policies written in prior years on to the syndicate's successor year in return for a premium. The profits or losses for the closed year are then paid out or collected from the Names. The determination of the size of the RITC is the decision of the syndicate's underwriter on whose judgment depends the profitability or otherwise of the syndicate for that year. The decision is subject to audit and to market regulations for reserving particular classes of business. However, it was not until 1985, that the audit had to be "true and fair". It has been said that the RITC figure is little more than "sheer guesswork."

11-048   Where syndicates specialise in short-term risks this system works well, however, when a syndicate is involved in long-tail risk it will not be possible to determine the liabilities. This can also arise in circumstances where a syndicate is closing down. The syndicate is thus unable to close that year.

11-049   This problem is at the heart of the crisis currently facing Lloyd's. Members wanting to resign from a syndicate cannot do so if the year remains open. At the end of 1994, some 584 syndicates had not been closed.

11-050   Lloyd's proposes to deal with the problem of open years by reinsuring long-tail syndicates into a limited company. Initially this was achieved by setting up Newco into which all old year claims prior to 1986 would be channelled. This would have the effect of protecting those syndicates which continued to trade from all claims on old year policies. The aim being to allow the on-going Lloyd's market to trade forward unencumbered by the problems of the past. This scheme has been expanded into "Equitas" which now provides a "firebreak" between the old and the new Lloyd's.

Judicial Review

11-051   The issue of whether Lloyd's was subject to judicial review was considered by the Divisional Court in the case of *R. v. Lloyd's of London, ex p. Briggs and others* [1993] 1 Ll.R. 176, which arose out of the losses made by syndicates managed by Gooda Walker. These syndicates had made substantial losses in run-off reinsurance of asbestosis and pollution claims form the USA and from London Excess of Loss Market (LMX) business. Gooda Walker went into liquidation in October 1991 and Lloyd's appointed G.W. Run-off Ltd as substitute agents. G.W. Run-off Ltd made cash calls on a number of Names. There had previously been actions brought by a number of Names seeking injunctions for the purpose of putting off until the hearing of the actions the procedure laid down by Lloyd's to obtain money to meet claims by the draw down procedure. The application for the injunction was refused and Savill J. held in those proceedings that under the contracts between the Names and their agents they were obliged to pay cash calls made by the managing agents in good faith.

A number of the Names sought judicial review against Lloyd's, the **11-052** Committee of Lloyd's, the Chairman and Deputy Chairman of Lloyd's and against G.W. Run-off Ltd. One of the issues which was considered by the Divisional Court (Leggatt J. and Popplewell J.) was whether Lloyd's was subject to judicial review. The court came to the view that Lloyd's was not a public law body. It operated within one section of the insurance market and its powers were derived from a private Act of Parliament which did not extend to any person in the insurance business other than those who wished to operate in the section of the market governed by Lloyd's. There could not, therefore, be any public law element about the relationship between Lloyd's and its Names which would place it within the public domain and for this reason Lloyd's was not susceptible to judicial review.

Chapter 12

The Stock Exchange

History

From very small beginnings the London Stock Exchange today plays a pivotal role in the United Kingdom economy. By the end of 1995 there were 2,078 listed United Kingdom companies with an equity market value of some £900 billion and 525 listed foreign companies with a total equity market value of £2,357 billion. Over 10 million people in the United Kingdom now own shares. **12–001**

The first joint stock company was established in London in 1553 to seek funding by subscription for an expedition to search for a north-east passage to China. Although the expedition was not successful in opening a new trade route to China, it did establish freedom of trade for English ships to Russia and the Muscovy Company and the first joint stock company was born. By the late seventeenth century, the Government had begun to issue loan stock through the Bank of England to raise money through public subscription. The trade in government loan stock took place in the coffee houses situated around the Bank of England. By 1773, the first "Stock Exchange" had been established on the same site as the present day. **12–002**

Need for Regulation

The need for regulation of the markets was recognised at a very early stage, the first legislation "to restrain the number of ill practices of brokers and stockjobbers" having been introduced in 1697. The South Seas Bubble scandal destroyed the reputation of the joint stock company. The Bubble Act 1720 placed barriers in the way of the legal transfer of shares in incorporated bodies and it was not until the middle of the nineteenth century with the need to fund major industrial developments, such as the railways, that the joint stock company made a come back. Company legislation originates from this time and with the growth in limited companies came a greater volume of trade in the stocks and shares of those companies. A new Stock Exchange was opened in 1884 which was 10,000 square feet bigger than its predecessor. Regulation of the stock market was also a matter which the Government thought worthy of attention; in 1877 the Government set up a Royal Commission "to inquire into the origins, objects, present constitution, customs and usages of the London Stock Exchange". **12–003**

12–004 The regulation of the market has traditionally been left to the market itself. However, attempts to undermine the fair workings of the market have been with us as long as the markets themselves. An early reported example of an attempt to manipulate the market was the *De Berenger Case* 3 M&S 66; 105 E.R. 536 where De Berenger and his associates were convicted of a criminal conspiracy to raise the price of government funds by spreading false rumours about the death of Napoleon.

12–005 As the workings of the markets have become progressively more sophisticated the need for tighter regulation has grown. The most revolutionary change came with Big Bang in 1986 which saw a radical shake up of the markets and particularly of the ownership of the membership of the Stock Exchange and the growth of the electronic markets has changed the face of the Stock Exchange. The most important electronic market is the Stock Exchange's computerised quotation system SEAQ (Stock Exchange Automated Quotations), which carries prices for over 2,000 securities and allows for up to the minute share price information to be viewed by market participants.

Financial Services Act 1986

12–006 The Financial Services Act 1986 established a new regulatory system for the conduct of investment business in the United Kingdom including business conducted on the Stock Exchange. Traditionally the Stock Exchange had assumed responsibility for the total regulation of its members. The major change brought about by the Financial Services Act 1986 was that to carry out business on the Exchange today, a firm needs to have gained authorisation to carry on investment business from a SRO (for firms operating on the Exchange this will be the SFA) as well as being a member of the Stock Exchange. Under the Financial Services Act 1986 the Exchange continues to regulate the operation of the market place as a Recognised Investment Exchange (RIE). The role of the Stock Exchange and the regulation of the market place forms the subject matter of this chapter.

Europe

12–007 It is the objective of the European Community to harmonise the regulations governing the listing of securities throughout the Member States and this is being achieved through a number of directives—see the Admissions Directive (79/279), the Listing Particulars Directive (80/390) and the Interim Reports Directive (82/121) which have been given effect in this country through the Part IV of the Financial Services Act 1986 and through the passage of various sets of regulations.

12–008 It is right to bear in mind that the European Directives do not afford the investor with any directly enforceable rights. The scope of Article 15 of the E.C. Directive (79/279) which requires that Member States shall ensure decisions of the competent authorities shall be subject to the right to apply to the Courts was considered in the case of *R. v. International Stock Exchange of the United Kingdom and the Republic of Ireland Ltd, ex p. Else (1982) Ltd* [1993] Q.B. 534. It was held in that case that the primary purpose of the Directive was to co-ordinate the listing practices of competent authorities in Member States and not directly to provide additional protection for investors. The Directive was concerned with relations between competent authorities and companies and issuers, not between those authorities and investors. The Directive conferred no enforceable rights on investors. The right to apply to the courts under Article 15 applied only to companies and issuers.

In 1995, the Dublin Stock Exchange separated from the London Stock Exchange (at midnight on December 8, 1995). The separation was the result of European legislation decreeing that each Member State must have its own statutory regulation. The Exchanges are now known as The London Stock Exchange Limited and the Irish Stock Exchange Limited. **12-009**

Structure of the Stock Exchange

Outline

The Stock Exchange was originally constituted by Deed of Settlement in 1802 and this continued until 1986 when the Exchange became a private limited company. The original Deed of Settlement was replaced in 1991 with a Memorandum and Articles of Association. The governing Council of the Exchange was replaced with a board of directors drawn from the Exchange's executive and its customers and users. The intention behind these changes was to create a more flexible organisation which is better able to react to changes in the financial world. **12-010**

The Financial Services Act 1986 provides the framework for the regulation of the United Kingdom securities markets. The Stock Exchange is a Recognised Investment Exchange ("RIE") under the Act and as such is answerable to the SIB. As an RIE the Exchange has the responsibility to regulate the users of its markets and to ensure that the operation of each market is orderly and provides proper protection to investors. The Exchange, in its role as regulator, has responsibility for vetting new applicants for membership, monitoring members compliance with its rules, providing services to aid trading and settlement of members business and investigating suspected abuse of its markets. **12-011**

The London Stock Exchange is the designated "competent authority" by virtue of section 142(6) of the Financial Services Act 1986. The "Official List" is the main or first tier market of the London Stock Exchange. An applicant for listing must comply with the requirements of Part IV of the Financial Services Act 1986 and with the Stock Exchange's own requirements for listing which are set out in the Listing Rules which have been amended to reflect the implementation of the **12-012**

Public Offers of Securities Regulations 1995 which came into force in June 1995. The Listing Rules are commonly known as the Yellow Book. The Yellow Book has statutory backing under Part IV of the Financial Services Act 1986.

12–013   The Listing Department acts as the competent authority for the London Stock Exchange. It has delegated authority from the Exchange's board.

Three Tiers

12–014   The Exchange's main market is the Official List, for which the criteria for official listing are broadly, the length of time a firm has been trading, the value of securities for which listing is sought and the proportion of securities that will be held by the public once listing has taken place.

12–015   A second tier market was established in 1980 to meet the needs of smaller and/or newer companies initially as the Unlisted Securities Market (USM). The USM has been replaced by the Alternative Investment Market (AIM) which was established to meet the needs of smaller and growing companies on June 19, 1995. Unlike new fully listed companies, AIM companies are not obliged to show a minimum trading record or market value, nor need they offer a set percentage of their shares to outside holders. AIM companies must have a nominated adviser and broker who are responsible for much of the day-to-day regulatory work and the company must make trading and other price sensitive information available in the usual way. In just over one year, the AIM has attracted 186 companies with a combined market value of £3.9 billion.

12–016   A third tier market was briefly established in 1987 but was phased out in 1991. This market was intended for less established companies. It has been replaced by OFEX, which was set up by J. P Jenkins, a specialist market maker in small company shares. OFEX is not regulated by the Stock Exchange but only Stock Exchange member firms can deal directly on it. Companies are required to make all relevant information available on J. P. Jenkins' newstrack information system. OFEX serves two functions. First, it offers a market place for the shares of unlisted companies that have no interest in coming into AIM but where the facility to deal may be important for their shareholders. More importantly, perhaps, it has evolved into a starter market for companies keen to minimise flotation and other costs at the outset. As such, it acts in part as a feeder market for AIM. To date 108 companies have joined OFEX with a combined market capitalisation of £1.53 billion.

Market Regulation Department

12–017   The Stock Exchange's market regulation department develops, monitors and enforces the rules affecting market makers and brokers in domestic equities and related products, international equities, gilts and fixed interest securities. The department regulates trading on the Exchange by monitoring market maker's quotations, the prices at which business is done, stock borrowing, trade reporting and compliance with the dealing rules. This is done using a computer system called IMAS (integrated monitoring and surveillance) which was introduced in June 1993 for all domestic securities. IMAS is designed to "alert" the Exchange to irregularities such as large fluctuations in share prices or volumes. During 1995 IMAS identified over 9,000 price movements, 1,100 of which needed more detailed investigation. In 1995, Market Supervision carried out nearly 900 investigations into potential breaches of the trading and reporting rules as a result of which 43 firms were fined, 68 firms were warned about their future conduct and 237 fines were imposed automatically for failures to open quotes on time.

The Rules of the London Stock Exchange

Membership

12–018 An applicant for membership of the London Stock Exchange must be authorised or exempted under the Financial Services Act 1986, an overseas person as defined by the Financial Services Act 1986 or a European authorised institution as defined by the Banking Co-ordination Regulations 1992. The Stock Exchange will assess the suitability of an applicant on the basis of the scope of the applicant's proposed business activities and relevant dealing capacity, the adequacy of its transaction recording, reporting and settlement procedures and systems (Chapter 1—Rules of the London Stock Exchange). The Stock Exchange is also concerned that member firms continue to satisfy the requirements for membership, failure to do so may lead to the firm being suspended from trading.

Core rules

12–019 The core rules are set out in Chapter 2 of the Rules of the London Stock Exchange and cover, amongst other things, transactions, market makers, the conduct of business and charges. A summary of the main core rules follows.

Transactions

12–020 Transactions must be "on exchange" transactions unless they fall within one of the exceptions. A transaction is "on exchange" if one or both of the parties to it is a member firm and the transaction is in securities which fall within the scope of rule 2.1(a). A member firm shall not effect a transaction in securities that are the subject of an application for admission to the Official List, to trading on the USM or listing or quotation on an approved organisation before the application is accepted except in certain specified circumstances (see rule 2.3(a) to (f)).

Market Makers

12–021 Member firms which wish to act as market makers must register with the Exchange. Registration in the case of the domestic equity market, the international equity market and for a fixed interest market makers is effective per security. Registration may be withdrawn at the market maker's request or by the Exchange (see rule 2.4). A firm may appeal against a refusal or withdrawal of registration to the Exchange appeal committee (see rules 2.5 and 1.33).

Conduct of Business

Contract Notes

12–022 A member firm must issue a contract note in respect of every transaction effected on the Exchange for or with a client. The contract note must state that the firm is a member of the London Stock Exchange and that the transaction is subject to the rules of the London Stock Exchange (rule 2.8).

Misleading Acts, Conduct and Prohibited Practices

12–023 A member firm must not intentionally, recklessly or without due care do any act or engage in any course of conduct which creates a false or misleading impression as to the market in or the price or value of any security which may induce another person to effect or refrain from effecting any transaction or to exercise or refrain from exercising any rights. Nor may the member firm engage in any course of conduct which may give rise to any artificial transaction; cause a fictitious transaction or a false price to be input into any Exchange system or to be printed as business done in the Official list; or effect a transaction at any price which differs to an unreasonable extent from the price at which market makers registered in that security are prepared to trade. The only exceptions to these prohibitions is if the conduct falls within the scope of any practice which is permitted under sections 48 (6) and 48 (7) of the Financial Services Act 1986 (rule 2.9).

Conditional Transactions

12–024 A member firm must not effect a transaction on Exchange subject to a condition precedent or condition subsequent without the prior consent of the Exchange (rule 2.11).

The Rules of the London Stock Exchange

Prohibited or Suspended Activities

12–025 The Stock Exchange may prohibit any transaction or class of transaction for any reason (rule 2.12).

Stabilisation

12–026 A member firm intended to act as or on behalf of a stabilising manager in accordance with SIB rules in a security to be traded on the Exchange must inform the Exchange and request it to publish a statement that stabilising transactions may be made by the member firm or on its behalf during the stabilising period (rule 2.13).

Transaction Charges

12–027 A member firm must pay a charge on every Exchange transaction (except those specified in rule 2.17(b)) at an *ad valorem* rate on the consideration payable for a transaction reported to be determined by the Exchange (rule 2.17).

Revenue Charges

12–028 Revenue charges are payable by inter dealer brokers and money brokers at the rates set out in the Exchange's price list (rule 2.18).

PTM Levy

12–029 This is the levy payable to the Panel on Take-overs and Mergers and must be included on each contract note issued by a member firm unless it falls within one of the exceptions set out in rules 2.19 (a) to (g) (rule 2.19).

Responsibility of Member Firms

12–030 A member firm is bound as a principal notwithstanding that it may be acting for a client in respect of its dealings with other member firms and its dealings with the Exchange. A member firm is responsible for the genuineness of transfer documents and certificates submitted by it (rule 2.20).

Action to Correct Erroneous Statement

12–031 A member firm which becomes aware that a client or counterparty has released for publication a materially inaccurate statement concerning any transaction effected through or with the firm must draw this to the attention of the client or counterparty and if no appropriate corrective statement is forthcoming, the member must take all reasonable steps to secure publication of such a statement (rule 2.21).

The International Equity Market

12–032   The rules concerning the functioning of the International Equity market are set out in Chapter 3 of the Rules of the Stock Exchange. The rules cover the display of prices on SEAQ International (rule 3.3), market makers as agents for non-member principals (rule 3.4), the obligations of market makers (rules 3.6–3.8), the obligations of members (rules 3.13–3.18), reporting (rules 3.19–3.22), and settlement (rules 3.23–3.32).

The Domestic Equity Market

12–033   The rules concerning the functioning of the Domestic Equity market are set out in Chapter 4 of the Rules of the Stock Exchange. The rules cover applications for permission to effect transactions (rule 4.2), participants including the registration of market makers (rules 4.3–4.4), the obligations of market makers (rules 4.5–4.19), trading activities (rules 4.20–4.22), limit orders (rules 4.23–4.32), SEAQ (the Stock Exchange Automated Quotation system), and the Automatic Execution Facility (SAEF) (rules 4.33–4.38), the Stock Exchange Alternative Trading Service (SEATS) (rules 4.39–4.49), and reporting (rules 4.50–4.60).

Compliance and discipline

12–034   The Stock Exchange rules concerning compliance and discipline are contained in Chapter 14 of the Stock Exchange rules. A member firm is required to provide the Exchange with information about its business, transactions and off-market transactions for the purpose of satisfying the Exchange that its rules are being complied with and for the protection of the integrity of the Exchange's markets. A member firm must comply with a request by the Exchange for explanation, verification or otherwise of information provided to it. The member firm must supply the Exchange with information if required to do so about any employee or agent of the firm engaged in its business (rules 14.1–14.4). In furtherance of its role of monitoring and investigating member firms the Exchange may visit the offices of member firms, require the production of information in the form of documents and other material, interview any employee or agent of a member firm, and require the attendance of an employee or agent of a member firm to answer questions (rules 14.5–14.6). The Exchange may bring proceedings against a former member firm for up to one year after that firm's membership has ceased (rule 14.9). The Exchange may institute disciplinary proceedings against a member firm in respect of acts of misconduct which includes breach of the rules of the Exchange, failure to comply with a decision or direction of the Exchange, conduct detrimental to the interests of the Exchange, provision to the Exchange of information which is false, misleading or inaccurate in a material particular, a breach of the Take-over code or the Substantial Acquisition rules, being knowingly concerned in or improper conduct which cause or contributes to an act of misconduct by another person or failure to pay a fine or order for costs imposed by the Exchange (rule 14.10).

12–035 The disciplinary process of the London Stock Exchange begins with an initial investigation, if this shows that there are grounds for believing that a member firm has or may have committed an act of misconduct these may be reported to the Professional Standards Panel which considers whether the matter should be referred to the Disciplinary Committee. The Disciplinary Committee hears and determines charges against a member firm in respect of misconduct at first instance. The Committee may also hear and determine appeals against findings or penalties imposed by Appeals Committees. The Disciplinary Committee sits in private and is usually comprised of three members. Appeals from the Disciplinary Committee are heard by the Disciplinary Appeals Committee (rules 14.12–14.23). The procedure to be followed in disciplinary hearings and appeals is set out in rules 14.24–14.68. The Disciplinary Committee may impose a fine, it may order that a member firm make restitution to any person when the member firm has benefited from a breach of the Exchange's rules at that person's expense, it may censure the member firm, it may suspend the right to use any system of the Exchange, it may suspend the member firm from dealing in securities or any class of securities dealt on the Exchange and it may expel the member firm from membership of the Exchange (rule 14.46).

12–036 In addition, the Exchange has a summary procedure for breaches of dealing, reporting and settlement rules (rules 14.69–14.89). The penalties which may be imposed for any such breach include a formal warning, a fixed penalty or a fine of up to £25,000 for each breach (rule 14.81)

Judicial Review

12–037 Decisions of the Stock Exchange are subject to judicial review. This right has been specifically preserved by Article 15 of E.C. Directive (79/279) which requires that Member States shall ensure decisions of the competent authorities be subject to the right to apply to the courts. The scope of Article 15 was considered in the case of *R. v. International Stock Exchange of the United Kingdom and the Republic of Ireland Ltd, ex p. Else (1982) Ltd and another* [1993] Q.B. 534, where in December 1990 a Stock Exchange Committee upheld a decision of the quotations panel cancelling the official listing of shares in a company in which the applicants were shareholders. The applicants brought proceedings for judicial review of the decision on the ground that they were entitled to be notified and given an opportunity to make representations to the committee prior to the decision to cancel and thereafter, to challenge such a decision in the courts under Article 15 of the E.C. Directive

(79/279). The Court of Appeal held, allowing the appeal, that the primary purpose of the Directive was to co-ordinate listing practices of competent authorities in Member States and not directly to provide additional protection for investors. The Directive was concerned with relations between competent authorities, companies and issuers, not between those authorities and investors. The Directive conferred no enforceable rights on investors. The right to apply to the courts under Article 15 applied only to companies and issuers. Shareholders were not entitled to be notified of an impending decision on discontinuation of listing or to be heard before such a decision was made.

Listing Requirements

12–038   Different listing requirements apply, depending on where the security is to be listed. The majority of requirements are to be found in the Financial Services Act 1986 and the Companies Act 1985. With regard to listed securities (*i.e.*, those which are to be admitted to official listing), the requirements are contained in Part IV of the Financial Services Act 1986, as amended by the Public Offer of Securities Regulations 1995. Public offers of unlisted securities are regulated by the Public Offer of Securities Regulations 1995 (S.I. 1995 No. 1537). These regulations took effect on June 19, 1995. Offers of securities falling outside both Part IV of the Financial Services Act 1986 and the Public Offer of Securities Regulations 1995 continue to be subject to the provisions of section 57 of the Financial Services Act 1986 concerning the issue of investment advertisements. There are also provisions in the Companies Act 1985 which apply to the allotment of shares and debentures. Each category of requirement is considered in turn.

Listed Securities

12–039   The London Stock Exchange has responsibility for admitting to listing securities that are covered by Part IV of the Financial Services Act 1986 giving effect to E.C. Directives directed at the harmonisation of securities listing regulations throughout the E.C. It also admits to listing, on a non statutory basis, gilt-edged securities to which Part IV does not apply.

12–040   The listing rules made by the Exchange govern the admission to listing of securities, the continuing obligations of issuers, the enforcement of the issuer's obligations and the suspension and cancellation of listing.

12–041   In applying the listing rules the Exchange has stated in its Introduction to the listing rules that it will have regard to the following objectives and principles:

"The Exchange seeks a balance between providing issuers with ready access to the market for their securities and protecting investors.

Listing Requirements

Securities will be admitted to listing only if the Exchange is satisfied that the applicant is suitable and that it is appropriate for those securities to be publicly held and traded.

Securities should be brought to the market in a way that is appropriate too their nature and number and which will facilitate an open and efficient market for trading in those securities.

An issuer must make full and timely disclosure about itself and its listed securities, at the time of listing and subsequently.

The listing rules, and in particular the continuing obligations, should promote investor confidence in standards of disclosure, in the conduct of listed companies' affairs and in the market as a whole.

Holders of equity securities should be given adequate opportunity to consider in advance and vote upon major changes in the company's management and constitution."

Official Listing

Section 142 of the Financial Services Act 1986 stipulates that no investment to which the section applies may be admitted to the Official List of the Stock Exchange except in accordance with the provisions of Part IV of the Financial Services Act 1986. Section 142 refers to shares and debentures and certificates representing such securities and warrants or other instruments entitling the holder to subscribe for shares or securities (s.142 applies to investments falling within paragraphs 1, 2, 4 and 5 of Schedule 1 to the Financial Services Act 1986). **12–042**

An application for a listing has to be made "to the competent authority in such a way as the listing might require." The competent authority for the United Kingdom is the London Stock Exchange (see the Official Listing of Securities (Change of Competent Authority) Regulations 1991 (S.I. 1991 No. 2000) which transferred the status of competent authority from the Council of the Stock Exchange to the Stock Exchange itself). In practice the Listing department of the Stock Exchange acts as the Competent authority having delegated authority from the Exchange's board to do so. **12–043**

Section 142(6) gives the Stock Exchange power to make the listing rules and it is this which gives the rules statutory backing. The Stock Exchange has delegated power to make rules regulating the applications for listing and specifying the detailed criteria for admission to the Official List within the widely drawn enabling provisions of the Act. In performing its function, the Stock Exchange must comply with the E.C. Directives relating to listing. A person who is refused admission by the Stock Exchange has the right to judicial review of the Exchange's decision, but no action for damages will lie against the Stock Exchange or its members, officers or employees for any thing done or omitted in good faith on discharge of their functions by virtue of section 187(4). **12–044**

Applications for Listing

12–045 Applications must be made to the competent authority in such a manner as the listing rules require (s.143(1)). Application for the listing of any security must be made by or with the consent of the issuer of the securities (s.143(2)).

12–046 Section 144 defines the responsibilities of the Stock Exchange for "vetting" applications for listing. The circumstances in which an application may or must be refused are set out in sections 144 (1) and (3). Section 144 (2) requires publication of a prospectus or listing particulars. Admission may be refused if the Stock Exchange considers it would be detrimental to the interests of investors (s.144 (3)) or if the applicant has not complied with listing obligations imposed by another Member State.

12–047 A decision must be notified to the applicant within six months of the date of its receipt or from the receipt of any further information which may be required (s.144(4)). If the Stock Exchange does not give notification within six months it must be taken to have refused the application (s.144(5)).

12–048 The conditions for listing are set out in Chapter 3 of the listing rules. An applicant must be duly incorporated or otherwise established according to the law of its place of incorporation or establishment and be operating in accordance with its memorandum and articles of association (rule 3.2). The company must have a trading record of at least three years and audited accounts for three years (rule 3.3). A shorter period than three years may be accepted if the Exchange is satisfied that it is in the interests of the applicant or of investors (rule 3.4). The company must have had continuity of management over the period covered by the accounts (rule 3.7). The company's directors must collectively have appropriate expertise and experience for the management of its business and must in general be free of conflicts between their duties to the company and their personal interests, or other duties (rule 3.8). The company must satisfy the exchange that it has sufficient working capital (rule 3.10). If the company has a controlling shareholder the company must be capable of operating and making decisions independently of the controlling shareholder (rules 3.12 and 3.13).

12–049 In addition, the securities themselves must satisfy a number of conditions. The securities must conform to the law of the applicant's place of incorporation and be duly authorised according to the requirements of the applicant's memorandum and articles of association and have any necessary statutory or other consents (rule 3.14). The securities must be freely transferable (rule 3.15). The market value of the shares to be listed must be at least £700,000 (debentures £200,000) (rule 3.16). The Exchange may admit securities of lower value if it is satisfied that there will be an adequate market (rule 3.17). At least 25 per cent of the shares must be in the hands of the public after the flotation (rules 3.18–3.21).

Listing Requirements

Sanctions

12–050 The Stock Exchange has the power to discontinue and suspend listing which is a powerful weapon in enforcing compliance with its rules, particularly the continuous reporting and dealing requirements (s.145). The rules concerning the compliance with and the enforcement of the listing rules are set out in Chapter 1 of the listing rules. Sanctions may be imposed by the Exchange if it considers that an issuer has contravened the listing rules. The Quotations Committee may censure the issuer and it may publish such censure or it may suspend or cancel the listing of the issuer's securities or any class of those securities. The 12–051 Quotations Committee may also censure any of the directors of the issuer if it finds that contravention of the listing rules is due to a failure of all or any of the issuer's directors to discharge their responsibilities. The Committee may also state publicly that retention of office by the director is prejudicial to the interests of investors and if the director continues in office following the issuing of such a statement, the Quotations Committee may suspend or cancel the listing of the issuer's securities or any class of those securities (see rules 1.8–1.10 and 1.11–1.23).

No Action for Damages

12–052 The Stock Exchange as the competent authority, and its members, officers and servants are not liable in damages for anything done or omitted to be done in the discharge or purported discharge of any functions of the competent authority under Part IV of the Financial Services Act 1986 unless the act or omission is shown to be in bad faith—see section 187(4).

Methods of Bringing Securities to Listing

Rights Issue

12–053 The most common method of bringing securities to listing and of raising more capital for listed companies is the rights issue (rule 4.16). A rights issue is defined by rule 4.16 as "an offer to existing holders of securities to subscribe or purchase further securities in proportion to their holdings by means of the issue of a renounceable letter (or other negotiable instrument) which may be traded (as "nil paid" rights) for a period before payments for the securities is due"—see rules 4.16–4.21.

12–054 When making a rights issue, regard must also be had to the rights as between holders of securities. A company proposing to issue equity securities for cash must offer these securities to existing equity shareholders first, in proportion to their existing holding (rules 9.18 and 9.19). Such pre-emption rights may be disapplied for a maximum of 15 months to the extent that shareholders of a company give their authorisation by way of special resolution for their disapplication (rule 9.20 and sections 95 and 89(1) of the Companies Act 1985).

Open Offer

12–055 Similar to the rights issue but less commonly used is the open offer which is "an invitation to existing holders of securities to subscribe or purchase securities in proportion to their holdings, which is not made by means of a renounceable letter (or other negotiable instrument)"—see rules 4.22–4.26.

Other Types of Issue

12–056 Other types of issue which are less common include:
— an offer for sale or subscription, sometimes known as an offer by tender which is a method often used in the U.S. but less often used in the United Kingdom (rule 4.4);
— placing, which is a marketing of securities already in issue but not listed or not yet in issue to specified persons or clients of the sponsor or any securities house assisting in the placing which does not involve an offer to the public (rule 4.7);
— intermediaries offer, which is a marketing of securities already or not yet in issue by means of an offer by or on behalf of the issuer to intermediaries for them to allocate to their own clients (rule 4.10);
— acquisition or merger issue or vendor consideration issue, which is an issue of securities in consideration for an acquisition of assets or an issue of securities on an acquisition of or merger with another company as consideration for the securities of that other company (rule 4.27);
— vendor consideration placing, which is a marketing by or on behalf of vendors of securities that have been allocated to them as consideration for any acquisition (rule 4.29);
— capitalisation issue or bonus issue, which is often used in lieu of dividend or otherwise is used as an issue to existing holders of securities in proportion to their holdings of further shares credited as fully paid out of the issuer's reserve (rule 4.31);
— issues for cash, which is the issue of securities for cash to persons who are specifically approved by shareholder in general meeting or an issue pursuant to a general disapplication of section 89 of the Companies Act 1985 approved by shareholders in general meeting (rule 4.33).

Market Makers

12–057 Where an application is made for listing of securities of a class not already listed there must normally be at least two market makers willing to make a market in those securities (rule 4.35).

Disclosure of Adviser's Interests

Advisers to any new applicant for listing must disclose an interest of 3 per cent or more in any class of equity shares being marketed to the Company Announcements Office before dealings in the securities commence (rule 4.38). **12–058**

Sponsors

In major public issues a company will have a sponsor who is normally a corporate broker or investment bank. The requirements relating to sponsors are set out in the listing rules—Chapter 2. A sponsor undertakes to the Exchange to accept certain responsibilities. A failure to carry out these responsibilities may lead to the Exchange referring the sponsor to the Quotations Committee who may impose certain sanctions (see rules 2.24 and 2.25). The sponsor acts as financial adviser to the company and the sponsor will also direct the strategy of the issue and co-ordinate the activities of other professional advisers. The sponsor has a duty to the Stock Exchange to ensure that the company satisfies the listing criteria and that the company is guided through the listing process. Over and above the requirements set out in Chapter 2 of the listing rules, the Exchange encourages the appointment of a sponsor who is fully experienced in market practice to give advice on a continuing basis regarding the application of the listing rules, particularly those continuing obligations and to give advice in the case of any unforeseen event. **12–059**

A sponsor must be an authorised person under the Financial Services Act or a European institution as defined by the Second Banking Co-ordination Directive Regulations 1992. The sponsor must satisfy the Exchange that it is competent to discharge the responsibilities of a sponsor and must make an undertaking to the Exchange in the form set out in Schedule 1 to the listing rules and be entered on the Exchange's register of sponsors (rule 2.1). It is necessary to appoint a sponsor when (a) an issuer makes any application for listing which requires the production of listing particulars, (b) there has been a breach of the listing rules and the Exchange requires the appointment of a sponsor, or (c) a sponsor is required by the listing rules to report to the Exchange in relation to any transaction or matter (rule 2.3). The responsibilities of a sponsor are set out in rules 2.6 to 2.18. **12–060**

Listing Agents

A listing agent's responsibilities are less onerous than those of a sponsor but like a sponsor, a listing agent must be an authorised person under the Financial Services Act 1986 (or a European institution) (rule 2.2). The responsibilities of a listing agent are set out in rule 2.19. **12–061**

Underwriting

Underwriting is an agreement under which the whole or part of an issue, if not applied for by the public, will be taken up by the underwriters. Underwriters are paid commission which is limited by sections 97 and 98 of the Companies Act 1985. **12–062**

Prospectus and Listing Particulars

12–063 Section 144(2) of the Financial Services Act 1986 as amended by the Public Offers of Securities Regulations 1995 (effective from June 19, 1995) implementing the E.C. Public Offers Directive and the Listing Particulars Directive, empowers the Stock Exchange to require the publication of a prospectus or a set of listing particulars as a condition of admission of securities to listing. A prospectus is mandatory if securities are sought to be offered to the public in the United Kingdom for the first time prior to their admission to the Official List unless the securities fall within an exception under Schedule 11A to the Financial Services Act 1986 as amended by the Public Offer of Securities Regulations 1995. However, in practice an offer of shares for sale or subscription is unlikely to fall within an exemption and a typical rights issue is also likely to be too large to benefit from any of the exemptions—see rule 5.1(a). Applications for listing of securities in all other circumstances require the issuer to prepare listing particulars (rule 5.1(b)). Exceptions to the requirement to produce listing particulars include securities which have been the subject of a public issue or issued in connection with a take-over offer or issued in connection with a merger or where the securities have been listed in a Member State for not less than three years or where the shares have been traded on the AIM and/or the USM for a period covering at least two years (rules 5.1(e) and 5.23A and 5.27).

12–064 The detailed requirements concerning the contents of prospectuses and of listing particulars are set out in Chapters 5 and 6 of the listing rules. Broadly, listing particulars must include information about the applicant and its share capital, financial information about the applicant and its recent development and prospects, and the applicant's group structure and management.

Form and Content of Prospectuses

12–065 The form and content of what should be contained in a prospectus is laid down in regulation 8 and Schedule 1 to the Public Offers of Securities Regulations 1995. Regulation 8(3) provides that information must be presented in an easily comprehensible form. A prospectus must include a number of general pieces of information, including: the name and address of the issuer and its registered office, the names and functions of the directors of the issuer, the date of publication of the prospectus, a statement that the prospectus has been delivered to the registrar of companies for registration, a statement that the prospectus accords with the regulations and perhaps most importantly from the point of view of the investor, the prospectus must include the words:

> "If you are in any doubt about the contents of this document you should consult a person authorised under the Financial Services Act

1986 who specialises in advising on the acquisition of shares and other securities."

12-066 In addition to the requirements set out in regulation 8 and Schedule 1 as to the contents of a prospectus there is a general duty of disclosure imposed by regulation 9 on the issuer of a prospectus that the prospectus must include all such information as investors would reasonably require for the purpose of making an informed assessment of the assets and liabilities, the financial position, profit and losses and the prospects of the issuer of the securities and of the rights attaching to those securities.

12-067 A supplementary prospectus must be published where there is a significant change affecting any matter contained in the prospectus which was required to be included by regulations 8 or 9, or where as significant new matter arises which would have been so required if it had arisen when the prospectus was prepared or there is a significant inaccuracy in the prospectus (see regulation 10). "Significant" means significant for the purpose of making an informed assessment of the financial standing of the issuer as mentioned in regulation 9.

Pre-publication Vetting of Listing Particulars and Prospectus

12-068 Under section 144(2) of the Financial Services Act 1986 and rule 5.1 of the listing rules, listing particulars and prospectuses must be submitted and approved by the Exchange prior to publication. Obviously such pre-publication vetting can provide an important safeguard for investors, in that the pre-publication vetting can make sure that all necessary information has been included and has been stated in a way which is not likely to give a false impression. Vetting may also have the effect of deterring those inclined to mislead or conceal information—see rules 5.9-5.13.

Compensation for False or Misleading Information

12-069 Section 150 of the Financial Services Act 1986 provides that compensation may be payable to any person who has acquired securities and suffered loss in respect of them as a result of any untrue or misleading statement or omission in the listing particulars.

The Issuer's General Duty to Disclose

12-070 In addition to the information specified to be included in the listing particulars, section 146(1) of the Financial Services Act 1986 imposes a further duty on the issuer of listed securities that listing particulars must also contain all such information as investors and their professional advisers would reasonably require for the purpose of making an informed assessment of the assets and liabilities, financial position, profits and losses and prospects of the issuer and the rights attaching to the securities.

12–071   Section 146(2) qualifies this obligation by saying that what is required is information which is within the knowledge of any person responsible for the listing particulars or which it would be responsible for him to obtain by making enquiries. In determining what information is required to be included, section 146(3) requires that regard is to be had to the nature of the securities and of the issuer, the nature of the persons likely to consider their acquisition (*i.e.* professional investment managers), and that persons may reasonably be expected to consult professional advisers who will have specialist knowledge in the field. In practice, professional advisers are likely to receive more detailed documentation than ordinary investors.

12–072   Section 148(1) of the Financial Services Act 1986 allows the Stock Exchange to exempt from the obligation to disclose in listing particulars certain information which would be contrary to the public interest or seriously detrimental to the issuer of securities. There is no authority for an exemption to be given where non-disclosure would be likely to mislead a person considering the acquisition "as to any facts the knowledge of which it is essential for him to have in order to make an informed decision"—see section 148(2).

Supplementary Listing Particulars

12–073   Where the circumstances show a significant change in any matter or the emergence of a significant new matter which would have been disclosed had it arisen at the time of the preparation of the original prospectus or listing particulars, section 147 of the Financial Services Act 1986 requires the issuing of supplementary listing particulars after admission to the official list but before the commencement of dealings . "Significant" in this context is defined as "significant for the purpose of making an informed assessment of the matters mentioned in section 146(1)" (see s.147(2) and rules 5.14-16).

Publication and Circulation of Listing Particulars

12–074   Listing particulars and supplementary listing particulars must not be published, advertised or circulated until they have been formally approved by the Exchange, and must be published in accordance with the rules of the Exchange (rule 8.1). A formal notice must be inserted in at least one national newspaper no later than one business day after publication of the listing particulars (rule 8.7).

Advertisements

12–075   In addition to meeting the requirements concerning advertisements contained in the Listing Rules, regard must also be had to the regulation of investment advertisements by section 57 of the Financial Services Act 1986 and to section 154 which concerns advertisements in connection with listing applications.

12–076 Section 154 of the Financial Services Act 1986 gives the Stock Exchange the power to control advertisements issued in connection with applications for listing. Under section 154(1) there must be no publication of an advertisement in the United Kingdom where the contents of the advertisement have not been submitted to the Stock Exchange for approval (rules 8.23-26). Contravention of this requirement by authorised persons will be treated as an infringement of the conduct of business rules in Part I, Chapter V of the Financial Services Act 1986 and the SIB can use its section 61 powers to seek injunction to restrain contravention.

12–077 Private investors may also seek damages for losses arising out of contravention of the conduct of business rules. In addition, section 154(3) imposes a criminal sanction for infringement of section 154 by persons who are not authorised. The penalty for contravention on conviction on indictment is one of two years' imprisonment and/or a fine, and if convicted in the magistrates' court a fine not exceeding the statutory maximum. It is a defence to a charge brought under section 154(3) to show that the person who issues the advertisement in the ordinary course of business other than investment business and to the order of another person reasonably believed that the advertisement had been approved by the Stock Exchange (s.154(4)). If the advertisement is approved by Stock Exchange, there is no civil liability if the advertisement turns out to be misleading (s.154(5)).

12–078 Listing particulars and supplementary listing particulars must be delivered to the registrar of companies prior to their publication and a statement that a copy has been so delivered must be included in the particulars (s.149).

Offers of securities falling outside both Part IV and the regulations are subject to provisions of section 57 of the Financial Services Act 1986 regulating the issue of investment advertisements and section 58 exemptions.

Unlisted Securities—Alternative Investment Market

12–079 The Unlisted Securities Market (USM) was first established in 1980 to meet the needs of smaller and newer companies. The USM has been replaced by the Alternative Investment Market (AIM) which was launched on June 19, 1995. Regulation of the unlisted securities markets was envisaged by the provisions of Part V of the Financial Services Act 1986. However, this Part of the Act was never brought into force because of the need to implement E.C. Prospectus Directive 89/298. This has been implemented by the Public Offers of Securities Regulations 1995.

Admission to the Alternative Investment Market

12–080   In general the requirements which must be met for admission to the AIM are more relaxed than for admission to the Official List. The AIM admission rules form Chapter 16 of the Rules of the London Stock Exchange and the AIM trading rules are set out in Chapter 17. There are six main requirements for admission.

12–081   The company must be duly incorporated or otherwise validly established according to the laws of its place of incorporation. and the company must be permitted by its national law to offer its securities to the public. In the United Kingdom, it must be a public limited company. (See the Rules of the London Stock Exchange—rule 16.1(a)).

The securities to be traded on the market must be freely transferable (rule 16.1(b)).

12–082   The company must appoint and retain a nominated adviser and a nominated broker (rule 16.1(d)). The nominated adviser must be independent of the issuer and must be a member firm of the Exchange or a person authorised under the Financial Services Act 1986 (rules 16.28-30). If at any time the issuer ceases to have a nominated adviser or a nominated broker the Exchange will suspend trading in its securities. Failure to appoint replacement advisers or brokers within one month will result in discontinuance of admission to AIM (rule 16.34).

The application for admission to AIM must be made in the form prescribed by the Exchange (rule 16.4).

12–083   When an issuer applies for the admission of securities to trading on AIM it must publish an admission document which must contain certain information set out in the Stock Exchange rules and information required by the Public Offers of Securities Regulations (rules 16.10 and 16.11).

12–084   There is a general and continuing obligation of disclosure for an issuer whose securities have been admitted to trading on AIM and issuer must accept continuing obligations with regard to such matters as the preparation of accounts, completion of transfers of securities and dealings in securities by directors and other employees (rules 16.14–16.27).

Sanctions Against an Issuer

12–085   If the Exchange considers that an issuer has contravened any of the rules set out in Chapter 16 of the Stock Exchange Rules it may censure the issuer, publish the fact that the issuer has been censured or suspend trading or discontinue the admission of the issuer's securities to trading—rules 16.31 and 16.38.

12–086   The Exchange may require an issuer to provide information to it and to publish such information in such form and within such time-limits as the Exchange considers appropriate for the purpose of protecting investors and maintaining the smooth operation of the market. Failure by the issuer to publish the information may lead to the Exchange itself publishing it (rules 16.32 and 16.33).

The Exchange has a general power to suspend or discontinue the admission of securities to trading on AIM where dealings in those securities are not being conducted in an orderly manner or where the protection of investors so requires (rule 16.35).

The Exchange may also impose sanctions on the directors of issuing companies where it considers that all or any of the directors of that company have failed to discharge their responsibilities (rule 16.36). **12–087**

If a nominated adviser is in breach of its responsibilities the Exchange may also impose sanctions on it (rule 16.37).

Appeals

Any decision by the Exchange in relation to the rules set out in Chapter 16 of the Stock Exchange Rules may be appealed to an appeal committee appointed by the Exchange and composed of persons not employed by the Exchange (rule 16.39). **12–088**

Prospectuses

It is a requirement under the Public Offers of Securities Regulations 1995 that when securities are offered to the public in the United Kingdom for the first time the offeror shall publish a prospectus by making it available to the public, free of charge, at an address in the United Kingdom, from the time he first offers the securities until the end of the period during which the offer remains open (reg. 4(1)). The prospectus must be delivered to the Registrar of Companies for registration prior to publication (reg. 4(2)). Unlike the requirement for listing particulars for listing on the official list, there is no obligation for mandatory pre-publication vetting which may be a major shortcoming of the AIM when viewed from the perspective of the protection of the investor. However, a contravention of regulation 4 by a person authorised by an SRO will be treated as a breach of the conduct of business rules made under the Financial Services Act 1986 (reg. 16(1)). Contravention of regulation 4 by an unauthorised person is an offence punishable by up to two years' imprisonment and/or a fine if convicted on indictment or a maximum of three months' imprisonment and/or a fine on of the statutory maximum if convicted in a magistrates' court (reg. 16(2)). Contravention of regulation 4 is also actionable at the suit of any person who suffers loss as a result subject to the defences applying to actions for breach of statutory duty (reg. 16(4)). **12–089**

As we have already seen in the context of prospectus's issued in connection with securities listed on the Official list the form and content of prospectuses must comply with requirements set out in Schedule 1 to the regulations—see above and regulations 8, 9 and Schedule 1. **12–090**

Supplementary Prospectuses

As with listed securities, it is necessary to publish a second or subsequent prospectus where there is a significant change affecting any matter contained in the prospectus which was required to be included or **12–091** where a significant new matter arises which would have been so required if it had arisen when the prospectus was prepared or there is a significant inaccuracy in the prospectus (reg. 10).

Offer of Securities to the Public

12–092 An offer of securities is defined by regulation 5 of the Public Offers of Securities Regulations 1995 as:

> "a person is to be regarded as offering securities if as a principal (a) he makes an offer which, if accepted, would give rise to a contract for the issue or sale of the securities by him or by another person with whom he has made arrangements for the issue or sale of the securities; or (b) he invites a person to make such an offer; but not otherwise; and except where the context otherwise requires, in this Part of these Regulations 'offer' and 'offeror' shall be construed accordingly."

12–093 An "offer to the public" is defined by regulation 6 as an offer which:

> "is made to the public, and for this purpose, an offer which is made to any section of the public, whether selected as members or debenture holders of a body corporate, or as clients of the person making the offer, or in any other manner, is to be regarded as made to the public."

Exempted Offers

12–094 Certain securities are deemed not to be offered to the public by virtue of regulation 7. Such exempted offers include:

— offers to persons in the context of their trade, profession of occupation;

— offers to no more than 50 people, which enables small scale offers to be made without excessive regulation. However, such offers would still be covered by the provision of sections 57 and 58 of the Financial Services Act 1986 on advertising;

— offers made to a restricted circle of person whom the offeror reasonably believes to be sufficiently knowledgeable to understand the risks involved;

— offers in connection with underwriting;

— offers of securities by a private company to its existing members, employees or debenture holders or to members of the families of existing members and employees;

— offers where the total consideration payable for all the securities offered does not exceed ECU 40,000;

— offers where the securities are denominated in amounts of at least ECU 40,000.

Advertisements

12–095 An advertisement in connection with an offer of securities must not be issued unless it states that a prospectus is or will be published and gives an address in the United Kingdom from which it can be obtained or will be obtainable (reg. 12). In addition, advertisements in relation to investment businesses are subject to section 57 of the Financial Services Act 1986.

Mutual Recognition

12–096 The Public Offer of Securities Regulations have adopted the mutual recognition of prospectuses and listing particulars between Member States of the E.C. This has been done so as to allow securities to be offered, or admitted to listing in a number of Member States on the basis of a prospectus or listing particulars which has satisfied the requirements imposed by one of the Member States (reg. 20 and Sched. 4).

Over the Counter Trading

12–097 A company is not obliged to seek admission to one of the official markets to trade its shares. The advantage of admission to a formal market is that it increases the number of potential investors and can increase a company's status which can make it easier to raise capital from other sources. However, as we have seen it also requires the company to adhere to the rules of the market which may prove to be expensive and restrictive. As we have seen, offers of securities to fewer than 50 people may be exempted from the requirements of the official markets under regulation 7 of the Public Offer of Securities Regulations 1995.

Companies Act 1985

12–098 The Companies Act 1985 is a source of regulation relating to the allotment of shares and debentures. The most important of these provisions are covered elsewhere in this book. The prohibitions on a company acquiring its own shares contained in section 143 of the Companies Act 1985 and the prohibition on the provision of financial assistance by a company to assist in the purchase of its own shares under section 151 of the Companies Act 1985 are covered in Chapter 21. Other Companies Act provisions intended to enhance fair dealing and foster and maintain investor confidence in the markets are discussed in Chapter 19, the provisions designed to counter market manipulation and those relating to insider dealing are discussed in Chapter 20.

Remedies for False Misleading or Incomplete Statements in Connection with Offers of Securities

Statutory Remedy

12–099   Section 150 of the Financial Services Act 1986 provides that the person or persons responsible for any listing particulars or supplementary listing particulars shall be liable to pay compensation to any person who has acquired any of the securities and suffered loss in respect of them as a result of any untrue or misleading statement in the particulars or the omission from them of any matter required to be included by section 146 or 147. This liability extends to supplementary prospectuses listing particulars under section 154A.

12–100   Section 151 sets out a number of exemptions from this liability to pay compensation. These include:

— where the person responsible reasonably believed that he made such enquiries as were reasonable that the statement was true and not misleading and that he continued in that belief until the securities were acquired;

— that the securities were acquired before it was reasonably practical to take steps to bring a correction to attention of those likely to acquire securities;

— that before the securities were acquired all reasonable steps had been taken to bring a correction to attention of those acquiring;

— that he continued to believe the statement was true;

— that there had been reasonable reliance on statements made by an expert;

— it is a defence to rely on a statement made by an official or in an official document.

12–101   Compensation is payable to a person who has acquired securities and suffered loss. The section does not specify how this should be quantified. It is expected that principles by which loss will be quantified will be the subject of future litigation. The persons responsible for the particulars are those who may be liable under section 150 of the Financial Services Act 1986 and are defined by section 152 as the issuer of the securities or the directors of the issuing company. Also liable are those who accept as stated in the particulars responsibility for the document. Such persons may include an issuing house, or an expert such as a valuer or accountant who is responsible for part of the contents of the document.

A person is not responsible for the contents of any particulars if they are published without his knowledge or consent and on becoming aware of their publication he gives reasonable public notice that they were published without his knowledge or consent (s.152(2)). Those who may seek a remedy under section 150 include "any person who has acquired any of the securities in question", and section 150(5) includes references to person contracting to acquire securities or an interest in them. This includes those who become the registered owners of securities, and those who have agreed to purchase or subscribe or buy options in securities. It is unresolved whether this extends to "market purchasers." 12–102

Virtually identical provisions apply in respect of unlisted securities under regulations 14 and 15 of the Public Offers of Securities Regulations 1995. 12–103

Common Law Remedies

Section 150(4) of the Financial Services Act 1986 specifically preserves "any liability which any person may incur apart from this section." This clearly leaves the way open for an investor to pursue claims based on misrepresentation or negligence. 12–104

Common law remedies in the investor protection context are discussed fully in Part 6 of this book.

Criminal Offences

Criminal offences which may be committed in the context of Stock Exchange fraud are discussed in Part 5 of this book. 12–105

Conclusion

As we have seen, the Financial Services Act 1986 established a new regulatory system for the conduct of investment business in the United Kingdom including business conducted on the Stock Exchange. The requirements of the Financial Services Act 1986 mean that a firm needs to have gained authorisation to carry on investment business from a SRO as well as being a member of the Stock Exchange. In practice, this means that firms operating on the Exchange are regulated by two bodies which can lead to confusion as to which body is to police the firm's activities and confusion as to where an aggrieved investor should turn for redress. Some commentators have suggested that the two tier system 12–106

Chapter 12: The Stock Exchange

of regulation now in force has led to an "identity crisis" for the Stock Exchange. This is a charge which has been strongly refuted by the Exchange itself. There have been calls for the replacement of the system with a more formal legal framework of Stock Market regulation.

Chapter 13

The Panel on Take-overs and Mergers

"The Panel on Take-overs and Mergers is a truly remarkable body. Perched on the 20th floor of the Stock Exchange building in the City of London, both literally and metaphorically it oversees and regulates a very important part of the United Kingdom financial market. Yet it performs this function without visible means of legal support"—*per* Sir John Donaldson M.R. in *R. v. Panel on Take-overs, ex p. Datafin* [1987] 2 W.L.R. 699 at 702.

Background

13–001 The Take-over Panel was set up in 1968, following proposals by the Governor of the Bank of England and the Chairman of the Stock Exchange, in response to concerns about unfair practices relating to shareholders and because it was widely recognised that the proper regulation of take-overs and mergers was essential in maintaining fairness and investor confidence in the markets. Between 1968 and 1990, the Panel handled some 5,500 announced offers and about half as many cases where no offer was announced.

13–002 The Take-over Panel administers and implements the City Code on Take-overs and Mergers which is a voluntary code comprised of a body of self-regulatory rules. It is voluntary in the sense that it is without direct statutory force. Unlike other self-regulatory bodies the Panel does not rely on either statutory or contractual powers to enforce the Code. Neither does the Panel have a membership in the way that the Stock Exchange or the SROs have and it is in this sense that the Code is voluntary.

13–003 The Code is very far from voluntary in the sense that the ambit of the Code administered by the Take-over Panel extends to all those involved in take-over bids or mergers. The individual players cannot opt out of supervision by the Panel. The functions of the Panel are performed with abundant invisible or indirect support from other regulatory bodies. Although the Code itself does not have a statutory basis, adherence to the Code is mandatory and its implementation is enforceable against their members by the Stock Exchange, the SIB and SROs and in certain circumstances the RPBs. There is a great area of overlap between the

CHAPTER 13: THE PANEL ON TAKE-OVERS AND MERGERS

Code and the Stock Exchange rules, the Financial Services Act 1986, and Companies legislation.

13–004 The Take-over Panel is concerned with take-overs of public (and certain private) companies where there is to be a change in control of companies whose shares are held by the public. The purpose of the Panel and the Code is to oversee and ensure the fair conduct of a take-over bid from the perspective of the shareholders. The spirit of the Code is expressed in 10 general principles and the practical implementation of the Code is achieved through the 38 rules. The commercial or financial merits of a take-over do not form part of the considerations of the Panel. However, there may be situations in which wider issues of public interest arise and the Panel may refer the take-over or merger for further consideration by the Monopolies and Mergers Commission, the Office of Fair Trading (see the Fair Trading Act 1973, Pt V), the Department of Trade and Industry or the E.C. Commission (under Article 86 of Treaty of Rome).

A Common Law Vacuum

13–005 The regulation of take-overs and mergers is an area where in practice, the common law has had little part to play and few remedies to offer. An attempt to obtain an injunction to prevent a take-over bid from being made was rejected by the Court of Appeal in the case of *Dunford and Elliott Ltd v. Johnson and Firth Brown Ltd* [1977] 1 Ll.Rep. 505. In this case, the plaintiffs were a steel making company who had sustained severe losses for a number of years. They decided to make a rights issue to their shareholders of whom some 43 per cent were institutional shareholders. The institutional shareholders were invited to form a consortium to underwrite the issue and to this end the plaintiff's financial advisers prepared a confidential report giving the company's financial prospects for the future. The consortium, without consulting the plaintiff, approached a rival steel making company and a second company to invite them to join the consortium. In doing so, the two further companies were shown the confidential financial document. The rival company declined to join the consortium but instead launched a take-over bid for the plaintiff company. The plaintiffs applied for an injunction to restrain the take-over bid. At first instance Mocatta J. granted the injunction but this was overturned by the Court of Appeal. The court held that the grant of an interlocutory injunction would have the effect of frustrating a take-over bid forever, and, having regard to the general principles of the Take-over Code, nothing should be done to frustrate the making of a bid. It followed that an injunction was not an appropriate remedy in an action arising out of a take-over bid. The Court of Appeal also held that when one gives confidential information to another on the understanding that the information will not be passed on to others, such a stipulation is normally enforced by the law.

However, the courts will not enforce such a stipulation if it is wider than what is reasonable. In this case it was held that it would not be reasonable for the stipulation of confidentiality to be enforced because the possession of the confidential information had placed the shareholder members of the consortium in a preferential position to the other shareholders. This would give effect to the requirement of the City Code that shareholders should be treated equally and possess sufficient information on which to base their decisions.

Europe

The draft thirteenth Directive on Take-overs was drafted with the aim of achieving the harmonisation of the law of Member States on take-over bids and the imposition of minimum standards throughout the E.C. ([1990] O.J. C240/7). However, this directive has not been implemented. When the E.C. proposals were published a number of bodies in the United Kingdom including the Take-over Panel and the Law Society's influential Company Law Committee expressed concern that, if implemented, the Directive would remove the flexibility of the existing system and lead to extensive litigation in the course of take-over bids. Further reading on this topic is contained in a report from Coopers and Lybrand commissioned by the Department of Trade and Industry: "Barriers to Take-overs in the European Community" and the Department of Trade and Industry consultative document "Barriers to Take-overs in the European Community: A Consultative document". 13–006

Definition of Terms

The Take-over Code contains a definitions section and for the purposes of this chapter certain terms which are used in the context of take-overs and mergers may require some clarification. An "offer" is defined by the Code as including take-over and merger transactions including reverse take-overs, partial offers, court schemes and offers by a parent company for shares in its subsidiary. An "offeror", is usually seen, as "a predator" in contrast to an "offeree" who is usually seen as "a victim." However, only the term "offeror" receives any note of definition in the Code which states that "an offeror" includes companies wherever incorporated and individuals wherever resident. 13–007

The Panel on Take-overs and Mergers

The Panel itself is purely a supervisory body with day-to-day administration of the Code being carried out by the Panel's Executive. The Panel draws its members from major financial and business institutions, 13–008

CHAPTER 13: THE PANEL ON TAKE-OVERS AND MERGERS

it's Chairman and a number of other members are appointed by the Governor of the Bank of England whilst the remaining members are representatives of various financial and professional organisations including the Chairman of the Stock Exchange, the Chairman of IMRO and the Chairman of the SFA.

Membership

13–009   Membership of the Panel includes representatives of the following associations:

> The Association of British Insurers;
> The Association of Investment Trust Companies;
> British Bankers Association;
> The British Merchant Banking and Securities Houses Association;
> The Confederation of British Industry;
> The Institute of Chartered Accountants in England and Wales;
> The London Stock Exchange;
> The London Investment Banking Association;
> The London Investment Banking Association Corporate Finance Committee;
> The National Association of Pension Funds;
> The SFA;
> Association of Unit Trusts and Investment Funds.

13–010   The Executive consists of a Director-General, Deputy Director Generals, Secretaries and staff all of whom report to the Chairman of the Panel. The main supervisory function of the Panel itself is to consider matters of policy and to hear appeals against rulings of the Director General, references by the Panel's executive, disciplinary cases and cases of exceptional importance. In 1994/1995 there were six appeals to the Panel against rulings of the Executive of which one was successful and there was one appeal from a decision of the Panel to the Appeal Committee, which was unsuccessful.

13–011   The Executive monitors take-overs by checking that all aspects of the take-over comply with the code. In addition it is an important function of the Executive that it is available for consultation both before and during take-overs.

Sanctions

13–012   Where there appears to have been a breach of the Code, the person involved is asked to appear before the full Panel which may hand out a private reprimand or public censure or which may take action to restrict or remove the miscreant's ability to enjoy the facilities of the securities markets. There is a right to appeal the decision of the Panel to the Appeal Committee where the Panel has found a breach of the Code and intends to impose disciplinary measures. However, no appeal lies against a finding of fact or against a decision of the Panel on the interpretation of the Code.

13–013 In practice, however, it is the overlap with other regulatory regimes and bodies which gives the Take-over Code its bite. The Code overlaps with the Stock Exchange Listing Rules which must also be complied with in the event of a take-over or merger (see Chapter 12). The Code overlaps with companies legislation which must be complied with, (namely the Companies Act 1985 and the Insolvency Act 1986), and with the provisions of the Financial Services Act 1986. In particular, the SIB has endorsed the Code in its Statements of Principle requiring those authorised under the Financial Services Act 1986 to comply with any code or standard to the extent endorsed for the purpose of the Principle and to adhere to any rulings made under it—see the "Endorsement of Take-over Code—Financial Services (Statements of Principle) (Endorsement of Codes and Standards) Instrument 1995" which came into effect on January 19, 1995, set out at Appendix 3.

13–014 Where a breach of the Code is also an act of misconduct by a member of the Stock Exchange it may result in the admission of shares on the Official List being withheld or suspended. Breaches of the Code by authorised persons who are members of any of the SROs will result in disciplinary action being taken by the individual SROs. For the scope of disciplinary action available to SROs, see Chapter 4. However, disciplinary action and the exercise of powers of intervention by the SIB or SROs for failure to comply with the Take-over Code may only be implemented on the request of the Take-over Panel—see paragraph 5 of the Endorsement of Take-over Code—Financial Services (Statements of Principle) (Endorsement of Codes and Standards) Instrument 1995.

Judicial Review

13–015 Decisions of the Panel and of the Appeal Committee are subject to judicial review. The leading case on judicial review of non-statutory bodies is *R. v. Panel on Take-overs, ex p. Datafin* [1987] 2 W.L.R. 699 which considered whether decisions of the Take-over Panel were susceptible to judicial review. The case arose where a company which had been in competition with Norton Opax plc over bidding for a target company, McCorquodale plc. The target company complained to the Take-over Panel that the bidder had been acting in concert with other parties in breach of the Take-over Code. The Panel dismissed the complaint. The applicants, Datafin plc and Prudential Bache Securities Inc., applied to the High Court for leave for judicial review to quash the Panel's decision and for mandamus to compel the Panel to reconsider the complaint. At first instance the judge refused leave for judicial review on the basis that the Panel's decisions were not susceptible to judicial review. This was overturned by the Court of Appeal which held that the supervisory jurisdiction of the High Court was flexible and could be extended to any regulatory body which performed public law duties supported by sanctions, and which was under an obligation to act judicially. Accordingly, the source of its powers were not derived simply from the consent of those over whom it exercised those powers. The Panel operated as an integral part of a governmental framework for the regulation of financial activity in the City of London and was supported by a periphery of statutory powers.

13–016 In argument in *R. v. Panel on Take-overs, ex p. Datafin* the concern was expressed that judicial review could be used as a method of obstructing or thwarting a take-over. This point was considered by Lord Donaldson in his judgment who expressed the expectation that the relationship between the Panel and the court would be historic rather than contemporaneous, with the courts allowing contemporary decisions to take their course and intervening retrospectively by way of declaratory orders. This approach enabled market confidence to be maintained.

13–017 An example of a situation where the courts refused to intervene occurred in *R. v. Panel on Take-overs, ex p. Guinness plc* [1990] 1 Q.B. 146. Following the DTI's inspection into the conduct of Guinness plc in the bid for Distillers it emerged that the conduct of Guinness plc had infringed the Take-over Code despite the Panel having been given assurances by Guinness at the time of the bid that its conduct had been within the rules of the Code. Guinness requested the Panel to adjourn its hearing into the alleged breaches until after the conclusion of the outstanding criminal proceedings and the publication of the DTI report. The Panel refused an adjournment and at the hearing found that Guinness had indeed infringed the Code. Guinness sought judicial review of the Panel's finding arguing that the company had been prevented from properly presenting its case because the Panel had not allowed its request for an adjournment. The Court of Appeal held that the non-statutory status of the Panel meant that the courts would only intervene by way of judicial review where it was satisfied that there had been an injustice and that no such injustice had taken place in the particular circumstances of this case.

13–018 The same point was demonstrated in *R. v. Panel on Take-overs, ex p. Fayed* [1993] 5 Admin. L.R.; [1992] B.C.C. 524 which arose in the wake of the successful bid made by the Fayed brothers for House of Fraser in which Lonrho had been prevented from bidding because of undertakings it had given to the Secretary of State. Lonrho brought an action against the Fayeds which alleged that the Secretary of State had been induced into not referring the Fayed's bid to the Monopolies and Mergers Commission by fraudulent misrepresentations. A 1991 report by DTI inspectors concluded that the Fayed's had dishonestly represented their origins, their wealth, their business interests and their resources to the Secretary of State, the shareholders of House of Fraser and others. The executive of the Panel on Take-overs sought to bring disciplinary proceedings against the Fayeds on the grounds that they had at the time of the bid made misleading statements in breach of general principle 12 of the City Code. The Fayeds sought an adjournment of the disciplinary proceedings until after the conclusion of the Lonrho action on the basis that disciplinary proceedings should not take place whilst there was other outstanding proceedings. The application was rejected by the Panel on the basis that the Lonrho hearing was to be based on the findings of the DTI report which had already been published. The Fayed's sought judicial review of the Panel's decision which was refused both at first instance and by the Court of Appeal on the basis that the trial of the Lonrho complaint would be heard by a judge rather than a jury and action would not be prejudiced by the judicial review. The Court of Appeal also held that there could be no legitimate expectation that the Panel would not proceed with its disciplinary hearing on the basis of a statement in the Panel's 1977 Annual Report which had said that in most circumstances the Panel would delay a disciplinary hearing until after the conclusion of any other outstanding litigation. Due to the time scale of events in this particular case and the publication of the DTI report upon which the disciplinary hearing was to be based, there was no need for the Panel to postpone the disciplinary hearing.

Panel's Liability in Defamation

The non-statutory status of the Panel was considered in the case of **13–019** *Graff v. Shawcross, Macdonald and Frazer*, October 10, 1980, unreported. In this case the Panel sent a copy of a press article together with a covering letter to the shareholders of a target company. The press article alleged that the bidder had offered inducements to one of the target company's shareholders in return for her selling him her shares. This, if true, would have been in breach of the Take-over code prohibiting the favourable treatment of only some of the shareholders. The bidder brought a libel action against the Chairman, Director General and a Deputy Director General of the Panel. The High Court held that the covering letter which had been sent to shareholders to accompany the press article was not defamatory because it was balanced between verifying and demolishing the allegation contained in the article. However, the court went on to consider the wider question of whether the Panel in conducting its investigations enjoyed qualified privilege. Although the Panel was not under a legal duty to investigate because of its non-statutory status it was under a moral duty to do so. The same principle would seem to apply to all supervisory bodies which operate in the regulatory context.

The City Code on Take-overs and Mergers

The Code is intended to provide a framework within which take-overs **13–020** are conducted in accordance with the observance of good business standards. The Code of Take-overs and Mergers comprises 10 General

CHAPTER 13: THE PANEL ON TAKE-OVERS AND MERGERS

Principles and 38 Rules and a number of guidance notes as to interpretation and implementation of the individual rules. The introduction to the Code makes it clear that the General Principles are: "expressed in broad general terms and the Code does not define the precise extent of, or the limitations on their application."

13–021 Similarly, the Rules:

"are not expressed in technical language and like the General Principles are to be interpreted to achieve their underlying purpose. Therefore, their spirit must be observed as well as their letter and the Panel may modify or relax the application of a Rule if it considers that, in the particular circumstances of the case, it would operate unduly harshly or in an unnecessarily restrictive or burdensome, or otherwise inappropriate manner" (see the Introduction to the Code, para. 3(a), The Code in Practice: General Principles and Rules).

13–022 An example of where the Code has been interpreted in a flexible way in practice was the BP flotation where following the collapse of the market during the privatisation sale the Government decided to buy back shares to compensate the private investors who had subscribed but incurred losses. Such a buy-back would have triggered rule 9 of the Code requiring the Government to make an offer for the whole company. The Panel agreed to waive rule 9 for the purposes of this case.

13–023 The Code applies to take-over transactions, partial offers and offers by a parent company for shares in its subsidiary. The Code applies to offers for all listed and unlisted public companies considered by the Panel to be resident in the United Kingdom, the Channel Islands or the Isle of Man. It also applies to offers for private companies resident in the United Kingdom in certain circumstances.

The General Principles

13–024 The general principles are intended to achieve a fair balance between the interests of the offeror and of the offeree company and its shareholders. The general principles are intended to be statements of good standards of commercial behaviour and apply to all transactions with which the Code is concerned. They are expressed in broad terms and may be applied by the Panel in such a way as to accord with their spirit to achieve their underlying purpose. The general principles are intended to ensure the equality of treatment and opportunity for all shareholders in take-over bids, that shareholders are supplied with adequate information and advice to enable them to assess the merits of the offer, that there is no action which might frustrate an offer is taken by a target company during the offer period without shareholders voting on it and the maintenance of fair and orderly markets in the shares of the companies concerned throughout the period concerned. The General Principles appear in full in Appendix 5.

The City Code on Take-overs and Mergers

The Code imposes a duty to act in the best interests of their **13–025** shareholders on the boards of an offeror and the offeree company and on their respective advisers (especially their financial advisers). The responsibility falls on each director of an offeror and offeree company to ensure that the Code is complied with as far as he reasonably can. Financial advisers, in addition to their own compliance with the Code, have a particular responsibility to ensure that directors are aware of their responsibilities—see Introduction to General Principles at B1. Guidance notes as to directors responsibilities and financial advisers and conflicts of interests are contained in Appendix 3 to the Code.

The Rules

There are 38 rules contained in the Code, in addition to which there **13–026** are guidance notes concerning the rules which are intended to assist in the application of the rules. The rules are intended to regulate the whole process by which a take-over or merger is conducted from the first approach to the conclusion of the deals.

Approach, Announcement and Independent Advice

These aspects are covered in rules 1, 2 and 3, the main points of which **13–027** are that in respect of the approach, the offer must be put forward to the board of the offeree company or to its advisers and the identity of the offeror must be disclosed at the outset (rule 1). Rule 2 sets out when an announcement of an offer is required, and the timing and contents of such announcement. It also emphasises the importance of secrecy before the making of an announcement. Rule 3 imposes the obligation on the board of an offeree company to seek competent independent advice on any offer and stipulates that the substance of such advice should be made known to its shareholders. The independence of the adviser is of paramount importance. A prospective adviser might not be considered sufficiently independent if it has had a recent advisery role with the offeror or has had a close advisery relationship with a large shareholder in the offeree company. The Panel recommends that if there is any doubt as to the independence of an adviser that the Panel is consulted at the earliest opportunity. (See page 10 of the 1994-1995 Take-over Panel annual report.)

Restrictions on Dealings and Restrictions on the Acquisition of Shares and Rights over Shares

The dealing of shares prior to or during an offer can cause significant **13–028** prejudice to shareholders. The various restrictions on dealings and on the acquisition of shares and of rights over shares are set out in rules 4 to 8. Of these, rule 4, contains the main restrictions in that it sets out the prohibition on dealings by persons who are privy to confidential price-sensitive information concerning an offer or contemplated offer other than by the offeror. During an offer period an offeror and those acting in concert with the offeror must not sell any securities in the offeree company except with the prior consent of the Panel and following 24 hours' public notice of such sales.

13–029 In addition to the restrictions imposed by rule 4, a person may be precluded from dealing or procuring others to deal by virtue of the insider dealing laws. This aspect is covered in more detail in Chapter 20.

13–030 A person who holds less than 30 per cent of the voting shares of a company may not acquire more voting shares if by doing so his holding would increase to 30 per cent or more (rule 5.1(a)). When a person holds between 30 per cent and 50 per cent of the voting shares of a company he may not acquire further shares which would amount to more than 1 per cent of the voting shares in the company in a 12 month period (rule 5.1(b)). The exercise of options and the acquisition of new shares, subscription rights, convertibles and options are not affected by this rule. In addition to this rule, the Substantial Acquisition Rules (SARs) will apply. Rule 5.2 sets out certain exceptions to these restrictions which include the acquisition of shares from a single shareholder in a seven day period which must be notified to the company and the Stock Exchange by 12 noon on the business day following the acquisition (rule 5.4).

13–031 Certain purchases result in an obligation to offer a minimum level of consideration and these are set out in rule 6. An immediate announcement is required if the offer has to be amended (rule 7.1).

13–032 Rule 8 requires that there be disclosure of dealing during the offer period by the offeror and offeree companies and by their associates if the dealing is on their own account or if the dealing is for discretionary clients. Dealings by those who own or control one per cent or more of any class of relevant securities in the offeror or offeree company must disclose any dealing. Public disclosure is to the Stock Exchange, the Panel and the press. Dealings by the parties and by associates for non-discretionary clients must be privately disclosed to the Panel.

Remaining Shareholders, the Mandatory Offer and its Terms

13–033 A problem arises where shareholders are left following a take-over are "locked-in." Rule 9 exists to prevent this problem from arising. A mandatory offer is required when any person acquires shares which carry more than 30 per cent of the voting rights of a company or a person who together with persons acting in concert with him, holds more than 30 per cent but less than 50 per cent of the voting shares of a company acquires in a 12 month period additional shares carrying more than one per cent of the voting rights such a person must make an offer to the holders of any class of equity share capital whether voting or non-voting. Offers for different classes of equity shares must be comparable. The Panel should be consulted in advance of such cases.

13–034 Acting in concert is defined by the Code as:

"persons who pursuant to an agreement or understanding (whether formal or informal) actively co-operate through the acquisition by any of them of shares in a company, to obtain or consolidate control of that company."

Certain persons are presumed to be acting in concert unless it is established to the contrary. These include: a company, its parent, subsidiaries and fellow subsidiaries and their associated companies, a company with its directors, a company with its pension funds, a fund manager with any investment company, unit trust or person whose funds the manager manages on a discretionary basis, a financial or other professional adviser with its client, directors of a company which is subject to an offer or where the directors have good reason to believe that an offer for their company may be imminent. Offers made through a consortium will also usually be treated as acting in concert.   13–035

The Voluntary Offer and its Terms

Rule 10 (in conjunction with Appendix 4, "Receiving agent's code of practice") requires that it must be a condition of any offer which would result in the offeror holding over 50 per cent of the voting rights of the offeree, that the offer will not become or be declared unconditional as to acceptances unless the offeror has acquired or agreed to acquire shares carrying over 50 per cent of the voting rights attributable to (a) the equity capital alone and (b) the equity share capital and the non-equity capital combined.   13–036

Rule 11 sets out the cases when a cash offer is required. The offer must be in cash (or accompanied by a cash alternative) at a price which is at least, the highest price paid by the offeror or any person acting in concert with him for shares of that class in the 12 months prior to the offer period when the shares of any class under offer in the offeree company carry 10 per cent or more of the voting or where in the view of the Panel there are circumstances which render such a course necessary to give effect to General Principle 1 that all shareholders of the same class of an offeree company must be treated similarly by an offeror. If the offeror considers that the highest price paid in the 12 months prior to the offer should not apply then he must consult the Panel which has a discretion to agree to an adjusted price (rule 11.2).   13–037

The Monopolies and Mergers Commission and the European Commission

When an offer comes within the statutory provision for possible reference to the Monopolies and Mergers Commission or to the European Commission, it must be a term of the offer that it will lapse if there is a reference before the first closing date or the date on which the offer is declared unconditional as to acceptances. The offeror may also make it a condition of the offer that there be no reference, issue of proceedings or referral (rule 12).   13–038

13–039 An offer must not normally be subject to conditions which depend solely on subjective judgments by the directors of the offeror or the fulfilment of which is in their hands although the Panel will accept an element of subjectivity where it would be impracticable not to do so (rule 13).

Provisions Applicable to All Offers

13–040 These provisions are set out in rules 14 to 18. Where a company has more than one class of equity share capital, a comparable offer must be made for each class whether each class carries voting rights or not. However, a comparable offer does not mean an identical offer. Where the offer concerns two or more classes of listed shares the ratios of the offer value should be equal to the average of the ratios of the middle market quotations taken from the Official List over the previous six months (rule 14.1). There must be separate offers for each class (rule 14.2) and the offeror must make an appropriate offer for any convertible securities outstanding of the offeree company (rule 15(a)). The board of the offeree company is required to obtain competent independent advice on the offer or proposal to the stockholders, the substance of which must be made known to the stockholders (rule 15(b). A copy of the offer or proposal must be lodged with the Panel at the time of issue (rule 15(c)).

13–041 Rule 16 prohibits special deals with favourable conditions which are not extended to all shareholders unless the Panel consents.

13–042 There must be an announcement by 8.30 am on the latest day of business following the day on which the offer is due to expire of acceptance levels. The Stock Exchange must also be informed unless the securities are not traded on the Exchange (rule 17.1). A failure to make such an announcement may result in the Stock Exchange temporarily suspending listing of the offeree's shares and, if appropriate the offeror's shares. A failure to comply with the requirements of rule 17.1 by 3.30 p.m. allows an acceptor to withdraw his acceptance (rule 17.2(a)–(c)).

Rule 18 sets out the circumstances in which proxies and other authorities in relation to acceptances may be employed.

Conduct During the Offer

13–043 Rules 19 to 22 concern conduct during an offer. One of the most important areas which the Code regulates is that of the equality of the availability and dissemination of information to concerned parties during the course of a take-over or merger implementing the General Principles. There are strict rules concerning the dissemination of information about an offer which are set out in Rule 19. First, each document, advertisement or statement made during the course of an offer must all satisfy the highest standards of accuracy and be adequately and fairly presented (rule 19.1). This applies equally, whether the statement, document or advertisement is issued by the company or by an adviser. Particular areas of sensitivity on which the guidance notes suggest that comment should be avoided are future profits and prospects, asset values and the likelihood of a revision of an offer. Unambiguous language must be used, sources for information must be clearly stated and quotations from newspapers, etc., must not be used out of context. Secondly, documents issued to shareholders or advertisements published in connection with an offer must state that the directors of the offeror and/or the offeree company accept responsibility for the information contained in the document or advertisement (rule 19.2). Thirdly, parties to an offer and their advisers must also take care not to make statements which, whilst factually accurate, are or may be misleading or create uncertainty (rule 19.3). Fourthly, the publication of advertisements connected with an offer or potential offer is prohibited unless that advertisement falls within one of the categories specified by rule 19.4 which must be submitted to the Panel for clearance prior to publication. Rule 19 also covers telephone campaigns (rule 19.5), interviews and debates undertaken by parties to an offer (rule 19.6), the distribution and availability of documents and announcements (rule 19.7), and what information should be released following the collapse of an offer following referral to the Monopolies and Mergers Commission or the European Commission (rule 19.8).

Rule 20 requires that information about companies involved in an offer must be made equally available to all shareholders as nearly as possible at the same time and in the same manner (rule 20.1). It is also a requirement that there be equality of information given to competing offferors or potential offerors (rule 20.2) and to independent directors in the case of management buy-outs (rule 20.3). **13–044**

Rule 21 contains restrictions on behaviour by the board of an offeree company which believes that an offer is imminent or once an offer has been made designed to frustrate the offer. The board of an offeree company may only act in pursuance of an earlier contract or with the approval of shareholders following a general meeting (the notice of which meeting must include information about the offer or anticipated offer)to issue any unissued shares, issue or grant options in respect of any unissued shares, create or issue any securities carrying rights of conversion into or subscription for shares, sell, dispose of or acquire assets of a material amount or enter into contracts otherwise than in the ordinary course of business. **13–045**

The offeree company must take action to ensure that the registrar of the company complies fully with the procedures set out in Appendix 4 of the Code and that there is prompt registration of transfers during an offer (rule 22). **13–046**

Documents from the Offeror and the Offeree Board

The rules concerning the documentation required in the course of an offer from the offeror and the offeree's board are set out in rules 23 to 27. The most important of these rules is rule 23 which requires that shareholder must be given sufficient information and advice to enable **13–047** them to reach a properly informed decision as to the merit or demerit of an offer.

13–048 Rule 24 sets out what must be contained in the offerors' documents including what financial information must be included (rule 24.2). Rule 25 concerns the contents of offeree board circulars setting out what may be included in these including the views of the offeree board and the substance of independent advice given to the board by independent advisers. Rule 27 requires that shareholders be informed of any material changes in information previously sent to them.

Rule 26 sets out the documents which must be made available for inspection during the offer period unless the Panel consents otherwise.

Profit Forecasts

13–049 Rule 28 sets out the requirements pertaining to profits forecasts made in the course of an offer. It is essential that a profit forecast must be compiled with scrupulous care and objectivity by the directors, whose sole responsibility it is. The financial advisers must satisfy themselves that the forecast had been prepared with scrupulous care and objectivity by the directors (rule 28.1). Any document addressed to shareholders in connection with an offer which contains a profit forecast must set out the assumptions upon which the forecast has been made as must any press release containing a profit forecast (rule 28.2). Unless the offer is solely for cash, the accounting policies and calculations for the profit forecasts must be examined and reported upon by auditors or consultant accountants (rule 28.3) Statements which amount to profit forecasts are set out in rule 28.6.

Asset Valuations

13–050 Rule 29 requires that when a valuation of assets is given in connection with an offer it should be supported by the opinion of a named independent valuer. This rule applies to land, buildings, process plant and machinery, stocks, ships, T.V. rental contracts and individual parts of a business. The valuer must be independent and a corporate member of the Royal Institution of Chartered Surveyors, The Incorporated Society of Valuers and Auctioneers or the Institute of Revenues Rating and Valuation or some other person approved by the Panel.

Timing and Revision

13–051 Rules 30 to 34 set out the timetable for the posting of offer documents and for timing of the offer. These rules include: that the offer document should normally be posted within 28 days of the announcement of a firm intention to make an offer. If the document is not to be posted within this period the Panel must be consulted (rule 30.1). The offeree board's circular to shareholders of the offeree company advising them of the offeree board's views should be sent as soon as practicable after publication of the offer document (normally within 14 days) (rule 30.2) The offer must be open for at least 21 days following the date on which the offer document was posted (rule 31.1), any extension of an offer must state a further closing date (rule 31.2) but there is no obligation to extend an offer the conditions of which are not met by the first or any subsequent closing date (rule 31.3). An offer must remain open for 14 days following the date on which a revised offer document is posted (rule 32.1). Rules 30 and 31 apply equally to alternative offers (rule 33.1). An acceptor is entitled to withdraw his acceptance within 21 days of the first closing date of the initial offer if the offer has not by such a date become or been declared unconditional as to acceptance (rule 34).

Restrictions Following Offers and Possible Offers

Where an offer has been announced or posted but has not become or been declared wholly unconditional and has been withdrawn or lapsed neither the offeror nor any person acting in concert with him may make an offer for the offeree company, or buy shares in the offeree company if to do so would put the buyer in the position of having to make a mandatory offer under rule 9, or acquire any shares of the offeree company if the offeror holds shares carrying over 49 per cent but not over 50 per cent of the voting rights of the company within 12 months of the date on which the original offer is withdrawn of lapses (rule 35.1) These restrictions also apply to partial offers which could result in a holding of not less than 30 per cent and not more than 50 per cent (rule 35.2). There must be a delay of 6 months before any person or persons acting in concert holding more than 50 per cent of the voting rights may make a second offer to shareholders on better terms than the original offer (rule 35.3). **13–052**

Partial Offers

Partial offers can be the cause of significant prejudice to shareholders. Rule 36 seeks to regulate the making of partial offers to diminish the risk of prejudice to shareholders. The SARs are also relevant when considering the regulation of partial offers. Rule 36 concerns partial offers for which the Panel's consent is required. Consent will normally be granted for offers which will result in the offeror holding shares carrying less than 30 per cent of the voting rights (rule 36.1). But consent will not normally be granted where the offeror holds shares carrying more than 30 per cent but less than 100 per cent of the voting rights where the offeror or those acting in concert with him, have selectively or in significant numbers acquired shares in the offeree company during the 12 months preceding the application for consent (rule 36.2). The offeror and person acting in concert with it may not purchase shares in the offeree company during the offer period or within 12 months after the end of the offer period (rule 36.3). If the offer is for between 30 per cent and 50 per cent of the voting shares the precise **13–053** number of shares offered for must be stated (rule 36.4) and an offer giving the offeror more than 30 per cent of the voting shares requires 50 per cent approval of existing shareholders (rule 36.5).

Redemption or Purchase by a Company of its own Securities

13–054   When a company redeems or purchases its own voting shares, a resulting increase in the percentage of voting rights carried by shareholdings of the directors and persons acting in concert with them shall be treated as an acquisition for the purpose of rule 9—mandatory offers (rule 37.1). An offeree company may not purchase or redeem its own shares if during the course of an offer or if it believes that an offer is imminent (rule 37.3).

Dealings by Connected Exempt Market Makers

13–055   Rule 38 prohibits an exempt market-maker connected with an offeror or the offeree company from carrying out any dealings with the purpose of assisting the offeror or the offeree company.

Substantial Acquisitions Rules

13–056   The Substantial Acquisition Rules were introduced in an attempt to meet the problem of "dawn raids". "Dawn raids" occur when there is rapid and organised early trading to acquire a substantial interest in a target company. In order to maintain secrecy, raids are often conducted using foreign nominees and a complex web of subsidiary and associate companies. In December 1980, the Council for the Securities Industry (which no longer exists), produced a set of Rules Governing Substantial Acquisition of Shares (SARs) in an attempt to counter the problem of "dawn raids". The SARs are issued on the authority of the Panel on Take-overs and Mergers and are administered through the Panel's executive.

The Scope of the Rules

13–057   The SARs are designed to slow down the speed with which a person (or persons acting together) can increase their shareholding to between 15 per cent and 30 per cent of the shares holding voting rights in a company resident in the United Kingdom whose shares are listed or otherwise traded on the Stock Exchange.

There are five SARs which are accompanied by guidance notes as to their interpretation and application.

13–058   A person may not in any period of seven days, acquire shares carrying voting rights in a company or rights over such shares, representing 10 per cent or more of the voting rights if such an acquisition, when aggregated with any shares or rights over shares which he already holds, would carry 15 per cent or more but less than 30 per cent of the voting rights of that company (rule 1). This rule does not apply to the acquisition of new shares or the rights to subscribe in new shares or to the exercise of options over existing shares (rule 1, note 5). The rule applies to market makers and other dealers in the same way as to any other person except where there is a block trade or when a market maker or other dealer purchases a portfolio without knowledge of its contents (rule 1, note 7).

Rule 2 provides certain exemptions from the application of rule 1, **13–059** these include the acquisition of shares from a single shareholder, or where the acquisition is pursuant to a tender offer or where the offer will be publicly recommended by, or the acquisition is made with, the agreement of the board of the offeree company and the acquisition is conditional on the announcement of the offer.

Following the acquisition of shares carrying voting rights in a **13–060** company which increases a person's holding to more than 15 per cent of the total or, if he already holds 15 per cent, where the acquisition is of more than 1 per cent of the total voting shares, the person acquiring the shares must notify the acquisition and his total holding to the company and to the Stock Exchange which in turn notifies the Panel (rule 3).

Rule 4 applies to tender offers and sets out the procedure and the **13–061** clearance which is required when a tender offer is made. A tender offer must be advertised in two national newspapers and must be notified to the listing department of the Stock Exchange which must clear the text of the advertisement, and to the company concerned. A tender offer must be for cash and must treat all shareholders equally. What must be contained in a tender offer advertisements is set out in rule 4.2. A buyer may circulate copies of the tender announcement to shareholders of the company whose shares are sought (rule 4.3). The result of a tender offer must be announced by 8.30 am on the day following the close of tender (rule 4.4). The buyer in a tender offer may not acquire or dispose of voting shares in the company between the time of the publication of the tender offer and the announcement of the result of the tender offer (rule 4.5).

Where two or more persons act together, their holdings and acquisitions are aggregated and treated as a single holding or acquisition for the purpose of the SARs (rule 5).

Appeals

If a person wishes to contest a ruling of the Panel executive, he may **13–062** ask for the matter to be referred to the Panel using the same procedure as for appeals against decisions of the executive in respect of take-overs and mergers.

Conclusion

13–063 The Take-over Code is generally seen as one area of self-regulation that has proved to be effective in practice. The non-statutory structure of the Code allows for a rapid and flexible response to particular situations as does the way in which the Panel imposes the rules according to their spirit in response to particular cases rather than sticking rigidly to the letter in every case. The 1987 review of the Panel instigated by the Secretary of State for Trade and Industry considered the status of the Panel and decided that the advantages of its non-statutory basis in terms of flexibility and speed of response far outweighed the advantages of giving it a statutory basis. The need for speed and certainty in the decision making process in the financial markets is a recurrent factor in the way in which the courts have approached litigation concerning take-overs.

13–064 An illustration of the awareness of the courts of the special needs of the financial markets for speed on the part of decision makers and for being able to rely on those decisions as a sure basis for dealing in the market is the case of *R. v. Monopolies and Mergers Commission, ex p. Argyll Group plc* [1986] 1 W.L.R. 763, which was a case arising out of the rival bids in 1985/1986 by Argyll Group plc and Guinness plc put for Distillers Co plc. The Guinness proposal was referred to the Monopolies and Mergers Commission under section 75 of the Fair Trading Act 1973. Whilst resolution of the reference was pending, Guinness was prohibited from making a further bid by the Take-over Code. However, before the Monopolies and Mergers Commission embarked on its investigation, representatives of Guinness met the Chairman of the Commission and gave him information about certain activities of Distillers which would not form part of the take-over. The Chairman decided that "the proposal to make an arrangement such as was mentioned in the reference had been abandoned" and recommended that Secretary of State to give his consent to the reference being laid aside. Guinness made a revised bid for Distillers which was not referred to the Commission. Argyll, as minority shareholders in Distillers, sought judicial review by certiorari to quash the decision that the proposal had been abandoned and the Secretary of State's consent to the laying aside of the reference. It was held that where the arrangements were in progress or in contemplation at the time of the reference, it was a question of fact and degree whether any new arrangements subsequently put forward were sufficiently different from the arrangements which were the subject of the reference so that it could be said that the proposed or contemplated arrangements had been abandoned. In this case, bearing in mind the concept of merger under the Act related to the merger of activities and not of corporations, the decision that the proposals had been abandoned was held to be correct.

13–065 The effectiveness of the Panel is also greatly enhanced because its staff is drawn from those with a knowledge of the markets they are regulating rather than by civil servants or those with no practical experience of the marketplace. Importantly, over the years the Panel has built up wide support both from the Government and from City institutions.

Future Developments

In February 1996 the European Commission published the text of a directive aimed at establishing general principles throughout the Community governing takeover bids. The DTI is currently consulting widely on the effects of, and benefits or disadvantages which might result from the implementation of the directive into English law. The House of Lords is also carrying out its own inquiry as part of parliamentary scrutiny procedures. The Financial Law Panel, sponsored jointly by the Corporation of London and the Bank of England, has given written evidence to the House of Lords on the implications for the conduct of takeover bids in the United Kingdom of the proposal for a European directive. The Financial Law Panel believes that the Commission has made out a case for legislation at Community level, to set a benchmark for takeover regulation and to carry on the process of harmonisation of corporate activity. If this does occur, it is unlikely that the attitude of the courts will change after the implementation of the directive.

13–066

Chapter 14

Banking Act 1987

Background

Traditionally the Bank of England has had an important role in supervising banks operating in the United Kingdom. This role became the statutory responsibility of the Bank of England with the passage of the Banking Act 1979. Before this, the Bank of England's supervisory role had been on an informal basis but the secondary banking crisis of the 1970s had effectively undermined confidence in the informal system of supervision and in the interests of restoring confidence, particularly international confidence in United Kingdom banking, the 1979 Banking Act was introduced. The growth in banking in the last two decades has also contributed significantly to the need for proper regulation of banking. **14–001**

The Banking Act 1979 provided the first statutory framework for the authorisation and supervision of deposit-taking businesses under the regulation of the Bank of England. However, the rapid changes in banking and in particular the Johnson Matthey affair in 1984 required a further review of banking supervision and resulted in the passage of the 1987 Banking Act. The Johnson Matthey affair threatened banking stability in the United Kingdom and required the Bank of England to mount a massive support operation. In September 1984, the Bank of England discovered that Johnson Matthey Bank has substantially misreported certain large single exposures in its loan book. Investigations revealed that Johnson Matthey's assets were not sufficient to cover these exposures. Before the news broke, the Bank of England felt impelled to take over Johnson Matthey Bank as a matter of urgency because it was considered that the failure of one of the five participants in the London bullion market would had have had the effect of undermining the stability of the whole banking system. **14–002**

The main purpose of the 1987 Act is the protection of depositors and potential depositors in banks. One of the main features of the 1987 Act was that it did away with the distinction between banks and licensed deposits takers which had existed under the 1979 Act, the distinction which had allowed for different levels of supervision which had been a factor in the Johnson Matthey affair. **14–003**

Before anyone may take deposits from the public as part of a deposit taking business they must be authorised to do so. The "authorised population" comprises of institutions authorised under the Banking Act 1987 by the Bank of England and European authorised institutions **14–004**

(EAIs) under the Second Banking Co-ordination Directive which are banks incorporated in other E.C. Member States which may take deposits in the United Kingdom on the basis of authorisation given by their home supervisor. The only exception to this are Building Societies which are authorised and supervised by the Building Societies Commission. The "authorised population" in 1994/1995 was 525 of which 379 were institutions authorised under the Banking Act 1987 and 146 were EAIs.

Scheme of Banking Act 1987

14–005   The Banking Act 1987 is primarily concerned with banking supervision in the interests of depositors. It does not seek to regulate transactions between banks and their customers nor is it concerned with consumer protection. The main purpose of the Banking Act 1987 is to regulate the acceptance of deposits in the course of a business and to protect depositors.

Duties

14–006   Part I of the 1987 Act sets out the duties and powers of the Bank of England which has both general supervisory powers and specific regulatory functions. Section 1 of the Act confers on the Bank of England the duty to supervise authorised institutions, and to keep under review the operation of the Act and developments in the field of banking which appear to be relevant to the Bank of England's exercise of its powers and duties under the Act. The Bank of England must report annually to the Chancellor of the Exchequer who in turn lays copies of the Bank of England report before Parliament. Under section 1(4), the Bank of England and its directors, officers or employees are not liable in damages for anything done or omitted in the discharge or purported discharge of the functions of the Bank of England unless it can be shown that they acted in bad faith.

Board of Banking Supervision

14–007   The Banking Act 1987, section 2 and Schedule 1, established the Board of Banking Supervision which, although not a part of the decision making process of the Bank of England, has a duty to give advice to the Bank of England in respect of supervisory issues. The Board comprises the Governor of the Bank of England, the Deputy Governor and the Director responsible for banking supervision together with six independent members with experience of banking, law and accountancy. The Chancellor of the Exchequer must be informed of any advice given by

Scheme of Banking Act 1987

the Board of Banking Supervision which is not followed (s.2(5)). In 1994/1995 there was no instance when this section had to be invoked. The Board meets monthly. At each meeting the Board receives a report from Supervision and Surveillance setting out matters of general supervisory policy and matters relating to specific organisations.

Acceptance of Deposits

14–008 Section 3(1) restricts the taking of deposits to institutions authorised under the provisions of the Act to accept deposits in the course of carrying on (whether in the United Kingdom or elsewhere) a deposit-taking business. Contravention of section 3(1) is a criminal offence under section 3(2) carrying a penalty of two years imprisonment and/or a fine if convicted on indictment or six months imprisonment and/or a fine not exceeding the statutory maximum (currently £5,000) if convicted in the magistrates' court. Contravention of section 3(1) does not affect any civil liability in respect of the deposit or the money deposited (s.3(3)). Section 4 and Schedule 2 sets out those who are exempt from the requirement for authorisation imposed by section 3. Exempted persons include the Bank of England, the Central banks of other E.C. Member States, the National Savings Bank, penny savings banks, municipal banks, Building Societies incorporated under the Building Societies Act, Friendly Societies, any institution authorised under sections 3 or 4 of the Insurance Companies Act 1982 to carry out insurance business, loan societies under the Loan Societies Act 1840, credit unions under the Credit Unions Act 1979, certified school banks, local authorities, Crown agents for overseas governments and administrations, the European Atomic Energy Community, the European Coal and Steel Community, the European Economic Community, the European Investment Bank, the International Bank for Reconstruction and Development, the International Finance Corporation, the International Monetary Fund, the African Development Bank, the Asian Development Bank, the Caribbean Development Bank, the Inter-American Development Bank, the European Bank for Reconstruction and Development and the Council of Europe Resettlement Fund.

14–009 The meaning of "Deposit" is defined by section 5(1) as:

"a sum of money [(whether denominated in currency or ECU's)] paid on terms (a) under which it will be repaid, with or without interest or a premium, and either on demand or at a time or in circumstances agreed by or on behalf of the person making the payment and the person receiving it; and(b) which are not referable to the provision of property or services or the giving of security."

14–010 "Deposit" does not include a sum paid by the Bank of England or an authorised institution, a sum paid by an exempted person who falls within Schedule 2 of the Act, a sum paid by a person in the course of

CHAPTER 14: BANKING ACT 1987

carrying on a business wholly or mainly of lending money, sums paid between companies within the same group of companies or which have the same person as their majority or principal shareholder, or a sum paid by a close relative or by the close relative of a director, controller or manager of that person, where a close relative is a spouse, children or their spouse, step-children or their spouse, parents, step-parents, siblings or their spouse and step-siblings or their spouse.

14–011 The meaning of "Deposit-taking business" is defined by section 6(1) as:

> "a business is a deposit-taking business for the purposes of this Act if (a) in the course of the business money received by way of deposit is lent to others; or (b) any other activity of the business is financed, wholly or to any material extent, out of the capital of or the interest on money received by way of deposit."

14–012 A business is not a deposit-taking business if the person carrying it on does not hold himself out as accepting deposits on a day-to-day basis and any deposits accepted are accepted only on particular occasions (depending on the frequency and characteristics of the occasions) (s.6(2) and (4)).

14–013 The Court of Appeal considered the meaning of "deposit" and of "deposit taking business" in *SCF Finance Co. Ltd v. Masri (No. 2)* [1987] 1 All E.R. 175. The facts of this case were that SCF carried on business as licensed brokers in commodity and financial futures. They held themselves out as willing to deal in the market on a client's behalf and for this purpose required clients to place funds with them to cover the transaction as well as "margins" to cover the risk of loss on the transactions. The margins proved inadequate in Masri's case and SCF Finance incurred substantial losses in the course of trading on his behalf. Masri failed to settle his account and SCF brought an action against him for the amount due. Masri argued that his agreement with SCF Finance contravened the provisions of the Banking Act 1979 (now s.3 of the 1987 Act) in that the payments constituted the acceptance of "deposits" in the course of an unauthorised "deposit taking business." Accordingly Masri argued that the transactions were illegal and SCF Finance were not entitled to sue him on the agreements. Masri's arguments were rejected both at first instance and in the Court of Appeal. The Court of Appeal considered the meaning of "deposit" and "deposit taking business." In relation to deposit, the court found that the amounts paid by Masri to SCF Finance had been paid by way of security for payment for the provision of property or services to be provided by SCF Finance and thus were not deposits for the purposes of the Banking Act. If a futures contract resulting in actual delivery of the commodity, then SCF Finance had provided services by insuring risk and consequent losses. In the event, the payments made by Masri were to be regarded as security to protect SCF against the risk that Masri might default in reimbursing them for expenses incurred on his behalf.

Accordingly SCF Finance fell within the exclusion to the definition of deposit if the money paid is referable to the provision of property or services or the giving of security. Further, the Court of Appeal held that:

"in our judgment, on the ordinary meaning of the words, a person 'holds himself out to accept deposits on a day-to-day basis' only if (by way of an express or implicit invitation) he holds himself out as being generally willing on any normal working day to accept such deposits from those persons to whom the invitation is addressed who may wish to place moneys with him by way of deposit" (*per* Slade L.J. at 190). **14–014**

The Court of Appeal held that a request by SCF Finance for specific payments to be made by a client did not come within this concept. **14–015**

Authorisation

Authorisation is the central feature of the whole system of regulation under the Banking Act and the key question for the Bank of England when considering authorisation is whether the bank is financially sound. Banks and institutions that are authorised are known as "authorised institutions" whilst the title "bank" is reserved for institutions with more than £5 million of capital (or which are incorporated abroad.) **14–016**

Decisions on authorisation and revocation of authorisation and on the exercise of Banking Act powers are reached through a formal assessment and review process involving committees of managers and senior officials in the Bank of England's Supervision and Surveillance area. The committees recommend a course of action to the Director of the Bank of England. Decisions of the Bank of England are subject to judicial review and there are provisions for appeal to a Tribunal which can review the decision. **14–017**

Applications for Authorisation

The procedure for applying for the granting or refusal of an application for authorisation and the minimum criteria required for authorisation are set out in sections 8–10 and Schedule 3 of the Act. The Bank of England is required by section 16 to publish a statement of principles in accordance with which it acts in carrying out its functions and duties under the Act. In addition the Bank of England must make available a list of authorised institutions (s.17). A full list of authorised institutions is to be found in the Bank of England Banking Act Report and includes all institutions authorised by the Bank of England and European authorised institutions (see 1994/1995 Banking Act Report, Appendix 4). The necessity of having a central list of authorised institutions was **14–018** demonstrated in the so called "Egyptian Sheikh" case (reported in the national press, see *The Guardian*, December 12, 1995) where the High Court granted an injunction to the Bank of England on four illegal self styled banks which it was believed were controlled by an Egyptian "sheikh". The existence of the "banks" came to light when enquiries were made to the Bank of England in early 1995 to check the "banks" credentials.

14–019 Any institution may make an application to the Bank of England for authorisation except a credit institution incorporated in or formed under the law of any part of the United Kingdom whose principal place of business is outside the United Kingdom and a credit institution incorporated or formed in another E.C. Member State (s.8(1)).

14–020 Applications for authorisation must be accompanied by a statement setting out the nature and scale of the deposit taking business which the applicant intends to carry on and any plans of the applicant for the future development of the business and the applicant's arrangements for the management of the business and any other information required by the Bank of England. Information provided to the Bank of England must be in the form specified by the Bank of England (s.8(2) and (5)).

14–021 It is a matter for the Bank of England whether to grant an application for authorisation, but before making such a grant the Bank of England must be satisfied that the minimum criteria set out in Schedule 3 of the Act are satisfied (s.9(1) and (2)). Part 2 of the Statement of Principles sets out the way in which the Bank of England interprets the minimum criteria. In deciding whether to grant or refuse an application the Bank of England may take into account any matters relating to any person who is or will be employed by or associated with the applicant for the purposes of the applicant's deposit-taking business and if the applicant is a body corporate, any other body corporate in the same group or to any director or controller of any such other body (s.9(4)).

No authorisation will be granted to a partnership or unincorporated association if the whole of the assets available to it are owned by a single individual (s.9(5)).

14–022 Where the Bank of England decides to grant authorisation the applicant for authorisation will receive a written notice to this effect (s.10(1)). Similarly, when the Bank of England decides to refuse an application for authorisation it must give the applicant written notice of its decision stating the reasons for the refusal within six months of receipt of the application or, where additional information is requested by the Bank of England, within 12 months from the application or within six months of the receipt of any additional information requested by the Bank whichever is the sooner (s.10(5) and (6)). Where the Bank of England proposes to refuse an application it must inform the applicant of its reasons for doing so in writing and give the applicants the opportunity to make written representations to the Bank of England within 28 days (s.10(2) and (4)).

Minimum Criteria for Authorisation: Schedule 3 and the Statement of Principles

14–023 The way in which the Bank of England interprets and applies the minimum criteria for authorisation is set out in Part 2 of the Statement of Principles. The Bank of England will consider the requirement for prudent conduct set out in paragraph 4 of Schedule 3, before any other criteria. The reason for this is that this sets the standard with the most obvious relevance to the interests of depositors, actual and potential, and for assessing whether an institution's directors, controllers and managers are fit and proper persons to hold their positions. The Bank of England then goes on to consider the other criteria set out in Schedule 3 concluding with the fit and proper criterion. Where the applicant is a foreign bank whose principal place of business is outside the United Kingdom, the Bank of England has a discretion in certain circumstances to rely on the assurance of the home supervisor of the institution that the supervisor is satisfied as to the prudential management and the overall financial soundness of the institution (see Pt 4 of the Statement of Principles).

"Fit and Proper"

14–024 Schedule 3(1) requires that every person who is or is to be a director, controller or manager of the institution is fit and proper to hold the particular position which he holds or is to hold. In determining whether a person is fit and proper to hold a position in an authorised institution regard must be had to his probity, competence, soundness of judgment and diligence for fulfilling his position. Account must also be taken of whether he is likely to fulfil his position in the interests of depositors or potential depositors of the institution and whether the interests of such depositors are in any way threatened by his holding that position.

The interpretation placed on the term "fit and proper" by the Bank of England is set out in the Statement of Principles. The considerations are probity, diligence and soundness of judgment.

14–025 In the case of a shareholder controller there is also a financial condition. Shareholder controllers of United Kingdom incorporated banks must be approved by the Bank of England which has the power to object to their investing (see—Statement of Principles, paras. 2.42–2.59).

"Four Eyes"—Two Individuals Directing Business

14–026 There must be at least two individuals effectively directing the business of the institution (Sched. 3(2)). Where there are only two individuals involved they must both be involved in directing strategy and have knowledge of the way in which strategy is being implemented through day-to-day policy (see—Statement of Principles, paras. 2.32–2.33).

Non Executive Directors

14–027 For institutions incorporated in the United Kingdom the directors must include a number, as the Bank of England considers appropriate, of non-executive directors (Sched. 3(3)). The Bank of England considers that non-executive directors can play a valuable role in bringing an outsider's independent perspective to the running of the business and in questioning the approach of the executive directors and other management. Non-executive directors are seen as having an important role as members in effect of an institution's audit committee (see—Statement of Principles, paras. 2.34 to 2.36).

Prudent Manner

14–028 Paragraph 4(1) of Schedule 3 requires an institution to conduct its business in a prudent manner (see—Statement of Principles paragraphs 2.3-2.31).

Whether an institution is conducting its business in a prudent manner will depend on a number of factors specified in paragraph 4(2) to (8) each of which must be fulfilled before an institution can be regarded as conducting its business in a prudent manner. The requirements, which are not exhaustive, (para. 4(9)), include a capital requirement, a liquidity requirement, and adequate provisions and systems of controls.

A Capital Requirement

14–029 An institution must maintain adequate capital, defined as its own funds, in such a nature and amount as the Bank of England considers appropriate given the nature and scale of the institution's operations and to safeguard the interests of depositors. (But in any event own funds must not be less than 5 million ECUs or an equal amount denominated wholly or partly in another unit of account.) In deciding whether depositor's interests are being safeguarded, account will be taken of the nature and scale of the institution's operations, the risks inherent in those operations and in the operations of any other undertaking in the same group which are capable of affecting the institution.

14–030 An institution's capital base is made up of a number of elements, these fall into two tiers: Tier 1 is core capital which essentially comprises of shareholder's equity and published accumulated profits. Core capital is considered to be more permanent and therefore of higher quality than tier 2 capital. At least 50 per cent of the bank's capital base must be made up of tier 1 capital. Tier 2 is supplementary capital which includes unpublished or undisclosed profits, "general" provisions which the bank has set aside against unidentified future losses and medium or long term subordinated debt issued by the bank. Subordinated term debt may not exceed 50 per cent of tier 1. This definition accords with the definition set out in the European Own Funds Directive implemented in the United Kingdom from December 1990.

Authorisation

The Bank of England's method of calculating the level of capital **14–031** required by an institution is based on the Risk Asset Ratio (RAR) system now set out in the E.C. Solvency Ratio Directive implemented in the United Kingdom in December 1990. The purpose of the Risk Asset Ratio system is to weight an institution's assets in broad categories according to their riskiness. The capital base is then measured against the weighted portfolio of risk and taken as a percentage of it, which is the institution's Risk Asset Ratio. Each institution is set a minimum target capital below which its RAR must not fall based on its individual circumstances. The absolute minimum set by international agreement is 8 per cent.

The RAR system works well if the institution has a diversified **14–032** portfolio but if the institution lends heavily to a single borrower the risk factors increase and there are special provisions in the 1987 Act requiring an institution to report large exposures to the Bank of England. (See also the E.C. Large Exposures Directive implemented in the United Kingdom from January 1, 1994.)

Liquidity

An institution must have at least enough ready money or liquidity to **14–033** meet its obligations as they fall due. An institution will not be regarded as conducting its business in a prudent manner unless it maintains adequate liquidity having regard to the relationship between liquid assets and its actual and contingent liabilities, to the time when those liabilities may fall due and its assets mature. The Bank of England may take into account assets of the institution which are capable of providing liquidity within a reasonable period.

Provisions

The institution must make adequate provision for depreciation or **14–034** diminution in the value of its assets (including provision for bad or doubtful debts), for liabilities which will or may fall to be discharged by it and for losses which it will or may incur.

Systems and Controls

An institution must maintain adequate accounting records and other **14–035** records of business and adequate systems of control of its business and records to enable the management to be continuously aware of the institution's condition and the risks to which it is exposed.

Integrity and Skills

The business of the institution must be carried out with integrity and **14–036** the professional skills appropriate to the nature and scale of its activities. The integrity element requires the institution to observe high ethical standards in carrying on its business particularly in respect of any provisions aimed at protecting the public from financial loss due to dishonesty, incompetence or malpractice and in respect of adherence to relevant codes of conduct. (These may include London Code of Conduct, the Code of Banking Practice, the Take-over code and guidance notes on money laundering.) Professional skills cover the general skills which bankers should have in conducting their business. The level of skills required will vary according to the nature and scale of a particular institution's activities. The integrity and skills requirement is distinct from the requirement that the directors, managers or controllers of an institution are fit and proper (see—Statement of Principles, paras. 2.37 to 2.39).

Minimum Net Assets

14–037   The institution must at the time that authorisation is granted have initial net capital of not less than five million ECU (or an amount of equal value denominated wholly or partly in another unit of account). If the institution is not a United Kingdom incorporated credit institution it must have the equivalent of £1 million in net assets at the time it is authorised (see—Statement of Principles, paras. 2.40–2.43).

Revocation or Restriction of Authorisation

14–038   The Bank of England has powers to revoke or restrict authorisation which are exercisable in a wide range of circumstances and enables the Bank of England to exercise its powers before the threat to the interests of depositors or potential depositors becomes great or immediate. The Bank of England has a wide discretion concerning the exercise of its powers of revocation or restriction. The only exception to this is in two cases which give rise to mandatory revocation; the first is in the case of an authorised institution which is not a credit institution and which has its place of business in another Member State of the E.C. and the banking supervisory authority in that Member State withdraws the institution's authorisation; the second case is where a winding-up order has been made against the institution in the United Kingdom or a resolution for a winding-up order has been passed or where analogous proceedings have occurred in other jurisdictions.

14–039   The circumstances in which the Bank of England may revoke the authorisation of an institution are set out in section 11 of the Act and include; if any of the criteria in Schedule 3 has not been or may not have been fulfilled, if the institution has not complied with any obligation imposed upon it by the Act, if a person has become the controller of the institution in contravention of the requirements of the Act, if the Bank of England has been provided with false, misleading or inaccurate information by or on behalf of the institution, and if the interests of depositors or potential depositors of the institution are in any other way threatened whether by the way in which the institution conducts its affairs or for any other reason (see—ss.11–14). Revocation of authorisation is unusual, in 1994/1995 no institution had its authorisation revoked but restrictions were put on the authorisation of one institution and remained in force in relation to another institution.

The Bank of England may restrict the scope if an institution's authorisation in circumstances where the Bank of England has the power to revoke authorisation but the circumstances are not such that revocation is justified (s.12(1)). Authorisation may be restricted by imposing such limit on its duration as the Bank of England thinks fit, by imposing such conditions as are desirable for the protection of the institution's depositors or potential depositor or a combination of these measures (s.12(2)). In particular the Bank of England may restrict authorisation by requiring the institution to take or refrain from taking certain steps, by imposing limits on the acceptance of deposits, the granting of credit or the making of investments, it may prevent the institution from soliciting deposits, from entering into any other transaction, the Bank of England may require the removal of any director, controller or manager and it may specify requirements to be fulfilled otherwise than by action taken by the institution (s.12(4)). **14–040**

Failure to comply with any requirement or any contravention of any prohibition imposed on an institution by a condition under section is an offence triable either way and punishable by a fine which is unlimited in the Crown Court and of the statutory maximum in the magistrates' court (s.12(6)). Failure to comply with any condition imposed under section 12 is also a ground for the revocation of authorisation but does not invalidate any transaction (s.12(7)). **14–041**

Where the Bank of England proposes to revoke or restrict an authorisation, it must give written notice of its intention to the institution concerned (s.13). **14–042**

The principles which the Bank of England will apply in considering the revocation of authorisation or the restriction of authorisation are set out in the Statements of Principles, paragraphs 5.1 to 5.18 and 6.1 to 6.10. **14–043**

An authorised institution may surrender its authorisation by written notice to the Bank of England (s.15).

Changes in Control

No person shall become a minority, 10 per cent, 20 per cent, 33 per cent, majority or principal shareholder controller, a parent controller or an indirect controller of an authorised institution unless he serves on the Bank of England a written notice stating that he intends to become such a controller of the institution and the Bank of England has notified him in writing within three months that he has no objection to his becoming a controller of the institution or a period of three months has elapsed **14–044** without the Bank of England having served upon him a written notice of objection to his becoming a controller of the institution (s.21(1)). The Bank of England may request further information from the applicant to assist it in making a determination (s.21(3)).

14–045 Before granting an application for new or changed control the Bank of England must be satisfied that the person concerned is fit and proper to become a controller of the description in question of the institution, that the interests of depositors and potential depositors of the institution are not threatened by that person becoming a controller, and that the criteria set out in Schedule 3 would continue to be fulfilled.

14–046 The Bank of England may object to an application for new or increased control by serving a notice of objection under section 22. The Bank of England must warn the person to whom it objects, in a preliminary written notice, that it intends to so object and that person may make written representations to the Bank of England accordingly within one month of the warning having been given, the preliminary notice must specify which matters the Bank of England is not satisfied about and give particulars of that applicant's rights under section 27.

14–047 Where a person has already become a controller without giving notice to the Bank of England, the Bank of England may serve him with notice of objection within three months after it becomes aware of his having become such a controller.

14–048 Under section 23, the Treasury may direct the Bank of England to serve a notice of objection on a person who has given notice under section 21 of his intention to become a shareholder controller of an institution (which is not a credit institution) or who has become such a controller without giving the required notice under that section if it appears to the Treasury that a notice could have been served under section 183 of the Financial Services Act 1986—disqualification or restriction of persons connected with overseas countries which do not afford reciprocal facilities for financial business.

14–049 Section 24 covers the procedure to be followed by the Bank of England where it objects to an existing shareholder controller because that person appears no longer to meet the requirement to be a fit and proper person to be a controller of an institution. The person must be served with a preliminary notice of the Bank of England's intention and afforded the opportunity to make written representations concerning the Banks' objections. If the objection is sustained the person must be served with a written notice specifying the reasons why he is no longer a fit and proper person unless to do so would involve the disclosure of confidential information prejudicial to a third party.

14–050 Section 25(1) makes it an offence to contravene section 21 by failing to give the notice required in section 21 (1) (a) or by becoming a controller of any description to which section 21 applies before the end of the period specified in section 21(1) (b). It is a defence to this offence if the person shows that he did not know of the acts of circumstances by virtue of which he became a controller of the relevant description. However, as soon as a person does become aware of becoming a controller he must give the Bank of England written notice within 14 days, failure to do so amounts to an offence (s.25(2)).

A person guilty of an offence under section 25 (1) or (2) shall be liable to a fine of up to the statutory maximum on summary conviction.

It is also an offence to become or continue to be a controller of any description after the service of a preliminary notice of objection or a notice of objection (s.25(3)(a)-(c)). 14–051

A person guilty of an offence under section 25 (3) shall be liable on conviction on indictment to imprisonment of two years maximum and/or a fine and on summary conviction to a fine not exceeding the statutory maximum and for offences within section 25(3)(c) to a fine not exceeding one tenth of the statutory maximum for each day on which the offence has continued. 14–052

Section 26 imposes restrictions on the sale of shares where a person has contravened section 21.

Impact of Single Market—Second Banking Co-ordination Directive D89/646 EEC O.J. L361/1

The Second Banking Co-ordination Directive took effect from January 1, 1993. It was intended to bring about the co-ordination and harmonisation of laws, regulations and administrative provisions relating to the taking up and pursuit of the business of credit institutions. The Directive introduced freedom of establishment for United Kingdom incorporated banks in the EEA on the basis of their United Kingdom authorisation. Supervision of United Kingdom banks' branches in other member sates of the EEA remains the responsibility of the Bank of England with the exception of supervision of liquidity. Also under this Directive banks incorporated in other E.C. Member States (European authorised institutions) do not require authorisation from the Bank of England to accept deposits in the United Kingdom. European authorised institutions may accept deposits in the United Kingdom upon the basis of authorisation granted by their home supervisor. The Bank of England has a duty to co-operate with other E.C. Member State banking supervisors. From January 1994, this scheme was extended to all the countries of the European Economic Area (EEA) which includes all E.C. Member States and Norway and Iceland. 14–053

Procedural Proprieties

It is accepted that the Bank of England's regulatory activities are subject to judicial review. The Bank of England's application of its powers to grant and revoke authorisation and the minimum criteria for 14–054 authorisation were considered by Schiemann J. in *R. v. Bank of England, ex p. Mellstrom* [1995] C.O.D. 161, Q.B.D. In this case Mr Mellstrom sought judicial review of the Bank of England's decision to issue a notice of its intention to revoke authorisation of National Guardian Mortgage Corporation Ltd on the grounds that Mr Mellstrom was not a fit and proper person to hold the position of executive controller and principal shareholder of National Guardian Mortgage Corporation Ltd. In the event, Mr Mellstrom resigned as a director and the authorisation for the company was not revoked but was merely restricted.

14–055   Where the Bank of England is minded to revoke authorisation on the grounds that a director is not a fit and proper person, the director must be given an opportunity to make representations to the Bank of England and if ultimately appeal to the Banking Appeals Tribunal. Mr Mellstrom argued that the procedure followed by the Bank of England was unfair because he was only able to make his statutory representations in response to the matters disclosed in the Bank of England's notice to him and not other matters in the Bank of England's files which were not disclosed to Mr Mellstrom and upon which he was therefore unable to comment. The Bank of England argued that it had done all that was required by the Act. It was held that the bank had not relied on any material which had not been disclosed, there was no requirement to disclose material not relied upon, and Mr Mellstrom had not been denied natural justice.

Unauthorised Deposit Taking

Consequences in Civil Law

14–056   Section 3 of the Banking Act 1987 restricts the acceptance of deposits in the course of carrying on a deposit taking business to institutions which are authorised under the Act (s.3(1)). However, the fact that a deposit has been taken in contravention of section 3(1) does not affect any civil liability in respect of the deposit or the money deposited.

14–057   The consequences of the unauthorised acceptance of deposits is specifically addressed in sections 48 and 49 of the Act. Section 48 requires on the application of the Bank of England to a court, the repayment of unauthorised deposits by the person whom it appears to the court to have accepted deposits in contravention of section 3 or by a person who appears to the court to have been knowingly concerned in the contravention. In making an order for repayment the court must have regard to the effect of the repayment on the solvency of the person concerned and on his ability to carry on his business in a manner satisfactory to his creditors.

14–058   Under section 49, the Bank of England may apply to the court for an order that profits from unauthorised deposits be paid into court or be recovered by way of the appointment of a receiver. Again the court must have regard to the effect of the repayment on the solvency of the person concerned and on his ability to carry on his business in a manner satisfactory to his creditors. Amounts paid into court will be distributed at the direction of the court to the person or persons appearing to the court to have made the deposits. The court also has the power to require the person taking the unauthorised deposit to furnish the court with such accounts or information as the court requires for the determination of any profits.

Consequences in Criminal Law

Contravention of the restriction in section 3(1) is an offence under section 3(2) punishable by imprisonment for a maximum of two years and/or a fine if convicted on indictment or six months' imprisonment and/or a fine of the statutory maximum if convicted in the magistrates' court. **14–059**

The mental ingredient of the offence was considered by the Court of Appeal in *Attorney General's Reference No. 1 of 1995, The Times,* January 30, 1996. This case concerned two directors of a company which had accepted deposits from clients in the course of business without being authorised by the Bank of England so to do. The directors were charged with offences of consenting to the company accepting deposit when not authorised to do so (s.3 and s.96(1)). The issue which the Court of Appeal was asked to consider was what state of mind had to be proved against a company director charged with consenting to the company accepting a deposit without authorisation. The elements of the offence were set by the trial judge as (i) that there was a deposit taking, (ii) that it was in the course of a deposit taking business and (iii) that there was no licence. The trial judge ruled that it was necessary for the appellants to have applied their minds to the fact that there was no licence for them to be guilty of the offence. It was plain from police interviews that the directors had never heard of licensed deposit taking and were in ignorance of the requirement for authorisation. The Court of Appeal rejected the final part of the trial judge's ruling, holding that it was necessary to prove simply that a director knew the material facts which constituted the offence by the body corporate and to have agreed to its conduct of business on the basis of those facts but that ignorance of the law was in itself no defence. **14–060**

In 1994/1995 the Bank of England investigators investigated 52 cases of suspected illegal deposit taking, a number of which reached the Crown Court. In one case of Ian Craig Reuben and Lawrence Michael Reuben who were directors of Syclon Finance Ltd. which was a company that had taken deposits, each director received sentences of imprisonment totalling one year for five offences under section 3 of the Act.

There are other criminal offences created by the Banking Act 1987 in addition to the offence under section 3.

False Statements as to Authorised Status

14–061 It is an offence under section 18 of the Banking Act to make false statements as to authorised status. Under this section it is possible to commit this offence in one of three ways: first, under section 18(1)(a) by a person describing himself as an authorised institution when he is not, or, secondly, under section 18(1)(b) by a person holding himself out as to indicate or be reasonably understood to indicate that he is an authorised institution and thirdly, under section 18(2) it is an offence to falsely state or do anything which falsely indicates that the person is entitled, although not an authorised institution, to accept a deposit in the course of carrying on a business which for the purposes of the Act is a deposit taking business.

14–062 The penalty for contravention of section 18 is one of imprisonment for a maximum of two years and/or a fine if convicted on indictment or six months imprisonment and/or a fine of the statutory maximum if convicted in the magistrates' court.

Fraudulent Inducement to make a Deposit

14–063 It is an offence under section 35(1) for any person to make a statement, promise or forecast which he knows to be misleading, false or deceptive or which dishonestly conceals material facts or recklessly makes dishonestly or otherwise a statement, promise or forecast which is misleading false of deceptive for the purpose of inducing, or is reckless as to whether it may induce another person (whether or not the person to whom the statement, promise of forecast is made or from whom the facts are concealed) to make or refrain from making a deposit with him or any other person or to enter or refrain from entering into an agreement for the purpose of making such a deposit.

14–064 Section 35(1) only applies if the statement, promise or forecast or the facts are concealed in the United Kingdom, and the person on whom the inducement is intended to have effect is in the United Kingdom or the deposit is or would be made or the agreement is or would be entered into in the United Kingdom (s.35(2)).

14–065 It is unnecessary to prove that the statement, promise or forecast induced the making of a deposit or agreement to deposit. It is sufficient that it is intended to be made for that purpose or made recklessly for that purpose—see *Finnegan and Braund*, October 13, 1995, unreported.

14–066 The penalty for contravention of section 35(1) is seven years imprisonment and/or a fine if convicted on indictment or six months' imprisonment and/or a fine of the statutory maximum if convicted in the magistrates' court (s.35(3)).

Supervisory Controls

14–067 Once authorisation has been granted, the Bank of England has a continuing role in supervising the institutions it has authorised. This is achieved by the collection of information from statistical returns, through reporting accountants' reports and through regular formal prudential interviews. In 1994/1995 the Bank of England held approximately 3,000 meetings of which 1,800 were non-routine meetings held to discuss specific issues. Routine meetings consist of prudential interviews to discuss the institution's performance and any attendant supervisory issues and trilateral meetings attended by the Bank of England, the institution and the reporting accountants.

The Bank of England surveillance department conducts regular review visits to authorised institutions. The Bank of England must be satisfied that risks are adequately assessed and that the interests of depositors are protected. The ultimate sanction if the interests of depositor are threatened is the removal of authorisation from an institution or the placing of restrictions the scope of the institution's authorisation. Decisions on the revocation or restriction of authorisation are reached through a formal assessment and review process involving committees of managers and senior officials in the Supervision and Surveillance area who make recommendations to the Director of the Bank of England responsible for banking supervision. These decisions may be appealed to the Banking Appeals Tribunal and are also subject to judicial review. **14–068**

Supervisory Notices Issued by the Banking Supervision Division

As already noted, the way in which the Bank of England interprets the provisions of the Banking Act 1987 relating to the grant, revocation and restriction of authorisation is set out in its Statement of Principles. In addition to the Statement of Principles, the Banking and Supervision Division of the Bank of England issues policy and practice notices from time to time which are intended to clarify and give guidance as to the way in which particular issues should be dealt with. A full list of current supervisory notices appears as an appendix to the Bank of England Banking Act Report. **14–069**

Information and Investigation

Power to Obtain Information and to Require the Production of Documents

Section 39 of the Banking Act 1987 gives the Bank of England powers to require an institution to provide such information as the Bank of England may reasonably require for the performance of its functions under the Act or to require the institution to commission reports from accountants or other suitably qualified professionals on any aspect of any matter about which the Bank of England has required or could require **14–070** the institution to provide information under section 39(1)(a). This is most commonly used by the Bank of England to establish the adequacy of the institution's systems and controls and the accuracy of its prudential returns. Section 39 reports are commissioned regularly as part of the Bank of England's routine supervision of United Kingdom authorised institutions, special reports may be commissioned if a specific area of concern is identified. In 1994/1995 610 section 39 reports were commissioned including 11 special reports.

14-071 Failure to comply with a requirement imposed by section 39 without reasonable excuse is an offence triable in the magistrates' court and punishable by six months' imprisonment and/or a fine of up to the statutory maximum (s.39(11)).

14-072 A statement made by a person in compliance with section 39 may be used in evidence against him (s.39(12)), but there is no power to compel the production by a legal representative of a document containing a privileged communication (s.39(13)).

14-073 Section 40 gives the Bank of England the right of entry into premises occupied by a person on whom a section 39 notice has been served or on whom a section 39 notice could be served (where the Bank of England has reasonable grounds for suspecting that if such a notice were served it would not be complied with or documents to which it relates would be removed, tampered with or destroyed) for the purpose of obtaining information or documents required under that notice.

Investigations on Behalf of the Bank of England

14-074 Section 41 empowers the Bank of England to appoint one or more competent persons to investigate and report on the nature, conduct or state of an authorised institution's (or a former authorised institution's) business or the ownership and control of the institution. The investigation may also extend to parent, subsidiary and related companies of the authorised institution. The Bank of England must give the institution written notice of such an investigation. It is the duty of all those who are or have been directors, controllers, managers, employees, agents, bankers, auditors or solicitors of a body under investigation to assist the investigation by the production of documents and by attending before the persons appointed as the investigator (s.41(5)).

14-075 It is an offence to fail to produce documents, to fail to attend before the person appointed to investigate and to fail to answer any questions relating to the institution under investigation without reasonable excuse. It is also an offence to intentionally obstruct an investigator in the exercise of his powers of entry into premises occupied by the institution under investigation granted under section 41(7) (s.41(9)(a)–(d)). An offence under section 41(9) is triable in the magistrates' court and is punishable by a maximum of six months' imprisonment and/or a fine of up to the statutory maximum.

14-076 A statement made by a person in compliance with section 39 may be used in evidence against him (s.41(10)). There is no power to compel the production by a legal representative of a document containing a privileged communication (s.41(11)).

Section 41 powers are utilised by the Bank of England where areas of concern have been identified and where it is in the interest of depositors to do so. No such reports were commissioned during 1994/1995.

14–077 The Bank of England may use its section 39 and section 41 investigatory powers in relation to European authorised institutions in order to carry out its supervision of local liquidity under the Second Banking Co-ordination Directive.

14–078 Section 42(1) provides that where the Bank of England has reasonable grounds for suspecting that a person is guilty of contravening section 3 or section 35 of the Act it is entitled to require that person, by way of a notice in writing, to provide such information or to produce such documents or to attend at a specified time and place to answer such questions as are relevant for determining whether a contravention has occurred. The Bank of England has the power to enter any premises occupied by a person on whom a notice has been served for the purpose of obtaining information or documents or for putting questions required by the notice (s.42(3). Failure to comply with a notice under section 42 without reasonable excuse is an offence triable in the magistrates' court and punishable by six months' imprisonment and/or a fine of the statutory maximum (s.42(4)). A statement made by a person in compliance with section 42 may be used in evidence against him (s.42(5)). There is no power to compel a legal representative to disclose privileged communications (s.42(6)).

14–079 Section 43 covers the powers of entry in cases of suspected contraventions and allows for the application by the Bank of England to a magistrate for a warrant to enter the premises of an authorised institution where there are reasonable grounds for suspecting that a person is guilty of a contravention and where that person has failed to comply with a section 42 notice or where there are reasonable grounds for suspecting the completeness of any information provided or document produced under a section 42 notice or where there are reasonable grounds for suspecting that if a section 42 notice was served it would not be complied with or that documents would be removed, tampered with or destroyed. Intentional obstruction of the exercise of any right conferred by such a warrant is an offence punishable by two years' imprisonment and/or a fine in the crown court or six months' imprisonment and/or a fine not exceeding the statutory maximum in the magistrates' court.

14–080 The Court of Appeal considered the scope of section 42 in *Bank of England v. Riley* [1992] 1 All E.R. 769. Between 1983 and 1989 the defendant ran two organisations which obtained money from members of the public. In 1989, she was arrested and charged with 53 offences of obtaining money by deception or theft. The Bank of England instituted proceedings for injunctions restraining the defendant from contravening section 3 of the Banking Act and for orders directing the repayment of monies already received. The Bank of England also obtained an order under section 42 requiring the defendant to answer interrogatories designed to ascertain what assets she had and to disclose certain documents. Although the defendant accepted that section 42 powers applied to the circumstances of her case, she sought to rely on the privilege against self-incrimination. The Court of Appeal held that the effect of section 42 is to impose a duty on a person required to provide information under section 42 powers and that it is no excuse to say that in providing such information the person might have contravened section 3 or any other provision of the criminal law nor did self-incrimination, a reasonable excuse defence within section 42(4), amount to a defence of reasonable excuse.

14–081 In *A. v. B. Bank* [1992] 1 All E.R. 778, the court considered the scope of the Bank of England's public duty to supervise banks and other deposit taking institutions authorised by it. Hirst J. said in the conclusion to his judgment that:

> "I cannot stress too strongly the importance which should be attached to the Bank of England having, within the limits laid down by the 1987 Act and the general law, unfettered and unimpeded scope for the exercise of their most important public duties of regulation under the 1987 Act in the interests of the public."

14–082 The case followed investigations by the U.S. Federal Reserve Board into the acquisition of three U.S. banks by the defendant bank allegedly in violation of U.S. banking regulations. A subpoena was issued by a New York court requiring the defendants to produce certain documents. The plaintiff's who were customers of the defendant bank obtained an injunction in the High Court restraining the defendant from delivering up or disclosing to any third party otherwise than in connection with the plaintiff's business any documents or information held by the defendant concerning the plaintiffs. The Bank of England served a notice on the defendant under section 39(3)(a) requiring the production of specific documents some or all of which were covered by the injunction. The defendant bank applied for a variation of the injunction to allow it to comply with the Bank of England notice which was opposed by the plaintiffs. The Bank of England argued that the documents were reasonably required by it in the exercise of its power to regulate and supervise banks and other deposit taking institutions. The court held that the Bank of England's powers to require the production of documents in the exercise of its public duty overrode the terms of an injunction and that the existence of the injunction did not amount to a reasonable excuse not to comply with the terms of the Bank of England notice.

14–083 A person who knows or suspects that an investigation under section 41 or into a suspected contravention of sections 3 or 35 is being carried out is guilty of an offence if he falsifies, conceals, destroys or otherwise disposes of or causes or permits the falsification, concealment, destruction or disposal of documents which he knows or suspects are or would be relevant to such an investigation. It is a defence for a person to prove that he had no intention of concealing facts disclosed by the documents from persons carrying out the investigation. An offence under section 44 is punishable by two years' imprisonment and/or a fine in the crown court or six months' imprisonment and/or a fine not exceeding the statutory maximum in the magistrates' court.

The exercise of the Bank of England's powers under the 1987 Act to compel the production of documents and information overrides the duty of confidence between a bank and its customer. An authorised institution's public duty also overrides its duty of confidence to its customers— see *R. v. IRC, ex. p Taylor No. 2* [1989] 3 All E.R. 353. However, sections 82 to 84 of the Act impose guidelines for the preservation of confidence by the recipients of information under the 1987 Act subject to certain specified exceptions. Section 82 restricts the disclosure of information received under or for the purposes of the Act relating to the business or other affairs of any person without the consent of the person to whom it relates. Section 83 stipulates that section 82 does not preclude the disclosure of information in any case in which disclosure is for the purpose of enabling the Bank of England to discharge its functions under the 1987 Act. Section 84 provides that section 82 does not preclude the disclosure of information by the Bank of England to certain specified persons including disclosure for the purpose of enabling or assisting an authority in a country or territory outside the United Kingdom to exercise functions corresponding to the Bank of England's under the Act. **14–084**

Role of Auditor in Policing Banks

Section 47 is a particularly significant provision in the Act in that it relaxes the auditor's and the reporting accountant's duty of confidentiality in situations where a matter which is relevant to any function of the Bank of England under the Act comes to light. **14–085**

Section 47(1) states: **14–086**

"No duty to which—
(a) an auditor of an authorised institution ; or
(b) a person appointed to make a report under sections 8(5) or 39(1)(b) above,
may be subject shall be regarded as contravened by reason of his communicating in good faith to the Bank, whether or not in response to a request made by it, any information or opinion on a matter to which this section applies and which is relevant to any function of the Bank under the Act."

This section applies to any matter of which an auditor or reporting auditor becomes aware in his capacity as auditor or reporting auditor and which relates to the business or affairs of the authorised institution or any associated body (ss.47(2) and (3)). **14–087**

14-088 In permitting auditors to waive their duty of confidentiality to their clients and report irregularities to the Bank of England, section 47 is a useful tool in placing auditors at the forefront of policing the banking system. However, there is no obligation on auditors under the Act as it is presently drafted to make reports to the Bank of England. It was one of the recommendations of the Treasury and Civil Service Committee report on the collapse of BCCI (Treasury and Civil Service Committee, Fourth Report; Banking Supervision and BCCI, International and National Regulation) that the auditors of an authorised institution should be obliged to report to the Bank of England if they uncover anything unusual in the course of their audit. The Bank of England initially asked BCCI's auditors, Price Waterhouse, to conduct an investigation of BCCI's U.K. activities under section 39 of the Banking Act 1987. In the light of further revelations, the Bank of England ordered Price Waterhouse to carry out a further investigation under section 41 of the 1987 Act and it was this report which showed evidence of "massive and wide spread fraud going back a number of years" and lead to the decision to close BCCI.

14-089 Accounts must be available for inspection. An authorised institution is required to keep a copy of its audited accounts (including the auditor's report) open for inspection at each of its offices in the United Kingdom at which it holds itself out as accepting deposit (s.45(1)). Failure to comply with this requirement is an offence triable in the magistrates' court and punishable by a fine not exceeding £5,000 (s.45(2)).

14-090 Under section 46 any change in the auditor of an authorised institution must be notified to the Bank of England by both the authorised institution and by the auditor. Failure to do so is an offence triable in the magistrates' court and punishable by a fine not exceeding £5,000.

Appeals

14-091 An institution that is aggrieved by a decision of the Bank of England may appeal to the Banking Appeals Tribunal. The right to appeal lies against a decision to refuse an application for authorisation, against a decision to revoke authorisation (unless revocation is mandatory), against a decision to restrict or vary authorisation and against a decision to give directions under section 19. The decision of the Bank of England will not take effect until the expiry of the period during which an appeal may be made or the determination of such an appeal. The time-limits for appealing a decision are set out in paragraph 4 of the Banking Appeal Tribunal Regulations 1987 (S.I. 1987 No. 1299) which set out the procedure for appealing to the Banking Appeal Tribunal. If the decision of the Bank of England relates to a particular person, *i.e.* a direction requiring the removal of a director, controller or manager of the institution, then that person also has the right to appeal to the Tribunal (s.27).

14-092 The Banking Appeals Tribunal is composed of a Chairman appointed by the Lord Chancellor and two others, appointed by the Chancellor of the Exchequer, who have experience of accountancy and banking (s.28).

14-093 The Tribunal determines an appeal on the basis of whether the original decision was lawful or whether it was not justified by the evidence on which it was based. The Tribunal may confirm or reverse a decision of the Bank of England but it has no power to vary the terms of any decision except where the decision was to revoke authorisation, the Tribunal may direct the Bank of England to restrict it instead and where the decision was to impose restrictions or make directions, the Tribunal may direct the Bank of England to impose different restrictions or directions (s.29(2)). Notice of the Tribunal's determination together with its reasons must be given to the appellant and to be Bank of England (s.29(7)).

14-094 An appellant who has appealed to a Tribunal or the Bank of England may appeal to the High Court on any question of law arising from the decision of the Tribunal (s.31(1)). This was what happened in the case of the Mount Banking Corporation Ltd (in administration) in May 1994 where two directors of Mount Banking Corporation had been found not to be fit and proper for their positions by the Bank of England. One of the directors appealed the decision of the Tribunal to the High Court, where the decision of the Tribunal was upheld. In giving his judgment, Vinelott J. found that "it cannot possibly be said that the decision of the Tribunal contradicted the true and only conclusion of the evidence before it". This judgment clarifies the test to be applied by the Banking Appeal Tribunal, namely, that it must make its own evaluation of the evidence and, having done so, it must decide whether the Bank of England's decision went beyond the range of what could have been said to have been justified by the evidence. Vinelott J. commented that the Tribunal was entitled "to give the policies and approach of the Bank of England, as the statutory regulator with unrivalled experience in the field, very considerable weight".

Compensation

14-095 Part II of the Banking Act is concerned with the Deposit Protection scheme. The Deposit Protection fund was originally established under the 1979 Act and its continuation was preserved by section 50(1) of the 1987 Act. The purpose of the Deposit Protection fund is to provide compensation to depositors on the insolvency of an institution authorised to accept deposits under the Act. The Fund is administered by a Board set up under the Banking Act and it is funded by levies made by the Board on contributory institutions these being authorised institutions and participating institutions being either a participating EEA institution or a participating non-EEA institution. The level of funds in the scheme should not be allowed to fall below £3 million and should normally be between £5 and £6 million.

14-096 Depositors are entitled to compensation from the fund in the event of an institution to which section 58 applies becomes insolvent. Institutions to which this applies are United Kingdom institutions, or participating institutions, former United Kingdom institutions or former participating institutions or former authorised institutions not being a recognised bank or licensed institution excluded by an order under section 23(2) of the 1979 Banking Act. The implementation of the E.C. Deposit Guarantee Directive from July 1995 results in a number of changes—United Kingdom branches of E.C. banks are covered by their home country scheme rather than the United Kingdom scheme. The United Kingdom scheme is extended to cover branches of United Kingdom incorporated banks throughout the EEA. The rate of compensation is 90 per cent (previously it was 75 per cent) of the depositor's protected deposits with a maximum payout to any depositor of £18,000. Deposits in other E.C. currencies will also be protected. See—sections 58(1) and (2) and section 60(1)).

14-097 The scope of deposits and depositors within the context of the Deposit Protection Fund was considered by the Court of Appeal in the case of *Deposit Protection Board v. Dalia* [1994] 2 All E.R. 577, H.L., which also arose out of the BCCI collapse. The Bank of England presented a petition for a winding-up order against BCCI on the ground that it was insolvent. Before the petition was heard, certain depositors took steps to maximise the amount of compensation they could claim from the Deposit Protection Board. These steps took the form of assigning sums of £20,000 from their deposits to family members or close friends with the intention that each could then make a claim on the fund for £15,000 in respect of the £20,000 deposit assigned on them, the Board being required by sections 58 and 60 to pay out of the deposit protection fund to each depositor with a protected deposit a sum equal to three-quarters of his protected deposit up to a maximum of £20,000. The question arose of whether the assignees of the deposits were entitled to payment out of the deposit protection fund pursuant to section 58(1) of the Act. The Court of Appeal held that it was inconsistent with the purpose of section 58 to confine the term "depositor" to the person who made the original deposit and that an assignee should be treated as having made a deposit provided the assignment was unimpeachable and made before the winding-up order. The House of Lords overturned the decision of the Court of Appeal, and held that a "depositor" entitled to compensation from the deposit protection fund meant a person who originally made the deposit. An assignee of part of the deposit was not a depositor.

If a depositor has placed his money with an unauthorised firm the protection of the Fund is not available to him.

Common Law Remedies

14-098 Investors who have been failed by the supervisory system may attempt to turn to common law remedies. However, the case of *Minories Finance Ltd v. Arthur Young* [1989] 2 All E.R. 105, established that there is no common law remedy in respect of a failure to supervise an authorised institution competently. This case was brought following the insolvency of Johnson Matthey Bank's commercial banking business and its financial rescue by the Bank of England. Minories Finance Ltd, the new owners, claimed damages in negligence against Arthur Young who were Johnson Matthey Bank's auditors on the grounds that the latter failed to discover and report on the state of Johnson Matthey Bank's loan portfolio. Arthur Young denied liability but joined as third party the Bank of England on the basis that the Bank of England had failed to exercise its supervisory powers under the Banking Act 1979 with reasonable care. On an application to strike out the third party claim, Saville J. held that the Bank of England was not under a legal obligation to an individual commercial bank to exercise reasonable care and skill in carrying out its functions of supervising the operations of commercial banks and that it would be contrary to common sense to suggest that an individual bank could look to the Bank of England to make good losses arising from its own imprudent conduct on the ground that the Bank of England should have discovered its shortcomings. Further the Bank of England did not owe a duty of care to the depositor of the money where the depositor was Johnson Matthey Bank's parent company. In this context, reference may also be made to *Yuen Kun Yeu v. Attorney General of Hong Kong* [1988] 1 A.C. 175 and *Three Rivers District Council v. Bank of England* [1996] 3 All E.R. 558.

Aggrieved investors may still attempt to utilise common law remedies in the banking context, particularly when there is a third party with deep pockets involved such as another authorised institution or the institution's auditors. In connection with the Barings collapse, the administrators (Ernst & Young) issued proceedings in the High Court in January 1996 claiming damages rumoured to be up to £1 billion against the bank's auditors (Coopers and Lybrand auditors in London and Singapore and Deloitte & Touche auditors in Singapore). The claim was based on the alleged negligence of the auditors in the conduct of audits between 1991 and 1994. In a separate action, a number of Barings bondholders issued writs against three former senior executives of the bank and against three City institutions which had participated in a bond issue with Barings in January 1994. The action was aimed at recovering £100 million of lost investments plus a further £9 million of lost interest payments. **14–099**

Technically, a civil action may lie against a supervisory body such as the Bank of England for misfeasance in a public office, but the cause of action will be extremely difficult, if not impossible, to establish in practice. It was said in *Three Rivers District Council v. Bank of England* that before a public officer can be held liable for misfeasance, it must be established that he has actual knowledge that the act complained of is unlawful, or that he has failed to take such steps as an honest and reasonable man would to ascertain whether the act is beyond his powers. The tort of misfeasance in public office is concerned with a deliberate and wrongful abuse of the powers given to a public officer. Malice and **14–100** knowledge that the act complained of will probably injure the plaintiff are alternative rather than cumulative ingredients of the tort.

Supervision in Practice

Harrods Bank

14-101 In 1991, the Bank of England approved the surrender of control of Harrods Bank by the Fayed brothers in favour of Law Debenture Trust. The surrender of control by the Fayeds came following the DTI report on their take-over of the House of Fraser. The approval of this change in ownership by the Bank of England was seen by many at the time as the Bank of England attempting to avoid imposing sanctions on an authorised institution.

BCCI

14-102 The BCCI collapse raised a large number of questions about the supervision of the banking system both in the United Kingdom and internationally. BCCI was unusual in the recent history of banking collapses in that a large financial institution was allowed by the Bank of England to default on ordinary depositors. Previously, in the various banking crises of the 1970s and 1980s, the Bank of England has tended to step in via its function of lender of last resort to prevent the default on investors by troubled banking institutions. Unusually, the failure of BCCI did not represent an immediate threat to the banking system generally because of its unusual corporate structure and funding arrangements. However, it did raise questions over the effectiveness of regulation in preventing losses on depositors through the maintenance of the solvency of regulated institutions. Before its collapse, BCCI was one of the largest private banks in the world with branches in 70 countries but it had a poor financial record having recorded losses in 1988 and 1989 and it was at the centre of money laundering allegations in the U.S. in 1988. The bank was managed through a parent holding company in Luxembourg with the main banking business split between two subsidiaries incorporated in Luxembourg and the Cayman Islands. The bank's shareholders were based in the Middle East and the operational headquarters were in London. This corporate structure raised difficult questions about corporate and regulatory control which led to the setting up of a college of international regulators in 1987. In the years following this, the Bank of England asked BCCI's auditors, Price Waterhouse, to conduct an investigation into BCCI's United Kingdom activities under section 39 and later under section 41 of the Banking Act 1987. As already noted, the section 41 report showed evidence of "massive and widespread fraud going back a number of years", which ultimately lead to the decision to close BCCI. The closure of BCCI was co-ordinated by regulators in the United Kingdom, Luxembourg, the U.S., Switzerland, Spain, France and the Cayman Islands on July 5, 1991 and resulted in criminal indictments being brought in New York in July 1991 in what the Manhattan District Attorney described as "the largest bank fraud in world financial history."

The BCCI affair raised many questions for regulators world-wide. In particular, it showed that the Bank of England was (and is) virtually powerless to prevent the problems of a foreign bank's parent company infecting its United Kingdom branches. In the case of foreign subsidiaries operating in the United Kingdom, the Bank of England has the power to intervene. In practice it seems likely that the Bank of England would expect the parent company or the parent bank's home supervising authority to step in but this pre-supposes that the home regulator is both active and effective in exercising supervisory powers. **14–103**

Barings Bank

The collapse of Barings Bank in 1995 received massive media attention. Barings was the oldest established banking institution in the City of London with assets of £6 billion and deposits of £3 billion. It collapsed because of the massive losses incurred on unauthorised derivatives transactions undertaken by Nick Leeson in Singapore. When the losses first became apparent the Bank of England attempted to mount a rescue package with the assistance of the clearing banks and merchant banks. The rescue package had to address three problems which arose out of the collapse: first, how to cap the open ended derivatives positions; secondly, how to recapitalise the bank to allow it to stay in business; and thirdly, how to ensure adequate liquidity. In the event the problem of the open-ended derivatives positions proved insurmountable and there was no alternative but for Barings to be placed into administration. The derivatives losses finally crystallised at £860 million. The various businesses of Barings were acquired by ING (Internationale Nederlanden Group) for the nominal sum of £1. ING took responsibility for Baring's losses and injected £660 million into Barings and this together with the original shareholders funds meant that the net asset position was £240 million. **14–104**

In the aftermath of the Barings collapse, the Board of Banking Supervision reported on the reasons for the collapse. The report was highly critical of senior Barings managers for their failure to properly control the activities of Nick Leeson. The report concluded that executives at Barings had been uncertain of their responsibilities and did not understand the derivatives arbitrage business conducted by Leeson. The Bank of England was criticised for its role in the collapse of Barings including the way in which the Bank of England monitored the capital adequacy and large exposures of Baring's banking and securities business. **14–105**

14–106 The Barings collapse also shows up the relatively narrow scope of the Bank of England's supervisory powers where a bank is part of a larger group of companies. In the case of Barings, only Barings Bank and Barings Sterling Bonds were the responsibility of the Bank of England as regulators. Other companies within the group were subject to regulation by other regulatory authorities both in the United Kingdom and abroad. Indeed, in the light of disciplinary action subsequently taken against former Barings executives by the SFA, it can be argued that other regulatory bodies are more effective than the Bank of England when it comes to imposing discipline. This issue also raises questions about the day-to-day co-ordination and co-operation that can and should exist between both domestic and international regulators. Many commentators have suggested that the only way to avoid similar problems in the future is to move towards a system whereby the whole of the financial services sector is regulated under the umbrella of a single co-ordinating organisation.

Relationship Between Banking Act and other Supervisory Regimes

Domestic Liaison Between Supervisory Authorities

14–107 Increasingly, the types of business undertaken by banks is diversifying from what has traditionally been seen as banking business, and banks are becoming more involved in the securities and other investment businesses which are supervised by the SIB and SROs. As a matter of policy, the Bank of England works with the Financial Services Act 1986 supervisors and has established arrangements designed to cut out duplication and to pinpoint where supervisory responsibility lies. This is especially important in area of capital adequacy. For example, in relation to Barings, where there was an overlap between the Bank of England and the SFA as the regulatory authority, the Bank of England had responsibility for overseeing Barings capital adequacy. In a more general area, an example of liaison between the Bank of England and other supervisory regimes are the discussions which took place between the Bank of England and the SIB and the SROs concerning the implementation of the Capital Adequacy Directive and the Investment Services Directive.

14–108 As we have already seen, in practice the trend appears to be to allow the SROs and the SFA in particular to impose discipline in the event of irregularities coming to light as was the case with the Barings executives.

International Liaison Between Supervisory Authorities

14–109 In the world of international banking, regular liaison and exchange of information between domestic supervisory bodies is essential for the effective regulation of international banking. To this end, regular liaison takes place between the Bank of England and other national and international supervisory bodies. International bodies with whom there is regular liaison include; the Basle Committee on Banking Supervision, European Union supervisory bodies—the Banking Advisory Committee (BAC), the Contact Committee of European Union Supervisory Authorities ("Group de Contact") and the EMI Banking Supervisory Sub-Committee all of which meet at intervals throughout the year. The work of the Banking Advisory Committee includes approving technical amendments to existing European Union legislation and working alongside the European Union Commission in the preparation, application and interpretation of European Union Banking legislation. The Group de Contact acts as a forum for reviewing developments in Member States' supervisory systems, conducting comparative studies of different aspects of these systems and for the exchange of confidential information of mutual interest to European Union banking supervisory authorities.

The Bank of England also holds bilateral meetings with the banking supervisory authorities of other EEA states the purpose of which is to exchange information on banks with a presence in both countries, to resolve any bilateral difficulties arising from the administration of the Second Banking Co-ordination Directive and to exchange views on supervisory developments and other issues of mutual interest. 14-110

The Future

There can be no doubt that the Bank of England treats its role as a supervisory body seriously and wishes to take steps to avoid further major embarrassments. In July 1996 a review was published by Arthur Anderson which had been commissioned following the Board of Banking Supervision's inquiry into the Barings collapse. In response to the report the Bank of England stated that it planned to recruit up to 50 front-line supervisors and increase spending by up to £8 million over the next three years. 14-111

In its report into the collapse of Barings the Board of Banking Supervision recommended that the Bank should establish an overarching quality assurance function. The new quality control mechanisms are aimed not just at improving the Bank's own surveillance and supervisory roles. They are just as much about telling the banks authorised to take deposits that their supervisory body is operating effectively. Professionals such as external auditors are also expected to take clearer responsibility for the figures they compile on behalf of their clients. 14-112

There remains, however, a conflict between the supervisory role of the Bank of England and its position as central banker which is difficult to resolve. After the Barings collapse the Governor of the Bank of England (Mr Eddie George) said that failure was "an essential discipline on the banking system". It is difficult to see how aggrieved depositors and investors could share this view. 14-113

Chapter 15

Building Societies

Background

Building Societies have their roots in the early nineteenth century together with the Friendly Societies and the Co-operative movement. Their first regulation came with the Friendly Societies Act 1834 but it was the 1874 Building Societies Act which laid the foundation for the modern Building Societies. Traditionally, Building Societies have been agencies designed to promote the ideals of thrift and home-ownership, taking deposits from savers to finance loans to borrowers for the purpose of purchasing a home. The difference in the interest rates charged to borrowers and that paid to lenders was intended to cover the costs of administration for the Societies. **15–001**

The scope of Building Societies' business has been tightly monitored and restricted by legislation dating from the 1874 Act and Building Societies have, as a result, been confined to their traditional role between making mortgage advances and taking the deposits of small individual savers. As we shall see, the business of Building Societies has changed radically in the last two decades. The regulation of Building Societies is covered in this chapter because traditionally a Building Society has been treated by savers as a repository for prudent investment. **15–002**

Building Society regulation has been one of the most effective areas of regulation in practice due in very large part to the prescriptive nature of the regulation which has traditionally imposed strict limits on the scope of their business. **15–003**

A Period of Change

In 1980, Building Societies accounted for 95 per cent of new mortgage lending. However, this was the year in which the banking sector was allowed to compete for mortgage lending business for the first time as a result of which the Building Societies' market share of mortgage lending was dramatically eroded. The Building Societies were permitted to diversify out of their traditional savings and mortgage markets for the first time by the Building Societies Act 1986. However, the recession in the housing market has seen a massive reduction in traditional Building Society business and this coupled with increased competition from the banking sector has led to calls for a major overhaul of the whole approach to Building Society business. The last 10 years has also seen a **15–004** number of Building Societies giving up their mutual status by floating on the stock market and effectively becoming banks (*e.g.* Abbey National) or by societies merging with existing banks (*e.g.* the Cheltenham and Gloucester with Lloyds Bank).

15–005 It is now widely felt that the 1986 legislation can no-longer meet the needs of this changing sector. The industry has made it plain that it feels that the 1986 Act is unduly restrictive in the modern market place in that it specifies precisely the nature of the activities that a Building Society can undertake restricting their activities to those areas for which there is express power in the legislation. Any activities beyond those expressly catered for in the legislation are effectively illegal.

15–006 In addition the 1986 Act has been repeatedly amended by the introduction of secondary legislation which has made its implementation cumbersome and difficult. The inflexibility of the current legislation has the result that Building Societies find it difficult to react with flexibility to the changing needs of the customer and the fast moving demands of the market place. When contrasted with the position of banks and companies regulated by the Banking Act and companies legislation the Building Societies feel that they are acting under an unfairly restrictive regime.

15–007 It is anticipated that there will be a new Building Societies Act in 1997 (a draft Bill has recently been published) which is intended to meet the concerns of the Building Societies by moving away from the old style prescriptive legislation by introducing a new and more permissive approach which will allow the Building Societies to react to changes in the markets in a more flexible way and which will avoid the necessity of regular amendment by secondary legislation. Since major new legislation is expected in 1997, no more than an outline of the existing legislation is set out in this Chapter.

The Building Societies Act 1986

15–008 The Building Societies Act 1986 gave Building Societies a completely new legal framework replacing the Building Societies Act 1962 which was in large measure a codifying act which in its turn had drawn many of its provisions from the legislation of 1874 which had established the basis for regulation of the Building Societies. Under the 1986 Act it was intended that Building Societies would maintain their traditional spheres of operations. The 1986 Act applies to all Building Societies throughout Great Britain and Northern Ireland.

The Building Societies Commission

15–009 Section 1 of the Act established a Building Societies Commission consisting of between four and 10 members appointed by the Treasury. The Building Societies Commission took over many of the functions of the Registry of Friendly Societies. The Commission has responsibility for both Building Societies and Friendly Societies. The Commission oversees the Building Societies with the aim of promoting the protection by each Building Society of the investments of its shareholders and depositors to ensure the financial stability of Building Societies generally to secure that the principal purpose of Building Societies remains that of raising funds from their members for making advances to members secured on residential land to administer the system of regulation provided by the Act and to advise and make recommendations to the Treasury or other government departments on any matters relating to Building Societies.

The Commission is funded by way of a general levy on Building Societies to cover the general expenses of the Commission and from fees in respect of the exercise of the Commission's functions in relation to a particular Building Society.

The Establishment of a Building Society

The object of a Building Society is defined by section 5(1) of the Act which states that:

"A society may be established under this Act if its purpose or principal purpose is that of raising, primarily by the subscriptions of the members, a stock or fund for making to them advances secured on land for their residential use."

A new Building Society can be established by 10 or more people and must have a minimum capital of £100,000. A Building Society must have a memorandum similar to that of a limited company which must be agreed and adopted by its members. (See Sched. 2.)

Authorisation

Authorisation may be granted by the Building Societies Commission when a society accords with the minimum requirements which include qualifying capital of at least £100,000, that the directors and senior executives are fit and proper persons capable of directing the affairs of the society in accordance with the criteria of prudent management (s.9 and Pts I-III of Sched. 3).

Prudent Management

The criteria for prudent management lies at the heart of the system of prudential supervision instituted by the 1986 Act. The criteria are set out in section 45 and include:

   (a) maintenance of adequate reserves and other designated capital resources;

(b) maintenance of a structure of commercial assets which satisfies the specified requirements;
(c) maintenance of adequate liquid assets;
(d) maintenance of the requisite arrangements for assessing the adequacy of securities for advances secured on land;
(e) maintenance of the requisite accounting records and systems of control of business and of inspection and report;
(f) direction and management of the society by a sufficient number of persons who are fit and proper to be directors or officers, this to be conducted by them with prudence and integrity;
(g) conduct of business with adequate professional skills.

In pursuance of the criteria of prudent management the Commission issues a series of Prudential notes. Eleven Prudential notes have been issued to date.

Accounts and Audit

15–015 Section 71 of the Building Societies Act 1986 contains the basic provisions for a Building Society's accounting records and its systems of control of its business and records.

15–016 Section 79(1) requires that the auditors, when preparing their report, must consider whether section 71 has been complied with. The auditors are afforded a "whistle blowing" role under section 82 which requires the auditors to make an annual report to the Building Society Commission on the society's compliance. In addition the auditors of a Building Society may provide information to the Building Society Commission about the Building Society without breaching any relationship of confidence they may have with the Society.

Maintenance of proper accounting records and systems of control is also one of the criteria of prudent management required under section 45.

Fund Raising

15–017 Section 7 of the Act gives Societies the power to raise funds. Section 7(3) provides that non-retail funds and deposits must not exceed at any time a prescribed percentage of the society's total funds. As from January 1, 1988, the limit was 40 per cent.

Advances Secured on Land

15–018 Section 10 of the Building Societies Act 1986 gives Building Societies the power to lend on mortgage of an estate in land. Societies also have the power to lend in respect of index-linked and equity-linked schemes.

Other Advances

Section 16 makes provision for unsecured loans to be made. There is a limit of £10,000 on the aggregate of any unsecured loan which can be made to one person.

15–019

Designated Bodies

Section 18 gives Societies the power to acquire and hold shares in corporate bodies or to take part in or to form corporate bodies to do anything which the Society itself is empowered to do. Examples of where this power has been used by the Building Societies is in joint ventures with appropriate insurance companies and for the formation of estate agencies.

15–020

Liquid Assets

Section 21 requires Building Societies to keep an adequate proportion of its funds in liquid form up to a maximum of $33^{1}/_{3}$ per cent.

15–021

Investor Protection Scheme

Part IV of the Act is concerned with measures intended to protect investors. In many ways the provisions are similar to the provisions contained in the Banking Act 1987. The Buildings Societies Act provides for the establishment of a statutory scheme for the protection of Building Society investors to be administered by the Building Societies Investor Protection Board established under section 24. Section 25 establishes the Investor Protection Fund and section 26 concerns funding of the scheme. The Investor Protection Board has the power to call up contributions from all authorised Building Societies in the event of a Building Society becoming insolvent which can then be used by the Board to make payments to investors in the insolvent society under section 27. However, the protection of investors is limited in two ways under this scheme; firstly, a person is only protected by the scheme to the extent of his "protected investment" (limited to £20,000) and second, the investor will get only 90 per cent of the protected investment back from the fund.

15–022

Services

The services which a Building Society may provide are set out in Schedule 8 of the Act and include banking services, investment services, insurance services, trusteeship, executorship and land services. The Schedule also sets out the various restrictions that are imposed on the provision of such services.

15–023

Sanctions and Discipline

15–024 The Commission has powers under sections 36 and 37 of the Act where a Society exceeds any of the limits applying to the categories of assets or liabilities or where its principal purpose has ceased to fall within that required by section 5(1). The Commission may direct the Society to submit for approval a restructuring plan to bring it within the limits, and the Commission may direct the Society to call a general meeting for the purpose of considering a proposal to convert to company status. In the final resort, the Commission may present a petition for the winding up of the Society.

15–025 Section 38 gives the Commission power to determine whether an activity of a Society is within the powers of that Society. Section 40 allows for prohibition orders to be issued where an activity is considered *ultra vires*.

15–026 Section 42 allows the Commission to impose conditions on a Society with which it must comply in order to retain its authorisation if the Commission considers it in the interests of investors to impose such conditions. Section 43 lays down the circumstances in which the Commission may revoke authorisation.

15–027 Sections 46 to 49 provides for a system of appeals against decisions of the Commission to refuse to grant authorisation, to revoke authorisation or to impose conditions for continued authorisations.

15–028 Section 50 gives the Commission power to control the advertising of a Society if it considers it necessary in the interests of investors to do so. Section 51 allows the Commission to direct a Society to remove a misleading association between the Society and another body. Sections 52 and 54 give the Commission power to obtain information and documents and section 53 covers the confidentiality of information obtained by the Commission.

15–029 Sections 55 to 57 give the Commission power to appoint inspectors to investigate any aspect of a Society or its affairs generally or to summon a meeting of members.

Complaints and Disputes

15–030 Sections 83 to 85 cover the requirement on societies to belong to an ombudsman scheme recognised by the Commission for the investigation of complaints.

Building Societies Ombudsman

15–031 The Building Societies Ombudsman Scheme was set up in 1987. The purpose of the scheme is to help private individuals in the settlement of their disputes with Building Societies once they have exhausted the individual Building Societies' internal complaints procedure. The Ombudsman can award up to £100,000 in compensation. The Scheme is funded from contributions from all the Building Societies.

The Proposed Legislation

As we have already seen, the Building Societies Act 1986 and all previous Building Society legislation has been prescriptive in its nature, setting out strict limits on the business that a Building Society could undertake. This has had the effect of inhibiting the Building Societies' ability to react to changes in the market, particularly in the housing recession of the late 1980s and 1990s and in meeting the increased competition from the banks. In an effort to meet this, the proposals for the new legislation include a relaxation of the sources from which Building Societies can raise funds. It is expected that the new legislation will require Building Societies to raise only 50 per cent of their funds from individual members. 15–032

The major change likely to be included in the proposed legislation is expected to come in respect of Building Society assets. At present at least 75 per cent of loans must be made to owner-occupiers and secured on residential property, with the remaining 25 per cent being put into assets specified by the legislation. The new position is expected to allow Societies to hold 75 per cent of their funds in housing related loans but without the additional requirement that these be secured on owner-occupied properties. The Society will be able to put the remaining 25 per cent into any asset as long as it can satisfy the Building Society Commission that it has sufficient financial and managerial resources to take on the proposed activity. It is expected that the Commission will be given wider powers to intervene in the affairs of a society to safeguard depositors funds. 15–033

Other changes anticipated include measures designed to make Building Societies more accountable to their members than at present. It is also expected that there will be moves to allow Societies to give greater benefits to their members in the form of some sort of "dividend." However, the proposed legislation may also contain some limitations on the windfall profits made by Building Society members in the event of the Society floating on the Stock Exchange or being taken-over by another financial institution. 15–034

Part 5

Investor Protection in Criminal Law

Chapter 16

Theft Act Offences

Until 1968 the law of stealing had developed in an arcane and random manner. The old law of larceny was abolished in that year and replaced by a new generic offence of theft created by the Theft Act 1968 which Parliament intended to embrace all manner of dishonest conduct. Twenty seven years in the development of English criminal law is perhaps a handbreadth, but against the sophistication of contemporary investor fraud the inadequacies of the existing law are regrettably as great today as those which the 1968 Act set out to remedy. 16–001

The practical application of the Theft Act 1968 has not proved to be as simple and effective as the legislators had hoped or intended, and as Beldam L.J. remarked recently in *Hallam and Blackburn* [1995] Crim.L.R. 323, C.A: 16–002

"Once again the law of theft is in urgent need of simplification and modernisation, so that a jury of twelve ordinary citizens do not have to grapple with concepts couched in the antiquated *franglais* of *choses in action*, and scarce public resources in time and money are not devoted to hours of semantic argument divorced from the true merits of the case."

Not before time the Law Commission has embarked upon a review of the workings of the legislation in this field and its recommendations are awaited with some alacrity. In a letter to *The Times*, February 1, 1996, Mr Stephen Silber Q.C. acknowledged on behalf of the Law Commission that the review was needed because "there had been radical and multifarious technological advances" and that "it was likely that some acts of dishonesty might not be effectively covered by present legislation". The Law Commission hopes to produce a series of Consultation Papers followed by a report. The urgency of the task cannot be understated. In *Preddy* [1996] 3 All E.R. 481, a case involving the obtaining of a mortgage advance by deception, Lord Jauncey acknowledged (at p. 496j) that: 16–003

"it is singularly unfortunate that Parliament has achieved ... the result of legalising fraudulent conduct of the type involved in these appeals—conduct which was almost certainly criminal prior to the 1968 Act. Building Societies may ... derive small comfort from the fact that in Scotland common law and common sense rather than

Parliamentary wisdom still prevail. It is almost certain that conduct such as that of the appellants would constitute the common law offence of fraud in that country."

16–004 A broad examination of Theft Acts 1968 and 1978 is beyond the scope of this work. Instead this chapter focuses on the ways in which prosecutors have sought to utilise the provisions of the Theft Acts 1968 and 1978 and the Forgery and Counterfeiting Act 1981 against those who have perpetrated investor fraud. A review of the cases demonstrates that the existing law is a blunt weapon in the armoury of investor protection.

Theft Act 1968

Theft

16–005 Theft is defined in section 1(1) of the Theft Act 1968 in the following terms: "a person is guilty of theft if he dishonestly appropriates property belonging to another with the intention of permanently depriving the other of it." Megaw L.J. spelt out the ingredients of the offence in *Lawrence* (1971) 55 Cr. App. R. 73 at 76:

> "Theft ... involves four elements: (i) a dishonest (ii) appropriation (iii) of property belonging to another (iv) with the intention of depriving the other of it."

Dishonesty

16–006 Dishonesty is an essential ingredient of the offence of theft. It is also an ingredient of a number of other offences which are covered in this chapter, these offences being: under the 1968 Theft Act; obtaining property by deception contrary to section 15, obtaining a pecuniary advantage by deception contrary to section 16, false accounting contrary to section 17, suppression of documents contrary to section 20(1), procuring the execution of a valuable security by deception contrary to section 20(2) and handling stolen goods contrary to section 22. And under the 1978 Theft Act; obtaining services by deception contrary to section 1 and evasion of a liability by deception contrary to section 2. The test to be applied when determining the issue of dishonesty was set out by Lord Lane C.J. in the leading case of *R. v. Ghosh* [1982] Q.B. 1053; 75 Cr.App.R. 154 as follows:

> "In determining whether the prosecution has proved that the defendant was acting dishonestly, a jury must first of all decide whether

according to the standards of reasonable and honest people what was done was dishonest. If it was not dishonest by those standards, that is the end of the matter and the prosecution fails. If it was dishonest by those standards, then the jury must consider whether the defendant himself must have realised that what he was doing was by those standards dishonest."

Subject to this test, however, there are a number of circumstances in which Parliament has declared that a person's actions will not be regarded as dishonest. If property is taken in the belief that the taker has in law the right to deprive the owner of it or if property is taken in the belief that the taker would have the owner's consent if the owner knew of the appropriation and the circumstances of it, the person's appropriation of the property will not be regarded as dishonest. Also, if a person takes property in the belief that a person to whom the property belongs cannot be discovered by taking reasonable steps, the appropriation is not to be regarded as dishonest. **16–007**

In the context of investor fraud, issues concerning dishonesty have tended to arise where a director takes money from his own company. In *Attorney General's Reference (No. 2 of 1982)* (1984) 78 Cr.App.R. 131, the Court of Appeal rightly rejected an argument that where a defendant was the sole directing mind of the company he could not be guilty of theft from the company because the company must have necessarily consented to his actions. Such knowledge should not be imputed to the company for the essence of such an arrangement was to deprive the company improperly of a large part of its assets. The company was a victim, and it would be irrational to treat the directors notionally as having transmitted this knowledge to the company. **16–008**

Appropriation

Parliament sought to encapsulate the notion of an appropriation in section 3. However, the statutory definition of the term has not proved to be comprehensive, not because of any drafting difficulties but rather because of the diversity of circumstances in which property can be appropriated. The statutory provision defines appropriation as any assumption by a person of the rights of an owner and includes circumstances where a person keeps or deals with property which has come into his possession (innocently or not) without stealing it. The keeping or dealing with property will amount to an assumption of the rights of an owner in those circumstances. Again, as with the issue of dishonesty, problems in the commercial context have focused on the position where a person (often a corporate person) might be said to have consented to the appropriation. **16–009**

This thorny issue was considered by the House of Lords in *Gomez* [1992] 3 W.L.R. 1067 in a case where an owner was induced to authorise the taking of property by a fraudulent deception. Deciding between conflicting Court of Appeal cases on the point the House of Lords held **16–010** that it was the actual taking of property in circumstances where it was intended to assume the rights of the owner which amounted to an appropriation. The question of whether the owner had consented or not was irrelevant to whether there had been an appropriation. There were obvious policy considerations which led the House of Lords to this conclusion. As Lord Browne-Wilkinson said in a passage at the end of his judgment which resonates in the investor context:

> "The pillaging of companies by those who control them is now all too common. It would offend both common sense and justice to hold that the very control which enables such people to extract the company's assets constitutes a defence to a charge of theft from the company. The question in each case must be whether the extraction of the property from the company was dishonest, not whether the alleged thief has consented to his own wrongdoing."

16–011 No doubt Lord Browne-Wilkinson may have had the case of *Asil Nadir*, 1992, in mind. The defendant had been charged with 46 counts of theft involving some £119.5 million. The charges alleged theft by the transfer of funds from a parent company bank account to an account of a wholly owned subsidiary based in Northern Cyprus. Mr Nadir held a controlling interest in the parent company. The charges were dismissed at a preliminary stage following a submission that there had been no appropriation of funds because Mr Nadir had been authorised to transfer them. The judge ruled that the transfer of funds from parent to subsidiary was a preparatory act which was not capable of amounting to an appropriation. Appropriation took place only when the funds were withdrawn from the subsidiary's bank account in Northern Cyprus. Mr Nadir was charged with other offences but he absconded from the jurisdiction of the court.

16–012 Had the same submission on the theft charges been made after *Gomez* had been decided, the submission would have failed. A company director with authority to transfer the company's funds to a foreign subsidiary will commit theft if he transfers funds with the dishonest intention of using them dishonestly for his own private purposes. Appropriation can now take place irrespective of the consent of the owner.

16–013 Acute difficulties concerning appropriation may arise in a case where an investor has paid money to an adviser to invest the money on the investor's behalf. If the adviser does not invest the money or invests it in some way other than that intended by the investor, is he guilty of theft? Has the investment adviser appropriated the money within the meaning of section 3 of the Theft Act 1968?

16–014 This question was raised directly in the case of *Hallam and Blackburn* [1995] Crim.L.R. 323, which concerned the sale of investment products by financial advisers through the medium of a company. In some cases the investor's money was not invested on the investor's behalf but was paid into the defendants' or the company's business account. In other cases policy surrender cheques from insurance companies were not paid to investors. The defendants appealed with the leave of the trial judge who certified a question of law for the Court of Appeal to decide whether a payment into a defendant's bank account of a cheque with the consent or approval of the drawer of the cheque amounted to an appropriation of those funds by reason of the fact that it is made with a dishonest intent and as a preliminary step to the misuse of those funds.

By the time the case came to be heard by the Court of Appeal the answer to the certified question had been given by the House of Lords, *Gomez*. However, this was not the end of the matter. It remained to be determined exactly when the appropriation took place. The prosecution alleged that the appropriation took place on the date when the cheques from the clients or the insurers were paid into the personal or company bank accounts. If this allegation was correct, so the defendants argued, the funds were not the investor's property and therefore the investor did not have any rights to appropriate at the time when the funds were paid into the personal or company bank accounts. Instead of charging the defendants with theft of monies, the appellants submitted that they should have been charged with theft of the cheque or chose in action it represented. **16–015**

The Court of Appeal circumvented the point by relying on section 5(2) of the Theft Act 1968, this being a special provision enacted to deal with such technical points. This section is considered later in this chapter. Suffice it to note here that the court held that the defendants had been entrusted with funds to invest on behalf of their clients. After the investors had passed the cheques to the defendants the investors retained an equitable interest in the funds which attached not only to the cheque but to its proceeds and any balance in the accounts operated by the defendants or the company to which payment could be traced. It was this equitable interest which was appropriated at the time when the funds were paid into the personal or company bank accounts as a preliminary step to the dishonest misuse of those funds. **16–016**

Whilst the Court of Appeal's decision is to be welcomed, it by no means eradicates the myriad of technical problems in this area. Suppose an investment adviser intends to invest funds on the investor's behalf at the time when he pays the investor's cheque into the company account but due to commercial pressures he subsequently decides to use the funds to discharge the company's business liabilities. The dishonest intention will not coincide with the appropriation. Nor will the investment adviser be guilty of obtaining property by deception, because at the time when the property was obtained there was no deception. **16–017**

Appropriation of a Chose in Action

A chose in action is a legal phrase which is used to describe all personal rights over property which can be claimed or enforced by an action in law. Typically in this context, a debt is a chose in action. In respect of monies held by a deposit-taking institution (such as a bank or **16–018** building society), although the monies paid into the account belong to the deposit-taking institution, the latter owes a debt to the depositing customer which it undertakes (subject to special terms) to repay on demand. It is this debt which is capable of appropriation. For example, if a person draws a cheque on a bank account on which he has no authority to draw, the act of causing the cheque to be drawn and issued will constitute an appropriation of the debt owed by the bank to the account holder. It is a usurpation of the account holder's rights. The leading cases on appropriation of a chose in action are *Wille* [1988] 86 Cr.App.R. 296 and *Kohn* (1979) 69 Cr.App.R. 395.

16–019   Cheques remain the most common type of chose in action encountered in the courts but the development of new types of financial instrument in the commercial sector has resulted in a wider range of methods by which money may be transferred. Other types of choses in action are rights which belong to a shareholder as a result of his holding of shares in a company or the rights of an owner in copyright. The problems associated with reconciling the concept of property within the Theft Act 1968 with these new methods of money transfer are considered later in this chapter.

Appropriation by Innocent Agent

16–020   A defendant is guilty of theft if he uses an innocent agent to carry out the appropriation for him. In *Stinger* (1991) 94 Cr.App.R. 13 a dishonest company employee signed bogus invoices which initiated company procedures and caused innocent employees to authorise payment. The company's bank account was debited in consequence. Whilst the defendant did not authorise payment, he was guilty of theft from the company bank accounts under the ordinary principles of criminal law.

Multiple Assumptions of the Rights of an Owner

16–021   The need to identify the precise time of appropriation is important when drafting charges. A mistake cannot be saved by resorting to a second appropriation where the circumstances of an earlier appropriation by the same defendant can be substantiated. In *Atakpu* [1994] Q.B. 69, the defendants hired cars abroad and brought them to England where they were sold. The Court of Appeal held that once the cars had been stolen abroad they could not be appropriated again in England by the same thief. Difficulties were encountered in this case because the initial assumption of the rights of the owner occurred outside the jurisdiction. This same problem has often been met in the commercial context where instructions to transfer funds are given in one jurisdiction and the funds are held in another. Part I of the Criminal Justice Act 1993 was enacted to resolve these problems. This is discussed at the end of this chapter.

Property

16–022   Property is given an inclusive but not an exhaustive definition by section 4(1) of the Theft Act 1968. It is defined to include "money and all other property, real or personal, including things in action and other intangible property." Before 1968 the property that could be stolen was property which was capable of being carried away, in other words tangible property which had a physical existence. Intangible property could not be stolen because it had no physical existence. Section 4(1) of the Theft Act 1968 changed the position by including intangible property in the definition of property which was capable of being stolen. This change had major significance in the commercial context since it embraced the amorphous chose in action as a species of intangible property which was capable of being stolen. In consequence the focus of attention has shifted away from concentration on the physical attributes of the nature of property to an examination of the legal incidents of relationships which arise when commercial arrangements of this nature are made.

Cheques

The degree of scrutiny to which commercial arrangements have been subject under the present law is well demonstrated by a consideration of the leading case involving theft of cheques. In *Kohn* (1979) 69 Cr.App.R. 395, a defendant drew cheques on various company bank accounts, the proceeds of which were intended for the defendant's personal benefit. The thefts fell into three categories. First, there was the situation where the company bank account was in credit. In this instance the drawing of a cheque on the company bank account amounted to theft of a chose in action which was identified as the debt owed by the bank to the company. Secondly, there were occasions where the balance of the company bank account was in overdraft but the amount dishonestly drawn did not exceed the agreed limit. Again, the drawing of a cheque was held to amount to theft of a chose in action which was identified as an obligation owed by the bank to the company to meet the cheque if the balance on the account did not exceed the overdraft limit. Thirdly, there were occasions where the overdraft limit was exceeded. Here, however, there could not be any theft of a chose in action because there was no relationship of debtor and creditor between the bank and the company. The bank had no obligation to meet the cheque in excess of the overdraft limit. Even though the bank met the cheque as a matter of grace it made no difference to the legal incidents of the arrangement. The meeting of the cheque could not retrospectively create any personal right of property in the customer nor any retrospective duty on the bank. **16–023**

Credit Balances

Following the decision in *Kohn*, there was some concern that the breadth of its effect had been restricted by the Court of Appeal in *Thompson (Michael)* (1984) 79 Cr.App.R. 191; [1984] 3 All E.R. 565, where a bank operator in Kuwait programmed the bank computer to credit accounts opened by him in Kuwait with amounts dishonestly **16–024** debited from the accounts of customers with corresponding amounts. On his return to England the bank operator instructed the Kuwaiti bank to transfer the funds from his accounts in Kuwait to his English bank accounts. The bank operator was charged with obtaining property by deception from the Kuwaiti bank. In a cleverly worded indictment the particulars of the charges alleged that he had obtained the transferred sum by falsely representing that the amount credited to his account was a genuine and accurate credit and that he was entitled to receive payment of the sum. On appeal the bank operator argued that the court lacked jurisdiction to try him because he had not committed any offences in England. He said that he had obtained the property abroad when he obtained control of the credit balances in Kuwait. No offence had been committed in England.

16–025 In an effort to defeat this argument the Court of Appeal held that the bank operator had not obtained a chose in action against the bank when the funds were transferred from the customer accounts to his personal accounts in Kuwait because an apparent credit balance on a customer's bank account could not properly be described as a chose in action in English law. May L.J. said that it was not possible to describe as a chose in action a liability which had been brought into existence by fraud where the action to enforce that liability is capable of immediate defeasance as soon as the fraud is pleaded.

16–026 Whilst the decision in *Thompson* was unimpeachable in its application of civil law, there were concerns about its consequences in criminal law, lest fraudsters sought to apply the same reasoning in cases where there was no extra-jurisdictional aspect. Suppose the events in Kuwait had happened in England? If the first part of the fraudulent scheme was to be reflected in a criminal charge the charge would have to be directed towards the dishonest programming of the bank computer (*i.e.* false accounting) rather than the transfer of funds from the customer accounts. Yet the real vice of the fraud was the theft of the credit balances from the customer accounts. Some astute drafting on the part of prosecutors would be needed to avoid the pitfalls.

16–027 Following the Privy Council decision in *Chan Man-sin v. Att.-Gen. of Hong Kong* [1988] 1 W.L.R. 196; [1988] 1 All E.R. 1, it no longer seems open to a defendant to raise such an unmeritorious point in his defence. In *Chan Man-sin* a company accountant drew forged cheques on a company's bank account. He was charged with theft of choses in action, namely debts owed by the company's bank to the company. In his defence the accountant argued that a forged cheque was a nullity so far as the customer was concerned and the bank was not entitled to debit the customer's account with the amount of the forged cheque. Accordingly, so he submitted, there was no intangible property which was capable of appropriation. The leading civil banking case of *Tai Hing Cotton Mill Ltd v. Lui Chong Hing Bank* [1985] 2 All E.R. 947; [1986] A.C. 80, was cited in support. The Privy Council robustly rejected this argument, saying that it was entirely immaterial whether the end result of the transaction may be a legal nullity. It is not possible to read into the definition of appropriation any requirement that the assumption of rights there envisaged should have a legally efficacious result. It has to be said that this decision sits uneasily with established principles of banking law. The theft in *Chan Man-sin* was artificial in the sense that, applying these principles of civil law, the customer did not suffer any loss. If loss is suffered in this type of case, it is borne by the deposit-taking institution. The problems caused by the interaction between principles of civil law and criminal law are considered at the end of this chapter.

Electronic transfers

The bank credit created by a CHAPS order (clearing house automated payment system order) is recognised as a chose in action. As Lord Lane C.J. said in *King* [1991] Crim.L.R. 906; [1991] 3 All E.R. 705, if the payee's right to the bank credit were to be called into question, the CHAPS order could be relied upon as his document of title to the credit. To similar effect, the reduction of a sum standing in one customer's bank account and the corresponding increase in the sum standing to the credit of another customer's bank account will constitute the obtaining of property even though the transfer between the bank accounts was effected by electronic means—*Crick, The Times,* August 18, 1993. It follows that intangible property will include a sum of money represented by a figure in an account maintained by a deposit-taking institution. **16–028**

Documents

In the age of electronic banking it will be the exception rather than the norm for charges to be based on theft of documents rather than a chose of action in cases which involve the loss of an investor's funds. Nevertheless, where a person dishonestly obtains a document which gives rise to certain legal rights on the part of the holder of the document, it is open to the prosecutor to allege theft of the document in question. As Megaw L.J. said towards the end of his judgment in *Duru* [1973] 3 All E.R. 715: **16–029**

"so far as [a] cheque is concerned, true it is a piece of paper. But it is a piece of paper which changes its character completely once it is paid, because then it receives a rubber stamp on it saying that it has been paid and it ceases to be a thing in action, or at any rate, ceases to be, in substance, the same thing as it was before: that is, an instrument on which payment falls to be made."

The same principles apply to documents of title. A person entrusted with shares in his capacity as trustee or stockbroker will commit theft of tangible property (*i.e.* the shares and not just a piece of paper) if he wrongfully pledges the shares as security or sells them when not authorised to do so—*Smith* [1963] 36 DLR 2d 613; [1963] 1 C.C.C. 68. **16–030**

Precise Identification of Property Stolen

16–031 Another problem which frequently occurs in investor fraud cases concerns the precise identification of the stolen property where the case involves the repeated taking of small amounts of money over a long period of time. Where there is an appropriation of a number of sums but no evidence as to when the individual appropriations took place the prosecution is entitled to charge the appropriation of the aggregate amount on a day within the period during which the appropriations took place—*D.P.P. v. McCabe* [1992] Crim.L.R. 885.

16–032 Sometimes a different problem arises where there is doubt as to whether a defendant stole the property or the proceeds arising from sale of the stolen property. In this situation a prosecutor may properly allege that the defendant has stolen the property or its proceeds. It is immaterial that it cannot be shown whether the defendant stole the original property or its proceeds as long as the jury is sure that he stole one or the other. In *Hallam and Blackburn*, above, the defendants argued that they should have been charged with theft of a cheque or chose in action represented by the cheque rather than theft of a specified sum of money. The Court of Appeal said that although it was not possible to prove whether the defendants had stolen a chose in action or the proceeds of a chose in action, it would nevertheless be sufficient to show that the defendants had failed to account for the sums with which they had been entrusted.

Belonging to Another

16–033 The prosecution must establish that the appropriated property belongs to another person before an offence of theft is committed. At first blush this additional statutory requirement may seem unnecessary since the essence of appropriation is an assumption of another's rights. In fact, this additional requirement is vital because of the various categories of ownership which exist in English law. A person may own the legal and/or equitable interest in personal property in the same way as ownership of land is classified. Also, a person may have property in his possession not because he owns any legal or equitable interest over it but because he has been entrusted with possession of it as bailee. It would be absurd if the law of theft were to apply only to cases where property had been taken from the custody and control of its legal owner. Section 5 of the Theft Act 1968 was enacted to deal with these points and it provides as follows:

16–034 "(1) Property shall be regarded as belonging to any person having possession or control of it, or having any proprietary right or interest (not being an equitable interest arising from an agreement to transfer or grant an interest).

(2) Where property is subject to a trust, the persons to whom it belongs shall be regarded as including any person having a right to enforce the trust, and an intention to defeat the trust shall be regarded accordingly as an intention to deprive of the property any person having that right.

(3) Where a person receives property from or on account of another, and is under an obligation to the other to retain and deal with that property or its proceeds in a particular way, the property or proceeds shall be regarded (as against him) as belonging to the other.

(4) Where a person gets property by another's mistake, and is under an obligation to make restoration (in whole or in part) of the property or its proceeds or of the value thereof, then to the extent of that obligation in the property or proceeds shall be regarded (as against him) as belonging to the person entitled to restoration, and an intention not to make restoration shall be regarded accordingly as an intention to deprive that person of the property or proceeds.

(5) Property of a corporation sole shall be regarded as belonging to the corporation notwithstanding a vacancy in the corporation."

Sub-sections (2) and (3) have proved to be a fertile breeding ground for fraudsters seeking to escape liability in criminal law in cases of investor loss. **16–035**

Naylor and Clowes—Investors' Funds Held on Trust

In a case following the well publicised collapse of the Barlow Clowes group of companies, the Court of Appeal had to consider the application of section 5 in the context of England's largest investor swindle. The case is reported as *Clowes and another* [1994] 2 All E.R. 316. Barlow Clowes had advertised for funds to be deposited in investment schemes which were said to be based on investment in British Government stocks. The monies were not invested and Clowes was charged with theft of investor funds which he had used for his own purposes. The principal issue argued in the Court of Appeal turned on whether Clowes was a trustee of the invested funds or a beneficial owner of the funds. If a trustee of the funds, Clowes would have taken property deemed to belong to investors by virtue of section 5(2), thereby rendering him guilty of theft as charged. If on the other hand Clowes was not a trustee of the funds but beneficially entitled to them, and subject only to a contractual obligation to pay back on demand equivalent sums to those who invested, Clowes would not have appropriated property belonging to another. In this event he would not have been guilty of the charges of theft which had been brought against him. **16–036**

Clowes argued that on a proper construction of the investment brochures and application forms the relationship between Barlow **16–037**

CHAPTER 16: THEFT ACT OFFENCES

Clowes and each investor was not that of a trustee and beneficiary but simply that of a creditor and debtor. The investment clause in the application form attached to each brochure did not limit Barlow Clowes to investing in British Government stock but also authorised it to invest the funds in, amongst other things, the purchase of shares of any public or private company or by lending it to anybody or person in the discretion of Barlow Clowes. In support of his argument Clowes relied upon a well-established line of civil cases in which the courts had demonstrated a reluctance to construe a relationship of trust in commercial transactions, particularly where the terms of the transaction did not require segregation of funds.

16–038 It required some deft judicial footwork to uphold the convictions for theft. Notwithstanding the fact that an investor's funds were not to be held in a segregated account but mixed with other investors' funds, the court held that there were clear indicators which showed that Barlow Clowes had received the investment funds on trust to invest them in British Government stocks. In the court's view the authority to place the monies elsewhere was limited to a temporary placement pending investment, re-investment or return of the money to the investor.

16–039 Naylor was a co-defendant in the Clowes case and he took a related point in the Court of Appeal. Naylor had been convicted of theft of a chose in action which was identified as a debt constituted by a credit in a sum of money held in a Barlow Clowes bank account. The bank account was a mixed account, in the sense that it consisted in part of money contributed by investors and in part of money coming from other sources. Focusing again on the concept of property belonging to another, Naylor argued that the credit sum was not property which belonged to the investors. Relying on a well known principle in trust law that where a trustee mixes his own money with the trust money, he is deemed to draw out his own money first, leaving the trust money in tact. The Court of Appeal rejected this argument by relying on the terms of section 5(1). Naylor could not possibly distinguish between investor and non-investor funds in the particular circumstances of the case.

16–040 The Court of Appeal's rejection of the appeals in *Naylor and Clowes* was broadly sound in principle. Nonetheless, it is somewhat disconcerting that Naylor and Clowes were able to mount a credible attack on one of the fundamental planks of the prosecution case by relying on esoteric principles of trusts law.

16–041 In any case where the prosecution seeks to rely on the section 5 provisions, it is essential for the judge to direct the jury on the essential elements of the arrangement which has to be proved. In *McHugh*, January 28, 1993, unreported, where a financial consultant was charged with theft of part of investors' funds the jury should have been directed that section 5(3) would apply only where the jury was satisfied that the defendant and the investor understood that the investor's funds were to be kept separate from the financial consultant's own money and that of his business.

Intention to Permanently Deprive

16–042 The final ingredient of theft identified by Megaw L.J. in *Lawrence* (1971) 55 Cr. App. R. 73, is the intention of permanently depriving the other of the property in question. The defendant's intention is a question of fact to be determined in each case and no particular problems have been encountered in the investor fraud context. Defendants are commonly heard to assert that they took monies with the intention of repaying the investor in the fullness of time. Whilst this assertion goes to the issue of their dishonesty in taking the monies in the first place, section 6 of the Theft Act 1968 effectively precludes a defendant from raising the matter in connection with his intention to permanently deprive. The section reads as follows:

"(1) A person appropriating property belonging to another without meaning the other permanently to lose the thing itself is nevertheless to be regarded as having the intention of permanently depriving the other of it if his intention is to treat the thing as his own to dispose of regardless of the other's rights; and a borrowing or lending of it may amount to so treating it if, but only if, the borrowing or lending is for a period and in circumstances making it equivalent to an outright taking or disposal.
(2) Without prejudice to the generality of subsection (1) above, where a person, having possession or control (lawfully or not) of property belonging to another, parts with the property under a condition as to its return which he may not be able to perform, this (if done for purposes of his own and without the other's authority) amounts to treating the property as his own to dispose of regardless of the other's rights."

Property by Deception

Obtaining Property by Deception

16–043 The offence of obtaining property by deception contrary to section 15 is the next offence which is often utilised in cases of investor fraud. By this section:

"(1) A person who by any deception dishonestly obtains property belonging to another, with the intention of permanently depriving the other of it, shall on conviction on indictment be liable to imprisonment for a term not exceeding 10 years.
(2) For the purposes of this section a person is to be treated as obtaining property if he obtains ownership, possession or control of it, and "obtain" includes obtaining for another or enabling another to obtain or retain."

16-044 A deception is defined in section 15(4) as "any deception (whether deliberate or reckless) by words or conduct as to fact or as to law, including a deception as to the present intentions of the person using the deception or any other person." Dishonesty and property mean the same as they do in the case of theft, and section 6 is expressly stated to apply when considering whether there was any intention to permanently deprive. It follows that the same considerations apply to the use of section 15 in the investor fraud context. Practical problems have been encountered when seeking to prove that property was obtained by deception. The dishonest deception must precede the obtaining of the property and operate on the mind of the person deceived. Unfortunately, with the sophistication of some investor frauds, this causative aspect is not always easy to prove. In cases involving a company, a company is fixed with the knowledge acquired by one of its employees only if the employee had its authority to act in relation to the particular transaction in question. Where the company had been the victim of fraud, an employee who was party to the fraud would not be acting with its authority. Knowledge acquired by such an employee which was relevant to the fraud was not therefore to be attributed to the company—*Rozeik* [1996] Crim.L.R. 271.

Multiple Share Applications

16-045 Some years ago, during the heyday of share privatisation, a number of successful prosecutions were brought under section 15 for multiple share applications. One case involved a barrister and former M.P., Keith Best, *The Times*, October 6, 1987. Best was convicted of three specimen offences of attempting to obtain property by deception after he had made six applications in the British Telecom flotation for a total of 39,000 shares. The applications were made in variations of Best's name and address. Initially Best had been charged with the full offence under section 15 but the charge was altered to an attempt after the prosecution failed to call the scrutineer who considered the Best applications to testify that he or she was deceived. Best contested the case on the basis that he was not acting dishonestly but he was convicted by a majority verdict. The trial judge sentenced him to four months imprisonment and a fine but on appeal the sentence was reduced to a fine of £4,500. Lord Lane C.J. commented that all types of stock market dishonesty were easy to commit, difficult to detect, and potentially very lucrative for the perpetrator:

> "Let it be clearly understood that from now on those who indulged in such or any other sort of cheating connected with the stock market were on notice that it was not only their assets which were at risk but also their liberty."

16-046 In an earlier case, *Greenstein* [1976] 1 All E.R. 1, the Court of Appeal had upheld convictions for obtaining property by deception where multiple share applications had been made and the cheques accompanying the share applications were at risk of bouncing. The jury had been asked in that case to decide whether it was merely irregular or a breach of contract to make applications for shares in this way, or whether a dishonest deception was involved.

Preddy

At the time of writing it is too early to assess the effect of the House of Lords decision in the case of *Preddy* [1996] 3 All E.R. 481, handed down on July 10, 1996. The case concerned the obtaining of a mortgage advance by deception. The House of Lords held that section 15 was inapt to cover the prosecution of a case of deception which involved the debiting of one person's bank account and the corresponding crediting of another's bank account. The House of Lords held that section 15 could not be used to cover this situation because no property which "belonged to another" was obtained by the person practising the deception. Lord Jauncey explained (at 496g) the underlying reasoning for this decision in the following terms: **16–047**

> "I start with the proposition that the money in a bank account standing at credit does not belong to the account holder. He has merely a chose in action which is the right to demand payment of the relevant sum from the bank . . . When a sum of money leaves A's account his chose in action quoad that sum is extinguished. When an equivalent sum is transferred to B's account there is created in B a fresh chose in action being the right to demand payment of the sum from his bank. Applying these simple propositions to the cases where sums of money are transferred from the lender's account to the account of the borrower or his solicitor, either by telegraphic transfer or CHAPS, the lender's property, which was his chose in action in respect of the relevant sum, is extinguished and a new chose in action is created in the borrower or his solicitor. Thus, although the borrower has acquired a chose in action, quoad a sum of money of equal value to that which the lender had a right, he has not acquired the property of the lender which was the latter's right against his own bank. It follows that section 15(1) has no application to such a situation."

In terms of the prosecution of mortgage frauds, this decision is significant indeed because it exposes a lacuna in the law which it will not be possible to fill by the use of alternative offences such as procuring a valuable security by deception or by obtaining services by deception. Problems involving both offences are discussed later in this chapter. **16–048**

The real question of concern, however, is the extent to which this case impacts on the ability of prosecutors to charge theft of property where the property in question is represented by a chose in action, as occurred in the cases of *Wille, Kohn, Thompson, Chan Man-sin, King, Crick*, and *Clowes and Naylor*, all of which have been discussed earlier in this **16–049**

Chapter 16: Theft Act Offences

chapter. None of these decisions was mentioned in the opinions delivered by House of Lords in *Preddy*, and at first blush it would seem extraordinary to suppose that the House of Lords intended to establish that there can be no theft of a chose in action because at the time of theft there was no longer any property belonging to another which was capable of being stolen.

16–050 The problem, however, rests with the logical force of the approach taken by the House of Lords, when considered within the terms of the certified question which it was asked. The principal question which the House of Lords was asked to answer was couched in the following terms:

> "Whether the debiting of a bank account and the corresponding credit of another's bank account brought about by dishonest misrepresentation amounts to the obtaining of property within section 15 of the Theft Act 1968."

16–051 Having answered this question in the affirmative, it is not difficult to see how defendants will seek to assert that the same answer follows if the word "appropriation" is substituted for the word "obtaining."After all, as Lord Goff said (at p. 490), the critical question did not concern the identity of the property obtained (here the word "appropriated" may be substituted), but "whether the defendant obtained (or attempted to obtain) property belonging to another".

16–052 Some light can be shed on the answer to this question by considering the way in which Lord Goff dealt with the decision in the case of *Att.-Gen of Hong Kong v. Nai-Keung* [1987] 1 W.L.R. 1339, where the Privy Council had decided that an export quota surplus to a particular exporter's requirements could constitute intangible property which was capable of theft. The sums standing to the credit of the lending institution in its bank account represented debts owed by the bank to the lending institution which, as choses in action belonging to the lending institution, fell within the definition of property which was capable of being stolen under section 4(1) of the Theft Act 1968. This situation, said Lord Goff (at p. 489h), could be differentiated from the situation in *Preddy* because the property which was the subject of the theft, namely the export quota surplus represented as a credit entry owed by the bank to the lending institution, was an asset which was capable of being traded on a market.

16–053 In reality, though, it is not easy to see what difference the marketability of the asset makes when considering whether it amounts to "property belonging to another" which is capable of being appropriated or obtained under section 1 or section 15 of the Theft Act 1968.

16–054 One possible response to this situation, it is suggested, is for prosecutors to exercise extreme care when drafting charges for theft under the principles set out in *Gomez*. Following *Preddy*, a charge alleging theft of a chose in action will remain good provided that it alleged that the act of appropriation takes place at a time when the sum of money continues to be held by the bank to the victim's order. An allegation that an appropriation takes place at a later stage, *i.e.* after the sum of money has been transferred to another account whether by cheque, telegraphic transfer or CHAPS, will be too late.

There will undoubtedly be further developments in this unnecessarily complicated area of the law. This was recognised in *Hawkins, The Times*, August 6, 1996, when, whilst rejecting an application for leave to appeal out-of-time on the basis that a guilty plea had been entered prior to the change in the law, Lord Bingham C.J. acknowledged that there was an argument that convictions of theft could have been sustained and that "it seemed overwhelmingly likely that the time would come when the correctness of these propositions would have to be decided."

False Accounting

False accounting is an extremely useful offence in the prosecution of investor fraud. Whether details of the fraud are recorded in the business records, it is axiomatic that the business records will not provide a true and genuine picture of the business activity in question. It is not uncommon for fabricated invoices to be recorded in business records in a manner which artificially inflates expenses and enables funds to be extracted by dishonest directors or employees in an irregular fashion. It is equally not uncommon for income to be omitted from business records in an effort to reduce the declared income and conceal the appropriation of business funds by a dishonest director or employee for his private use. In both cases the business records will conceal the fraudulent activity which has been perpetrated to the prejudice of the shareholders or business creditors. Section 17 of the Theft Act 1968 exposes the falsifiers of business records to a maximum punishment of seven years' imprisonment and unlimited fine. 16–055

Section 17 provides as follows: 16–056
"(1) Where a person dishonesty, with a view to gain for himself or another or with intent to cause loss to another,

(a) destroys, defaces, conceals or falsifies any account or any records or document made or required for an accounting purpose; or
(b) in furnishing information for any purpose produces or makes use of any account, or any such record or document as aforesaid, which to his knowledge is or may be misleading, false or deceptive in a material particular;

he shall, on conviction on indictment, be liable to imprisonment for a term not exceeding seven years.
(2) For the purposes of this section a person who makes or concurs in making in an account or other document an entry which is or may be misleading, false or deceptive in a material particular, or who omits or

concurs in omitting a material particular from an account or other document, is to be treated as falsifying the account or document."

16–057 The word "record" is wide enough to cover a mechanical account such as a meter—*Edwards v. Toombs* [1983] Crim.L.R. 43. It follows that business accounts and records kept on computer will constitute a record within the meaning of this section. This was confirmed in *Re Levin*, March 1, 1996, unreported, when the Divisional Court held that where a person made an entry made into a continuous record stored on computer disc which was false or misleading, he was to be treated as having falsified an account for the purposes of section 17. In *Scot-Simmonds* [1994] Crim.L.R. 933, the Court of Appeal confirmed that the word "account" has its meaning in ordinary usage and that the words "made or required for an accounting purpose" do not qualify the word "account". An entirely bogus set of accounts will constitute a false account within the meaning of this section.

16–058 Documents which are made or required for some purpose other than an accounting purpose fall within section 17 if the documents are required for an accounting purpose as a subsidiary purpose. The fact that the falsified information is contained in a different part of the document from that required for an accounting purpose is irrelevant since the document must be examined as a whole—*Attorney General's Reference (No. 1 of 1980)* (1980) 72 Cr.App.R. 60.

With a View to Gain or with Intent to Cause Loss

16–059 Section 34(2)(a) of the Theft Act 1968 provides that:

"gain" and "loss" are to construed as extending only to gain or loss in money or other property, but as extending to any such gain or loss whether temporary or permanent; and
(i) 'gain' includes a gain by keeping what one has, as well as a gain by getting what one has not; and
(ii) 'loss' includes a loss by not getting what one might get, as well as a loss by parting with what one has."

16–060 Although generally not problematic this statutory definition is unduly restrictive in a case where a financial services consultant falsifies an accounting document, for example an investment portfolio valuation, with the intention of inducing the investor to forbear from starting legal proceedings against him.

16–061 In *Goleccha and Choraria* (1989) 90 Cr.App.R. 241 the Court of Appeal held that where a debtor dishonestly falsifies documents required for an accounting purpose, intending to induce his creditor to forbear from suing on the debt, he does not have "a view to gain" or an "intent to cause loss" within the meaning of section 34(2). Therefore in this type of case the financial services consultant (the debtor) will not be possessed of any proprietary rights. He will not have money and the chose in action represented by the debt will be owned by the investor (the creditor).

Valuable Securities

16–062 There are two offences contained in section 20 of the Theft Act 1968 which concern dealing with a valuable security. It is an offence contrary to section 20(1) to dishonestly destroy or deface a valuable security, and contrary to section 20(2) it is an offence to dishonestly procure the execution of a valuation security by deception. In both cases the offence has to be committed with a view to gain or with intent to cause loss. Commonly the offence has been used to prosecute cases of travellers cheque fraud, banking fraud and mortgage fraud.

16–063 A valuable security is defined in section 20(3) as:

"any document creating, transferring, surrendering or releasing any right to, in or over property, or authorising the payment of money or delivery of any property, or evidencing the creation, transfer, surrender or release of any such right, or the payment of money or delivery of any property, or the satisfaction of any obligation."

16–064 An irrevocable letter of credit is a valuable security—*Benstead and Taylor* (1982) 75 Cr.App.R. 276. Likewise, a CHAPS (Clearing House Automated Payment System) order—*King* [1992] 1 Q.B. 20; 93 Cr.App.R. 259—and all forms of electronic transfer—*Bolton* (1991) 94 Cr.App.R. 74; and *Crick, The Times*, August 18, 1993. The prosecution must be able to specify the valuable security which was procured. It is insufficient to allege that the valuable security was "a cheque or telegraphic transfer authority" without bringing evidence to prove that it was one or the other—*Mensah Lartey and Relevy* [1996] Crim.L.R. 203. In *Preddy*, Lord Goff (at p.492h) declined to speculate on whether the defendants could have been charged with dishonestly procuring the execution of a valuable security by deception since the issue did not arise for consideration in the appeal.

16–065 As with an offence of obtaining property by deception, the element of causation has to be established. Under section 20(2) the execution of the valuable security must be procured by the dishonest deception. The Court of Appeal held in *Beck* (1984) 80 Cr.App.R. 355, that the word "procure" has no special meaning for the purpose of section 20(2). It means simply to cause or bring about. "Execution" means doing something to the face of the document, such as signing it, or the due performance of all formalities to give it validity—*Kassim* [1992] 1 A.C. 9. The offences under sections 20(1) and (2) are each punishable by a maximum sentence of seven years' imprisonment and unlimited fine on indictment and six months' imprisonment and a fine of up to £5,000 if convicted summarily.

Theft Act 1978

16–066 There are two offences contained in the Theft Act 1978 which have marginal relevance in the investor context.

16–067 A person who by deception dishonestly obtains services from another contravenes section 1(1) of the Act. Deception has the same meaning as for section 15(1) of the Theft Act 1968 and once again the deception must be operative in relation to the services which are obtained. By section 1(2) a person is deemed to obtain services where the other is induced to confer a benefit by doing some act, or causing or permitting some act to be done, on the understanding that the benefit has been or will be paid for.

16–068 In *Shortland* [1995] Crim.L.R. 893 the Court of Appeal held that a benefit could include the provision of banking facilities but it had to be established evidentially that the defendant would have been required to pay for the banking services. Otherwise, no benefit had been established. A hire purchase agreement was held to be capable of amounting to a service in *Widdowson* (1986) 82 Cr.App.R. 314, but, according to the decision in *Halai* [1983] Crim.L.R. 624 a mortgage advance is not. There is some doubt as to whether *Halai* was correctly decided. In *Preddy* the House of Lords was invited to hear argument on the correctness of the decision in *Halai* but it declined to do so because the question did not arise for decision in the appeal. Lord Goff said (at p.495j) that he recognised that this left prosecuting authorities in a difficult position, and that the problem would best be solved by the enactment of a short Act of Parliament which declared that dishonestly inducing another to make a loan could constitute the offence of dishonestly obtaining services by deception.

16–069 The second relevant offence is created by section 2(1) of the Theft Act 1978 which provides that a person commits a criminal offence where, by deception, he:

"(a) dishonestly secures the remission of the whole or any part of any existing liability to make a payment, whether his own or another's; or
(b) with intent to make permanent default in whole or in part on any existing liability to make a payment, or with intent to let another do so, dishonestly induces the creditor or any person claiming on behalf of he creditor to wait for payment (whether or not the due date for payment is deferred) or to forgo payment; or
(c) dishonestly obtains any exemption from or abatement of liability to make a payment."

16–070 For purposes of this section "liability" means any legally enforceable liability. The Law Commission intended that section 2(1) should create three distinct offences but in practice there is considerable overlap. The decided cases emphasise that the defendant must intend to gain a permanent remission of liability before any one of three offences is committed. If convicted on indictment a person is liable to a maximum of five years' imprisonment and/or an unlimited fine if convicted of an offence under section 1 or 2 of the Theft Act 1978. The maximum penalty on summary conviction is six months' imprisonment and/or a fine of up to £2,000.

Forgery and Counterfeiting Act 1981

16–071 Like the offence of false accounting contrary to section 17 of the Theft Act 1968, offences of forgery are often committed during the course of an investor fraud. "The essence of forgery . . . is the making of a false document intending that it be used to induce a person to accept and act upon the message contained in it, as if it were contained in a genuine document" (Law Commission Report on Forgery and Counterfeit Currency (Law Com. No. 55) para. 22). The Forgery and Counterfeiting Act 1981 covers this area of the law. The purpose of Act is to preserve confidence in the authenticity of documents on which reliance might be placed.

16–072 By section 1, a person is guilty of forgery if he makes a false instrument, with the intention that he or another shall use it to induce somebody to accept it as genuine, and by reason of so accepting it to do or not to do some act to his own or any other person's prejudice. The meaning of an "instrument" is defined by section 8 (1) as any document, whether of a formal or informal character but the definition is artificially extended to include "electronic" documents which appear in or on a disc, tape, sound track or other device on or in which information is recorded or stored by mechanical, electronic or other means. It was held in *Re Levin*, March 1, 1996, unreported, that a magnetic disc fell within the term of "instrument" within the meaning of section 8(1)(d) and embraced the information stored as well as the medium on which it was stored. A disc could be falsified by entering false instructions on to the disc.

16–073 The House of Lords placed a gloss on the wording of section 8(1) in *Gold and Schifreen* [1988] A.C. 1063, when their Lordships held that the information must be preserved for an appreciable time with the object of subsequent retrieval or recovery. *Gold and Schifreen* was a case in which the defendants gained access to a Prestel computer data bank by a dishonest trick. They were charged with an offence under section 1 of the Forgery and Counterfeiting Act 1981 but it was held on appeal that the language of the Forgery and Counterfeiting Act 1981 did not cover the facts of the case. The facts of the case would now fall within the Computer Misuse Act 1990.

16–074 The meaning of "false" is defined in section 9 and follows the recommendations of the Law Commission. Essentially an instrument will be false if it tells a lie about itself—*Jeraj* [1994] Crim.L.R. 595. "Prejudice" is defined in section 10. The prejudice must be directed at someone other than the deceiver—*Utting* (1987) 86 Cr.App.R. 164. There is no direct authority on whether a person might be guilty of forgery by omission. The issue was left unresolved in *Hopkins and Collins* (1957) 41 Cr.App.R. 231.

16–075 There are four other offences created by the Forgery and Counterfeiting Act 1981.

Copying a false instrument is an offence under section 2 where the person makes a copy of an instrument which is, and which he knows or believes to be, a false instrument with the intention that he or another shall use it to induce somebody to accept it as a copy of a genuine instrument, and by reason of so accepting it to do or not to do some act to his own or any other person's prejudice.

16–076 Using a false instrument is an offence contrary to section 3 of the Act. Under the terms of this section it is an offence for a person to use an instrument which is, or which he knows or believes to be false, with the intention that he or another shall use it to induce somebody to accept it as genuine, and by reason of so accepting it to do or not to do some act to his own or any other person's prejudice.

16–077 Using a copy of a false instrument is an offence under section 4, and by section 5 it is an offence to have custody or control of certain false instruments and manufacture, custody or control of equipment or materials with which such instruments may be made.

16–078 Section 5(5) sets out the instruments to which the offences created in sections 1 to 4 apply. These include money orders, postal orders, share certificates, cheques, travellers cheques, cheque cards and credit cards. Custody means physical custody, whilst control imports some notion of the power to direct what shall be done with the things in question.

A person convicted on indictment of an offence contrary to section 5 of the Act will be liable to a maximum sentence of 10 years' imprisonment and an unlimited fine. A maximum sentence of six months' imprisonment and a fine of up to £5,000 can be imposed if convicted summarily.

Jurisdiction

16–079 There have been a number of problems concerning the jurisdiction of the court to try cases of theft and obtaining property by deception where either the subject-matter of the offence was located abroad or the conduct giving rise to the offence was committed abroad. A significant change in the law was made by sections 1 to 6 of the Criminal Justice Act 1993, which were enacted by Parliament to overcome the technical problems which had arisen. Under these sections, Theft Act offences (theft, obtaining property by deception, false accounting, procuring execution of a valuable security, etc.) and offences under the Forgery and Counterfeiting Act 1981 can be tried in the United Kingdom where any one of the constituent elements of the offence occurs in England and Wales. Section 3(1) states that a person may be guilty of an offence, whether or not he was in England and Wales at any material time, and whether or not he was a British citizen at any such time.

16–080 For an instructive consideration of the law as it applied before Part 1 of the Criminal Justice Act 1993, see the decision of the Court of Appeal in *Smith* [1996] Crim.L.R. 326. The old law will remain relevant until the new provisions are brought into effect. Surprisingly, this has yet to occur.

Conclusion

It is axiomatic that the interests sought to be protected by the Theft 16–081
Act 1968 and associated legislation are essentially property rights. The nature and scope of these property rights have been refined over many years by the civil courts and in some cases they are complex indeed. Traditionally the criminal courts have tried to shy away from introducing concepts of civil law into criminal cases in an effort, no doubt, to spare the jury from having to decide complex legal issues. With reference to the Theft Act 1968 this sentiment was powerfully expressed by Sachs L.J. in *Baxter* [1971] 2 All E.R. 359 in the following terms:

"... the Theft Act 1968 was designed to simplify the law—it uses words in their natural meaning and is to be construed thus to produce sensible results; when that Act is under examination this Court deprecates attempts to bring into too close consideration the finer distinctions in civil law as to the precise moment when contractual communications take effect or when property passes."

Similar sentiments were echoed in *Morris* [1984] A.C. 320, when Lord 16–082
Roskill expressed concern that it was:

"on any view wrong to introduce into this branch of the law [the meaning of appropriation] questions of whether particular contracts are void or voidable on the grounds of mistake or fraud or whether any mistake is sufficiently fundamental to vitiate a contract."

Yet, notwithstanding these judicial protestations, some interaction 16–083
between the civil and criminal law is inevitable. When the question whether property belongs to another is raised in the course of a criminal prosecution for theft, how else are the nature of relationships to be determined if not by reference to civil law? Consider, for example, the position in *Tillings and Tillings* [1985] Crim.L.R. 393. In that case the defendants were held to be not guilty of theft where they induced a patient in a residential home to alter her will in their favour because those disinherited had no interest in the property covered by the will until after the testator's death. The identification of a property right capable of appropriation was an essential ingredient which the prosecution had to prove before the defendants could be found guilty of theft. Clearly it is absurd that the criminal law should be impotent to embrace this dishonest behaviour, but it is wrong to blame the application of established civil law principles for this outcome. Parliamentary draughtsman should ensure that the provisions of the criminal law are sufficiently broad to ensure that crooks and swindlers do not escape from the consequences of dishonest behaviour by reliance on well established principles of civil law. Experience since the enactment of the Theft Act 1968 has demonstrated that the enactment of a general fraud

offence is needed to obviate these problems. It is unacceptable that prosecutions for fraudulent conduct should founder on an application of the niceties of civil law.

Chapter 17

Fraudulent Trading

Increasingly, the offence of fraudulent trading is being used to prosecute the perpetrators of investor fraud. Prosecution of offenders under other provisions of the criminal law is bedeviled with pitfalls in the context of investor fraud, and in recent years, in the absence of a generic "catch all" offence of fraud, prosecutors have striven to expand the width of fraudulent trading to encompass a multitude of investor sins. A typical case of fraudulent trading in this context might involve a financial intermediary who has supported his failing business by the retention of investor funds. It is difficult to convict the financial intermediary under the law of theft because the investor deposits his funds with the intermediary to be used in the course of his investment business. An offence of obtaining property by deception is also problematic because the financial intermediary invariably asserts that he intended to invest the funds at the time when they were paid to him by the investor. 17–001

With the benign approval of Parliament, fraudulent trading has been utilised by prosecutors to circumvent these difficulties, the offence having started life as a technical insolvency offence under earlier legislation. The principal restriction with the offence is that it can be committed only by a defendant who uses a company as a vehicle for his fraudulent activities. This restriction was considered by the Cork Committee which recommended the creation of a parallel offence of fraudulent trading by an individual (Cork Committee, Cmnd. 8558, at para. 1890). 17–002

The Legislative History

Fraudulent trading was introduced into company law by section 75 of the Companies Act 1928, only to be replaced by section 275 of the Companies Act in 1929. The provision survived the post-war reforms and during this period of its history it was to be found in section 332 of the Companies Act 1948. The 1948 legislation created a civil and criminal liability with the same constituent elements and some of the cases decided under section 332 continue to be relevant to an understanding of the contemporary law. Until 1981 the scope of the fraudulent trading was artificially restricted by the requirement that the fraudulent conduct had to occur in the course of winding up a limited liability company. This requirement was abolished by section 96 of the Companies Act 1981 and from this time onwards fraudulent trading has been detached from its roots as an insolvency offence. 17–003

CHAPTER 17: FRAUDULENT TRADING

17–004 The Companies Act 1985 recast the provision by separating civil and criminal liability for fraudulent trading. Today the civil provisions are contained in the Insolvency Act 1986 under which civil liability can accrue under two heads of fraudulent trading, either as fraudulent trading contrary to section 213 or wrongful trading contrary to section 214. These civil provisions are discussed in Chapters 26 and 30 respectively. The criminal offence is contained in section 458 of the Companies Act 1985 which forms a separate part of the Act, Part XVI, under the rubric "fraudulent trading by a company". Following conviction on indictment the offence is punishable by a maximum period of seven years' imprisonment plus an unlimited fine. On summary conviction the maximum period of imprisonment is six months' imprisonment and a fine of the statutory maximum, presently £5,000.

The Criminal Offence

17–005 Section 458 of the Companies Act 1985 provides as follows:

"If any business of a company is carried on with intent to defraud creditors of the company or creditors of any other person, or for any fraudulent purpose, every person who was knowingly a party to the carrying on of the business in that manner is liable to imprisonment or a fine or both. This applies whether or not the company has been, or is in the course of being, wound up."

17–006 To establish an offence of fraudulent trading it must be proven that: (1) there was conduct which formed part of the carrying on of the business of the company; (2) the defendant played an active role in this conduct; (3) the defendant intended to defraud the creditors of the company or the creditors of some other person, or alternatively intended some fraudulent purpose; and (4) the defendant acted dishonestly. In this context an intention to defraud may be inferred from circumstances which are considered to be dishonest. In *R. v. Grantham* [1984] 1 Q.B. 647; 79 Cr.App.R. 86, the Court of Appeal approved the terms of the trial judge's direction to the jury that if a trader obtained or helped to obtain credit when he knew there was no good reason for thinking funds would become available to repay the debt when it became due or shortly thereafter, a jury could properly conclude that this conduct was dishonest and the defendant intended to defraud.

If any Business of a Company is Carried On

17–007 The Courts have tended to give a generous construction to the statutory requirement that the conduct must form part of the carrying on of the business of the company. In *Re Gerald Cooper Chemical Limited*

[1978] Ch. 262; [1978] 2 All E.R. 49, a court held that a single transaction was capable of amounting to the carrying on of a business with intent to defraud creditors. What is more, the conduct need not relate to the carrying on of the company's trade. In *Re Sarflax* [1979] 1 All E.R. 529, a company had gone into liquidation and its assets were used to discharge its business liabilities. Oliver J. held that the use of proceeds from the sale of the company's assets to discharge business liabilities could constitute the carrying on of a business. In the context of investor fraud, however, the liberality of this approach may be misleading since in practical terms proof of an isolated dishonest act will be unlikely to satisfy the threshold requirement that the business of the company has been carried on with intent to defraud.

As Oliver J. said in *Re Murray Watson*, unreported, April 6, 1977, the section was: "aimed at the carrying on of a business . . . and not at the execution of individual transactions in the course of carrying on the business." 17–008

The director of a financial services company may make false representations about the security of an investment or its rate of return. This, to use Oliver J.'s language, may make him a "fraudulent rascal", but whilst it is true that the director carries on a particular business transaction in a fraudulent manner, it does not necessarily follow that the director carries on the company's business for a fraudulent purpose. 17–009

In this type of case a judge must give a clear direction to the jury on the meaning of "carrying on the business of the company" and counsel should be invited to address him on the legal issues before he sums up—*Miles* [1992] Crim.L.R. 657; [1992] T.L.R. 195. What amounts to "carrying on the business of the company" will vary depending on the circumstances of each case. To take but one example, a distinction can be drawn between an enterprise conceived in fraud and the bona fide trading company which runs into difficulties. The financial intermediary who sells bogus shares on behalf of a company acquired for the purpose of selling bogus shares is much more obviously carrying on the business of the company with intent to defraud than the registered market maker who sells stock which he does not hold on an isolated occasion. 17–010

A Party to the Carrying On of a Business

In order to be guilty of an offence of fraudulent trading the prosecution has to prove not just that a person has taken an active step in furthering the activity of the business but also that he was a party to the carrying on of the business in a managerial or supervisory sense. In *Re Maidstone Building Provisions Ltd* [1971] 1 W.L.R. 1085, in the context of a civil case for fraudulent trading, Pennycuick V.-C. rejected an attempt to attach liability to the company secretary on the grounds that, knowing the company was insolvent, he failed to advise the directors that the company should cease trading. Participation involves taking 17–011

CHAPTER 17: FRAUDULENT TRADING

some step of a positive nature. Inertia or omission is not enough. What is more, the participating step must be taken by a person who exercised a controlling or managerial function. A salesman employed by a company who sells worthless shares in a non-existent enterprise participates in the business of the company but he is not guilty of fraudulent trading if he does not exercise a controlling or managerial function over the business.

17-012 A person will not be a party to the carrying on of a business if he participates in the business on the instructions of others and a judge should direct a jury to this effect—*Miles, supra*. Of course this is not to say that the ordinary principles of secondary liability will not apply in a fraudulent trading case. If a salesman of bogus shares knows that the controllers of the business are defrauding its creditors, the salesman will assist and encourage the fraudulent trading and his position is no different to the accomplice who keeps a look out whilst the burglar uses a jemmy to open the door. Just as the look out is guilty of burglary as an aider and abetter, so the salesman is guilty of fraudulent trading. The salesman is guilty of fraudulent trading not as a principal offender but as an aider and abetter, a secondary party. Support for this view may be derived from a consideration of the decision in *Re Gerald Cooper Chemical Limited* [1978] Ch. 262; [1978] 1 All E.R. 49, where in a civil case the court held that a creditor was a party to the carrying on of a business where he accepted money in fraudulent preference to other creditors. There was no suggestion that the creditor was involved in the running or management of the company.

With Intent to Defraud Creditors . . . or for any Fraudulent Purpose

17-013 In *R. v. Inman* [1967] 1 Q.B. 140, the Court of Appeal held that section 332 of the Companies Act 1948 encompassed two different offences, namely fraudulent trading with intent to defraud creditors (either the company's or those of some other person) and fraudulent trading for the purpose of achieving certain objectives.

Intent to Defraud

17-014 The phrase "with intent to defraud" is used to denote a state of mind whereby a person dishonestly prejudices or takes the risk of prejudicing another's right, knowing that he has no right to do so. In the context of fraudulent trading, a good working definition of the phrase was put forward by Maugham J. in *Re William C Leitch Bros Ltd* [1932] 2 Ch. 71, which forms the basis of its meaning in contemporary times:

> "With regard to the meaning of the phrase 'carrying on business with intent to defraud creditors', if a company continues to carry on

business and to incur debts at a time when there is to the knowledge of the directors no reasonable prospect of the creditors ever receiving payment of those debts it is, in general, a proper inference that the company is carrying on business with intent to defraud."

In the leading House of Lords case of *Welham v. D.P.P.* [1961] A.C. 103, it was held that "to defraud" was "to act to the prejudice of another's right", which would include carrying on business (to the potential prejudice of creditors) when the defendant knew there was a risk that the company would not be able to meet its debts as they fell due. The following passage, approved by the Court of Appeal in *Grantham* (1984) 79 Cr.App.R. 86, reflects the standard direction which is given to a jury in a case involving fraudulent trading with intent to defraud creditors: 17–015

"Some fraudulent traders intend from the outset never to pay or never to pay more than a fraction of the debt. If that is true in your view in this case then the intent to defraud would be made out but a trader can intend to defraud if he obtains credit when there is a substantial risk of the creditor not getting his money or not getting the whole of his money and the defendant knows that is the position and knows he is stepping beyond the bounds of what ordinary decent people engaged in business would regard as honest."

The potential liability for company receivers where they continue to operate parts of the business is relieved in the normal case by the requirement to prove an intention to defraud creditors. For example, in *Brown v. City of London Corporation* [1996] 22 E.G. 118, the court held that there was no fraudulent trading by receivers when they decided to postpone sale of various properties during the course of business. 17–016

Creditors

Section 458 envisages that fraudulent trading will be directed to the prejudice of the company's creditors or creditors of any other person. Who are creditors for the purposes of this section? Notwithstanding the use of the plural, the term includes the defrauding of a single creditor— *Re Gerald Cooper Chemical Limited* [1978] Ch. 262; [1978] 2 All E.R. 49. It appears that the term includes a potential creditor where the liability will come into existence in the future. 17–017

In *Seillon* [1982] Crim.L.R. 679 the Court of Appeal held that a reference to creditors in an indictment alleging conspiracy to defraud would include potential creditors because "if the law were otherwise it would mean that nobody could be found guilty of conspiracy to defraud his creditors until the creditor had obtained judgment against him." 17–018

It was thought that the same reasoning would apply to section 458, particularly after the legislative change in 1981 when the criminal offence was detached from the insolvency section of the Companies Act. 17–019

CHAPTER 17: FRAUDULENT TRADING

This has recently been confirmed by the Court of Appeal in *Smith*, [1996] Crim.L.R. 329. The word "creditor" in its ordinary meaning denoted one to whom money was owed; whether that debt could found an action in debt was immaterial. The court observed that section 458 was a continuing offence and future as well as present creditors might be prejudiced by fraudulent trading.

For any Fraudulent Purpose

17–020 If a prosecution is brought for fraudulent trading in a case where investors have suffered losses, the allegation is likely to be laid under the second limb of fraudulent trading, namely fraudulent trading for the purpose of achieving certain objectives. Customers of financial services companies are rarely creditors of the company, and for this reason an allegation of fraudulent trading has to be couched in different terms.

17–021 *Kemp* (1988) 87 Cr.App.R. 95 is the seminal case on point, where the Court of Appeal upheld a conviction for fraudulent trading after the appellant had dishonestly supplied between 20 and 30 customers with carbon paper which the customers had not ordered but had paid for. The allegation of fraudulent trading did not contain any reference to creditors but instead asserted that the appellant had been a party to carrying on the business of a named company trading for a fraudulent purpose, namely the obtaining of property by deception. The court concluded that the mischief of section 458 was directed at fraudulent trading and not fraudulent trading just in so far as it affects creditors. The Court of Appeal certified that a point of general public importance had arisen but leave to appeal to the House of Lords was refused. A similar conclusion was reached in *Phillipou* (1989) 89 Cr.App.R. 290.

Chapter 18

Conspiracy

Introduction

18–001 Section 1 of the Criminal Law Act 1977 replaced most offences of common law conspiracy with a statutory offence. Only conspiracy to defraud, conspiracy to cheat and conspiracy to do acts tending to corrupt public morals or outrage public decency survived as common law offences. Where serious cases of investor fraud are discovered, prosecuting authorities often bring charges of conspiracy, and therefore to this extent the use of these offences is relevant to any consideration of investor protection. The general principles concerning conspiracy are set out fully in all the standard criminal textbooks and it is beyond the scope of this chapter to offer more than a cursory summary of the essential principles.

Statutory Conspiracy

18–002 Section 1(1) of the Criminal Law Act 1977 sets out the statutory offence of conspiracy:

"Subject to the following provisions of this Part of this Act, if a person agrees with any other person or persons that a course of conduct shall be pursued which, if the agreement is carried out in accordance with their intentions, either

(a) will necessarily amount to or involve the commission of any offence or offences by one or more of the parties to the agreement, or

(b) would do so but for the existence of facts which render the commission of the offence or any of the offences impossible,

he is guilty of conspiracy to commit the offence or offences in question."

18–003 The maximum penalty on conviction for conspiracy to commit an indictable offence is the same as the maximum sentence that could be imposed for the indictable offence itself.

CHAPTER 18: CONSPIRACY

18–004 A conspiracy requires that two or more persons enter into an agreement which will necessarily amount to or involve the commission of a criminal offence or would do so but for the existence of facts which render the commission of the offence impossible. It is what is agreed to be done not what is actually done which is important in a charge of conspiracy. In *R. v. Aspinall* (1876) 2 Q.B.D. 731 Brett J.:

> "The crime of conspiracy is completely committed the moment two or more have agreed that they will do, at once or at some future time, certain things. It is not necessary in order to complete the offence that any other thing should be done beyond the agreement. The conspirators may repent and stop, or may have no opportunity, or may be prevented, or may fail. Nevertheless the crime is complete: it was completed when they agreed."

18–005 A husband and wife cannot conspire together, neither can the sole director of a company conspire with his company although a company is capable of entering into a conspiracy. It is not necessary that a conspirator be a party throughout the duration of the agreement. It must be shown, however, that all the conspirators joined together in a single agreement. In *R. v. Griffiths* (1965) 49 Cr.App.R. 279, Paull J. said:

> ". . . in law all must join in the one agreement, each with the others, in order to constitute one conspiracy. They may join at various times, each attaching himself to that agreement; any one of them may not know all the other parties, but only that there are other parties; any one of them may not know the full extent of the scheme to which he attaches himself; but what each must know is that there is coming into existence, or is in existence, a scheme which goes beyond the illegal act which he agrees to do."

18–006 The mental element of conspiracy requires proof of an intention to be a party to an agreement to do an unlawful act. The leading case is *R. v. Anderson* [1986] 1 A.C. 27, H.L. There are situations where the mental element to commit the substantive offence would not be sufficient to prove a conspiracy to commit that offence. The usual text book example is the offence of murder where an intent to cause grievous bodily harm would be sufficient to prove the substantive offence but would not be sufficient to prove a charge of conspiracy to murder.

18–007 The advantage of charging conspiracy is that it often allows the prosecution to place before a court a course of criminal conduct whereas substantive offences may show only a small aspect of the behaviour complained of.

18–008 Where the course of conduct complained of reveals more than one conspiracy these must not be charged as one "rolled-up" count.

Conspiracy to Defraud

When the Criminal Law Act 1977 replaced offences of common law conspiracy with a statutory offence, conspiracy to defraud was retained as a common law offence. The law was considerably complicated by the decision of the House of Lords in *R. v. Ayres* [1984] A.C. 447, where it was held that a charge of conspiracy to defraud contrary to common law was inappropriate if the evidence also supported the commission of a conspiracy to commit a substantive criminal offence. This decision severely dented the range of offences available to the prosecuting authorities. Prosecutors did not like to prosecute for statutory conspiracy because the penalties which could be imposed for conspiracy were no greater than those which could be imposed for the substantive offence. The decision in *Ayres* was overturned by Parliament in section 12 of the Criminal Justice Act 1987 and today, once again, prosecutions for conspiracy to defraud are commonly brought in investor fraud cases. 18–009

Section 12 (1) Criminal Justice Act 1987 provides that: 18–010

"If

(a) a person agrees with any other person or persons that a course of conduct shall be pursued; and

(b) that course of conduct will necessarily amount to or involve the commission of any offence or offences by one or more of the parties to the agreement if the agreement is carried out in accordance with their intentions,

the fact that it will do so shall not preclude a charge of conspiracy to defraud being brought against any of them in respect of the agreement."

Section 12 (3) limits the penalty for a person guilty of conspiracy to defraud to 10 years' imprisonment and/or a fine.

Conspiracy to defraud is indictable only. Guidance on the drafting of an indictment alleging conspiracy to defraud was given by the Court of Appeal in the case of *R. v. Landy* (1981) 72 Cr.App.R. 237, C.A. The need to particularise the indictment to enable the defence and the court to know the nature of the prosecution's case was emphasised. The Court of Appeal referred to *Landy* in *R. v. Cohen* (1992) 142 N.L.J. 1267, when it was said that the particulars "must not be more than is necessary having regard to the limitations imposed by a jury trial." 18–011

The usual starting point when considering what amounts to a conspiracy to defraud is the case of *Scott v. Metropolitan Police Commissioner* [1975] A.C. 819; [1974] 3 All E.R. 1032: 18–012

"An agreement by two or more dishonesty to deprive a person of something which is his or to which he is or would be or might be entitled and an agreement by two or more dishonesty to injure some proprietary right of his, suffices to constitute the offence of conspiracy to defraud."

18–013 This definition cannot be treated as exhaustive but it is undoubtedly authoritative, having been accepted by the Law Commission in its recent consideration of conspiracy to defraud (Law Com. 228).

18–014 The meaning of defraud was considered by the Court of Appeal in *R. v. Sinclair* (1968) 52 Cr.App.R. 618 at 621, where it was said that to prove fraud it had to be established that the conduct was deliberately dishonest. It is fraud if it is proved that there was the taking of a risk which there was no right to take which would cause detriment or prejudice to another.

Conspiracy to Defraud a Regulatory Body

18–015 In most cases of investor fraud there will be an obvious and identifiable economic loss but this does not always follow. Situations can be envisaged where there is no economic loss but there is an obvious intention to defraud. One such example is where the allegation relates to the activities of a financial adviser or company offering financial advice and the fraudulent behaviour complained of amounts to the deception of a regulatory body in order to ensure that the regulatory body allows the financial adviser to continue trading.

18–016 The leading case on the need to prove economic loss is *Welham v. D.P.P* [1961] A.C. 103, where the House of Lords was concerned with the meaning of "intent to defraud" in the Forgery Act 1913. The question arose whether an intent to defraud was confined to an intent to cause or take the risk of causing pecuniary loss to another. The House of Lords found that an intent to cause pecuniary loss was not necessary to prove an intent to defraud. The fraud consisted of taking a risk of injuring another's right which the accused knows he has no right to take. Lord Radcliffe set out the position in his speech at p.124:

> "There is nothing in any of this that suggests that to defraud is in ordinary speech confined to the idea of depriving a man by deceit of some economic advantage or inflicting upon him some economic loss. Has the law ever so confined it? In my opinion, there is no warrant for saying that it has. What it has looked for in considering the effect of cheating upon another and in so defining the criminal intent is the prejudice of that person: what Blackstone (4 Comm. 245) called 'to the prejudice of another's right'."

18–017 In *Scott v. Metropolitan Police Commissioner* [1975] A.C. 819, the House of Lords considered the question of whether fraud necessarily required deceit, and found unanimously that it did not. Lord Diplock suggested (erroneously, it is thought) that if the victim of the fraud was an individual then it was necessary that the fraudster intended to cause that person economic loss. Lord Diplock's view was not accepted by the other judges in *Scott* nor has it been followed in subsequent cases. Lord Denning, giving his judgment in *Scott*, explained his approach in the following terms:

> "To defraud, they say involves economic loss. I cannot agree with them on this. If a drug addict forges a doctor's prescription so as to enable him to get drugs from a chemist, he has, I should have thought, an intent to defraud, even though he intends to pay the chemist the full price and no one is a penny the worse off."

Lord Denning's approach was supported by the Court of Appeal in *R. v. Allsop* (1976) 64 Cr.App.R. 29, which was approved by the Privy Council in *Wai Yu-Tsang v. R.* [1992] 1 A.C. 269, P.C., and more recently in *Adams v. R.* [1995] 1 W.L.R. 52, P.C. In *Adams* the Privy Council confirmed that cases of conspiracy to defraud are not confined to cases of intention to cause economic loss. The prosecution must prove that the victim had a right which was capable of being prejudiced either by actual loss or by being put at risk. The Privy Council went on to say that if a person was entitled to have information disclosed to him or that a person was under a duty to disclose information and that information was withheld, then the person who should have disclosed the information could be guilty of fraud. In practice this would apply in the situation where a person was under a duty to disclose information to a regulatory body—for example to demonstrate compliance with solvency requirements to be allowed to continue trading—and the information disclosed was false or misleading. 18–018

The deception of a public body was also considered in *R. v. Moses and Ansbro* [1991] Crim.L.R. 617 C.A., where the defendants had been charged with conspiracy to defraud by facilitating applications by immigrants to get work permits. It was held that where the intended victim of a conspiracy to defraud was a person performing public duties, it was sufficient if the purpose was to cause him to contravene that duty, and the intended means of achieving it was dishonest. It was not necessary that the purpose involved causing economic loss to anyone. 18–019

"Fraudulently" or "Dishonestly"

It is clear from the line of authorities from *Welham* onwards that the appellate courts have not considered that the addition of the word "dishonesty" adds anything to the meaning of intention to defraud. It is, however, conventional for judges when summing up to add the word "dishonesty" to their definition of "with intent to defraud" and "fraudulently." See in this context the direction given by Henry J. to the jury in *R. v. Saunders, The Independant,* May 17, 1991. 18–020

CHAPTER 18: CONSPIRACY

Jurisdiction

18–021 In these days of electronic communication and global markets, conspiracy to defraud like other commercial crimes, is increasingly likely to have a significant foreign element. The position at common law was that conspiracies formulated abroad but intended to result in the commission of a criminal offence in England or Wales were triable by the English courts. The increasingly international face of crime has been recognised by Parliament in Part I of the Criminal Justice Act 1993 which widens the jurisdiction of the English courts, by giving them jurisdiction to try certain cases of fraud and related offences where there is a significant foreign element. This has been effected by designating conspiracy to defraud as a Group B offence by virtue of section 1(3) of the Act. The Act has extended the jurisdiction of the English courts to cases where there is an agreement made abroad amounting to a conspiracy to defraud where the substantive fraud is intended to be effected in England. Jurisdiction has also been extended over conspiracy to defraud where the fraud is intended to take place in a foreign jurisdiction—see section 5(3). Section 6 requires that a person may only be convicted in this country by virtue of the provisions of section 5 if the objective of the offence represents an offence in the territory where it is intended to take place.

Reform of the Law of Conspiracy to Defraud

18–022 The Law Commission report on Conspiracy to Defraud (Law Com. No. 228) recommends that conspiracy to defraud should be retained for the time being. The Law Commission's recommendation to retain conspiracy to defraud appears to be based on the need for an offence which enables the prosecution to present the "overall criminality" and the recognition that its abolition might leave large areas of criminal activity which may not be covered by any other existing substantive offence. The Commission also sees the retention of conspiracy to defraud as "a means of simplifying and shortening fraud trials and enabling individual defendants to be convicted of an offence appropriate to their conduct." The subject will, no doubt, be reviewed again during the course of the Law Commission's study of offences involving dishonesty.

Chapter 19

Companies Act Offences

The directors control the company and its dealings with third parties, and they are responsible for proper management of the company's assets. Investor confidence depends on the effective regulation of directors' conduct in the management of companies, particularly with regard to their personal interests *vis-à-vis* the company. As is discussed in Chapter 26, the courts recognise that breach of a director's fiduciary duty to deal with the company in good faith gives rise to a cause of action against the director in civil law. Parliament has sought to set additional standards of good conduct and breach of these standards will expose a director to criminal as well as civil sanctions. Many requirements, however, are rather technical and there is considerable scope to undermine the Parliamentary intention by paying lip-service to the statutory provisions.

19–001

Restrictions on Directors Taking Financial Advantage

In the interests of investor protection it is critical to ensure that the directors of the company do not take an unfair financial advantage of their position within the company. Sections 311 to 322 of the Companies Act 1985 contain various provisions designed to prevent directors of a company from taking financial advantage of their position within the company which include provisions relating to directors' remuneration and the duty to disclose any interest, direct or indirect, in a contract with his company. The penalties for non-compliance are financial.

19–002

Interest in Contracts

By section 317(1) of the Companies Act 1985 a duty is imposed on a director of a company who is in any way, whether directly or indirectly, interested in a contract or a proposed contract to declare the nature of his interest at a meeting of the directors of the company. By section 317(7) a director who fails to comply with this section is liable to a fine. The requirement to make disclosure to a meeting of the directors has been construed strictly by the courts. In *Guinness plc v. Saunders* [1988] 2 All E.R. 940, the Court of Appeal held that the requirement could not be satisfied by a disclosure to a sub-committee of the directors. Although the reasoning of the Court of Appeal was rejected by the House of Lords

19–003

on appeal, the Court of Appeal determination on this point continues to be accepted as good law.

19–004   In *Runciman v. Walter Runciman plc* [1992] B.C.L.C. 1084, Simon Brown J. held that the obligation to make disclosure applied to a director's contract of service although the judge did express some doubt in that case as to whether section 317 extended to a variation concerning salary or some other term of employment. Certainly the stringency, and perhaps the absurdity, of the requirement was demonstrated more recently in *Re Neptune (Vehicle Washing Equipment) Ltd* [1995] T.L.R. 132, where a court held that it was the duty of a sole director no less than a co-director to comply with the obligations imposed by the statutory provision. Lightman J. said that when holding the meeting on his own, the director had still to make the declaration to himself and have the statutory pause for thought. Although the declaration need not be read out loud, the judge advised that it should be recorded in the minutes because a court might find it hard to accept that the declaration had been made if it was not so recorded. Who said the payment of lip-service was not enough!

Share Dealings by Directors and their Families

19–005   Share dealings by directors and those connected with them in companies in which the director may be thought to have some inside knowledge or unfair advantage over the investor are strictly regulated by the Companies Act. The regulation by the Companies Act is supplemented and strengthened by legislation specifically designed to counteract market manipulation by those who may be thought to be "in the know" and thus have an unfair advantage. These provisions are discussed in Chapter 20. The obligations of a company director and the obligations of a board of directors are discussed in Chapter 26.

Prohibition on Directors Dealing in Share Options

19–006   Section 323(1) renders it an offence for the director (including a shadow director) of a company to deal in share options in the company of which he is a director, or in any subsidiary company, holding company or any subsidiary company of its holding company where the shares are listed (whether in United Kingdom or abroad). This prohibition is absolute, the prosecution do not have to prove that the defendant had any inside knowledge of any likely future price movements. The prohibition does not apply to the purchase of a right to subscribe in shares or debentures of the company (s.323(5)).

19–007   This prohibition extends to the spouse and children aged under 18 of directors who are not themselves directors of the relevant companies (s.327). It is a defence for a person charged under section 327 to prove that he had no reason to know of their spouse's or parent's status as directors of the company in question.

The maximum sentence for contravention of section 323(1) is two years' imprisonment and/or an unlimited fine if convicted on indictment and six months' imprisonment and/or a fine of the statutory maximum (£5,000) if convicted summarily. **19–008**

Director Failing to Notify Interest in Company's Shares or Making False Statement in Purported Notification

Section 324 imposes a duty on a director (including a shadow director) to disclose shareholdings in his own company to that company in writing. Failure to disclose such a shareholding is rendered an offence by section 324(7)(a). It is also an offence for a director to make what he purports to be disclosure to the company knowing the disclosure to be false or recklessly making a statement which is false (s.324(7)(b)). **19–009**

Section 328 extends the obligations imposed under section 324 to the spouse and children under the age of 18 of the director who are not themselves directors of the company. Failure to notify the company of any interests held by the family of a director is an offence with the same punishment as for contravention of section 324 (s.328(6)). **19–010**

Register of Directors' Interests

A company is under an obligation to keep a register of directors' interests for the purposes of section 324 which may be inspected by anyone on payment of a fee. The company is also under a duty to provide a copy of the register if requested to do so, again on payment of a fee (s.325 and Part IV of Sched. 13). If default is made in complying with the requirements of section 325 and Part IV of Schedule 13 those in default may be punished by the imposition of a fine. Continued contravention may lead to the imposition of a daily default fine (s.326 (2)–(5)). **19–011**

Loans to Directors

Sections 330 to 347 of the Companies Act 1985 set out restrictions on a company's power to make loans (including quasi-loans, guarantees and other forms of credit transactions) to directors and persons connected with them. **19–012**

The prohibitions on the making of loans to directors and persons connected with them are set out in section 330 of the Companies Act 1985. The prohibitions apply to certain identified transactions, namely, loans (s.330 (2)(a)), quasi-loans (s.330(3)(a) and (b)), credit transactions (s.330(4)(a)), guarantees for the provision of security in connection with loans, quasi-loans and credit transactions (s.330(2)(b), 330(3)(c), 330(4)(b)), arrangements for the assignment to the company or the assumption by the company of any rights, obligations or liabilities under **19–013** a prohibited transaction (s.330(6)) and back-to-back arrangements where a person enters into an arrangement which would have been prohibited by section 330 if it had been entered into by the company, and that person obtains some benefit from the company or from another company in the same group (s.330(7)(a) and (b)). Breaches of the section 330 prohibitions are rendered offences by section 342.

19–014 Those who may commit a criminal offence in breach of section 330 are (1) a director of a relevant company who authorises or permits the company to enter into a prohibited transaction knowing or with reasonable cause to believe that the company was thereby contravening the provisions set out in section 330; (2) the relevant company, though the company has a defence if it's directors did not know the relevant circumstances at the time it entered into the transaction; and (3) a person who procures the relevant company to enter into a prohibited transaction knowing or having reasonable cause to believe that the transaction is prohibited. The offence is punishable by a maximum sentence of two years' imprisonment and/or an unlimited fine if convicted on indictment and six months' imprisonment and/or a fine of the statutory maximum (£5,000) if convicted summarily. The offence may also be committed by a "shadow director" who is deemed to be treated as a director by section 330 (5).

19–015 Connected persons are defined by section 346 and include a director's spouse, a director's child under the age of 18 (including a step child) but not a child over the age of 18, a body corporate with which the director is associated, a person acting in his capacity as trustee of any trust the beneficiaries of which include the director or persons connected to him, a person acting in his capacity as partner of the director or of any person connected with the director and any Scottish firm with which the director is connected.

19–016 Sections 332 to 338 create eight exceptions to the section 330 prohibition. Broadly these exceptions are transactions within a group of companies (ss.333 and 336), transactions in the ordinary course of business (ss.335(2), 337 and 338), and other transactions permitted up to certain specified limits (ss.332, 334 and 335(1)).

Allotment of Shares

19–017 The rules governing the allotment of shares and debentures are set out in Part IV of the Companies Act 1985. Part IV of the 1985 Act has created a number of criminal offences in support of these regulatory provisions.

Prohibition on Shares being Allocated at a Discount

19–048 Sections 99 to 107 of the Companies Act 1985 regulate the amount to be paid for shares and the means of payment. Contravention of any of the provisions of sections 99 to 104 and 106 renders the company or any defaulting officer liable to a fine.

Section 104 relates to the transfer to a public company of non-cash **19–019** assets in the initial period after its formation. A new public company is prohibited from making certain agreements with certain persons unless a stipulated procedure is followed. One of the requirements of the stipulated procedure is that of an independent valuer making a report to the company. It is an offence contrary to section 110(2) to knowingly or recklessly make to the valuer an oral or written statement which is misleading false or deceptive in a material particular and which conveys (or purports to convey) any information or explanation which he requires or is entitled to require.

Other Offences in Part IV of the Companies Act 1985

There are over 60 offences contained in the Companies Act 1985 **19–020** which are directed towards the protection of the investor. The list of offences with maximum punishments and mode of trial is set out in Schedule 24 to the Act as amended. Schedule 24 is reproduced as Appendix 6.

Who May Commit Criminal Offences Under the Companies Act

Offences in the Companies Acts may be committed by the company, a **19–021** company officer and on occasions by other persons such as the company auditors. It is necessary to look at the wording of each offence to see who may be liable. Section 733(2) of the Companies Act specifies certain offences (ss.210, 216(3), 394A(1) and ss. 447-451) for which the company and the director, manager, secretary or other similar officer of the body corporate or any other person who was purporting to act in such a capacity may incur criminal liability. In addition to these specifically mentioned sections, joint liability of the company and individuals is imposed under the Act by the inclusion in specific offences of the words "and every officer in default." Criminal proceedings may be brought against unincorporated bodies (s.734) in respect of offences alleged under sections 389A, 394A(1) and sections 447-451.

The Company

It is well-established in criminal law that a company may be directly **19–022** liable for the commission of a criminal offence, liability being attached by the imputation of wrongdoing on the part of the senior officers of the company. The leading case is *Tesco v. Nattrass* [1971] 2 W.L.R. 1166; [1972] A.C. 153, where the House of Lords held that corporate liability was derived from a concept of the company in which there existed a nerve-centre of command represented by the board of directors, the company secretary and perhaps the managing director. Only the wrong-doing of those who belonged to the nerve centre can be imputed to the company.

The Company Officers

19–023 The liability of company officers was considered in the case of *Boal* (1992) 95 Cr.App.R. 272, where the statutory phrase "any director, manager, secretary or other similar officer of the body corporate" fell to be construed. Simon Brown J. said that the expression was intended to fix with criminal liability "only those who are in a position of real authority, the decision makers within the company who have both the power and responsibility to decide corporate policy and strategy."

Consent to Prosecute

19–024 Certain offences under the Companies Act 1985 (ss.210, 324, 329, 447–451 and 455) may be prosecuted only with the consent of the Secretary of State, the Director of Public Prosecutions or the Industrial Insurance Commissioner (s.732).

Accounting Records

19–025 The content, accuracy and availability of company accounting records are of paramount importance to investors and are regulated by the provisions of the Companies Act. Failure to meet these requirements gives rise to criminal sanctions. Indeed, by far the greatest number of prosecutions brought by the Department of Trade and Industry under its Companies Acts powers concerned offences relating to company accounts and annual returns. In 1993-1994 the DTI launched 4,031 prosecutions for failure to deliver company accounts to Companies House and 2,212 prosecutions for failure to deliver annual returns. Failure to keep or preserve accounting records was the next most frequently charged offence, 118 prosecutions having been brought in 1993–1994. To put these figures into some context, during the same period the DTI brought 68 charges of fraudulent trading and 13 further charges under other provisions of the Companies Act 1985. (These figures taken from Tables D2 and D3 of the DTI's report on Companies for 1993-94.)

Duty to Keep Accounting Records

19–026 Pursuant to section 221 of the Companies Act 1985 every company, whatever its size, is required to keep accounting records which are sufficiently detailed to disclose with reasonable accuracy the financial position of the company and to enable the directors to ensure that any balance sheet or profit and loss accounts are correctly prepared. Failure to keep such accounting records in accordance with section 221 is rendered an offence by section 221(5) and the offence will be committed by every officer of the company who is in default. The penalty following conviction on indictment is two years' imprisonment and/or an unlimited fine. If convicted summarily the penalty is six months' imprisonment and/or a fine of the statutory maximum (£5,000). It is a defence to this offence to show that the officer of the company acted honestly and that the default was excusable in the circumstances. The burden of proving the statutory defence rests on the company officer and it must be established on the balance of probabilities.

Section 222 of the Companies Act 1985 provides that the accounting records must be kept at the registered office of the company or such other place as the directors think fit. The accounting records must be open to inspection at all times by the company's officers. Again it is a defence to show on the balance of probabilities that the company officer acted honestly and that the default was excusable in the circumstances. By section 222(5) company accounts must be preserved for at least three years for a private company and six years for a public limited company. An officer of the company is guilty of an offence if he fails to take all reasonable steps to secure compliance by the company or if he intentionally causes any default by the company. Contravention is visited by the same penalties which may be imposed for an offence contrary to section 221. **19–027**

Failure to Deliver Annual Accounts

Under section 242(1) of the Companies Act 1985 company accounts, a copy of the director's report and a copy of the auditor's report must be delivered annually to Companies House. Failure to deliver company documents amounts to a criminal offence under section 242 (2) which is committed by every person who was a director of the company immediately before the end of the period allowed for the delivery of the accounts. The penalty is a fine and if the contravention continues a daily default fine can be imposed. Under section 242(4) it is a defence for the director to prove that he took all reasonable steps for securing that the requirements would be satisfied. It is not a defence to show that company accounts had not been prepared. **19–028**

Failure to Deliver an Annual Return

By section 363(1) every company is under a duty to deliver an annual return to the Registrar of Companies at Companies House. Failure to deliver the annual return within the specified period (28 days from the company's return date as statutorily defined) renders the company guilty of an offence and liable to a fine and in the case of continuing **19–029** contravention a daily default fine. Where a company is guilty of the offence, under section 363(4) every director or company secretary is also guilty unless he can show that he took all reasonable steps to avoid the commission or continuation of the offence.

Rights of Auditors

19–030 Every company is under a duty to appoint an auditor or auditors in accordance with section 384(1) of the Companies Act 1985. As from April 1, 1990 the company auditors have a right of access at all times to the company's accounting records and they are entitled to require from the company's officers such information and explanations as they think necessary for the performance of their duties as auditors. These provisions, brought into law by section 389A of the Companies Act 1985, are important in the context of investor protection because they confer on the company auditor an opportunity to act in a pro-active way if fraudulent conduct is suspected.

19–031 Company auditors need not be confined to the information with which they have been supplied by dishonest directors. It is an offence under section 389A(2) for a company officer to make false, misleading or deceptive statements to company auditors. Contravention of this section exposes a company officer to the same penalties as commission of an offence under section 221 or 222. Similar provisions apply to the supply of information concerning subsidiaries or parent companies of the company being audited.

Company Investigations

19–032 Under the Companies Acts, the Secretary of State for Trade and Industry has the power to appoint investigators to investigate the affairs of a company—see sections 431, 432, 442 and 446 of the Companies Act 1985. The objective of these investigations is to increase confidence in corporate integrity through effective enforcement action. The conduct of a DTI investigation is covered in Chapter 26. To assist in the effective conduct of investigations the DTI is empowered by the Companies Act 1985 to require documents (however recorded, including computer records) to be produced to it by companies and company officers. Failure to assist in the course of an investigation may give rise to a number of criminal offences (ss.444(3), 447(6), 448(7), 449(2), 451).

Destroying or Mutilating Company Documents

19–033 It is an offence under section 450(1) of the Companies Act 1985 for a company officer to destroy, mutilate, falsify or be privy to the destruction, mutilation or falsification of document relating to the company's property or affairs or to make or be privy to the making of a false entry in such a document. It is a defence to show that there was no intention to conceal the state of the company's affairs or to defeat the law. By section 450(2) it is also an offence for an officer of the company to fraudulently part with, alter or make an omission to a company document or be privy to the fraudulent parting with, alteration or making of omission from such a document.

There can be little doubt that Parliament intended the commission of these offences to be taken seriously since the maximum penalty if convicted on indictment is seven years' imprisonment and/or an unlimited fine. If convicted summarily the maximum penalty is six months' imprisonment and/or a fine of the statutory maximum (£5,000). These penalties are the same as the maximum penalties which can be imposed for fraudulent trading contrary to section 458 of the Act. This offence has been used surprisingly rarely, notwithstanding the fact that a person will be vulnerable to conviction for an offence under section 450(1) unless, reversing the usual rule on the burden of proof in a criminal case, he can establish an absence of dishonest intent. The dearth of prosecutions under this section is probably explained by the fact that a prosecution can be brought only with the consent of the Secretary of State, the Director of Public Prosecutions or the Industrial Assurance Commissioner. Consideration should be given to the abolition of this restriction. **19–034**

False Statements in a Company's Prospectus

Sections 70 and 71 of the Companies Act 1985 created offences relating to the issuing of a prospectus which contains an untrue statement. The provisions were repealed by the Financial Services Act 1986 (Sched. 17) and the making of false statements to induce investment is now covered by section 47 of the Financial Services Act 1986. This provision will be discussed in some detail in Chapter 20. **19–035**

The Efficacy of Companies Act Regulation

As already noted the Companies Acts bring together a large number of disparate criminal offences. The majority of these offences are of a largely technical nature and apart from failure to file company documents and fraudulent trading these offences are rarely if ever prosecuted in practice. The figures available from the DTI for prosecutions brought by them reveal the extremely narrow range of offences which are actually prosecuted. Of course there is always going to be a tension between the concerns of investor protection and the ability of company officers to function commercially in their field of activity, but instead of creating a myriad of technical criminal offences which are satisfied by **19–036** lip service and little else, perhaps it is time to give some consideration to the introduction of some alternative coercive mechanisms which might encourage errant companies to obey the rules. As the Council of Europe has suggested, these alternative sanctions could include warnings, reprimands, recognisances, confiscation of property and illegal profits, prohibitions on certain activities, exclusion from government subsidies and benefits, prohibitions on advertising, annulment of licences, removal of managers, appointment of provisional caretaker managers, closure, restitution and the publication of decisions imposing sanctions. (See Council of Europe Recommendation No. R. (88) (1990).) In November 1992 the DTI announced that it would set up a review of selected areas of the Companies Act and related legislation. Although a number of areas have been considered further legislative changes are awaited.

Chapter 20

Market Manipulation

In this chapter we consider the various legal provisions which seek to offer investors some protection against manipulation of the financial markets. There are two principal provisions which we shall consider in turn: the legislation against insider dealing, and the making of false statements to induce investment contrary to section 47 of the Financial Services Act 1986. The application of conspiracy to defraud to cases where the victim is an investor and the crime involves market manipulation or some other improper practice such as the deception of a regulatory body has been considered in Chapter 18.

20–001

Introduction

By comparison with other jurisdictions where there has been a sophisticated and developed market in the purchase and sale of financial securities, English law has been slow to regulate against market manipulation. The first reported English case of market manipulation occurred during the Napoleonic wars. In *De Berenger* 3 M & S 66; 105 E.R. 536, a man dressed as a soldier arrived at Winchester and spread a false rumour that Napoleon had been killed. The news caused a rise in the price of government securities. De Berenger and his associates were convicted of conspiring by false rumours to raise the price of government funds, in contemporary terms a conspiracy to defraud.

20–002

Over 100 years later, section 13 of the Prevention of Fraud (Investments) Act 1958 Parliament made it an offence to make false and misleading statements for the purpose of inducing investment, but this offence, subsequently to be replaced by section 47 of the Financial Services Act 1986, was not directed specifically at market manipulation.

20–003

It was not until 1980 that legislation was introduced which focused on market manipulation when insider dealing was made a criminal offence by sections 68 to 73 of the Companies Act 1980. By comparison, there has been anti-manipulation legislation in the United States for the last 60 years in the form of the American Securities Exchange Act 1934 which was enacted in the wake of the Wall Street crash. Certain share dealings had been subject to regulation under the City Code on Takeovers and Mergers but it was not until 1973 that the Stock Exchange and Takeover Panel issued a joint statement calling for criminal sanctions against insider dealers. Regulation against market manipulation was perceived to be necessary in order to protect investors

20–004

against unfair practices and to safeguard the public interest in maintaining open and fair markets thereby preserving public confidence. As Mason J. said in the Australian case of *North v. Marra Developments Ltd* [1982] 56 A.L.J.R. 106, regulation is necessary:

"to ensure that the market reflects the forces of genuine supply and demand. By genuine supply and demand I exclude buyers and sellers whose transactions are undertaken for the sole or primary purpose of setting or maintaining the market price. It is in the interests of the community that the market for the securities should be real and genuine, free from manipulation."

Insider Dealing

Nature of Insider Dealing

20–005 In essence insider dealing involves the use of restricted information about a company by a buyer or seller of its securities to gain an advantage.

"Insider dealing is understood, broadly, to cover situations where a person buys or sells securities when he, but not the other party to the transaction, is in possession of confidential information which affects the value to be placed on those securities. Furthermore, the confidential information will generally be in his possession because of some connection which he has with the company whose securities are to be dealt in (*e.g.* he may be a director, employee or professional advisor of that company) or because someone in such a position has provided him, directly or indirectly, with the information"—Conduct of Company Directors (1977) (Cmnd. 7037).

20–006 It is sometimes said that insider dealing is a "victimless" crime. Whilst no individual "victim" can usually be identified in any particular insider dealing transaction, the general perception of the probity of those involved in the market is undermined. This point has been underlined in the recitals to the European Communities Council Directive 89/592 on Insider Dealing where the importance of the smooth operation of the market is emphasised. The smooth operation of the market is said to be dependant to a large extent on the confidence it inspires in investors:

"The factors on which such confidence depends include the assurance afforded to investors that they are placed on an equal footing and that they will be protected against the improper use of inside information."

The provisions of the Companies Act 1980 concerning the regulation of insider dealing were replaced by the provisions of the Company Securities (Insider Dealing) Act 1985. Today the offence is contained in Part V of the Criminal Justice Act 1993. This last legislative change was made in order to ensure that the law complied with the requirements of the 1989 European Communities Council Directive. The Criminal Justice Act 1993 came into force on March 1, 1994.   **20–007**

A Criminal Sanction

The Criminal Justice Act 1993 imposes criminal liability but it does not include provision for any civil remedy for the company or an unwitting outsider. Although the inside information comes from the company, the victims of insider dealing are usually outsiders who bought or sold shares in ignorance of the information which, if made public, would affect their price.   **20–008**

There is some discussion in the leading texts about the availability of civil remedies on the basis of constructive trusteeship, fiduciary accountability or breach of confidence, but the position is far from clear. Directors are entitled under existing civil law to buy shares without disclosing an intended takeover offer or to sell shares knowing that the company is in difficulties—*Percival v. Wright* [1902] 2 Ch. 421. Readers are referred to Chapters 26 and 27 for a more detailed discussion of these principles. The situation is significantly different in the U.S. where comprehensive civil and criminal sanctions have existed since the 1930s.   **20–009**

The Offence

Section 52 of the Criminal Justice Act 1993 sets out three forms of the offence: acquiring and disposing of securities, encouraging another person to do so, and disclosing inside information to someone else. Proof of an offence under section 52 has retained the two step approach of the Company Securities (Insider Dealing) Act 1985, whereby commission of the offence rests on the status of the person charged as an insider and on the type of information in his possession being inside information.   **20–010**

Section 52 provides as follows: **20–011**

"(1) An individual who has information as an insider is guilty of insider dealing if, in the circumstances mentioned in subsection (3), he deals in securities that are price-affected securities in relation to the information.

(2) An individual who has information as an insider is also guilty of insider dealing if—

(a) he encourages another person to deal in securities that are (whether or not that other knows it) price-affected securities in relation to the information, knowing or having reasonable cause to believe that the dealing would take place in the circumstances mentioned in subsection (3); or

(b) he discloses the information, otherwise than in proper performance of the functions of his employment, office or profession, to another person.

(3) The circumstances referred to above are that the acquisition or disposal in question occurs on a regulated market, or that the person dealing relies on a professional intermediary or is himself acting as a professional intermediary.

(4) This section has effect subject to section 53."

An Individual

20–012 The prohibition in section 52 applies to "an individual." The use of the word "individual" excludes limited companies and other institutions like local authorities. However, an unincorporated partnership or firm could commit insider dealing since it is no more than a collection of individuals. This is not to say that a company can escape liability completely. A company may be liable for the secondary offence of encouraging another person to deal.

An Insider

20–013 Under section 52 an individual must have information "as an insider", the meaning of which is defined by section 57 as follows:

"(1) . . . a person has information as an insider if and only if

(a) it is, and he knows that it is, inside information, and

(b) he has it, and knows that he has it, from an inside source.

(2) For the purposes of subsection (1), a person has information from an inside source if and only if—

(a) he has it through

(i) being a director, employee or shareholder of an issuer of securities; or

(ii) having access to the information by virtue of his employment, office or profession; or

(b) the direct or indirect source of his information is a person within paragraph (a)."

20–014 It follows that section 57 has established a distinction between a person who knows inside information (often referred to as a primary insider) and a person who comes to know information from an inside source (often referred to as a secondary insider). A primary insider is a person who has information through being a director, employee or shareholder of an issuer of securities or any person who has information because of his employment, office of profession. A secondary insider is someone whose source of information is directly or indirectly a primary insider. Brokers and analysts who rely on market intelligence could be caught by the provisions of section 57 if they know that the intelligence comes from a primary insider.

Inside Information

Section 56 defines the meaning of inside information: 20–015

"(1)... inside information means information which—

(a) relates to particular securities or to a particular issuer of securities or to particular issuers of securities and not to securities generally or to issuers of securities generally;

(b) is specific or precise;

(c) has not been made public; and

(d) if it were made public would be likely to have a significant effect on the price of any securities.

(2)... securities are 'price-affected securities' in relation to inside information, and inside information is 'price-sensitive information' in relation to securities, if and only if the information would, if made public, be likely to have a significant effect on the price of the securities.
(3) For the purposes of this section 'price' includes value."

It is interesting to note that section 56 has been drafted more widely 20–016 than the E.C. Directive 89/592 in respect of the requirement that the inside information has to be specific or precise. Article 1 of the Directive requires the inside information to be "of a precise nature" which is narrower than information which is "specific." As section 56 passed through the House of Commons, the Economic Secretary to the Treasury explained the variation in the following way:

"... if somebody were to say during ... lunch ... 'Our results will be much better than the market expects or knows', that would not be precise. The person would not have disclosed what the results of the company were to be. However, it would certainly be specific because he would be saying something about the company's results, and making it pretty obvious that the information had not been made public ... It would be insider information because it would be specific"—Standing Committee B, col. 175, June 10, 1993.

CHAPTER 20: MARKET MANIPULATION

Public Information

20–017 Information loses its confidential quality for the purposes of section 56 if it is made public or is to be treated as made public. Sections 58(2) and (3) provide examples of information which has entered the public domain but, as the language of sub-section (3) demonstrates, the list is by no means exhaustive:

"(2) Information is made public if—

(a) it is published in accordance with the rules of a regulated market for the purpose of informing investors and their professional advisers;

(b) it is contained in records which by virtue of any enactment are open to inspection by the public;

(c) it can be readily acquired by those likely to deal in any securities—

(i) to which the information relates, or

(ii) of an issuer to which the information relates; or

(d) it is derived from information which has been made public.

(3) Information may be treated as made public even though—

(a) it can be acquired only by persons exercising diligence or expertise;

(b) it is communicated to a section of the public and not to the public at large;

(c) it can be acquired only by observation;

(d) it is communicated only on payment of a fee; or

(e) it is published only outside the United Kingdom."

20–018 It is important to note that information may be treated as public even though steps have to be taken in order to obtain the information. There is little doubt that, in due course, the courts will be asked to consider the scope of section 58(3). Whilst each case will turn on its particular facts, it is unfortunate that the statutory language should be ambiguous with regard to a provision which goes to the heart of mischief which the legislation has been enacted to prevent. The E.C. Directive 89/592 makes it clear that information collated from *publicly available data* cannot be regarded as inside information and any transaction carried out on the basis of such information would not constitute insider dealing within the meaning of the Directive. The domestic courts are likely to construe section 58(3) widely in the light of this recital.

Price-affected Securities

20–019 Price-affected securities are defined in Schedule 2 to the Criminal Justice Act 1993. The range of securities to which the insider dealing provisions apply has been extended and now covers shares, bonds, gilts, warrants, depositary receipts, options, futures and contracts for differences. The range of securities to which the insider dealing legislation applies closely mirrors the list of investments within the scope of the Financial Services Act 1986.

It is worth noting that dealings in derivatives by directors is proscribed by section 323 of the 1985 Companies Act discussed in Chapter 19.   **20–020**

Deals On and Off Market

To be caught by the legislation, dealings must take place on a regulated market or off-market but involving a professional intermediary.   **20–021**

Section 55 defines "dealing" in securities: **20–022**

"(1) For the purposes of this Part, a person deals in securities if—

(a) he acquires or disposes of the securities (whether as principal or agent); or

(b) he procures, directly or indirectly, an acquisition or disposal of the securities by any other person."

There is no need to establish any causal link between the information and the dealing—see Lord Lane C.J. (at pp. 979–980) in *Attorney General's Reference (No. 1 of 1988)* [1989] 1 A.C. 971: "[T]he offence is not one of using information but of dealing in the securities whilst being in possession of the relevant information."   **20–023**

Professional Intermediaries

Section 59 puts forward a definition of a professional intermediary in the following terms: **20–024**

"(1) For the purposes of this Part a 'professional intermediary' is a person—

(a) who carries on a business consisting of an activity mentioned in subsection (2) and who holds himself out to the public or any section of the public (including a section of the public constituted by persons such as himself) as willing to engage in any such business; or

(b) who is employed by a person falling within paragraph (a) to carry out any such activity.

(2) The activities referred to in subsection (1) are—

(a) acquiring or disposing of securities (whether as principal or agent); or

(b) acting as an intermediary between persons taking part in any dealing in securities."

Takeovers

20–025　Extending the statutory prohibition to off-market deals can cause difficulty when there is a takeover bid. The involvement of a professional intermediary taints the transaction so that if the bidder and its financial adviser have inside information about the target, being itself a listed company, the dealing restriction could potentially apply. The value of the bidder's own securities is price-affected by the approach to the target. A bidder may seek to adopt the solution of making the bid in their own name rather than through the financial institution. However, the offer document is an investment advertisement within section 57 of the Financial Services Act 1986 and must be issued by an authorised person.

Defences

20–026　Section 53 repeats a number of defences available under the old legislation. Broadly, these are that there was no intention in that the accused did not expect the deal to result in a profit attributable to the fact that the information in question was price-sensitive. Profit in this context may be taken to include the avoidance of a loss. It is also a defence to show that the defendant reasonably believed that the information had been disclosed. Lastly, it is a defence if it can be shown that the defendant would have acted as he did irrespective of whether he was in possession of the price sensitive information.

20–027　The burden of proving a defence under section 53 rests on the defendant and is to the civil standard on the balance of probabilities.

20–028　Section 53 provides:

"(1) An individual is not guilty of insider dealing by virtue of dealing in securities if he shows—

(a) that he did not at the time expect the dealing to result in a profit attributable to the fact that the information in question was price sensitive information in relation to the securities; or

(b) that at the time he believed on reasonable grounds that the information had been disclosed widely enough to ensure that none of those taking part in the dealing would be prejudiced by not having the information; or

(c) that he would have done what he did even if he had not had the information.

(2) An individual is not guilty of insider dealing by virtue of encouraging another person to deal in securities if he shows—

(a) that he did not at the time expect the dealing to result in a profit attributable to the fact that the information in question was price sensitive information in relation to the securities; or

(b) that at the time he believed on reasonable grounds that the information had been disclosed widely enough to ensure that none of those taking part in the dealing would be prejudiced by not having the information; or

(c) that he would have done what he did even if he had not had the information.

(3) An individual is not guilty of insider dealing by virtue of a disclosure of information if he shows—

(a) that he did not at the time expect any person, because of the disclosure, to deal in securities in the circumstances mentioned in subsection (3) of section 52; or

(b) that, although he had such an expectation at the time, he did not expect the dealing to result in a profit attributable to the fact that the information was price sensitive in relation to the securities."

Special Defences

Schedule 1 to the Criminal Justice Act 1993 sets out a number of specific defences to an allegation of insider dealing. It is a defence for an individual dealing in securities or encouraging another person to deal if he acted in good faith in his capacity as a market maker. To come within the provisions of the special defence it is necessary for the market maker to be regulated by an "approved organisation" meaning a self-regulating organisation approved under paragraph 25B of Schedule 1 to the Financial Services Act 1986. **20–029**

It is also a defence to insider dealing for an individual to show that the information he had as an insider was market information. In deciding whether the information was market information, regard must be had to the content of the information, the circumstances in which the information was first obtained and the capacity in which the insider now acts. **20–030**

It is a defence for an individual to show that his actions were in conformity with the price stabilisation rules made under section 48 of the Financial Services Act 1986. **20–031**

Penalties

An individual guilty of insider dealing is liable to a maximum of seven years' imprisonment and/or an unlimited fine if tried on indictment or to a maximum of six months' imprisonment and/or a fine not exceeding the statutory maximum (being £5,000) if tried summarily—see section 61(1). **20–032**

20-033 Proceedings alleging insider dealing may be instituted only with the consent of the Secretary of State or the Director of Public Prosecutions—section 61(2).

Jurisdiction

20-034 Provisions relating to jurisdiction are contained in section 62 of the Criminal Justice Act 1993. For the United Kingdom courts to have jurisdiction, some element of the offence under section 52(1) or (2) must have taken place within the United Kingdom—*i.e.* the tippee was located in the United Kingdom or the dealing was on a United Kingdom regulated market, or the broker or market maker was carrying on business in the United Kingdom.

20-035 Where a United Kingdom individual seeks to avoid the territorial scope of the legislation by causing a company which he controls outside Europe to effect the trade, he cannot be a primary insider but could be an encourager or discloser of the inside information. An example occurred in the case involving Geoffrey Collier, former head of securities at Morgan Grenfell, who was convicted in 1987 on the basis of counselling and procuring a Cayman Island company which he controlled to deal in shares on the London Stock Exchange. He was fined £25,000 and received a 12 month suspended prison sentence, having admitted using confidential information to buy shares before a bid in which he actually lost £10,000.

Effectiveness of legislation

20-036 A prosecution will only succeed if all of the components mentioned in the definition are proved. The effectiveness of the legislation rests on the interpretation of section 56. It is difficult to distinguish in practice between specific and general information.

20-037 Between January 24, 1980 and January 17, 1994 there were 33 prosecutions for insider dealing involving 52 individuals of which 18 of the prosecutions resulted in the convictions of some 24 individuals. In roughly the same period about 100 cases are said to have been reported to the DTI by the London Stock Exchange Surveillance Unit.

20-038 Prosecution is not made easier by the inherently secretive nature of financial life, the complexity of financial life, and the increasing globalisation of markets making insider dealing a transnational crime. It has frequently been argued that the burden of proof renders the offence of insider dealing difficult if not impossible to prove to a criminal standard. This has been met by calls to replace the criminal sanction with a civil offence which would be easier to prove. In June 1996 the Foundation for Business Responsibilities recommended that insider dealing should be subject to a civil sanction.

20-039 As a result of efforts to promote the success of the legislation, it has been suggested that the scope of the insider dealing legislation is now too wide. The Financial Law Panel sponsored by the Corporation of

London and the Bank of England pointed out in a paper issued in April 1996 that the legislation was so wide that banks might be prevented from enforcing their security merely because they have price sensitive information, even if it has come into their hands without any suggestion of impropriety. It was pointed out that the legislation does not differentiate between a mortgagee of shares and any other market participant.

20–040 The Secretary of State but not the SIB has the power to investigate insider dealing under section 177 of the Financial Services Act 1986. Inspectors may be appointed by the Department of Trade and Industry and have similar powers to those of inspectors appointed under section 432 or 442 of the Companies Act and may require any person to give evidence to them and produce documents. Department of Trade and Industry investigations are discussed more fully in Chapter 26. Investigations are not normally announced and the reports resulting from them are not published.

20–041 When inspections reveal that insider dealing offences have been committed the Secretary of State may prosecute the offenders or take other appropriate action. The Department of Trade and Industry works closely with the Surveillance Department of the Stock Exchange. In the summer of 1993, the Stock Exchange introduced the Integrated Monitoring and Surveillance (Imas) system which is designed to draw the attention of the Stock Exchange's Surveillance Department to unusual trades. There have, however, been numerous calls for the investigation of insider dealing to be taken away from the Stock Exchange and for it to be given to the Securities and Investments Board. In 1995 the Stock Exchange investigated more than 1,500 cases of unusual share trading but only 43 cases were referred to the prosecuting authorities.

Inducing an Investment

20–042 There are two offences created by section 47 of the Financial Services Act 1986. Section 47(1) makes it an offence for an investor to be induced dishonestly or recklessly into making an investment on the basis of a misleading, false or deceptive statement. Most cases arise in circumstances where the investment is transferable on a recognised securities market, but the section is not confined to this situation. Section 47(2) is aimed at an act or a course of conduct which creates a false or misleading impression as to the market in or the price or value of any investments.

Section 47(1)

20–043 Section 47(1) of the Financial Services Act 1986 provides that:

"(1) Any person who

(a) makes a statement, promise or forecast which he knows to be misleading, false or deceptive or dishonestly conceals material facts: or

(b) recklessly makes (dishonestly or otherwise) a statement, promise or forecast which is misleading false or deceptive,

is guilty of an offence if he makes the statement, promise or forecast or conceals the facts for the purpose of inducing, or is reckless as to whether it may induce, another person (whether or not the person to whom the statement, promise or forecast is made or from whom the facts are concealed) to enter or offer to enter into, or refrain from entering into, an investment agreement or to exercise, or refrain from exercising any rights coffered by an investment."

Several statements

20–044　Where several statements are made together, it is the effect of the statements taken together which has to be considered. Several statements taken together could be misleading even if each individually was true—see *Aaron's Reefs Ltd v. Twiss* [1896] A.C. 273.

Recklessness

20–045　A statement will be reckless in the context of section 47(1) if it is a rash statement to make and the person who made the statement had no real basis of fact on which he could support the statement. This was established in *R. v. Grunwald* [1963] 1 Q.B. 935, which concerned the making of reckless statements within the meaning of section 13 of the Prevention of Fraud (Investments) Act 1958.

Dishonesty

20–046　The meaning of dishonesty has been considered in Chapter 16. The same meaning applies here.

Investment

20–047　An investment is defined by section 1(1) and Part I, Schedule 1 to the Financial Services Act which is set out in Appendix 2.

Section 47(2)

20–048　Section 47(2) of the Financial Services Act 1986 contains the second offence, known as creating a false or misleading impression. The subsection reads as follows:

"(2) Any person who does any act or engages in any course of conduct which creates a false or misleading impression as to the market in or the price or value of any investments is guilty of an offence if he does it for the purpose of creating that impression and of thereby inducing another person to acquire, dispose of, subscribe for or underwrite those investments or to refrain from doing so or to exercise, or refrain from exercising, any rights conferred by those individuals."

A False or Misleading Impression

An impression is to be regarded as the perception received by the investor. A false impression is one which is objectively incorrect. It will be necessary to assess the effect of the impression on the particular class of person at whom the impression was aimed and not on an average investor. In *North v. Marra Developments Ltd*, the New South Wales Court of Appeal suggested that the following questions could be asked when seeking to determine whether a false or misleading impression had been created: **20–049**

— what is the apparent state of affairs, with respect to the market or the price for the securities in question, conveyed by the transactions or the conduct impugned?
— was that the true state of affairs?
— if it was not, was the apparent state of affairs false or misleading?
— if it was, were the transactions or the conduct impugned calculated to create that false or misleading appearance?

Examples of artificial devices by which a false impression as to the market in a security may be created and which would be prohibited by section 47 (2) are: **20–050**

— wash sales. These are transactions effected through the market which involve no change in beneficial ownership of the shares. The transaction is a fiction and the buyer incurs no real financial obligation to the seller. It does however, create a false appearance of active trading in those shares. An example of a wash sale can be seen in the the Canadian case of *R. v. Lampard* [1968] 2 O.R.
— matched orders. A matched order occurs where a transaction (purchase or sale) is entered in the knowledge that a mirror transaction is to be entered into by another of substantially the same size, price and type again creating the impression of active trading.

Potentially the scope of section 47(2) is very wide. It has been suggested that almost any action by a market maker would potentially be caught by section 47(2) because the market maker's job is to create an impression of the market. For example, section 47(2) would catch the situation where traders enter into share purchases legitimately in order to create the impression of active trading. This often occurs in circumstances where the trader holds a large number of the same shares which are unsubscribed. **20–051**

Chapter 20: Market Manipulation

Engaging in Conduct

20–052   This will include acts and omissions to act. The concept that an omission to act may lead to a criminal sanction is unusual since the criminal law has been traditionally reluctant to impute criminal liability for omissions except in cases where there is a recognised duty to act. It may be said that a market maker has a duty to act in accordance with the rules of the market. In the case of *Adams v. R.* [1995] 1 W.L.R. 52, the Privy Council held that a person could be guilty of fraud when he dishonestly concealed information from another which he was under a duty to disclose to that other or which that other was entitled to require him to disclose.

False Price or Value

20–053   In the case of a security listed on an exchange the correct value is the market price which is arrived at by a concensus of the bona fide purchasers and sellers. A false price or value will be created when there is a shift in the equilibrium of the market. One of the most obvious situations where there is a tampering with the correct market price is in a takeover where a share support operation is mounted or where tactics are employed to resist a dawn raid.

Intent

20–054   Section 47(2) requires proof of an intention to create an impression as to the market in or the price or value of a security. The intent required by section 47(2) is subjective. If no reasonable person in the position of the defendant would have held the belief, this is powerful evidence that he did not honestly hold that belief—see *R. v. MacKinnon* [1959] 1 Q.B. 150, which concerned the now repealed Prevention of Fraud (Investment) Act 1939.

Inducing Another to Act

20–055   It must be shown that the defendant's act was for the purpose of inducing another to deal in the securities. It would not be an offence under section 47(2) if the defendant could show that he was merely shuffling his own investments. The court will be obliged to look at the primary motive of the defendant. It is probably enough to show that the defendant intended to affect investors generally or a class of investors and not that he had some specific person in mind.

Defences

20–056   Section 47(3) of the Financial Services Act 1986 contains a statutory defence which applies to an offence under section 47(2) which reads as follows:

"In proceedings brought against any person for an offence under subsection (2) above it shall be a defence for him to prove that he reasonably believed that his act or conduct would not create an impression that was false or misleading as to the matters mentioned in that subsection."

The defence has to be established by the defendant on the balance of probabilities.

20–057 A second defence is afforded by section 48(7) where a defendant can establish that he was acting in conformity with the rules for the purpose of price stabilisation. The scope of the exception has been extended by the Financial Services Act 1986 (Stabilisation) Order 1988 (S.I. 1988 No. 717). Price stabilisation is most commonly employed in the Eurobond markets and is not applicable to the domestic equities market.

Jurisdiction

20–058 Section 47(4) requires that some facet of an offence under sections 47(1) or (2) must take place within the United Kingdom.

Penalties

20–059 An individual who is convicted of an offence under section 47(1) or (2) is liable to a maximum of seven years' imprisonment and/or an unlimited fine if tried on indictment or to a maximum of six months' imprisonment and/or a fine not exceeding the statutory maximum (being £5,000) if tried summarily.

Problems

20–060 Section 47 of the Financial Services Act 1986 does not work well in practice. It is too widely drawn, and unlike fraudulent trading, for example, it does not provide a direct civil remedy. It is only where a defendant is an authorised person that a civil action can be brought under section 62 of the Financial Services Act—see Chapter 4 on this point. In other cases aggrieved investors have to resort to the common law—see Chapters 28 and 29.

20–061 The section 47 criminal offences are also difficult to prosecute. In the prosecution against Peter Marks (a director of stockbrokers, Branston & Gothard), Mr Marks was charged with making a misleading, false or deceptive statement to induce share dealing. It was alleged that Mr Marks had telephoned Goldman Sachs on October 12, 1990 and told the then head of United Kingdom equity sales that Maxwell Communications Corporation would be filing for bankruptcy that day knowing this to be untrue. The trial was stopped because the evidence suggested that Mr Marks had relayed his own opinion rather than a statement of fact.

Chapter 21

A Company's Purchase of its Own Shares

This chapter examines the provisions contained in the Companies Acts which prohibit the purchase by a company of its own shares, the prohibition on a company giving financial assistance to purchase its own shares, and the exemptions to the general prohibitions set out in the legislation. In particular this chapter will look at the way in which these provisions regulate corporate conduct so as to protect the interests of an investor, in this context a shareholder, who has bought shares in a limited liability company. The provisions regulate corporate behaviour through a combination of civil and criminal sanctions. The way in which the provisions have been applied by the courts will be considered in the context of investor protection **21–001**

The Fundamental Prohibition on the Acquisition by a Company of its Own Shares

It is a fundamental principle of English company law that a limited liability company shall not reduce its capital or purchase its own shares save in accordance with some specific statutory provisions which permit this course. **21–002**

This fundamental principle is set out in section 143(1) of the Companies Act 1985 which provides that: "... a company limited by shares or limited by guarantee and having a share capital shall not acquire its own shares whether by purchase, subscription or otherwise." **21–003**

The rationale underlying this fundamental principle was explained by Lord Watson in the House of Lords case of *Trevor v. Whitworth* (1887) 12 App. Cases 409, in the following terms: **21–004**

> "Paid up capital may be diminished or lost in the course of the company's trading; that is a result which no legislation can prevent; but persons who deal with and give credit to the limited company naturally rely upon the fact that the company is trading with a certain amount of capital already paid, as well as upon the responsibilities of its members for the capital remaining at call; and they are entitled to assume that no part of the capital which has been paid into the coffers

CHAPTER 21: A COMPANY'S PURCHASE OF ITS OWN SHARES

of the company has been subsequently paid out except in the legitimate course of its business. When a share is forfeited or surrendered the amount which has been paid upon it remains with the company, the shareholding having been relieved of liability for future calls, the share itself reverts to the company, bears no dividend, and may be reissued. When shares are purchased at par and transferred to the company the result is very different. The amount paid up on the shares is returned to the shareholder; and in the event of the company continuing to hold the shares (the amount) is permanently withdrawn from its trading capital."

21–005 Breach of the prohibition in section 143(1) of the Companies Act 1985 gives rise to an actionable cause of action in the civil courts. In addition, enforcement of this prohibition is bolstered by the criminal law. Section 143(2) of the Companies Act 1985 makes it a criminal offence to contravene section 143(1).

21–006 The offence may be committed by the company or any of its officers. The term "company officers" is defined by section 744 of the Companies Act 1985 as being a director, manager or secretary of a body corporate. Although the point has yet to be confirmed judicially, it appears that the criminal offence can also be committed by a shadow director of the company. A "shadow director" is defined by section 741(2) of the Companies Act 1985 as "a person in accordance with whose directions or instructions the directors of the company are accustomed to act."

21–007 The offence created by section 143(2) is triable either on indictment (in the Crown Court) or summarily (in the magistrates' court). If tried on indictment the penalty is, where the company is convicted, an unlimited fine. If an officer of the company is convicted, the maximum sentence is two years' imprisonment and/or an unlimited fine. When tried summarily the penalty is, where the company is convicted, a fine of the statutory maximum (presently £5,000) and where an officer of the company is convicted, six months' imprisonment and/or a fine of the statutory maximum.

Exceptions to the Fundamental Principle

21–008 Section 143(3) provides that the general prohibition on the acquisition by a company of its own shares does not apply in a number of limited circumstances. There are express provisions to permit the redemption or purchase of shares in circumstances sanctioned in sections 159 to 181 of the Act. The general prohibition will not apply where the purchase of shares is made pursuant to an order of the court (*i.e.* relief to members unfairly prejudiced, authorised reduction of share capital, etc.), or where there is a permitted forfeiture or surrender of shares. The prohibition will not apply to the redemption of redeemable shares—section 143(3)(a) and section 160(4).

21–009 In addition to the statutory exceptions, it was recently established by the High Court in *Acatos & Hutcheson plc v. Watson*, December 13, 1994, unreported, that the prohibition in section 143(1) of the Companies Act

1985 may not prevent a company from acquiring shares in a target company where the target company's sole asset is shares in the acquiring company. In that case the acquiring company, Acatos & Hutcheson plc, sought to purchase the entire issued share capital of Acatos Ltd. The problem arose because the sole asset of Acatos Ltd was a holding of 29.4 per cent of the voting share capital in Acatos & Hutcheson plc. The court was asked to decide whether the corporate veil should be lifted so as to expose the commercial reality underlying the transaction. In the particular circumstances of this case the court was satisfied that the corporate veil did not need to be lifted but in other cases the position might be different. However, the decision in *Acatos and Hutcheson plc* is limited in its effect. The judge was aware of the ramifications of this decision in the context of investor protection, and at the end of his judgment he added this warning:

"... whilst such a purchase by one company of a shareholding in it is not absolutely prohibited, in view of the potential for abuse and for adverse consequences for shareholders and creditors, the Court will look carefully at such transactions to see that the directors of the acquiring company have acted with an eye solely to the interests of the acquiring company (and not *e.g.* to the interests of the directors) and have fulfilled their fiduciary duties to safeguard the interests of shareholders and creditors alike." **21–010**

Suppose, for example, the intended subsidiary company was set up as the first of two stages in a single scheme. The first stage could involve the acquisition by the intended subsidiary of shares in the holding company. The second stage could involve the subsequent acquisition by the holding company of the intended subsidiary. In such a case the corporate veil would almost certainly be lifted, because the arrangement would be a façade or sham—see Mitchell J. in *August Investments Pty Ltd v. Poseidon Ltd and Samin Ltd* [1971] 2 S.A.S.R. 71 at 90. **21–011**

Provision by a Company of Financial Assistance for the Acquisition of its Own Shares

History of the Rule

Prior to the passing of the Companies Act 1981 it was unlawful for a company to give financial assistance for the purchase of, or subscription for, its own shares. Section 54 of the Companies Act 1948 made the giving of financial assistance a criminal offence. The prohibition was expressed in wide terms and included financial assistance whether given "directly or indirectly and whether by means of a loan, guarantee, the provision of security or otherwise." The giving of assistance by a **21–012** subsidiary company to anyone wanting to acquire shares or subscribing in shares in the holding company was also prohibited.

21–013   The purpose of this prohibition was considered by the Jenkins Committee (Report of the Company Law Committee Cmnd. 1749) and expressed in the following terms:

> "If people who cannot provide the funds necessary to acquire control of a company from their own resources, or by borrowing on their own credit, gain control of a company with large assets on the understanding that they will use the funds of the company to pay for their shares it seems to us all to likely that in many cases the company will be made to part with its funds either on inadequate security or for an illusory consideration. If the speculation succeeds, the company and therefore its creditors and minority shareholders may suffer no loss, although their interests will have been subjected to an illegitimate risk; if it fails, it may be little consolation for creditors and minority shareholders to know that the directors are liable for misfeasance" (at para. 171).

21–014   The Jenkins Report recognised that there may be legitimate commercial reasons why a company might wish to offer financial assistance in the purchase its own shares and it recommended that there should be limited provision to allow such transactions. The Companies Act 1981 repealed section 54 of the Companies Act 1948 and replaced it with provisions which are now contained in Chapter VI (ss.151 to 158) of the Companies Act 1985.

The Prohibition

21–015   The provision of financial assistance by a company in the purchase of its own shares continues to be generally prohibited. Sections 151(1) and (2) of the Companies Act 1985 repeat the prohibition by rendering it unlawful for a company or any of its subsidiaries to give financial assistance directly or indirectly to a person acquiring or proposing to acquire shares in that company prior to, or at the time of, the acquisition. The prohibitions are as follows:

> Section 151(1) —
> " . . . where a person is acquiring or is proposing to acquire shares in a company, it is not lawful for the company or any of its subsidiaries to give financial assistance directly or indirectly for the purpose of that acquisition before or at the same time as the acquisition takes place.
> Section 151(2)—
> " . . . where a person has acquired shares in a company and any liability has been incurred (by that or any other person), for the purpose of that acquisition, it is not lawful for the company or any of

its subsidiaries to give financial assistance directly or indirectly for the purpose of reducing or discharging the liability so incurred."

Section 151(3) provides that breach of the prohibitions in sections 151(1) and (2) will constitute a criminal offence which may be tried on indictment or summarily. The offence may be committed by the company and by an officer of the company who is in default. The definition of an officer of the company and the potential liability of shadow directors has already been set out in this chapter. If tried on indictment the penalty is, where the company is convicted, an unlimited fine and where an officer of the company is convicted two years' imprisonment and/or an unlimited fine. When tried summarily the penalty is, where the company is convicted, a fine of the statutory maximum (presently £5,000) and where an officer of the company is convicted six months' imprisonment and/or a fine of the statutory maximum. **21–016**

Breach of the prohibitions has consequences in civil law also. Breach will render the transaction void (in whole or in part) and unenforceable in civil law. The courts may enforce a contract of sale where there has been provision of financial assistance if the financial assistance is severable in some way. Financial assistance will be severable if it is ancillary to the overall transaction and its elimination would leave the subject matter of the transaction unchanged. The directors involved in an unlawful transaction could be sued for breach of trust to compensate the company for any loss suffered (see Chapter 27). Also, a director who is party to a breach of the prohibitions in section 151(1) and (2) could be vulnerable to an action for breach of fiduciary duty (see Chapter 26), or where the company has been wound up, an action for misfeasance to recover the loss (see Chapter 30). **21–017**

Meaning of Financial Assistance

"Financial assistance" is defined by section 152(1)(a) as follows: **21–018**

"(i) financial assistance given by way of gift,
(ii) financial assistance given by way of guarantee, security or indemnity, other than an indemnity in respect of the indemnifier's own neglect or default, or by way of release or waiver,
(iii) financial assistance given by way of a loan or any other agreement under which any of the obligations of the person giving the assistance are to be fulfilled at a time when in accordance with the agreement any obligation of another party to the agreement remains unfulfilled, or by way or the novation or, or the assignment of rights arising under, a loan or such other agreement, or
(iv) any other financial assistance given by a company the net assets of which are thereby reduced to a material extent or which has no net assets."

CHAPTER 21: A COMPANY'S PURCHASE OF ITS OWN SHARES

21-019   The definition is widely drawn and is inclusive rather than exhaustive. The definition includes direct financing by a company and what is more common in practice, indirect financing.

21-020   Examples of the types of transaction prohibited by section 151 can be found in cases decided under the old legislation. The Court of Appeal held in the leading case of *Belmont Finance Corporation v. Williams Furniture Ltd (No. 2)* [1980] 1 All E.R. 393, that financial assistance was afforded where a company, without regard to its own commercial interests, bought something from a third party with the sole purpose of putting the third party in funds to acquire shares in the company. Financial assistance was given irrespective of whether the company received a fair price for its assets if the transaction was not in the ordinary course of the company's business and did not enable the company to acquire anything which it genuinely needed for its own purposes.

21-021   A loan made by a company to finance the borrower's purchase of shares in the company was held to amount to financial assistance in *Selangor United Rubber Estates v. Craddock (No 3)* [1968] 1 W.L.R. 1555. In *Wallersteiner v. Moir (No. 1)* [1974] 1 W.L.R. 991, the Court of Appeal considered unlawful an arrangement under which a purchaser of shares undertook a liability as part of the consideration which he would never discharge or cause the company to discharge. (See also *Armour Hick Northern Limited v. Whitehouse* [1980] 1 W.L.R. 1520, where it was held to be sufficient that assistance was given "in connection with" an acquisition.)

21-022   In *Parlett v. Guppys (Bridport) Ltd, The Times,* February 8, 1996, the Court of Appeal held that the section 151 prohibition did not apply to an agreement whereby four private companies together assumed liability for making future payments of salary, bonus and pension to one of their shareholders in return for that shareholder transferring shares in one of the companies. The critical aspect in this case was the fact that there was no reduction in the net assets of the company in respect of which the shareholder transferred his shares.

21-023   In order for a company to be liable under section 152(1)(a)(ii) for giving assistance by way of indemnity, the Court of Appeal has recently held that the indemnity in question must give assistance of a financial nature for the purpose of the acquisition of the shares. The fact that there was a contract under which a party might recover the same amount by way of damages as he would have recovered under an indemnity was not sufficient to convert that contract into an indemnity—*British and Commonwealth Holdings v. Barclays Bank* [1996] 1 All E.R. 381.

21-024   Ultimately, each case will depend on its particular facts, and unless declaratory of some point of principle, the influence of past decisions will be limited. As Hoffman J. said in *Charterhouse Investment Trust Ltd v. Tempest Diesels Ltd* [1985] 1 B.C.C. 99544, the question of financial assistance has to be considered against the commercial realities of the particular transaction. On the facts of that case, where a letter surrendering tax losses of one company to other companies within the group formed a collateral contract which was part of a composite transaction, the court determined that the surrender could not in any acceptable commercial sense be regarded as a giving of financial assistance when the transaction was considered as a whole.

Financial Assistance from Foreign Subsidiaries

In the case of *Arab Bank plc v. Mercantile Holdings Ltd* [1994] 2 All E.R. 7, the court held that section 151 did not have extra-territorial effect and that a foreign subsidiary was not prohibited from giving financial assistance for the purpose of an acquisition of shares in its parent company. Nonetheless, the court was concerned to safeguard the interests of investors in this context. Towards the end of his judgment Millett J. noted that the hiving down of the assets by an English company to a foreign subsidiary in order that they may be available for the purpose of assisting in the financing of a contemplated purchase of the parent company's own shares would constitute the indirect provision of financial assistance by the parent company.

21–025

Exceptions

Section 153(1) and (2) exempt certain transactions from the prohibitions in section 151 against the giving of financial assistance directly or indirectly for the acquisition of shares by a company in itself or in its holding company. A company is not prohibited from giving financial assistance for the purpose of acquiring shares in itself or its holding company if:

21–026

"(i) the company's principal purpose in giving the assistance is:
  (a) where the assistance is caught by section 151(1), not to give that assistance for the purpose of any such acquisition of shares; OR
  (b) where the assistance is caught by section 151(2), not to reduce or discharge any liability incurred by a person for the purpose of the acquisition of shares in the company or its holding company; OR
(ii) where the assistance is caught by either section 151(1) or (2), where the assistance is but an incidental part of some larger purpose of the company, AND
(iii) the assistance is given in good faith and in the interests of the company."

The alternative exceptions are referred to as "the principal purpose" exception and "the larger purpose" exception. In each case it must be shown that the assistance was given in good faith and in the interests of the company.

21–027

The Company's Principal Purpose

21-028   The principal purpose of the transaction must be a bona fide commercial purpose which can be divided from the share acquisition. The transaction must be capable of being justified commercially in the company's own interests. A transaction under which a company purchases from another goods in the ordinary course of its business but also with the intention of putting the seller in a position to acquire shares in the purchasing company will not be prohibited if the latter purpose is not the principal purpose of the transaction—*Belmont Finance Corporation v. Williams Furniture Ltd (No. 2)* [1980] 1 All E.R. 393.

Some Larger Purpose

21-029   The House of Lords has given the phrase "some larger purpose" a narrow interpretation by drawing a distinction between a "purpose" and the "reason" why a purpose is formed. In order to establish some larger purpose, it is necessary to show some overall larger corporate purpose in which the resultant financial assistance to purchase shares is merely incidental. The purpose must be a corporate purpose and it must be immediate or proximate and well defined. A non-specific or long term business strategy may not be enough.

21-030   The meaning of the phrase "some larger purpose" was considered at some length in the leading case of *Brady v. Brady* [1988] B.C.L.C. 579; [1989] A.C. 755. The case concerned the corporate reorganisation of a family company following a quarrel between directors. To prevent winding up of the company it was agreed that the business should be divided equally between the directors with a cash adjustment being made to bring about equality between the two sides. The scheme involved merger of the family company with its wholly owned subsidiary company. The assets of the merged companies would then be divided and transferred to two new companies. Transfer of assets was to be achieved by the issuing of fully paid up shares in the new companies, to be paid for by the issue of loan stock. In the course of the merger the family company had to provide financial assistance to the subsidiary company in order to reduce the subsidiary company's liabilities. It was this aspect of the transaction which fell foul of the prohibition in section 151(2) and the question arose as to whether the transaction could be saved by the larger purpose exception. It was in this context that the House of Lords came to construe the phrase "some larger purpose" in comparatively narrow terms:

> "In applying sub-section 1(a) one has . . . to look for some larger purpose in the giving of financial assistance than the mere purpose of the acquisition of the shares and to ask whether the giving of assistance is a mere incident of that purpose . . . The ultimate reason for forming the purpose of financing an acquisition may, and in most

cases probably will, be more important to those making the decision than the immediate transaction itself. But 'larger' is not the same thing as 'more important' nor is 'reason' the same as 'purpose'. If one postulates the case of a bidder for control of a public company financing his bid from the company's own funds, the obvious mischief at which this section is aimed, the immediate purpose which it is sought to achieve is that of completing the purchase and vesting control of the company in the bidder. The reasons why that course is considered desirable may be many and varied ... These may be excellent reasons but they cannot, in my judgment, constitute a 'larger purpose' of which the provision of assistance is merely an incident."—*per* Lord Oliver.

Lord Oliver explained that the purpose of financial assistance in this case was to enable the shares to be acquired. Whilst the commercial advantages flowing from the acquisition were laudable, they remained a by-product of the financial assistance rather than an independent purpose for which the financial assistance had been provided. The principles set out in *Brady v. Brady* were applied by Morritt J. in *Plaut v. Steiner* (1989) 5 B.C.C. 352, which was also concerned with the division of a business in order to resolve management deadlock. 21–031

Other Statutory Exceptions to the Section 151 Prohibitions

Additional express exemptions from the section 151 prohibitions are set out in sections 153(3) and (4). These include: 21–032

(1) the payment of a lawful dividend—s.153(3) (a);
(2) the allotment of bonus shares—s.153(3)(b);
(3) loans in the ordinary course of business by money lending institutions—s.153(4)(a). Both the lending of money and the particular loan must be within the ordinary course of the company's business. Loans made with the purpose of an acquisition in mind are unlikely to be regarded as loans made in the usual course of business—see *Steen v. Law* [1964] A.C. 287;
(4) arrangements in connection with employee share schemes— s.153(4)(b) as amended by s.196 of the Financial Services Act 1986 and s.132, Schedule 18, paragraph 33 of the Companies Act 1989. The provision of financial assistance for the purpose of an employee share scheme must be given in good faith and in the interests of the company. The section covers provision of financial assistance as distinct from money;
(5) loans to employees to permit them to acquire fully paid shares—s.153(4)(c). This does not apply to directors. There are restrictions on loans to directors and persons connected with them—see Chapter 19.

Special Restrictions for Public Companies

21–033 There are special restrictions for public limited liability companies. Section 154 authorises the giving of financial assistance only if the company has net assets which are not thereby reduced or, to the extent that net assets are reduced, if the assistance rendered is provided out of distributable profits. "Net assets" are defined as the amount by which the aggregate of the company's assets exceeds the aggregate of its liabilities. "Liabilities" are defined to include any amount retained as reasonably necessary for the purpose of providing for any liability or loss which is either likely to be incurred or certain to be incurred but uncertain as to amount or as to the date on which it will arise.

Private Companies

21–034 Sections 155 to 158 contain a general exemption for private companies from the prohibition on giving financial assistance for the acquisition of its own shares. The exemption is obtained by compliance with a prescribed procedure and timetable set out in sections 155 to 158. The Act makes specific provision for the protection of creditors in section 155(2) and minority shareholders in section 157. Private companies may rely on the exceptions in section 153 as well as the specific exemption in sections 155 to 158. In *Brady v. Brady*, where the transaction was not saved by the larger purpose exception in section 153(2), the House of Lords concluded that the conditions of section 155(2) had been fulfilled, and on this basis the transaction was not prohibited. The private company exemption applies for the purposes of the acquisition of shares by a company in itself or in its holding company provided that the holding company is also a private company.

21–035 Financial assistance can only be given if:

(1) there is no reduction of net assets—s.155(2);
(2) there is a statutory declaration by the directors of the company as to its solvency prior to giving assistance—s.155(6);
(3) a special resolution is passed approving the giving of financial assistance by the company—s.155(4);
(4) the timetable for compliance with the requirements of sections 156 to 158 is adhered to.

21–036 The statutory declaration must be in the prescribed form—see the Companies (Forms) Regulations 1985 (S.I. 1985 No. 854), reg. 4(1), Sched. 3 and Part II of Schedule 4. The declaration must include details of the assistance to be given, the business of the company giving assistance, and it must identify the recipient of the assistance—section 156(1). The courts have considered the question of how detailed the particulars contained in such a statutory declaration must be to comply with the prescribed form. The principal purpose of the statutory declaration is to ensure that the company providing financial assistance meets with the solvency requirements. The statutory declaration must therefore, contain information which gives "particulars" of the form of assistance to be provided and of the principal terms on which the assistance will be given—*Re S.H. & Co. (Realisations) 1990 Ltd* [1993] B.C.L.C. 1309; [1993] B.C.C. 60.

21–037 Although the statutory declaration must be in the prescribed form, it is not a requirement that the declaration made be on a prescribed form but, if it is not, it must contain all the statutory requirements—*Re NL Electrical* [1994] 1 B.C.L.C. 22. Directors must state that in their opinion the company will be able to pay its debts both immediately after the rendering of assistance and as the debts fall due within the year following the rendering of assistance. If the company is to be wound up, the directors must state that the company is in a position to pay its debts in full. Section 156(5) requires the statutory declaration to be registered at Companies House. Failure to register the statutory declaration is a criminal offence which is triable summarily and for which a director if found guilty may be fined—section 156(6).

21–038 The declaration must have annexed to it an auditor's report to the effect that the auditors have made inquiry into the affairs of the company and are not aware of anything to contradict the opinion of the directors as to its solvency position—section 156(4). It is a criminal offence for the directors of a company to make a statutory declaration if they do not have reasonable grounds for giving the opinion expressed—section 156(7). The penalty is, on indictment, a maximum of two years' imprisonment and/or an unlimited fine. On summary conviction the maximum penalty is six months' imprisonment and/or a fine of the statutory maximum (presently £5,000). The auditors of a company are not subject to any criminal sanction in respect of any report they may provide.

21–039 A special resolution must approve the giving of financial assistance by the company. If the financial assistance is for the purpose of the acquisition of shares in a holding company there must be a special resolution passed by both the holding company and the assisting company and any intermediate company between them in the group—section 155(5). Wholly owned subsidiaries are, by their very nature, exempt from the requirement to pass a special resolution.

21–040 The various requirements are subject to a strict timetable which is contained in the respective provisions. Non-compliance with the statutory requirements is not a mere procedural irregularity capable of waiver and it cannot be validated by unanimous agreement of all members entitled to vote at meetings of the company—*Precision Dippings Ltd v. Precision Dippings Marketing Ltd & Ors* (1985) 1 B.C.C. 539 at 543, *per* Dillon L.J.

21–041 The legislation has made specific provision for the protection of minority shareholder interests. After the passing of any of the requisite special resolutions, a dissentient minority may apply to the court to have the resolution set aside. A dissentient minority must hold at least 10 per cent of the issued share capital or if the company is not limited by shares by at least 10 per cent of its members. The application must be made within 28 days of the passing of the special resolution. The court has wide powers in the event of such an application, including ordering that the minority be bought out or ordering that the resolution be cancelled—section 157(2). Reference may also be made in this context to the power of the court to protect minority shareholders more generally (see Chapter 26).

Section 151 in Practice and Calls for Reform

21–042   Although the courts have endeavoured to uphold the width of the prohibitions in section 143 and section 151, the prohibitions have proved a blunt tool in the context of investor protection. The statutory language is technical and difficult to apply, and the exceptions to both sets of prohibitions are sufficiently wide to deprive shareholders of any effective protection.

21–043   In so far as the criminal sanctions are concerned, these are rarely utilised, and the courts have proceeded on the assumption that in order to establish an offence under section 151(3) the prosecution must show that a defendant has contravened one of the section 151 prohibitions dishonestly and that none of the section 153 exemptions apply in the case. The point is well demonstrated by a consideration of the Court of Appeal decision in *R. v. Saunders and others, The Independent,* May 17, 1991. The court held that it was necessary to explain that proof of a substantive offence depended in part on the ability of the prosecution to show the absence of any section 153 exemption. Since the section 153 exemption brings the issue of a defendant's good faith into question, it follows that the prosecution has to prove a defendant's dishonesty before the defendant can be convicted of the criminal offence. This is difficult to establish in practice, since directors will quite sensibly take detailed legal advice before entering into any arrangement of this nature. In practical terms, unless the arrangement takes place under the cloak of false documentation, dishonesty will be impossible to prove. Where more than one person is a party to a dishonest transaction it is possible for the prosecution to charge a conspiracy to defraud (see Chapter 18), but again the prosecution has to prove an intention by the defendant to be party to an agreement to commit an unlawful act—*Churchill v. Walton* [1967] 2 A.C. 224, H.L; *R. v. Anderson* [1986] 1 A.C. 27, H.L. It follows that a prosecution under section 151(3) will not enhance the prospects of conviction.

21–044   There have been calls for reform of this area of the law, and suggestions have included the decriminalisation of section 151 and its replacement by a more effective civil sanction. There is much to support this line of thought. The origin of the current provisions on maintenance of capital came from the Second EEC Directive (77/91; [1977] O.J. L26/1), and it is from Europe that further initiatives in the reform of company law are likely to come.

Chapter 22

Directors' Disqualification

Introduction

Section 1 of the Company Directors Disqualification Act 1986 empowers a court to make an order for a specified period against a person that he shall not be a director of a company or an administrator or liquidator of a company, a receiver or manager of a company's assets or in any way whether directly or indirectly be concerned in or take part in the promotion, formation or management of a company. As Sir Donald Nicholls V.-C. said in *Secretary of State for Trade and Industry v. Ettinger* [1993] B.C.L.C. 896:

22–001

> "The procedure for disqualifying directors was an important sanction ... Those who took advantage of limited liability had to conduct their companies with due regard to the ordinary standards of commercial reality."

Directors disqualification is a sanction which is exercised in the investor context and the circumstances in which an order for disqualification may be made is considered in this chapter.

22–002

The definition of a director is set out in Chapter 26. Suffice it to note that a director will include any person occupying the position of a director and for the purposes of sections 6 to 9 of the Company Directors Disqualification Act 1986 it will include a shadow director. In *Re Lo-Line Electric Motors Ltd* [1988] Ch. 477, it was held that a person acting as a de facto director was a director for the purposes of this Act.

22–003

Disqualification on Conviction for an Indictable Offence

Section 2(1) of the Act allows a court to make a disqualification order against a person where he is convicted of an indictable offence (whether on indictment or summarily) in connection with the promotion, formation, management or liquidation of a company, or with the receivership or management of a company's property.

22–004

The Court

For the purposes of section 2, a court includes (a) any court having jurisdiction to wind up the company in relation to which the offence was committed, (b) the court by or before which the person is convicted of

22–005

the offence; and (c) in the case of a summary conviction in England and Wales, any other magistrates' court acting for the same petty sessional area.

Discretion

22–006 The extent of the court's discretion to make a disqualification order was considered in *R. v. Young* (1990) 12 Cr.App.R.(S). The appellant pleaded guilty to managing a company as an undischarged bankrupt and was disqualified from being a director for two years and conditionally discharged. The judge accepted that there had been no fraud or dishonesty on the part of the defendant. The disqualification was appealed on the basis that there had been no finding that the appellant was unfit to be a company director. The Court of Appeal held that under section 2 of the Company Directors Disqualification Act 1986 there was an unfettered discretion to make a disqualification order against a person convicted of an indictable offence committed in connection with the promotion, formation, management or liquidation of a company.

In Connection with the Management of a Company

22–007 The meaning of "in connection with the management of a company" has been considered in a number of cases. A good statement of the principles to be applied was set out by Mann J. in *R. v. Austen* (1985) 7 Cr.App.R.(S.) 214, where fraudulent hire purchase transactions had been carried out by the appellant through a number of limited companies. The Court of Appeal considered whether the phrase "in connection with the management of a company" was restricted to the internal management of the company. In giving judgment Mann J. said at 216:

> "In our judgment the words of the section when they refer to 'the management of the company' refer to the management of the company's affairs and there is no reason in language for differentiating between internal affairs and external affairs. Indeed as a matter of policy it may be thought appropriate that management should extend to both internal and external affairs. The section should cover activity in relation to the birth, life and death of a company."

22–008 There are a number of cases which demonstrate the application of these principles. In *R. v. Corbin* (1984) 6 Cr.App.R.(S.) 17, an earlier decision, the appellant was convicted on six counts of obtaining property by deception. He and his father operated a business dealing in yachts using three limited companies. Through deception they obtained money and boats. On appeal it was argued that "in connection with the management of a company" related only to the internal management of a company. The Court of Appeal held that the management of a company was not restricted to the management of a company's affairs internally.

Similarly, in *R. v. Georgiou* (1988) 87 Cr.App.R. 207, the appellant pleaded guilty to an offence of carrying on insurance business without the authorisation of the Secretary of State contrary to sections 2 and 14 of the Insurance Companies Act 1982 He was sentenced to six months' imprisonment, a fine of £1,000 and disqualified from being a director for a period of five years. In the course of his appeal against sentence the Court of Appeal considered what was meant by "in connection with the management of a company." The court held that carrying on an insurance business through a limited company is a function of management and if that function is performed unlawfully in any way which makes the person guilty of an indictable offence it can properly be said that it is in connection with the management of a company. 22–009

What amounted to the management of a company was again considered in *R. v. Goodman* [1993] 2 All E R. 789; [1994] 1 B.C.L.C. 349, where the defendant was a director and chairman of a public company who was convicted in relation to insider dealing offences. The court included in sentence a disqualification from being a director under section 2(1) of the Act. The defendant appealed on the basis that his conviction was not relevant to his involvement in the management of a company. The Court of Appeal held that the conviction was indeed relevant to involvement with the management of a company. 22–010

Period of Disqualification

Under section 2(3) of the Act, the maximum period of disqualification is five years where the disqualification order is made by a magistrates' court and 15 years in any other case. 22–011

The appropriate length of disqualification was considered in *Re Seven Oaks Stationery (Retail) Ltd* [1991] Ch. 164 where (at p. 174) Dillon L.J. gave the following guidelines: 22–012

"I . . . endorse the division of the potential 15 year disqualification period into three brackets . . . viz: (i) the top bracket of disqualification for periods over 10 years should be reserved for particularly serious cases. These may include cases where a director who has already had one period of disqualification imposed on him falls to be disqualified again. (ii) The minimum bracket of two to five years' disqualification should be applied where, though disqualification is mandatory, the case is relatively not very serious. (iii) The middle bracket of disqualification for six to 10 years should apply for serious cases which do not merit the top bracket."

Although set out in a "civil" case, these guidelines have been applied by the criminal courts. In the case of *R. v. Millard* (1994) 15 Cr.App.R.(S.), for example, the original sentence of 15 years' disqualification in respect of nine counts of fraudulent trading was reduced to eight years on appeal. 22–013

22–014 A significant period of disqualification may be imposed in a case where there is no dishonesty on the part of the defendant. In *Secretary of State for Trade and Industry v. Ettinger* [1993] B.C.L.C. 896, *The Times*, February 18, 1993 the Court of Appeal increased a period of disqualification from three to five years and stressed that persistent failure to file accounts was to be viewed seriously even where there was no dishonest intent.

Imposition of Disqualification when Coupled with Compensation Orders

22–015 In *R. v. Holmes* (1992) 13 Cr.App.R.(S.), the Court of Appeal considered whether it was appropriate to impose a compensation order at the same time as imposing disqualification from being a director. The court held that when a compensation order is made it is generally wrong in principle to inhibit a defendant from freely engaging in business activities which must have been contemplated as necessary for the purposes of fulfilling the obligations of the compensation order.

Disqualification for Persistent Breach of Companies Legislation

22–016 Under section 3 of the Act a disqualification order may be made against a person who has been persistently in default of any requirements under the companies legislation. This includes a persistent failure to file audited accounts for the company—*Secretary of State of Trade and Industry v. Ettinger* [1993] B.C.L.C. 896, and failure to maintain proper accounting records for a company—*Re New Generation Engineers Ltd* [1993] B.C.L.C. 435 and *Re Firedart Ltd, Official Receiver v. Fairall* [1994] 2 B.C.L.C. 340.

The maximum period of disqualification under section 3 is five years.

Disqualification for Unfitness

22–017 Section 6 of the Act imposes a duty on a court to disqualify a director who is or has been a director of a company which has at any time become insolvent (whether while he was a director or subsequently) and where his conduct as director of that company (either taken alone or taken together with his conduct as a director of any other company or companies) makes him unfit to be concerned in the management of a company.

22–018 Applications for disqualification under section 6 may be made by the Secretary of State, by the official receiver or the liquidator. The application must normally be made within two years of the date on which the company became insolvent.

22-019 There is a growing body of decided cases dealing with the circumstances in which a court must make a disqualification order under section 6. The standard to be applied on the question of whether a person is unfit to be concerned in the management of the company was considered in the case of *Secretary of State of Trade and Industry v. Lewinsohn*, March 19, 1996, unreported. It was held that the court must ask whether the standard of conduct fell below the standard which is today expected of a director who enjoys the privilege of limited liability. The standard of proof is the balance of probabilities rather than the criminal standard but regard has to be had to the seriousness of the issues raised. This is particularly so in the case of professional men where the complaints are as to lack of probity rather than negligence.

22-020 In *Re Continental Assurance Company of London plc*, June 14, 1996, unreported, Chadwick J. held that incompetence may justify the making of an order under section 6. A failure to read and understand statutory accounts amounted to sufficient incompetence and neglect to justify the making of an order. The court referred to *Re Lo-Line Electric Motors Ltd* and *Re Grayan Ltd* [1995] Ch. 241 in this context.

22-021 It is not open to a director to avoid disqualification by contending that at the material time he did not know that the company was insolvent. Where it can be demonstrated that a company has continued trading for a substantial period of time while it was insolvent and as a result has put the claims of existing and new creditors at unwarrantable risk of not being repaid, it is not open to a director to avoid responsibility by arguing that he was not aware of the company's financial position. It is the duty of all directors to ensure that they have a reasonably clear picture of the financial state and trading profitability of their companies. It they are unable to ascertain the state of the company it is incumbent on them to procure that immediate steps are taken to put the books and records in a reasonable state or to bring trading to an end—*Secretary of State for Trade and Industry v. Harry Laing*, June 20, 1996, unreported.

22-022 Under section 6(4) the minimum period of disqualification is two years and the maximum is 15 years. The principles concerning the length of disqualification as set out in *Re Seven Oaks Stationary Retail Ltd* will apply.

Procedure

22-023 By analogy with other situations such as a plea of guilty in criminal cases, the court has jurisdiction to deal with an application under section 6 summarily without requiring a full trial and without requiring the parties to contest every point provided some evidence, and not merely an assertion of no evidential value or an admission which was unsupported by evidence, was presented to the court which established unfitness—*Re Carecraft Construction Co Ltd* [1993] 4 All E.R. 499. It must be remembered in this context that it was a condition precedent to the making of a disqualification order under section 6 that the court was satisfied that the conduct of a director in relation to a particular company or companies made him unfit to be concerned in the management of a company.

22-024 In *Secretary of State for Trade and Industry v. Rogers*, July 30, 1996, unreported, a case came before the court on agreed facts in which no allegation of dishonesty had been made. In his written judgment the judge included a finding of dishonesty which the Court of Appeal held it was not open for him to make. However, the Court of Appeal was concerned to note that by using the *Carecraft Construction Co Ltd* procedure, parties cannot oblige the judge to approach the case in a particular way. It is important in cases where this procedure is to be used that the judge has the opportunity to read the papers in advance and to voice any doubts that he has about either the need for disqualification or its length at the earliest possible moment so that the parties can consider whether they or either of them would prefer a full trial.

Disqualification in the Public Interest

22-025 Following an investigation by the DTI, the Secretary of State has power to apply to the court for a disqualification order where it appears to be in the public interest that such an order be made. The court has power to order disqualification under section 8.

22-026 The maximum period of disqualification under section 8 is 15 years. The principles concerning the length of disqualification as set out in *Re Seven Oaks Stationary Retail Ltd* will apply.

Disqualification Following a Declaration of Fraudulent or Wrongful Trading

22-027 Section 10 provides that disqualification may also follow a declaration of fraudulent or wrongful trading under sections 213 and 214 of the Insolvency Act 1986 which are covered in Chapters 26 and 30 respectively.

22-028 The maximum period of disqualification under section 10 is 15 years. The principles concerning the length of disqualification as set out in *Re Seven Oaks Stationary Retail Ltd* will apply.

Disqualification where an Undischarged Bankrupt Acting as a Director

22-029 Under section 11 it is an offence for an undischarged bankrupt to act as a director or to take part in or be concerned in, either directly or indirectly, the promotion, formation or management of a company except with leave of the court.

The Consequences of Contravention of an Order for Disqualification

Under section 13 of the Act, if a person acts in contravention of a disqualification order or of section 12(2), or is guilty of an offence under section 11, he is liable on conviction on indictment, to imprisonment for not more than two years or a fine, or both; and on summary conviction, to imprisonment for a maximum of six months or a fine not exceeding the statutory maximum, or both. **22–030**

Register of Disqualification Orders

Under section 18 of the Act the Secretary of State maintains a register which is open to inspection of disqualification orders which remain in force. **22–031**

Chapter 23

Confiscation of Assets and Compensation

Introduction

Confiscation of the proceeds of crime has two aspects both of which 23–001
attract popular support and approval; the first is to deprive criminals of the fruits of their criminal activity (a tradition recognised by the common law under which the property of anyone convicted of a felony was forfeit to the Crown until 1870) and the second is to allow for the compensation of the victims of crime. Following the Hodgson Committee report on "Forfeiture of the Proceeds of Crime" in 1984 a number of pieces of broadly parallel legislation were passed—the Drug Trafficking Offences Act 1986 aimed at the removal of the proceeds of drug trafficking, the Prevention of Terrorism (Temporary Provisions) Act 1989 aimed at the removal of the proceeds of terrorism, and Part VI of the Criminal Justice Act 1988 which introduced confiscation orders aimed at the removal of the proceeds of other areas of lucrative crime.

Whilst the drug trafficking legislation has been widely applied (£5.3 23–002
million confiscated in the year 1993-1994), Crown Courts have not made confiscation orders in non-drug related cases. In the year 1993-1994 only 13 confiscation orders were made realising £265,000 in non-drugs cases. The Proceeds of Crime Act 1995 which came into force on the November 1, 1995 is intended to widen the powers of the courts to confiscate the proceeds of criminal activity which are not the result of drug trafficking or terrorism. This Act has significant potential application in cases of investor fraud.

Confiscation Orders

The Proceeds of Crime Act 1995 is somewhat cumbersome in that it 23–003
operates by making amendments to the Criminal Justice Act 1988 (already heavily amended by the Criminal Justice Act 1993). The amendments introduced by the 1995 Act provide two procedures for the making of confiscation orders; a "simple procedure" and a "complex procedure", as they have come to be known.

The "simple procedure" allows for confiscation limited to the amount 23–004
of benefit derived from the offences for which the defendant is to be sentenced. These are the offences of which the defendant has been

convicted and any offences which have been taken into consideration. The confiscation order cannot be for amounts over and above this, for example where the charges are sample or specimen counts but where there are no other offences taken into consideration. This represents the position as it was under the unamended 1988 Act which gave rise to the Court of Appeal commenting in the case of *R. v. Crutchley and Tonks* (1994) 15 Cr.App.R.(S.) 627, that it might be desirable to devise a procedure by which, when a defendant was accepting his guilt of a whole series of frauds, an order could properly be made in a sum reflecting the total losses suffered by those who had been defrauded. This was a case where the indictment represented specimen counts but where the defendants accepted the full amount obtained from their fraudulent behaviour. Notwithstanding, the Court of Appeal held that the amount of the order which could be made by the court was limited to the amounts in the counts on the indictment and to offences taken into consideration.

23–005 An attempt to remedy this anomaly has been made by the introduction of the "complex procedure" which allows the court to confiscate the proceeds of offences with which the defendant has not been charged and of which he has not been convicted and which he has not admitted but which form a course of criminal conduct.

The Simple Procedure

23–006 Section 1 of the 1995 Act (which becomes section 71(1) of the Criminal Justice Act 1988) allows that where an offender is convicted, in any proceedings before the Crown Court or a magistrates' court, of an offence of a relevant description, it shall be the duty of the court to impose a confiscation order in respect of that offence or any other relevant criminal conduct. This duty arises where (a) the prosecutor has given written notice to the court that he considers it would be appropriate for the court to proceed under this section, or (b) if the court considers, even though it has not been given such notice, that it would be appropriate for it to so proceed.

23–007 Section 71(1) does not apply in the case of proceedings against a person in which that person is convicted of an offence committed before the commencement of the section. This section introduces two major changes to the previous law; the first is that it places a duty on the court to exercise its powers to order confiscation in every case where written notice has been given by the prosecution. It also allows the court to make a confiscation order of its own volition where appropriate, whereas previously the court had no such power where the prosecution had not served a notice. Secondly, the 1995 Act abolishes the requirement that a confiscation order could only be made in cases where at least £10,000 could have been expected to be recovered. Baroness Blatch indicated in the course of a debate during the passage of the Bill through Parliament that £10,000 may continue to be the effective practical starting point. It remains to be seen whether this power will be any more widely used than the powers it replaces.

An offence of a relevant description means an indictable offence other **23–008** than a drugs trafficking offence or an offence under Part III of the Prevention of Terrorism (Temporary Provisions) Act 1989 and certain summary only offences listed in Schedule 4 to the 1988 Act.

Relevant criminal conduct means the offence of which the offender **23–009** has been convicted taken together with any other offences of a relevant description of which he is convicted in the same proceedings (*i.e.* on the indictment), or which the court is taking into consideration.

Determination of Benefit under the Simple Procedure

The court is required, first to determine whether the offender has **23–010** benefited from any relevant criminal conduct. Under the simple procedure the court is not entitled to make assumptions but it has power under section 4 (section 73A(2)) to order a defendant to give the court such information as may be specified in the order to assist the court in carrying out its functions. Under section 73A(5) the court is entitled to draw such inferences as it considers appropriate if the defendant fails without reasonable excuse to comply with such an order.

It is by no means clear what will amount to a reasonable excuse in **23–011** these circumstances. In particular, it is not clear whether it would be a reasonable excuse for a defendant to say that compliance with the order would result in self incrimination in respect of other crimes. This is especially pertinent as there does not appear to be any limit on the way in which information gained in response to an order under section 73A(2) can be used.

Amount to be Recovered

Once the court has determined that the offender has benefited from **23–012** relevant criminal conduct, it must then go on to determine the amount to be recovered and make an order accordingly. The amount of the order must not exceed the amount of the benefit nor must it exceed the amount which appears to the court that may be realisable at the time the order is made.

The court has a power but not a duty to make a confiscation order where it is satisfied that a victim of any relevant criminal conduct has already instituted or intends to institute civil proceedings against the defendant in respect of loss, injury or damage sustained in connection with the conduct.

The Complex Procedure

Section 2 of the 1995 (which becomes section 72AA of the Criminal **23–013** Justice Act 1988) gives the court power to make a confiscation order, following the service of a written notice by the prosecution, where an offender is convicted in any proceedings before the Crown Court or a magistrates' court of a qualifying offence. The written notice must contain a declaration that it is the prosecutor's opinion that the case is one in which it is appropriate for this section to be applied and the offender is (i) convicted in those proceedings of at least two qualifying offences (*i.e.* two offences in the same indictment) or (ii) the offender has been convicted of a qualifying offence on at least one previous occasion during the relevant period (six years before the institution of the current proceedings). Unlike section 71, the court can only make a confiscation order in relation to a course of criminal conduct where there has been a notice served by the prosecution.

A Qualifying Offence

23–014 This is any indictable or either way offence which is not a drug trafficking offence or an offence under Part III of the Prevention of Terrorism (Temporary Provisions) Act 1989. The qualifying offence must have been committed after the commencement of section 2 (section 72AA) and the court must be satisfied that it is an offence from which the defendant has benefited, *i.e.* the defendant has obtained property or a pecuniary advantage as a result of or in connection with the offence.

Assessing Benefit

23–015 Under section 2 (s.72AA) the court is entitled to make either or both of two assumptions as to a defendant's benefit. The court may assume, first, that any property held by the defendant at the date of conviction or at any time between the date of conviction and the making of the order was received by him as a result of or in connection with the commission of offences to which the Act applies. Secondly, the court may assume that any property which has passed through the defendant's hands (both property transferred to him and his own expenditure) within the six years prior to the present proceedings being started represents the proceeds of crime. In applying these assumptions the court may conclude that the defendant has benefited from crimes other than the ones with which he has been charged. The court must treat these crimes as if they comprised part of the defendant's relevant criminal conduct and the court must determine the amount of the defendant's benefit and thus of the confiscation order on the basis of the benefit derived from all those offences, irrespective of the fact that the defendant has never been charged with them.

23–016 The court will not make the assumptions in relation to particular property or expenditure if the assumption is shown to be incorrect in the defendant's case; if the assumption relates to property which has already been the subject of a confiscation order; or if the court is satisfied that there would be a serious risk of injustice in the defendant's case if the assumption was made (s.72AA(5)).

Written Notice by the Prosecution

23–017 Section 3 (section 73A of the 1988 Act) requires the prosecutor to tender to the court a statement containing information relevant to whether the defendant has benefited from relevant criminal conduct and the value of any such benefit. Where such a statement is tendered the defendant should be asked specifically whether what the prosecution says is true. An admission by the defendant as to the truth of the allegations in the written notice is to be taken as conclusive proof of their accuracy.

Provision of Information by the Defendant

Section 4 (section 73) empowers the court to order the defendant to give it information to assist in carrying out its functions under Part VI of the 1988 Act. Failure to comply with such an order would be punishable as a contempt of court. The order may specify such information as may be required by the court. There is no provision in the Act limiting the use to which information received in this way may be put. If the information discloses other criminal offences, there appears to be no reason why the defendant should not find himself open to further prosecution. The defendant may only refuse to comply with the order to supply information if he has a reasonable excuse. Refusal to comply with an order without reasonable excuse allows the court to draw such inference as it considers appropriate. Plainly such inferences will depend to a very large extent on the individual facts of each case but are not likely to be favourable to the defendant.

23–018

Provision for the Review of Cases

Section 5 (section 74A), section 6 (section 74B), and section 7 (section 74C) of the 1995 Act insert into the 1988 Act provisions which allow for the review of cases where the court has either made no assessment as to the proceeds of crime, or where the court has made an assessment of no benefit or of limited benefit and subsequent evidence comes to light that the defendant has benefited from crime to a greater extent than had originally been put before the court.

23–019

The procedure is broadly the same whether there has been no assessment, an assessment of no benefit or an under-assessment. Where further evidence showing benefit comes to light within a period of six years from the date of conviction, it is for the prosecution to apply to the court to consider new evidence. Having considered the evidence and all the circumstances of the case the court may then proceed to make a confiscation order. The court is under no duty to make an order and it has a discretion as to the amount of any such order. The court must take into account any fine or order for compensation which was imposed upon the defendant. The court may take into account any payments or other rewards received by the defendant after he was sentenced. Where there is an upward revision of a confiscation order, the period of imprisonment in default of payment shall also be revised in accordance with section 31(2) of the Powers of the Criminal Courts Act 1973.

23–020

Enforcement of Confiscation Orders

23–021   Confiscation orders are enforced by the magistrates' court as if they were fines. (See section 75 of the 1988 Act and ss.31(1)–(3C) and s.32(1) and (2) of the Powers of the Criminal Courts Act 1973.) The court may allow time for payment of an order and it may direct that payment of an order be made in instalments. The court must make an order fixing a term of imprisonment in default of payment of the confiscation order. Section 31 (3A) of the Powers of the Criminal Courts Act 1973 sets out the maximum periods of imprisonment applicable which go up to 10 years' imprisonment for orders in excess of £1 million. In the event of a failure to pay the confiscation order, the court will issue a warrant of commitment specifying the period of imprisonment that the defendant is to serve. This term shall take into account any payment made towards the confiscation order. A term of imprisonment imposed in default of payment will run consecutively to any other custodial sentence. The 1995 Act introduces an amendment which means that periods of imprisonment served in default of payment of confiscation order do not wipe out the obligation to pay. This is in contrast with the position as far as fines are concerned where serving a period of imprisonment in default wipes out the fine.

23–022   Section 9 (section 75A) of the 1988 Act provides that where a sum is required to be paid under a confiscation order and the sum is not paid by a date specified by the court, the court may charge interest on the outstanding sum.

23–023   Where a confiscation order has been made, the High Court may appoint a receiver in respect of realisable property (s.80). Section 81 of the 1988 Act concerns the application of the proceeds of realisation. Such sums shall first be applied in payment of such expenses incurred by a person acting as an insolvency practitioner, thereafter any balance is to be applied on the defendant's behalf towards the satisfaction of the confiscation order. If any sum is left after the payment of the confiscation order it must be distributed amongst the persons who held the property which has been realised.

Investigations into the Proceeds of Criminal Conduct

23–024   The purpose of section 11 (section 93H) is to permit the police and Customs and Excise to make an application to a Circuit Judge for an order permitting the obtaining of relevant materials (including information from bank accounts and material held on computer) relevant for use in making an assessment for the purposes of an investigation into the extent or whereabouts of the proceeds of any criminal conduct. A judge in making such an order must be satisfied that there are reasonable grounds for suspecting that a specified person has benefited from criminal conduct, that the material sought is likely to be of substantial value to the investigation and does not consist of material which is excluded material or material to which legal professional privilege applies and that there are reasonable grounds for believing that production of the material is in the public interest.

In pursuance of an investigation under section 93H a constable may apply to a Circuit Judge for the issuing of a search warrant in relation to specified premises.

23-025

These powers are additional to the general powers of seizure conferred upon the police by sections 19 to 22 of the Police and Criminal Evidence Act 1984.

23-026

Disclosure of Information held by Government Departments

Section 13(1) (section 93J(1)) of the 1988 Act allows for the making of an order by a High Court judge requiring the production to the court of any document currently in the possession of a government department where the document appears to the High Court Judge to be relevant to the exercise of powers under the 1988 Act to the making of a confiscation order. Such an order may be made on the application of a person appearing to the court to have conduct of any prosecution. This would appear to be wide enough include a person bringing a private prosecution. The court may make an order under section 93J(1) only where proceedings have been instituted in England and Wales and have not yet been concluded or where the court is satisfied that the proceedings in which a confiscation order may be made are to be instituted (ss.76(1) and (2)).

23-027

The material which may be the subject of a section 93J(1) order is material which has been submitted to an officer of a government department by the defendant or a person holding realisable property; material made by an officer of a government department in relation to the defendant or a person holding realisable property; or is material contained in correspondence which passed between an officer of a government department and the defendant or a person holding realisable property (s.93J(3)).

23-028

The court may under section 93J(5) order disclosure of material obtained under section 93J(1) to a receiver appointed by the High Court in pursuance of a restraint or charging order, as to which see below.

23-029

The court may also order disclosure of material obtained under an order under section 93J(1) by virtue of section 93J(7) to a police officer, a member of the Crown Prosecution Service or a Customs officer where an officer of the government department from whence the material came, has had a reasonable opportunity to make representations to the court and it appears to the court that the material is likely to be of substantial value in the investigation of crime.

23-030

Under section 93J(9) material which has been disclosed under an order pursuant to section 93J(7) may be further disclosed (subject to any conditions in the order) for the purposes of functions relating to the investigation of crime, of whether any person has benefited from any criminal conduct or the extent or whereabouts of the proceeds of any such conduct.

23-031

23–032 Disclosure under section 93J(9) to a private prosecutor would appear to be restricted to investigations relating to the extent and whereabouts of any proceeds arising out of criminal conduct. This has significant implications for any aggrieved investor who is considering use of this material in support of a private prosecution.

Restraint Orders and Charging Orders

23–033 The 1988 Act allows for quasi-civil action to be taken in advance of or during trial to ensure that assets which may be the subject of a confiscation order remain available to meet any such order. The High Court has powers to make restraint orders (under s.77) and charging orders (under s.78) where proceedings against the defendant have been instituted. In making such an order the court must be satisfied that the defendant has benefited or may have benefited from the proceeds of crime. The High Court may also exercise its powers under section 77 and 78 where it is satisfied that a person is to be charged with an offence to which the confiscation provisions apply.

23–034 Restraint orders and charging orders are plainly of enormous practical importance in that their use can prevent dissipation of the proceeds of criminal conduct at a very early stage of the criminal process, thereby enhancing the possibility that the victims of crime will recover at least some of their losses.

Restraint Orders

23–035 A restraint order may be made on the *ex parte* application of the prosecutor to a judge in Chambers and must provide for notice to be given to persons affected by the order. Under section 77 of the 1988 Act the High Court may prohibit any person from dealing with any realisable property. The procedure for the making of an application for a restraint order is set out in Order 115, rule 4 of the Rules of the Supreme Court.

23–036 The provisions of the Act which confer jurisdiction on the court to make restraint and charging orders are civil in character. Although the Act does not contain express provisions empowering the court to order a defendant to make full disclosure of all his assets there is inherent a power to make any order necessary to make a restraint order effective, including a power to order a defendant to make such disclosure. This power, however, is discretionary and is exercisable subject to certain conditions and exceptions. The Act does not abrogate the common law rule against self-incrimination. Hence, it is customary to insert in a restraint order a clause which indicates that any information disclosed in the course of the proceedings will not be used in evidence in support of a criminal prosecution—*Re O (disclosure order)* [1991] 1 All E.R. 330.

23-037 The court may make provision for reasonable living and legal expenses as it thinks fit—see *Re Peters* [1988] 3 All E.R. 46. However, a restraint order is not in all respects equivalent to a Mareva injunction (as to which, see Chapter 31). There is no jurisdiction either under the statute or the court's inherent jurisdiction to provide for the payment of compensation to innocent third parties—see *Re R. (restraint order)* [1990] 2 All E.R. 569. However, section 89 of the 1988 Act provides for the payment of compensation to persons who have been caused loss because they hold realisable property which is subject to restraint or charging orders. Compensation may only be paid if the defendant is acquitted.

23-038 A restraint order may apply to all realisable property held by a specified person whether the property is described in the order or not and it also applies to all realisable property held by a specified person being property transferred to him after the making of an order. The restraint order may be varied or discharged on the application of any person affected by it in relation to any property—see, for example, *Re K* [1990] 2 W.L.R. 1224, where a bank was entitled to obtain variation, it having a right of set off where several accounts were restrained including overdrawn ones.

23-039 A restraint order must be discharged at the conclusion of proceedings for the offence. Where the High Court has made a restraint order, the High Court may appoint a receiver to take possession of any realisable property and who may manage or deal with such property as the court directs. Property the subject of a restraint order may be seized by a constable for the purpose of preventing its removal from Great Britain.

Charging Order

23-040 Where a defendant or third party (including a trustee) holds land and specified securities, the High Court may make a charging order over such property under section 78 of the Act. The procedure for making an application for a charging order is the same as that for a restraint order.

23-041 The procedure allowing for the grant of restraint and charging orders fills a gap which may otherwise be left in the light of the courts' reluctance to grant injunctions to freeze assets which may be the proceeds of crime pending the outcome of criminal cases—see *Chief Constable of Kent v. V.* [1983] Q.B. 34; *Chief Constable of Hampshire v. A Ltd* [1985] Q.B. 132; *Constable of Leicestershire v. M and another* [1989] 1 W.L.R. 20, and *Chief Constable of Surrey v. A and another, The Times,* October 27, 1988. For the requirements which have to be met before a Mareva injunction can be granted, see Chapter 31.

Compensation Orders

General Principles

23-042 The power to order compensation is contained in sections 35 and 36 of the Powers of the Criminal Courts Act 1973 as amended by section 104 of the Criminal Justice Act 1988. A compensation order may be made in respect of personal injury, loss or damage resulting from the offence of which the defendant is convicted or from any offence taken into consideration. As noted, in *R. v. Crutchley and Tonks* the Court of Appeal held that a compensation order could only be made in relation to offences appearing on the indictment or taken into consideration.

23–043 Where a court has power to make a compensation order and does not do so it must give its reasons for not doing so when passing sentence. The amount of a compensation order is the amount that the court thinks appropriate having regard to any evidence and any representations made by the prosecution or the defendant. Where, for example, property which has been stolen has been recovered undamaged then the court cannot make a compensation order in respect of the value of the goods.

23–044 In ordering compensation the court does not have to find that the loss, damage or personal injury was inflicted intentionally—see *R. v. Corbett* (1993) 14 Cr.App.R.(S.) 101. Nor is it necessary that the loss, damage or personal injury is actionable in the civil courts—see *R. v. Chappell* (1984) 6 Cr.App.R.(S.) 214.

23–045 A compensation order should not be made in conjunction with a custodial penalty unless the court is satisfied that the defendant has the means from which to pay it. An inability to pay compensation should not be a factor affected the length of a custodial sentence.

23–046 A compensation order made by the Crown Court is enforced like a fine by the magistrates' court. The Crown Court has no power to fix a term of imprisonment in default of payment of a compensation order. The magistrates' court has the power to commit a defendant to custody in the event of default of payment, the term of imprisonment is determined from the table in Schedule 4 to the Magistrates' Courts Act 1980. The Crown Court may direct that a longer maximum term of imprisonment in default is available to the magistrates' court where the order for compensation exceeds £20,000. The Crown Court may allow time for payment of a compensation order and it may allow for payment by instalments.

Procedure

23–047 In making a compensation order the court should have before it either an agreed figure as to the amount of the loss or it should hear evidence as to the extent of the loss. However, the Court of Appeal in a series of cases has discouraged the criminal courts from embarking on a complicated investigation as to the extent of loss which is more properly the province of the civil courts. A compensation order may include an amount in respect of interest.

A compensation order may be made following the application of the prosecution or by the court of its own motion.

Amount

23–048 A separate compensation order should generally be made for each offence, although where there have been a series of offences against a victim forming a course of conduct a single compensation order may be made. Where there is more than one defendant, the level of compensation payable by each must be determined individually for a portion of the loss. Where there are a number of victims and the defendant's means are not enough to compensate each victim in full, the amount of compensation payable to each victim should usually be assessed on a pro rata basis, although there may be circumstances where it may be preferable to pay one victim in full rather than small amounts to a number of victims.

The determination of the amount of a compensation order must take into account the means of the defendant and an order should only be made when it is realistic that the defendant will be in a position to pay it following an inquiry into the means of the defendant. However, when considering a defendant's means the court is not restricted to funds which appear to be the proceeds of crime nor does the court have to be satisfied that the defendant has derived any profit from his crimes. Where there is a change in the defendant's financial circumstances after the imposition of a compensation order it is open to the defendant to apply to the enforcing court to vary the compensation order accordingly. However, the change must be a genuine and unforeseen one. In the case of *R. v. Dando* [1995] Crim.L.R. 750, the defendant, who had given evidence on oath as to his means, claimed his assets were in truth more limited than he had originally claimed. The Court of Appeal held that the defendant could not complain about the amount of compensation order imposed because he had lied to the Crown Court on oath about his means in an effort to mitigate his sentence. **23–049**

Compensation or Confiscation

Where the court has power to make both a confiscation order and a compensation order, the position prior to the 1995 Act was that the court could decline to make a confiscation order on the grounds that the matter can be dealt with by making a compensation order. Since the 1995 Act imposes a duty on the court to impose a confiscation order where there is a finding of benefit, this is a course which is no longer open to the court. **23–050**

It is still possible for a court to make both a confiscation order and a compensation order. The court may direct that such amounts of the compensation order which cannot be met out of the defendant's means may be paid out of the amount recovered under a confiscation order. Section 72 (7) of the 1988 Act (and s.81(7)) allows that where a court has made both a compensation and a confiscation order and it appears that the defendant will have insufficient means to pay both in full, the court may direct that the amount of the compensation order which would not be recoverable because of the insufficiency of the means of the defendant be paid out of any sums recovered under a confiscation order. **23–051**

CHAPTER 23: CONFISCATION OF ASSETS AND COMPENSATION

Restitution Orders

23–052 A restitution order may be made where goods have been stolen, obtained by criminal deception or blackmail and the defendant has been convicted of an offence "with reference to" the theft or such an offence has been taken into consideration. The power to make a restitution order is to be found in section 28 of the Theft Act 1968 and section 6 of the Criminal Justice Act 1972.

23–053 There are four types of restitution order. The court may order whoever has the property which has been stolen to return it to the owner. If the victim applies to the court, the court may order the defendant to deliver to the victim any other property which he has which directly or indirectly represents the stolen goods. If any money has been taken from the defendant on his arrest, the court may order an amount not exceeding the value of the property stolen to be given to the victim. If a third party is ordered to return property to a victim which he had purchased in good faith or has made a loan secured against the stolen property, that third party may receive a sum equal to the amount he paid or loaned from any money which was taken from the defendant at the time of his arrest.

23–054 Failure to comply with a restitution order will be treated as a contempt of court and will be treated accordingly.

Deprivation Orders

23–055 Section 43 of the Powers of the Criminal Courts Act 1973 as amended by section 69 of, and Schedule 15 to the Criminal Justice Act 1988, empowers a court to make orders depriving offenders of property used in connection with the commission of an offence. Before making a deprivation order the court must be satisfied that the property was taken from the defendant at the time of his arrest or that it has been lawfully seized from the offender, or that the property was in the possession of the offender when a summons was issued. The court must have regard to the likely financial effects on the offender of making the order. A deprivation order may be made in addition to any other form of sentence. A court which has made a deprivation order under section 43 is empowered to order that any proceeds of sale of the property seized may be paid to the victim of the offence (s.43A). The Court of Appeal has held that it is inappropriate to make a deprivation order where the property is the subject of multiple ownership—*R. v. Troth* (1979) 1 Cr.App.R.(S.) 341.

Chapter 24

Money Laundering

Introduction

At its most basic, money laundering is the concealment of the criminal origins of money by its use in legitimate financial activity. There are usually three stages to money laundering: the placement stage; the layering or agitation stage; and the integration or re-integration stage. Money laundering is an international activity, and increasingly so, with the increase in cross-border financial crime. It is estimated that approximately £200 billion non-drugs related money is laundered each year. An element of money laundering is likely to be found in every serious investor fraud.   24–001

In an effort to meet this problem there have been a number of initiatives aimed at co-ordinating an international response. These have included initiatives by the United Nations in the form of the United Nations Convention Against Illicit Traffic in Narcotics Drugs and Psychotropic Substances (the Vienna Convention) and the setting up of the Financial Action Task Force under the auspices of the G7 countries. The European Community has responded by issuing Directive 91/308 which followed the Council of Europe Convention on Laundering, Tracing, Seizure and Confiscation of Proceeds of Crime (1990). Part III of the Criminal Justice Act 1993 was passed in an effort to implement the recommendations of the Directive.   24–002

Sections 29 to 33 and 35 of the Criminal Justice Act 1993 inserted seven new sections (numbered 93A–93G) into Part VI of the Criminal Justice Act 1988 which came into force on the April 1, 1994. The 1993 Act extends the scope of money laundering to the proceeds of crime in general and is not restricted to serious crimes as originally suggested by the Council of Europe. The provisions of the 1993 Act are augmented by the Money Laundering Regulations 1993. The mechanism of regulation is through the creation of a series of criminal offences.   24–003

Assisting Another to Retain the Benefit of Criminal Conduct

The Offence

Section 29 of the 1993 Act (which becomes section 93A of the 1988 Act) makes it an offence: 24–004 "if a person enters into or is otherwise concerned in an arrangement whereby—

(a) the retention or control by or on behalf of another (A) of A's proceeds of criminal conduct is facilitated (whether by concealment, removal from the jurisdiction, transfer to nominees or otherwise); or

(b) A's proceeds of criminal conduct—

(i) are used to secure that funds are placed at A's disposal; or
(ii) are used for A's benefit to acquire property by way of investment,

knowing or suspecting that A is a person who is or has been engaged in criminal conduct or has benefited form criminal conduct."

24–005 The prosecution must prove that the defendant knew or suspected that A had engaged in or had benefited from criminal conduct. The notion that a defendant's suspicion will be enough to render him guilty of an offence is unusual in terms of criminal law. In this context it would seem that suspicion must have been intended to embrace the situation where a person deliberately shuts his eyes to the obvious and perhaps the situation where a person deliberately refrains from making inquiries, the results of which he might not care to know. Having said that, there must clearly be some limit to the elasticity of the notion of suspicion. Mere neglect to ascertain what could have been found out by making reasonable inquiries will presumably not be sufficient to establish the necessary mental ingredient under this section.

Penalty

24–006 On conviction on indictment, a person is liable to a maximum period of 14 years' imprisonment and/or to payment of an unlimited fine. On summary conviction a person is liable to a maximum of six months' imprisonment and/or a fine of the statutory maximum.

Breach of Confidence

24–007 Under section 93A(3)(a), where there is disclosure to a constable of any suspicion or belief that funds represent the proceeds of criminal conduct, the disclosure shall not be treated as a breach of any restriction upon the disclosure of information imposed by statute or otherwise.

This section is necessary because, having imposed a positive duty on professional advisors to report suspicious transactions, disclosure might be said to amount to a breach of the duty of confidentiality owed to another.

The protection afforded by section 93A(4) stops short of giving protection against liability of any kind, as was originally suggested in the E.C. Directive. This might leave the way open for an aggrieved person to bring an action in defamation, although a defence of qualified privilege would almost certainly be raised. **24–008**

In respect of information obtained under section 93A, there appears to be no limit on the use to which information obtained by a constable may be used. In theory at least, there is no reason why this information could not be passed to other regulatory or taxation authorities such as the Inland Revenue. **24–009**

Defences

It is a defence under section 93A(3)(b) to any act which would be an offence under section 93A(1) to show that the act was done following disclosure to the constable and with the constable's consent or that the disclosure was made after the act but was made on his own initiative and as soon as it was reasonable for him to make it. **24–010**

Under section 93A(4) it is a defence to prove (a) that the defendant did not know or suspect the arrangement related to any person's proceeds of criminal behaviour; or (b) that he did not know or suspect that by the arrangement the retention or control by or on behalf of A of any property was facilitated or, as the case may be, that by the arrangement any property was used, as mentioned in subsection (1); or (c) that he intended to disclose to a constable such a suspicion, belief or matter as is mentioned in subsection (3) in relation to arrangement but there is reasonable excuse for his failure to make disclosure in accordance with subsection (3b). **24–011**

If the defendant was an employee he may afford himself of the defences set out in subsections (3) and (4) if he has complied with the appropriate internal procedures of his employers as regards disclosure under the Act (s.93A(5)). **24–012**

The burden of proof when raising a statutory defence under the Act rests with the defendant and is on the balance of probabilities. What amounts to a reasonable excuse in section 93A(4)(c)(ii) is largely a question of fact. Ignorance of the statutory provisions would not amount to a reasonable excuse nor would a mistake as to the provisions. It may be arguable that reliance on the advice of a professional amounts to a reasonable excuse in this context. Once evidence of a reasonable excuse has been raised it is for the prosecution to demonstrate that it does not in fact amount to a reasonable excuse. **24–013**

Acquisition, Possession or Use of the Proceeds of Criminal Conduct

The Offence

24–014   A person is guilty of an offence if he acquires or uses property or has possession of property knowing that the property is, either in whole or in part, directly or indirectly represents another person's proceeds of criminal conduct (s.93B).

Possession of property means, for the purposes of this section, doing any act in relation to it.

Defences

24–015   It is a defence to show that the person acquired or used the property or had possession of it for adequate consideration. Inadequate consideration would be consideration which is significantly less than the value of the property or significantly less than the value of the use of the possession of the property.

24–016   As for section 93A, disclosure under this section to a constable does not amount to a breach of any restriction on the disclosure of information imposed by statute or otherwise and no offence is committed if it is done with the knowledge and consent of a constable or the disclosure is made as soon after the act as is reasonable.

It is also a defence to show that there was a reasonable excuse for failing to make such disclosure to a constable.

24–017   An employee is not guilty of an offence under this section if he has complied with his employers internal disclosure procedures.

Penalties

24–018   The same penalties apply as under section 93A.

Concealing or Transferring the Proceeds of Criminal Conduct

The Offence

24–019   Section 93C creates an offence where a person conceals or disguises any property which is, or represents in whole or in part whether directly or indirectly, his proceeds of criminal conduct; or where he converts or transfers property or removes it from the jurisdiction for the purpose of avoiding prosecution for an offence to which the Act applies or to avoid the making or enforcement of a confiscation order.

Concealing or Transferring the Proceeds of Criminal Conduct

A person is guilty of an offence if he conceals or disguises, converts or transfers property, knowing or having reasonable grounds to suspect that the property represents, either in whole or in part whether directly or indirectly, another person's proceeds of criminal conduct. A person would also commit an offence if he removes property from the jurisdiction for the purpose of assisting any person to avoid prosecution for an offence under the money laundering provisions of the Act or to avoid the making or enforcement of a confiscation order.

24–020

Concealing or disguising includes concealing or disguising the nature, source, location, disposition, movement or ownership of any rights in respect of the property.

Penalties

The same penalties apply as under sections 93A and 93B.

24–021

Tipping Off

Offences

Section 93D creates three offences in relation to tipping-off another person:

24–022

Under section 93D(1) a person is guilty of an offence if:

24–023

"(a) he knows or suspects that a constable is acting or is proposing to act, in connection with an investigation which is being, or is about to be, conducted into money laundering; and

(b) he discloses to any other person information or any other matter which is likely to prejudice that investigation or proposed investigation."

Under section 93D(2) a person is guilty of an offence if:

24–024

"(a) he knows or suspects that a disclosure (the disclosure) has been made to a constable under section 93A or 93B; and

(b) he discloses to any other person information or any other matter which is likely to prejudice any investigation which might be conducted following the disclosure."

Under section 93D(3) a person is guilty of an offence if:

24–025

"(a) he knows or suspects that a disclosure of a kind mentioned in section 93A(5) or 93B(8) (the disclosure) has been made; and

(b) he discloses to any person information or any other matter which is likely to prejudice any investigation which might be conducted following the disclosure."

Defences

24–026   A legal adviser does not commit an offence of tipping-off if disclosure takes place in the course of giving advice to a client, in the contemplation of, or in connection with, legal proceedings and for the purpose of those proceedings. However, it is not a defence if the information is disclosed with a view to furthering any criminal purpose—see sections 93D(4) and (5). There have been a number of recent cases on the scope of legal professional privilege as it relates to the furtherance of a criminal purpose. The House of Lords in *R. v. Central Criminal Court, ex. p. Francis and Francis (a Firm)* [1989] A.C. 346, affirmed the common law rule set out in the leading case *R. v. Cox and Railton* (1884) 14 Q.B.D. 153, in which it was decided that legal professional privilege did not extend to advice given by the innocent lawyers to a client who wanted guidance in the commission of a crime or a fraud.

24–027   A constable or any other person acting in connection with the enforcement or intended enforcement of any provisions of the Act is not guilty of an offence under section 93D (s.93D(10)).

24–028   Section 93D(6) provides a defence for any person who proves that he did not know or suspect that disclosure was likely to be prejudicial in the ways mentioned in section 93D(1) to (3).

Penalties

24–029   A person guilty of an offence under section 93D is liable, if convicted on indictment to maximum of five years' imprisonment and/or an unlimited fine or, if convicted summarily, to a maximum of six months' imprisonment and/or a fine of the statutory maximum.

The Money Laundering Regulations 1993

24–030   The regulations came into force on April 1, 1994. The purpose of the regulations is to require financial institutions to put in place systems intended to deter money laundering, and to assist the relevant authorities to detect money laundering activities. The regulations seek to implement this goal by requiring financial institutions to participate in:

— the creation and maintenance of a system for the identification of new customers;

— the creation and maintenance of appropriate training for all those who may come into contact with money laundering;

— the appointment of a compliance officer to receive all reports of suspicious money laundering and to make reports to the authorities where appropriate;

— the creation and maintenance of a system for employees to make reports of suspicious transactions.

Application

24-031 The regulations apply to all businesses which are engaged in activities which amount to relevant financial business which is defined by regulation 4. Although the definition includes investment business as defined by the Financial Services Act 1986, it is considerably wider in its scope in that it includes nine forms of business activity which fall within the scope of financial business. It also lists five exemptions which include activities carried out by the Bank of England.

Internal Procedures

24-032 Regulation 5 requires anyone whose activities come within the definition of relevant financial business to implement internal procedures through which money laundering will be prevented. This includes the implementation of the appropriate identification, record keeping, internal reporting, control and communication procedures, and the putting in place of appropriate staff training. In determining whether a person has complied with the requirements of this regulation the court may take account of any relevant supervisory or regulatory guidance that applies to that person or, if no such guidance does apply, to any other relevant guidance issued by a body that regulates or is representative of any trade, profession, business or employment carried out by that person.

24-033 Contravention of this regulation constitutes an offence carrying a maximum penalty of two years' imprisonment and/or a fine if convicted on indictment and six months' imprisonment and/or a fine of the statutory maximum if convicted summarily. It is a defence for the defendant to show that he took all reasonable steps and exercised all due diligence to avoid committing the offence.

Regulation 6 provides the mechanism through which individuals and bodies corporate may be prosecuted for offences under regulation 5.

Identification Procedures

24-034 Regulations 7 to 11 set out the procedures for the creation and maintenance of a system for the identification of applicants for business. In this context, applicants for business are defined in regulation 2 as a person seeking to form a business relationship, or carrying out a one-off

CHAPTER 24: MONEY LAUNDERING

transaction, with a person who is carrying out relevant financial business in the United Kingdom.

24–035 Regulation 7 sets out the identification procedures which must be implemented so as to comply with the requirements of regulation 5. Essentially, a person must make sure that applicants for business, whether in a business relationship or in a one-off transaction, have given satisfactory evidence of identity or that such measures as will produce satisfactory evidence of his identity have been taken as soon as is reasonably practicable after contact is first made by an applicant for business. If satisfactory evidence as to identity is not obtained the business relationship or one-off transaction should not proceed any further.

24–036 Regulation 8 allows that where it is reasonable that there is payment by post or an electronic means is utilised to transfer funds, the fact that payment is debited from an account held in the applicant's name at a recognised bank or building society is capable of constituting relevant evidence of identity.

24–037 Regulation 9 applies where a person who falls under the obligations imposed by regulation 5 is dealing with an applicant's who appears to be acting otherwise than as a principal. Reasonable measures must be taken to establish the identity of the principal. What is reasonable is determined by having regard to regard to all the circumstances of the case and best practice.

24–038 Regulation 10 sets out the exemptions where it is unnecessary to take steps under the identification procedures. There is no requirement to take steps to obtain a person's identity where there are reasonable grounds for believing that:

    (a) the applicant for business is bound by regulation 5(1);
    (b) the applicant for business is someone covered by the Money Laundering Directive;
    (c) where a one-off transaction is carried out with or for a third party where a person introduces that party and has provided an assurance that he will record their identity;
    (d) where a person to whom the proceeds of a one-off transaction are payable but to whom no payment is made because all of those proceeds are directly reinvested on his behalf in another transaction. A record must be kept of this transaction;
    (e) where an insurance policy in connection with an employer's pension scheme contains no surrender clause and cannot be used a security for a loan;
    (f) where single premium insurance business is involved not exceeding 2,500 ECU;
    (g) where the insurance business is payable in instalments not exceeding a total of 1,000 ECU per year.

24–039 Evidence of identity will be satisfactory if (i) the evidence of identity is reasonably capable of establishing that the applicant is who he claims to be and (ii) the person who obtains the evidence of identity is satisfied that it establishes the fact of identity (reg. 11).

All the circumstances must be taken into account when deciding what is a reasonable time scale for obtaining evidence of an applicant's identity.

Record Keeping Procedures

Those who are subject to the money laundering regulations must maintain minimum standards of record keeping. These procedures are set out in regulations 12, 13 and 14. 24–040

Regulation 12 sets out the record keeping procedures and is supplemented by regulation 13 which sets out the recording keeping procedures in the event of insolvency of a person carrying on the relevant business. 24–041

Regulation 14 sets out internal reporting procedures which must: 24–042

(a) identify the person ("an appropriate person"—in practice usually called a compliance officer) to whom handlers of financial business within the organisation must report their initial knowledge or suspicion of money laundering activity;
(b) the appropriate person must fully evaluate such information to determine whether it does reveal such a knowledge of suspicion;
(c) in evaluating information the appropriate person must have reasonable access to other information in order to assist in the assessment of the situation;
(d) the appropriate person must disclose the matter to a constable where he knows or suspects that the matter constitutes money laundering activity.

Supervisory Authorities

The supervisory authorities are listed in regulation 15 and include the Bank of England, the Building Societies Commission, the SROs and other bodies recognised under the Financial Services Act 1986, the Secretary of State, Lloyd's, the Director General of Fair Trading and various bodies governing Friendly Societies. 24–043

Under regulation 16 supervisory authorities are under a duty as secondary recipients of information to disclose to a constable any information which indicates that a person has or may have been engaged in money laundering, as soon as reasonably practicable. 24–044

Money Laundering in Practice

It was initially thought that there would be about 250 reports of suspicious transactions a year, however, in 1994, 15,000 suspicious transactions were reported to the National Criminal Intelligence Service 24–045

Economic Crimes Unit. About one in five was found to have some criminal connection. There is a widespread belief in the financial community that although they are diligently reporting money-laundering activities, they are seeing very little consequential action from the law enforcement agencies. No doubt in response to this perception, a new police fraud unit was established by the City of London police in May 1996, called the Financial Investigation Unit (FIU). The Unit has warned the legal profession that they may unwittingly be representing clients with connections to organised crime.

24–046 Certainly awareness of the money laundering provisions has increased in recent times. Herbert Smith (a leading firm of solicitors) recently reported that a number of their clients had sought guidance as to how best to recognise and respond to suspicious circumstances and so minimise the risk of prosecution under this legislation.

Chapter 25

Investor Protection and the Criminal Process

Although consideration of criminal procedure is generally beyond the scope of this book, there are two particular areas that are worthy of interest in the investor context. The first relates to the special powers given by Parliament to the Serious Fraud Office to obtain information by interviewing witnesses when a serious fraud has been committed. In such cases aggrieved investors will be concerned to know whether they can obtain access to the interview transcripts to use as evidence in support of civil proceedings. 25–001

The second area relates to the circumstances where an investor can seek relief against a prosecution authority if it decides not to bring criminal proceedings, notwithstanding the perpetration of a serious fraud. This situation occurred recently in the case of Nick Leeson and Barings Bank, when the Serious Fraud Office declined to bring criminal proceedings on the grounds that it was more appropriate for Mr Leeson to stand his trial in Singapore. Proceedings brought by aggrieved investors for judicial review against the Serious Fraud Office were abandoned before a court ruling was obtained. In other cases an aggrieved investor may wish to bring proceedings for judicial review against a regulatory body which has decided not to bring disciplinary proceedings or institute an inquiry into the circumstances of his case. 25–002

The Serious Fraud Office

Creation

The investigation of serious fraud creates greater problems for prosecuting authorities than the investigation of more straight-forward crimes. In 1976 the Roskill Committee was set up to consider the investigation and prosecution of fraud, and it recommended the establishment of a unified organisation responsible for all the functions of detection, investigation and prosecution of serious fraud cases (Fraud Trials Committee Report HMSO, 1986). The Committee also recognised that a fraud investigatory body required more extensive powers of investigation, if it was to be successful, than other investigatory bodies: 25–003

CHAPTER 25: INVESTOR PROTECTION AND THE CRIMINAL PROCESS

"An investigator naturally needs to be able to question witnesses, including suspects. Of even greater importance in fraud cases, an investigator needs access to the documents which were the vehicle of the fraudulent scheme and which will enable him to understand what has happened and piece together the case for the prosecution. The skilled fraudster is likely to do all he can to prevent the investigator from finding and using the documentation in the case; and a further problem for the investigator may be that some documents are in the hands of banks and other third parties in this country of abroad"—Fraud Trials Committee Report, para. 2.32.

25–004   Putting into effect some, but not all of the recommendations made by the Roskill Committee, Parliament established the Serious Fraud Office—by section 1(1) of the Criminal Justice Act 1987—and gave to the Director of the Serious Fraud Office special powers of investigation under section 2 of the Act.

Compulsory Interview and Production of Documents

25–005   Section 2(2) of the Criminal Justice Act 1987 confers power on the Director of the Serious Fraud Office to compel witnesses, including an accused, to attend for interview and to answer questions. Section 2(3) extends this power to include the production of documents. The draconian nature of these powers is illustrated by the case of *Smith v. Director of the Serious Fraud Office* [1992] 3 All E.R. 456, where the House of Lords held that the enactment of sections 2(2) and 2(3) of the Criminal Justice Act 1987 have overridden the common law privilege against self incrimination. The defendant was chairman and managing director of a company which was reported to the Bank of England as being in financial difficulties in 1991. The case was taken on by the Serious Fraud Office. The Director of the Serious Fraud Office issued a notice under section 2(2) of the Criminal Justice Act 1987 requiring the defendant to attend for interview after he had been charged with criminal offences for which he was being investigated. The House of Lords confirmed that the clear words of the 1987 Act showed that Parliament had intended to establish an inquisitorial regime in relation to serious or complex fraud in which the Director of the Serious Fraud Office could obtain by compulsion answers to questions that might be self-incriminating. There was no implied qualification that a person was entitled to invoke the privilege against self-incrimination after he had been charged. The privilege against self-incrimination is discussed fully in Chapter 31.

25–006   The powers of compulsion conferred on the Director of the Serious Fraud Office by section 2(2) and (3) of the Criminal Justice Act 1987 are supported by a number of criminal offences which have been created to deal with non-compliance.

25–007   It is a summary offence to fail to comply without reasonable excuse with a requirement under section 2. This is punishable by imprisonment of up to six months and/or to a fine not exceeding level 5 (s.2(13)). What may amount to a reasonable excuse for the purposes of a defence to a charge brought under section 2(13) will depend on the circumstances of the case. In the case of *R. v. Director of Serious Fraud Office, ex p. Johnson* [1993] C.O.D. 58, the court held that being the spouse of a person facing criminal charges did not amount to a reasonable excuse which allowed that person to refuse to answer questions posed under the section 2 powers. This contrasts with the position under section 80 of the Police and Criminal Evidence Act 1984 which prevents spouses from being compelled to give evidence against each other. Nor is it a reasonable excuse to refuse to answer questions posed under section 2 because the person being questioned has already been charged with criminal offences—see *Smith v. Director of the Serious Fraud Office*.

A person who purports to comply with a requirement under section 2, but who knowingly or recklessly makes a statement which is false or misleading in a material particular commits an offence which is punishable on conviction in the Crown Court by imprisonment up to a maximum of two years and/or a fine, and if convicted in the magistrates' court to imprisonment of up to six months and/or a fine not exceeding the statutory maximum (ss.2(14) and (15)). 25–008

Where a person deliberately falsifies, conceals, destroys or otherwise disposes of any documents or causes the same to be done to any document when he knows or suspects that an investigation by the police or Serious Fraud Office is being or is likely to be carried out he commits an offence which is punishable on conviction in the Crown Court by imprisonment up to a maximum of seven years and/or a fine, and if convicted in the magistrates' court to imprisonment of up to six months and/or a fine not exceeding the statutory maximum (ss.2(16) and (17)). 25–009

A person may refuse to produce information requested by the Director of the Serious Fraud Office under his section 2 powers where to do so would breach legal professional privilege or where such disclosure would undermine an obligation of confidence by virtue of carrying on banking business (s.2(9) and (10)). 25–010

Use of Information Obtained under Section 2 in Civil Proceedings

Section 2(8) of the Criminal Justice Act 1987 restricts the way in which information obtained under section 2 powers may be used. Information obtained under section 2(2) or 2(3) may only be used in a criminal trial against a defendant if in giving evidence in the course of a trial, the defendant gives evidence which is inconsistent with the information given in response to a section 2 investigation or where the defendant is being prosecuted for an offence under section 2(14) of the Criminal Justice Act 1987, as to which see below. 25–011

The provision in section 3 of the Act is of more interest to an aggrieved investor. This section concerns the ability of the Director of the Serious Fraud Office to disclose information obtained in the exercise 25–012

CHAPTER 25: INVESTOR PROTECTION AND THE CRIMINAL PROCESS

of section 2 powers to other parties. Under this section, information may only be disclosed to other government departments, or to a competent authority (as defined by section 3(6)), or for the purposes of a prosecution and for the purposes of assisting any public or other authority designated by the Secretary of State. The list of competent authorities includes several classes of persons appointed to carry out investigative functions under statutes, such as inspectors appointed under the Companies Act 1985, the Building Societies Act 1986 and the Financial Services Act 1986. The list includes any body having supervisory, regulatory or disciplinary functions in relation to any profession or area of commercial activity.

25–013 The scope of section 3 was considered in *Morris v. Director of Serious Fraud Office* [1993] 1 All E.R. 788, which arose in the aftermath of the BCCI collapse. The Serious Fraud Office had obtained documents concerning BCCI under its section 2(3) powers which it had exercised against Price Waterhouse (BCCI's auditors) and other third parties. The liquidators of BCCI applied for disclosure of these documents to use in the course of an investigation under section 236 of the Insolvency Act 1986. Accordingly, the court had to consider whether the Serious Fraud Office could make disclosure of documents which had come into its possession pursuant to the exercise of its section 2 powers. The court held that voluntary disclosure could not be made by the Serious Fraud Office since its powers were constrained by the language of section 3. Liquidators and administrators were not included in the list of bodies to whom disclosure could be made; accordingly, no voluntary disclosure could be made. Nicholls V.-C. said that:

> "The powers conferred by section 2 are exercisable only for the purposes of an investigation under section 1. When information is obtained in exercise of those powers the SFO may use the information for those purposes as may be authorised by statute, but not otherwise. Compulsory powers are not to be regarded as encroaching more upon the rights of individuals than is fairly and reasonably necessary to achieve the purpose for which the powers were created. That is to be taken as the intention as Parliament, unless the contrary is clearly apparent" (at p. 795b).

25–014 The court proceeded to consider whether the Director of the Serious Fraud Office could be ordered to disclose the transcripts under section 236(2) of the Insolvency Act 1986. The court came to the conclusion that there was no reason why disclosure should not be ordered, provided that a court took into account any prejudice that a third party might suffer if disclosure was ordered. Nicholls V.-C. held that persons from whom documents were seized or the true owners of the documents were in general entitled to be given an opportunity to present to the court any objections they might have to the disclosure of the documents.

25–015 It is interesting to consider whether, by analogy with this decision, business documents evidencing fraud could be obtained from the Serious Fraud Office if a subpoena were issued by an aggrieved investor in support of an action for damages. Regulatory bodies who fall within the definition of "competent authorities" could, subject to legal professional privilege and public interest immunity concerns, obtain the documents from the Serious Fraud Office by way of subpoena. But what about the position of the aggrieved investor?

The starting point, perhaps, is a dictum of Nicholls V.-C. in *Morris v.* 25–016 *Director of Serious Fraud Office* (at p. 797h) when he said that:

> "There is no sound distinction between production of documents in answer to a subpoena and production of documents pursuant to an order made under section 236."

Whether this passage is sufficient to open the door to the obtaining of 25–017 such information by an aggrieved investor remains to be seen. Support for a plaintiff investor's argument can be derived from the decision of the Court of Appeal in *Marcel v. Commissioner of Police* [1992] 1 All E.R. 72, where a defendant in a civil action issued a subpoena against the police to produce documents against the police officer in charge of investigations for use in the civil proceedings. The police had no objection to production. The Court of Appeal held that a police officer, like anybody else, is amenable to produce on subpoena any documents in his possession, subject to the true owner having the right to challenge the subpoena, or the production of documents, on any of the grounds on which a subpoena can be challenged. Such grounds would include, of course, legal professional privilege and public interest immunity. Different considerations might apply where an application for production of documents against the Director of the Serious Fraud Office where the documents were made expressly for the purpose of a criminal prosecution. Witness statements, for example, would fall into this category—*per* Nicholls V.-C. in *Morris v. Director of the Serious Fraud Office* at 798j and *Re Barlow Clowes Gilt Managers Ltd* [1991] 4 All E.R. 385.

The decision in *Marcel v. Commissioner of Police for the Metropolis* was 25–018 applied by Morritt J. in *Hoechst United Kingdom Ltd v. Chemiculture Ltd* [1993] F.S.R. 270, where the plaintiffs, who had brought an action for passing off and infringement of trade mark, obtained information from the Health and Safety Executive which had been obtained by the Executive under powers conferred by the Food and Environment Protection Act 1985. The defendant sought to set aside an Anton Piller order which the plaintiffs had obtained in reliance on the information which the Health and Safety Executive had supplied. Morritt J. dismissed the defendants' application, holding that there was no impropriety in disclosure to a person for whom, given the purposes of the statute, the information was of mutual interest and concern. The decision in *Marcel v. Commissioner of Police for the Metropolis* was also considered in *Bank of Crete SA v. Koskotas* [1992] 1 W.L.R. 919, where Millett J. had to consider the position where material had been disclosed in civil proceedings on the basis of an undertaking which confined the use of the material in support of the plaintiff's claim for misappropriation of funds. The order was varied to permit the plaintiff to disclose the material to an interested foreign party.

CHAPTER 25: INVESTOR PROTECTION AND THE CRIMINAL PROCESS

25–019   Once documents and interview transcripts have been passed from the Director of the Serious Fraud Office to another party, it will be much easier for an aggrieved litigant to obtain the documents from that other party. In *Wallace Smith Trust Co Ltd v. Deloitte*, July 10, 1996, unreported, the liquidator of a bank brought proceedings in professional negligence against the bank's auditors. The auditors had in their possession transcripts of interviews held with two of the auditor's employees which had been conducted by the Serious Fraud Office in exercise of its section 2 powers. The Court of Appeal held that discovery of the transcripts should be ordered only where the plaintiff can show that production is necessary to dispose fairly of the matter or to save costs. The auditors tried to resist discovery on the basis that the documents were protected by public interest immunity but this was rejected by the court. The documents were not protected in the hands of the auditors, since they could not be characterised as documents which by their nature would be protected regardless of whose possession they were in.

25–020   Most interestingly, on the question of whether the documents would have been protected in the hands of the Serious Fraud Office at the suit of the plaintiff, different views were expressed by members of the court on this point.

Reviewing a Decision not to Prosecute

Introduction

25–021   The second procedural area to be discussed in this chapter is whether an aggrieved investor can seek to judicially review a decision by the prosecuting authorities not to commence a prosecution in a case of investor fraud.

25–022   The decision whether or not to prosecute an individual is a serious step with far-reaching implications for all involved including the accused, the victims and the witnesses. In all cases the prosecuting authority must reach its decision of whether or not to prosecute by applying its prosecution policy to the circumstances of each individual case, in the light of its assessment about the sufficiency of evidence and the competency of criminal proceedings. The Crown Prosecution Service, for example, is bound to approach a decision about the commencement of criminal proceedings within the framework of principles set out in the Code for Crown Prosecutors which was issued in June 1994.

Jurisdiction

25–023   The jurisdiction of the Court to judicially review a decision not to prosecute was established by the case of *R. v. Metropolitan Police*

Commissioner, ex p. Blackburn [1968] 1 All E.R. 763. In that case the court drew a distinction between a review of the terms of policy which underlay a decision whether or not to commence criminal proceedings and the review of the way in which the terms of the policy had been applied in a particular case. The court held that there was no jurisdiction to review the terms of a policy but that its application to the facts could be judicially reviewed by the court in a particular case. This distinction between terms of policy and the application of policy has been confirmed in later cases, notably in *R. v. Chief Constable of the Kent Constabulary, ex p. L (a minor)* [1993] 1 All E.R. 756, where the court held that decisions whether or not to pursue a prosecution were reviewable only in as far as the applicant for judicial review could allege that the policy had been wrongly applied in the circumstances of the particular case.

Stuart-Smith L.J. conducted a review of the contemporary state of the law in this area in *R. v. Inland Revenue Commissioners, ex p. Mead and Cook* [1993] 1 All E.R. 772, where two taxpayers had been charged with tax evasion together with their accountant. The accountant was charged with a number of additional offences which named other taxpayers who had not been charged by the Inland Revenue even though it was clear that they had dishonestly benefited from the tax evasion scheme set up by the accountant. Instead, these taxpayers had been made the subject of civil penalties. The two taxpayers who had been charged with criminal offences sought to challenge the decision of the Inland Revenue to bring criminal proceedings against them. The issue for the court to decide was whether the decision by a prosecuting authority to prosecute an adult was judicially reviewable. In rejecting the application for judicial review, Stuart-Smith L.J. said (at p.782d) that the circumstances in which such jurisdiction would be invoked would be rare in the extreme: **25–024**

"Absurd examples, such as a policy only to prosecute black men or the political opponents of an outgoing government, which are virtually unthinkable, do however point to the theoretical existence of the jurisdiction to review. Fraud and corruption are perhaps other examples where the jurisdiction could be invoked."

These principles were applied by the court in *R. v. D.P.P., ex p. C* (1995) 1 Cr.App.R. 136 and *R. v. CPS, ex p. Waterworth*, December 1, 1995, unreported, where it was said by the Divisional Court that it was clear from the authorities that the court could only be persuaded to act in this case if it could be demonstrated that the CPS had arrived at a decision not to prosecute because they had failed to act in accordance with their own settled policy or because their decision was manifestly unreasonable. **25–025**

CHAPTER 25: INVESTOR PROTECTION AND THE CRIMINAL PROCESS

Reviewing a Decision not to Commence Disciplinary Proceedings or an Investigation

25–026 In addition to prosecutions brought in the criminal courts, investor protection is also achieved by the implementation of disciplinary actions and/or investigations by the regulatory authorities. The decision not to prosecute before a regulatory tribunal is subject to judicial review—see *R. v. General Council of the Bar, ex p. Percival* [1990] 3 All E.R. 137—and the same principles apply with regard to the way this jurisdiction will be exercised.

Part 6

Investor Protection in Civil Law

Chapter 26

Investor Protection in Company Law

Introduction

In this chapter consideration is given to the provisions of company law **26–001** which aggrieved investors should consider if there has been mismanagement of investor funds in the corporate context. Necessarily, in the context of company law it is the interests of the shareholder investor which forms the focus of attention in this chapter. This chapter is split into three sections, the first section focuses on directors' duties. The second section deals with minority shareholders actions and the concept of unfair prejudice. The third section examines the powers of the Department of Trade and Industry (DTI) to investigate companies.

In addition to the provisions of company law which form the subject **26–002** matter of this chapter, the Companies Acts impose a number of statutory obligations and restrictions on directors which are designed to promote fair dealing. These include restrictions as to directors dealings in shares and options, restrictions on directors loans and the disclosure of any interest in contracts, proposed contracts, transactions or arrangements with a company of which he is a director. These are discussed in Chapter 19.

Directors' Duties

Every company must have a director, public companies must have at **26–003** least two directors (see s.282(1) of the Companies Act 1985). The Companies Act 1985 does not define directors, it merely states that directors are "any persons occupying the position of director, by whatever name called" including those who act as directors even though not formally appointed as such (*de facto* as opposed to *de jure* directors) and shadow directors (see s.741(1) of the Companies Act 1985).

Directors manage the company in accordance with the Articles of **26–004** Association. Although the company is a separate corporate entity, its directors are often said to be its directing mind and will. The duties of directors in fulfilling the management of the company are therefore of critical importance in practice. Directors' duties may be either (a)

Chapter 26: Investor Protection in Company Law

fiduciary duties, which are often said to be duties of good faith, integrity and honesty, and which are strictly interpreted by the courts and (b) duties of skill, care and prudence in conducting the business of the company.

26–005 Directors must exercise their duties in such a way as to ensure that the interests of both the present and future shareholders of the company are maintained. It is a fundamental duty of directors not to place themselves in a position where their personal interests conflict with those of the company. The law imposes restrictions on the way in which directors may act which are designed to ensure fair dealing and to guard against directors taking financial advantage of their positions.

26–006 There has been considerable recent discussion about whether the courts should take into account regulatory rules when determining the existence or extent of a fiduciary duty. When regulatory rules are considered to be adequate, a court can be expected to decide that the fiduciary duty has been modified and that compliance with the rules is sufficient to meet the fiduciary obligations. The situation, however, might be different where the court considers that the regulatory rule is too stringent or lax; in this situation there will be a mismatch between the regulatory rules on the one hand and the scope of fiduciary duties on the other. The Law Commission has recently published a report in which these issues have been fully explored—Law Commission Report on Fiduciary Duties and Regulatory Rules, No. 236.

A Director's Fiduciary Duty

26–007 A director's fiduciary duty is usually described as a duty of good faith or integrity and honesty and is owed to the company alone. A director is under a duty to promote the interests of the company and must not let his personal interests intrude. A director does not owe a fiduciary duty to any subsidiary or associated company nor is such a duty owed to the individual shareholders of the company. That no fiduciary duty was owed to the shareholders of the company was established by the case of *Percival v. Wright* [1902] 2 Ch. 421, in which directors of a company had purchased shares from a number of shareholders, at the time of the purchase the directors, but not the shareholders, were in possession of information which significantly affected the value of the shares. The court held that the directors were not under any duty to disclose such information to the shareholders and that in the circumstances of the case there had been no "unfair dealing." Had the directors approached the shareholders seeking to purchase shares rather than the shareholders approaching the directors seeking to sell, the decision might have been rather different.

Duty to Act in Good Faith

26–008 The primary duty of a director is to act in good faith (bona fide) in the interests of the company. It was clearly established by the leading case of

Re Smith & Fawcett Ltd [1942] Ch. 304, that the test of what is bona fide in the interest of the company is subjective and not objective in that directors are required to exercise their powers "bona fide in what they consider—not what a court may consider—is in the interests of the company" (*per* Lord Greene M.R. at p. 306).

The Interests of the Company

The interests of the company are usually described as the interests of the company as a commercial entity. Strictly, a company's interests should be judged by reference to the interests of present and future shareholders. Where there are different classes of shareholder, the directors have a duty to act fairly having regard to the interests of all the shareholders. In reality, those running a company are likely to take into account the interests of a company's customers, creditors and employees when considering what is in the interests of a company and there is nothing in law which prevents directors from considering the interests of third parties with whom the company has a relationship. Indeed, under section 309 of the Companies Act 1985 the directors of a company are now obliged to have regard to the interests of employees. Additionally, where a company is insolvent or on the brink of becoming insolvent, the interests of creditors become paramount. 26–009

If a director is found to have exercised a power not bona fide in the interests of the company, the action may be declared void. If a third party is aware of the lack of bona fides, the action is avoidable as against that third party. If the action causes loss to the company, the director responsible may be liable to make good the loss. 26–010

Acting for Proper Purposes

Directors must exercise their powers in accordance with the Articles of Association. An exercise of powers for some purpose other than the purpose for which the power was granted, *i.e.* for some "collateral purpose", lays the conduct of the directors open to challenge. It is not open to a director who has exercised a power for a collateral purpose to argue that he believed he was acting in the interests of the company. 26–011

In *Hogg v. Cramphorn* [1967] Ch. 254, the directors of a company allotted shares to persons who would support them in office in an effort to avoid being taken over. The court found that the allotment of shares for the purpose of defeating a take-over was not within the purpose of the power of allotment conferred on the directors under the Articles of the company notwithstanding that the directors honestly believed that their action was in the best interests of the company. However, a meeting of the shareholders prior to allotment could have authorised such a course of action. In the later case of *Howard Smith v. Ampol Petroleum* [1974] A.C. 821, which again arose in circumstances relating to a take-over bid, the Privy Council set aside the allotment of shares to the 26–012 bidder for the company. The facts of *Howard Smith v. Ampol Petroleum* were that two shareholders held 55 per cent of the shares in a company between them. The two majority shareholders indicated that they would not accept any offer which amounted to a take-over bid. The directors allotted sufficient shares to the bidder for the company to reduce the majority shareholders holding to below 50 per cent. The decision of the directors was set aside on the basis that it had been made for an improper purpose even though there was no element of self-interest involved.

The Notion of Trusteeship

26–013 Directors are regarded as trustees of company property under their control. A director, is therefore answerable for any misapplication of the company's property in which he participated. The application of trust law in the context of investor protection is set out in Chapter 27.

26–014 Suffice it to note that a director will be considered to be a constructive trustee where he has received company money to which he is not entitled. In *Guinness plc v. Saunders* [1990] 1 All E.R. 652, a company director received payment of £5.2 million for services rendered in connection with a take-over bid for another company. The payment was received by the director in breach of section 317 of the Companies Act 1985 and of his own company's Articles of Association. In the Court of Appeal—[1988] 2 All E.R. 940, the company director was said to hold the money as a constructive trustee of the company and was obliged to account to the company for it. The basis of the constructive trust was, said Fox L.J. (at p. 945g):

> "the combination of three factors, namely a fiduciary relationship, a breach of a duty arising in respect of that fiduciary relationship and the receipt, in breach of duty, of property belonging to the person to whom such duty was owed."

The decision of the Court of Appeal was affirmed by the House of Lords on other grounds.

Conflict of Interest

26–015 It is a well-established principle that a director must not embark on a course of conduct which puts his personal interests in direct conflict with his duty to the company. If a court finds that a director has acted in such a way that a conflict arises, the court may order him to account to the company for any profits made. In the case of *Industrial Development Consultants v. Cooley* [1972] 2 All E.R. 162, the managing director of a company was asked to undertake work personally by the local gas board. The gas board indicated that it did not wish the work to be performed by the company. In order to take up the offer of work, the managing director obtained his release from his service contract by falsely representing ill-health. The court held that he was liable to account to the company for the profit he obtained from performing the contract as he had embarked on a course of conduct which put his personal conduct in direct conflict with his pre-existing duty as managing director of the company.

Secret Profits

Directors are under a duty not to make personal profits while acting as directors. It is a general principal that a director must account to the company for any profit acquired by him as a result of holding the office of director. The leading case on secret profits is *Regal (Hastings) Ltd v. Gulliver* [1942] 1 All E.R. 378. In that case it was held that the directors had used their special knowledge and opportunities as directors to make a secret profit for themselves and that they were accountable to the company for the profits made. The company in this case owned a cinema. The company directors wished to acquire two further cinemas but the company was unable to fund the acquisition. To avoid buying the leases in their own names, the directors formed a new limited company of which they were also shareholders, and this company made the acquisition. The three cinemas were subsequently sold together as a going concern and the directors each received a substantial profit as shareholders of the second company. Again, a director was held accountable to the company for the profit he made personally in the case of *Horcal Ltd v. Gatland* [1984] B.C.L.C. 549. In that case, the company was a building contractor. The director received an order for work to be done on a house and rather than executing the work through the company he took the benefit of the contract himself. The prohibition on directors receiving secret profits is equally applicable to the receipt by a director of a bribe or secret commission received in the course of negotiating a contract on behalf of the company. In *Att.-Gen. for Hong Kong v. Reid* [1994] 1 All E.R. 1, the Privy Council held that when a fiduciary accepted a bribe as an inducement to betray his trust he held the bribe in trust for the person to whom he owed the duty as fiduciary. If property representing the bribe increased in value, the fiduciary was not entitled to retain any surplus in excess of the initial value of the bribe because he was not allowed by any means to make a profit out of a breach of duty. 26–016

It has yet to be decided by a United Kingdom court whether a director may legitimately take the benefit of business opportunity which has already been rejected by the company. This point came before the Canadian Courts in the case of *Peso Silver Mines v. Cropper* [1966] 58 D.L.R. 281. The decision in that case suggests that it might be acceptable for a director to take the benefit of a business opportunity which has been rejected by the company as long as he has not influenced the decision. 26–017

Duty not to Compete

26–018   It is now common practice for a director's contract to indicate that competition with the company is prohibited. The only decided cases on this point date from the nineteenth century and seem to suggest that a director is free to compete with his company—see for example the case of *London & Mashonaland Exploration Co v. New Mashonaland Exploration Co* [1891] W.N. 165. A modern court would most probably take a different view.

Directors' Duties of Skill and Care

26–019   In contrast to directors' fiduciary duties, traditionally a directors' duties of skill and care have not been held to be onerous. The leading cases in this area were decided at a time when professional directors were unusual, and suggest that the courts will take a lenient view of directors' shortcomings of ability. The seminal review of the old authorities is contained in the case of *Re City Equitable Fire Insurance Co Ltd* [1925] Ch. 407. According to these cases, there is no objective standard of the reasonable director; a director is required only to exhibit that level of skill and care which may reasonably be expected from a person of his knowledge and experience. Applying this principle, a director who is a qualified accountant might be expected to exhibit a greater degree of skill and care in respect of the company's financial dealings than a director who was unqualified.

26–020   In practice, however, the law would seem to be moving towards a more objective standard. Parliament instituted an objective test for the personal liability of a director in wrongful trading cases—section 214 of the Insolvency Act 1986, discussed in Chapter 30—and there have been cases where the court has indicated its willingness to apply an objective standard more generally when considering the liability of a director. See, for example, the decisions in *Re D' Jan of London Ltd* [1993] B.C.C. 646 and *Norman v. Theodore Goddard* [1991] B.C.L.C. 1028. The courts have also tendency to apply an objective test in cases of disqualification brought under section 6 of the Company Directors Disqualification Act 1986—see Chapter 22.

26–021   This tendency is likely to be reflected in the drafting of obligations contained in a director's contract of service. In practice, a director's contract of service is likely to require him to exercise an objectively reasonable level of skill in the exercise of his duties. A director is not bound to give continuous attention to the affairs of the company although again in practice, the level of attention due from a director is likely to set out in his contract of service. Where it is permitted by the Articles of Association, a director may delegate the performance of his duties to some other official on whose honesty he may rely unless he has grounds for suspicion that the official is acting dishonestly.

Relieving a Director from Liability

26–022 There are a number of ways in which a director may be relived of liability for a breach of duty. The first of these is by ratification by the general meeting. The general meeting may "cure" a breach of duty by a director by the passing of an ordinary resolution. Breaches which may be cured in this way must be ones where the director has acted bona fide in the interests of the company and include a failure to disclose an interest in a contract, obtaining secret profits which does not include a misapplication of company funds, negligence and using a power for an improper purpose. Breaches which cannot be cured by ratification by the general meeting include any breach which involves a lack of bona fides on the part of the director, any breach which results in the company performing an illegal or *ultra vires* act, any breach which involves the company performing an act which is beyond the scope of the articles unless ratified by a special resolution, a breach which bears on the personal rights of individual shareholders, and any breach involving a fraud on the minority.

26–023 Alternatively, breaches of duty may be ratified by way of obtaining the consent of all members of the company. Such consent is not capable of ratifying a breach if it is *ultra vires* the company or involves a fraud on the creditors of the company.

26–024 Section 310 of the Companies Act 1985 makes any provision contained in the Articles of Association or in any contract which purports to exempt any officer of the company or any person employed by the company as auditor form, or indemnifying him against, any liability which by virtue of any rule of law would otherwise attach to him in respect of any negligence, default, breach of duty or breach of trust of which he may be guilty in relation to the company. Policies of professional indemnity insurance are specifically excluded from this restriction (see s.310(3)(a)).

26–025 The scope of section 310 was considered in the case of *Movitex Ltd v. Bulfield* [1986] 2 B.C.C. 99, in that case the Articles of Association of the company allowed a director to have interests in and profit from transactions in which the company was interested, if he made disclosure of such interest to his fellow directors and did not vote on the matter. The court held that the articles were valid and did not infringe section 310.

26–026 Section 727(1) of the Companies Act 1985 allows the court which has found a director or other officer liable for negligence, default, breach of duty or breach of trust to relieve him from liability, wholly or partly, on such terms as it thinks fit provided that the director established that he acted honestly, reasonably and having regard to all the circumstances.

Audit Committees/Non-executive Directors

26–027 Until recently the issue of corporate governance has been seen as an internal matter for each company which fell outside the scope of any form of external direction or regulation. The whole question of corporate governance was considered by the Cadbury Committee which reported in 1992 (The Report of the Committee on the Financial Aspects of Corporate Governance, December 1992). The Committee suggested that there should be greater reliance on the role of the non-executive director and on various committees including an audit committee, a nomination committee and a remuneration committee, in regulating companies from within. The Cadbury Code came into operation on June 30, 1994 and its long-term impact on the way in which companies operate has yet to be seen. However, the issue of directors remuneration continued to be the subject of widespread public disquiet which ultimately led to the setting up of the Greenbury Committee in January 1995 to identify good practice in determining directors' remuneration and to draw up a code of practice in respect of directors' remuneration which has now been done. A further committee was appointed in November 1995 under the chairmanship of Sir Ronald Hampel, to examine the progress made on the implementation of the Cadbury Code of Best Practice. The remit of the new committee is wide enough to allow for a fundamental review of all aspects of corporate governance. It is expected to look carefully at the structure of the board and to consider ways in which shareholders can be encouraged to exercise their rights to vote. The Hampel Committee is expected to report towards the end of 1997.

26–028 Suggestions for reform to allow for greater accountability of directors to the members of a company have included moving towards the German system whereby there is a two tier board structure which keeps the management functions and the supervisory functions of the board separate. In theory, the two tier system should ensure that there is an independent body policing the management of the company. Another method of exercising control over the directors of a company is to encourage greater participation of the company shareholders in the company's decision making process. In the U.S., for example, certain institutional investors such as pension funds, are required to exercise their vote at general meetings.

Minority Shareholders Actions

26–029 This section is concerned with the remedies available to minority shareholders which may often afford the only effective way of enforcing directors' duties in practice. The Companies Act creates two inter-related statutory remedies; first, a member of a company may petition the court on the ground of unfair prejudice under the provisions of sections 459 to 461 of the Companies Act 1985, and secondly, the court may be asked to have the company wound up on the ground that it would be just and equitable to do so under section 122 of the Insolvency Act 1986. Both of these remedies can be claimed in the alternative.

26–030 When considering the existing provisions which relate to unfair prejudice, it should be noted that the Law Commission is currently carrying out a review of shareholders' remedies including a considera-tion of the rule in *Foss v. Harbottle* and its exceptions; the provisions of sections 459 to 461 of the Companies Act 1985 concerning "unfair prejudicial conduct" including the orders available to an aggrieved shareholder under section 461; and the enforcement of the rights of shareholders under the articles of association.

The Rule in Foss v. Harbottle

26–031 The rule in *Foss v. Harbottle* (1843) 2 Hare 461, is that if a wrong is done to a company, only the company may sue for the damage caused to it. A shareholder has no right to bring an action on behalf of the company in order to protect the value of his shares. The rule preserves the rights of majority shareholders against an attempt by a minority shareholder to bring an action where the majority do not wish such an action to be brought. Minority shareholders cannot sue for wrongs done to their company or complain of irregularities in the conduct of the company's internal affairs. The rule rests on two propositions: first, the right of the majority to block a minority action where the majority is in a position to legally ratify alleged misconduct and secondly, the exclusive right of a company to sue upon a corporate cause of action.

The Exceptions to the Rule in Foss v. Harbottle

26–032 There are a number of exceptions to the general principal that minority shareholders cannot bring an action. The general rule does not apply where it is alleged that those in control of a company have defrauded it, *i.e.* where there has been fraud upon the minority, or where the action is *ultra vires* or where the action is unfair and oppressive upon the minority.

Fraud on a Minority

26–033 It was established in the case of *Burland v. Earle* [1902] A.C. 83, that a minority may bring an action where:

> "the acts complained of are of a fraudulent character or are beyond the power of the company. A familiar example is where the majority are endeavouring directly or indirectly to appropriate to themselves money or property, or advantages which belong to the company, or in which the other shareholders are entitled to participate."

26–034 What behaviour may amount to "fraud" in this context was the subject of consideration in the case of *Daniels v. Daniels* [1978] Ch. 406. The court held that "a minority shareholder who has no other remedy may sue where directors use their powers, intentionally or unintentionally, fraudulently or negligently in a manner which benefits themselves at the expense of the company". "Fraud" in this context was to be given a wider meaning than at common law.

Wrongdoer Control

26-035　An exception may be made to the rule in *Foss v. Harbottle* where the persons against whom relief is sought control the company and are in a position to stifle any attempt to institute proceedings in the name of the company. In the case of *Pavlides v. Jensen* [1956] Ch. 565, the directors who were alleged to have harmed the company by their negligence were a majority of the board although they did not in the strict legal sense control the company. The minority action against them failed because first, the directors' actions did not amount to fraud or to an *ultra vires* act but instead were merely negligent and thus open to ratification. Secondly, the action failed because the directors were held not to have sufficient control over the company to enable them to prevent the shareholders deciding in general meeting to an attempt to institute proceedings in the name of the company.

26-036　It is well established that if directors exercise their powers mala fides or for an improper purpose this is a matter of which the minority are entitled to complain as well as being a breach of duty. For example, if the directors were to use their powers to issue shares to take over majority control, a shareholder might seek an injunction to protect the rights of the existing shareholders. The use of directors powers for an improper or collateral purpose may also be the subject of a minority shareholders action. Such situations often arise in the context of take-over battles, where the directors issue shares in an effort to thwart the efforts of a potential bidder—see *Hogg v. Cramphorn* [1967] Ch. 254.

"Derivative Actions"

26-037　A plaintiff shareholder may seek to recover damages for the breach of duty of directors or for the restitution of property to the company where an action is brought under one of the exceptions to the rule in *Foss v. Harbottle, i.e.* where there has been fraud on the minority or there have been ultra vires acts. The distinctive feature of a minority shareholders' action is that damages awarded are not paid to the plaintiff but to the company. The defendants to the action will be those who have committed the act complained of and the company itself. The reasons for this were set out by Chitty L.J. in *Spokes v. Grosvenor Hotel Company* [1897] 2 Q.B. 124 at 128 when he said:

> "To such an action as this the company are necessary defendants. The reason is obvious: the wrong alleged is done to the company, and the company must be a party to the suit in order to be bound by the result of the action and to receive the money recovered in the action. If the company were not bound they could bring a fresh action for the same cause if the action failed, and there were subsequently a change in the board of directors and in the voting power. Obviously, in such an action as this, no specific relief is asked against he company; and

obviously, too, what is recovered cannot be paid to the plaintiff representing the minority, but must go into the coffers of the company."

26–038 Minority shareholders' actions must be brought by a present shareholder although the subject matter of the action may have taken place prior to the plaintiff becoming a shareholder. If the shareholder ceases to be a shareholder, the action may be continued by another shareholder. The plaintiff shareholder must not have participated in the wrong-doing complained of. The action must be brought in the interests of the company and not for the benefit of a rival company which has indemnified the plaintiff's costs. However, the courts have recognised that a minority shareholder who brings a derivative suit may have a right to an indemnity as against the company in respect of his costs—see *Wallersteiner v. Moir (No. 2)* [1975] Q.B. 373.

26–039 A minority shareholder must bring the action for the benefit of the company and not for an ulterior purpose see the case of *Nurcombe v. Nurcombe* [1984] B.C.L.C. 557, and more recently the case of *Barrett v. Duckett* [1995] 1 B.C.L.C. 243, in which the Court of Appeal held that a shareholder would be allowed to bring a derivative action on behalf of a company where the action was brought bona fide for the benefit of the company for wrongs to the company for which no other remedy was available but not for an ulterior purpose. Conversely, if the action was brought for an ulterior purpose or if another adequate remedy was available, the court would not allow the derivative action to proceed.

26–040 Once a company is in liquidation, redress must be sought from the liquidator, minority shareholders actions cannot be brought once a company is in liquidation.

Unfair Prejudice

26–041 The restrictions on minority shareholders' actions imposed by the rule in *Foss v. Harbottle* mean that derivative actions do not always lie in cases of minority oppression. The provisions contained in sections 459 to 461 of the Companies Act 1985 are intended to alleviate this restriction. Section 459(1) allows a member of the company to apply to the court by petition for an order on the ground that:

> "the company's affairs are being or have been conducted in a manner which is unfairly prejudicial to the interest of its members generally or of some part of its members (including at least himself) or that any actual or proposed act or omission of the company (including an act or omission on its behalf) is or would be so prejudicial."

26–042 The procedural rules to be followed in any action brought under this section are now contained in the Companies (Unfair Prejudice Application) Proceedings Rules 1986 (S.I. 1986 No. 2000).

26–043 The Companies Act 1985 does not define "unfair prejudice." The courts have considered what is meant by "unfair prejudice" in a number of cases. In the unreported case of *Re Bovey Hotels*, July 31, 1981, Slade J. said:

> "a member of a company will be able to bring himself within the section if he can show that the value of his shareholding in the company has been seriously diminished or at least seriously jeopardised by reason of a course of conduct on the part of those persons who have had de facto control of the company, which is unfair to the member concerned. The test of fairness must, I think, be an objective, not a subjective one. In other words it is not necessary for the petitioner to show that persons who have had de facto control of the company have acted as they did in the conscious knowledge that his was unfair to the petitioner or that they were acting in bad-faith; the test I think is whether a reasonable bystander observing the consequences of their conduct would regard it as having unfairly prejudiced the petitioner's interests."

26–044 The scope of "unfair prejudice" was considered in *Re Saul D Harrison & Sons Plc* [1995] 1 B.C.L.C. 14. In that case the petitioner sought a winding-up order on the just or equitable grounds or an order under section 459 that the controlling shareholders purchase the petitioners' shares. The petition alleged in essence that although the company had substantial net assets any reasonable board would have closed it down because of its poor prospects and distributed its assets to the shareholders. The Court of Appeal upheld the first instance decision to strike out the petition and in doing so considered what was meant by unfairness in the commercial context. Hoffman L.J. said (at 17):

> "In deciding what is fair or unfair for the purposes of section 459 it is important to have in mind that fairness is being used in the context of a commercial relationship. The articles of association are just what their name implies: the contractual terms which govern the relationships of the shareholders with the company and each other. They determine the powers of the board and the company in general meeting and everyone who becomes a member of a company is taken to have agreed to them. Since keeping promises and honouring agreements is probably the most important element of commercial fairness, the starting point in any case under section 459 will be to ask whether the conduct of which the shareholder complains was in accordance with the articles of association."

26–045 Exactly what will constitute a shareholders' interest which will fall within the scope of section 459 has been the subject of a number of decisions of the courts and has yet to be satisfactorily settled. As a general rule, in bringing a petition under section 459, the petitioner must be seeking to protect his interests as a member of the company and not interests which he may hold in some other capacity (*i.e.* as the freeholder of land). However, there have been some judicial decisions which have allowed a more liberal approach to be taken to the construction of the phrase "interests of some part of its members." In *Re a Company* [1986] B.C.L.C. 382, Hoffman J. observed that:

> "the interests of a member who had ventured his capital in a small private company might include the legitimate expectation that he would continue to be employed as a director—so that his dismissal would be unfairly prejudicial to his interests as a member."

For a consideration of the point in relation to a case of quasi-partnership, see the case of *Re London School of Electronics* [1986] Ch. 211. **26–046**

The courts are likely to take a broad view of what might properly be held to be regarded as a petitioner's interest as a member of the company. That interest is not necessarily limited to the member's strict legal rights under the constitution of the company but in the case of a small private company in which the petitioner had ventured capital might include legitimate expectation that he would continue to participate in the management of the company and be a director unless for some good reason a change in management and control became necessary. This view was expressed by the court in the case of *R & H Electric v. Haden Bill Electrical* [1995] 2 B.C.L.C. 280, in which the court concluded that the relationship between the parties in this case had broken down to such an extent that a change in the management of the company was inevitable, and accordingly an order would be made to purchase the shares of the party excluded from the management of the company pursuant to the powers conferred on the court under section 461. **26–047**

The test to be applied to by the courts was whether a reasonable bystander observing the consequences of the conduct complained of would regard it as having unfairly prejudiced the petitioner's interests was re-iterated in *Re Little Olympian Each-Ways Ltd (No. 3)* [1995] 1 B.C.L.C., in which the court considered the situations in which a member could bring an unfair prejudice petition under section 459 of the Companies Act 1985 were considered. A petitioner could bring such an action where he could show that the value of his shareholding in the company had been seriously diminished or at least seriously jeopardised by reason of a course of conduct on the part of those persons who had de facto control of the company, which conduct viewed objectively had been unfair to the member concerned. The test was whether a reasonable bystander observing the consequences of the conduct would regard it as having unfairly prejudiced the petitioner's interests. The petitioner was entitled to seek relief under section 461, against those in de facto control of the company at the relevant time but also against a second company which was effectively under the same control as the first to which the assets of the first company had been transferred at an undervalue. **26–048**

26–049 Breaches of directors' fiduciary duties may form the subject matter of a complaint under a petition for unfair prejudice brought under section 459. This may be a practical way of getting round the limitations of the exceptions of the fraud on the minority rule in *Foss v. Harbottle*. See also in this connection *Re a Company* [1986] 1 W.L.R. 281; *Re a Company* [1986] B.C.L.C. 382; and *Re a Company* [1986] B.C.L.C. 376.

26–050 In the recent case of *Popely v. Planarrive Limited*, March 28, 1996, unreported, the court was asked to rectify a Company register to record that the applicant owned certain shares in the Company which had been transferred to him. The directors of the company had themselves declined to register the shares in exercise of the powers conferred on them by the Articles. The court found that where it was being asked to set aside the exercise by directors of deliberately wide powers bestowed on them by the articles of the company, it was necessary to prove that the directors had acted outside the scope of their powers. If the power was unqualified, the only restriction on the directors was that they must act bona fide in the interests of the company.

Remedies for Unfair Prejudice

26–051 The remedies which may be granted by a court which has received a petition for unfair prejudice are set out in section 461 of the Companies Act 1985. Section 461(1), which is very widely drawn, allows the court to make such order "as it thinks fit for giving relief in respect of the matters complained of". Section 461(2) sets out specific remedies which may be imposed by the court. Under section 461(2) the court may regulate the conduct of the company's affairs in the future; or, the court may require the company to refrain from doing or continuing an act complained of, or it may order the company to carry out an act which it has omitted to carried out. The court may authorise the bringing of civil proceedings in the name of or on behalf of the company although this power is little used in practice. Finally, the court may provide for the purchase of the shares of any members of the company by other members of the company or by the company itself. This final power is the remedy most often sought in practice and is known as a "buy-out order". The provisions of section 461(2) are subject to section 461(1) which allows the court to "make such order as it thinks fit for the giving of relief in respect of the matters complained of".

26–052 "Buy-out" orders raise a number of practical problems in their implementation which have been subject to consideration by the courts. The first and most difficult problem is how to value the minorities' shares. The legal basis on which the minority's shares were valued where a buy-out order had been made was considered in *Re Bird Precision Bellows* [1986] 2 W.L.R. 158. In that case, the Court of Appeal emphasised that the overriding consideration is that the valuation must be fair and equitable. Valuation of shares may be either on a pro-rata basis according to the value of the shares as a whole or alternatively, on the basis that the price of the shares should be discounted to reflect the fact that the shares were a minority holding. Generally, where shares have been acquired on the incorporation of a quasi-partnership company the pro-rata method of valuations likely to be preferred. The date at which the valuation of the shares is to be made is also subject to what may considered fair. In practice a number of dates have been utilised for this purpose including the date of the unfair prejudice, the date of the petition and the date when the valuation was made, the date of a consent order that shares should be purchases.

Just and Equitable Winding-up

Under section 122(1)(g) of the Insolvency Act 1986 a member may petition for a just and equitable winding-up. The leading case on the scope of the "just and equitable" ground is the House of Lords decision in *Ebrahimi v. Westbourne Galleries* [1973] A.C. 360. The facts of that case were that A and B set up a business selling Persian carpets essentially as a partnership. After a time the business became a company with each partner receiving 500 shares. The son of one of the partners became a director and shareholder of the company receiving 100 shares from each partner by way of transfer. The company had only these three directors all of whom worked full time for the company. Profits were distributed as directors' remuneration. No dividends were ever paid. Relations between the directors deteriorated and B was removed from the board by the other two directors. At first instance, the court, allowing the petition for winding up, held that although the removal of the director was lawful, it still constituted an "abuse of the power and a breach of good faith which partners owe to each other" in that B's removal represented the exclusion of B from all participation in the business. The case went to the House of Lords which ordered winding-up. The mere fact that the exclusion of a director from participation in a company accords with the powers conferred by section 303 of the Companies Act 1985 and the articles of a company is not conclusive. Section 122(1)(g) of the Insolvency Act 1986 allows the court to "subject the exercise of legal rights to equitable considerations; considerations that is of a personal character arising between one individual and another, which make it unjust, or inequitable, to insist on legal rights, or to exercise them in a particular way". The court did not however, give an exhaustive definition of the circumstances in which a court would make such a decision. 26–053

The primary importance of this decision is the rejection of the view that the petitioner must prove that his exclusion was not bona fide in the interest of the company or such that no reasonable man could consider it to be in the interest of the company. The case established that the court might order winding-up where the circumstances of the case disclosed an underlying obligation in good faith and confidence that the petitioner should participate in management so long as the business continued. 26–054

26-055 The application of the decision in *Ebrahimi v. Westbourne Galleries* to situations which do not involve expulsion remains uncertain. Any course of dealing which produces a breakdown in mutual confidence may well suffice to justify the making of a winding-up order under section 122(1)(g) unless the breakdown is as a result of the behaviour of the complainant shareholders.

Overlap Between Unfair Prejudice and Just and Equitable Winding-up

26-056 The circumstances of the particular case will determine whether one or other or both the remedies of just and equitable winding-up and actions for unfair prejudice are available. When considering the relationship between these two types of action consideration should be given to the provisions of section 125(2) of the Insolvency Act 1986 which requires the court on hearing a just and equitable winding-up petition, to consider whether "some other remedy is available to the petitioners and that they are acting unreasonably in seeking to have the company wound up instead of pursing the other remedy".

Fraudulent Trading

26-057 In addition to the criminal offence of fraudulent trading created by section 458 of the Companies Act 1985 (see Chapter 17), section 213 of the Insolvency Act 1986 creates a civil sanction in the event of fraudulent trading.

26-058 Section 213 provides that if, in the course of the winding-up of a company, it appears that any business of the company has been carried on with intent to defraud creditors of the company or of any other person, or for any fraudulent purpose, the liquidator may apply to the court for a declaration that any persons who were knowingly parties to the carrying on of the business in such a manner are liable to make such contributions to the company's assets as the court thinks proper. This section has obvious implications as against directors personally who have been knowing parties to the carrying on of the business of the company in a manner which amount to fraudulent trading. The legislative history of fraudulent trading and the interpretation of the key concepts underlying it are discussed in Chapter 17.

26-059 The liability of a director for his negligence in circumstances where section 214 of the Insolvency Act 1986 concerning wrongful trading, applies, is discussed in Chapter 30.

Powers of the DTI to Investigate Companies

26-060 The Companies Act 1985 (as amended by the Companies Act 1989 Part III) gives the DTI powers to appoint inspectors to investigate the

POWERS OF THE DTI TO INVESTIGATE COMPANIES

affairs of a company. The Secretary of State for Trade and Industry has powers of investigation where fraud or other misconduct is suspected. Investigations into limited companies are mainly conducted under the Companies Acts, the Financial Services Act and the Insurance Companies Act 1982. The Secretary of State can also investigate companies, partnerships and individuals in those sectors.

The object of a Companies Act investigation is to find out what is going on by calling for the production of papers and by interviewing witnesses. Following investigation, action that may be taken includes criminal prosecution, winding up the company, the disqualification of directors and the imposition of sanctions by regulators. The ultimate purpose being the protection of investors and the promotion of efficient and honest markets. In the Third Report on Company Investigations of the Trade and Industry Committee (HMSO May 2, 1990), the Committee questioned whether the objectives of the Companies Act investigatory procedures to protect investors and promote confidence in the integrity of the markets worked when taken with the emphasis placed by company law on the duties of directors to their companies and the rights of shareholders. The Committee was particularly concerned with the efficacy of the system of DTI investigations in the light of experience following the Guinness, House of Fraser, County Nat West and Barlow Clowes investigations. The Committee recommended that "broader public interests than just the duties of directors and the rights of shareholders should be reflected in company law and the way in which it is applied" (see para. 15 of the Third Report). 26–061

Investigations are carried out by officials from the DTI's Investigations Division or by private sector lawyers, accountants or other specialists. On average, the Investigations Division receives about 1,000 requests for investigation a year (approximately two-thirds of requests are received from the public and the remainder come from various organisations working in the field of regulation). The Secretary of State has a discretion as to which complaints to pursue and about 250 requests are accepted for investigation a year. 26–062

One of the problems encountered in practice is that where malpractice arises (or may have arisen) it is often the case that more than one body has the right to investigate. There is considerable overlap between the powers of the DTI and the SIB, the SROs, the SFO, the Take-Over Panel and the other prosecution authorities. Where there are so many bodies charged with the task of investigating potential malpractice, there must be an efficient system for the exchange of information between them. The Trade and Industry Committee recommended in its Third report that these problems be combated by the setting up of a central clearing house to track all cases dealt with by different regulatory bodies and to maintain a database of people convicted of other publicly censured for commercial malpractice, fraud, insider dealing, disqualification as directors etc. (see para. 106 of the Third Report). 26–063

Inspections Under Section 447 of the Companies Act 1985

26–064 In practice, the vast majority of DTI investigations are carried out under section 447 of the Companies Act 1985 (as amended by section 63 Companies Act 1989). Section 447 confers on the Secretary of State the power to require the production of documents. A section 447 investigation is limited to an inspection of documents and is commonly referred to as a "calling for papers" inquiry. Section 447 investigations are confidential fact finding inquiries and they may be only the first step in a longer investigation using other powers. "Documents" include information recorded in any form so encompassing electronically stored information (s.447 (9)). Where a section 447 investigation produces evidence of corporate misconduct, a full investigation into the company's affairs may be ordered.

26–065 Failure to produce documents legitimately requested by a DTI inspector is a criminal offence punishable by a fine (s.447(6)). It is a defence to prove that the documents were not in the possession or control of the accused (s.447(7)).

26–066 Under section 447(5)(a)(ii), any past or present officer or employee of the company may be requested to provide an explanation for the contents of documents requested for inspection. It is an offence to furnish false information either knowingly or recklessly in purported compliance with a requirement to provide an explanation or to make a statement imposed under section 447. Such an offence is punishable by imprisonment or a fine (s.451).

Powers of Entry and Search of Premises

26–067 The Secretary of State may apply to a magistrate for a search warrant if he believes that documents which are he requires to be produced under his powers are being held on premises and would not otherwise be produced but would be removed, hidden, tampered with or destroyed (s.448(1) and (2) of the Companies Act 1985).

Investigations under Section 431 of the Companies Act 1985

26–068 The Secretary of State has a discretion to appoint inspectors to investigate the affairs of a company when asked to do so by the company itself or by a prescribed number of its shareholders (s.432(2)). Those asking for the inspection must satisfy the Secretary of State that there is good reason for an investigation and on the provision of security for the costs of the inquiry (not exceeding £5,000). Such an investigation will normally be conducted by two inspectors who are usually one senior accountant and a Q.C. or senior solicitor.

26–069 The application to the DTI for an investigation into the affairs of the company may be made by the following groups of members of a company:

- in the case of companies having a share capital, on the application of not less than 200 members or of members holding not less than one-tenth of the shares issued;
- in the case of a company not having share capital, on the application of not less than one-fifth of the company's members must apply; or
- on the application of the company.

Investigations under Section 432

In addition to his powers under section 431, the Secretary of State must order an inspection into the affairs of a company where there is a court order declaring that the company's affairs should be investigated (s.432(1)). The Secretary of State also has a discretion to appoint inspectors to investigate the affairs of a company under section 432(2) if he suspects that: 26–070

- the company's affairs are being or have been conducted with intent to defraud its creditors or the creditors of any other person, or for some fraudulent or unlawful purpose to some part of its members; or
- that any act of omission of or for the company would have such an effect or that the company was formed for a fraudulent or unlawful purpose; or
- that persons concerned with the company's formation or management have been guilty of fraud, misfeasance or other misconduct towards the company or its members;
- the members of the company have not been given all the information to which they are entitled.

An inspector appointed to conduct an investigation under section 431 or 432 may also inspect the affairs of subsidiary or holding companies (s.433). 26–071

Where a company is under investigation under section 431 or 432, its officers and agents have a duty to produce all documents relating to the company, a duty to attend on the inspectors and to render the inspectors all assistance they are reasonably able to give. The inspectors may examine a person on oath in the course of an investigation and answers given may be used in evidence against him (s.434). 26–072

A failure to comply with any of the requirements of section 434 will be treated as a contempt (s.436). 26–073

The Privilege Against Self-incrimination

During the course of an investigation a person called upon to answer questions by the inspectors must do so. The courts have considered the relationship between the DTI's powers of investigation and the 26–074 common-law privilege against self incrimination. In *Re London United Investments plc* [1992] 2 All E.R. 842, the Court of Appeal considered whether on a proper construction of the Companies Act 1985 the common law right to refuse to answer questions the answers to which may tend to incriminate had been abrogated. The case arose out of a DTI inspection in respect of London United Investments Plc under section 432(2) of the Companies Act 1985. The inspectors were appointed to investigate the circumstances surrounding the payment of commission on reinsurance contracts relating to a subsidiary company of LUI. The privilege against self-incrimination was held to be impliedly excluded where DTI inspectors have undertaken an investigation because the circumstances which give rise to the investigation will often include those where fraud is suspected. There is an obligation on those questioned to answer questions and the inspector's report may lead the Secretary of State to petition for the winding up of the company or to bring civil proceedings in the public interest. The privilege against self-incrimination is considered in greater detail in Chapter 31.

26–075 Following an inspection under section 431 or 432, the inspectors make a report to the Secretary of State (s.437(1)), the report is admissible in legal proceedings as evidence of the opinion of the inspectors. (s.441(1)). In proceedings under the Company Directors Disqualification Act 1986 the report is also admissible as evidence of any fact stated therein. The decision in the case of *Savings and Investment Bank Ltd v. Gasco Investments* [1984] 1 All E.R. 296, has been overruled by this legislation.

Civil Proceedings by the DTI

26–076 Once in receipt of a report, the Secretary of State may bring civil proceedings which are in the public interest and could have been brought by the company itself (s.438(1)). The DTI also has the power to petition for winding-up where it would be in the public interest (see the Insolvency Act 1986, s.124(4)(b)). The DTI may also seek relief under section 460 of the Companies Act 1985 where the affairs of the company are being conducted in a way which is unfairly prejudicial to some members' interests.

Investigations into the Ownership of a Company

26–077 The DTI has the power to investigate the ownership of shares of a company under section 442. The purpose of such investigations is to determine who has an interest in the success or failure of the company and who is able to control the company or materially influence its policy. Such investigations are generally conducted at the request of the shareholders in the case of companies having a share capital, on the application of not less than 200 members or of members holding not less than one tenth of the shares issued or in the case of a company not having share capital, on the application of not less than one fifth of the company's members must apply. The Secretary of State is permitted to proceed using his powers under section 444 allowing him to obtain information as to those interested in shares where he deems it more appropriate (s.442(3C)).

In connection with an investigation under sections 442 or 444, the DTI may impose restrictions on shares the transfer of shares, on the exercise of voting rights in connection with shares and on payments in relation to shares by the company (s.454). **26–078**

Investigations under Section 446

The Secretary of State can appoint inspectors to investigate share dealings by directors or their families in their own companies or related companies in contravention of section 323 or 324 and Schedule 13 to the Companies Act 1985. **26–079**

Privileged Information

Nothing in sections 431 to 446 of the Companies Act 1985 requires the production of information which is the subject of legal professional privilege. **26–080**

The Financial Services Act 1986

The DTI may investigate authorised persons within the meaning of the Financial Services Act under section 446 using the powers to require the production of documents and evidence granted under sections 434 to 436. **26–081**

Disclosure of Transcripts and Documents Obtained During the Course of Investigations

There has been considerable recent litigation concerning the production of documents and interview transcripts which have been obtained during the course of investigations. Production can be required for use in criminal or civil proceedings. It was established in *Re Arrows Ltd* (No 4) [1994] 3 All E.R. 814, that the material could be disclosed to the prosecution authorities and that its admissibility in criminal proceedings was subject to the exercise of the court's powers to exclude evidence where its admission would adversely prejudice the fairness of the proceedings under section 78 of the Police and Criminal Evidence Act 1984. The way in which a Crown Court should exercise this discretion **26–082** was considered by the Court of Appeal in *Saunders and others* [1996] Crim.L.R. 420. Similarly, where documents or interview transcripts were required by a defendant for use in a criminal trial, the crown court judge would have to consider whether disclosure was in the public interest, taking into account the competing interests—*Re Barlow Clowes Gilt Managers Ltd* [1991] 4 All E.R. 385.

26–083 The principles to be applied where material is sought for use in a civil action are considered in Chapter 25, in the context of material obtained by the Director of the Serious Fraud Office in exercise of powers under section 2 of the Criminal Justice Act 1987. The scope of the discretion to produce material obtained during the course of an inquiry was considered by the Court of Appeal in *Re British and Commonwealth Holdings plc (Nos 1 and 2)* [1992] 2 All E.R. 801, and more recently in *Re Murjani (a bankrupt)* [1996] 1 All E.R. 66.

26–084 Issues of confidence were considered in *Soden v. Burns* and *R. v. Secretary of State for Trade and Industry, ex p. Soden, The Times,* July 5, 1996, in which Walker J. recognised that there was a qualified duty of confidence and public interest immunity to be considered in respect of evidence given under compulsion. Certainly, before requiring any material to be disclosed for use in a civil case, the court had to take account of these qualified, but not absolute, concerns. In any event, the Judge added that documents belonging to a third party should not be disclosed before the third party had been heard.

26–085 A similar point can be derived from a consideration of the decision in *Re Atlantic Computers* May 23, 1996 unreported, where the court considered whether transcripts of oral evidence given to DTI inspectors pursuant to an inquiry conducted under section 432 should be disclosed to the administrators of a company in liquidation. The court held that section 236 of the Insolvency Act 1986 was binding on the Crown and that the transcripts of evidence of witnesses, but not any other documents, should be disclosed to the administrators but that disclosure should only take place after the witnesses had been notified that such a course of action was to take place so that they had the opportunity to apply to have the order for disclosure set aside.

Chapter 27

Investor Protection in Trust Law

Introduction

There are three ways in which trusts law may impinge in the area of investor protection. 27–001

In the first instance, there are occasions when an investor passes investment funds to another person in circumstances where the funds are to be used for a specific purpose, such as the purchase of shares, government securities, gold bullion or some other form of property or financial security. In this type of case the funds are held on trust for the investor, so that if the moneys are misapplied by the receiver and/or the receiver becomes insolvent, the receiver's duty to return the funds to the investor is founded not simply in terms of debt but also in breach of an obligation to account in terms of trust. The existence of the trust relationship has considerable significance in this context. In an insolvency the funds will not enter the general pool of assets from which a receiver's creditors will fall to be paid because the funds are "impressed" with a trust and held by the receiver on a different basis, on resulting trust for the investor. This means that if an investor's funds can be identified, the funds will be recoverable and protected from the claims of other creditors. The circumstances in which an investor's funds will be impressed with a trust will be considered in the first part of this chapter. 27–002

There is a second area in which trusts law may impinge in the context of investor protection law. In any modern case of investment fraud, persons other than the fraudster will almost certainly handle or assist in handling the misapplied funds, either at the time of misappropriation or during the laundering process. Third parties, such as banks, building societies, stockbrokers, estate agents, solicitors and accountants are potentially exposed in this regard. Where misapplied funds have been handled by a third party or a third party has assisted in the handling of funds, it will be important for an investor to know whether there is any actionable claim against the third party in respect of his conduct. A third party may become personally liable to an investor as a constructive trustee where, with regard to his action or inaction in relation to the investment funds (*i.e.* the trust property), a court considers it appropriate to order him to make good the investor's loss. Although a professional third party like a bank may not be an accomplice to a fraudulent scheme, this will not be sufficient to absolve the third party from personal liability where there were circumstances which should have put the third party on enquiry. In cases where the fraudster may have fled 27–003

Chapter 27: Investor Protection in Trust Law

the jurisdiction, or where he is resident but insolvent, the possibility of legal action against a professional third party can sometimes provide the aggrieved investor with his only realistic chance of recovering his lost investment. The circumstances where an aggrieved investor can recover his loss from a third party is the subject of consideration in the second part of this chapter.

27–004 Modern trusts law is also significant in procedural terms, because where an investor can establish a claim against a trustee for breach of trust or a third party for assisting in a breach of trust, an investor can utilise the extensive power of tracing monies which has been retained by the court in the exercise of its ancient equitable jurisdiction. The operation of these tracing remedies is considered in part three of this chapter.

1. Investor's Funds Held on Trust

Relationship in Contract and/or Trust

27–005 In the ordinary situation, when a person pays over his monies to another, the relationship between the payer and the payee is governed by the terms of the agreement which has been made between them. A contract for banking services is a classic example, where a payer pays money to a banker for the latter to hold on his behalf. The relationship is exclusively contractual, and it is the duty of the payee as debtor to repay the payer as creditor in accordance with the terms of the contract which have been agreed. The debtor's obligation is personal and not proprietary, which means that the obligation to repay arises in debt rather than in any obligation to deal with the money in a particular way. However, in cases where money is paid over for the purposes of investment, the position will probably be different, for in this type of case the purpose for which the money is paid will often be specified. For instance, where an investor pays money to a financial services company for the purchase of some specified form of investment, such as stocks or shares, government securities, bonds, or commodities, the words which are used when the payment is made will probably be capable of being construed as creating an obligation both in terms of contract and also in terms of trust. Indeed, if the financial services company is authorised under the terms of the Financial Services Act 1986 a relationship of trust will almost certainly be created since the authorised person will be obliged to hold the funds in a designated client account—see Chapter 3 on this point.

27–006 The essence of a trust relationship is the passing of property by one person (known as the beneficiary) into the possession and control of another person (known as the trustee) for the trustee to deal with the property on behalf of the beneficiary in a particular way. Unlike a contractual relationship, which is exclusively personal, a trust relationship is proprietary, in the sense that it arises independently of agreement and attaches to the property itself. There is no reason why, in terms of law, the relationship of debtor/creditor and trustee/beneficiary cannot co-exist in cases where the circumstances demonstrate that the parties intended to create both forms of obligation.

A good illustration of the confluence between a contractual and a trust relationship occurred in the Barlow Clowes case where the Barlow Clowes group marketed off-shore investment schemes, known as portfolios, for investment in gilt-edged stock. Investors were induced to invest in the portfolios by representations that their monies would be securely invested in British government securities. The brochure stated that investors cheques were to be paid to the Barlow Clowes group's international account, which on its face suggested that a relationship of debtor and creditor was to be created between the investor and the financial services company. However, the brochures went on to state that all monies were to be held in a designated clients account and "the clients are the beneficial owners of all securities purchased on their behalf", which strongly suggested that a relationship of trust between the investor as beneficiary and the financial services company as trustee was to be created as well. In these circumstances the Court of Appeal determined that it was clear from the brochures and the terms of the portfolio investments, construed as a whole, that the Barlow Clowes group had received funds from investors on trust to invest them in British government stocks—see *R. v. Clowes* [1994] 2 All E.R. 316. 27–007

The practical implications of a trust relationship were vividly demonstrated some years ago by a case which was heard in the House of Lords, *Barclays Bank Ltd v. Quistclose Investments Ltd* [1968] 3 All E.R. 651. A company needed to borrow a significant sum of money to pay dividends which had been declared on its shares. The company borrowed the money from Quistclose Investments under an arrangement whereby the loan was to be used only for that purpose. The money was paid into a separate account at Barclays Bank, the bank having notice of the nature of the arrangement. Before the dividend was paid the company went into liquidation. Barclays Bank sought to off-set the money against the company's overdraft liability but Quistclose Investments intervened and argued that the company had received the money as trustees and continued to hold it as trustee. The House of Lords held that the money had indeed been received on trust to be applied for the payment of dividends. That purpose having failed, the money was held on trust for the lender. The fact that the transaction was a loan, recoverable by an action at law, did not exclude the implication of a trust. The legal (*i.e.* debt) and equitable (*i.e.* trust) remedies could co-exist. As Lord Wilberforce explained in his judgment which continues to govern this area of law: 27–008

". . . when the money is advanced, the lender acquires an equitable right to see that it is applied for the primary designated purpose . . .; when the purpose has been carried out (*i.e.* the debt paid) the lender has his remedy against the borrower in debt; if the primary purpose cannot be carried out, the question arises if a secondary purpose (*i.e.* the repayment to the lender) has been agreed, expressly or by implication: if it has, the remedies of equity may be invoked to give effect to it, if it has not (and the money is intended to fall within the general fund of the debtor's assets) then there is the appropriate remedy for recovery of a loan. I can appreciate no reason why the flexible interplay of law and equity cannot let in these practical arrangements, and other variations if desired: it would be to the discredit of both systems if they could not".

Application in the Investor Context

27–009   The courts have permitted the "Quistclose trust" principle to apply quite broadly in cases where money has not been paid to a defendant to hold beneficially. In *Carreras Rothmans v. Freeman Mathews* [1985] 1 All E.R. 155, the plaintiff lent money to the defendant company for the specific purpose of settling invoices submitted by the plaintiff in the course of its business. The court, applying *Barclays Bank v. Quistclose Investments Limited*, held that a relationship of trust had been created because the money had not been paid to the defendant beneficially. Broadening the category of case to which the Quistclose trust principle will apply, Peter Gibson J. said (at p. 165f) that equity fastens onto the conscience of the person who receives property from another person for a specific purpose only and not for the recipients' own purpose—

> "If the common intention is that property is transferred for a specified purpose and not so as to become the property of the transferee, the transferee cannot keep the property if for any reason that purpose cannot be fulfilled."

27–010   The payment of monies into a designated bank account was a significant but not conclusive indication of a common intention to create a trust—*Re Kayford Ltd* [1975] 1 All E.R. 604. The Quistclose trust principle has been applied in other cases, such as *Barclays Bank plc v. Willowbrook International Ltd, The Times*, February 5, 1987 and *Re EVTR Ltd, Gilbert v. Barber, The Times*, June 24, 1987.

27–011   The significance of the application of these principles in the investor protection context, where investor's funds are misapplied and/or an investment scheme fails, will be readily appreciated. In *Re Nanwa Gold Mines Ltd* [1955] 3 All E.R. 219, a company issued a share form application to existing shareholders seeking fresh capital to resume its activities. The application contained a statement which said that shares would be issued on condition that a scheme for reduction of capital was approved by the company in general meeting and ratified by the court. The scheme was formally abandoned after existing members had subscribed for new shares. The court held that the money was repayable to the members because they had subscribed the money on the faith of a promise to refund the money if certain conditions were not fulfilled.

In a more recent case *Stanlake Holdings Ltd v. Tropical Capital* 27–012
Investment Ltd, FT Law Reports, June 25, 1991, a businessman lent
£70,000 to an investment company in order to assist an off-shore client
with a contract to buy tyres in the Ivory Coast. In fact the scheme was a
fraud and the director of the defendant company together with his
solicitor were convicted of obtaining property by deception. Of the
£70,000, £55,000 was found in a safe at the solicitor's office. Applying the
Quistclose Trust principle, the Court of Appeal ruled that the money was
held in trust for the plaintiff, the purpose of the loan having failed.

2. Knowing Receipt and Knowing Assistance in Breach of Trust

The General Principle

The foundation of liability in this complicated area of law is rooted in 27–013
the notion that persons, not appointed trustees, may be liable as if they
were so appointed, if they intermeddle with funds which are held on
trust. This important principle of trusts law was famously expressed long
ago by Lord Selborne L.C. in *Barnes v. Addy* [1874] LR 9 Ch.App. 244,
in terms which continue to express the present state of the law in this
area:

> "That responsibility [of a trustee] may no doubt be extended in
> equity to others who are not properly trustees, if they are found . . .
> actually participating in any fraudulent conduct of the trustee to the
> injury of the . . . [beneficiary]. But . . . strangers are not to be made
> constructive trustees merely because they act as the agents of trustees
> in transactions within their legal powers, transactions, perhaps of
> which a Court of Equity may disapprove, unless those agents receive
> and become chargeable with some part of the trust property, or unless
> they assist with the knowledge in a dishonest and fraudulent design
> on the part of the trustees."

In this passage Lord Selborne delineated two distinct limbs of 27–014
potential liability. The first limb, contained in the first sentence of the
citation, provided that a third party (*i.e.* stranger or non-trustee) may
become liable to account if he "actually participates in any fraudulent
conduct" by receiving funds which have been misapplied in breach of
trust. The second limb, reflected in the second sentence of the citation,
established that a third party may become liable where he "assists with
knowledge in a dishonest and fraudulent design", not necessarily where
he actually receives the trust funds but where he provides some other
form of assistance. The first limb has become known as "knowing
receipt", in contrast to the second limb which has become known as
"knowing assistance".

Chapter 27: Investor Protection in Trust Law

Problems

27–015 During the last 30 years there has been much litigation directed at defining more precisely the circumstances in which a third party can be held liable as a constructive trustee in application of the principles formulated by Lord Selborne. There have been two main areas of contention. The first area of dispute concerned the degree of dishonest knowledge which had to be imputed to a third party before he could be held liable as a constructive trustee. Was it necessary to prove that the third party was dishonest in a strictly subjective sense, or was a more objective standard sufficient, as where a third party "turned a blind eye" to the breach of trust or where there were circumstances which should have alarmed the third party by "putting him on notice" that he was assisting in the handling of funds in breach of trust?

27–016 The second area of dispute has focused not on the mental state of the third party's mind but on the state of mind of the trustee. In these cases litigants have sought to argue that a dishonest third party could not be held liable for dishonestly assisting in the handling of trust funds where the breach of trust committed by the trustee was innocent or negligent rather than dishonest. Dishonest conduct on the part of the trustee was, so litigants argued, a condition precedent to the liability of an (albeit dishonest) third party.

The Position Resolved

27–017 After a series of contradictory decisions in both these areas of dispute, the position was resolved by the Privy Council recently in the case of *Royal Brunei Airlines Sdn v. Tan* [1995] 3 All E.R. 97. Summarising the Privy Council's conclusion, Lord Nicholls said:

> "Drawing the threads together, their Lordships' overall conclusion is that dishonesty is a necessary ingredient of accessory liability. It is also a sufficient ingredient. A liability in equity to make good resulting loss attaches to a person who dishonestly procures or assists in a breach of trust or fiduciary obligation. It is not necessary that, in addition, the trustee or fiduciary was acting dishonestly, although this will usually be so where the third party who is assisting him is acting dishonestly. 'Knowingly' is better avoided as a defining ingredient of the principle . . ."

Within the formulation put forward by Lord Selborne in *Barnes v. Addy*, instead of referring to "knowing receipt" and "knowing assistance", "dishonest receipt" and "dishonest assistance" are more accurate epithets. 27–018

Dishonesty—An Objective Standard

Exploring the position a little further, the Privy Council considered what was meant by the notion of "dishonesty." Was dishonesty a subjective matter or, as some of the earlier cases had suggested, could dishonesty be established by a more objective standard? The answer, said the Privy Council, lay in keeping in mind that honesty is an objective standard. Irrespective of the position in criminal law, in the context of the accessory liability principle, acting dishonestly, or with a lack of probity, meant simply not acting as an honest person would in the circumstances. This was clearly, said Lord Nicholls, an objective standard. 27–019

Whilst it was right that there is a subjective aspect to dishonesty, in the sense that it is a description of a type of conduct assessed in the light of what a person actually knew at the time, honesty could not be measured on an optional scale. "If a person knowingly appropriates another's property, he will not escape a finding of dishonesty simply because he sees nothing wrong in such behaviour." An honest person does not, said Lord Nicholls, deliberately close his eyes and ears, or deliberately not ask questions, lest he learn something he would rather not know, and then proceed regardless: 27–020

"The individual is expected to attain the standard which would be observed by an honest person placed in those circumstances. It is impossible to be more specific. Knox J. captured the flavour of this, in a case with a commercial setting, when he referred to a person who is 'guilty of commercially unacceptable conduct in the particular context involved': see *Cowan de Groot Properties Ltd v. Eagle Trust plc* [1992] 4 All E.R. 700 at 761t . . . Ultimately, in most cases, an honest person should have little difficulty in knowing whether a proposed transaction, or his participation in it, would offend the normally accepted standards of honest conduct" (at p. 107c-f).

A Trustee's State of Mind

As regards the second area which had been the subject of dispute, Lord Nicholls explained by use of examples why the trustee's state of mind was not a relevant consideration to a third party's liability: 27–021

"Take a case where a dishonest solicitor persuades a trustee to apply trust property in a way the trustee honestly believes is permissible but which the solicitor knows full well is a clear breach of trust. The

CHAPTER 27: INVESTOR PROTECTION IN TRUST LAW

solicitor deliberately conceals this from the trustee. In consequence, the beneficiaries suffer a substantial loss. It cannot be right that in such a case the accessory liability principle would be inapplicable because of the innocence of the trustee" (at p. 101h).

27–022　The trustee, as Lord Nicholls pointed out, will be liable in any event for the breach of trust, even if he acted innocently, unless excused by an exemption clause in the trust instrument or relieved by the court. But his state of mind is essentially irrelevant to the question whether the third party should be made liable to the beneficiaries for the breach of trust.

Assessment of the Royal Brunei Airlines Decision

27–023　Seen within the context of investor protection, the Privy Council decision is helpful to an aggrieved investor in two respects. The objective standard of dishonesty by which a third party is to be judged is helpful in terms of investor protection because it means that third parties, such as the smaller merchant banks, will no longer be able to "turn a blind eye" and retain "dodgy" business without accepting responsibility to re-imburse the aggrieved investor if his investment is lost. So far as the trustee's state of mind is concerned, whilst it is right that in most cases of investment fraud the trustee, *i.e.* the fraudster to whom the investor paid his funds, will be acting dishonestly in subjective, let alone objective, terms, there will be other cases where, in the financial services arena, an investor may suffer loss at the hands of an honest, but recklessly incompetent, trustee of his funds. In these situations an action against a third party who handles or assists in handling the funds should not be ruled out. As Lord Nicholls pointed out (at p. 108b-c), professional advisors employed by trustees owe a duty to exercise reasonable skill and care. The rights flowing from that duty, in Lord Nicholls' view, form part of the trust property and can be enforced by the beneficiaries in a suitable case if the trustees are unable or unwilling to do so.

27–024　The facts of the *Royal Brunei Airlines* case usefully illustrate the application of the constructive trust principle in practical terms. The defendant was the principal shareholder and managing director of a travel company which had been appointed to act as a general travel agent for an airline. From time to time monies were transferred from the company's current account into fixed term deposits held in the name of the defendant. The company current account contained monies received by the company from sales of airline tickets, in respect of which the company was obliged to account to the airline within 30 days of receipt. The company terminated its agency agreement and became insolvent, whereupon the airline brought an action against the defendant on the basis that he had knowingly assisted in a fraudulent and dishonest design on the part of the company to deal with the funds in breach of trust. The defendant argued that he had not acted dishonestly in a subjective sense, and further the company, as trustee of the funds, had not been acting dishonestly. Asserting arguments which are commonly advanced in the context of fraudulent trading, the defendant said that he expected to pay the airline but that the funds had been lost in the ordinary course of a poorly run business with heavy overhead expenses. The Privy Council rejected these arguments, holding that the airline should succeed in its claim.

The Privy Council extensively reviewed the previous cases which had been decided in this area and reference should be made to Lord Nicholls' opinion for references to these cases. Suffice it to note that the circumstances in *Lipkin Gorman (a firm) v. Karpnale Ltd* [1992] 4 All E.R. 331 and *Barclays Bank plc v. Quincecare Ltd* [1992] 4 All E.R. 363, are of particular interest in the context of investor protection. 27–025

Funds Must Have Been Held on Trust

Liability as a constructive trustee will be imposed only where the trustee has "intermeddled" with funds which are held on trust. Of course, a trust does not need to have been formally, or expressly, established. There are many cases where the law imputes a relationship of trust where it can be seen that the parties intended the funds to be held in trust. As noted when considering the application of a *Quistclose* trust, this can usually be demonstrated by an analysis of the purpose for which the money was paid. Generally, investment funds will be received under some obligation to retain or deal with the funds in a particular way, as where, for example, the funds are to be invested in stocks and shares, government securities, unit trusts, bonds, commodities or real estate. 27–026

In the absence of an obligation on the part of the recipient to retain and deal with funds in a particular way, the principle of constructive trusteeship cannot apply. This requirement was satisfied in *Royal Brunei Airlines* because, albeit not an investment case, the company was obliged under the terms of its general agency agreement to account to the airline for ticket sales within 30 days of their receipt. An example of a case where the position was different occurred in *Goose v. Wilson & Sandford*, April 1, 1996, unreported, where the defendant had persuaded the plaintiff to become jointly involved in a venture with a third party who turned out to be a fraudster. The defendant was the accountant of the company in which the plaintiff invested, and on the basis of this relationship the plaintiff brought a claim against him as a constructive trustee as well as a claim in negligence. The court dismissed the claims because, so far as the constructive trustee allegation was concerned, a person could not be a trustee in the abstract. Since the company was not subject to account for the money which it had received from the plaintiff, there could be no trusteeship. No person can be liable for assisting in the performance of a dishonest design if the alleged trustee does not hold any property for the benefit of another. 27–027

Assistance

27–028 A third party has to afford some active assistance to the trustee if he is to become liable as a constructive trustee. Mere knowledge of a breach of trust is not enough, some participation in furtherance of the breach must be shown. In *Brinks Limited (formerly Brink's Mat Limited) v. Kamal Hassan Abu-Saleh*, October 10, 1995, unreported, the plaintiff sought to hold a defendant liable as a constructive trustee on the grounds that she had assisted in furtherance of a breach of trust by accompanying her husband on various journeys from England to Switzerland when her husband had been transporting approximately £3 million in cash. The money had been derived from the sale of melted down gold bullion which had been stolen from Heathrow Airport in a large robbery. The breach of trust had been committed not by the defendant's husband, who plainly assisted in the furtherance of the breach, but by a security guard at Heathrow Airport who, in breach of trust, had passed security information to the robbers. The court held that the security guard was employed in a position of trust, that he owed a duty not to divulge security information, that he breached that duty by disclosing this information to the robbers, but that the defendant's association with her husband did not amount to "assistance" in furtherance of the breach of trust to hold her liable as a constructive trustee. The plaintiff's claim against the defendant's husband was settled prior to the hearing.

Liability for Breach of Trust

27–029 Where a trustee (or a third party liable as if he were a trustee) is found to be under a liability to a beneficiary, it is necessary to consider the extent of the trustee's liability to compensate the beneficiary for such loss. Traditionally, the trustee is obliged to restore the assets or to pay compensation for the loss but this will apply only where there is some causal connection between the trustee's breach and the loss. There would be liability even if the direct cause of the loss was not caused by the trustee if, but for the trustee's breach, the loss could not have occurred—*Nestlé v. National Westminster Bank* [1994] 1 All E.R. 118. This is not to say that the courts will expect a trustee to act as an insurer for the assets held in trust. A trustee will not be liable to compensate the beneficiary for losses which the beneficiary would, in any event, have suffered even if there had been no breach of trust. This was established recently by the House of Lords in *Target Holdings Ltd v. Redferns (a firm)* [1995] 3 All E.R. 785, where solicitors acting for a client/mortgagee erroneously transmitted money to mortgagors before the charges were executed over the relevant properties. The properties were later (through no fault of the solicitors) found to be insufficient security for the loans. The purpose of equitable compensation for breach of trust was to make good loss suffered by the beneficiary which, using hindsight and common sense, could be seen to have been caused by the breach.

3. Tracing Remedies

General Principles

Whereas an action for breach of contract is personal, in the sense that 27–030
the action fixes on the liability of the person rather than the asset, an action for breach of trust will fix on the property where the property is capable of identification. The advantage of a proprietary remedy over a personal remedy is that the former does not depend on the defendant's solvency if the property is still in existence. In an investor fraud where funds have been lost, attention is focused on whether the funds are capable of identification for the purposes of the proprietary remedy. The position is relatively clear in a case where a defendant has exchanged one chattel for another, but suppose he has mixed investment funds with his personal monies. How can an investor's funds be traced and identified for the purpose of the proprietary remedy in these circumstances? These questions have been asked many times before, and the relevant principles were established long ago. It is the application of these principles to the complexities of modern commercial life which continue to occupy the time of the court on a daily basis.

The court first grappled with the problems engendered in this area by 27–031
an investor fraud over 180 years ago, in *Taylor v. Plumer* [1815] 3 M & S 562, where a defendant, an investor, paid money to his stockbroker to purchase exchequer bonds. The stockbroker used the funds to buy some American investments and sought to flee to the new country. He was arrested, and on his bankruptcy the plaintiff, his assignee in bankruptcy, tried to recover the American investments. The defendant resisted on the ground that the investments were the ascertainable product of the money which he had given to the stockbroker, and, in terms, they were owned by him. The court agreed and rejected the assignee's claim. The relevant principles to be applied in this type of case were elucidated by Lord Ellenborough in terms which continue to have considerable relevance today:

> "It makes no difference in reason or law into what form, different from the original, the change may have been made, whether it be into that of promissory notes for the security of the money which was produced by the sale of the goods of the principal, as in *Scott v. Surman* [1742] Willes 400, or into other merchandize, as in *Whitcomb v. Jacob* [1710] Salk 160, for the product of or in substitute for the original thing still follows the nature of the thing itself, as long as it can be ascertained to be such, and the right only ceases when the means of ascertainment fail, which is the case when the subject is turned into money, and mixed and confounded in a general mass of the same description. The difficulty which arises in such a case is a difficulty of fact and not law, and the dictum that money has no earmark must be understood in the same way; *i.e.* as predicated only of

an undivided and undistinguishable mass of current money. But money in a bag or otherwise kept apart from other money, guineas, or other coin marked, if the fact were so, for the purpose of being distinguished, and so far ear-marked as to fall within the rule on this subject, which applies to every other description of personal property whilst it remains (as the property in question did) in the hands of the factor [the bankrupt] or his general legal representatives."

27–032 The position is more complicated where a trustee has mixed trust funds with other monies. At common law the right to trace is considered to be lost because the funds are no longer identifiable, but equity has sought to overcome this problem by the application of some complex rules. Where trust funds have been mixed, equity has imposed an onus on the trustee to establish that part of his own money has been mixed with the trust funds. A beneficiary will be entitled to the funds which the trustee cannot prove to be his own. But suppose the trustee has drawn on mixed funds and/or replenished the funds from an outside source. The general rule is that the tracing remedy can be applied against a mixed fund only to the extent that the trust funds can still be shown to be there. If the account falls below that sum, that part of the trust money will be deemed to have been spent—*Roscoe v. Winder* [1915] 1 Ch. 62. Later payments into the mixed fund will not be treated as repayments of the trust fund unless the trustee shows an intention to do so. It is essential, therefore, to determine from the accounts the lowest intermediate balance in the fund to see if a tracing remedy is available.

27–033 In cases where funds have been mixed in a bank account, the courts are sometimes prepared to apply the rule in *Clayton's Case* [1817] 1 Mer. 572, which provides that the first payment into the account is appropriated to the earliest debt which is not statute-barred, in other words "first in, first out." An example of a situation where this rule will not apply, however, is a case where many small investors participated in a collective investment scheme by which their money would be mixed together and invested through a common fund. This is what happened in the Barlow Clowes case where the court concluded that the presumed intention of the parties must have been that the "first in, first out" rule would not apply and that all the assets available for distribution, whether monies already invested in British government stocks, monies awaiting investment and moneys diverted into other assets would be shared *pari passu* in proportion to the amounts due to them. The court said that the "first in, first out" rule would not apply where it would be impractical or where it would result in injustice between investors because a relatively small number of investors would get most of the funds. The "first in, first out" rule would be applied in an investor fraud case only where the rule provided a convenient method of determining competing claims where several beneficiaries' moneys had been blended in one account and there was a deficiency or where there had been a wrongful mixing of different sums of trust money in a single account—*Barlow Clowes International Limited (in liquidation) v. Vaughan* [1994] 2 All E.R. 22.

The leading trusts law textbooks are replete with further examples of 27–034
the application of these tracing principles. Suffice it in this context if
consideration is confined to some problems which have occurred
recently in the investor context.

Recent Applications in Investor Fraud Cases

The elasticity of the equitable tracing remedy was insufficient to assist 27–035
the trustees of the hapless Maxwell pension fund after money had been
improperly paid into the overdrawn bank account of Maxwell Communication Corporation plc. Equitable tracing, although devised for the
protection of misapplied funds, could not be pursued through an
overdrawn and therefore non-existent fund. As the Court of Appeal
explained, it was only possible to trace in equity funds which had
continued in existence, actual or notional, and which could be identified
at every stage of their journey through life—*Bishopsgate Investment
Management v. Homan* [1995] 1 All E.R. 347.

At one time it had been thought that the courts might have been 27–036
prepared to stretch the tracing remedy to cover all the assets of the
trustee, after Lord Templeman had said in *Space Investments Ltd v.
Canadian Imperial Bank of Commerce Trust Co* [1986] 3 All E.R. 75 (at
pp. 76-77), a case involving the position of an insolvent bank that had
been taking deposits and lending money, that equity would allow the
beneficiaries to trace the trust money "to all the assets of the
bank."These words were given a wide interpretation by the New
Zealand Court of Appeal in *Liggett v. Kensington* [1993] 1 N.Z.L.R. 257,
where in a case involving a gold bullion company which had become
insolvent, non-allocated claimants were permitted to assert a proprietary
claim to gold bullion which was held by the company. This decision,
however, was overturned by the Privy Council, reported as *Re Goldcorp
Exchange Ltd (in receivership)* [1994] 2 All E.R. 806, on the basis that an
equitable title could not pass under a simple contract for the sale of
unascertained goods merely by virtue of the sale because the buyer could
not acquire title until it was known to what goods the title related. These
established principles were affirmed by the Court of Appeal in *Bishopsgate Investment Management v. Homan*. As Buckley L.J. said in *Borden
(U.K.) Ltd v. Scottish Timber Products Ltd* [1979] 3 All E.R. 961 (at
p. 974), in a passage approved by Leggatt L.J. in *Bishopsgate Investment
Management v. Homan*: ". . . it is a fundamental feature of the doctrine of
tracing that the property to be traced can be identified at every stage of
its journey through life." The limitation imposed by this fundamental
feature on the efficacy of the tracing remedy in cases of investor fraud is
well demonstrated by the *Bishopsgate Investment Management v. Homan*
decision.

It follows from an application of these principles that there can be no 27–037
equitable remedy over an asset acquired before misappropriation of
funds takes place, unless there is a possibility of subrogation, since *ex
hypothesi* the funds cannot be followed into property which existed and

so had been acquired before the funds were was received and therefore without their aid—*Re Goldcorp Exchange Ltd (in receivership)* [1994] 2 All E.R. 806. The relationship between tracing and subrogation was explored by the Court of Appeal in *Boscawen v. Bajwa* [1995] 4 All E.R. 769, where the court noted that the remedies were quite distinct in law.

Application of the Tracing Remedy to a Constructive Trustee

27–038 Whilst the issues concerning the ability of a litigant to trace his assets have tended to arise during the course of litigation for breach of trust, the tracing remedy can be utilised against a constructive trustee who dishonestly handles or assists in handling the trust funds. As Millett L.J. said recently in *Boscawen v. Bajwa* (at p. 776g), in a case where a judgment creditor claimed to be entitled to property over which he had a charging order:

"Tracing properly so called . . . is neither a claim nor a remedy but a process. Moreover, it is not confined to the case where the plaintiff seeks a proprietary remedy; it is equally necessary where he seeks a personal remedy against the knowing recipient or knowing assistant. It is the process by which the plaintiff traces what has happened to his property, identifies the persons who have handled it or received it, and justifies his claim that the money which they have handled or received (and if necessary which they still retain) can properly be regarded as representing his property."

27–039 The unhappy experience of the Maxwell pensioners and the gold bullion investors may be contrasted with the experience of a wealthy Saudi Arabian investor who recently succeeded in recovering £2.325 million by an application of the tracing principles in a claim based on constructive trust, albeit after a protracted battle in the courts. The investor's money had been spent by his dishonest agent on the purchase of a large number of worthless shares which had been marketed by fraudulent salesmen in Amsterdam. The profits of the fraud were laundered through an elaborate international system and some of the proceeds eventually came to be represented by part of the interest which ostensibly belonged to the defendant, Dollar Land Holdings plc, a United Kingdom property company, in a site at Nine Elms, Battersea. This interest was acquired by another United Kingdom property company, Regalian plc, for £4.65 million. Regalian plc had been a joint venture partner of the defendant, Dollar Land Holdings, but had no knowledge of the fraud. The investor sued the defendant to recover his money based on the defendant's knowing receipt of assets traceable in equity as representing his misappropriated funds. The investor had invested approximately U.S. $6.673 in the company and on the strength of this investment he claimed to recover the total sum of £2.325 million, which represented one-half of the purchase price paid when the property was sold by the defendant to Regalian plc. Although the Court at First Instance held that the assets were traceable in equity, it rejected the plaintiff's claim on the basis that the knowledge of a former chairman of the defendant company did not amount to knowledge on the part of the company.

The Court of Appeal reversed this decision and remitted the case to the Chancery Division to determine the assessment of damages—*El Ajou v. Dollar Land Holdings plc* [1994] 2 All E.R. 685. Evidence presented before the Dutch court had shown that although the shares had been sold fraudulently to 4,000 investors, the plaintiff, as the largest investor by far, was the only victim whose lost assets could be specifically traceable to the defendant company through the laundering process. In these circumstances the plaintiff argued that his equitable right extended to recovery of the whole of his investment. The defendant company presented a contrary argument, contending that the plaintiff could recover only a fraction of the £2.325 million and that the balance belonged in equity to the other victims. The court held that since there was no other claimant who was seeking to assert a charge ranking rateably with the plaintiff's charge and that there was no realistic possibility of such a claim being made in the future, there was nothing inequitable in permitting the plaintiff to recover the whole of his investment. The court said that there could be no rigid rule as to whether or not the rights of a third party could be raised as a defence to a tracing claim because each case depended on its individual circumstances—*El Ajou v. Dollar Land Holdings (No 2)* [1995] 2 All E.R. 213. **27-040**

This case is significant in the investor protection context for two reasons. First, in terms of imputing dishonesty to a limited company for the purposes of establishing a claim based on constructive trust, the case demonstrates that an aggrieved investor will not be limited to reliance on the conduct of a company officer who holds office at the time of the misappropriation. Rather, the courts will examine the mind and will of the natural person or persons who manage and control the company. As Nourse L.J. acknowledged in the Court of Appeal (at p. 696c), "decided cases show that, in regard to the requisite status and authority, the formal position, as regulated by the company's articles of association, service contracts and so forth, though highly relevant, may not be decisive."Secondly, the decision draws attention to the unavoidable element of randomness which occurs in this type of case where an investor attempts to recover misapplied funds. As Robert Walker J. acknowledged when assessing the amount of damages (at pp. 221j and 222b), changes in the "state of investment" of the fund which is being traced may occur in a totally random way, and it is possible for one claimant to lose his right to trace and another claimant may in consequence be preferred through circumstances over which neither has any control. In this sense the position of a claimant in a constructive trust case is different from that of a beneficiary of a properly constituted trust fund. In the latter case the rights between beneficiaries will not **27-041** alter, whereas in the former case the rights between beneficiaries will alter, depending on changes in the composition of the trust fund.

Jurisdiction

27–042　A jurisdictional issue often arises in cases where restitutionary remedies are sought in respect of property which is situated outside the jurisdiction. The problem occurred in another aspect of the Maxwell case, in this instance concerning shares in a New York company which had been pledged in England to banks as security for loans without the shareholder's consent. The question arose as to whether the issue of priority of ownership of the shares should be determined according to English law or the law in the United States. The Court of Appeal held that the appropriate law to decide questions of title to shares was the law of the place where the shares were situated which was in the ordinary way the place where the company was incorporated. Since New York was also the place where the share register was maintained, the applicable law for determination of the issue of priority was the domestic law of the State of New York—*Macmillan v. Bishopsgate Investment Trust (3)* [1996] 1 All E.R. 585. Each of the three judges, Staughton, Auld and Aldous L.JJ., reviewed the principles which are to be applied in this type of case at some length.

Chapter 28

Investor Protection at Common Law

Introduction

This chapter is concerned with an aggrieved investor's ability to obtain 28–001
redress through the civil courts where he has been induced to make an
investment and/or his investment funds have been misapplied as a result
of another's fraud, or where the investor has suffered loss as a result of
another's misrepresentation and/or breach of contract. Other situations
where an investor can obtain redress, as where an investment has been
made on the basis of inaccurate financial information and/or incorrect
investment advice, or where loss can be attributed to some breach of
director's duty or breach of trust, are the subject of consideration in
other chapters, namely, Chapters 26 (breach of director's duties and
other company law remedies), 27 (breach of trust and constructive trust
remedies) and 29 (liability for negligent misstatement). Readers should
bear in mind that the civil remedies discussed in this chapter have been
considered in a number of learned works. Reference should be made to
these works where necessary.

Deceit

General Principle

An action for deceit involves: (1) the making of a false representation 28–002
by the defendant, who either knows the representation to be untrue or
who has no belief in its truth or who is reckless as to its truth; (2) an
intention by the defendant that the investor will rely on the representation; and (3) actual reliance by the investor on the representation. Each
ingredient has to be established before an action for the tort of deceit
can succeed.

The representation which is necessary to found an action must be a 28–003
representation as to a past or existing fact. A classic example of a false
representation occurred in *Edginton v. Fitzmaurice* [1885] 29 Ch.D. 459,
where directors issued a prospectus inviting subscriptions for debentures. The prospectus stated that the object of the loan was to enable the

Chapter 28: Investor Protection at Common Law

company to enlarge its premises and buy additional plant, but in fact the money was needed to discharge trading liabilities. The court held that the misrepresentation of the purpose was sufficient to found an action for deceit. Complicated issues sometimes arise in this area, as for instance where the substance of the representation reflects a person's opinion or concerns some future fact (*e.g.* "in the opinion of the auditors the profits of the company will exceed £5 million in the next accounting year"), or where non-disclosure of a critical fact impacts on the way in which a representation of existing fact may be understood. A detailed examination of the law in this area is beyond the scope of this book.

28–004   As regards the defendant's state of mind, the position was established long ago in the leading case of *Derry v. Peek* [1889] 14 App. Cas. 337, where Lord Herschell set out (at p. 376) the essential ingredients of an action of deceit:

> "First, in order to sustain an action of deceit, there must be proof of fraud and nothing short of that will suffice. Secondly, fraud is proved when it is shown that a false representation has been made (i) knowingly, (ii) without belief in its truth, or (iii) recklessly, careless whether it be true or false. Although I have treated the second and third as distinct cases, I think the third is but an instance of the second, for one who makes a statement under such circumstances can have no real belief in the truth of what he states. To prevent a false statement from being fraudulent, there must, I think, always be an honest belief in its truth."

28–005   Proof of the defendant's lack of honest belief will not be easy to achieve in cases of this nature. In forensic terms an investor will be assisted where the grounds of honest belief are obviously unreasonable, but in the majority of cases it will be difficult to tip the balance of the scales in the investor's favour. The facts of *Derry v. Peek* illustrate the point. In that case a private Act of Parliament had provided that cars provided by a tramway company could be propelled by steam power if the Board of Trade consented to this course. The directors, before obtaining consent, issued a prospectus stating that under the terms of the private Act the company had authority to use steam power. In the event the Board of Trade refused to grant consent and the company was wound-up. In an action brought by the shareholders against the directors for deceit, the House of Lords held that the directors, having no intention to deceive, were not liable. The shareholders had not proved that the directors lacked honest belief. Lord Herschell reached this conclusion with reluctance, exhorting directors who seek to raise funds from the public to be vigilant to see that the prospectus contains only such representations "as are in strict accordance with fact."

28–006   The difficulties involved in the proof of fraud are well engrained in the consciousness of the legal profession, and when considering an action on behalf of an aggrieved investor, legal advisers should reflect on the advice given by Hilbery J. in his book, *Duty and Art in Advocacy*, (1946) when he wrote (at p. 6):

"By a case of fraud a lawyer means a complete cause of action in fraud. A charge of fraud is a charge of dishonesty. A claim for the recovery of money lost through fraud is the criminal charge of obtaining money by false pretences made in civil form, and no more serious charge can be placed upon the Records of a Civil Court. The Barrister [sic: Advocate] is called upon in this instance to some extent to exercise the judicial function. If the material before him is not sufficient in his view to warrant the allegation he must advise his client that is his view and that he cannot put his signature to the pleading if it is to contain that charge."

The more stringent evidential standard of proof must also be considered when considering the sufficiency of evidence to sustain an allegation of fraud. In *Bater v. Bater* [1951] P. 35, Denning L.J. said (at p. 37) that: 28–007

"A civil court, when considering a charge of fraud, will naturally require for itself a higher degree of probability than that which it would require when asking if negligence is established. It does not adopt so high a degree as a criminal court, even when it is considering a charge of a criminal nature; but still it does require a degree of probability which is commensurate with the occasion."

Denning L.J. cited this passage with approval in *Hornal v. Neuberger Products Ltd* [1957] 1 Q.B. 247 (at p. 258).

Once, however, an action of deceit can be successfully established, compensation for an aggrieved investor will be assessed by the courts on a generous basis. The purpose of damages in the tort of deceit is to put the plaintiff into the position he would have been in had the representation not been made to him. The basic assessment will be the difference between the price actually paid and the market value of the property at the time of sale—*Saunders v. Edwards* [1987] 1 W.L.R. 1116. Any damage directly flowing from the fraudulent inducement, whether or not such damage is reasonably foreseeable may be recovered unless it is caused by the plaintiff behaving completely without prudence or common sense—*Doyle v. Olby (Ironmongers) Ltd* [1969] 2 Q.B. 158. 28–008

Misrepresentation

The practical difficulties in the establishment of a defendant's absence of honest belief were substantially alleviated by the Misrepresentation Act 1967 which artificially extended the scope of an action of deceit by casting the onus onto the defendant to establish that he had reasonable grounds for believing, and did believe, that the facts represented were true. 28–009

CHAPTER 28: INVESTOR PROTECTION AT COMMON LAW

28–010 Section 2(1) of the Act reads as follows:

"Where a person has entered into a contract after a misrepresentation has been made to him by another party thereto and as a result thereof he has suffered loss, then, if the person making the representation would be liable in damages in respect thereof had the misrepresentation been made fraudulently, that person shall be so liable notwithstanding that the misrepresentation was not made fraudulently unless he proves that he had reasonable ground to believe and did believe up to the time the contract was made that the facts represented were true."

28–011 In terms, therefore, the Misrepresentation Act 1967 imposes an obligation not to make representations which the representor cannot prove that he had reasonable grounds to believe. It will not be sufficient for a representator to show that he took reasonable care when he made the representation. The legislation requires the representator to go further and establish that he believed that the facts were true, and that there were reasonable grounds for that belief—see *Howard Marine and Dredging v. A. Ogden & Sons (Excavations)* [1978] Q.B. 574. Where liability can be established under the Act, the measure of damages was the same as the measure of damages in the tort of deceit, with the result that the plaintiff can recover all losses which flow from the misrepresentation even if the loss could not have been foreseen—*East v. Maurer* [1991] 2 All E.R. 733 and *Royscot Trust Ltd v. Rogerson* [1991] 3 All E.R. 294.

28–012 In practice, actions continue to be brought by aggrieved investors in the tort of deceit, with claims for misrepresentation under the Misrepresentation Act 1967 asserted in the alternative.

28–013 Whilst the Misrepresentation Act 1967 has considerably broadened the ability of the courts to make awards which compensate an investor who has lost his funds, certain limits about the scope of the statutory remedy should be noted. First, it applies only where the misrepresentation induced the investor into entering a contract. In investor loss cases, this requirement can usually be satisfied. Secondly, as with an action of deceit, it remains essential that a representation by assertion is made. Concealment of relevant facts may not be sufficient. Failure to make disclosure in breach of a duty to disclose will not amount to a misrepresentation that full disclosure has been made—*Banque Financiere v. Westgate Insurance* [1989] 2 All E.R. 952.

28–014 A recent illustration of the issues which can typically arise in an action for deceit and/or misrepresentation occurred in the case of *Witter Ltd v. TBP Industries* [1996] 2 All E.R. 573, where, in management accounts provided to a prospective purchaser of a company, a one-off expense of £120,000 was included which suggested that, in the absence of the one-off expense, the underlying profits of the company would have been higher. An action was brought against the seller of the company in deceit and for misrepresentation in the alternative. The court awarded damages to the purchaser for misrepresentation in respect of the one-off expense, but in the course of reaching its decision guidance was given on a number of practical issues which tend to arise in these cases. So far as proof of deceit was concerned, the court confirmed that the essence of deceit was dishonesty and that recklessness was not sufficient. Within the parameters set down by Lord Herschell in *Derry v. Peek*, it had to be shown that the defendant was reckless in the sense that he disregarded the truth in a manner which would be regarded as fraudulent. There was also discussion in the case about the scope of remedies under the Misrepresentation Act 1967 where a defendant can establish proof of belief under section 2(1). The case considered whether there was a further remedy for innocent misrepresentation under section 2(2) of the Act which could be exercised in circumstances where a right to rescind the contract had been lost, and whether liability for pre-contractual misrepresentations could be excluded under the terms of the contract. Consideration of these issues fall beyond the scope of this book. Suffice it to note that section 3 of the 1967 Act provides that if a contract contains a term which would exclude or restrict any liability for misrepresentation, the term shall be of no effect except in so far as it satisfies the requirement of reasonableness. In the circumstances of this case the clause was not considered to be reasonable because it sought to exclude liability for all types of misrepresentation, whether fraudulently, negligently or innocently made.

Conspiracy

In the most serious cases of investor fraud, where more than one person is involved, a civil action for conspiracy can be brought. Broadly, a civil conspiracy consists of two forms, a conspiracy to use unlawful means and a conspiracy to injure the interest of another. A conspiracy to use unlawful means is actionable if it causes damage, but a conspiracy to injure the interests of another will not be actionable unless the damage was done with the sole or dominant intention of injuring that other. As Lord Bridge explained in *Lonrho plc v. Fayed* [1991] 3 All E.R. 303: **28–015**

> "Where conspirators act with the predominant purpose of injuring the plaintiff and in fact inflict damage on him, but do nothing which would have been actionable if done by an individual acting alone, it is the fact of their concerted action for that illegitimate purpose that the law, however anomalous it may now seem, finds a sufficient ground to condemn their action as illegal and tortious. But when conspirators intentionally injure the plaintiff and use unlawful means to do so, it is no defence for them to show that their primary purpose was to further or protect their own interests; it is sufficient to make their actions tortious that the means used were unlawful" (at pp. 309j–310a).

28-016 When alleging an action against defendants for conspiracy, the Statement of Claim must describe the parties and the relationships between them. The agreement between the defendants must be alleged, together with the purpose of the agreement, and the overt acts performed by each defendant have to be alleged. The conspirators need not all join in the conspiracy at the same time, but it has to be shown that at some stage during the conspiracy a defendant must have performed an act which furthered the conspiracy. Where a number of people have been culpably involved in an investment fraud, in relation to each person the aggrieved investor will have to consider whether that particular person, having regard to his knowledge, utterances and actions, was sufficiently a party to the combination and the common design.

28-017 An example of the difficulties associated with an action for conspiracy in the context of fraudulent activity can be demonstrated by a consideration of the case of *Metall und Rohstoff AG v. Donaldson Lufkin* [1989] 3 All E.R. 14, where a company and its officers were alleged to have traded fraudulently on the London Metal Exchange. To protect its own position the company seized warrants and closed accounts owned by the plaintiff. After obtaining an unsatisfied judgment against the company, the plaintiff issued a writ against the company's American parent company in which it alleged conspiracy to steal the warrants. The claim failed because the predominant purpose of the agreement between the company and its American parent had been to close the plaintiff's positions in order to advance the parent companies' own commercial interests. There has been some doubt as to whether this case was correctly decided. The decision has been attacked because the Court of Appeal appeared to accept that it was an essential ingredient in the civil tort of conspiracy to establish that the predominant purpose of the conspirators was to injure the plaintiff, even in a case where the means used to effect that purpose were unlawful. It was against this background that the House of Lords were asked to overrule the *Metall* decision in *Lonrho plc v. Fayed*. The House of Lords accepted that the Court of Appeal had erred in its suggestion that the predominant purpose to injure needed to be established in a case where unlawful means were used to effect the purpose, but the House stopped short of saying that *Metall* was wrongly decided.

28-018 As Lord Templeman recognised, this complex area of law will inevitably be the subject of further litigation.

> "Without encouraging the continuation or initiation of litigation by the present or any future disputants, I apprehend that the ambit and ingredients of the torts of conspiracy and unlawful interference may hereafter require further analysis and reconsideration by the courts."

It may well be that, in due course, the courts will come to the view that the *Metall* case was wrongly decided.

Conversion

At first blush, where an investor swindle has occurred, it might be thought that a civil action could be brought for conversion under the Torts (Interference with Goods) Act 1977. In fact, in many cases no action can be brought because of the limited definition of "goods" in section 14 of the 1977 Act which broadly follows the common law. This section provides that "goods" are to be taken as including "all chattels personal other than things in action and money." This statutory exclusion rules out almost any action in a modern investor fraud where the misapplied funds will have been represented by some form of chose in action. Detailed consideration is given to the definition of chose in action in Chapter 16 when considering the definition of "property" which is capable of being stolen under the Theft Act 1968. Suffice it to note that the artificial limitation on the meaning of "goods" in civil law is replicated by the constricted meaning which is applied to "property" in the criminal context. In both civil and criminal jurisdictions, English law is out of step with modern times.

28–019

Money Had and Received

The deficiency in the law of conversion is made good by the traditional restitutionary remedies in contract and quasi-contract, which confer wide protection on an aggrieved investor who has suffered at the hands of fraudster. These restitutionary principles can be traced back to a famous judgment given by Lord Mansfield in *Moses v. Macferlan* [1760] 2 Burr. 1005, where he set out the principles which underlay an action for money had and received to the use of the plaintiff in the following terms:

28–020

> "This kind of equitable action to recover back money which ought not in justice to be kept is very beneficial, and therefore much encouraged. It lies for money which, *ex aequo et bono*, the defendant ought to refund ... It lies for money paid by mistake; or upon a consideration which happens to fail; or for money got through imposition (express or implied); or extortion; or oppression; or an undue advantage taken of the plaintiff's situation, contrary to the laws made for the protection of persons under those circumstances. In one word, the gist of this kind of action is that the defendant, upon the circumstances of the case, is obliged by the ties of natural justice and equity to refund the money."

For a more modern formulation of the restitutionary principle, see Lord Wright's opinion in *Fibrosa Spolka Akcyjina v. Fairbairn Lawson Combe Barbour Ltd* [1943] A.C. 32 at 61.

28–021

CHAPTER 28: INVESTOR PROTECTION AT COMMON LAW

28–022 There have been a number of occasions when the restitutionary principle has been applied in cases of fraud. In *Gurney v. Womersley* [1854] 4 E. & B. 133, where the names of the drawer and the acceptor were forged to a bill of exchange, and the bill was discounted by the plaintiffs for the defendants (who had indorsed it), it was held that, since the genuiness of the acceptance was of the essence of the description of a bill, there was a total failure of consideration entitling the plaintiffs to recover from the defendants the amount paid to them. Five years earlier, in *Vaughan v. Matthews* [1849] 13 Q.B. 187, a plaintiff was allowed to sue a defendant to recover his loss after the defendant had obtained payment of a promissory note payable to the plaintiff by means of a false or forged representation of authority purporting to emanate from the plaintiff.

28–023 A recent example of the use of money had and received occurred in *Agip (Africa) Ltd v. Jackson* [1992] 4 All E.R. 451, where the plaintiff's employee forged a payment order in favour of a nominee company which had been set up and controlled by the defendants. The ability of the plaintiff to trace this money at common law was also an issue in the case.

28–024 A defendant may be liable in a restitutionary action even where the fraud was committed by his partner and agent, and not by him personally. Where payments of premiums on a policy were continued by the plaintiff because of false representations by the defendant's agent, it was held in *Kettlewell v. Refuge Assurance Co.* [1908] 1 K.B. 545 that the premiums could be recovered by the plaintiff in a claim in restitution, although they might also have been recovered in an action of deceit.

28–025 The ability of a plaintiff to hold a defendant responsible for the fraud of his partner and agent has implications where a limited company is involved, and sometimes an application of this principle can allow an aggrieved investor to pursue a director in his personal capacity on the ground that the limited company is liable as his agent. This aspect is explored in more detail in Chapter 30.

28–026 The width of the restitutionary principal can also be demonstrated by the case of a defendant who, without intending to pay for it, fraudulently induces the plaintiff to perform a service for him. The plaintiff may sue either for the tort of deceit or in restitution for reasonable remuneration—*Rumsey v. NE Railway* [1863] 14 C.B. (NS) 641.

28–027 An aggrieved investor who has been induced by fraud to enter into a contract must, as soon as he discovers the fraud, elect to rescind the contract and seek to recover his funds. An investor must be careful not to affirm the contract in any shape or form. The right to rescind is lost by affirmation, and it is doubtful whether it would be revived by the subsequent discovery of another incident in the same fraud.

28–028 In practice, experience suggests that the courts continue to apply the spirit of Lord Mansfield's approach in cases where an aggrieved investor has lost some or all of his funds, and in any such case the pursuit of a restitutionary remedy must not be overlooked.

Illegal Transactions

The courts have repeatedly held that public policy precludes the bringing of a civil action for redress on the basis of an illegal act. So if an investor suffers loss as a result of dealings with a defendant which are intrinsically illegal, he will not be able to recover damages for his loss, irrespective of whether his loss was caused by a fraudulent representative or breach of contract. The principle has been fully articulated in the leading textbooks on Torts (Clerk & Lindsell) and Contracts (Chitty). Suffice it to mention here a dramatic and very recent application of this principle in the context of investor protection where, following the ruling of the Court of Appeal in the "Titan" case, investors are unlikely to be able to benefit from investments which they made in the scheme. The scheme was based on invitations to become a member of a business club. To take up the invitation, a person had to be interviewed and pay £2,500. The new recruit then had the right to introduce new members. For the first two new members he received £450 from each of the new members. If he introduced a third or subsequent member, he became a "senior partner" and received £1,250. In addition he received £770 for each new member introduced by members who were introduced by him. The balance of the membership fee was distributed amongst the members and the companies involved in the scheme. The scheme was best described as an enormous financial "chain letter." The Court of Appeal held that the scheme was unlawful because it was an unlicensed lottery and the Department of Trade and Industry was correct to bring proceedings for winding-up the scheme—*Re Senator Hanseatische Wertwaltungs Gesellschaft mbh,* July 24, 1996, unreported.

28–029

Chapter 29

Negligent Advice and Negligent Financial Information

This chapter focuses on the common law obligations of a person who, in the absence of any contract between the parties which defines their respective obligations, advises an investor or disseminates accounting information to an investor in relation to an investment. How does the law protect the investor against negligent advice or the dissemination of negligently prepared financial information? If negligent advice or incorrect financial information is given, what is the investors' remedy? Often the person giving the advice or disseminating the information will be a professional advisor, such as a financial consultant or intermediary, broker, accountant, banker or solicitor. **29–001**

Background

The ability of an investor to recover financial loss as a result of an accountant's professional negligence was raised directly in *Candler v. Crane, Christmas & Co* [1951] 2 K.B. 164; [1951] 1 All E.R. 426. There a potential investor wanted to see the accounts of a company before deciding whether to invest in it. The company accountants were told to complete the company's accounts as soon as possible because they were to be shown to the potential investor. Subsequently, the potential investor discussed the accounts with the accountants and he was allowed to take a copy. The accounts had been carelessly prepared and gave a wholly misleading picture. Not appreciating the errors, the potential investor subscribed £2,000 for shares in the company. The company went into liquidation and the investor lost his money. The Court of Appeal held, after an extensive review of the law, that in the absence of a contractual arrangement between the parties, the accountants did not owe any duty to the potential investor to exercise care in preparing the accounts. In a dissenting judgment, Denning L.J. expressed concern about the position of investors. The accountant, noted Denning L.J., was required to do more than certify accounts for the satisfaction of his client. Accounts were required for the guidance of shareholders, investors, revenue authorities, and others who may have to rely on the accounts in serious matters of business. **29–002**

In a passage which foreshadowed problems which have come to plague this area of the law, Denning L.J. questioned the scope of the duty of care which he wished to establish. Would the accountants be **29–003**

CHAPTER 29: NEGLIGENT ADVICE AND NEGLIGENT FINANCIAL INFORMATION

liable to any person in the land who chose to rely on the accounts in matters of business, or would they be liable only if the accounts were prepared for the guidance of a specific class of persons in a specific class of transactions?

29–004 It was over 30 years before these questions came to be addressed by the House of Lords, and today the answer to these questions remains far from clear. The law continues to develop on a case by case basis.

Hedley Byrne

29–005 The majority decision of the Court of Appeal in *Candler v. Crane, Christmas & Co* was disapproved by the House of Lords in *Hedley Byrne & Co Ltd v. Heller & Partners Ltd* [1963] 2 All E.R. 575. This decision is now the foundation of the modern law. In *Hedley Byrne & Co Ltd v. Heller* the House of Lords held that a person who made a negligent statement could owe a duty of care to a person who suffered economic loss through reliance upon the statement. The facts of this case did not involve a potential investor but a firm of advertising agents who sought a credit reference on one of their clients. The reference was sought from the client's bankers. A favourable reference was negligently given, and the advertising agents suffered heavy losses on the transactions which they entered in reliance on the reference. Since the credit reference was given "without responsibility", the advertising agents failed in their action for damages against the client's bankers, but as matter of principle the House of Lords was unanimous in holding that there were circumstances where damages could be awarded for financial loss brought about by a negligent misstatement.

29–006 Lord Morris expressed the principles succinctly as follows:

> "My Lords, I consider that it follows and that it should now be regarded as settled that if someone possessed of a special skill undertakes, quite irrespective of contract, to apply that skill for the assistance of another person who relies on such skill, a duty of care will arise. The fact that the service is to be given by means of, or by the instrumentality of, words can make no difference. Furthermore if, in a sphere in which a person is so placed that others could reasonably rely on his judgment or his skill or his ability to make careful inquiry, a person takes it on himself to give information or advice to, or allows his information or advice to be passed on to, another person who, as he knows or should know, will place reliance on it, then a duty of care will arise" (at p. 594B).

29–007 The law reports are replete with cases in which this principle has been applied during the last 30 years. In this chapter consideration is confined to cases which have arisen in the investment context.

Liability for Negligent Investment Advice or Conduct

The Lloyd's Litigation

The culmination of the litigation concerning the losses suffered by Names at Lloyd's of London are now the seminal cases in this area. The test case actions progressed to the House of Lords and are reported under the leading case of *Henderson and others v. Merrett Syndicates Ltd* [1994] 3 All E.R. 506.   29–008

The plaintiffs were Lloyd's Names and were members of syndicates managed by the defendant underwriting agents. The plaintiffs were either "direct Names", in which case the syndicates to which they belonged were managed by the members' agents (known as "managing agents"), or "indirect Names", in which case the members' agents placed Names with syndicates managed by other agents. Where Names were placed with other syndicates managed by other agents, the members agents entered into sub-agency agreements with the managing agents of those syndicates. Under these sub-agency agreements the managing agents of those syndicates were appointed to act as sub-agents in respect of the Names' business. The relationship between Names, members' agents and managing agents was regulated by the terms of agency and sub-agency agreements which gave the agent "absolute discretion" in respect of underwriting business conducted on behalf of the Name but it was accepted that it was an implied term of the agreements that the agents would exercise due care and skill in the exercise of their functions as managing agents. In the course of preliminary proceedings, notwithstanding the contractual relationship between the parties, legal issues arose concerning the nature and extent of care owed by the member's agents and the managing agents under the sub-agency agreements.   29–009

In a robust judgment the House of Lords rejected the defendant underwriting agents' contentions. Their Lordships held that the managing agents owed a duty of care to Names. By holding themselves out as possessing a special expertise to advise the names on the suitability of risks to be underwritten and the circumstances in which reinsurance should be taken out and claims settled, the managing agents had assumed responsibility towards the names in their syndicates. The managing agents well knew that the names placed implicit reliance on their advice, and the names gave authority to the managing agents to bind them in contracts of insurance and re-insurance and to the settlement of claims. The discretion given to managing agents in the agreements defined the scope of the agents' authority, not the standard of skill and care required of the agents in carrying on underwriting business on behalf of Names. The assumption of responsibility by a person rendering professional or quasi-professional services gave rise to a tortious duty of care irrespective of whether there was a contractual relationship between the parties.   29–010

The implications of this decision are quite far-reaching for investors who have suffered financial loss at the hands of a negligent financial adviser. The House of Lords reached its decision by applying the   29–011

CHAPTER 29: NEGLIGENT ADVICE AND NEGLIGENT FINANCIAL INFORMATION

principles set out in *Hedley Byrne & Co v. Heller & Partners Ltd*. Their Lordships noted that underlying principle rested on the assumption of responsibility by one party towards another party, and whilst this assumption of responsibility undoubtedly covered the provision of investment advice and information, it was said that there may be other circumstances in which there will be necessary reliance to give rise to the application of the principle.

29–012   As Lord Goff said:

"In particular, where the plaintiff entrusts the defendant with the conduct of his affairs in general or in particular, he may be held to have relied on the defendant to exercise due skill and care in such conduct" (at p. 520g).

29–013   In the context of investor protection, the same principles will apply to all professional or quasi-professional advisers who advise investors or undertake investment business on their behalf.

29–014   Covering similar ground, the first instance decision in *Brown v. KMR Services* [1994] 4 All E.R. 385 is interesting because, unlike the House of Lords ruling in *Henderson and others v. Merrett Syndicates Ltd*, the judgment was delivered after the facts of the case had been determined. The judge, Gatehouse J., concluded that where a Lloyd's Name obtained an assurance from his member's agent that only syndicates constituting a low risk conservative underwriting policy would be recommended, the agent would be in breach of his duty of care (as well as in breach of contract) if he subsequently recommended high risk excess of loss syndicates contrary to that assurance without first obtaining the Name's informed consent. A Lloyd's Name was entitled to expect a warning of the dangers inherent in excess of loss reinsurance syndicates from his members' agent, irrespective of whether he happened to be a sophisticated investor.

29–015   Interestingly, whilst this decision was affirmed on appeal, the Court of Appeal said that Gatehouse J.'s assessment of an agent's duty was too restrictive. A members' agent owed a duty to a Lloyd's Name to provide proper advice when recommending that he allocate a percentage of his premium in income limit to high risk excess of loss syndicates. Proper advice involved the giving of information and advice about the character and extra risk of the business underwritten by such syndicates, individually and collectively, as well as advice on maintaining a proper balance between allocation of premiums to such syndicates and the allocation of premiums to syndicates which were not high risk in order to ensure a prudent spread of risk—*Brown v. KMR Services Ltd* [1995] 4 All E.R. 598.

Ingredients of a Cause of Action

29–016   It follows that an investor may recover damages for financial losses in circumstances where the investor can show that: (i) he relied on a professional or quasi-professional advisor to provide investment advice or to conduct investment affairs on his behalf, and (ii) the professional or quasi-professional adviser realised that the investor was relying upon his skill and judgment in providing investment advice or conducting investment affairs. Establishment of these two elements gives rise to a "degree of proximity" between the parties which the courts deem sufficient to show that a duty of care is owed to the investor on the facts of a particular case.

In addition to the establishment of this relationship of proximity between the parties, an investor has to prove three further elements before he can recover damages for financial loss in this type of case. **29–017**

First, he must show that the professional or quasi-professional adviser acted negligently in the exercise of his skill and judgment. **29–018**

Secondly, he must show that the negligence caused him to suffer financial loss. The real test of whether the negligence was the effective cause of the loss is a pragmatic one based on common sense. Causation is a question of fact in each case—*Banque Bruxelles Lambert SA v. Eagle Star Insurance*, March 22, 1996, unreported. In the context of the Lloyd's litigation, the question of causation was approached by identifying first what advice the name ought to have received and then what the name could prove, on the balance of probabilities, would have been the consequence of his receipt of such information and advice—*Brown v. KMR Services Ltd* [1995] 4 All E.R. 598. **29–019**

Thirdly, the investor must prove that the loss was reasonably foreseeable in all the circumstances. On the issue of foreseeability of loss, the test for negligence is the same regardless of whether the victim complains of pure economic loss or damage to property. Either way, the victim has to show that the damage was reasonably foreseeable—*Marc Rich & Co AG v. Bishop Rock Marine Co*, [1994] 3 All E.R. 686. **29–020**

In most cases in the investment context, foreseeability of loss will not be difficult to prove once the other elements of the cause of action have been established. In *Aiken v. Stewart Wrightson Members Agency* [1995] 3 All E.R. 449, another case in the Lloyd's litigation, Potter J. held that it was reasonably foreseeable that syndicates would rely on run-off reinsurance for the benefit of names in future years. Those names were inevitably persons who would be affected if the run-off reinsurance were to be avoided for non-disclosure. **29–021**

Measure of Damages

The proper measure of damages in a case of where negligent advice had been given was the subject of consideration in *South Australia Asset Management Corp v. York Montague Ltd* [1996] 3 All E.R. 365, a case involving the negligent valuation of property. During the course of his judgment in which he reviewed the relevant principles at some length, Lord Hoffman confirmed that foreseeability of loss was the test by which recoverability of loss would be determined. A negligent supplier of information is responsible for all the foreseeable consequences of the information being wrong, and a negligent adviser is responsible for all **29–022**

CHAPTER 29: NEGLIGENT ADVICE AND NEGLIGENT FINANCIAL INFORMATION

the foreseeable losses which are a consequence of that course of action having been taken. The loss suffered by the plaintiff is compared with what his position would have been if he had received information which was correct or had not entered into the transaction in respect of which he negligently advised.

29–023   Applying these principles to the facts of the case before it, the House of Lords held that the compensation payable by a valuer who had negligently overvalued property on which a lender had secured a loan was restricted to the difference between the valuation negligently provided and the correct property value at the time of valuation. As Lord Hoffman acknowledged (at p. 373j), a different measure of damages is applied where the plaintiff has been induced to enter into the transaction by virtue of fraud—see Chapter 28 on this point.

29–024   In cases where an incorrect projection of profits is made, there is a prima facie assumption that the most likely forecast would have reflected the actual outcome. The nature of the problem is demonstrated by a consideration of the facts in *Lion Nathan Ltd v. CC Bottlers Ltd*, May 14, 1996, unreported, where the vendor of a company made a projected profit forecast of $2.223 million for the remaining two months of the financial year. In the event actual earnings were $1.233 million. The trial judge held that a properly prepared forecast would have been $1.6 million, but the Court of Appeal of New Zealand thought that a proper forecast would have been $1.2 million. The Privy Council concluded that a proper forecast should be taken as the actual outcome, and this would be taken as the basis for assessing damages. The Privy Council said that the uncertainty inherent in the process of forecasting may have led to reasonable forecasts both higher and lower than the actual outcome but since those uncertainties tended in both directions, the only way to deal with the matter was to regard the unpredictable factors as cancelling each other out.

29–025   Sometimes, where an investor is negligently advised not to make a particular investment, he will suffer the loss of a chance. This may occur, for example, where a plaintiff is negligently advised not to enter into a business venture with a third party, and because of the plaintiff's lack of support the third party does not proceed with the business venture. The loss of chance will be difficult to quantify in these circumstances. Certainly a plaintiff will be entitled to succeed if he can establish that there was a substantial, and not a speculative, chance that a third party would have taken action to confer some benefit on him. According to the Court of Appeal in *Allied Maples Group Ltd v. Simmons & Simmons* [1995] 4 All E.R. 907, the evaluation of a substantial chance was a question of quantification of damages, the range lying somewhere between something that just qualified as real or substantial on the one hand and near certainty on the other.

29–026   An example of a court's assessment of damages in this type of case occurred in *First Interstate Bank of California v. Cohen Arnold & Co.* [1995] E.G.C.S. 188, where the Court of Appeal considered the position where a bank claimed that it would have taken action to enforce its

408

security if it had known the true facts about the financial state of the borrower. In the event the bank sold the security for £1.4 million when, if it had enforced the security earlier, it would have received between £3.5 million and £4 million. The court concluded on the facts of the case that the bank had lost the opportunity to sell the property for £3 million. The chance should be valued at 2:1; accordingly the bank obtained judgment for £2 million less the £1.4 million actually received.

Contributory Negligence

Although unusual in an investor related case, there is no reason in principle why, if justified on the facts of a case, a deduction for contributory negligence on the part of a plaintiff could not be made. The possibility of a deduction for contributory negligence on the basis that a bank had negligently failed to assess the risks of a transaction was rejected in *Cavendish Funding Ltd v. Henry Spencer & Sons Ltd*, March 20, 1996, unreported.

29–027

Limitation of Action

Under the terms of the Limitation Act 1980 all actions for negligence seeking compensation for economic loss must be brought within six years from the date when the cause of action accrued. This date may sometimes be difficult to determine. The cause of action will accrue when an investor suffers loss, but is the loss suffered at the time of the negligent advice or at the time when financial loss is sustained? The latter date is the date which is usually taken. In *First National Commercial Bank plc v. Humberts, The Times*, January 27, 1995, bankers alleged that they financed a property acquisition on the basis of a negligent property valuation. The property was valued at £4.4 million when a value of £2.7 million should have been given. The Court of Appeal held that the cause of action accrued on the date when the bankers' loss crystallised, which was the date when the loan security was sold. The date of the advance was the date when prima facie the measure of loss might be established but this was the starting point. It did not follow that the loss occurred at this time since the loss might have been recoverable in other ways.

29–028

Practical Problems

The practical problems of establishing liability on the facts of a particular case can be quite formidable. First, the element of reliance has to be established. In *Anthony v. Wright* [1995] 1 B.C.L.C. 236, investors who were beneficiaries of a trust failed to establish liability against auditors of a trust because they did not rely on the audit, and in any event the beneficiaries were not sufficiently close to force such a duty on the auditors. To similar effect, in the Canadian case of *Bank Fur Handel*

29–029

und Effekten v. Davidson & Co Ltd [1975] 55 D.L.R. (3d) 303, a stockbroker escaped liability after negligently advising the bank as to its clients' investment transactions because the bank had not relied on the advice. In *Eagle Trust v. SBC Securities, The Independent*, September 28, 1994, it was held that a financial adviser to an acquiring company did not owe a duty of care to the company to ensure that the sub-underwriters were good for the money necessary for the underwriting.

29-030 The difficulties of establishing negligence and causation are illustrated by a consideration of the decision in *Stafford v. Conti Commodity Services Ltd* [1981] 1 All E.R. 691, where an investor brought proceedings against a commodity broker on the London commodities futures market. Between January and August 1976 the broker had carried out 46 transactions which had resulted in an overall loss of over £19,000 for the investor. Only 10 of the 46 transactions made a profit. The investor argued that the extent of the losses demonstrated that the broker had failed to exercise due care and diligence in the conduct of his affairs. Whilst the court accepted that the broker may have made an error of judgment in giving advice, the commodities market was unpredictable and a broker could not always be expected to be correct. "Losses in the ordinary course of things do occur even if proper care is used when one is dealing with transactions on the commodities futures market"—*per* Mocatta J. at p. 698d.

Examples of Successful Cases

29-031 There have been other cases where investors have been successful in recovering damages for financial loss. In *Cornish v. Midland Bank plc* [1985] 3 All E.R. 513, the Court of Appeal held Midland Bank liable in negligence for its failure to advise a customer as to the financial consequences of executing a mortgage in favour of the bank (*cf: Barclays Bank v. Khaira* [1992] 1 W.L.R. 623). A trust company which advised an investor that a co-operative was 100 per cent insured has been held liable in negligence where the co-operative failed and the money was not insured—*Blair v. Canada Trust Co* [1986] 32 D.L.R. (4th) 515. If a bank negligently gives advice as to specific investments, as opposed to referring the customer to a stockbroker, a duty of care will be owed. There is also an old Assize case in which Salmon J. held a bank liable for giving a prospective customer negligent investment advice—*Woods v. Martins Bank Ltd* [1958] 3 All E.R. 166. Canadian courts have held a mortgage broker liable for misrepresenting the value of property to an investor—*Herrington v. Kenco Mortgage & Investments Ltd* [1981] 125 D.L.R. (3d) 377—and a stockbroker liable for negligently giving the impression that he had inside information on the company which was the subject of his investment recommendation—*Elderkin v. Merrill Lynch Royal Securities Ltd* [1977] 80 D.L.R. (3d) 313.

29-032 A recent example of a successful claim occurred in *Verity and Spindler v. Lloyds Bank plc* [1995] N.P.C. 148, where the plaintiff had specifically sought the bank manager's advice on the prudence of a transaction. The manager advised the plaintiffs that the transaction was financially viable and encouraged them to proceed with it. In these circumstances the plaintiffs were not just seeking a loan but asking whether it was "a sensible thing to do" or whether they should "forget it."

The *Verity and Spindler* case can be contrasted with *Bankers Trust International plc v. PT Dharmala Sakti Sejahtera*, December 1, 1995, unreported, where it was held that a commercial bank did not owe an investor company any duty to explain the risks and effects of leveraged interest rate swaps. It would seem that unless asked to do so by its customer, a commercial bank owes no duty of care to assess a customer's suitability for the purchase of a derivative or to advise him on the risks involved. **29–033**

The Duties of a Financial Adviser to Advise its Client on a Takeover

In recent years questions have arisen concerning the scope of the duty of care owed by a financial adviser who has been instructed to advise on a takeover. To date, these questions remain largely unresolved. Inspectors appointed by the DTI to investigate the affairs of Atlantic Computers plc considered that a merchant bank acting as a financial adviser on a takeover did not impliedly assume a responsibility for giving advice on the question of whether an acquisition was in the best interests of the offer company's shareholders. The inspectors said that the financial adviser's duties were no higher than "to satisfy itself that the company has taken all reasonable steps to enable it to evaluate the target and judge whether the acquisition is in the best interests of shareholders". **29–034**

Whether the courts will adopt such a restrictive view remains to be seen. Preliminary indications suggest otherwise. In *Ginora Investments Ltd v. James Capel & Co Ltd*, February 10, 1995, unreported, Rimer J. held that a merchant bank had assumed a wide duty of care to the offeror company to advise on the financial implications, suitability, and terms of a proposed acquisition, and also to advise on the tactics to be employed, in particular whether the bid should be a recommended or hostile bid and whether it should be declared unconditional in all respects. **29–035**

The basis of this extended duty of care rested on the terms of the letter of engagement between the offeror company and the merchant bank, under which the merchant bank expressly assumed an obligation to advise on tactics and strategy. On the facts of the case, however, the court held that the merchant bank had not breached any of the duties which it owed. Those seeking investment advice can learn from this case about the importance of setting out clearly in the letter of engagement the scope of the duties and obligations which the financial adviser is to assume. **29–036**

Chapter 29: Negligent Advice and Negligent Financial Information

Negligent Statements in Accounts

Duty of Care to Shareholders, Existing and Potential

29-037 The House of Lords decided in *Caparo Industries plc v. Dickman* [1991] 1 All E.R. 568, that auditors who certified accounts for the purposes of the Companies Act 1985 owed no duty of care to a potential takeover bidder. It was not sufficient that it was foreseeable, even highly foreseeable, that a bidder might rely on the accounts. The House of Lords held that there was no relationship of proximity between auditors and bidder to found a duty of care. In *Caparo* the auditor's certificate had been required by the Companies Act 1985. An analysis of the company's legislation led to the conclusion that the statutory purpose of the auditor's certificate was to provide the shareholders and debenture holders with reliable information to enable them to exercise their rights as such and not to protect investors in the market. The legal limits of investor protection in this context are well demonstrated in the following passage from Lord Bridge's judgment (at p. 580j):

> "Assuming for the purposes of the argument that the relationship between the auditor of a company and individual shareholders is of sufficient proximity to give rise to a duty of care, I do not understand how the scope of that duty can possibly extend beyond the protection of any individual shareholder from losses in the value of the shares which he holds. As a purchaser of additional shares in reliance on the auditor's report, he stands in no different position from any other investing member of the public to whom the auditor owes no duty."

29-038 This decision caused some consternation in the commercial world which had relied heavily on the accuracy of an auditor's report in relation to a company's accounts.

Duty of Care to Bidders and Potential Lenders

29-039 In *James McNaughten Papers Group Ltd v. Hicks Anderson & Co (a firm)* [1991] 1 All E.R. 134, the Court of Appeal held that an accountant did not owe a duty of care to a bidder when preparing draft accounts at the request of the target company for use in takeover negotiations. The Court of Appeal said that the draft accounts were produced for the target company and not the bidder, the accounts were merely draft accounts and the accountants could not reasonably have foreseen that the bidder would treat the draft accounts as final accounts. In any event, the bidder was aware that the target company was in poor financial health and the bidder could reasonably have been expected to consult its own accountants.

29-040 The position with regard to a potential lender is the same. In *Al Saudi Banque v. Clark Pixley (a firm)* [1989] 3 All E.R. 361, Millett J. held that the auditors of a company owed no duty of care to a bank which lent money to the company, regardless of whether the bank was an existing creditor or a potential creditor of the company. Although the bank had relied on audited accounts when making loans to the company to enable it to finance business operations, there was not a sufficiently close or direct relationship between the auditors and the bank to give rise to the degree of proximity necessary to establish a duty of care. As the judge noted in that case, the potential liability of the auditors to a creditor was far greater than the potential liability to the company's shareholders. Where the value of a company is negligently overstated or understated in the accounts, the auditor's liability to investors and shareholders would be measured by, or at least related to, the extent of their own negligence. That is not so where creditors are concerned and the company is alleged to have been insolvent. In the case of a subsequent and irrecoverable advance, the auditors' maximum liability would fall to be measured by the amount of the advance, which would be unknown to the auditors and could not be foreseen by them. It would bear no necessary relationship to, and could be many times greater than, the value of the company as shown by its published accounts.

29–041 These decisions may be contrasted with the decision of the Court of Appeal in *Morgan Crucible Co v. Hill Samuel Bank* [1991] 1 All E.R. 148, where a profit forecast was issued by financial advisers to a target company in the course of a takeover bid. The court concluded that if the bidder could show that the financial advisers of the target company had intended the bidder to rely on the profit forecast for the purpose of deciding whether to make an increased bid, a relationship of proximity between the parties would be established. Distinguishing the decision in the *Caparo* case, Slade L.J. noted that in that case the relevant statement by the auditors had not been given for the purpose for which the plaintiff takeover bidder relied upon it.

29–042 The limits of the decision in *Morgan Crucible* are well illustrated by a consideration of the decision in *Al-Nakib Investments (Jersey) Ltd v. Longcroft* [1990] 3 All E.R. 321, where a company had issued a prospectus inviting shareholders to subscribe for shares by way of a rights issue. The shareholder applied for some shares, and some months later bought further shares through the stock market. In an action against the company for negligence following misrepresentations in the prospectus, the shareholder argued that it was reasonably foreseeable that a shareholder might rely on the prospectus when deciding to buy shares on the open market. The court rejected this argument on the basis of the *Caparo* decision. The prospectus was addressed to shareholders for the particular purpose of inviting a subscription for shares. If the prospectus was used by a shareholder for a different purpose of buying shares through the stock exchange there was not a sufficiently proximate relationship between the directors and the shareholder for a duty of care to arise on the part of the directors.

29–043 A different result was achieved in *Galoo Ltd (in Liquidation) v. Bright Grahame Murray (a firm)* [1995] 1 All E.R. 16, where company auditors had provided accounts to enable a purchaser to determine a purchase price of a target company. The purchaser subsequently purchased further shares and made loans to the company and a wholly owned subsidiary company. The Court of Appeal considered the decisions in *Caparo* and *Morgan Crucible*. Glidewell L.J. expressed the distinction between the cases in the following terms:

> "Mere foreseeability that a potential bidder may rely on the audited accounts does not impose on the auditor a duty of care to the bidder, but if the auditor is expressly made aware that a particular identified bidder will rely on the audited accounts or other statements approved by the auditor, and intends that the bidder should so rely, the auditor will be under a duty of care to the bidder for the breach of which he may be liable" (at p. 37d).

29–044　Glidewell L.J.'s summary of the principles represents a clear statement of the modern law in this area. The position concerning liability to a potential lender or creditor is the same.

29–045　An example of a case where subscribing and after-market investors have been allowed to proceed to trial against auditors who negligently shared responsibility for misrepresentations in a prospectus occurred recently in *Possfund Custodian Trustee Ltd v. Diamond* [1996] 2 All E.R. 774. Rejecting an application to strike out the Statement of Claim as disclosing no reasonable cause of action, the court held that it was arguable that the auditors owed a duty of care to both subscribing and after-market investors in the light of the way in which the prospectus had been worded. The case involved the flotation of a company's shares on the unlisted securities market, and the prospectus specifically stated that, as part of the exercise of allotment, the facility would be available for shares to be traded on this market. Lightman J. held that if the shareholders could establish that, at the date of preparation and circulation of the original share prospectus, the auditors intended to inform and encourage after-market purchasers, in addition to those investors who relied on the prospectus in making a decision whether to accept the allotment offer, it was at least arguable that the auditors had assumed and owed a duty of care to those investors who relied on the contents of the prospectus in making after-market purchases. The decision in *Al Nakib v. Longcraft* was distinguished on the ground that the purpose of the prospectus in that case was limited to inducing investors to take up the allotment of shares in respect of which the prospectus was issued.

Auditing Standards

29–046　It follows that, unless the auditor is made aware that a particular identified bidder or lender will rely on the accounts, no duty of care will arise to the potential equity or creditor investor. In many cases an investor who suffers financial loss as a result of negligently drawn accounting statements will not be able to recover compensation through the courts, and the most effective practical way to protect investors is to ensure that the standards of the accountancy profession are maintained. In December 1994 the Auditing Practices Board recommended that auditors should be asked to sign their reports on company accounts personally as part of a series of reforms to help re-establish their objectivity and bolster their authority. Whilst the Audit Agenda was careful to say that it did not want to extend auditors' duty to third-party readers of accounts or to potential stakeholders beyond shareholders, the implementation of the Auditing Practices Board recommendations would undoubtedly be welcomed as a step in the right direction.

An interesting case where auditors became liable to a bidder for a company occurred in the unreported case of *ADT v. Binder Hamlyn*, December 6, 1995, when Binder Hamlyn were asked by the bidder to confirm whether they stood by their audit of the company. Binder Hamlyn answered in the affirmative. May J.'s judgment is interesting because it provides a detailed analysis of the standards to be expected in the audit of a substantial group of companies. It identifies the problems which occur in joint audits and the measures which need to be taken if standards are to be met in these circumstances. More work is needed in this area if auditors are to avoid liability when asked to verify their reports personally. **29–047**

Overlap Between Claims for Negligent Advice or Misrepresentation and Breach of Contract

This chapter has focused on the circumstances in which the Courts will recognise liability for negligent advice or misstatement in the absence of a contractual relationship between the parties. Frequently, though, cases occur where claims for breach of contract and liability in tort under the *Hedley Byrne* principle arise concurrently. In most of these cases there will be no difference between the ability of a plaintiff to establish his case in contract or tort because the outcome depends upon the plaintiff's ability to prove the factual aspects of his case, *i.e.* whether the advice or representation was incorrect, whether the defendant failed to take reasonable care, whether the failure caused reasonably foreseeable damage or damage which was within the reasonable contemplation of the parties. **29–048**

In some cases, however, the difference can be important. The limitation period within which a cause of action can be brought starts to run at different times, depending on whether the action is brought for breach of contract or in tort. In contract, the limitation starts to run from the date when the breach occurred, whereas in tort the period runs from the date when financial loss has been sustained. Often loss is sustained some time after the breach of contract has taken place, and it is against this background that there have been a number of cases in **29–049** recent years where plaintiffs have sought to pursue a claim in tort where the incidents of their relationship has been governed by the terms of a contract made between them. In these situations defendants have been assiduous to challenge the plaintiff's ability to make out a concurrent cause of action in tort.

29–050   In *Henderson v. Merrett Syndicates Ltd* [1994] 3 All E.R. 506, the House of Lords held that where liabilities arose concurrently in tort and contract it was open to a plaintiff to assert the cause of action that appeared to him most advantageous, and in the circumstances of that case the House of Lords was satisfied that concurrent liability could be made out. However, this will not always follow; the mere fact that a contractual duty exists does not mean that there is a co-extensive duty owed in tort. As set out in this chapter liability in tort will depend on the nature of the relationship between the parties. It will be difficult to establish a tortious claim where the claim is derived from an obligation or duty which has been set out in a contract. For a more comprehensive consideration of the issues which arise in this context, see *Banque Financiere de la Cite SA v. Westgate Insurance Co* [1989] 2 All E.R. 952 and *Aiten v. Stewart Wrightson Members Agency* [1995] 3 All E.R. 449.

Chapter 30

Parties to a Civil Action

When an aggrieved investor considers the commencement of a civil action to recover his loss, it is essential for him to correctly identify the appropriate defendants. There are, of course, a number of different considerations to be taken into account. In cases where investment funds have been handled by a limited company, the investor plaintiff has to consider whether the pursuit of the company is worthwhile. Commonly, by the time litigation is envisaged a limited company will be insolvent and any judgment against it will almost certainly be worthless. In these circumstances it is necessary to consider whether any liability can attach to a director personally, because if it can, the chances of recovering the misapplied assets and/or damages will be considerably enhanced. 30–001

Personal Liability of Directors

The General Principle of Corporate Liability

It is trite law that a limited company duly formed and registered under the companies legislation is a separate legal entity and has to be treated like any other independent person with its own rights and liabilities as distinct from those of its directors and shareholders. This position was firmly established 100 years ago in *Salomon v. Salomon* [1897] A.C. 22, when the House of Lords refused to allow unsecured creditors to obtain judgment against Mr Salomon personally, even though Mr Salomon was the controlling shareholder and the principal secured creditor of the company. As Lord MacNaughton explained in this seminal case: 30–002

"The company is at law a different person altogether from the subscribers to the memorandum; and, though it may be that after incorporation the business is precisely the same as it was before, and the same persons are managers, and the same hands receive the profits, the company is not in law the agent of the subscribers or the trustees for them. Nor are the subscribers as members liable in any shape or form, except to the extent and in the manner provided by the Companies Act."

CHAPTER 30: PARTIES TO A CIVIL ACTION

30–003　To every rule, however, there are exceptions. In the case of company law there have been a succession of cases throughout the twentieth century in which the courts have been prepared to "lift the corporate veil" to identify the persons who directed and controlled the activities of the company and to hold these people accountable for their misdeeds. It is not possible to formulate any single principle as to the basis of these decisions, but their direction is reasonably clear. It is the purpose of this chapter to explore the boundaries of these exceptional cases to see when they might assist an investor plaintiff who seeks to recover his misapplied funds where those funds have been held by a limited company.

Fraud

30–004　Where a defendant uses a company to raise funds from an investor on a fraudulent basis, a court will be prepared to look behind the corporate entity and permit the investor to recover his funds. Authority for this proposition can be found in the old case of *Re Darby and Brougham* [1911] 1 K.B. 95, where Darby and Brougham arranged for a company prospectus to represent to potential investors that a corporation owned by the company was making profits from a mining contract when in fact the profits were being passed through the corporation to themselves. Darby and Brougham were prosecuted and convicted of making fraudulent and material misstatements in the prospectus, since they had failed to disclose that the corporation was simply an alias for themselves. The company went into liquidation and the liquidator sued Darby, who had considerable assets, for breach of trust and for return of the undisclosed profits which he had received. Phillimore J. allowed the liquidator's claim. The corporation was merely an alias for Darby and Brougham which they had used as a vehicle for fraud:

> "The fraud here is that what they did through the corporation they did themselves and represented it to have been done by a corporation of some standing and position, or at any rate a corporation which was more than different from themselves."

30–005　This decision has clear implications for an investor who wishes to sue a defendant to recover his loss in circumstances where the defendant has used a limited company for the purposes of fraud. An illustration of the contemporary application of this application can be found in the recent case of *Re H and others* [1996] 2 All E.R. 391, where, albeit in a reverse situation, the Court of Appeal confirmed its willingness to lift the corporate veil in the face of fraud. In *Re H and others* two companies had been utilised by three defendants to import a large volume of alcoholic liquor in breach of the excise duties. The defendants sought to resist an application by Customs and Excise to obtain restraint orders over the assets of the two companies on the basis that the company assets could not be said to form part of the realisable property of the defendants. In rejecting this argument the Court of Appeal said that it was willing to lift the corporate veil so as to treat the assets of the companies as the realisable property of the defendants because the companies had been used by the defendants as vehicles for fraud.

Device to Evade a Contractual or Legal Obligation

Consistent with the approach taken in cases of fraud, the Courts have also been prepared to lift the corporate veil where a company has been used as a device to evade a contractual or other legal obligation. This exceptional category may interest an investor plaintiff in a case where a defendant attempts to play "fast and loose" with the civil process. 30–006

The classic authority here is that of *Gilford Motor Co v. Horne* [1933] Ch. 935, where a defendant formed a limited company to carry on business in circumstances where he was prohibited from carrying on this business by virtue of a restrictive covenant. The court granted an injunction against the defendant on the grounds that the company was not a genuine, independent legal entity. The same principle was applied by the court in *Jones v. Lipman* [1962] 1 W.L.R. 832, where a defendant sought to escape from a conveyancing obligation by transferring the property to a nominee company. The company was, said Russell J., "the creature of the first defendant, a device and a sham, a mask which he holds before his face in an attempt to avoid recognition by the eye of equity." See also *Wallersteiner v. Moir (No. 1)* [1974] 3 All E.R. 217, *per* Lord Denning M.R. at 237/8 in this context. 30–007

An investor plaintiff will be interested in a recent application of these principles to the not uncommon situation where a defendant seeks to avoid liability by transferring his personal assets into a complicated network of offshore companies and trusts. This situation occurred in *Re A Company* [1985] B.C.L.C. 333, where the defendant was sued for fraud and breach of trust. He sought to conceal his true beneficial interests by transferring them into a complex corporate and trust network but the Court of Appeal restrained him from dealing with the assets held by these companies and trusts pending the outcome of the case. In the next chapter the way in which a plaintiff can seek to locate the whereabouts of the defendant's assets is addressed. 30–008

Holding Companies

In some cases the courts have concluded that a holding company has been carrying on business through the agency of its subsidiary company. There are a number of decided cases which illustrate the relevant principles (see, for example, *D H N Food Distributors Ltd v. Tower Hamlets L.B.C.* [1976] 1 W.L.R. 852) but they do not impact significantly in the area of investor protection. Perceived injustice in the face of insolvency will not be sufficient to cause a court to treat a subsidiary company and a holding company as one economic unit—*Re Polly Peck International plc (in administration)* [1996] 2 All E.R. 433. 30–009

Agency

30–010 Exceptionally, as with the relationship between an holding company and its subsidiary, the circumstances of a particular case may permit a plaintiff to circumvent the sanctity of the corporate personality by asserting that the company has acted as an agent for a director who is a principal. The decision in *Salomon v. Salomon* did not exclude the operation of principal and agent in this context but in reality this relationship will be difficult to establish because a plaintiff will have to show that, in terms of some tortious liability, the director is the employer or principal of the company. As Tomlin J. explained in *British Thomson-Houston Co Ltd v. Sterling Accessories* [1924] All E.R. 294:

> "It has been made plain by the House of Lords that, for the purpose of establishing contractual liability, it is not possible, even in the case of the so-called one-man companies, to go behind the legal corporate entity of the company and treat the creator and controller of the company as the real contractor merely because he is the creator and controller. If he is to be fixed with liability as a principal, the agency of the company must be established substantively and cannot be inferred from the holding of director's office and the control of the shares ... Any other conclusion would have nullified the purpose for which the creation of limited companies was authorised by the legislature."

30–011 Three recent cases where the courts have applied the agency principle to attach personal liability to a director are worthy of mention because they illustrate the increasing willingness of the courts to impose personal liability in this area.

30–012 In *Haley v. Northington Archives Ltd*, November 15, 1995, unreported, a deputy High Court Judge held that an employee of a company which traded in currency futures owed a non-contractual personal duty of care to the plaintiff when he gave investment advice upon which the plaintiff acted. Although employed by the company and acting on its behalf, the defendant held himself out as an adviser and specialist, and regarded himself as a professional man providing services to a client. This was enough to bring him within one of the existing categories where a personal duty of care was owed.

30–013 A few weeks later, in *Williams v. Natural Life Health Foods Ltd*, December 1, 1995, unreported, Langley J. held a managing director of a company liable for negligent mis-statements made in the name of the company concerning the company's financial projections. The judge said that the fact that the director controlled the company was not in itself sufficient to make him personally liable, but since he had personally directed the presentation to the plaintiff of the financial projections and assumed responsibility for them, personal liability had been established. It was found as a fact that, in considering the financial projections, the managing director had appreciated that the plaintiff would rely on his personal experience and expertise.

Lastly, in *Infante v. Charman*, July 31, 1996, unreported, a Court held that the defendant, who was a director of a company with whom the plaintiff had placed a building contract, had contracted with the plaintiff as principal and not as an agent of the company. The plaintiff and the defendant were long-standing friends. All the correspondence had been informal, although it had been written on the company's headed notepaper. The court said that use of company headed notepaper was not enough in itself to demonstrate that the defendant was contracting as the company's agent. Given the relationship between the plaintiff and the defendant, there had to be explicit wording to such effect in the correspondence. Applying *The Swan* [1968] Ll.Rep. 5, whether a director contracted as a principal or an agent depended on the objective intention of the parties, as evidenced by (1) the nature of the contract, (2) its surrounding terms and (3) the surrounding circumstances. **30–014**

Wrongful Trading

Until 1986 it used to be the case that directors could hide behind the corporate shelter unless they had been acting fraudulently or in some other way intending to evade a contractual or legal obligation. The enactment of section 214 of the Insolvency Act 1986 made a radical change in this position and today a negligent director of an investment company may be vulnerable where the company has become insolvent. Potentially, this legislative change significantly erodes the inviolability of the corporate entity in the investment context. **30–015**

The Cork Committee recommended the institution of a new remedy of wrongful trading in its report in 1982 (Cmnd. 8558) where a company went into liquidation in circumstances where the directors or shadow directors knew, or ought to have known, that the company could not pay its debts. This recommendation was adopted by Parliament in section 214 of the Insolvency Act 1986 which provides that a person will be liable for wrongful trading if: **30–016**

"(a) the company has gone into insolvent liquidation;
(b) at some time before the commencement of the company's winding-up that person knew or ought to have known, that there was no reasonable prospect that the company would avoid going into insolvent liquidation;
(c) he was a director or shadow director of the company at that time; and
(d) the court is not satisfied that he took every step that he ought to have taken with a view to minimising the potential loss to the company's creditors (assuming him to have known that there was no reasonable prospect that the company would avoid going into insolvent liquidation)."

The last criteria is the most difficult to satisfy. Further guidance on the meaning the requirement is contained in section 214(4) which reads as follows: **30–017**

" ... the facts which a director of a company ought to know or ascertain, the conclusions which he ought to reach and the steps which he ought to take are those which would be known or ascertained, or reached or taken, by a reasonably diligent person having both—

(a) the general knowledge, skill and experience that may reasonably be expected of a person carrying out the same functions as are carried out by that director in relation to the company;

(b) the general knowledge, skill and experience that that director has."

30–018 This test represents a curious mix of objective and subjective standards, and where the director or shadow director has particular expertise, for example in financial accounting, the standard will be higher than that required of his less highly trained counterpart. In *Re Produce Marketing Consortium Ltd (No. 2)* [1989] B.C.L.C. 520, the court held that a director or shadow director had to be judged by the standards that might reasonably be expected from somebody fulfilling his functions and showing reasonable diligence in doing so. Certain minimum standards would be assumed, such as knowledge on the part of the directors of information compiled by the company in accordance with its obligation under the Companies Act 1985 to publish annual accounts.

30–019 It was said in *Re Purpoint* [1991] B.C.L.C. 491, that the court is concerned to ensure that the director makes good the depletion in assets attributable to the period after the moment when he knew or ought to have known that there was no reasonable prospect of avoiding an insolvent winding-up. This, then, is the measure of compensation which a director will be required to pay in an appropriate case.

30–020 Initially there was some concern at the scope of persons who might fall into the definition of a shadow director, as where, for example, a bank supported an ailing company with a business plan which the company was obliged to follow. To some extent the point was resolved in *Re MC Bacon* [1990] B.C.L.C. 324, where the court said a liquidator's claim against a bank had been rightly abandoned. More recently, in *Re Hydrodam (Corby) Ltd* [1994] 2 B.C.L.C. 180, a court refused to accept that the directors of a holding company were shadow directors of a subsidiary company.

30–021 The most significant limitation on this innovative power is that a liquidator is the only person by whom an application may be made under this section. In a compulsory winding-up the official receiver acts as liquidator by virtue of section 136(2) of the Insolvency Act 1986, unless a different person is appointed by virtue of sections 139 or 140. In most cases the necessary evidence will be difficult to gather, and the liquidator is likely to be in the best position to decide whether the requirements of the section could be established to the satisfaction of the court. Unfortunately no procedure has been set up to deal with the situation where a liquidator fails to take action in the face of good evidence. Arguably, an aggrieved investor might have sufficient status to bring the matter before the court in proceedings for declaratory relief. If not, his remedy would be confined to the Parliamentary Ombudsman.

Costs

There is one further area in which a director may be personally **30–022** vulnerable where a limited company is involved. This area is exclusively procedural, focusing on the power contained in section 51(1) of the Supreme Court Act 1981 which confers power on the Court to determine by whom and to what extent the costs of any legal action are to be paid. The section contemplates the making of an order against a party who has not been joined as a party to an action, although in *Taylor v. Pace Developments Ltd*, [1991] B.C.C. 406, the court said that it would seldom be appropriate to make such an order against a director of an insolvent company.

Chapter 31

Pre-Emptive Civil Remedies

31–001 The purpose of this chapter is to address an important area of civil procedure which has particular relevance in cases where an investor plaintiff brings an action against a defendant to recover his losses following the discovery of an investor fraud. The area concerns the efforts which an investor plaintiff can make to identify, locate and freeze the misapplied funds. Reliance by a defendant on the privilege against self-incrimination can operate to thwart these efforts and the scope of the privilege is considered in the second part of this chapter. In the third section of this chapter brief mention is made of the ability of an investor plaintiff to obtain summary judgment in an investor fraud case.

1. The Mareva and Anton Piller Jurisdiction

General Principles

31–002 In cases where investor losses have been suffered, it is essential for investors to have swift recourse to the civil process so as to ensure that misapplied funds are identified, located and returned to the United Kingdom in cases where (as often occurs) they have been transferred abroad. There are two main ways in which this can be achieved. First, an aggrieved investor can seek to obtain an injunction which freezes the assets of the defendant. This is known as a Mareva injunction. Secondly, an investor can seek to obtain an order which enables him to enter the premises of the defendant and search for specified documents and property which he may then seize. This order is known as an Anton Piller order.

31–003 A plaintiff can apply for both orders in an appropriate case ("piling Piller on Mareva", as it has become known). Applications for a Mareva injunction and an Anton Piller are made *ex parte* since secrecy is essential for the success of the operation. Experience has shown time and again that these pre-emptive remedies provide the only realistic chance for an investor plaintiff to recover his loss where he has been a victim of investor fraud. The police, the Serious Fraud Office and the regulatory bodies seem to take an unconscionable time to decide whether to act on information which they receive, and by the time search warrants have been obtained through the criminal process the

CHAPTER 31: PRE-EMPTIVE CIVIL REMEDIES

misapplied monies have often been subjected to the laundering process. There is no other mechanism whereby an investor or a liquidator can require a defendant to disclose the whereabouts of misapplied funds at an early stage in the investigatory process. In a case of investor fraud, although it may be late and perhaps much of the money might have gone, the sooner that steps are taken to try and trace where it is the better. If steps are going to be taken, it is important that they are taken at the earliest possible moment.

31-004 A Mareva injunction will be granted where a plaintiff can be shown that there is a real risk that the defendant has dissipated the investment funds or that the funds have been removed from the jurisdiction. An investor plaintiff must show that he has a good arguable case and that there is a real risk that any judgment which he obtains will be unenforceable because of dissipation or secretion of the misapplied funds. It should be possible to satisfy these criteria in almost every serious fraud case. A Mareva injunction can be granted against any defendant in an action, whether inside or outside of the United Kingdom and whether or not the defendant has assets inside or outside the jurisdiction—*Derby & Co Ltd v. Weldon (Nos. 3 & 4)* [1990] Ch. 65.

31-005 There may be occasions where a plaintiff will be required to give an undertaking not to make any application to a foreign court without first obtaining leave of the United Kingdom court because the Court was concerned to ensure that the Mareva injunction would not be enforced by a multiplicity of actions in different countries throughout the world, but this will not occur in every case. In *Re Bank of Credit and Commerce International SA (9)* [1994] 3 All E.R. 764, the Court of Appeal recognised that it was undesirable for liquidators who were seeking material for the prosecution of fraud and the enforcement of regulatory procedures in international cases to be fettered by undertakings simply because they were seeking worldwide Mareva relief in domestic civil proceedings for the benefit of creditors.

31-006 One unresolved issue which is likely to recur in the future is whether a court can grant a Mareva injunction to restrain a defendant's assets in the United Kingdom where a plaintiff has brought proceedings in another jurisdiction and the subject matter of the action has no connection with the domestic jurisdiction. The issue was raised before the Privy Council in *Mercedes-Benz AG v. Herbert Heinz Horst Leiduck* [1995] 3 All E.R. 929, but the point was not decided because the plaintiff's claim failed on a different point. Whilst it is right that there is increasing emphasis on the importance of international co-operation in the battle against international fraud, it has to be remembered that the Mareva relief takes effect *in personam* and not *in rem*, which means that the injunction is not an attachment and does not confer on the plaintiff any proprietary rights in the assets seized. Bearing this in mind, a court may not find it easy to afford assistance to a foreign investor plaintiff where the matters in dispute have no connection with an English court, even though the defendant is present in the United Kingdom, perhaps because he has fled from another jurisdiction. The position is different where the court is asked to assist in aid of proceedings begun in another jurisdiction. Under section 25 of the Civil Jurisdiction and Judgments Act 1982 an English court has jurisdiction to give pre-trial or post-trial relief in aid of proceedings commenced in a Brussels Convention country.

An application for an Anton Piller order will be successful where an **31-007** investor plaintiff can show strong evidence that serious harm or serious injustice would be suffered by him if the order is not granted, and strong evidence that the defendant has in his possession inculpating documents or other property. There must be a strong prima facie case that the defendant may destroy or dispose of the documents or property before an *inter partes* application can be made. Again, in cases involving serious fraud, these criteria can usually be satisfied.

Disclosure of Assets

The critical importance of a Mareva injunction in the investor context **31-008** is that an ancillary disclosure order can be attached to the injunction which requires a defendant to make full disclosure of his assets, confirming by affidavit the existence, location and amount of these assets. This power is derived from section 37 of the Supreme Court Act 1981 which confers jurisdiction (albeit implicitly) to make all such orders as appear to the court to be just and convenient for the purpose of ensuring that the exercise of the Mareva jurisdiction is effective to achieve its purpose. A defendant may have more than one asset within or outside the jurisdiction—for example, he may have a number of bank accounts. A plaintiff will not know how much, if anything, is in any of them, nor will each of the defendant's bankers know what is in the other accounts. Without information about the state of each account it is difficult, if not impossible, to operate the Mareva jurisdiction properly—see *A. J. Bekhor & Co Ltd v. Bilton* [1981] 1 Q.B. 923, and *A. v. C. (Note)* [1981] Q.B. 956. When pursuing a tracing remedy to recover the misapplication of investor funds, it is vital that a defendant is ordered to disclose details of his foreign assets as well as assets which he holds within the jurisdiction.

Bankers' Trust Order

In the area of investor fraud in particular, the growth of Mareva **31-009** injunctions has led to an expansion of the equitable jurisdiction relating to the obtaining of details of a defendant's bank accounts. Frequently an investor plaintiff will seek a tracing order in relation to such accounts, in order to recover the misapplied funds. In *A. v. C.* [1981] Q.B. 956, Goff J. confirmed that a Court had inherent jurisdiction to obtain information about bank accounts so as to facilitate the operation of a Mareva injunction in this type of case. As Lloyd J. explained during the first instance hearing in *PCW (Underwriting Agencies) Ltd v. Dixon* [1983] 2

Chapter 31: Pre-emptive Civil Remedies

All E.R. 158 (at p. 164E-F), the distinction between an ordinary Mareva plaintiff and the case where a plaintiff is laying claim to a trust fund is that in the latter case the whole object of the action is to secure the trust fund itself so that it is available if the plaintiff proves his claim.

31-010   The power to obtain this type of order operates in addition to the powers to inspect bankers' books under the Bankers' Books Evidence Act 1879. As with the normal Mareva injunction, a bankers' order needs to be sought as a matter of urgency. It has been established that a bankers order will be made only if the order is likely to lead to the discovery of misapplied funds or alternatively where it is necessary to preserve such funds—*Arab Monetary Fund v. Hashim (No. 5)* [1992] 2 All E.R. 911. The investor plaintiff must establish that he has a proprietary claim to the funds which he is seeking to locate or preserve—*Lipkin Gorman (a firm) v. Cass, The Times*, May 29, 1985. In this type of case a bank may be ordered not simply to disclose details of bank accounts held in a defendant's name but also to disclose details of the balances standing in any account and to permit the plaintiff to take copies of banking documents which relate to the operation of the account.

31-011   The Court of Appeal upheld the making of such an order in *Bankers' Trust Co v. Shapira* [1980] 1 W.L.R. 1274, from which "the bankers' trust order" takes its name. In complicated cases a court will sanction the appointment of a specified firm of chartered accountants to prepare a schedule setting out the identity and whereabouts of all assets which are held or retained by the defendant. This occurred in the *PCW (Underwriting Agencies) Ltd* case.

31-012   Documents produced by a bank pursuant to a bankers' trust order can be used for the purposes of mounting personal claims against other persons and pursuing parallel remedies in other jurisdictions—*Mohamed Omar v. Chiiko Aikawa Omar, The Times*, December 27, 1994. The Court noted in this case that confidentiality in bankers' documents was broken when there was fraud.

Delivery up

31-013   In rare cases of serious fraud, a court can order a defendant to deliver up the misapplied assets to the court so that the assets can be held pending judgment in the action. This order will not be made unless a plaintiff can establish that the assets have been acquired by a defendant as a result of his wrong-doing and that he is likely to dispose of them in order to deprive the plaintiff of the fruits of any judgment he may obtain. The court must be able to specify as clearly as possible the identity of the assets in question—*CBS United Kingdom Ltd v. Lambert* [1983] Ch. 37.

Restraining a Defendant's Freedom of Movement

31-014   Rarely, a court may be prepared to take the ultimate step and restrain a defendant from leaving the country if there is a significant risk that he will flee the jurisdiction in order to frustrate an order which requires him to disclose the whereabouts of his assets. This occurred in *Bayer AG v. Winter (No 2)* [1986] 1 W.L.R. 540, where, after an order was made for disclosure of certain correspondence and documents in an Anton Piller case, the Court of Appeal ordered that the defendant should be restrained from leaving the jurisdiction for a period of two days following service of the order, and that he should deliver up his passport to the solicitor who served the order on him, with a requirement that the passport should be returned on the expiry of the two days in question.

31–015 This type of court order must be distinguished from the ancient writ of *ne exeat regno* under which a court can impose a power of arrest. There are four conditions which have to be satisfied before a writ of *ne exeat regno* can be issued, these being: (1) that the action is one in which the defendant would formerly have been liable to arrest at law; (2) that a good cause of action for at least £50 is established; (3) that there is probable cause for believing that the defendant is about to leave England unless arrested; and (4) that the defendant's absence would materially prejudice the plaintiff in the prosecution of his claim—*Felton v. Callis* [1969] 1 Q.B. 200. It is the fourth condition which prevents the writ of *ne exeat regno* being granted as an ancillary order in the Mareva jurisdiction.

31–016 As Leggatt J. explained in *Allied Arab Bank Ltd v. Hajjar* [1988] 22 W.L.R. 942, the primary purpose of a Mareva application is to identify assets in relation to which a Mareva injunction can operate. That is not part of the prosecution of the claim, and it follows that the fourth condition cannot be satisfied.

Cross-examination

31–017 If there are grounds for believing that a defendant has not made full disclosure in response to an order made in Mareva or Anton Piller proceedings, a court has power to order that the defendant is subjected to cross-examination on his affidavit—*House of Spring Gardens Ltd v. Waite* [1985] F.S.R. 173. Once again the jurisdiction to make such an order is derived from section 37 of the Supreme Court Act 1981 and the need for a court to ensure that its Mareva and Anton Piller jurisdiction is efficacious.

31–018 A judge has to exercise his discretion when deciding whether to make an order for cross-examination of a defendant on the disclosure of his assets. There are no hard and fast rules. As a general rule cross-examination will not be ordered unless a plaintiff can show that there are some grounds for believing that there are serious inaccuracies or omissions in a defendant's affidavit, in circumstances where an application for contempt of court might be appropriate.

31–019 In *CBS United Kingdom Ltd v. Perry* [1985] F.S.R. 421, Falconer J. expressed the view that it would not be right to allow a plaintiff the opportunity of a roving cross-examination merely because a plaintiff harbours suspicions that a defendant has not been entirely open in his disclosure. It is, after all, in the nature of an application for Mareva or

Anton Piller relief that a plaintiff harbours grave suspicions about a defendant who is served with an order. Also, the power to order cross-examination cannot be used for some ulterior purpose which goes beyond the efficacy of the Mareva and Anton Piller jurisdiction. In *Cloverbay Ltd (joint administrators) v. Bank of Credit and Commerce International SA* [1991] Ch. 90, the court refused to allow the administrators oral examination of certain BCCI employees in order to decide whether to bring claims of constructive trust against them. The court said that the administrators had considerable material, including material obtained in a bankers' trust order, on which to make this decision. Pre-trial oral depositions would be unduly oppressive for the employees concerned.

31–020 Guidance on the making of an order for cross-examination was given by the Court of Appeal in the *House of Spring* case. Slade L.J. explained the approach of the court in the following terms:

> "I can very well see that on the particular facts of many cases—perhaps most cases—the court might not consider it 'just and convenient' to order the cross-examination of a defendant who has filed an affidavit in purported compliance with a Mareva order, in a case where the plaintiff has not yet seen fit to issue a motion for contempt and is not seeking an order for the swearing of a second affidavit by the defendant concerned. The court will always seek to be careful to ensure that the Mareva jurisdiction is not used as a weapon to oppress a defendant; it will no doubt be particularly on guard against potential oppression in a case where it considers that there is no immediate issue before it which calls for decision."

31–021 On the other hand, as Slade L.J. went on to acknowledge:

> " . . . cases can . . . arise where, on the particular facts, the court may properly take the view that the calling or recalling of a defendant for cross-examination on his affidavit is the only just and convenient way of ensuring that the exercise of this jurisdiction will be effective to achieve its purpose, by ensuring that all the relevant assets are identified before any opportunity arises for their dissipation. And this may be so even if, procedurally, the only application before it is the application for cross-examination itself (made subsequent and ancillary to the making of the Mareva order) and the plaintiff has not yet seen fit to launch a motion for committal."

31–022 Cumming-Bruce L.J. agreed with Slade L.J.'s approach, declaring that there are situations where the circumstances demonstrate that it is more sensible, in the interests of speed and urgency, not to order further affidavits in order to fill the vacuum alleged to exist in the affidavits filed pursuant to the original order but to proceed at once to order that the defendant attends for cross-examination on his affidavit.

31–023 The proper scope of cross-examination in this type of case will be twofold. First, to ascertain whether or not a defendant has fully and properly complied with the obligations imposed on him in the Mareva and/or Anton Piller order to disclose the location of his assets and his dealings with them. Secondly, in so far as there has not been full and proper compliance, to elicit the missing information which should have been supplied. By Order 29, rule 1A of the Rules of the Supreme Court cross-examination can be ordered to take place before a judge, a Master of the Supreme Court or an examiner appointed by the court. On a purely practical point, no shorthand note of the cross-examination is taken by the court, so a plaintiff would be well advised to make his own arrangements.

The ability of the court to order cross-examination of a defendant in these circumstances will almost certainly be the subject of future litigation. The first instance judge in *House of Spring*, Scott J., came to the view that, notwithstanding the defendant's consent to be cross-examined, no cross-examination should take place because the plaintiff had not ascertained or clarified the specific issue which was disputed between the parties. The function of a civil court, said Scott J., was to decide issues between the parties and not to police the court's order. The Court of Appeal, of course, disagreed with this view, holding that Scott J. had taken too narrow a view of the width of the Mareva jurisdiction possessed by the court, but in the subsequent case of *Bayer AG v. Winter (No. 2)* [1986] 1 W.L.R. 540, Scott J. was clearly unrepentant. In that case a plaintiff had obtained *ex parte* an Anton Piller order which directed the defendant to disclose certain information relating to the alleged distribution by the defendant of a counterfeit product. The plaintiff was dissatisfied with the disclosure which it obtained and sought an order for cross-examination. Scott J. rejected the plaintiff's application on the basis, once again, that, in his view, the proper function of a judge in civil litigation is to decide issues between the parties and not preside over an interrogation. "Star Chamber interrogatory procedure", said the judge, "has formed no part of the judicial process in this country for several centuries." 31–024

As regards the decision in *House of Spring*, Scott J. said that it could be distinguished because the defendant in that case had consented to cross-examination. The judge said that for his part he found it very difficult to envisage any circumstances in which, as a matter of discretion, it would be right to make such an order as was sought in *Bayer AG v. Winter (No. 2)* and as was made by consent in *House of Spring*. Scott J.'s approach ignores not only the clear spirit of the judgments in the Court of Appeal, but also the protection afforded to a defendant by the privilege against self-incrimination, the operation of which is considered in the second part of this chapter. 31–025

Procedure

The procedure for a Mareva and/or Anton Piller application is set out in a Practice Direction, *Practice Direction (Mareva Injunctions and Anton Piller Orders)* [1994] 1 W.L.R. 1233; [1994] 4 All E.R. 52, and it is right to record that there is much learning on these pre-emptive civil 31–026 remedies which extends beyond the scope of this work. Suffice it that in the second part of this chapter focuses on the principal impediment to a successful application for a Mareva injunction and/or an Anton Piller order where a defendant seeks to exercise the privilege against self-incrimination. The successful assertion of this privilege can frustrate an investor plaintiff's attempts to locate the whereabouts of his misapplied funds, and since the privilege is commonly asserted in investor fraud cases, it is necessary to consider the matter in some detail.

2. The Privilege Against Self-incrimination

The Privilege

31-027   The privilege against self-incrimination has been described recently, by Lord Browne-Wilkinson, in *Re Arrows Ltd (No. 4) Hamilton v. Naviede* [1994] 3 All E.R. 814, as "one of the basic freedoms secured by English law." It has, said Lord Wilberforce in *Rank Film Distributors v. Video Information Centre* [1981] 2 All E.R. 76, been too long established in our law as a basic liberty of the subject to be denied. In *Rank Film Distributors* the plaintiff sought disclosure from the defendants of information which, if revealed, might expose them to a prosecution for conspiracy to defraud in respect of the unauthorised recording and sale of a large number of video cassettes. The question before the House of Lords was whether the defendants could avail themselves of the privilege against self-incrimination in order to resist the plaintiff's application for disclosure. Reluctantly, the House of Lords upheld the defendants' right to claim the benefit of the privilege and the plaintiff failed in his appeal to obtain disclosure of the incriminating information.

31-028   The decision was consistent with the position under Article 6(1) of the European Convention for the Protection of Human Rights and Fundamental Freedoms (Rome, November 4, 1950), which recognises that it is unlawful to render a demand to produce self-incriminating documents (see *Funke v. France* [1993] 16 E.H.R.R. 297; *Miailhe v. France* [1993] 16 E.H.R.R. 332; and *Cremieux v. France* [1993] 16 E.H.R.R. 357). Moreover, the European Court of Justice has held that under European Community law an individual cannot be compelled to give incriminating answers to the European Commission since to do so would infringe "the general principles of Community law, of which fundamental rights form an integral part."

31-029   The privilege against self-incrimination is derived from a Latin maxim, *"nemo tenetur prodere seipsum"* and came to be incorporated into English law in the sixteenth century in response to the compulsory interrogations then being conducted by the Star Chamber and the High Commission for Causes Ecclesiastical. The classic statement of the privilege is contained in the judgment of Goddard L.J. in *Blunt v. Park Lane Hotel* [1942] 2 K.B. 253, as follows:

"The rule is that no one is bound to answer any question if the answer thereto would, in the opinion of the judge, have a tendency to expose the deponent to any criminal charge, penalty or forfeiture which the judge regards as reasonably likely to be preferred or sued for."

Asserting the Privilege

The privilege has to be asserted by the defendant. However, it is not sufficient for him to merely state that his answer or production of documents would in his opinion render him liable to criminal prosecution. Affidavit evidence asserting the privilege will not be conclusive. The specific offence or offences have to be identified. This is not to say that the defendant will be required to set out the details of the incriminating evidence. He must provide sufficient information for the judge to make his ruling, but no more. 31–030

It is for the judge to satisfy himself that the defendant's claim to rely on the privilege against self-incrimination is properly made. The court will examine whether, taking into account the circumstances of the case and the nature of the evidence, there is reasonable ground to apprehend some danger if the defendant is compelled to answer the question or produce the documents in question. The privilege will not be available where the defendant is already at risk of prosecution and the risk will not be increased if he were to answer questions or provide information. However, once the danger of self-incrimination is apparent, great latitude will be allowed to the defendant in assessing for himself the effect of any particular question. The cases of *Rio Tinto Zinc Corp v. Westinghouse Electric Corporation* [1978] A.C. 547 and *Sociedade Nacional de Combustiveis de Angola v. Lundqvist* [1991] 2 Q.B. 310, are the seminal cases in point and authorities for these propositions. In *Sociedade* Staughton L.J. set out the test (at p. 324E) which is to be applied: "The substance of the test is this, that there must be grounds to apprehend danger to the witness, and those grounds must be reasonable, rather than fanciful." 31–031

A court will have regard to the petty nature of any offence and the fact that prosecutions are rare. In *Rank Film Distributors* the House of Lords held that the possibility of charges under section 21 of the Copyright Act 1956 which carried a maximum penalty of a £50 fine could not justify the claim for privilege. 31–032

By section 14(1) of the Civil Evidence Act 1968, Parliament has confirmed that the privilege against self-incrimination is to be taken to include any answer which would tend to expose the spouse of the defendant to proceedings for a criminal offence. A company, being a legal person, may also claim the privilege. In these circumstances it should be remembered that the privilege belongs to the company and not to its officers, although the officers can claim the benefit of the privilege in their own right. If a defendant elects not to claim the privilege, his answers cannot be recalled. 31–033

Chapter 31: Pre-emptive Civil Remedies

31-034   In recent times the courts have moved towards a situation where Mareva injunctions and Anton Piller orders will not be granted *ex parte* without a provision in the order which informs a defendant of his right to claim the benefit of the privilege against self-incrimination. Lord Wilberforce said in *Rank Film Distributors* that forms should be worked out which will enable the orders to be as effective as practicable whilst preserving the defendant's essential rights. Such a formula of words was incorporated into an Anton Piller order by Warner J. in *IBM United Kingdom Ltd v. Prima Data International Ltd* [1994] 1 W.L.R. 719, to the following effect:

> " . . . before any persons enter [the premises] pursuant to this order the supervising solicitor shall offer to explain to the [defendant] the meaning and effect of this Order in everyday language and shall also advise the [defendant] of his right to obtain legal advice before permitting entry provided that such advice is taken as once (such advice to include an explanation that the [defendant] may be entitled to avail himself of the privilege against self-incrimination) . . ."

31-035   This order was executed but the defendant subsequently complained that he had not fully understood the privilege against self-incrimination to which reference had been made. In the course of its judgment the Court approved the use of this formula, noting that defendants are bemused by the appearance of solicitors bearing 13 page orders in legal language. The judge, Sir Mervyn Davies Q.C., said that it would have been helpful to have seen cross-examination of the solicitor and the defendant as to exactly what was said when the order was executed but neither party had applied to take this course. In the event the court concluded that since the defendant was a businessman of some experience he must have understood the position which had been explained to him by the solicitor concerned. This type of clause protects the interests of a defendant but at the expense of a plaintiff who is seeking to recover losses as a result of an investment fraud.

Mareva Injunctions

31-036   The privilege is often asserted by defendants in applications for Mareva injunctions where the court orders the defendant to disclose the whereabouts of his assets and/or attend for cross-examination on the contents of his affidavit. In these circumstances it is sometimes difficult for a plaintiff to circumvent the operation of the privilege. The Court of Appeal held in *Sociedade* that a defendant in civil proceedings who is facing allegations of conspiracy to defraud is entitled to rely on the privilege against self-incrimination to resist an order requiring him to disclose the value of his assets overseas where the value of such assets might form a link in the chain of proof against him on a criminal charge. Moreover, it seems that a defendant can seek to rely on the privilege against self-incrimination as a secondary defence in circumstances where he disputes on the facts of the plaintiff's claim that he has conducted himself in a way which might expose him to criminal proceedings. It is not open to a plaintiff to say that a defendant, because he protests his innocence, he must be lying when he claims potential incrimination. A defendant in such a case may properly claim the benefit of the privilege against self-incrimination—*AT & T Istel Ltd v. Tully* [1993] A.C. 45.

In recent times there has been some litigation on whether the operation of the privilege against self-incrimination can be circumvented by an assurance that the disclosed material will not be used in a criminal prosecution. In *AT & T Istel Ltd* the House of Lords sanctioned this approach, deciding that a defendant cannot rely on the privilege where the prosecuting authorities have stated by letter that any disclosure made in civil proceedings will not be used as evidence in criminal proceedings. As Ralph Gibson L.J. pointed out in *Bank of England v. Riley* [1992] 2 W.L.R. 840, the question as to whether there was any misuse of information could be determined by a criminal court which was subsequently involved. The position is different, however, in the absence of an assurance from the prosecuting authorities. **31–037**

In *United Norwest Co-operatives Ltd v. Johnstone, The Times,* February 24, 1994, the first instance judge ordered disclosure of assets in a claim for fraudulent trading but sought to protect the interests of the defendants by ordering that the plaintiff was restrained from disclosing the information to any person who was not a party to the action and in particular to any police force or prosecuting authority. The Court of Appeal were unable to approve of this approach because it did not depend on any assurance from a prosecuting authority. It did not follow, the Court of Appeal said, that a court could withhold its assistance to a prosecuting authority where there had been no assurance given by the prosecuting authority and the court order had been made without notice to the prosecuting authority, let alone its consent. **31–038**

It is presently unclear whether the privilege against self-incrimination applies where a defendant is concerned about his exposure to prosecution in another country. Section 14(1) of the Civil Evidence Act 1968 provides that the privilege against self-incrimination "shall apply only as regards criminal offences under the law of any part of the United Kingdom", but it is difficult to see how, in these times of trans-border crime, this provision can sit easily with Article 6(1) of the European Convention. The Court of Appeal went some way to recognising to this point in *Arab Monetary Fund v. Hashim* [1989] 3 All E.R. 466 when it held that the possibility of self-incrimination in respect of criminal offences in foreign law was a factor to be taken into account by the court in deciding whether, and in what terms, a disclosure order in support of a Mareva injunction should be made. Where a defendant asserts that he is vulnerable to criminal proceedings in a foreign jurisdiction, it will be necessary for a plaintiff to obtain expert evidence on the law in that jurisdiction. **31–039**

CHAPTER 31: PRE-EMPTIVE CIVIL REMEDIES

31–040   In exceptional circumstances the court has limited jurisdiction to order that the facts required to be disclosed by a defendant should not be disclosed to the plaintiff provided that they are disclosed to someone on the plaintiff's side (such as the plaintiff's solicitor) who can effectively deal with the matter—*Arab Monetary Fund v. Hashim*. The propriety of this approach is far from clear. It is unsatisfactory that a plaintiff's solicitor should come into possession of information which he cannot disclose to his client.

Anton Piller orders

31–041   Similar considerations arise where a plaintiff obtains an Anton Piller order to search and seize documents from a defendant's premises. A court should not make an order at the *ex parte* stage if it is apparent on the facts alleged by a plaintiff that disclosure of documents or the immediate answer to questions might tend to incriminate the defendant on a criminal charge—see *Rank Distributors Limited* and *Tate Access Floors Inc v. Boswell* [1990] 3 All E.R. 303. Where a plaintiff obtains and executes an *ex parte* Anton Piller, a defendant can apply to set aside the order and may obtain return of his documents if he can satisfy the court that he is entitled to claim the privilege against self-incrimination, provided that the application to set aside the order is made before the documents have been adduced in evidence—*Universal City Studios Inc v. Hubbard* [1983] 2 All E.R. 596, on appeal [1984] Ch. 225.

Bankers' Trust Orders

31–042   At present there is no direct authority on whether the privilege against self-incrimination can be raised in answer to a tracing order where details of a defendant's bank accounts are required. Bankers' trust orders are necessarily concerned with the recovery of funds which are alleged to have been misapplied, so the same considerations which apply in cases of Mareva injunctions and Anton Piller orders can be expected to apply.

Bankers' Books Evidence Act

31–043   In the course of civil proceedings a plaintiff may seek to apply for discovery of a defendant's bank account under the provisions of the Bankers' Books Evidence Acts 1876 and 1879. Once again, the privilege against self-incrimination operates to impede an aggrieved plaintiff in his attempt to recover his losses where he has been the victim of an investment fraud. In *Waterhouse v. Wilson Barker* [1924] 2 K.B. 759, it was alleged that the defendant and her husband had fraudulently taken certain monies belonging to Mr Waterhouse. The plaintiff was the executrix of Mr Waterhouse's will and sought inspection of the defendant's bank account. The defendant successfully raised the privilege against self-incrimination to prevent the plaintiff's inspection of his bank account.

Exceptional Cases where the Privilege Against Self-incrimination has been Abrogated by Statute

31-044 The operation of the privilege against self-incrimination has been embraced by the courts with some equanimity, particularly in recent times. Whilst in the nineteenth century the Lord Chancellor, Lord Eldon, in *Ex p. Cossens, In the Matter of Worrall* [1820] *Cases in Bankruptcy* 53, accepted that the privilege was "one of the most sacred principles in the law of this country", the contemporary approach is more sceptical. As Lord Wilberforce pointed out in *Rank Film Distributors* it was a strange paradox that the worse, *i.e.* the more criminal, the activities of the defendants can be made to appear, the less effective is the civil remedy that can be granted.

31-045 Mindful of this paradox, Parliament has intervened in a number of situations to abrogate the operation of the privilege where this has been perceived to be in the public interest. Notwithstanding these statutory interventions, for some members of the judiciary nothing short of abolition would be sufficient. Lord Templeman in *AT & T Istel Ltd* described the privilege against self-incrimination as "an archaic and unjustifiable survival from the past", and said (at 53B) that:

> "it was difficult to see any reason why in civil proceedings the privilege ... should be exercisable so as to enable a litigant to refuse relevant and even vital documents which are in his possession or power and which speak for themselves."

Theft

31-046 Section 31(1) of the Theft Act 1968 provides that a witness, who may be a defendant in a civil action, shall not be excused from answering a question in proceedings for the recovery or administration of any property, for the execution of any trust or for an account of any property or dealings with property, or from complying with any order made in any such proceedings, on the ground that it would incriminate him or his spouse in an offence under the Theft Act 1968. The abrogation of the privilege is tempered by the fact that the section further provides that no statement or admission made by the witness shall be admissible in criminal proceedings for an offence under the Act. The provision is extended to cover offences under the Theft Act 1978.

31-047 Suppose a defendant falls within the scope of section 31(1) but he is liable to be prosecuted for some other offence outside the parameters of the Theft Acts, such as forgery under the Forgery and Counterfeiting

Act 1981. Will the privilege be abrogated in these circumstances? The Court of Appeal answered this question affirmatively in *Khan v. Khan* [1982] 2 All E.R. 60, where a defendant was obliged to swear an affidavit concerning the whereabouts of money removed from an account. The court upheld the order notwithstanding that a possible charge of forgery might have been brought as well.

31–048 This decision was applied by the Court of Appeal in *Renworth Ltd v. Stephansen*, December 21, 1995, unreported, where the defendant was required to swear an affidavit specifying certain matters in relation to the plaintiff's claim for breach of contract and conversion. The defendant claimed the privilege against self-incrimination because there was a risk of prosecution for offences under the Theft Acts and non-Theft Act offences. The correct approach, the court held, was for the matter to be considered from the point of view of separate claims to privilege in respect of both types of criminal offence. In each case the test was whether to answer the question would tend to expose the defendant to proceedings for the relevant offence by creating or increasing the risk of proceedings for that offence. If the test was satisfied in the case of a Theft Act offence, section 31 applied. In the case of the non-Theft Act offence, the test was whether the question would create or increase the risk of proceedings for that offence separate and distinct from its connection with the Theft Act offence. If the answer was "no", there was no privilege. If the answer was "yes", the privilege subsisted in relation to the non-Theft Act offence notwithstanding the availability of the Theft Act charges.

31–049 The prohibition set out in section 31 concerning the use in criminal proceedings of answers obtained in civil proceedings does not extend to cover answers given in proceedings for bankruptcy. In *R. v. Kansal* [1993] Q.B. 244, the Court of Appeal held that evidence given by a bankrupt in bankruptcy proceedings was admissible against him in his subsequent prosecution for offences under the Theft Act 1968. The court held that section 31 related to civil proceedings, *inter partes*, where a claim was made in relation to property which had been acquired in circumstances of an incriminating nature. The normal privilege against self-incrimination was abrogated by the terms of section 31 in such proceedings.

Copyright

31–050 After the decision in *Rank Film Distribution*, Parliament intervened and by section 72 of the Supreme Court Act 1981 it removed the privilege against self-incrimination in actions for breach of copyright. The courts have held that this provision is not to be construed restrictively—*Universal City Studios Inc v. Hubbard*—but there have been difficulties in establishing what is a "related offence" for the purposes of the section—see *Crest Homes plc v. Marks* [1987] 2 All E.R. 1074, *per* Lord Oliver at pp. 1079b-1081a. Again, however, the abrogation of the privilege against self-incrimination was tempered by a restriction against the use of admissions in criminal proceedings.

Bankruptcy

31-051 The effect of section 290 of the Insolvency Act 1986 is more draconian, in the sense that there is no tempering provision so far as admission of evidence in criminal proceedings are concerned. Where a bankruptcy order has been made and the Official Receiver applies for a public examination of the bankrupt under section 290 of the Insolvency Act 1986, rule 9.4(3) of the Insolvency Rules provides that the bankrupt shall be examined on oath and shall answer all such questions as the court may put to him. In *Re Paget* [1927] 2 Ch. 85, a case decided under earlier legislation, it was held that a witness could not refuse to answer questions on the ground that his answers might incriminate him. Answers given in bankruptcy proceedings will be admissible in evidence against an accused in a criminal case. Rule 6.175(5) of the Insolvency Rules provides that "the written record may, in any proceedings . . . be used as evidence against the bankrupt of any statement made by him in the course of his public examination".

Business Fraud

31-052 Procedures have been established under section 432 of the Companies Act 1985 and section 236 of the Insolvency Act 1986 for examinations to be conducted by inspectors and/or liquidators in order to elicit the true facts from those who know them. Although the statutory provisions establishing such inquisitorial rights for the purpose of discovering the true facts about the conduct of a company or an individual are silent on the question of whether the privilege against self-incrimination is to apply, the courts have been ready to hold in recent years that Parliament has impliedly overridden the ancient privilege against self-incrimination by their enactment of these provisions. It has been held that a witness cannot rely on the privilege so as to refuse to answer questions put by inspectors under the Companies Act 1985—*Re London United Investment plc* [1992] 2 All E.R. 842—or by liquidators on an examination under the Insolvency Act 1986—*In Re Jeffrey S Levitt Ltd, The Times,* November 6, 1991 and *Bishopsgate Investment Management Ltd v. Maxwell* [1992] 2 All E.R. 856.

31-053 What is more, answers will be admissible against a defendant in any criminal proceedings. In *R. v. Saunders* [1996] Crim.L.R. 420, the defendant was interviewed by inspectors appointed to conduct an investigation into the Guiness acquisition of Distillers under sections 432 and 442 of the Companies Act 1985. The defendant was subsequently prosecuted for criminal offences and the trial judge admitted into evidence the transcripts of interview which the accused had given to the inspectors before he was charged in order to establish his dishonest state of knowledge and to contradict his testimony to the jury. The Court of Appeal, Lord Taylor C.J. presiding, upheld the trial judge's decision, having come to the view that Parliament intended to override the privilege against self-incrimination in the fields of insolvency and company fraud. The European Commission of Human Rights

CHAPTER 31: PRE-EMPTIVE CIVIL REMEDIES

has, however, taken a different view, saying that the admission into evidence of the interview transcripts offended against Article 6(1) of the Convention. The European Court of Human Rights usually adopts the opinion of the European Commission, and this can be expected to happen in the *Saunders* case.

31–054 Whether an unfavourable ruling by the European Court of Human Rights will persuade the Government to intervene and alter the law remains to be seen. Certainly it is right to note that section 31 of the Theft Act 1968 would not fall foul of Article 6(1) of the European Convention because of the tempering provision against the admission of answers into evidence in criminal proceedings. It might be thought that a similar limitation could be applied to the use of interview transcripts obtained under the Companies Act and Insolvency Act powers.

The Effect of Asserting the Privilege

31–055 Traditionally, no adverse inference can be drawn from a defendant's assertion of the privilege against self-incrimination. For as Staughton L.J. said in *Sociedade* (at p. 319F): "to comment adversely about a person who claims privilege to avoid incriminating himself is plainly wrong."

31–056 The opponents of the privilege have sought to advance a contrary view, exemplified by Templeman L.J.'s comments in *Rank Film Distributors* when the case was heard in the Court of Appeal:

> "The plaintiff is not wholly or necessarily defeated and the defendant is not necessarily assisted by the defendant relying on the privilege against self-incrimination. The civil court may draw conclusions where a criminal court may not. If the privilege is raised in connection with an inquiry as to damages the court will be driven to draw conclusions as to the scope and harm caused by the defendant's activities and, in the face of silence and concealment on the part of the defendant, will not be slow to make assumptions and draw inferences which will enable damages to be awarded on a scale which will do justice to the plaintiff".

31–057 Whether this contrary view can be said to undermine the efficacy of the privilege to such an extent that it contravenes Article 6(1) of the European Convention on Human Rights remains to be seen, but an investor plaintiff can undoubtedly contend that the time has now come for the courts to depart from the traditional position and draw adverse inferences from a defendant's silence. On April 10, 1995, English law was altered by section 35 of the Criminal Justice Act 1994 and a criminal court is now allowed to draw an adverse inference from the exercise by an accused of his right to silence. In these circumstances an investor plaintiff may argue with some considerable force that it is absurd for a defendant to be better protected in a civil court than a criminal court.

31–058 Whether or not the concomitant effect of section 35 of the Criminal Justice Act 1994 has been to allow a civil court to draw an adverse inference of liability in an action where the defendant asserts the privilege against self-incrimination, cases will continue to occur where the raising of the privilege can be used to thwart recovery of misapplied funds. Unless an aggrieved plaintiff has knowledge of the whereabouts of the misapplied funds, in all probability any judgment against the defendant will be unenforceable. This begs the question as to whether Parliament should extend the operation of section 31 of the Theft Act 1968 to all criminal offences. As Sir Nicholas Browne Wilkinson observed in *Sociedade*, "if [this] is not done, I fear that the effectiveness of civil remedies designed to redress fraud will be seriously impaired". The section 31 approach is to be preferred to the approach taken by Parliament in the Companies Act 1985 and the Insolvency Act 1986 because it provides protection for the defendant against the admission of incriminating answers in criminal proceedings.

Fear of Physical Violence

Although it is a factor to be taken into account when deciding whether to set aside a Mareva injunction or an Anton Piller order, the risk of violence to the defendant by another party whose wrongdoing will be exposed by compliance with a court order will rarely outweigh a plaintiff's pressing need for the information in question. The point arose in *Coca-Cola v. Gilbey* [1995] 4 All E.R. 711, where the plaintiff obtained an Anton Piller order against a defendant in a breach of trade mark case. Documents disclosed the existence of another party against whom the plaintiff subsequently obtained a further Anton Piller order. This party sought to set aside the order on the basis that his documents would disclose the names of others involved which would place his safety in danger. Lightman J. rejected the submission: "I cannot think that in any ordinary case where the plaintiff has a pressing need for the information in question, the existence of the risk of violence against the potential informant should outweigh the interest of the plaintiff in obtaining the information". **31–059**

Summary Judgment

Since 1992 it has been possible to obtain summary judgment in a civil case under Order 14 of the Rules of the Supreme Court where a defendant has no defence to the claim in the writ. The advantage of the procedure is that it enables a plaintiff to obtain a quick judgment without incurring significant costs in the pursuit of a defendant who does not have a *bona fide* defence. **31–060**

In order to obtain summary judgment it will be necessary for the evidence of investor fraud to be overwhelmingly clear, and in practice this may occur only after a defendant has been convicted of fraud offences in a criminal court. Nevertheless, if a plaintiff is successful in **31–061**

Chapter 31: Pre-emptive Civil Remedies

securing the freezing of the misapplied funds under the Mareva jurisdiction, the summary judgment procedure can be usefully employed as soon as the criminal case has concluded. By section 11(1) of the Civil Evidence Act 1968 a criminal conviction is admissible in a civil court to prove that a person committed the offence in question, and by section 11(2) a person is deemed to have committed the offence unless the contrary is proved. Therefore, if a defendant is to resist an application for summary judgment, he bears a heavy onus to show that he was wrongly convicted by the criminal court.

31–062 The summary judgment procedure was successfully utilised in the Brinks-Mat bullion case when summary judgment was entered against a total of 57 defendants who had been involved in varying ways with the stolen gold or laundering the stolen gold. Two of the defendants sought to resist summary judgment but without success. Jacobs J. held that before a convicted robber or money launderer could raise a defence under Order 14 he had to raise a real or *bona fide* defence to the claim. A defence that was "practical moonshine" would not do—*Brinks Ltd v. Abu-Saleh and others* [1995] 4 All E.R. 65. The court also held that delay in making an application for summary judgment was not of itself a relevant matter in determining the application in circumstances where there was no defence to the claim.

31–063 In *Brinks Ltd v. Abu-Saleh (No. 2)* [1995] 4 All E.R. 74, on a different but tangentially relevant point, Rimer J. held that a transcript of a judge's summing up in criminal proceedings was at least potentially relevant in subsequent civil proceedings as a means of identifying the factual basis on which a defendant was convicted of the offence with which he had been charged. The admission of the transcript would clearly be helpful where a defendant contests the relevance of a criminal conviction on an application for summary judgment under Order 14.

Part 7

Conclusion

Chapter 32

The Future

The Need for Reform

There can be no doubt at all that significant reforms have to be made if investor protection is to be effective in the twenty first century. Instead of the re-active recognition of investor interests, the law must encourage a pro-active approach. It is no longer acceptable for regulatory bodies to respond to new cases of investor malpractice with swathes of new legislation to close the stable door long after the horse has bolted. 32–001

The time has come for Parliament to demand that the scope and application of the regulatory system is sufficiently comprehensive to protect the interests of investors so as to ensure the security of their investments in the years to come. It is incumbent on the legislators, and in particular the House of Commons Treasury and Civil Service Committee which concerns itself with supervisory affairs, to take the lead in this regard. 32–002

The scale of fraud today is truly massive. It is estimated that in 1992 losses from reported fraud totalled £8,500 million, as compared with losses from reported burglary of just under £500 million, and the Director General of the National Criminal Intelligence Service has estimated that fraud costs British industry £10 billion a year. Indeed, a 1992 survey by Ernst & Young of 100 leading British companies found that 54 per cent had reported a fraud over £50,000 in the last two years. How many more investor disasters will have to occur before a comprehensive regulatory system is put in place? One only has to think of the Barlow Clowes investors, the Mirror group pensioners, the BCCI and Barings Bank depositors to demonstrate the point. 32–003

Looking into the future, there can be little doubt that sales of pensions and long-term care insurance policies will provide a significant part of the financial services market in the next 10 years. There have, of course, been significant problems with sales of non-occupational personal pensions (see Chapter 5) and it was not until the passing of the Pensions Act 1995 that a comprehensive system for the regulation of occupational pensions was created in the wake of the Maxwell affair. At least today these forms of investment have the benefit of regulation under one or other of the supervisory regimes. But Parliament has not afforded the same protection to purchasers of long-term care insurance policies. The selling of long-term care insurance policies is presently unregulated, notwithstanding the avowed objective of Government to 32–004

CHAPTER 32: THE FUTURE

shift the cost of care from the State to the individual. There is, it is feared, another financial disaster waiting to happen if the area continues to be open to unauthorised persons who can work alongside those who are authorised to sell other forms of insurance policy for which authorisation is necessary.

A Co-ordinated Approach

32–005   As the Centre for the Study of Financial Innovation acknowledged in a paper entitled "U.K. financial supervision: a blueprint for change" published in May 1994, the new regulatory creatures in the form of the Securities and Investments Board with its associated bodies have added to the complexity and untidiness of the supervisory control. The paper suggests that a new Financial Services Supervisory Commission is needed to act as a centralised supervisor.

> "The aim behind this restructuring would be to remove the conflicts which are built into the present set-up, and to streamline the supervisory practices in place across different financial sectors. It would also create a supervisory structure which was well adapted to handle the broader financial institutions which are emerging in the liberalised E.U. markets. The [Commission] would be created as a statutory Commission, answerable to Parliament. It would be headed by a Commissioner and a Board of Supervision including representatives of the financial services industry, the business community and the Bank of England, which would be closely involved both in policy and in the day-to-day running of the Commission. The main duty of the [Commission] would be to ensure the soundness of the financial system as a whole, for which purpose it would have the power to license and regulate financial institutions."

32–006   A consideration of the disparate statutory and non-statutory systems for the regulation of investment as described in Parts 2, 3 and 4 of this book bears out the good sense of this recommendation.

32–007   A suggestion along similar lines has come from the Institute of Chartered Accountants Audit Faculty in a paper entitled "Taking Fraud Seriously" issued in January 1996. The Audit Faculty recommends the establishment of an independent standing body, to be called the Fraud Advisory Panel, with responsibility for (i) providing a forum for discussion and improved co-operation between government, law enforcement, the private sector and other interested parties, and (ii) increasing overall awareness of the problem of fraud. The paper suggests that the Panel's membership should be drawn from the legal and accounting professions, law enforcement, regulatory agencies, business and academia, and that the Panel should report to ministers as necessary.

Strengthening the Policing Role of Auditors

The Audit Faculty also recommended that a legal duty should be created for regulators to report suspected fraud to auditors, and that the law against knowingly misleading an auditor should be strengthened. Section 389A of the Companies Act 1985 presently gives auditors right of access to the company's records and requires its officers to provide such explanation or information as the auditors need to perform their duties. This, the Audit Faculty believes, is too limited in its application. The Faculty recommends that:

— the maximum penalty should be increased from two years' imprisonment to five years' imprisonment;

— the provision should be extended to cover unincorporated bodies or associations, pension schemes, partnerships and individuals;

— the provisions should be extended to cover persons carrying on unauthorised investment business;

— the term "officer" should be deleted from the legislation and that the term "any person" should be substituted;

— the provisions should be extended to cover reporting engagements for prospectus and profit forecast purposes;

— it should be an offence to destroy or suppress accounting or other records which are relevant to the enquiries of auditors or reporting accountants.

Additionally, the Audit Faculty alighted on the way in which the civil law could be utilised in the cause of investor protection by recommending that a new civil penalty should be created which provides that a person who knowingly deceives an auditor would be liable to the company for any damage or loss which might arise. As the Audit Faculty points out, punishment of serious fraud in the criminal courts has proved to be a poor deterrent. There were only seven sentences of more than five years' duration for serious fraud in 1992 and only one in 10 defendants was sentenced to a period of more than two years' imprisonment.

Enforcement

The inadequacy of the criminal process in the context of investor protection has been well documented. In 1986 Lord Roskill said in his report on Fraud Trials that:

"the public no longer believes that the legal system in England and Wales is capable of bringing the perpetrators of serious frauds

Chapter 32: The Future

expeditiously and effectively to book. The overwhelming weight of the evidence laid before us suggests that the public is right. In relation to such crimes, and to the skilful and determined criminals who commit them, the present legal system is archaic, cumbersome and unreliable."

32–011 Consideration of the matters discussed in Part 5 of this book shows that the situation has not improved in the 10 years which have passed since these words were written, notwithstanding the passing of the Criminal Justice Act 1987 which was designed to make special provision for the speedy trial of serious fraud. The images of the defendants in the Guinness, Blue Arrow, Brent Walker and Roger Levitt trials hover over the void which characterises the impotence of the criminal law in this area. As *The Times* recognised in its leading editorial on the January 20, 1996:

"The Government must initiate a serious inquiry into the laws and regulations which govern financial dealing ... The common law offences of fraud and theft are simply not appropriate to cover the complicated transactions and chains of contractual relationships which arise in the biggest financial mishaps ... The idea of creating a powerful financial regulator, modelled on the U.S. Securities and Exchange Commission, is finding growing support even within the City and the Bank of England, which have traditionally insisted on the lightest possible financial supervision, based on self-regulation. Whichever of the many possible options are ultimately enacted, the Government and the City cannot afford to ignore the evidence that the present system of financial regulation has failed."

Part 8

Appendices

Appendix 1

Regulatory Structure for Financial Services in the United Kingdom

H.M. Treasury—Securities and Investments Board A1–001
    Securities and Futures Authority
    Personal Investment Authority
    Investment Management Regulatory Organisation
Department of Trade and Industry—The insurance industry

Recognised Professional Bodies

Chartered Association of Certified Accountants A1–002
Institute of Actuaries
Institute of Chartered Accountants in England and Wales
Institute of Chartered Accountants in Ireland
Institute of Chartered Accountants in Scotland
Insurance Brokers Registration Council
The Law Society
The Law Society of Northern Ireland
The Law Society of Scotland

Recognised Investment Exchanges

International Petroleum Exchange of London Ltd A1–003
International Stock Exchange of the United Kingdom
LIFFE Administration and Management
London Commodity Exchange
London Metal Exchange Ltd
OMLX, The London Securities and Derivatives Exchange Ltd

APPENDICES

Appendix 2

Financial Services Act 1986

Sections 1 and 2   SCHEDULE 1

INVESTMENTS AND INVESTMENT BUSINESS

COMMENCEMENT
A2–001 This Schedule came into force on December 18, 1986 except for paras. 23, 25(2), (3) (see S.I. 1986 No. 2246 (c. 88)).
Para. 23 came into force on December 1, 1987 (S.I. 1987 No. 1997 (c. 58) Art. 6, Sched. 2 and para. 22(2)).

PART I

INVESTMENTS

Shares etc.

A2–002 1. Shares and stock in the share capital of a company.
Note. In this paragraph "company" includes any body corporate and also any unincorporated body constituted under the law of a country or territory outside the United Kingdom [but does not, except in relation to any shares of a class defined as deferred shares for the purposes of section 119 of the Building Societies Act 1986, include a building society incorporated under the law of, or any part of the United Kingdom, nor does it include an open-ended investment company or any body incorporated under the law of, or any part of, the United Kingdom relating to industrial and provident societies or credit unions].

AMENDMENTS
A2–003 The amendment to the Note in square brackets was made by the Financial Services Act 1986 (Extension of Scope of Act) Order 1991, S.I. 1991 No. 1104, Art. 2.

Debentures

A2–004 2. Debentures, including debenture stock, loan stock, bonds, certificates of deposit and other instruments creating or acknowledging indebtedness, not being instruments falling within paragraph 3 below.
Note. This paragraph shall not be construed as applying—
  (a) to any instrument acknowledging or creating indebtedness for, or for money borrowed to defray, the consideration payable under a contract for the supply of goods or services;

Appendices

(b) to a cheque or other bill of exchange, a banker's draft or a letter of credit; or

(c) to a banknote, a statement showing a balance in a current, deposit or savings account or (by reason of any financial obligation contained in it) to a lease or other disposition of property, a heritable security or an insurance policy.

Government and public securities

3. Loan stock, bonds and other instruments creating or acknowledging indebtedness issued by or on behalf or a government, local authority or public authority. **A2–005**

Notes

(1) In this paragraph "government, local authority or public authority" means—
   (a) the government of the United Kingdom, of Northern Ireland, or of any country or territory outside the United Kingdom;
   (b) a local authority in the United Kingdom or elsewhere;
   (c) any international organisation the members of which include the United Kingdom or another Member State.

(2) The Note to paragraph 2 above shall, as far as applicable, apply also to this paragraph.

[(3) This paragraph does not apply to any instrument creating or acknowledging indebtedness in respect of money received by the Director of Savings as deposits or otherwise in connection with the business of the National Savings Bank or in respect of money raised under the National Loans Act 1968 under the auspices of the Director of Savings or in respect of money treated as having been so raised by virtue of section 11(3) of the National Debt Act 1972.]

Amendment

Note (3) was added by S.I. 1990 No. 349, Art. 2(1). **A2–006**

Instruments entitling to shares or securities

4. Warrants or other instruments entitling the holder to subscribe for investments falling within paragraph 1, 2 or 3 above. **A2–007**

Notes

(1) It is immaterial whether the investments are for the time being in existence or identifiable.

(2) An investment falling within this paragraph shall not be regarded as falling within paragraph 7, 8 or 9 below.

Certificates representing securities

5. Certificates or other instruments which confer— **A2–008**
   (a) property rights in respect of any investment falling within paragrah 1, 2, 3 or 4 above;
   (b) any right to acquire, dispose of, underwrite or convert an investment, being a right to which the holder would be entitled if he held any such investment to which the certificate or instrument relates; or
   (c) a contractual right (other than an option) to acquire any such investment otherwise than by subscription.

APPENDICES

Note. This paragraph does not apply to any instrument which confers rights in respect of two or more investments issued by different persons or in respect of two or more different investments falling within paragraph 3 above and issued by the same person.

Units in collective investment scheme

A2–009   6. Units in a collective investment scheme, including shares in or securities of an open-ended investment company.

Options

A2–010   7. Options to acquire or dispose of—
   (a) an investment falling within any other paragraph of this Part of this Schedule;
   (b) currency of the United Kingdom or of any other country or territory;
   (c) gold, [palladium, platinum,] or silver; or
   (d) an option to acquire or dispose of an investment falling within this paragraph by virtue of (a), (b) or (c) above.

AMENDMENT

A2–011   The words in subpara. (c) in square brackets were added by the Financial Services Act 1986 (Extension of Scope of Act and Meaning of Collective Investment Scheme) Order 1988, S.I. 1988 No. 496, Art. 2.

Futures

A2–012   8. Rights under a contract for sale of a commodity or property of any other description under which delivery is to be made at a future date and at a price agreed upon when the contract is made.

Notes

(1) This paragraph does not apply if the contract is made for commercial and not investment purposes.

(2) A contract shall be regarded as made for investment purposes if it is made or traded on a recognised investment exchange or made otherwise than on a recognised investment exchange but expressed to be as traded on such an exchange or on the same terms as those on which an equivalent contract would be made on such an exchange.

(3) A contract not falling within Note (2) above shall be regarded as made for commercial purposes if under the terms of the contract delivery is to made within seven days.

(4) The following are indications that any other contract is made for a commercial purpose and the absence of any of them is an indication that it is made for investment purposes—
   (a) either or each of the parties is a producer of the commodity or other property or uses it in his business;
   (b) the seller delivers or intends to deliver the property or the purchaser takes or intends to take delivery of it.

(5) It is an indication that a contract is made for commercial purposes that the price, the lot, the delivery date or the other terms are determined by the parties for the purposes of the particular contract and not by reference to regularly published prices, to standard lots or delivery dates or to standard terms.

APPENDICES

(6) The following are also indications that a contract is made for investment purposes—
  (a) it is expressed to be as traded on a market or on an exchange;
  (b) performance of the contract is ensured by an investment exchange or a clearing house;
  (c) there are arrangements for the payment or provision of margin.

(7) A price shall be taken to have been agreed upon when a contract is made—
  (a) notwithstanding that it is left to be determined by reference to the price at which a contract is to be entered into on a market or exchange or could be entered into at a time and place specified in the contract; or
  (b) in a case where the contract expressed to be by reference to a standard lot and quality, notwithstanding that provision is made for a variation in the price to take account of any variation in quantity or quality on delivery.

Contracts for differences etc.

9. Rights under a contract for differences or under any other contract the purpose or pretended purpose of which is to secure a profit or avoid a loss by reference to fluctuations in the value or price of property of any description or in an index or other factor designated for that purpose in the contract. **A2–013**

Notes

(1) This paragraph does not apply where the parties intend that the profit is to be obtained or the loss avoided by taking delivery of any property to which the contract relates.

[(2) This paragraph does not apply to rights under any contract under which money is received by the Director of Savings as deposits or otherwise in connection with the business of the National Savings Bank of raised under the National Loans Act 1968 under the auspices of the Director of Savings or under which money raised is heated as having been so raised by virtue of section 11(3) of the National Debts Act 1972.]

AMENDMENT
Note (2) was added by S.I. 1990 No. 349, Art. 2(2). **A2–014**

Long term insurance contracts

10. Rights under a contract the effecting and carrying out of which constitutes long term business within the meaning of the Insurance Companies Act 1982. **A2–015**

Notes

(1) This paragraph does not apply to rights under a contract of insurance if—
  (a) the benefits under the contract are payable only on death or in respect of incapacity due to injury, sickness or infirmity;
  (b) to benefits are payable under the contract on a death (other than a death due to accident) unless it occurs within ten years of the date on which the life of the person in question was first insured under the contract or before that person attains a specified age not exceeding seventy years;
  (c) the contract has no surrender value or the consideration consists of a single premium and the surrender value does not exceed that premium; and

APPENDICES

(d) the contract does not make provision for its conversion or extension in a manner that would result in its ceasing to comply with paragraphs (a), (b) and (c) above.

(2) Where the provisions of a contract of insurance are such that the effecting and carrying out of the contract—
    (a) constitutes both long term business within the meaning of the Insurance Companies Act 1982 and general business within the meaning of that Act; or
    (b) by virtue of section 1(3) of that Act constitutes long term business notwithstanding the inclusion of subsidiary general business provisions, references in this paragraph to rights and benefits under the contract are references only to such rights and benefits as are attributable to the provisions of the contract relating to long term business.

(3) This paragraph does not apply to rights under a re-insurance contract.

(4) Rights falling within this paragraph shall not be regarded as falling within paragraph 9 above.

Rights and interests in investments

A2–016   11. Rights to and interests in anything which is an investment falling within any other paragraph of this Part of this Schedule.
Notes
(1) This paragraph does not apply to interests under the trusts of an occupational pension scheme.
(2) This paragraph does not apply to rights or interests which are investments by virtue of any other paragraph of this Part of this Schedule.

PART II

ACTIVITIES CONSTITUTING INVESTMENT BUSINESS

A2–017   *NOTE: For the purposes of section 47A (Statements of Principle) and 48 (Conduct of Business Rules), Part II of this Schedule has effect as if amongst the activities falling within this Part of Schedule I were those listed services falling within Section C of the Annex to the Investment Services Directive; and for these purposes none of the exclusions in Part III of Schedule I shall have effect: see the Financial Services Act 1986 (Investment Services) (Extension of Scope of Act) Order 1995, S.I. 1995 No. 3271, Art. 5 (in force, January 1, 1996, implementing the Investment Services Directive).*

Dealing in investments

A2–018   12. Buying, selling, subscribing for or underwriting investments or offering or agreeing to do so, either as principal or as an agent.
[*Notes*
(1) This paragraph does not apply to a person by reason of his accepting, or offering or agreeing to accept, whether as principal or as agent, as instrument creating or acknowledging indebtedness in respect of any loan, credit, guarantee or other similar financial accommodation or assurance which he or his principal has made, granted or provided or which he or his principal has offered or agreed to make, grant or provide.
(2) The references in (1) above to a person accepting, or offering or agreeing to accept, an instrument include references to a person becoming,

or offering or agreeing to become, a party to an instrument otherwise than as a debtor or a surety.]

AMENDMENT

Notes (1), (2) were added by the Financial Services Act 1986 (Restriction of Scope of Act and Meaning of Collective Investment Scheme) Order 1988, S.I. No. 803, Art. 2.

Arranging deals in investments

13. Making or offering or agreeing to make—
    (a) arrangements with a view to another person buying, selling, subsecribing for or underwriting a particular investment; or
    (b) arrangements with a view to a person who participates in the arrangements buying, selling, subscribing for or underwriting investments.

Notes

(1) This paragraph does not apply to a person by reason of his making, or offering or agreeing to make, arrangements with a view to a transaction to which he will himself be a party as principal or which will be entered into by him as agent for one of the parties.

(2) The arrangements in (a) above are arrangement which bring about or would bring about the transaction in question.

[(3) This paragraph does not apply to a person ("the relevant person") who is either a money-lending company within the meaning of section 338 of the Companies Act 1985 or a body corporate incorporated under the law of, or of any part of, the United Kingdom relating to building societies or a person whose ordinary business includes the making of loans or the giving of guarantees in connection with loans by reason of the relevant person making, or offering or agreeing to make, arrangements with a view to a person ("the authorised person") who is either authorised under section 22 or 23 of this Act or who is authorised under section 31 of this Act and carries on insurance business which is investment business selling an investment which falls within paragraph 10 above or, so far as relevant to that paragraph, paragraph 11 above if the arrangements are either—
    (a) that the authorised person or a person on his behalf will introduce persons to whom the authorised person has sold or proposes to sell an investment of the kind described above, or will advise such persons to approach, the relevant person with a view to the relevant person lending money on the security of that investment; or
    (b) that the authorised person gives an assurance to the relevant person as to the amount which will or may be received by the relevant person, should that person lend money to a person whom the authorised person has sold or proposes to sell an investment of the kind described above, on the surrender or maturity of that investment if it is taken as security for that loan.]

[(4) This paragraph does not apply to a person by reason of his making, or offering or agreeing to make, arrangements with a view to a person accepting, whether as principal or as agent, an instrument creating or acknowledging indebtedness in respect of any loan, credit, guarantee or other similar financial accommodation or assurance which he or his principal has made, granted or provided or which he or his principal has offered or agreed to make, grant or provide.

(5) Arrangements do not fall within (b) above by reason of their having as their purpose to provision of finance to enable a person to buy, sell, subscribe for or underwrite investments.

Appendices

(6) This paragraph does not apply to arrangements for the introduction of persons to another person if—
   (a) the person to whom the introduction is made is an authorised or exempted person or is a person whose ordinary business involves him in engaging in activities which fall within this Part of this Schedule or would do apart from the provisions of Part III or Part IV and who is not unlawfully carrying on investment business in the United Kingdom; and
   (b) the introduction is made with a view to the provision of independent advice or the independent exercise of discretion either—
      (i) in relation to investments generally; or
      (ii) in relation to any class of investments if the transaction or advice is or is to be with respect to an investment within that class.

(7) The references in (4) above to a person accepting an instrument include references to a person becoming a party to an instrument otherwise than as a debtor or a surety.]

AMENDMENT

A2–021   Note (3) was added by the Financial Services Act 1986 (Restriction of Scope of Act) Order 1988, S.I. 1988 No. 318, Art. 2.

Notes (4)–(7) were added by the Financial Services Act 1986 (Restriction of Scope of Act and Meaning of Collective Investment Scheme) Order 1988, S.I. 1988 No. 803, Art. 3.

Managing investments

A2–022   14. Managing, or offering or agreeing to manage, assets belonging to another person if—
   (a) those assets consist of or include investments; or
   (b) the arrangements for their management are such that those assets may consist of or include investments at the discretion of the person managing or offering or agreeing to manage them and either they have at any time since the date of the coming into force of section 3 of this Act done so or the arrangements have at any time (whether before or after that date) been held out as arrangements under which they would do so.

Investments advice

A2–023   15. Giving, or offering or agreeing to give, to persons in their capacity as investors or potential investors advice on the merits of their purchasing, selling, subscribing for or underwriting an investment, or exercising any right conferred an investment to acquire, dispose or, underwrite or convert an investment.

Establishing etc. collective investment schemes

A2–024   16. Establishing operating or winding up a collective investment scheme, including acting as trustee of an authorised unit trust scheme.

Appendices

Part III

Excluded Activities

Dealings as principal

17.—(1) Paragraph 12 above applies to a transaction which is or is to be entered into by a person as principal only if— A2–025
  (a) the holds himself out as willing to enter into transactions of that kind at prices determined by him generally and continuously rather than in respect of each particular transaction; or
  (b) he holds himself out as engaging in the business of buying investments with a view to selling them and those investments are or include investments of the kind to which the transaction relates; or
  (c) he regularly solicits members of the public for the purpose of inducing them to enter as principals or agents into transactions to which that paragraph applies and the transaction is or is to be entered into as a result of his having solicited members of the public in that manner.
(2) In sub-paragraph (1) above "buying" and "selling" means buying and selling by transactions to which paragraph 12 above applies and "members of the public", in relation to the person soliciting them ("the relevant person"), means any other person except—
  (a) authorised persons, exempted persons, or persons holding a permission under paragraph 23 below;
  (b) members of the same group as the relevant person;
  (c) persons who are, or propose to become, participators with the relevant person in a joint enterprise;
  (d) any person who is solicited by the relevant person with a view to—
    (i) the acquisition by the relevant person of 20 per cent or more of the voting shares in a body corporate (that is to say, shares carrying not less than that percentage of the voting rights attributable to share capital which are exercisable in all circumstances at any general meeting of the body); or
    (ii) if the relevant person (either alone or with other members of the same group as himself) holds 20 per cent or more of the voting shares in a body corporate, the acquisition by him of further shares in the body or the disposal by him and shares in that body to the person solicited or to a member of the same group as that person;
  (e) any person whose head office is outside the United Kingdom, who is solicited by an approach made or directed to him at a place outside the United Kingdom and whose ordinary business involves him in engaging in activities which fall within Part II of this Schedule or would do so apart from this Part or Part IV.
(3) Sub-paragraph (1) above applies only—
  (a) if the investment to which the transaction relates or will relate falls within any of paragraphs 1 to 6 above or, so far as relevant to any of those paragraphs, paragraph 11 above; or
  (b) if the transaction is the assignment (or, in Scotland, the assignation) of an investment falling within paragraph 10 above or is the assignment (or, in Scotland, the assignation) of an investment falling within paragraph 11 above which confers rights to or interests in an investment falling within paragraph 10 above.]

APPENDICES

(4) Paragraph 12 above does not apply to [any transaction [. . .] which relates or is to relate to an investment which falls within paragraph 10 above or, so far as relevant to that paragraph, paragraph 11 above nor does it apply to a transaction which relates or is to relate to an investment which falls within any of paragraphs 7 to 9 above or, so far as relevent to any of those paragraphs, paragraph 11 above being a transaction which, in either case,] is or is to be entered into by a person as principal if he is not as authorised person and the transaction is or is to be entered into by him—
- (a) with or through an authorised person, an exempted person or a person holding a permission under paragraph 23 below; or
- (b) through an office outside the United Kingdom, maintained by a party to the transaction, and with or through a person whose head office is situated outside the United Kingdom and whose ordinary business is such as is mentioned in sub-paragraph (2)(e) above.

AMENDMENTS AND REPEALS

A2–026 The amendments to sub-paras. (3) and (4) in square brackets were effected by the Financial Services Act 1986 (Restriction of Scope of Act) Order 1988, S.I. 1988 No. 318, Art. 3.

The repeal in sub-para. (4) was effected by the Financial Services Act 1986 (Restriction of Scope of Act and Meaning of Collective Investment Scheme) Order 1990, S.I. 1990 No. 349, Art. 3.

Groups and joint enterprises

A2–027 18.—(1) Paragraph 12 above does not apply to any transaction which is or is to be entered into by a person as principal with another person if—
- (a) they are bodies corporate in the same group; or
- (b) they are, or propose to become, participators in a joint enterprise and the transaction is or is to be entered into for the purposes of, or in connection with, that enterprise.

(2) Paragraph 12 above does not apply to any transaction which is or is to be entered into by any person as agent for another person in the circumstances mentioned in sub-paragraph (1)(a) or (b) above if—
- (a) where the investment falls within any of paragraphs 1 to 6 above or, so far as relevant to any of those paragraphs, paragraph 11 above, the agent does not—
  - (i) hold himself out (otherwise that to other bodies corporate in the same group or persons who are or propose to become participators with him in a joint enterprise) as engaging in the business of buying investments with a view to selling them and those investments are or include investments of the kind to which the transaction relates; or
  - (ii) regularly solicit members of the public for the purpose of inducing them to enter as principals or agents into transactions to which paragraph 12 above applies;

  and the transaction is not or is not to be entered into as a result of his having solicited members of the public in that manner.
- (b) where the investment is not as mentioned in paragraph (a) above—
  - (i) the agent enters into the transaction with or through an authorised person, an exempted person or a person holding a permission under paragraph 23 below; or
  - (ii) the transaction is effected through an office outside the United Kingdom, maintained by a party to the transaction, and with or

through a person whose head office is situated outside the United Kingdom and whose ordinary business involves him in engaging in activities which fall within Part II of this Schedule or would do so apart from this Part or Part IV.

(3) Paragraph 13 above does not apply to arrangements which a person makes or offers or agrees to make if—
  (a) that person is a body corporate and the arrangements are with a view to another body corporate in the same group entering into a transaction of the kind mentioned in that paragraph; or
  (b) that person is or proposes to become a participator in a joint enterprise and the arrangements are with a view to another person who is or proposes to become a participator in the enterprise entering into such a transaction for the purposes of or in connection with that enterprise.

(4) Paragraph 14 above does not apply to a person by reason of his managing or offering or agreeing to manage the investments of another person if—
  (a) they are bodies corporate in the same group; or
  (b) they are, or propose to become, participators in a joint enterprise and the investments are or are to be managed for the purposes of, or in connection with, that enterprise.

(5) Paragraph 15 above does not apply to advice given by a person to another person if—
  (a) they are bodies corporate in the same group; or
  (b) they are, or propose to become, participators in a joint enterprise and the advice is given for the purpose of, or in connection with, that enterprise.

(6) The definition in paragraph 17(2) above shall apply also for the purposes of sub-paragraph (2)(a) above except that the relevant person referred to in paragraph 17(2)(d) shall be the person for whom the agent is acting.

Sale of goods and supply of services

19.—(1) [Subject to sub-paragraph (9) below,] this paragraph has effect where a person ("the supplier") sells or offers or agrees to sell goods to another person ("the customer") or supplies or offers or agrees to supply him with services and the supplier's main business is to supply goods or services and not to engage in activities falling within Part II of this Schedule.

A2–028

(2) Paragraph 12 above does not apply to any transaction which is or is to be entered into by the supplier as principal if it is or is to be entered into by him with the customer for the purposes of or in connection with the sale or supply or a related sale or supply (that is to say, a sale or supply to the customer otherwise than by the supplier but for or in connection with the same purpose as the first-mentioned sale or supply).

(3) Paragraph 12 above does not apply to any transaction which is or is to be entered into by the supplier as agent for the customer if it is or is to be entered into for the purpose of or in connection with the sale or supply or a related sale or supply and—
  (a) where the investment falls within any of paragraphs 1 to [5] above or, so far as relevant to any of those paragraphs, paragraph 11 above, the supplier does not—
    (i) hold himself out (otherwise than to the customer) as engaging in the business of buying investments with a view to selling them and those investments are or include investments of the kind to which the transaction relates; or

APPENDICES

(ii) regularly solicit members of the public for the purpose of inducing them to enter as principals or agents into transactions to which paragraph 12 above applies;

and the transaction is not or is not to be entered into as a result of his having solicited members of the public in that manner;

(b) where the investment is not as mentioned in paragraph (a) above, the supplier enters into the transaction—

(i) with or through an authorised person, an exempted person or a person holding a permission under paragraph 23 below; or

(4) Paragraph 13 above does not apply to arrangements which the supplier makes or offers or agrees to make with a view to the customer entering into a transaction for the purposes of or in connection with the sale or supply or a related sale or supply.

(5) Paragraph 14 above does not apply to the supplier by reason of his managing or offering or agreeing to manage the investments of the customer if they are or are to be managed for the purposes of or in connection with the sale or supply or a related sale or supply.

(6) Paragraph 15 above does not apply to advice given by the supplier to the customer for the purposes of or in connection with the sale or supply or a related sale or supply or to a person with whom the customer proposes to enter into a transaction for the purposes of or in connection with the sale or supply or a related sale or supply.

(7) When the supplier is a body corporate and a member of a group sub-paragraphs (2) to (6) above shall apply to any other member of the group as they apply to the supplier, and where the customer is a body corporate and a member of a group references in those sub-paragraphs to the customer include references to any other member of the group.

(8) The definition in paragraph 17(2) above shall apply also for the purposes of sub-paragraph (3)(a) above.

[(9) This paragraph does not have effect where either—

(a) the customer is an individual; or
(b) the transaction in question is the purchase or sale of an investment which falls within paragraph 6 or 10 above, so far as relevant to either of those paragraphs, paragraph 11 above; or
(c) the investments which the supplier manages or offers or agrees to manage consist of investments falling within paragraph 6 to 10 above or, so as relevant to either of those paragraphs, paragraph 11 above; or
(d) the advice which the supplier gives is advice on an investment falling within the paragraphs 6 to 10 above, or so far as relevant to either of those paragraphs, paragraph 11 above.]

AMENDMENTS

A2–029 The amendments in sub-para. (1) in square brackets and sub-para. (9) were added by the Financial Services Act 1986 (Extension of Scope of Act and Meaning of Collective Investment Scheme) Order 1988, S.I. 1988 No. 496, Art. 3.

The Financial Services Act 1986 (Restriction of Scope of Act and Meaning of Collective Investment scheme) Order 1990, S.I. 1990, No. 349, Art. 4 attempted to substitute the number 5 of the number 6 in sub-para. (3)(a) but due to a misprint, failed to achieve this. A later order, the Financial Services Act 1986 (Restriction of Scope of Act and Meaning of Collective Investment Scheme) (No. 2) Order 1990, Art. 3, S.I. 1990 No. 1493. finally substituted "5" for a "6" in sub-para. (3)(a).

Appendices

Employees' share schemes

20.—(1) Paragraphs 12 and 13 above do not apply to anything done by a body corporate, a body corporate connected with it or a relevant trustee for the purpose of enabling or facilitating transactions in shares in or debentures of the first-mentioned body between or for the benefit of any of the person mentioned in sub-paragraph (2) below or the holding of such shares or debentures by or for the benefit of any such person.

(2) The persons referred to in sub-paragraph (1) above are—
  (a) the bona fide employees or former employees of the body corporate or of another body corporate in the same group; or
  (b) the wives, husbands, widows, widowers, or children or step-children under the age of eighteen of such employees or former employees.

(3) In this paragraph "a relevant trustee" means a person holding shares in or debentures of a body corporate as trustee in pursuance of arrangements made for the purpose mentioned in sub-paragraph (1) above by, or by a body corporate connected with, that body corporate.

(4) In this paragraph "shares" and "debentures" include any investment falling within paragraph 1 or 2 above and also include any investment falling within paragraph 4 or 5 above so far as relating to those paragraphs or any investment falling within paragraph 11 above so far as relating to paragraph 1, 2, 4 or 5.

(5) For the purposes of this paragraph a body corporate is connected with another body corporate if—
  (a) they are in the same group; or
  (b) one is entitled, either alone or with any other body corporate in the same group, to exercise or control the exercise of a majority of the voting rights attributable to the share capital which are exercisable in all circumstances at any general meeting of the other body corporate or of its holding company.

Sale of [body corporate]

21.—(1) Paragraphs 12 nd 13 above do not apply to the acquisition or disposal of, or to anything done for the purposes of the acquisition or disposal of, shares in a [body corporate other than an open-ended investment company], and paragraph 15 above does not apply to advice given in connection with the acquisition or disposal of such shares, if—
  (a) the shares consist of or include shares carrying 75 per cent or more of the voting rights attributable to share capital which are exercisable in all circumstances at any general meeting of the [body corporate]; or
  (b) the shares, together with any already held by the person acquiring them, carry not less than that percentage of those voting rights; and
  (c) in either case, the acquisition and disposal is, or is to be, between parties of whom is a body corporate, a partnership, a single individual or a group of connected individuals.

(2) For the purposes of subsection (1)(c) above "a group of connected individuals", in relation to the party disposing of the shares, means persons each of whom is, or is a close relative of, a director or manager of the [body corporate] and, in relation to the party acquiring the shares, means persons each of whom is, or is a close relative of, a person who is to be a director or manager of the [body corporate].

APPENDICES

(3) In this paragraph [. . .] "close relative" means a person's spouse, his children and step-children, his parents and step-parents, his brothers and sisters and his step-brothers and step-sisters.

AMENDMENTS

A2–032　The amendments in square brackets were effected by the Financial Services Act 1986 (Restriction of Scope of Act) Order 1988, S.I. 1988 No. 318, Art. 4.

Trustees and personal representatives

A2–033　22.—(1) Paragraph 12 above does not apply to a person by reason of his buying, selling or subscribing for an investment or offering or agreeing to do so if—
  (a) the investment is or, as the case may be, is to be held by him as bare trustee or, in Scotland, as nominee for another person;
  (b) he is acting on the person's instructions; and
  (c) he does not hold himself out as providing a service of buying and selling investments.

(2) paragraph 13 above does not apply to anything done by a person as trustee or personal representative with a view to—
  (a) a fellow trustee or personal representative and himself engaging in their capacity as such in an activity falling within paragraph 12 above; or
  (b) a beneficiary under the trust, will or intestacy engaging in any such activity,
unless that person is remunerated for what he does in addition to any remuneration he receives for discharging his duties as trustee or personal representative.

(3) Paragraph 14 above does not apply to anything done by a person as trustee or personal representative unless he holds himself out as offering investment management services or is remunerated for providing such services in addition to any remuneration he receives for discharging his duties as trustee or pesonal representative.

(4) Paragraph 15 above does not apply to advice given by a person as trustee or personal representative to—
  (a) a fellow trustee or personal representative for the purposes of the trust or estate; or
  (b) a beneficiary under the trust, will or intestacy concerning his interest in the trust fund or estate.
unless that person is remunerated for doing so in addition to any remuneration he receives for discharging his duties as trustee or personal representative.

(5) Sub-paragraph (1) above has effect to the exclusion of paragraph 17 above as respects any transaction in respect of which the condition in sub-paragraph (1)(a) and (b) are satisfied.

Dealings in course of non-investment business

A2–034　23.—(1) Paragraph 12 above does not apply to anything done by a person—
  (a) as principal;
  (b) if that person is a body corporate in a group, as agent for another member of the group; or
  (c) as agent for a person who is or proposes to become a participator with him in a joint enterprise and for the purposes of or in connection with that enterprise,

APPENDICES

if it is done in accordance with the terms and conditions of a permission granted to him by the Secretary of State under this paragraph.

(2) Any application for permission under this paragraph shall be accompanied or supported by such information as the Secretary of State may require and shall not be regarded as duly made unless accompanied by the prescribed fee.

(3) The Secretary of State may grant a persmission under this paragraph if it appears to him—
   (a) that the applicant's main business, or if he is a member of a group the main business of the group, does not consist of activities for which a person is required to be authorised under this Act;
   (b) that the applicant's business is likely to involve such activities which fall within paragraph 12 above; and
   (c) that, having regard to the nature of the applicant's main business and, if he is a member of a group, the main business of the group taken as a whole, the manner in which, the persons with whom and the purposes for which the applicant proposes to engage in activities that would require him to be an authorised person and to any other relevant matters, it is inappropriate to require him to be subject to regulation as an authorised person.

(4) Any permission under this paragraph shall be granted by a notice in writing, and the Secretary of State may by a further notice in writing withdraw any such permission if for any reason it appears to him that it is not appropriate for it to continue in force.

(5) The Secretary of State may make regulations requiring persons holding permissions under this paragraph to furnish him with information for the purpose of enabling him to determine whether those permissions should continue in force; and such regulations may, in particular, require such persons—
   (a) to give him notice forthwith of the occurence of such event as are specified in the regulations and such information in respect of those events as is so specified;
   (b) to furnish him at such times or in respect of such periods as are specified in the regulations and such information as is so specified.

(6) Section 61 of this Act shall have effect in relation to a contravention of any condition imposed by a permission under this paragraph as it has effect in relation to any such contravention as is mentioned in subsection (1)(a) of that section.

(7) Section 104 of this Act shall apply to a person holding a permission under this paragraph as if he were authorised to carry on investment business as there mentioned; and sections 105 and 106 of this Act shall have effect as if anything done by him in accordance with such permission constituted the carrying on if investment business.

Advice given [or arrangements made] in course of profession or non-investment business

24.—(1) Paragraph 15 above does not apply to advice—   A2–035
   (a) which is given in the course of the carrying on of any profession or of a business not otherwise constituting investment business; and
   (b) the giving of which is a necessary part of other advice or services given in the course of carrying on that profession or business.

[(2) Paragraph 13 above does not apply to arrangements—
   (a) which are made in the course of the carrying on of any profession or of a business not otherwise constituting investment business; and

(b) the making of which is a necessary part of other services provided in the course of carrying on that profession or business.

(3) Advice shall not be regarded as falling within sub-paragraph (1)(b) above and the making of arrangements shall not be regarded as falling within sub-paragraph (2)(b) above if the giving of the advice or the making of the arrangements is remunerated separately from the other advice or services.]

AMENDMENTS

A2–036   The amendments in square brackets were effected by the Financial Services Act 1986 (Restriction of Scope of Act and Meaning of Collective Investment Scheme) Order 1988, S.I. 1988 No. 803, Art. 4.

Newspapers

A2–037   25.—(1) Paragraph 15 above does not apply to advice given in a newspaper, journal, magazine or other periodical publication if the principal purpose of the publication, taken as a whole and including any advertisements contained in it, is not to lead persons to invest in any particular investment.

(2) The Secretary of State may, on the application of the proprietor of any periodical publication, certify that it is of the nature described in sub-paragraph (1) above and revoke any such certificate if he considers that it is no longer justified.

(3) A certificate given under sub-paragraph (2) above and not revoked shall be conclusive evidence of the matters certified.

COMMENCEMENT

A2–038   Para. (1): December 18, 1986 (S.I. 1986 No. 2246 (c. 88)), Art. 2 and Sched. 1.

[Advice given in television, sound or teletext services

A2–039   25A.—(1) Paragraph 15 above does not apply to any advice given in any programme included, or made for inclusion, in—
   (a) any television broadcasting service or other television programme service (within the meaning of Part I of the Broadcasting Act 1990); or
   (b) any sound broadcasting service or licensable sound programme service (within the meaning of Part III of that Act); or
   (c) any teletext service.

(2) For the purposes of this paragraph, "programme", in relation to a service mentioned in sub-paragraph (1) above, includes an advertisement and any other item included in the service.]

AMENDMENT

A2–040   Para. 25A was added by the Financial Services Act 1986 (Restriction of Scope of Act) Order 1988 S.I. 1988 No. 318, Art. 5. A new para. 25A (extending the old para. 25A to direct broadcasting by satellite) was substituted by the Financial Services Act 1986 (Restriction of Scope of Act and Meaning of Collective Investment Scheme) Order 1991, S.I. 1990 No. 349, Art. 5. A new para. 25A was substituted by the Broadcasting Act 1990, from January 1, 1991. A revised (and narrower) version was substituted by the Financial Services Act 1986 (Extension of Scope of Act) Order 1992, S.I. No. 273, from June 1, 1992.

[International Securities Self-regulating Organisation

A2–041   25B.—(1) An activity within paragraph 13 above engaged in for the purposes of carrying out functions of a body or association which is approved under this paragraph as an international securities self-regulating organisation, whether by

APPENDICES

the organisation or by any person acting on its behalf, shall not constitute the carrying on of investment business in the United Kingdom for the purposes of Chapter II of Part I of this Act.

(2) In this paragraph—

"International securities business" means the business of buying, selling, subscribing for or underwriting investments (or offering or agreeing to do so, either as principal or agent) which fall within any of the paragraphs in Part I above other than paragraph 10 and, so far as relevant to paragraph 10, paragraph 11 and which, by their nature, and the manner in which the business is conducted, may be expected normally to be bought or dealt in by persons sufficiently expert to understand any risks involved, where either the transaction is international or each of the parties may be expected to be indifferent to the location of the other, and, for the purposes of this definition, the fact that the investments may ultimately be bought otherwise than in the course of international securities business by persons not so expert shall be disregarded; and

"international securities self-regulating organisation" means a body corporate or unincorporated association which
  (a) does not have its head office in the United Kingdom;
  (b) is not eligible for recognition under section 37 or section 39 of this Act on the ground that (whether or not it has applied, and whether or not it would be eligible on other grounds) it is unable to satisfy the requirements of section 40(2)(a) or (c) of this Act;
  (c) has a membership composed of persons falling within any of the following categories, that is to say, authorised persons, exempted persons, persons holding a permission under paragraph 23 above and persons whose head offices are outside the United Kingdom and whose ordinary business is such as is mentioned in paragraph 17(2)(e) above; and
  (d) which facilitates and regulates the activity of its members in the conduct of international securities business.

(3) The Secretary of State may approve as an international securities self-regulating organisation any body or association appearing to him to fall within sub-paragraph (2) above if, having regard to such matters affecting international trade, overseas earnings and the balance of payments or otherwise as he considers relevant, it appears to him that to do so would be desirable and not result in any undue risk to investors.

(4) Any approval under this paragraph shall be given by notice in writing, and the Secretary of State may by a further notice in writing withdraw any such approval if for any reason it appears to him that it is not apropriate for it to continue in force.]

AMENDMENT

Para. 25B was added by the Financial services Act 1986 (Restriction of Scope of Act) Order 1988, S.I. No. 318, Art. 6 **A2–042**

PART IV

ADDITIONAL EXCLUSION FOR PERSONS WITHOUT PERMANENT PLACE OF BUSINESS IN UNITED KINGDOM

Transactions with or through authorised or exempted persons

26.—(1) Paragraph 12 above does not apply to any transaction by a person not falling within section 1(3)(a) of this Act ("an overseas person") with or through— **A2–043**

APPENDICES

   (a) an authorised person; or
   (b) an exempted person acting in the course of business in respect of which he is exempt.
(2) Paragraph 13 above does not apply if—
   (a) the arrangements are made by an overseas person with, or the offer or agreement to make them is made by him to or with, an authorised person or an exempted person and, in the case of an exempted person, the arrangements are with a view to his entering into a transaction in respect of which he is exempt; or
   (b) the transactions with a view to which the arrangements are made are, as respects transactions in the United Kingdom, confined to transactions by authorised persons and transactions by exempted persons in respect of which they are exempt.

Unsolicited or legitimately solicited transactions etc with or for other persons

A2–044   27.—(1) Paragraph 12 bove does not apply to any transaction entered into by an overseas person as principal with, or as agent for, a person in the United Kingdom, paragraphs 13, 14 and 15 above do not apply to any offer made by an overseas person to or agreement made by him with a person in the United Kingdom and paragraph 15 above does not apply to any advice given by an overseas person to a person in the United Kingdom if the transaction, offer, agreement or advice is the result of—
   (a) an approach made to the overseas person by or on behalf of the person in the United Kingdom which either has not been in any way solicited by the overseas person or has been solicited by him in a way which has not contravened (section 56 or 57 of this Act); or
   (b) an approach made by the overseas person which has not contravened either of those sections.
(2) Where the transaction is entered into by the overseas person as agent for a person in the United Kingdom, sub-paragraph (1) above applies only if—
   (a) the other party is outside the United Kingdom; or
   (b) the other party is in the United Kingdom and the transaction is the result of such an approach by the other party as is mentioned in sub-paragraph (1)(a) above or of such an approach as is mentioned in sub-paragraph (1)(b) above.

PART V

INTERPRETATION

A2–045   28.—(1) In this Schedule—
   (a) "property" includes currency of the United Kingdom or any other country or territory;
   (b) references to an instrument include references to any record whether or not in the form of a document;
   (c) references to an offer include references to an invitation to treat;
   (d) references to buying and selling include references to any acquisition or disposal for valuable consideration.
(2) In sub-paragraph (1)(d) above "disposal" includes—
   (a) in the case of an investment consisting of rights under a contract or other arrangements, assuming the corresponding liabilities under the contract or arrangement;

(b) in the case of any other investment, issuing or creating the investment or granting the rights or interests of which it consists;

(c) in the case of an investment consisting of rights under a contract, surrendering, assigning or converting those rights.

(3) A company shall not by reason of issuing its own shares or share warrants, and a person shall not by reason of issuing his own debentures or debenture warrants, be regarded for the purposes of this Schedule as disposing of them or, by reason of anything done for the purpose of issuing them, be regarded as making arrangements with a view to a person subscribing for or otherwise acquiring them or underwriting them.

(4) In sub-paragraph (3) above "company" has the same meaning as in paragraph 1 above, "shares" and "debentures" include any investments falling within paragraph 1 or 2 above and "share warrants" and "debenture warrants" means any investment which falls within paragraph 4 above and relates to shares in the company concerned or, as the case may be, to debentures issued by the person concerned.

29. For the purposes of this Schedule a transaction is entered into through a person if he enters into it as agent or arranges for it to be entered into by another person as principal or agent. **A2–046**

[**30.**—(1) For the purposes of this Schedule a group shall be treated as including any body corporate in which a member of the group holds a qualifying capital interest. **A2–047**

(2) A qualifying capital interest means an interest in relevant shares of the body corporate which the member holds on a long-term basis for the purpose of securing a contribution to its own activities by the exercise of control or influence arising from that interest.

(3) Relevant shares means shares comprised in the equity share capital of the body corporate of a class carrying rights to vote in all circumstances at general meetings of the body.

(4) A holding of 20 per cent or more of the nominal value of the relevant shares of a body corporate shall be presumed to be a qualifying capital interest unless the contrary is shown.

(5) In this paragraph "equity share capital" has the same meaning as in the Companies Act 1985 and the Companies (Northern Ireland) Order 1986.]

AMENDMENT
A new paragraph 30 was inserted by the Companies Act 1989, s. 23 and Sched. 10 from April 1, 1990 (see S.I. 1990 No. 355 (c. 13), Art. 3). **A2–048**

31. In this Schedule "a joint enterprise" means an enterprise into which two or more persons ("the participators") enter for commercial reasons related to a business or businesses (other than investment business) carried on by them; and where a participator is a body corporate and a member of a group each other member of the group shall also be regarded as a participator in the enterprise. **A2–049**

32. Where a person is an exempted person as respects only part of the investment business carried on by him anything done by him in carrying on that part shall be disregarded in determining whether any paragraph of Pt. III or IV of this Schedule applies to anything done by him in the course of business respect of which he is not exempt. **A2–050**

33. In determining for the purposes of this Schedule whether anything constitutes an investment or the carrying on of investment business section 18 of the Gaming Act 1845, section 1 of the Gaming Act 1892, any corresponding **A2–051**

Appendices

provision in force in Northern Ireland and any rule of the law of Scotland whereby a contract by way of gaming or wagering is not legally enforceable shall be disregarded.

A2–052 [34.—(1) For the purposes of this Schedule arrangements are not a collective investment scheme if—
  (a) the property to which the arrangements relate (other than cash awaiting investment) consists of shares;
  (b) they constitute a complying fund;
  (c) each participant is the owner of a part of the property to which the arrangments relate and, to the extent that his part of that property—
    (i) comprises relevant shares of a class which are admitted to the Official List of any Member state or to dealing on a recognised investment exchange, he is entitled to withdraw it at any time after the end of the period of five years beginning with the date on which the shares in question were issued;
    (ii) comprises relevant shares which do not fall within sub-paragraph (i) above, he is entitled to withdraw it at any time after the end of the period of two years beginning with the date upon which the period referred to in sub-paragraph (i) above expired;
    (iii) comprises any other shares, he is entitled to withdraw it at any time after the end of the period of six months beginning with the date upon which the shares in question ceased to be relevant shares; and
    (iv) comprises cash which the operator has not agreed (conditionally or unconditionally) to apply in subscribing for shares, he is entitled to withdraw it at any time; and
  (d) the arrangements would meet the conditions described in section 75(5)(c) of this Act were it not for the fact that the operator is entitled to exercise all or any of the rights conferred by shares included in the property to which the arrangements relate.
(2) For the purposes of this paragraph—
  (a) "shares" means investments falling within paragraph 1 of this Schedule;
  (b) shares shall be regarded as being relevant shares if and so long as they are shares in respect of which neither—
    (i) a claim for relief made in accordance with section 306 of the Income and Corporation Taxes Act 1988 has been disallowed; nor
    (ii) an assessment has been made pursuant to section 307 of that Act withdrawing or refusing relief by reason of the body corporate in which the shares are held having ceased to be a body corporate which is a qualifying company for the purposes of section 293 of that Act; and
  (c) arrangements shall be regarded as constituting a complying fund if they provide that—
    (i) the operator will, so far as practicable, make investments each of which, subject to each participant's individual circumstances, qualify for relief by virtue of Chapter III of Part VII of the Income and Corporation Taxes Act 1988; and
    (ii) the minimum subscription to the arrangements made by each participant must be not less than £2,000.]

General Note

A2–053 This paragraph was added by the Financial Services Act 1988 (Restriction of Scope of Act and Meaning of Collective Investment Scheme) Order 1990, S.I. 1990 No. 349 Art. 7.

The provision of this paragraph wre originally in s. 75(5A) and (5B). This paragraph excludes from the definition of collective investment scheme (as to which see s. 75) certain business expansion schemes.

[35. For the purposes of this Schedule the following are not collective investment schemes—   A2–054
  (a) arrangements where the entire contribution of each participant is a deposit within the meaning of section 5 of the Banking Act 1987 or a sum of a kind described in subsection (3) of that section;
  (b) arrangements under which the rights or interests of the participants are represented by the following—
    (i) investments falling within paragraph 2 of this Schedule which are issued by a single body corporate which is not an open-ended investment company or which are issued by a single issuer which is not a body corporate and are guaranteed by the government of the United Kingdom, of Northern Ireland, or of any country or territory outside the United Kingdom; or
    (ii) investments falling within sub-paragraph (i) above which are convertible into or exchangeable for investments falling within paragraph 1 of this Schedule provided that those latter investments are issued by the same person as issued the investments falling within sub-paragraph (i) above or are issued by a single other issuer; or
    (iii) investments falling within paragraph 3 of this Schedule issued by the same government, local authority or public authority; or
    (iv) investments falling with paragraph 4 of this Schedule which are issued otherwise than by an open-ended investment company and which confer rights in respect of investments, issued by the same issuer, falling within paragraph 1 of this Schedule or within sub-paragraph (i), (ii) or (iii) above;
  (c) arrangements which would fall within paragraph (b) above were it not for the fact that the rights or interests of a participant ('the counterparty') whose ordinary business involves him in engaging in activities which fall within Part II of Schedule or would do so apart from Part III or IV are or include rights or interests under a swap arrangement, that is to say, an arrangement the purpose of which is to facilitate the making of payments to participants whether in a particular amount or currency or at a particular time or rate of interest or all or any combination of those things, being an arrangement under which—
    (i) the counterparty is entitled to receive amounts (whether representing principal or interest) payable in respect of any property subject to the scheme or sums determined by reference to such amounts; and
    (ii) the counterparty makes payments (whether or not of the same amount and whether or not in the same currency as those referred to in sub-paragraph (i) above) which are calculated in accordance with an agreed formula by reference to the amounts or sums referred to in sub-paragraph (i) above;
  (d) arrangements under which the rights or interests of participants are rights to or interests in money held in a common account in circumstances in which the money so held is held on the understanding that an amount representing the contribution of each participant is to be applied either in making payments to him or in satisfaction of sums owed by him or in the acquisition of property or the provision of services for him;

Appendices

(e) arrangements under which the rights and interests of participants are rights and interests in a fund which is a trust fund within the meaning of section 42(1) of the Landlord and Tenant Act 1987.]

[(f) arrangements where—
  (i) each of the participants is a bona fide employee or former employee (or the wife, husband, widow, widower, or child (including in Northern Ireland, adopted child) or step-child under the age of eighteen of such an employee or former employee) of any of the following bodies corporate, that is to say, The National Grid Company plc, Electricity Association Services Limited or any other body corporate in the same group as either of them [being arrangements which] operated by any of those bodies corporate; and
  (ii) the properly to which the arrangements relate consists of shares or debentures (as defined in paragraph 20(4) above) in or of a body corporate which is an electricity successor company for the purposes of Part II of the Electricity Act 1989 or a body corporate which would be regarded as connected with such an electricity successor company for the purposes of paragraph 20 above,

and for the purposes of this paragraph references to former employees shall have the same meaning as in the Financial Services Act 1986 (Electricity Industry Exemptions) Order 1990.]]

General Note

A2–055 Sub-paras. (a)–(e) of this paragraph were added by the Financial Services Act 1986 (Restriction of Scope of Act and Meaning of Collective Investment Scheme) Order 1990, S.I. 1990 No. 349, Art. 7, para. 4–344, *post*. Sub-para. (f) was added later (see "Amendment" below).

Amendments

A2–056 Sub-para. (f) (in double square brackets) was added by the Financial Services Act 1986 (Restriction of Scope of Act and Meaning of Collective Investment Scheme) (No. 2) Order 1990, S.I. 1990 No. 1493.

In sub-para. (f)(i) the words in square brackets were substituted by the Financial Services Act 1986 (Schedule 1 (Amendment) and Miscellaneous Exemption) Order 1991, S.I. 1991 No. 1516, Art. 2.

Appendix 3

The SIB's Statements of Principle

Note: This statement of principle was issued by SIB on March 15, 1990 under section 47A of (and, in relation to friendly societies, paragraph 13A of Schedule 11 to) the Financial Services Act 1986.

Introduction

1. These principles are intended to form a universal statement of the standards expected. They apply directly to the conduct of investment business and financial standing of all authorised persons ("firms"), including members of recognised self-regulating organisations and firms certified by recognised professional bodies.   A3–001

2. The principles are not exhaustive of the standards expected. Conformity with the principles does not absolve a failure to observe other requirements, while the observance of other requirements does not necessarily amount to conformity wth the principles.

3. The principles do not give rise to actions for damages, but will be available for purposes of discipline and intervention.

4. Where the principles refer to customers, they should be taken to refer also to clients and to potential customers, and where they refer to a firm's regulator, they mean SIB, or a self-regulating organisation or professional body which regulates the firm.

5. Although the principles may be taken as expressing existing standards, they come into force formally, with additional sanctions resulting, on April 30, 1990.

THE PRINCIPLES

Integrity

1. A firm should observe high standards of integrity and fair dealing.   A3–002

Skill, Care and Diligence

2. A firm should act with due skill, care and diligence.   A3–003

Market Practice

3. A firm should observe high standards of market conduct. It should also, to the extent endorsed for the purose of this principle, comply with any code or standard as in force from time to time and as it applies to the firm either according to its terms or by rulings made under it.   A3–004

Information about Customers

A3–005 4. A firm should seek from customers it advises or for whom it exercises discretion any information about their circumstances and investment objectives which might reasonably be expected to be relevant in enabling it to fulfil its responsibilities to them.

Information for Customers

A3–006 5. A firm should take reasonable steps to give a customer it advises, in a comprehensive and timely way, any information needed to enable him to make a balanced and informed decision. A firm should similarly be ready to provide a customer with a full and fair account of the fulfilment of its responsibilities to him.

Conflicts of Interest

A3–007 6. A firm should either avoid any conflict of interest arising or, where conflicts arise, should ensure fair treatment to all its customers by disclosure, internal rules of confidentiality, declining to act, or otherwise. A firm should not unfairly place its interests above those of its customers and, where a properly informed customer would reasonably expect that the firm would place his interests above its own, the firm should live up to that expectation.

Customer Assets

A3–008 7. Where a firm has control of or is otherwise responsible for assets belonging to a customer which it is required to safeguard, it should arrange proper protection for them, by way of segregation and identification of those assets or otherwise, in accordance with the responsibility it has accepted.

Financial Resources

A3–009 8. A firm should ensure that it maintains adequate financial resources to meet its investment business commitments and to withstand the risks to which its business is subject.

Internal Organisation

A3–010 9. A firm should organise and control its internal affairs in a responsible manner, keeping proper records, and where the firm employs staff or is responsible for the conduct of investment business by others, should have adequate arrangements to ensure that they are suitable, adequately trained and properly supervised and that it has well-defined compliance procedures.

Relations with Regulators

A3–011 10. A firm should deal with its regulator in an open and co-operative manner and keep the regulator promptly informed of anything concerning the firm which might reasonably be expected to be disclosed to it.

THE FINANCIAL SERVICES (STATEMENTS OF PRINCIPLE) (ENDORSEMENT OF CODES AND STANDARDS) INSTRUMENTS 1995

Introduction

1. The Securities and Investments Board ("SIB") has issued statements of principle ("the Principles") under section 47A of (and, in relation to friendly societies, paragraph 13A of Schedule 11 to) the Financial Services Act 1986 ("the Act").   **A3–012**
2. Principle 3 (Market Practice) of the Principles requires a firm, to the extent endorsed for the purposes of the Principle, to comply with any code or standard as in force from time to time and as it applies to the firm either according to its terms, or by rulings made under it.
3. Accordingly, SIB now issues this instrument to endorse the Takeover Code for the purposes of Principle 3.

Endorsement of the Takeover Code

4. For the purposes of Principle 3 (Market Practice) of the Principles, SIB endorses, to the extent specified in this instrument, the Takeover Code.   **A3–013**

Restrictions on enforcement

5. The Principles enable disciplinary action to be taken, or powers of intervention to be exercised, for failure to comply with the Takeover Code only at the request of the Takeover Panel.   **A3–014**
6. The Principle do not enable the taking of disciplinary action for failure to comply with the Takeover Code if that action consists in an application to the Court under section 61(1) of the Act.

Firms certified by or otherwise regulated by a recognised professional body

7. A firm which is certified by a recognised professional body, or which is a member of a recognised self-regulating organisation but is also regulated by a recognised professional body in relation to the firm's professional practice generally, should comply with the Takeover Code (in so far as it would, by its terms, apply to such a firm) unless the firm would thereby be in breach of any rule of principle of, or any requirement of a published guidance note relating to, professional conduct applying generally to members of the profession regulated by that body.   **A3–015**

Other firms

8. A firm to which paragraph 7 does not apply should comply with the Takeover Code, in so far as it would, by its terms, apply to such a firm.   **A3–016**

Supplementary

A3–017 9. This instrument forms part of the Principles and is issued, under the same powers, on January 19, 1995. It comes into force on the date of issue.
10. In this instrument:

- "the Takeover Code" means the City Code on Takeovers and Mergers and the Rules Governing Substantial Acquisitions of Shares, published by the Takeover Panel;
- "the Takeover Panel" means the Panel on Takeovers and Mergers;
- "disciplinary action" means disciplinary action which may be taken by SIB by virtue of section 47A(3) of the Act; and
- "powers of intervention" means the powers conferred by Chapter VI of Part 1 of the Act.

Appendix 4

The Core Conduct of Business Rules

Note: A4–001

The Core Conduct of Business Rules were designated so as to apply to members of IMRO and SFA under section 63A of the Financial Services Act 1986. They were to apply to persons directly regulated by the Board.

They came into force on dates specified in commencement instruments made by the Board. The Board's intention was that the rules should be brought into force, as respect the members of a particular SRO, when that SRO was ready to bring its "third tier" rules into force. There were appropriate transitional arrangements.

However, the Financial Services (Dedesignation) Rules and Regulations 1994 "dedesignated" the core rules (with the exception of core rule 36 as well as core rule 40(4)(a) and (b) in so far as relevant to rule 36) and revoked the IMRO and SFA commencement orders. Thus the core rules (with those exceptions) are no longer directly applicable to SRO members. However, the core rules have been incorporated into the SRO rule-books (with appropriate derogations) and thus apply to SRO members by virtue of the contract of membership which includes the SRO rules.

CONTENTS

A4–002

Rule	Title
	Independence
1.	Inducements
2.	Material interest
3.	Soft commission
4.	Polarisation
	Advertising and marketing
5.	Issue and approval of advertisements
6.	Issue or approval of advertisements for an overseas person
7.	Overseas business for United Kingdom private customers
8.	Business conducted from an overseas place of business with overseas customers
9.	Fair and clear communications
10.	Customers understanding
11.	Information about the firm
12.	Information about packaged products
13.	Appointed representatives

Rule	Title
	Customer relations
14.	Customer agreements
15.	Customers' rights
16.	Suitability
17.	Standards of advice on packaged products
18.	Charges and other remuneration
19.	Confirmations and periodic information
	Dealing for customers
20.	Customer order priority
21.	Timely execution
22.	Best execution
23.	Timely allocation
24.	Fair allocation
25.	Dealing ahead of publications
26.	Churning and switching
27.	Certain derivatives transactions to be on exchange
	Market integrity
28.	Insider dealing
29.	Stabilistion of securities
30.	Off-exchange market makers
31.	Reportable transactions
	Administration
32.	Safeguarding of customer investments
33.	Scope of business
34.	Compliance
35.	Complaints
36.	Chinese walls
37.	Cessation of business
	General
38.	Reliance on others
39.	Classes of customer
40.	Application of the Core Conduct of Business Rules

APPENDICES

THE CORE CONDUCT OF BUSINESS RULES

INDEPENDENCE

1. Inducements

A firm must take reasonable steps to ensure that neither it nor any of its **A4–003** agents:
  (a) offers or gives, or
  (b) solicits or accepts,
either in the course of regulated business or otherwise any inducement which is likely significantly to conflict with any duties of the recipient (or the recipient's employer) owed to customers in connection with regulated business.

2. Material interest

Where a firm has a material interest in a transaction to be entered into with or **A4–004** for a customer or a relationship which gives rise to a conflict of interest in relation to such a transaction, the firm must not knowingly either advise, or deal in the exercise of discretion, in relation to that transaction unless it takes reasonable steps to ensure fair treatment for the customer.

3. Soft commission

A firm which deals for a customer on an advisory basis or in the exercise of **A4–005** discretion may not so deal through a broker pursuant to a soft commission agreement unless:
  (a) the only benefits to be provided under the agreement are goods or services which can reasonably be expected to assist in the provision of investment services to the firm's customers and which are in fact so used;
  (b) the broker has agreed to provide best execution to the customer;
  (c) the firm is satisfied on reasonable grounds that the terms of business and methods by which the relevant broking services will be supplied do not involve any potential for comparative price disadvantage to the customer;
  (d) in transactions in which the broker acts as principal, he is not remunerated by spread alone; and
  (e) adequate prior and periodic disclosure is made.

4. Polarisation

1. A firm which advises a private customer on packaged products must either: **A4–006**
  (a) be a product company or its marketing group associate; or
  (b) do so as an independent intermediary.
2. A firm which is a product company or its marketing group associate must not advise private customers to buy packaged products which are not those of the marketing group.
3. A firm which acts as an independent intermediary in advising a private customer on packaged products must act as an independent intermediary

whenever it advises private customers on packaged products in the course of regulated business.

4. But where a firm acts as an investment manager for a customer, the core rule on polarisation does not prevent the firm from advising the customer on any packaged product.

Advertising and marketing

5. Issue and approval of advertisements

A4–007
1. When a firm issues or approves an investment advertisement, it must:
    (a) apply appropriate expertise; and
    (b) be able to show that it believes on reasonable grounds that the advertisement is fair and not misleading.

2. Where a firm issues or approves a specific investment advertisement it must ensure that the advertisement identifies it as issuer or approver, and also identifies its regulator.

3. A firm must not approve a specific investment advertisement if it relates to units in an unregulated collective investment scheme.

4. A firm must take reasonable steps to ensure that it does not issue or approve a direct offer advertisement for the sale of investments or the provision of investment services to a private customer unless the advertisement:
    (a) gives information about the investments or investment services, the terms of the offer, and the risks involved, which is adequate and fair having regard to the (UK or overseas) regulatory protections which apply and the market to which the advertisement is directed; and
    (b) offers derivatives or warrants only where the firm itself issues the advertisement and does so only to a customer for whom it believes on reasonable grounds the investment or investment services to be suitable.

6. Issue or approval of advertisements for an overseas person

A4–008
A firm must not issue or approve a specific investment advertisement which is calculated to lead directly or indirectly to an overseas person carrying on investment business:
    (a) which is not regulated business; and
    (b) with or for a private customer who is in the United Kingdom;
unless both the advertisement contains the prescribed disclosure and the firm has no reason to doubt that the overseas person will deal with investors in the United Kingdom in an honest and reliable way.

7. Overseas business for UK private customers

A4–009
1. A firm must not carry on investment business:
    (a) which is not regulated business; and
    (b) with or for a private customer who is in the United Kingdom;
unless it has made the prescribed disclosure to the customer.

2. A firm must not give an introductionor advice, or make arrangements, with a view to another person carrying on such business with or for such a customer, unless it has both made the prescribed disclosure and has no reason to doubt that the customer will be dealt with in an honest and reliable way.

8. Business conducted from an overseas place of business with overseas customers

If many communication made or advertisement issued to a private customer outside the United Kingdom in connection with investment business which is not regulated business, a firm indicates that it is an authorised person, it must also, and with equal prominence, make the prescribed disclosure. **A4–010**

9. Fair and clear communication

1. A firm may make a communication with another person which is designed to promote the provision of investment services ony if it can show that it believes on reasonably grounds that the communication is fair and not misleading. **A4–011**
2. A firm must take reasonable steps to ensure that any agreement, written communication, notification or information which it gives or sends to a private customer to whom it provides investment services is presented fairly and clearly.

10. Customers' understanding

A firm must not recommend a transaction to a private customer, or act as a discretionary manager for him, unless it has taken reasonable steps to enable him to understand the nature of the risks involved. **A4–012**

11. Information about the firm

1. A firm must take reasonable steps to ensure that a private customer to whom it provides investment services is given adequate information about its identity and business address, the identity and status with the firm of employees and other relevant agents with whom the customer has contact and the identity of the firm's regulator. **A4–013**
2. Unless a firm is acting as an investment manager, it must take reasonable steps to ensure that a private customer it advises to buy a packaged product is also given adequate information about the firm's polarisation status, the buying process and any limits on the packaged products on which it can advise.

12. Information about packaged products

1. Before or when making a personal recommendation to a private customer to buy a packaged product, a firm must give him information about the product which is adequate to enable him to make an informed investment decision. **A4–014**
2. Before or as soon as practicable after a private customer buys a packaged product in a transaction recommended, effected or arranged by a firm, the firm must provide him with appropriate written product particulars unless:
   (a) the firm buys the packaged product as a discretionary investment manager; or
   (b) the transaction is effected or arranged on an execution-only basis.

AMENDMENT

From a date yet to be specified in a separate commencement instrument (which is expected to contain a derogation clause providing for exceptions) to be made by the SIB, the following new core Rule 12 will be substituted for the original. **A4–015**

APPENDICES

"12. Information about packaged products

1. Before or when making a personal recommendation to a private customer to buy a packaged product, a firm must:
   (a) give him information about the product which is adequate to enable him to make an informed investment decision; and
   (b) provide him in particular with general written information about the key features of the product.
2. Before or as soon as practicable after a private customer buys a packaged product in a transaction recommended, effected or arranged by a firm, the firm must provide him with appropriate written particular of his specific purchase unless:
   (a) the firm buys the packaged product as a discretionary investment manager; or
   (b) the transaction is effected or arranged on an execution-only basis."

13. Appointed representative

A4–016 1. A firm must satisfy itself on reasonable grounds and on a continuing basis that any appointed representative it appoints is fit and proper to act for it in that capacity.
2. A firm must also satisfy itself on reasonable grounds and on a continuing basis that it has adequate resources to monitor and enforce compliance by its appointed representatives with high standards of business conduct.
3. A firm must ensure that any of its appointed representatives carries on regulated business for which the firm has accepted responsibility only:
   (a) in circumstances where the representative does not carry on (or purport to carry on) in the United Kingdom any investment business for which the representative is not an authorised or exempted person; and
   (b) in a way which ensures that the business for which the firm has accepted responsibility is, and is held out as being, clearly distinct from any financial business which the representative carries on which is not investment business, unless that other financial business is covered by authorisation under an enactment as a bank or building society;
but a firm does not break this requirement if it can show it has taken reasonable steps to comply with it.
4. Subject to any exceptions contained in the rules of an SRO of which it is a member, a firm must ensure that its employment of any of its appointed representatives can be terminated only with the authority of its regulator.

CUSTOMER RELATIONS

14. Customer agreements

A4–017 1. Where a firm provides investment services to a private customer (other than an indirect customer) on written contractual terms, the agreement must set out in adequate detail the basis on which those services are provided.
2. Where a firm provides to a private customer (other than an indirect customer) investment services involving:
   (a) contingent liability transactions; or
   (b) the discretionary management of the customer's assets;

it must do so under a two-way customer agreement unless the customer is ordinarily resident outside the United Kingdom and the firm believes on reasonable grounds that he does not wish a two-way agreement to be used.

15. Customers' rights

1. A firm must not, in any written communication or agreement, seek to exclude or restrict any duty or liability to a customer which it has under the Act, or under the act, or under the regulatory system.
2. Similarly, unless it is reasonable to do so in the circumstances, a firm must not, in any written communication or agreement, seek to exclude or restrict:
    (a) any other duty to act with skill, care and diligence which is owed to a private customer in connection with the provision to him of investment services in the course of regulated business; or
    (b) any liability owed to a private customer in connection with regulated business for failure to exercise the degree of skill, care and diligence which may reasonably be expected of it in the provision of investment services in the course of that business.
3. A firm must not seek unreasonably to rely on any provision seeking to exclude or restrict any such duty or liability.

16. Suitability

1. A firm must taken reasonable steps to ensure that it does not in the course of regulated business or associated business:
    (a) make any personal recommendation to a private customer of an investment or investment agreement; or
    (b) effect or arrange a discretionary transaction with or for a private customer or, subject to any exceptions contained in the rules of an SRO of which the firm is a member, any other customer,
unless the recommendation or transaction is suitable for him having regard to the facts disclosed by that customer and other relevant facts about the customer of which the firm is, or reasonably should be, aware.
2. But where, with the agreement of the customer, a firm has pooled his funds with those of other with a view to taking common management decisions, the firm must instead take reasonable steps to ensure that the transaction is suitable for the fund, having regard to the stated investment objectives of the fund.

AMENDMENT
From a date yet to be specified in a separate commencement instrument to be made by the SIB, the following new core rule 16 will be substituted for the original:

"16. Suitability

(1) A firm must take reasonable steps to ensure that it does not in the course of regulated business or associated business:
    (a) make any personal recommendation to a private customer of an investment or investment agreement; or
    (b) effect or arrange a discretionary transaction with or for a private customer or, subject to any exceptions contained in the rules of an SRO of which the firm is a member, any other customer;

unless the recommendation or transaction is suitable for him having regard to the facts disclosed by that customer and other relevant facts about the customer of which the firm is, or reasonably should be, aware.

(2) But where, with the agreement of the customer, a firm has pooled his funds with those of others with a view to taking common management decisions, the firm must instead take reasonable steps to ensure that the transaction is suitable for the fund, having regard to the stated investment objectives of the fund.

(3) Before or as soon as practicable after a firm recommends to a private customer that he should—
  (a) take on a long term commitment which is or appears to be acceptable to him, or
  (b) relinquish a long term commitment,
the firm must explain to him in writing the reasons why (on the basis of the facts about the customer of which it is aware) it believes the commitment (or relinquishment) to be suitable for the customer."

17. Standards of advice on packaged products

A4–021 1. A firm which advises private customers to buy packaged products must take reasonble steps to inform itself and relevant agents:
  (a) where the firm is a product company or its marketing group associate, about packaged products available from the marketing group; or
  (b) where the firm is an independent intermediary, about packaged products which are generally available on the market and on which it can advise.

2. Where a firm is a product company or its marketing group associate, it must not advise a private customer to buy a packaged product, or buy a packaged product for him in the exercise of discretion, if it is aware of a packaged product of the marketing group which would better meet his needs.

3. Where a firm is acting as an independent intermediary, it must not advise a private customer to buy a packaged product, or buy a packaged product for him in the exercise of discretion, if it is aware of a generally available packaged product which would better meet his needs.

4. Where a firm is a product company or its marketing group associate and is acting as an investment manager, it must not advise a private customer to buy a packaged product of a product company outside the marketing group, or buy such a product for him in the exercise of discretion, if it is, or reasonably should be, aware of a generally available packaged product which would better meet his needs.

5. Where a firm is acting for a private customer as an independent intermediary but not as an investment manager, it must not advise him to buy a packaged product from its extended group if it is aware of a generally available packaged product which is not a product of the extended group and which would meet his needs as well as the extended group product.

6. In assessing the merits of a packaged product to be held as the plan investment of a personal equity plan, a firm must take into account the characteristics (including charging arrangements) of the plan, as well as those of the product.

18. Charges and other remuneration

A4–022 1. The amount of a firm's charges to a private customer for the provision of investment services to him must not be unreasonable in the circumstances.

2. Subject to any exceptions contained in the rules of an SRO of which it is a member, before a firm provides investment services to a private customer (other than an indirect customer), it must disclose to him the basis or amount of its charges for the provision of those services and the nature or amount of any other remuneration receivable by it (or, to its knowledge, by its associate) and attributable to them.

19. Confirmations and periodic information

1. Subject to any exceptions contained in the rules of an SRO of which it is a **A4–023** member, a firm which effects a sale or purchase of an investment (other than a life policy) with or for a customer must ensure that he is sent with due despatch a note containing the essential details of the transaction.
2. Subject to any exceptions contained in the rules of an SRO of which it is a member, a firm which acts as an investment manager for a customer must ensure tht he is sent at suitable intervals a report stating the value of the portfolio or account at the beginning and end of the period, its composition at the end, and, in the case of a discretionary portfolio or account, changes in its composition between those dates.

DEALING WITH CUSTOMERS

20. Customer order priority

A firm should deal with customer and own account orders fairly and in due **A4–024** turn.

21. Timely execution

1. Once a firm has agreed or decided in its discretion to effect or arrange a **A4–025** current customer order, it must effect or arrange the execution of the order as soon as reasonably practicable in the circumstances.
2. But the core rule on timely execution does not preclude a firm from postponing execution of an order where it believes on reasonable grounds that this is in the best interests of the customer.

22. Best execution

1. Where a firm deals with or for a private customer, it must provide best **A4–026** execution.
2. A firm must also provide best execution where it fulfils an order from a non-private customer.
3. A firm may rely on another person who executes the transaction to provide best execution, but only if it believes on reasonable grounds that he will do so.
4. For the purposes of the core rule on best execution, a firm provides best execution if:
   (a) it takes reasonable care to ascertain the price which is the best available for the customer in the relevant market at the time for transactions of the kind and size concerned; and

(b) unless the circumstances require it to do otherwise in the interests of the customer, it deals at a price which is no less advantageous to him;
and in applying the core rule on best execution, a firm should leave out of account any charges disclosed to the customer which it or its agent would make.

5. The core rule on best execution does not require a firm to provide best execution on a purchase of a life policy or on a purchase from the operator of a regulated collective investment scheme of units in the scheme.

23. Timely allocation

A4–027   A firm must ensure that a transaction it executes is promptly allocated.

24. Fair allocation

A4–028   Where a firm has aggregated an order for a customer transaction with an order for an own account transaction, or with another order for a customer transaction, then in the subsequent allocation:
    (a) it must not give unfair preference to itself or to any of those for whom it dealt; and
    (b) if all cannot be satisfied, it must give priority to satisfying orders for customer transactions unless it believes on reasonble grounds that, without its own participation, it would not have been able to effect those orders either on such favourable terms or at all.

25. Dealing ahead of publications

A4–029   Subject to any exceptions contained in the rules of an SRO of which it is a member, where a firm or its associate intends to publish to customers a recommendation or a piece of research or analysis, it must not knowingly effect an own account transaction in the investment concerned or any related investment until the customers for whom the publication was principally intended have had (or are likely to have had) a reasonable opportunity to react to it.

26. Churning and switching

A4–030   1. A firm must not:
    (a) make a personal recommendation to a private customer to deal; or
    (b) deal or arrange a deal in the exercise of discretion for any customer;
if the dealing would reasonably be regarded as too frequent in the circumstances.
2. A firm must not:
    (a) make a personal recommendation to a private customer to switch within a packaged product or between packaged products; or
    (b) effect such a switch in the exercise of discretion for a private customer;
unless it believes on reasonable grounds that the switch is justified from the customer's viewpoint.

27. Certain derivatives transactions to be on exchange

A4–031   A firm must not effect, arrange or recommend a contingent liability transaction with, for or to a private customer unless:

(a) the transaction is made on a recognised or designated investment exchange; or
(b) the firm believes on reasonable grounds that the purpose of the transaction is to hedge against currency risk involved in a position which the customer holds.

Market integrity

28. Insider dealing

1. A firm must not effect (either in the United Kingdom or elsewhere) an own account transaction when it knows of circumstances which mean that it, its associate, or an employee of either, is prohibited from effecting that transaction by the statutory restrictions on insider dealing. **A4–032**
2. A firm must use its best endeavours to ensure that it does not knowingly effect (either in the course of regulated business or otherwise) a transaction for a customer it knows is so prohibited.
3. But the core rule on insider dealing does not apply where:
(a) the prohibition applies only because of knowledge of the firm's own intentions;
(b) the firm is a recognised market maker with obligations to deal in the investment; or
(c) the firm is a trustee or personal representative who acts on the advice of a third party appearing to be an appropriate adviser who is not so prohibited.

29. Stabilisation of securities

Where a firm takes action (either in the course of regulated business or otherwise) for the purpose of stabilising the price of securities, it must comply with any applicable provisions of the statutory stabilisation rules. **A4–033**

30. Off-exchange market makers

Where a firm sells to a private customer any securities which are not quoted on a recognised or designated investment exchange, whilst giving the customer the impression that the firm is a market maker in the investment concerned, it must: **A4–034**
(a) give notice to the customer that it is required to ensure that a reasonable price for repurchase of the investment is available to him for a specified period which must not be less than three months after the date the notice is given; and
(b) ensure that such a price is available to him for that specific period.

31. Reportable transactions

Unless otherwise provided by the rules of an SRO of which it is a member, a firm must make available to its regulator details about transactions (including own account transactions) in securities which it effects other than on a recognised investment exchange. **A4–035**

APPENDICES

ADMINISTRATION

32. Safeguarding of customer investments

A4–036   A firm which has custody of a customer's investments in connection with or with a view to regulated business must, subject to any exceptions contained in the rules of an SRO of which it is a member:
  (a) keep safe, or arrange for the safekeeping of, any documents of title relating to them;
  (b) ensure that any registrable investments which it buys or holds for a customer in the course of regulated business are properly registered in his name or, with the consent of the customer, in the name of an eligible nominee; and
  (c) where title to investments is recorded electronically, ensure that customer entitlements are separately indentifiable from those of the firm in the records of the person maintaining records of entitlement.

33. Scope of business

A4–037   A firm must maintain a business profile describing the kind of investment business it carries on in the United Kingdom and may carry on (and hold itself out as carrying on) investment business in the United Kingdom of that kind only.

34. Compliance

A4–038   1. A firm must take reasonable steps, including the establishment and maintenance of procedures, to ensure that its officers and employees and officers and employees of its appointed representatives act in conformity with:
  (a) their own and their employer's relevant responsibilities under the regulatory system;
  (b) where relevant, the requirements of the statutory restrictions on insider dealing; and
  (c) appropriate arrangements on proprierty in personal dealings.
  2. A firm must take reasonable steps, including the estabishment and maintenance of procedures, to ensure that sufficient information is recorded and retained about its regulated business and complicance with the regulatory system.
  3. Records required to be maintained by the regulatory system may be inspected by a person appointed for the purpose by the firm's regulator.

35. Complaints

A4–039   1. A firm must have procedures to ensure.
  (a) the proper handling of complaints from customers relevant to its compliance with the regulatory system;
  (b) that any appropriate remedial action on those complaints is promptly taken; and
  (c) where the complaint is not promptly remedied, that the customer is advised of any further avenue for complaint available to him under the regulatory system.

2. A firm must co-operate with a person appointed by its regulator to investigate complaints.

36. Chinese walls

1. Where a firm maintains an established arrangement which requires information obtained by the firm in the course of carrying on one part of its business of any kind to be withheld in certain circumstances from persons with whom it deals in the course of carrying on another part of its business of any kind, then in those circumstances:
   (a) that information may be so withheld; and
   (b) for that purpose, persons employed in the first part may withhold information from those employed in the second;
but only to the extent that the business of one of those parts involves investment business or associated business.
2. Information may also be withheld where this is required by an established arrangement between different parts of the business (of any kind) of a group, but this provision does not affect any requirement to transmit information which may arise apart from the Core Conduct of Business Rules.
3. Where the Core Conduct of Business Rules apply only if a firm acts with knowledge, the firm is not for the purposes of the Core Conduct of Business Rules to be taken to act with knowledge if none of the relevant individuals involved on behalf of the firm acts with knowledge.
4. In addition, in order to avoid the attribution of information held within a firm to that firm for the purposes of section 47 of the Act, the effect of section 48(6) of the Act is that nothing done in conformity with paragraph (1) of the core rule on Chinese walls is to be regarded as a contravention of section 47 of the Act.

37. Cessation of Business

1. Where a firm or its appointed representative decides to withdraw from providing any investment or related custodian services to private customers, the firm must ensure that any such business which is outstanding is properly completed or is transferred to another firm.
2. Where the interests of private customers of a firm would be significantly affected by the death or incapacity of an individual within the firm, the firm must make arrangements to protect the interests of those customers in that event.

GENERAL

38. Reliance on others

1. A person is to be taken to act in conformity with the Core Conduct of Business Rules to the extent that:
   (a) the relevant regulator has issued formal guidance on compliance with them; and
   (b) in reliance on standards set in that guidance, the person concerned believes on reasonable grounds that he is acting in conformity with the rules.

2. A person is to be taken to act in conformity with any of the Core Conduct of Business Rules as to information, to the extent that he can show that he reasonably relied on information provided to him in writing by a third party whom he believed on reasonable grounds to be independent and competent to provide the information.

3. Any communication required under the Core Conduct of Business Rules to be sent to a customer may be sent to the order of the customer, so long as the recipient is independent of the firm; and there is no need for a firm to send a communication itself where it believes on reasonable grounds that this has been or will be supplied direct by another person.

39. Classes of customer

A4–043 1. The Core Rule on Conduct of Business apply subject to any exceptions contained in the rules of an SRO of which the firm is a member which enable it to treat a customer who would otherwise be a private customer as a non-private customer for the purposes of the Core Conduct of Business Rules if:
  (a) it can show that it believes on reasonable grounds that the customer has sufficient experience and understanding to waive the protections provided for private customers;
  (b) it has given a clear written warning to the customer of the protections under the regulatory system which he will lose; and
  (c) the customer has given his written consent after a proper opportunity to consider that warning.

2. But SRO rules need not require written consent where the customer is ordinarily resident outside the United Kingdom and is reasonably believed not to wish to consent in writing.

40. Application of the Core Conduct of Business Rules

1. Business

A4–044 (a) The general application of the Core Conduct of Business Rules is that, as far as they relate to business, they relate to business which is regulated business, and accordingly, where a rule relating to business applies only in particular circumstances, the rule applies only if those circumstances apply in the course of regulated business.
  (b) To the extent indicated, the Core Conduct of Business Rules also apply to the carrying on (whether in the United Kingdom or elsewhere) of other business if that other business is investment business, associated business or business which is held out as being for the purposes of investment.
  (c) The Core Conduct of Business Rules do not apply to authorised persons to the extent that they are acting as authorised persons certified by recognised professional bodies (since these persons are subject to regulation by those bodies) or to the extent that they are acting as exempted persons.
  (d) The Core Conduct of Business Rules are limited in their application to regulated insurance companies (by paragraph 4 of Schedule 10 to the Act), to regulated friendly societies (by paragraph 14 of Schedule 11 to the Act) and to certain UCITS operators and trustees (by section 86(7) of the Act).

(e) The Core Conduct of Business Rules apply to an oil market participant subject to exceptions contained in the rules of an SRO of which the firm is a member.
(f) Where the firm is:
   (i) a journalist, broadcaster, author or publisher;
   (ii) whose only investment business is the provision of investment advice;
   the Core Conduct of Business Rules apply subject to exceptions contained in the rules of an SRO of which the firm is a member.

2. Advertisements

(a) Where the Core Conduct of Business Rules govern the issue or approval of an investment advertisement then, except to the extent indicated, they govern issue of an investment advertisement in the United Kingdom and approval (whether in the United Kingdom or elsewhere) of an investment advertisement for issue in the United Kingdom. **A4–045**

(b) The Core Conduct of Business Rules on issue and approval of advertisements and on issue or approval of advertisements for an overseas person do not apply:
   (i) to the issue by an authorised person of an exempt advertisement; or
   (ii) to the issue or approval of a DIE advertisement, a takeover advertisement, or (unless they constitute a direct offer advertisement) scheme particulars.

(c) The Core Conduct of Business Rules do not apply to the reissue of an investment advertisement which has been prepared and issued by another person and which the firm believes on reasonable grounds:
   (i) is an exempt advertisement, a DIE advertisement, a takeover advertisement, or (unless they constitute a direct offer advertisement) scheme particulars; or
   (ii) is already issued or approved by an authorised person and is issued to a market for which it was intended at the time of its issue or approval by the authorised person.

3. Time

The application of the Core Conduct of Business Rules as to time is that they apply to a firm from the date specified for firms of the relevant class in a separate commencement instrument made by the Board (subject to any transitional provisions contained in that instrument). **A4–046**

4. Interpretation

(a) The Financial services [Core] Glossary 1991 [Third Edition] applies, unless the context otherwise requires, for the interpretation of the Core Conduct of Business Rules. **A4–047**

(b) Any other expression defined for the purposes of the Act, or in the Interpretation Act 1978, have the same meanings in the Core Conduct of Business Rules.

(c) These rules may be cited as the Core Conduct of Business Rules. They are made under section 48 of and, for friendly societies, paragraph 14 of Schedule 11 to, the Act. They are designated so as to apply directly to members of recognised self-regulating organisations under section 63A of and, for friendly societies, paragraph 22B of Schedule 11 to, the Act.

Appendix 5

General Principles of the Panel for Takeovers and Mergers

Introduction

A5–001　It is impracticable to devise rules in sufficient detail to cover all circumstances which can arise in offers. Accordingly, persons engaged in offers should be aware that the spirit as well as the precise wording of the General Principles and the ensuing Rules must be observed. Moreover, the General Principles and the spirit of the Code will apply in areas or circumstances not explicity covered by any Rules.

While the boards of an offeror and the offeree company and their respective advisers have a duty to act in the best interests of their respective shareholders, these General Principles and the ensuing Rules will, inevitably, impinge on the freedom of action of boards and persons involved in offers; they must, therefore, accept that there are limitations in connection with offers on the manner in which the pursuit of those interests can be carried out.

Each director of an offeror and of the offeree company has a responsibility to ensure, so far as he is reasonably able, that the Code is complied with in the conduct of an offer (see Appendix 3 for Guidance Note). Financial advisers have a particular responsibility to comply with the Code and to ensure, so far as they are reasonably able, that an offeror and the offeree company, and their respected directors, are aware of their responsibilities under the Code and will comply with them. Financial advisers should ensure that the Panel is consulted whenever relevant and should co-operate fully with any enquiries made by the Panel. Financial advisers must also be mindful of conflicts of interest (see Appendix 3 for Guidance Note).

General Principles

A5–002　1. All shareholders of the same class of an offeree company must be treated similarly by an offeror.

2. During the course of an offer, or when an offer is in contemplation, neither an offeror, nor the offeree company, nor any of their respective advisers may furnish information to some shareholders which is not made available to all shareholders. This principle does not apply to the furnishing of information in confidence by the offeree company to a bona fide potential offeror or vice versa.

3. An offeror should only announce an offer after the most careful and responsible consideration. Such an announcement should be made only when the offeror has every reason to believe that it can and will continue to be able to

implement the offer: responsibility in this connection also rests on the financial adviser to the offeror.

4. Shareholders must be given sufficient information and advice to enable them to reach a properly informed decision and must have sufficient time to do so. No relevant information should be withheld from them.

5. Any document or advertisment addressed to shareholders containing **A5–003** information or advice from an offeror or the board of the offeree company or their respective advisers must, as is the case with a prospectus, be prepared with the highest standards of care and accuracy.

6. All parties to an offer must use every endeavour to prevent the creation of a false market in the securities of an offeror or the offeree company. Parties involved in offers must take care that statements are not made which may mislead shareholders or the market.

7. At no time after a bone fide offer has been communicated to the board of the offeree company, or after the board of the offeree company has reason to believe that a bona fide offer might be imminent, may any action be taken by the board of the offeree company in relation to the affairs of the company, without the approval of the shareholders in general meeting, which could effectively result in any bona fide offer being frustrated or in the shareholders being denied an opportunity to decide on its merits.

8. Rights of control must be exercised in good faith and the oppression of a minority is wholly unacceptable.

9. Directors of an offeror and the offeree company must always, in advising their shareholders, act only in their capacity as directors and not have regard to their personal or family shareholdings or to their personal relationships with the companies. It is the shareholders' interests taken as a whole, together with those of employees and creditors, which should be considered when the directors are giving advice to shareholders. Directors of the offeree company should give careful consideration before they enter into any commitment with an offeror (or anyone else) which would restrict their freedom to advise their shareholders in the future. Such commitments may give rise to conflicts of interest or result in a breach of the directors' fiduciary duties.

10. Where control of a company is acquired by a person, or persons acting in concert, a general offer to all other shareholders is normally required; a similar obligation may arise if control is consolidated. Where an acquisition is contemplated as a result of which a person may incur such an obligation, he must, before making the acquisition, ensure that he can and will continue to be able to implement such an offer.

Appendix 6

The Companies Act 1985, Sched. 24 (as amended)

Section 730

SCHEDULE 24

Punishment of Offences Under the Companies Act 1985

Note: [. . .]

Section of Act creating offence	General nature of offence	Mode of prosecution	Punishment	Daily default fine (where applicable)
6(3)	Company failing to deliver to registrar notice or other document, following alteration of its objects.	Summary.	One-fifth of the statutory maximum.	One-fiftieth of the statutory maximum.
18(3)	Company failing to register change in memorandum of articles.	Summary.	One-fifth of the statutory maximum.	One-fiftieth of the statutory maximum.
19(2)	Company failing to send to one of its members a copy of the memorandum or articles, when so required by the member.	Summary.	One-fifth of the statutory maximum.	
20(2)	Where company's memorandum altered, company issuing copy of the memorandum without the alteration.	Summary.	One-fifth of the statutory maximum for each occasion on which copies are so issued after the date of the alteration.	
28(5)	Company failing to change name on direction of Secretary of State.	Summary.	One-fifth of the statutory maximum.	One-fiftieth of the statutory maximum.
31(5)	Company altering its memorandum or articles, so ceasing to be exempt from having "limited" as part of its name.	Summary.	The statutory maximum.	One-tenth of the statutory maximum.
31(6)	Company failing to change name, on Secretary of State's direction, so as to have "limited" (or Welsh equivalent) at the end.	Summary.	One-fifth of the statutory maximum.	One-fiftieth of the statutory maximum.
32(4)	Company failing to comply with Secretary of State's direction to change its name, on grounds that the name is misleading.	Summary.	One-fifth of the statutory maximum.	One-fiftieth of the statutory maximum.

APPENDICES

A6–002

Section of Act creating offence	General nature of offence	Mode of prosecution	Punishment	Daily default fine (where applicable)
33	Trading under misleading name (use of "public limited company" or Welsh equivalent when not so entitled); purporting to be a private company.	Summary.	One-fifth of the statutory maximum.	One-fiftieth of the statutory maximum.
34	Trading or carrying on business with improper use of "limited" or "cyfyngedig".	Summary.	One-fifth of the statutory maximum.	One-fiftieth of the statutory maximum.
54(1)	Public company failing to give notice, or copy of court order, to register, concerning application to re-register as private company.	Summary.	One-fifth of the statutory maximum.	One-fiftieth of the statutory maximum.
56(4)	Issuing form of application for shares or debentures without accompanying prospectus.	1. On indictment. 2. Summary.	A fine. The statutory maximum.	
61	Issuing prospectus with expert's statement in it, he not having given his consent; omission to state in prospectus that expert has consented.	1. On indictment. 2. Summary.	A fine. The statutory maximum.	
64(5)	Issuing company prospectus without copy being delivered to registrar of companies, or without requisite documents endorsed or attached.	Summary.	One-fifth of the statutory maximum.	One-fiftieth of the statutory maximum.
70(1)	Authorising issue of prospectus with untrue statement.	1. On indictment. 2. Summary.	Two years or a fine; or both. Six months or the statutory maximum; or both.	
78(1)	Being responsible for issue, circulation of prospectus, etc. contrary to Part III, Chapter II (overseas companies).	1. On indictment. 2. Summary.	A fine. The statutory maximum.	
80(9)	Directors exercising company's power of allotment without the authority required by section 80(1).	1. On indictment. 2. Summary.	A fine. The statutory maximum.	
81(2)	Private limited company offering shares to the public, or alloting shares with a view to their being so offered.	1. On indictment. 2. Summary.	A fine. The statutory maximum.	

82(5)	Alloting shares or debentures before third day after issue of prospectus.	1. On indictment. 2. Summary.	A fine. The statutory maximum.
86(6)	Company failing to keep money in separate bank account, where received in pursuance of prospectus stating that stock exchange listing is to be applied for.	1. On indictment. 2. Summary.	A fine. The statutory maximum.
87(4)	Offeror of shares for sale failing to keep proceeds in separate bank account.	1. On indictment. 2. Summary.	A fine. The statutory maximum.
88(5)	Officer of company failing to deliver return of allotments, etc., to registrar.	1. On indictment. 2. Summary.	A fine. The statutory maximum.	One-tenth of the statutory maximum.
95(6)	Knowingly or recklessly authorising or permitting misleading, false or deceptive material in statement by directors under section 95(5).	1. On indictment. 2. Summary.	Two years or a fine; or both. Six months or the statutory maximum; or both.
97(4)	Company failing to deliver to registrar the prescribed form disclosing amount or rate of share commission.	Summary.	One-fifth of the statutory maximum.
110(2)	Making misleading, false or deceptive statement in connection with valuation under section 103 or 104.	1. On indictment. 2. Summary.	Two years or a fine; or both. Six months or the statutory maximum; or both.
111(3)	Officer of company failing to deliver copy of asset valuation report to registrar.	1. On indictment. 2. Summary.	A fine. The statutory maximum.
111(4)	Company failing to deliver to registrar copy of resolution under section 104(4), with respect to transfer of an asset as consideration for allotment.	Summary.	One-fifth of the statutory maximum.
114	Contravention of any of the provisions of sections 99 to 104, 106.	1. On indictment. 2. Summary.	A fine. The statutory maximum.	One-tenth of the statutory maximum.
117(7)	Company doing business or exercising borrowing powers contrary to section 117.	1. On indictment. 2. Summary.	A fine. The statutory maximum.	One-fiftieth of the statutory maximum.

A6–004

Section of Act creating offence	General nature of offence	Mode of prosecution	Punishment	Daily default fine (where applicable)
122(2)	Company failing to give notice to registrar of reorganisation of share capital.	Summary.	One-fifth of the statutory maximum.	One-fiftieth of the statutory maximum.
123(4)	Company failing to give notice notice to registrar of increase of share capital.	Summary.	One-fifth of the statutory maximum.	One-fiftieth of the statutory maximum.
127(5)	Company failing to forward to registrar copy of court order, when application made to cancel resolution varying shareholders' rights.	Summary.	One-fifth of the statutory maximum.	One-fiftieth of the statutory maximum.
128(5)	Company failing to send to registrar statement or notice required by section 128 (particulars of shares carrying special rights).	Summary.	One-fifth of the statutory maximum.	One-fiftieth of the statutory maximum.
129(4)	Company failing to deliver to registrar statement or notice required by section 129 (registration of newly created class rights).	Summary.	One-fifth of the statutory maximum.	One-fiftieth of the statutory maximum.
141	Officer of company concealing name of creditor entitled to object to reduction of capital, or wilfully misrepresenting nature or amount of debt or claim, etc.	1. On indictment. 2. Summary.	A fine. The statutory maximum.	
142(2)	Director authorising or permitting non-compliance with section 142 (requirement to convene company meeting to consider serious loss of capital).	1. On indictment. 2. Summary.	A fine. The statutory maximum.	
143(2)	Company acquiring its own shares in breach of section 143.	1. On indictment. 2. Summary.	In the case of the company, a fine. In the case of an officer of the company who is in default, two years or a fine, or both. In the case of the company, the statutory maximum.	

498

APPENDICES

A6–005

149(2)	Company failing to cancel its own shares, acquired by itself, as required by section 146(2); or failing to apply for re-registration as private company as so required in the case there mentioned.	Summary.	In the case of an officer of the company who is in default, six months or the statutory maximum; or both. One-fifth of the statutory maximum.	One-fiftieth of the statutory maximum.
151(3)	Company giving financial assistance towards acquisition of its own shares.	1. On indictment.	Where the company is convicted, a fine. Where an officer of the company is convicted, two years or a fine; or both.	
		2. Summary.	Where the company is convicted, the statutory maximum. Where an officer of the company is convicted, six months or the statutory maximum; or both.	
156(6)	Company failing to register statutory declaration under section 155.	Summary.	The statutory maximum.	One-fiftieth of the statutory maximum.
156(7)	Director making statutory declaration under section 155, without having reasonable grounds for opinion expressed in it.	1. On indictment. 2. Summary.	Two years or a fine; or both. Six months or the statutory maximum; or both.	
169(6)	Default by the company's officer in delivering to registrar the return required by section 169 (disclosure by company of purchase of own shares).	1. On indictment. 2. Summary.	A fine. The statutory maximum.	One-tenth of the statutory maximum.

APPENDICES

A6–006

Section of Act creating offence	General nature of offence	Mode of prosecution	Punishment	Daily default fine (where applicable)
169(7)	Company failing to keep copy of contract, etc., at registered office, refusal of inspection to person demanding it.	Summary.	One-fifth of the statutory maximum.	One-fiftieth of the statutory maximum.
173(6)	Director making statutory declaration under section 173 without having reasonable grounds for the opinion expressed in the declaration.	1. On indictment. 2. Summary.	Two years or a fine; or both. Six months or the statutory maximum; or both.	
175(7)	Refusal of inspection of statutory declaration and auditors' report under section 173, etc.	Summary.	One-fifth of the statutory maximum.	One-fiftieth of the statutory maximum.
176(4)	Company failing to give notice to registrar of application to court under section 176, or to register court order.	Summary.	One-fifth of the statutory maximum.	One-fiftieth of the statutory maximum.
183(6)	Company failing to send notice of refusal to register a transfer of shares or debentures.	Summary.	One-fifth of the statutory maximum.	One-fiftieth of the statutory maximum.
185(5)	Company default in compliance with section 185(1) (certificates to be made ready following allotment or transfer of shares, etc.)	Summary.	One-fifth of the statutory maximum.	One-fiftieth of the statutory maximum.
189(1)	Offences of fraud and forgery in connection with share warrants in Scotland.	1. On indictment. 2. Summary.	Seven years or a fine; or both. Six months or the statutory maximum; or both.	
189(2)	Unauthorised making of, or using or possessing apparatus for making, share warrants in Scotland.	1. On indictment. 2. Summary.	Seven years or a fine; or both. Six months or the statutory maximum; or both.	
191(4)	Refusal of inspection or copy or register of debenture-holders, etc.	Summary.	One-fifth of the statutory maximum.	One-fiftieth of the statutory maximum.

APPENDICES

A6–007

210(3)	Failure to discharge obligation of disclosure under Part VI; other forms of non-compliance with that Part.	1. On indictment. 2. Summary.	Two years or a fine; or both. Six months or the statutory maximum; or both.	One-fiftieth of the statutory maximum.
211(10)	Company failing to keep register of interests disclosed under Part VI; other contraventions of section 211.	Summary.	One-fifth of the statutory maximum.	
214(5)	Company failing to exercise powers under section 212, when so required by the members.	1. On indictment. 2. Summary.	A fine. The statutory maximum.	
215(8)	Company default in compliance with section 215 (company report of investigations of shareholdings on members' requisition).	1. On indictment. 2. Summary.	A fine. The statutory maximum.	
216(3)	Failure to comply with company notice under section 212; making false statement in response, etc.	1. On indictment. 2. Summary.	Two years or a fine; or both. Six month or the statutory maximum; or both.	
217(7)	Company failing to notify a person that he has been named as a shareholder; on removal of name from register, failing to alter associated index.	Summary.	One-fifth of the statutory maximum.	One-fiftieth of the statutory maximum.
218(3)	Improper removal of entry from register of interests disclosed; company failing to restore entry improperly removed.	Summary.	One-fifth of the statutory maximum.	For continued contravention of section 218(2) one-fiftieth of the statutory maximum.
219(3)	Refusal of inspection of register or report under Part VI; failure to send copy when required.	Summary.	One-fifth of the statutory maximum.	One-fiftieth of the statutory maximum.
223(1)	Company failing to keep accounting records (liability of officers).	1. On indictment. 2. Summary.	Two years or a fine; or both. Six months or the statutory maximum; or both.	

APPENDICES

A6–008

Section of Act creating offence	General nature of offence	Mode of prosecution	Punishment	Daily default fine (where applicable)
223(2)	Officer of company failing to secure compliance with, or intentionally causing default under section 222(4) (preservation of accounting records for requisite number of years).	1. On indictment. 2. Summary.	Two years or a fine; or both. Six months or the statutory maximum; or both.	
231(3)	Company failing to annex to its annual return certain particulars required by Schedule 5 and not included in annual accounts.	Summary.	One-fifth of the statutory maximum.	One-fiftieth of the statutory maximum.
231(4)	Default by director or officer of a company in giving notice of matters relating to himself for purposes of Schedule 5 Part V.	Summary.	One-fifth of the statutory maximum.	
235(7)	Non-compliance with the section, as to directors' report and its content; directors individually liable.	1. On indictment. 2. Summary.	A fine. The statutory maximum.	
238(2)	Laying or delivery of unsigned balance sheet; circulating copies of balance sheet without signatures.	Summary.	One-fifth of the statutory maximum.	
240(5)	Failing to send company balance sheet, directors' report and auditors' report to those entitled to receive them.	1. On indictment. 2. Summary.	A fine. The statutory maximum.	One-tenth of the statutory maximum.
243(1)	Director in default as regards duty to lay and deliver company accounts.	Summary.	The statutory maximum.	
[...] [...] 246(2)	Company failing to supply copy of accounts to shareholders on his demand.	Summary.	One-fifth of the statutory maximum.	
254(6) [...] [...]	Company or officer in default contravening section 254 as regards publication of full individual or group accounts.	Summary.	One-fifth of the statutory maximum.	One-fiftieth of the statutory maximum.

APPENDICES

A6–009

288(4)	Default in complying with section 288 (keeping register of directors and secretaries, refusal of inspection).	Summary.	The statutory maximum.	One-tenth of the statutory maximum.
291(5)	Acting as director of a company without having the requisite share qualification.	Summary.	One-fifth of the statutory maximum.	One-fiftieth of the statutory maximum.
294(3)	Director failing to give notice of his attaining retirement age; acting as director under appointment invalid due to his attaining it.	Summary.	One-fifth of the statutory maximum.	One-fiftieth of the statutory maximum.
305(3)	Company default in complying with section 305 (directors' names to appear on company correspondence, etc.)	Summary.	One-fifth of the statutory maximum.	
306(4)	Failure to state that liability of proposed director or manager is unlimited; failure to give notice of that fact to person accepting office.	1. On indictment. 2. Summary.	A fine. The statutory maximum.	
314(3)	Director failing to comply with section 314 (duty to disclose compensation payable on takeover, etc.); a person's failure to include required particulars in a notice he has to give of such matters.	Summary.	One-fifth of the statutory maximum.	
317(7)	Director failing to disclose interest in contract.	1. On indictment. 2. Summary.	A fine. The statutory maximum.	
318(8)	Company default in complying with section 318(1) or (5) (directors' service contracts to be open to inspection); 14 days' default in complying with section 319(4) (notice to registrar as to where copies of contracts and memoranda are kept); refusal of inspection required under section 318(7).	Summary.	One-fifth of the statutory maximum.	One-fiftieth of the statutory maximum.
[322B(4)	Terms of unwritten contract between sole member of a private company limited by shares or by guarantee and the company not set out in a written memorandum or recorded in minutes of a directors' meeting.	Summary.		Level 5 on the standard scale.]
323(2)	Director dealing in options to buy or sell company's listed shares or debentures.	1. On indictment. 2. Summary.	Two years or a fine; or both.	

503

A6–010

Section of Act creating offence	General nature of offence	Mode of prosecution	Punishment	Daily default fine (where applicable)
324(7)	Director failing to notify interest in company's shares; making false statement in purported notification.	1. On indictment. 2. Summary.	Six months or the statutory maximum; or both. Two years or a fine; or both. Six months or the statutory maximum; or both.	
326(2), (3), (4), (5)	Various defaults in connection with company register of directors' interests.	Summary.	One-fifth of the statutory maximum.	Except in the case of section 326(5), one-fiftieth of the statutory maximum.
328(6)	Director failing to notify company that members of his family have, or have exercised, options to buy shares or debentures; making false statement in purported notification.	1. On indictment. 2. Summary.	Two years or a fine; or both. Six months or the statutory maximum; or both.	
329(3)	Company failing to notify [investment exchange] of acquisition of its securities by a director.	Summary.	One-fifth of the statutory maximum.	One-fiftieth of the statutory maximum.
342(1)	Director of relevant company authorising or permitting company to enter into transaction or arrangement, knowing or suspecting it to contravene section 330.	1. On indictment. 2. Summary.	Two years or a fine; or both. Six months or the statutory maximum; or both.	
342(2)	Relevant company entering into transaction or arrangement for a director in contravention of section 330.	1. On indictment. 2. Summary.	Two years or a fine; or both. Six months or the statutory maximum; or both.	
342(3)	Procuring a relevant company to enter into transaction or arrangment known to be contrary to section 330.	1. On indictment. 2. Summary.	Two years or a fine; or both.	

APPENDICES

A6–011

343(8)	Company failing to maintain register of transactions, etc., made with and for directors and not disclosed in company accounts; failing to make register available at registered office or at company meeting.	1. On indictment. 2. Summary.	Six months or the statutory maximum; or both. A fine. The statutory maximum.
348(2)	Company failing to paint or affix name; failing to keep it painted or affixed.	Summary.	One-fifth of the statutory maximum. In the case of failure to keep the name painted or affixed, one-fiftieth of the statutory maximum.
349(2)	Company failing to have name on business correspondence, invoices, etc.	Summary.	One-fifth of the statutory maximum.
349(3)	Officer of company issuing business letter or document not bearing company's name.	Summary.	One-fifth of the statutory maximum.
349(4)	Officer of company signing cheque, bill of exchange, etc. on which company's name not mentioned.	Summary.	One-fifth of the statutory maximum.
350(1)	Company failing to have its name engraved on company seal.	Summary.	One-fifth of the statutory maximum.
350(2)	Officer of company, etc., using company seal without name engraved on it.	Summary.	One-fifth of the statutory maximum.
351(1)(a)	Company failing to comply with section 351(1) or (2) (matters to be stated on business correspondence, etc.).	Summary.	One-fifth of the statutory maximum.
351(5)(b)	Officer or agent of company issuing, or authorising issue of, business document not complying with those subsections.	Summary.	One-fifth of the statutory maximum.
351(5)(c)	Contravention of section 351(3) or (4) (information in English to be stated on Welsh company's business correspondence, etc.).	Summary.	One-fifth of the statutory maximum. For contravention of section 351(3), one-fiftieth of the statutory maximum.

505

A6–012

Section of Act creating offence	General nature of offence	Mode of prosecution	Punishment	Daily default fine (where applicable)
352(5)	Company default in complying with section 352 (requirement to keep register of members and their particulars).	Summary.	One-fifth of the statutory maximum.	One-fiftieth of the statutory maximum.
[352A(3)	Company default in complying with section 352A (statement that company has only one members).	Summary.	Level 2 on the standard scale.	One-tenth of level 2 of the standard scale.]
353(4)	Company failing to send notice to registrar as to place where register of members is kept.	Summary.	One-fifth of the statutory maximum.	One-fiftieth of the statutory maximum.
354(4)	Company failing to keep index of members.	Summary.	One-fifth of the statutory maximum.	One-fiftieth of the statutory maximum.
356(5)	Refusal of inspection of members' register; failure to send copy on requisition.	Summary.	One-fifth of the statutory maximum.	
363(7)	Company with share capital failing to make annual return.	Summary.	The statutory maximum.	One-tenth of the statutory maximum.
364(4)	Company without share capital failing to complete and register annual return in due time.	Summary.	The statutory maximum.	One-tenth of the statutory maximum.
[...] 366(4)	Company default in holding annual general meeting.	1. On indictment. 2. Summary.	A fine. The statutory maximum.	
367(3)	Company default in complying with Secretary of State's direction to hold company meeting.	1. On indictment. 2. Summary.	A fine. The statutory maximum.	
367(5)	Company failing to register resolution that meeting held under section 367 is to be its annual general meeting.	Summary.	One-fifth of the statutory maximum.	One-fiftieth of the statutory maximum.
372(4)	Failure to give notice, to member entitled to vote at company meeting, that he may do so by proxy.	Summary.	One-fifth of the statutory maximum.	
372(6)	Officer of company authorising or permitting issue of irregular invitation to appoint proxies.	Summary.	One-fifth of the statutory maximum.	
376(7)	Officer of company in default as to circulation of members' resolutions for company meeting.	1. On indictment. 2. Summary.	A fine. The statutory maximum.	

APPENDICES

A6–013

380(5)	Company failing to comply with section 380 (copies of certain resolutions etc. to be sent to registrar of companies).	Summary.	One-fifth of the statutory maximum.	One-fiftieth of the statutory maximum.
380(6)	Company failing to include copy of resolution to which section 380 applies in articles; failing to forward copy to member on request.	Summary.	One-fifth of the statutory maximum for each occasion on which copies are issued or, as the case may be, requested.	
382(5)	Company failing to keep minutes of proceedings at company and board meetings, etc.	Summary.	One-fifth of the statutory maximum.	One-fiftieth of the statutory maximum.
[382B(2)]	Failure of sole member to provide the company with a written record of decision.	Summary.	Level 2 on the standard scale.]	
383(4)	Refusal of inspection of minutes of general meeting; failure to send copy of minutes on member's request.	Summary.	One-fifth of the statutory maximum.	
[...]				
[...]				
[387(2)	Company failing to give Secretary of State notice of non-appointment of auditors.	Summary.	One-fifth of the statutory maximum.	One-fiftieth of the statutory maximum.]
389(10)	Person acting as company auditor knowing himself to be disqualified; failing to give notice vacating office when he becomes disqualified.	1. On indictment. 2. Summary.	A fine. The statutory maximum.	One-tenth of the statutory maximum.
[389A(2)	Officer of company making false, misleading or deceptive statement to auditors.	1. On indictment. 2. Summary.	Two years or a fine; or both. Six months or the statutory maximum; or both.	
389A(3)	Subsidiary undertaking or its auditor failing to give information to auditors of parent company.	Summary.	One-fifth of the statutory maximum.	
389A(4)	Parent company failing to obtain from subsidiary undertaking information for purposes of audit.	Summary.	One-fifth of the statutory maximum.	
[...]				

A6–014

Section of Act creating offence	General nature of offence	Mode of prosecution	Punishment	Daily default fine (where applicable)
[391(2)]	Failing to give notice to registrar of removal of auditor.	Summary.	One-fifth of the statutory maximum.	One-fiftieth of the statutory maximum.]
[...] [392(3)]	Company failing to forward notice of auditor's registration to registrar.	1. On indictment. 2. Summary.	A fine. The statutory maximum.	One-tenth of the statutory maximum.
392A(5)	Directors failing to convene meeting requisitioned by resigning auditor.	1. On indictment. 2. Summary.	A fine. The statutory maximum.]	
[...] 394A(1)	Person ceasing to hold office as auditor failing to deposit statement as to circumstances.	1. On indictment. 2. Summary.	A fine. The statutory maximum.	
394(4)	Company failing to comply with requirements as to statement of person ceasing to hold office as auditor.	1. On indictment. 2. Summary.	A fine. The statutory maximum.	One-tenth of the statutory maximum.
399(3)	Company failing to send to registrar particulars of charge created by it, or of issue of debentures which requires registration.	1. On indictment. 2. Summary.	A fine. The statutory maximum.	One-tenth of the statutory maximum.
400(4)	Company failing to send to registrar particulars of charge on property acquired.	1. On indictment. 2. Summary.	A fine. The statutory maximum.	One-tenth of the statutory maximum.
402(3)	Authorising or permitting delivery of debenture or certificate of debenture stock, without endorsement on it of certificate of registration of charge.	Summary.	One-fifth of the statutory maximum.	
405(4)	Failure to give notice to registrar of appointment of receiver or manager, or of his ceasing to act.	Summary.	One-fifth of the statutory maximum.	One-fiftieth of the statutory maximum.
407(3)	Authorising or permitting omission from company register of charges.	1. On indictment. 2. Summary.	A fine. The statutory maximum.	
408(3)	Officer of company refusing inspection of charging instrument, or of register of charges.	Summary.	One-fifth of the statutory maximum.	One-fiftieth of the statutory maximum.

APPENDICES

A6–015

415(3)	Scottish company failing to send to registrar particulars of charge created by it, or of issue of debentures which requires registration.	1. On indictment. 2. Summary.	A fine. The statutory maximum.	One-tenth of the statutory maximum.
416(3)	Scottish company failing to send to registrar particulars of charge on property acquired by it.	1. On indictment. 2. Summary.	A fine. The statutory maximum.	One-tenth of the statutory maximum.
422(3)	Scottish company authorising or permitting omission from its register of charges.	1. On indictment. 2. Summary.	A fine. The statutory maximum.	
423(3)	Officer of Scottish company refusing inspection of charging instrument, or of register of charges.	Summary.	One-fifth of the statutory maximum.	One-fiftieth of the statutory maximum.
425(4)	Company failing to annex to memorandum court order sanctioning compromise or arrangement with creditors.	Summary.	One-fifth of the statutory maximum.	
426(6)	Company failing to comply with requirements of section 426 (information to members and creditors about compromise or arrangement.)	1. On indictment. 2. Summary.	A fine. The statutory maximum.	
426(7)	Director or trustee for debenture holders failing to give notice to company of matters necessary for purposes of section 426.	Summary.	One-fifth of the statutory maximum.	
427(5)	Failure to deliver to registrar office copy of court order under section 427 (company reconstruction or amalgamation).	Summary.	One-fifth of the statutory maximum.	One-fiftieth of the statutory maximum.
[429(6)	Offeror failing to send copy of notice or making statutory declaration knowing it to be false, etc.	1. On indictment. 2. Summary.	Two years or a fine; or both. Six months or the statutory maximum; or both.	One-fiftieth of the statutory maximum.
430A(6)	Offeror failing to give notice or rights to minority shareholders.	1. On indictment. 2. Summary.	A fine. The statutory maximum.	
444(3)	Failing to give Secretary of State, when required to do so, information about interests in shares, etc.; give false information.	1. On indictment. 2. Summary.	Two years or a fine; or both. Six months or the statutory maximum; or both.	One-fiftieth of the statutory maximum.]

APPENDICES

A6–016

Section of Act creating offence	General nature of offence	Mode of prosecution	Punishment	Daily default fine (where applicable)
447(6)	Failure to comply with requirement to produce [documents] imposed by Secretary of State under section 447.	1. On indictment. 2. Summary.	A fine. The statutory maximum.	
[448(7)]	[Obstructing the exercise of any rights conferred by a warrant or failing to comply with a requirement imposed under subsection (3)(d)].	1. On indictment. 2. Summary.	A fine. The statutory maximum.	
449(2)	Wrongful disclosure of information or document obtained under section 447 or 448.	1. On indictment. 2. Summary.	Two years or a fine; or both. Six months or the statutory maximum; or both.	
450	Destroying or mutilating company documents; falsifying such documents or making false entries; parting with such documents or altering them or making omissions.	1. On indictment. 2. Summary.	Seven years or a fine; or both. Six months or the statutory maximum; or both.	
451	Making false statement or explanation in purported compliance with section 447.	1. On indictment. 2. Summary.	Two years or a fine; or both. Six months or the statutory maximum; or both.	
455(1)	Exercising a right to dispose of, or vote in respect of, shares which are subject to restrictions under Part XV; failing to give notice in respect of shares so subject; entering into agreement void under section 454(2), (3).	1. On indictment. 2. Summary.	A fine. The statutory maximum.	
455(2)	Issuing shares in contravention of restrictions of Part XV.	1. On indictment. 2. Summary.	A fine. The statutory maximum.	
458	Being a party to carrying on company's business with intent to defraud creditors, or for any fraudulent purpose.	1. On indictment. 2. Summary.	Seven years or a fine; or both.	

510

APPENDICES

A6–017

461(5)	Faiure to register office copy of court order under Part XVII altering, or giving leave to alter, company's memorandum.	Summary.	Six months or the statutory maximum; or both. One-fifth of the statutory maximum.	One-fiftieth of the statutory maximum.
[...] 651(3)	Person obtaining court order to declare company's dissolution void, then failing to register the order.	Summary.	One-fifth of the statutory maximum.	One-fiftieth of the statutory maximum.
652E(1)	Person breaching or failing to perform duty imposed by section 652B or 652C.	1. On indictment. 2. Summary.	A fine. The statutory maximum.	
652E(2)	Person failing to perform duty imposed by section 652B(6) or 652C(2) with intent to conceal the making of application under section 652A.	1. On indictment. 2. Summary.	Seven years or a fine; or both. Six months or the statutory maximum; or both.	
652F(1)	Person furnishing false or misleading information in connection with application under section 652A.	1. On indictment. 2. Summary.	A fine. The statutory maximum.	
652F(2)	Person making false application under section 652A.	1. On indictment. 2. Summary.	A fine. The statutory maximum.	
697(1)	Oversea company failing to comply with any of sections 691 to 693 or 696.	Summary.	For an offence which is not a continuing offence, one-fifth of the statutory maximum. For an offence which is a continuing offence, one-fifth of the statutory maximum.	One-fiftieth of the statutory maximum.
697(2)	Oversea company contravening section 694(6) (carrying on business under its corporate name after Secretary of State's direction).	1. On indictment. 2. Summary.	A fine. The statutory maximum.	One-tenth of the statutory maximum.
[697(3)	Oversea Company failing to comply with section 695A or Schedule 21A.	Summary.	For an offence which is not a continuing offence, one-fifth of level 5 of the standard scale.	£100]

511

A6–018

Section of Act creating offence	General nature of offence	Mode of prosecution	Punishment	Daily default fine (where applicable)
703(1)	Oversea company failing to comply with s. 700 as respects delivery of annual accounts.	1. On indictment. 2. Summary.	For an offence which is a continuing offence one fifth of level 5 of the standard scale. A fine.	One-tenth of the statutory maximum.
[703R(1)	Company failing to register winding up or commencement or insolvency proceedings etc.	1. On indictment. 2. Summary.	The statutory maximum. A fine.	£100]
[703R(2)	Liquidator failing to register appointment, termination of winding up or striking-off of company.	1. On indictment. 2. Summary.	The statutory maximum. A fine. The statutory maximum.	£100]
710(4)	[Repealed by the Insolvency Actr 1986, Sched. 12.]			
720(4)	Insurance company etc. failing to send twice-yearly statement in form of Schedule 23.	Summary.	One-fifth of the statutory maximum.	One-fiftieth of the statutory maximum.
720(3)	Company failing to comply with section 722(2), as regards the manner of keeping registers, minute books and accounting records.	Summary.	One-fifth of the statutory maximum.	One-fiftieth of the statutory maximum.
Sched. 14, Pt. II, para. 1(3)	Company failing to give notice of location of overseas branch register, etc.	Summary.	One-fifth of the statutory maximum.	One-fiftieth of the statutory maximum.
Sched. 14, Pt. II, para. 4(2)	Company failing to transmit to its registered office in Great Britain copies of entries in overseas branch register, or to keep a duplicate of overseas branch register.	Summary.	One-fifth of the statutory maximum.	One-fiftieth of the statutory maximum.
[Sched. 21C, Pt. I, para. 7	Credit or financial institution failing to deliver accounting documents.	1. On indictment. 2. Summary.	The statutory maximum. A fine.	£100]
[Sched. 21C, Pt. II, para. 15	Credit or financial institution failing to deliver accounts and reports.	1. On indictment. 2. Summary.	The statutory maximum. A fine.	£100]

| [Sched. 21D, Pt. I, para. 5] | Company failing to deliver accounting documents. | 1. On indictment. 2. Summary. | A fine. The statutory maximum. | £100] |
| [Sched. 21D, Pt. I, para. 13] | Company failing to deliver accounts and reports. | 1. On indictment. 2. Summary. | A fine. The statutory maximum. | £100] |

Amendments

A6–020   The Note to Schedule 24 was repealed by the Statute Law (Repeals) Act 1993.

The words in square brackets were inserted by Sched. 16 para. 27 of the Financial services Act 1986.

The words omitted from this Schedule were repealed by the Insolvency Act 1986, Sched. 12, and by the Companies Act 1989, Sched. 24.

The words in square brackets relating to s. 387(2) were inserted by the Companies Act 1989, s. 119.

The words in square brackets relating to ss. 389A(2), (3) and (4) were inserted by the Companies Act 1989, s. 120.

The words in square brackets relating to ss. 391(2), 392(3) and 392A(5) were inserted by the Companies Act 1989, s. 122.

The words in square brackets relating to ss. 394A(1) and (4) were inserted by the Companies Act 1989, s. 123.

The words in square brackets relating to s. 447(6) were substituted by the Companies Act 1989, s. 63(8).

The words in square brackets relating to s. 448(7) were substituted by the Companies Act 1989, s. 64(2).

For the repeal of references to ss. 56(4), 61, 64(5), 70(1), 78(1), 81(2), 82(5), 86(6), 87(4) and 97(4) see S.I. 1986 No. 2246 (para. B–700 below), S.I. 1988 No. 740 (para. B–760, below), and S.I. 1988 No. 1960 (para. B–766, below).

The references to ss. 245(1) and (2) were repealed by the Companies Act 1989, Sched. 24, subject to transitional provisions in S.I. 1990 No. 2569, para. A–3639, below.

The words in square brackets relating to ss. 322B(4), 352A(3) and 382B(2) were inserted by S.I. 1992 No. 1699.

The words in square brackets relating to ss. 697(3), 703R(1) and 703R(2) and to Scheds. 21C and 21D were inserted by S.I. 1992 No. 3179.

The entries relating to s. 652E(1), 652E(2), 652F(1), and 652F(2) were inserted by the Deregulation and Contracting Out Act 1994, Sched. 5.

Index

Accounts,
building societies, 15–015
company. *See* **Company**
Council of Lloyd's, 11–019
insurance company,
    deposited documents, 10–028, 10–029
    filing, 10–025
    non-compliance with requirements, 10–026
    preparation, 10–025
    separate accounting, 10–030
negligent statements. *See* **Professional negligence**
professional negligence. *See* **Professional negligence**
Acquisition issue, 12–056
Acting in good faith, directors, 26–008
Actuaries,
appointment, insurance company, by, 10–027
occupational pension scheme,
    appointment, 7–043
    liability, 7–043
    requirement, 7–043
    whistle blowing, 7–045—7–047
personal pensions, whistle blowing, 7–048
trustees, as, 7–012—7–014
Adequacy test, 3–018
Administration,
occupational pension scheme, 7–053
Pensions Compensation Board, 9–013
Administration order, 4–037
Advertising,
AIM, 12–095
approval of contents, 20–039
approved exchanges, 2–044
authorised, 3–056
building societies, 15–028

Advertising,—*cont.*
complaints, 2–044
defences, 2–039
enforcement of related agreement, 2–040, 2–041
E.U. Member State national issuing, 2–043
exceptions from restrictions, 2–042
influenced by, 2–041
insurance companies, 10–047
"investment advertisement", 2–039
issuing, 2–040, 3–056
listing particulars, 2–044, 12–075—12–078
offences, 2–039
prospectuses, 2–044
regulated insurance company, 10–050
restrictions, 2–039—2–044
sanctions, 2–039
standards,
    basic standards, 3–055
    core rule, 3–055
    FIMBRA, 3–059
    general, 3–055, 3–056
    IMRO, 3–057
    LAUTRO, 3–059
    PIA, 3–059
    SFA, 3–058
Advice, negligent. *See* **Professional negligence**
Advising on investments,
investment business, 2–021
negligently. *See* **Professional negligence**
Agency,
parties to civil action, 30–010—30–014
Agents, listing, 12–061
Agreement, customer. *See* **Customer agreement**

INDEX

AIM,
  admission, 12–080—12–084
  advertisements, 12–095
  adviser, nominated, 123–082
  appeals, 12–088
  application for admission, 12–082
  background, 12–079
  breach of responsibilities, 12–087
  broker, nominated, 12–082
  contravention of rules,
    12–085—12–087
  directors, sanctions imposed on,
    12–087
  disclosure, 12–084
  discontinuance of trading, 12–086
  document, admission, 12–083
  establishment, 12–015
  false or misleading statements,
    12–103
  freely transferable securities,
    12–081
  incorporation requirement, 12–081
  information required, 12–086
  market value, 12–015
  minimum trading requirements,
    12–015
  nominated adviser, 12–082
  nominated broker, 12–082
  offer to public, 12–092, 12–093
  over the counter trading, 12–097
  prospectuses, 12–089, 12–090
  public, offer to, 12–092, 12–093
  purpose, 12–015
  recognition, 12–096
  requirements, 12–015
  requirements for admission,
    12–080
  sanctions against issuer,
    12–085—12–087
  supplementary prospectuses,
    12–091
  suspension of trading, 12–082,
    12–086
  trading rules, 12–080
  USM, replacing, 12–079
  valid company, 12–081
Allotment of shares,
  discounted, 19–048
  non-cash, 19–019
  offences, 19–017
  prohibition on discounted, 19–048

Allotment of shares,—*cont.*
  rules, 19–017
  valuation, 19–019
Alternative Investment Market. *See*
  AIM
Amendment of pension schemes.
  See **Occupational pensions**
Anton Piller order,
  application for, 31–003, 31–007
  criteria for, 31–007
  cross-examination. *See*
    Cross-examination order
  effect, 31–002
  ex parte application, 31–003
  fear of physical violence, 31–059
  grant of, 31–007
  inter partes application, 31–007
  meaning, 31–002
  Practice Direction, 31–026
  procedure, 31–026
  purpose, 31–002
  self incrimination, 31–041
APP,
  contracting out for, 8–010, 8–011
  meaning, 8–005
Appeals,
  AIM, 12–088
  OPRA, 6–039
  PTM, 13–062
  substantial acquisition rules,
    13–062
Appointed representatives,
  carrying on investment business
    exclusion, 2–031
Appointment of trustees,
  OPRA, by, 6–028
**Appropriate personal pensions
  (APP),** 8–005
Appropriation. *See* **Theft**
Arranging deals,
  investment business, as, 2–020
Assets,
  confiscation. *See* **Confiscation of
    assets**
  insurance company,
    custody of, 10–039
    maintenance in U.K., 10–038
  mergers, 13–050
  occupational pension schemes. *See*
    Occupational pensions
  restraint orders. *See* **Injunctions;
    Restitution orders**

INDEX

Assisting another to retain the benefit of criminal conduct. *See* **Money laundering**
Association of Lloyd's Members, 11–025
Audit,
  auditors. *See* **Auditors**
  building societies, 15–015, 15–016
  client money, 3–032
Auditors,
  banking, role in policing. *See* **Banking**
  occupational pension scheme,
    appointment, 7–043
    liability, 7–043
    requirement, 7–043
    whistle blowing, 7–045—7–047
  personal pensions, 7–048
  policing role. *See* **Banking**
  rights of, 19–030, 19–031
  strengthening role, 32–008, 32–009
  trustees, as, 7–012—7–014
Authorisation,
  See also **Carrying on investment business**
  applications,
    contents, 3–003
    direct authorisation, 3–003
    grant of, 3–003
    responsibility, 3–003
    statutory provisions, 3–002
  automatic, 10–021, 10–022
  banking. *See* **Banking**
  body granting, 3–003
  building societies, 14–004, 15–013
  Central Register, SIB, 3–002
  direct, 3–003, 3–004
  E.U.Member State, by, 3–003
  Europersons, 3–015—3–017
  IMRO, 3–012, 3–013
  insurance. *See* **Insurance companies**
  methods, 2–013, 3–002
  personal pensions, 5–003
  register, 3–002
  requirement for, 3–002
  responsibility for applications, 3–003
  RPB, 3–014
  SFA, 3–008

Authorisation,—*cont.*
  SIB, by,
    applications, 3–003
    Central Register, 3–002
    generally, 3–002
  SRO membership, by,
    definition of SRO, 3–005
    effect of membership, 3–005
    generally, 3–002
    recognition of SRO, 3–005
    requirements for SRO, 3–005
    simplification of system, 3–006
  suspension, 3–004, 4–031—4–033
  unit trust. *See* **Unit trusts**
  withdrawal, 3–004
    effective date, 4–032
    insurance, 10–020
    notice, 4–032
    reasons, 4–031
    requested by authorised person, 4–033

Balance sheets,
  insurance companies, 10–028
Bank account,
  margined transaction, 3–033
  occupational pension scheme, 7–054
  settlement, 3–033
Bank of England,
  annual reports, 14–006
  bad faith, acting in, 14–006
  Board of Banking Supervision, 14–007
  carrying on investment business exclusion, 2–030
  continuing supervision, 14–067
  duties, 14–006
  entry, right of, 14–073, 14–079
  future of, 14–111—14–113
  information, power to require, 14–070—14–073, 14–084
  interviews, 14–067
  investigations on behalf of, 14–074—14–084
    appointment of competent person, 14–074
    concealment of documentation, 14–083
    destruction of documentation, 14–083

Bank of England,—*cont.*
　disposal of documentation,
　　14–083
　documentation offences, 14–083
　entry powers, 14–079
　European authorised
　　institutions, 14–077
　evidential use of statement,
　　14–076
　falsification of documents,
　　14–083
　information provision, 14–084
　non-attendance, 14–075
　non-production of documents,
　　14–075
　obstruction, 14–075
　offences, 14–075
　production of documents,
　　14–084
　reasonable grounds for
　　suspicion, 14–078, 14–080
　scope of duty to investigate,
　　14–081, 14–082
　statutory basis, 14–074
　utilisation of powers, 14–076
　judicial reivew, 14–054, 14–055
　liability, 14–006
　meetings, 14–0367
　notices, supervisory, 14–069
　powers, 14–006
　production of dcouments,
　　14–070—14–073, 14–084
　prudential interviews, 14–067
　reporting, 14–006
　review of legislation, 14–006
　review visits, 14–068
　role, 14–001
　sanctions, 14–068
　supervisory role, 14–001, 14–006,
　　14–067—14–069
　surveillance department, 14–068
Bankers' trust orders,
　31–009—31–012. *See also*
　　Self-incrimination
Banking,
　acceptance of deposits,
　　14–008—14–015
　authorisation requirement,
　　14–008
　Bank of England payments,
　　14–010
　deposit, meaning of, 14–009

Banking,—*cont.*
　acceptance of deposits,—*cont.*
　　"deposit-taking business",
　　　14–011—14–015
　　exempted persons, 14–008,
　　　14–010
　　family payments, 14–010
　　groups of companies, 14–010
　　lending money, 14–010
　　occasional, 14–012
　　offences, 14–008
　　penalties, 14–008
　　restrictions, 14–008
　　unauthorised. *See* **unauthorised deposit taking** *below*
　accounting records, 14–035
　appeals,
　　High Court, 14–094
　　Tribunal. *See* **Appeals Tribunal** *below*
　Appeals Tribunal,
　　Bank of England directions,
　　　14–093
　　composition, 14–092
　　determination of appeal, 14–093
　　options available to, 14–093
　　powers, 14–093
　　right of appeal to, 14–091
　　subject matter of appeal, 14–091
　　time limits, 14–091
　auditor's role,
　　accounts' inspection, 14–089
　　availability of accounts, 14–089
　　BCCI scandal, 14–088
　　change in auditor, 14–090
　　duty, 14–086
　　obligations, 14–088
　　policing role, 14–085—14–090
　　statutory basis, 14–085, 14–086
　　waiver of duty of
　　　confidentiality,
　　　14–086—14–088
　authorisation,
　　accompanying statement, 4–020
　　accounting records, 14–035
　　applicants, 14–019
　　applications, 14–018—14–022
　　"authorised institutions",
　　　14–016
　　capital requirement. *See* **capital requirement** *below*
　　credit insitutions, 14–019
　　criteria, 14–018, 14–021,
　　　14–023—14–027

518

INDEX

Banking,—*cont.*
  authorisation,—*cont.*
    decisions on, 14–017
    fit and proper, 14–024, 14–025
    foreign banks, 14–023
    formal assessment, 14–017
    "four eyes", 14–026
    generally, 14–004
    integrity, 14–036
    key questions, 14–016
    liquidity, 14–033
    minimum criteria, 14–018, 14–021, 14–023—14–027
    minimum net assets, 14–037
    nature of business, 14–020
    non executive directors, 14–027
    procedure for applications, 14–018—14–022
    provisions, 14–034
    prudent manner, 14–028
    restriction. *See* **restriction of authorisation** *below*
    review process, 14–017
    revocation, 14–017
    revocation. *See* **revocation of authorisation** *below*
    scale of business, 14–020
    skills, 14–036
    statment of principles, 14–018, 14–023
    surrender, 14–043
    systems, 14–035
    two individuals directing business, 14–026
    written notice, 14–022
  authorised population, 14–004
  background, 14–001—14–004
  Bank of England. *See* **Bank of England**
  Barings collapse, 14–099, 14–104—14–106
  Basle Committee, 14–109
  BCCI, 14–102, 14–103
  Board of Banking Supervision, 14–007
  capital requirement,
    amount, 14–029
    calculations, 14–031
    capital base, 14–030
    core capital, 14–030
    nature, 14–029
    need for, 14–029
    Risk Asset Ratio (RAR), 14–031

Banking,—*cont.*
  capital requirement,—*cont.*
    supplementary capital, 14–030
    tiers, 14–030
  changes in control,
    general rule, 14–044
    grant of application, 14–045
    intention of objecting, 14–046
    notice of objection, 14–046, 14–047
    notification, 14–044
    objection to application, 14–046
    offences, 14–050—14–052
    preliminary warning notice, 14–046
    procedure for objection, 14–049
    Treasury directions, 14–048
    unauthorised, 14–047
  common law remedies, 14–098—14–100
  compensation, 14–095—14–098
  criminal offences, 14–059—14–056
  Deposit Protection Fund,
    administration, 14–095
    "depositor", 14–097
    entitlement to compensation, 14–096
    establishment, 14–095
    funding, 14–095
    institutions applicable, 14–096
    purpose, 14–095
    statutory basis, 14–095
    unauthorised funds, 14–097
  Directive. *See* single market *below*
  domestic liaison between supervisory authorities, 14–107, 14–108
  EAI, 14–004
  European Authorised Institutions (EAI), 14–004
  false statements as to authorised status, 14–061, 14–062
  fit and proper, 14–024, 14–025
  foreign banks, 14–023
  "four eyes", 14–026
  fraudulent inducement to make a deposit, 14–063—14–066
  growth, 14–001
  Harrods Bank, 14–101
  High Court, appeals to, 14–094
  inducement to make a deposit, 14–063—14–066
  integrity, 14–036

519

Banking,—*cont.*
Johnson Matthey affair, 14–002
judicial review, 14–054—14–055
liaison between supervisory authorities,
  Basle Committee, 14–109
  domestic, 14–107, 14–108
  international, 14–109, 14–110
liquidity, 14–033
negligence claim, 14–098
non executive directors, 14–027
offences, 14–059—14–056
practical supervision,
  Barings Bank, 14–104—14–106
  BCCI, 14–102, 14–103
  Harrods Bank, 14–101
procedural proprieties, 14–054, 14–055
provisions, 14–034
prudent manner, 14–028
purpose of legislation, 14–003
RAR, 14–031, 14–032
restriction of authorisation,
  circumstances, 14–040
  criteria, 14–039
  discretion, 14–038
  non-compliance, 14–041
  powers, 14–038
  principles applied, 14–042
  written notice, 14–042
revocation of authorisation, 14–017
  circumstances, 14–039
  criteria, 14–039
  discretion, 14–038
  justification, 14–040
  mandatory, 14–038
  non-compliance, 14–041
  powers, 14–038
  principles applied, 14–043
  written notice, 14–042
Risk Asset Ratio (RAR), 14–031, 14–032
scheme of legislation, 14–005—14–015
SIB supervision, 14–107
single market,
  basis, 14–053
  freedom of establishment, 14–053
  implementation, 14–053
skills, 14–036

Banking,—*cont.*
surrender of authorisation, 14–043
two individuals directing business, 14–026
unauthorised deposit taking,
  civil law consequences, 14–056—14–058
  criminal law, 14–059—14–056
  false statements as to authorised status, 14–061, 14–062
  fraudulent inducement to make a deposit, 14–063—14–066
  inducement to make a deposit, 14–063—14–066
  mental element, 14–060
  offences, 14–059—14–056
  payment into court, 14–058
  profits from, 14–058
  receiver appointed, 14–058
  sanctions, 14–059
Bankrupt,
directors, 22–029
disqualification of directors, 22–029
self-incrimination, 31–051
undischarged, 22–029
Barings collapse, 14–099, 14–104, 14–105
Barlow Clowes affair, 16–036—16–040
Basle Committee, 14–109
BCCI, 14–088, 14–102, 14–103
Betting, 2–017
"Big Bang", 2–006, 12–005
Blowing whistle. *See* **Whistle blowing**
"Blue chip" property, 1–020
Board of Banking Supervision, 14–007
Board of Trade,
inspectors, 2–005
unit trust investigation, 2–005
Bonus issue, 12–056, 21–032
Brussels Convention, 31–006
Building Societies,
accounts, 15–015
administration costs, 15–001
advances,
  secured on land, 15–018
  unsecured, 15–019
advertising, 15–028
amendment of legislation, 15–006

520

Building Societies,—cont.
audit, 15–015, 15–016
authorisation, 14–004, 15–013
background, 15–001—15–003
banking sector competition, 15–004
becoming banks, 15–004
changing role, 15–004—15–007
Commission, 14–004, 15–009, 15–010, 15–024—15–029
company status, conversion to, 15–024
complaints, 15–030
conditions imposed, 15–026, 15–027
costs of administration, 15–001
criticisms of legislation, 15–005
designated bodies, 15–020
discipline, 15–024—15–029
disputes, 15–030
diversification of role, 15–004
draft Bill, 15–007
equity-linked schemes, 15–018
establishment, 15–011, 15–012
estate agencies, joint ventures with, 15–020
fund raising, 15–017
index-linked schemes, 15–018
inspectors' investigation, 15–029
insurance companies, joint ventures with, 15–020
Investor Protection Fund, 15–022
land, advances secured on, 15–018
liquid assets, 15–021
management, 15–014
market share, 15–004
meeting summoned, 15–029
memorandum, 15–012
merging with banks, 15–004
minimum capital, 15–012
non-retail funds, 15–017
objects, 15–011
ombudsman, 15–031
powers of Commission, 15–024—15–029
prescriptive nature of regulation, 15–003
prohibition orders, 15–025
proposed legislation, 15–032—15–034
protected investment, 15–022

Building Societies,—cont.
prudent management, 15–014
Prudential notes, 15–014
raising funds, 15–017
reform proposals, 15–007, 15–032—15–034
sanctions, 15–024—15–029
scope of business, 15–002
services, 15–023
statutory regulation, 15–008
stock market flotation, 15–004
supervision, 14–004
traditional role, 15–001
unsecured loans, 15–019

CAD,
commencement, 3–017
harmonisation through, 3–017
purpose, 3–017, 3–064
Cadbury Committee, 26–027
Calling for papers inquiry, 26–064—26–066
Capital,
financial resources rules. *See* **Financial resources rules**
qualifying, 3–063
Capital Adequacy Directive. *See* **CAD**
Capitalisation issue, 12–056
Carrying on insurance business, 10–011—10–016
Carrying on investment business,
appointed representatives, 2–031
authorisation. *See* **Authorisation**
Bank of England, 2–030
Central Board of Finance of the Church of England, 2–031
clearing houses, 2–030
court officials, 2–031
definition, 2–028
exemptions, 2–030, 2–031
investment business. *See* **Investment business**
liquidators, 2–031
listed institutions, 2–031
Lloyd's, 2–031, 11–016
meaning, 2–028
official receivers, 2–031
overseas investment exchanges, 2–030
recognised investment exchanges, 2–030

Carrying on investment business,—*cont.*
  scope, 2–029
  trustee in bankruptcy, 2–031
Central Board of Finance of the Church of England, 2–031
CHAPS, 16–028, 16–064
Charging orders. *See* **Confiscation of assets**
Cheat, conspiracy to, 18–001
Cheques, theft of, 16–023
Chose in action,
  appropriation of, 16–018
  cheques as, 16–019
  credit balances, 16–025
  debts as, 16–018
  meaning, 16–018
  types, 16–019
City Code. *See* **Code on Take-overs and Mergers**
City Disputes Panel, 4–064
City of London,
  Court of the Alderman of the City, 2–002
  regulation of workers in, 2–002
Clayton's Case, rule in, 27–033
Clearing house automated payment system order, 16–028, 16–064
Clearing houses,
  carrying on investment business exclusion, 2–030
Client accounts. *See* **Client money**
Client money,
  accounting properly for, 3–032
  application of rules, 3–031
  audit requirements, 3–032
  fiduciary, holding as, 3–032
  generally, 3–029
  IMRO, 3–035
  interest on, 3–032
  margined transaction bank account, 3–034
  misuse, 3–029
  PIA, 3–037
  regulation of dealings with, 3–031
  requirements, 3–032
  separation of, 3–029
  settlement bank account, 3–033
  SFA, 3–036
  Statement of Principle, 3–030
Co-operative movement, 15–001
Co-ordinated approach to regulation, 32–005—32–007

Code on Take-overs and Mergers,
  acquisition of shares, 13–028
  acting in concert, 13–034, 13–035
  announcement, 13–027
  application of, 13–023
  approach, 13–027
  asset valuations, 13–050
  cash offers, 13–037
  compliance, 13–025
  conduct during offer, 13–043—13–046
  connected exempt market makers, 13–055
  dealings, restrictions on, 13–028, 13–032
  documents,
    offeror, from, 13–047, 13–048
    requirements for, 13–043
  duty to act in best interests, 13–025
  European Commission, 13–038, 13–039
  flexible interpretation, 13–022
  general principles,
    13–024-55, App 5
    function, 13–024
    nature of, 13–024
    purpose, 13–024
  independent advice, 13–027
  information about companies, 13–044
  interpretation, 13–021, 13–022
  locked in shareholders, 13–033
  market makers, 13–055
  Monolpolies and Mergers Commission, 13–038, 13–039
  offeror's documents, 13–047, 13–048
  partial offers, 13–053
  possible offers, 13–052
  profit forecasts, 13–049
  provisions applicable to all offers, 13–040—13–042
  purchase of own shares, 13–054
  purpose, 13–020
  redemption, 13–054
  remaining shareholders, 13–033
  restrictions following offers, 13–052
  revision of offer, 13–051
  rights over shares, 13–028

INDEX

Code on Take-overs and Mergers,—*cont.*
rules,
acquisition of shares, 13–028
acting in concert, 13–034, 13–035
announcement, 13–027
approach, 13–027
asset valuations, 13–050
cash offers, 13–037
conduct during offer, 13–043—13–046
connected exempt market makers, 13–055
dealings, restrictions on, 13–028, 13–032
European Commission, 13–038, 13–039
function, 13–026
generally, 13–026
independent advice, 13–027
locked in shareholders, 13–033
market makers, 13–055
Monopolies and Mergers Commission, 13–038, 13–039
offeror's documents, 13–047, 13–048
partial ofers, 13–053
possible offers, 13–052
profit forecasts, 13–049
provisions applicable to all offers, 13–040—13–042
purchase of own shares, 13–054
purpose, 13–026
redemption, 13–054
remaining shareholders, 13–033—13–035
restrictions following offers, 13–052
revision of offer, 13–051
rights over shares, 13–028
terms of offer, 13–036, 13–037
timing of offer, 13–051
voluntary offer, 13–036, 13–037
structure, 13–020
terms of offer, 13–036, 13–037
timing of offer, 13–051
voluntary offer, 13–036, 13–037
Codes of practice,
SIB, 3–025

Cold calling,
enforcement of agreements, 2–045
freedom of establishment, 2–010
restrictions, 2–045
unenforceability of agreement, 2–045
Collective investment scheme,
characteristics required, 2–035
day to day control, 2–035
definition, 2–034
intervention powers, 4–030
investment business, 2–021
participants, 2–035
requirements, 2–035
Commission,
underwriters, 12–062
Common law,
background to protection, 28–001
conversion, 28–019
deceit. *See* **Deceit**
illegal transactions, 28–029
misrepresentation. *See* **Misrepresentation**
money had and received. *See* **Money had and received**
Common law actions,
breach of statutory obligation, 4–065
lack of remedies, 4–065—4–069
Company,
accounting records,
accuracy, 19–025
annual return, failure to deliver, 19–029
availability, 19–025
content, 19–025
defences, 19–028
delivery failure, 19–028
DTI prosecutions, 19–025
duty to keep, 19–026
failure to meet requirements, 19–025
inspection, 19–027
penalties, 19–026
registered office, at, 19–027
requirement to keep, 19–026
allotment of shares. *See* **Allotment of shares**
auditors' rights, 19–030, 19–031
consent to prosecute, 19–024
defendants, potential, 19–21
destruction of documents, 19–033

523

Company,—*cont.*
   directors. *See* **Directors**
   efficacy of regulation, 19–036
   false statements in prospectus, 19–035
   falsification of documents, 19–033
   financial assistance. *See* **Financial assistance for purchase of own shares**
   investigations,
      consent of Secretary of State for prosecution, 19–034
      destruction of documents, 19–033
      DTI powers, 19–032
      falsification of documents, 19–033
      mutilation of documents, 19–033
      objective, 19–032
      penalties, 19–034
      power, 19–032
   mutilation of documents, 19–033
   offences by company, 19–022
   officers, 19–023
   order of court, 21–008
   propsectus, false statements in, 19–035
   purchase of own shares. *See* **Purchase of own shares**
Company law. *See* **DTI; Directors; Minority shareholders interests**
Compensation,
   damages, 4–042, 4–043
   deceit, 28–008
   ICS. *See* **ICS**
   Investors Compensation Scheme. *See* **ICS**
   orders. *See* **Compensation orders**
   pension. *See* **Pensions Compensation Board**
   unauthorised trading, 4–005
Compensation orders,
   amount, 23–043, 23–048, 23–049
   application, 23–047
   changing financial circumstances, 23–049
   civil court action, 23–044
   confiscation and, 23–050, 23–051
   Crown Court enforcement, 23–046
   custodial penalty and, 23–045
   determination of amount, 23–049

Compensation orders,—*cont.*
   enforcement, 23–046
   extent of loss, 23–047
   general principles, 23–042
   imprisonment for default, 23–046
   inability to pay, 23–045
   intention, 23–044
   interest, 23–047
   more than one defendant, 23–048
   multiple victims, 23–048
   power to make, 23–042, 23–043
   procedure, 23–047
   reasons for not making, 23–043
   subject matter, 23–042
   time for payment, 23–046
Complaints,
   advertising, 2–044
   building societies, 15–030
   City Disputes Panel, 4–064
   IMRO, 4–060
   PIA,
      award, 4–058
      case fees, 4–057
      consideration of complaint, 4–055
      establishment of procedure, 4–054
      funding, 4–057
      impartiality, 4–054
      jurisdiction, 4–058
      mandatory jurisdiction, 4–058
      maximum compensation, 4–058
      Ombudsman Bureau, 4–054—4–059
      powers of Ombudsman, 4–056
      procedure, 4–055
      recommendations, 4–058
      rules, 4–055
      statistics, 4–059
      subject matter, 4–059
      time limits, 4–056
      voluntary jurisdiction, 4–058
   requirement for scheme, 4–052
   RPB, 4–053
   SFA,
      arbitration, 4–061
      compliance officer, 4–061
      cost, 4–061
      fines, 4–063
      procedure, 4–061
      review, 4–062
   suitability of investment, 3–038
   time limits, PIA, 4–056

INDEX

Complex procedure. *See*
Confiscation of assets
COMPS. *See* **Money purchase schemes**
Confidence, promoting, 2–010
Confiscation of assets,
amounts, 23–004
assessing benefit,
complex procedure, 23–015, 23–016
simple procedure, 23–010, 23–011
background, 23–001, 23–002
charging orders,
compensation, 23–037
conditions, 23–033
effect, 23–041
importance, 23–034
jurisdiction, 23–036
procedure, 23–041
statutory basis, 23–030, 23–033
uses, 23–034
compensation orders. *See*
Compensation orders
complex procedure,
assessing benefit, 23–015, 23–016
assumptions, 23–016
benefit, 23–015, 23–016
condition of offence, 23–014
introduction, 23–005
power of court, 23–013
purpose, 23–005
qualifying offence, 23–013, 23–014
statutory basis, 23–003
written notice by prosecution, 23–013, 23–017
defendant providing information, 23–018
deprivation orders, 23–055
drug trafficking legislation, 23–001
enforcement of order,
distribution of proceeds, 23–023
fines, 23–021
High Court, 23–023
imprisonment, 23–021
instalments, payment by, 23–021
interest, 23–022
magistrates' court, 23–021

Confiscation of assets,—*cont.*
enforcement of orders,—*cont.*
proceeds of realisation, 23–023
sanctions, 23–021
function, 23–001
government departments'
disclosure of information,
application, 23–027
conditions for, 23–027
CPS members, 23–030
Customs officer, 23–030
investigating crimes, 23–031
police officers, 23–030
private prosecuter, 23–032
receivers, 23–029
requirement, 23–027
statutory basis, 23–027
subject matter, 23–028
Hodgson Committee report, 23–001
information provided by defendant, 23–018
introduction of legislation, 23–001
investigations into proceeds of criminal conduct,
conditions for, 23–024
purpose, 23–024
search warrant, 23–025
seizure and, 23–026
orders,
amounts, 23–004
procedure, 23–004
statutory basis, 23–003
prevention of terrorism, 23–001
provision of information by defendant, 23–018
purpose, 23–001
restitution orders. *See* **Restitution orders**
restraint orders,
application, 23–035
conditions for, 23–033
dicretionary nature, 23–036
discharge, 23–039
ex parte application, 23–035
importance, 23–034
innocent third parties, 23–037
jurisdiction, 23–036
living and legal expenses, 23–037
scope of, 23–038

Confiscation of assets,—*cont.*
  restraint orders,—*cont.*
    seizure by constable, 23–039
    self-incrimination, 23–036
    statutory basis, 23–033
    uses, 23–034
  review of cases,
    factors affecting, 23–020
    procedure, 23–020
    provision for, 23–019
    reasons for, 23–019
    revision, 23–020
    upward revision, 23–020
  revision of order, 23–020
  self incrimination, 23–011
  simple procedure,
    amount to be recovered, 23–012
    appropriate uses, 23–006
    assumptions made, 23–010
    benefit, determination of, 23–010, 23–011
    civil proceedings, 23–012
    court initiating, 23–007
    determination of benefit, 23–011, 23–010
    duty of court, 23–006
    exceptions, 23–006
    limitations, 23–004
    offence of a relevant description, 23–008
    purpose, 23–004
    reasonable excuse, 23–010, 23–011
    relevant criminal conduct, 23–009
    self incrimination, 23–011
    statutory basis, 23–0003, 23–006
    written notice by prosecution, 23–006, 23–007
  written notice by prosecution,
    accuracy, 23–017
    complex procedure, 23–013, 23–017
    content of statement, 23–017
    information provided by defendant, 23–018
    requirement, 23–017
    simple procedure, 23–006, 23–007

Conflict of interest,
  directors, 26–015

Conflict of interests,
  nominated trustees, 7–010, 7–020, 7–021

Conspiracy,
  availability of remedy, 28–015
  cheat, to, 18–001
  common law offences, 18–001
  corrupting public morals, 18–001
  defraud, to,
    abolition proposals, 18–022
    definition, 18–012—18–014
    deliberate dishonesty, 18–014
    detriment to other, 18–014
    development of law, 18–009
    generally, 18–001
    indictable offences, 18–011
    Law Commission report, 18–022
    meaning, 18–012—18–014
    penalty, 18–010
    prejudice to another, 18–014
    reform of law, 18–022
    regulatory body. *See* regulatory body, defrauding *Below*
    retention of offence, 18–009
    statutory provisions, 18–010
  difficulties of action, 28–017, 28–018
  "dishonestly", 18–020
  forms, 28–015
  "fraudulently", 18–020
  general principles, 18–001
  generally, 18–001
  injuring interest of another, 28–015
  intention, 18–006
  jurisdiction, 18–021
  Law Commission, 18–022
  mental element, 18–006
  outraging public decency, 18–001
  predominant purpose, 28–015
  proving, 18–006
  reform of law, 18–022
  regulatory body, defrauding, 18–015—18–019
    deceit, 18–017
    disclosure of information, 18–018
    economic loss, 18–015—18–019
    example, 18–015
    "intent to defraud", 18–016
    public body, 18–019
  relationship between parties, 28–016

Conspiracy,—*cont.*
  sole director of company, 18–005
  spouses, 18–005
  Statement of Claim, 28–016
  statutory,
    advantages of charge, 18–007
    definition, 18–002
    duration of agreement, 18–005
    intention, 18–006
    meaning, 18–002
    mental element, 18–006
    offence, 18–002
    penalty, 18–003
    proving, 18–006
    requirements, 18–004
    rolled up count, 18–008
    sole director of company, 18–005
    spouses, 18–005
  unlawful means, using, 28–015
Constructive trusts,
  assistance, 27–028
  dishonest assistance, 27–018
  dishonest knowledge, 27–015
  dishonest receipt, 27–018
  funds held on trust, 27–026, 27–027
  intermeddling with funds, 27–026
  knowing assistance, 27–018
  knowing receipt, 27–018
  liability for breach of trust, 27–029
  problems, 27–015, 27–016
  resolution of problem, 27–015, 27–018
  state of mind of trustee, 27–016
Consumer Arbitration Scheme,
  SFA, 4–061
Contempt of court, 4–014
Contract notes, 12–022
Contracting out,
  APP, 8–010, 8–011
    exception to requirement, 8–007
  buying back guaranteed minumum pensions, 8–002
  certificates, 8–006
  commencement of provisions, 8–002
  COMPS, 8–005, 8–010, 8–011
  COSRS, 8–004, 8–005
  criteria, 8–006
  effect, 8–003

Contracting out,—*cont.*
  GMP,
    deferment, 8–012, 8–013
    exception to requirement, 8–007
    indexation, 8–013
    meaning, 8–002
    revaluation, 8–012, 8–013
  guaranteed minimum pensions,
    deferment, 8–012, 8–013
    exception to requirement, 8–007
    indexation, 8–013
    meaning, 8–002
    revaluation, 8–012, 8–013
  introduction of provisions, 8–002
  money purchase schemes, 8–005, 8–010, 8–011
  new requirements, 8–006, 8–007
  PAD, 8–002
  prescribed requirements, 8–007
  Principal Appointed Day, 8–002
  quality test, 8–007
  rebate, 8–003
  requirements of scheme, 8–006
  salary related schemes, 8–04, 8–005
  scheme-based test,
    actuarial certification, 8–009
    certificates, 8–009, 8–014, 8–015
    generally, 8–007
    Occupational Pensions Board role, 8–009
    practice, 8–014, 8–015
    procedure, 8–014, 8–015
    renewal of certificates, 8–015
    requirements, 8–008
    transitional provisions, 8–015
Contracts for differences,
  betting contracts, 2–017
  investment, as, 2–016
  meaning, 2–017
Contributions, schedule of,
  money purchase schemes, 7–034
  occupational pensions, 7–031
Contributory negligence, 29–027
Conversion, 28–019
Cooling off period,
  insurance companies, 10–049
Copying a false instrument, 16–075
Copyright,
  self-incrimination, 31–050
Core Conduct of Business Rules.
  See **Core rules**

Core rules,
adaption, 3–023
ambit, 3–024
application of, 3–022
breaches, 3–024
burdensome compliance, 3–023
changing, 3–024
content, App 4
contravention, 3–024
customer agreements, 3–048, 3–051
financial resources rules, 3–060
general effect, 3–023
list of, App 4
objectives, 3–023
second tier of regulation, 3–022—3–024
subject matter, 3–022
Cork Committee, 17–002, 30–016
Corporate bodies, transactions between,
investment business exclusion, 2–024
Corrupting puplic morals,
conspiracy to, 18–001
COSRS, 8–004, 8–005
Costs,
investigations, 4–024
parties to civil action, 30–022
Council of Lloyd's. *See* **Lloyd's**
Counterfeiting. *See* **Forgery**
Court of the Alderman of the City, 2–002
Court intervention. *See* **Enforcement of financial services regulation**
Court officials, 2–031
Creating a false or misleading impression. *See* **Inducing an investment**
Creditors,
fraudulent trading, 17–013, 17–015—17–017, 26–058
Criminal law,
See also **Offences**
conspiracy. *See* **Conspiracy**
fraud. *See* **Fraud**
non-investment specific offences, 1–015
range of offences, 1–015
recognition of investor interests, 1–015

Criminal law,—*cont.*
sources of law, 1–015, 1–016
theft. *See* **Theft Act offences**
unauthorised trading, 4–003, 4–004
Criminal procedure,
generally, 25–001
Serious Fraud Office. *See* **Serious Fraud Office**
Cromer Report, 11–002, 11–038
Cross-examination order,
availability, 31–024
consent, 31–024—31–035
exercise of discretion, 31–018
grounds, 31–017
guidance on making, 31–020—31–023
reasons, 31–017
scope, 31–023
shorthand note of, 31–023
suspicions as ground for, 31–019
ulterior purpose, 31–019
Crown Prosecution Service,
code, 25–022
decision not to prosecute,
generally, 25–021, 25–022
implications of decision, 25–022
jurisdiction of court, 25–023
reaching decision, 25–022
Custody of false instrument, 16–077
Customer agreement,
contents, 3–049
core rule, 3–048, 3–051
general, 3–048, 3–049
IMRO, 3–050, 3–051
key feature document, 3–054
nature of, 3–048
PIA, 3–053, 3–054
presentation, 3–050, 3–054
purpose, 3–048
SFA, 3–052
subject matter, 3–049

Damages, 4–042, 4–043
compensation, 4–042
deceit, 28–008
defence, 4–042
seeking, 4–042
"Dawn raids", 13–056

INDEX

Deceit,
careless, 28–005
compensation, 28–008
damages, 28–008
evidence, 28–006, 28–007
false representation, 28–002, 28–003
forseeability of loss, 28–008
general principal, 28–002—28–008
ingredients, 28–002
lack of honest belief, 28–005
proof of fraud, 28–006, 28–007
reckless, 28–004
representation, false, 28–002, 28–003
requiremants, 28–002
standard of proof, 28–007
state of mind of defendant, 28–002, 28–004, 28–005
Deception. See **Obtaining property by deception**
Deeds of trust, construction, 1–007
Delegation,
occupational trustees' investment power, 7–037, 7–039
Department of Trade and Industry. See **DTI**
Deposit Protection Fund. See **Banking**
Deposits. See **Banking**
Deprivation orders, 23–055
Derivates, directors' dealings in, 20–020
Directors,
acting in good faith, 26–008
Audit Committees, 26–027, 26–028
bankrupt, 22–029
Cadbury Committee, 26–027
care and skill, duty of,
ability of director, 26–019
contract of service, 26–021
drafting obligations, 26–021
meaning, 26–019
objective test, 26–020
practical operation, 26–020
collateral purposes, 26–011
compete, not to, 26–018
conflict of interest, 26–015
conviction for indictable offence. See **Disqualification of directors**

Directors,—*cont.*
de facto, 26–003
de jure, 26–003
definition, 22–003
derivates, dealing in, 20–020
dishonesty, 16–008
disqualification. See **Disqualification of directors**
duties,
acting in good faith, 26–008
care and skill,
ability of director, 26–019
contract of service, 26–021
drafting obligations, 26–021
meaning, 26–019
objective test, 26–020
practical operation, 26–020
compete, not to, 26–018
conflict of interest, 26–015
exercise, 26–005
fiduciary. See **fiduciary duty** *below*
generally, 26–003
good faith, acting in, 26–008
importance, 26–004
interests of company, 26–009, 26–010
nature of, 26–004
proper purposes, acting for, 26–011, 26–012
regulatory rules, 26–006
scope, 26–005
secret profits,
duty not to make, 26–016
general rule, 26–016
rejected opportunities, 26–017
skill and care, meaning, 26–019
trusteeship, 26–013, 26–014
false statement in notification, 19–009, 19–010
families, share dealings by, 19–005
fiduciary duty, 19–001, 21–017
associated company, 26–007
Law Commission report, 26–006
meaning, 26–007
regulatory rules, 26–006
shareholders, 26–007
subsidiary company, 26–007
financial advantage, taking, 19–002
fraudulent trading, 22–027, 22–028

529

Directors,—*cont.*
good faith, acting in, 26–008
Hampel Committee, 26–027
incompetence, 22–019
insider dealing, 20–009
insolvent, 22–017
interest in contracts, 19–003, 19–004
interest in shares, 19–009, 19–010
interests of company, 26–009, 26–010
loans to,
   connected persons, 19–015
   credit transaction, 19–012, 19–013
   defence, 19–014
   exceptions, 19–016
   fines, 19–014
   group companies, 19–016
   guarantees, 19–012, 19–013
   ordinary course of business, 19–016
   penalties, 19–014
   prohibited transaction, 19–013
   quasi-loans, 19–012, 19–013
   restrictions, 19–012
   shadow directors, 19–014
   statutory provisions, 19–012
making false statement in notification, 19–009, 19–010
management of company by, 26–004
meaning, 26–003
negligence, disqualification for, 22–019
non-executive, 26–027, 26–028
notification of interest in shares, 19–009, 19–010
number required, 26–003
options, prohibition on dealing in, 19–006, 19–007
parties to civil action. *See* **Parties to civil action**
personal liability, 30–002 *et seq.*
probity, lack of, 22–019
proper purposes, acting for, 26–011, 26–012
purpose, 19–001, 26–004
register of interests, 19–011
relieving from liability, 26–022—26–026
   consent of members, 26–023

Directors,—*cont.*
relieving from liability,—*cont.*
   honest and reasonable actions, 26–026
   professional indemnity insurance, 26–024
   ratification of general meeting, 26–022
remuneration, 19–002
requirement to have, 26–003
secret profits,
   duty not to make, 26–016
   general rule, 26–016
   rejected opportunities, 26–017
shadow directors, 19–014, 26–003
share dealings, 19–005
share options, prohibition on dealing in, 19–006, 19–007
taking financial advantage, 19–002
trust, breach of,
   constructive trustee, 26–014
   financial assistance for purchase of own shares, 21–017
   generally, 26–013
undischarged bankrupt, 22–029
unfitness, disqualification. *See* **Disqualification of directors**
Discipline. *See* **Enforcement of financial services regulation**
Dishonesty. *See* **Theft**
Dispute resolution of pensions,
compensation. *See* **Pensions Compensation Board**
establishing, 9–002
exclusions, 9–002
Industrial Tribunals, 9–020
non-compliance with requirements, 9–002
Occupational Pensions Advisory Service (OPAS). *See* **OPAS**
ombudsman. *See* **Pensions Ombudsman**
OPAS. *See* **OPAS**
operation, 9–002
penalties, 9–002
prescribed persons, 9–002
procedural requirements, 9–002
requirements, 9–002
Disqualification,
automatic, 6–026
directors. *See* **Disqualification of directors**
occupational pension scheme trustees, 6–025—6–028

INDEX

Disqualification,—*cont.*
register, 6–027
trustees, 6–025—6–028, 7–016, 7–017
Disqualification of directors,
bankrupt, 22–029
compensation order coupled with, 22–015
conduct, 22–019
contravention of order, 22–030
conviction for indictable offence,
  compensation order coupled with, 22–015
  connection with management of company, 22–007—22–010
Court, 22–005
discretion, 22–006
internal management of company, 22–007, 22–008
length of disqualification, 22–011—22–014
management of company, 22–007—22–010
period of, 22–011—22–014
persistent failure to file accounts, 22–014
statutory provisions, 22–004
de facto directors, 22–0032
definition of director, 22–003
fraudulent trading, 22–27, 22–028
generally, 22–001
importance of procedure, 22–001
incompetence, 22–019
insolvent, 22–017
nature of, 22–002
negligence, 22–019
period,
  conviction for indictable offence, when, 22–011—22–014
  fraudulent trading, 22–028
  persistent breach of companies legislation, 22–014
  public interest disqualification, 22–026
  unfitness, 22–022
  wrongful trading, 22–028
persistent breach of companies legislation,
  period of disqualification, 22–014
scope, 22–016
statutory provisions, 22–016

Disqualification of directors,—*cont.*
powers of court, 22–001
probity, lack of, 22–019
public interest, 22–025, 22–26
register, 22–031
shadow directors, 22–033
statutory basis, 22–001
undischarged bankrupt, 22–029
unfitness,
  applications, 22–018
  conduct, 22–017
  duty of court, 22–017
  incompetence, 22–019
  insolvency, 22–017
  negligence, 22–019
  no knowledge of insolvency, 22–021
  period of disqualification, 22–022
  probity, lack of, 22–19
  procedure, 22–023, 22–024
  proving, 22–019
  standard, 22–019
wrongful trading, 22–027, 22–028
Divorce,
occupational pension scheme, 8–017—8–021
court's duty, 8–017
factors affecting court order, 8–020
importance, 8–017
jurisdiction of court, 8–017
lump sums, 8–021
maintenance, 8–018
Scotland, 8–023
Scotland, 8–023
Domestic Equity Market, 12–033
DTI,
action following investigation, 26–061
application for investigation, 26–068
authorised persons, 26–081
calling for papers inquiry, 26–064—26–066
civil proceedings, 26–076
confidential issues, 26–084
court order, 26–070
disclosure of transcripts, 26–082—26–085
documents,
  disclosure of, 26–082—26–085
  required, 26–064—26–066

INDEX

DTI,—*cont.*
  entry powers, 26–067
  holding companies investigated, 26–071
  inspections, 26–064—26–066
  inspectors, 26–060
  investigation,
    action following, 26–061
    application, 26–069
    authorised persons, 26–081
    central clearing house proposals, 26–063
    confidence, 26–084
    disclosure of documents obtained during, 26–082—26–085
    failure to comply with requirements, 26–073
    holding companies, 26–071
    inspectors, by, 26–060
    object, 26–061
    ownership of company, 26–077, 26–078
    privileged information, 26–080
    requests, 26–062
    responsibility, 26–062
    restrictions on shares, 26–078
    Secretary of State discretion, 26–068
    self-incrimination. *See* **Self-incrimination**
    share dealings, 26–079
    subsidiary companies, 26–071
    transcripts obtained during, 26–082—26–085
  object of investigation, 26–061
  ownership of company investigated, 26–077, 26–078
  powers, 26–060 *et seq.*
  privileged information, 26–080
  reasons for investigation, 26–070
  responsibility for investigations, 26–062
  restrictions on shares, 26–078
  search of premises, 26–067
  Secretary of State discretion, 26–068
  share dealings, 26–079
  share restrictions, 26–078
  subsidiary companies, 26–071
  transcripts, disclosure of, 26–082—26–085

EAI, 14–004
Electronic transfers,
  theft, 16–028
  valuable securities, 16–064
Employee's share scheme, 2–026
Employer's associations,
  authorisation, 10–011
Enforcement,
  compensation orders, 23–046
  confiscation orders. *See* **Confiscation orders**
  contract of sale, 21–017
  financial services regulation. *See* **Enforcement of financial regulation**
  inadequacy in, 32–010, 32–011
  listing obligations, 12–040
  PTM code, 13–002
  Yellow Book, 12–050
Enforcement of financial services regulation,
  administration order, 4–037
  court intervention,
    compelling investigation, 4–041
    judicial review, 4–041
    reluctance, 4–038
    representations, 4–040
    restraining enforcement action, 4–038—4–041
    urgent, 4–039
  discipline,
    examples, 4–034
    non-compliance, 4–034
    publicity, 4–035
    range of powers, 4–034
    requirements of SFA, 4–034
    SFA Disciplinary Tribunal, 4–034
    SRO Disciplinary Tribunals, 4–035
    tribunals, 4–034, 4–035
    types, 4–034
  generally, 4–001
  inadequacy in, 32–010, 32–011
  informant,
    identity, 4–026
    journalist, obtaining identity from, 4–026
    liability, 4–025
  information provision, 4–020, 4–021

Enforcement of financial services regulation,—*cont.*
injunctions. *See* **Injunctions**
inspections, 4–017
intervention powers,
  authorised person, prohibition on, 4–028
  collective investment schemes, 4–030
  conditions for exercise, 4–027
  RPB, 4–027
  sanctions, 4–028
  scope, 4–027
  SIB, 4–027, 4–028
  SRO, 4–029
investigations. *See* **Investigations**
levels of, 4–001
liability of informant, 4–025
methods, 4–015, 4–016
monitoring, 4–016
resources for, 4–015
restraint of assets orders. *See* **Injunctions; Restraint of assets** orders
unauthorised trading. *See* **Unauthorised trading**
winding up, 4–036
withdrawal of authorisation, 4–031—4–033

Entry power,
Bank of England, 14–073, 14–079
DTI, 26–067
OPRA, 6–034

Equal treatment,
occupational pensions, 8–024—8–035

Equitas, 11–047—11–050
establishment, 11–046
function, 11–046
reasons for establishing, 11–047
RITC, 11–047

Estate agencies, 15–020
Eurobondmarkets, 20–057
European Authorised Institutions (EAI), 14–004, 14–077
European Commission,
Code on Take-overs and Mergers, 13–038, 13–039

European Community law,
development of law, 1–024

European Convention for the Protection of Human Rights and Fundamental Freedoms, 31–028, 31–053, 31–058

European Economic Area,
jurisdiction, 2–048

European law,
CAD. *See* **CAD**
financial resources rules, 3–064
insider information, 20–016
insurance companies, 10–031
ISD. *See* **ISD**
listing, 12–044, 12–063
money laundering, 24–002
PTM, 13–006

European Union,
Directive,
  capital adequacy, 2–009, 3–017. *See also* **CAD**
  investment services, 2–009, 3–017. *See also* **ISD**
harmonisation of financial services regulation, 2–009, 3–017
unit trusts, 2–036

Europersons,
authorisation, 3–015—3–017
criminal offences by, 3–016
definition, 3–015
meaning, 3–015

Evidence,
bankers trusts orders, 31–043
deceit, 28–006, 28–007
investigation, statements from, 4–024
money laundering, 24–039
summary judgment, 31–061

Expenses,
trustees, occupational pensions, 7–061

False accounting,
accounting purpose, documents required for, 16–058
definition, 16–056
gain, view to, 16–059—16–061
intent to cause loss, 16–059—16–061
problem of, 16–055
punishment, 16–055

False accounting,—*cont.*
  records, 16–056, 16–057
  sanctions, 16–055
  statutory provisions, 16–056
  uses, 16–055
  view to gain, 16–059—16–061
Fiduciary duty, breach of,
  financial assistance for purchase of own shares, 21–017
FIMBRA, 3–010
  risk, 3–046
  suitability of investments, 3–041
FIMBRO,
  advertising standards, 3–059
Financial assistance for purchase of own shares,
  asset reduction, 21–018, 21–022
  background to rule, 21–012—21–014
  bonus shares allotment, 21–032
  breach of prohibition, 21–016
  breach of trust, 21–017
  civil law consequences of breach, 21–017
  commercial justification, 21–028
  commission of offence, 21–016
  criminal offence, 21–016
  criticisms, 21–042—21–044
  decriminalisation proposals, 21–044
  directors, 21–017
  dividend payment, 21–032
  employee share schemes, 21–032
  employees, loans to, 21–032
  enforcement of contract of sale, 21–017
  examples, 21–020
  exceptions,
    bonus shares allotment, 21–032
    dividend payment, 21–032
    employee share schemes, 21–032
    employees, loans to, 21–032
    larger purpose. *See* larger purpose exception *below*
    loans to employees, 21–032
    money lending institutions, 21–032
    principal purpose, 21–026—21–028
  fact, question of, 21–024
  fiduciary duty, breach of, 21–017

Financial assistance for purchase of own shares,—*cont.*
  financial assistance,
    asset reduction, 21–018, 21–022
    definition, 21–018
    examples, 21–020
    fact, question of, 21–024
    gifts, 21–018
    guarantees, 21–018
    indemnity, 21–018, 21–023
    loans, 21–018, 21–021
    scope of definition, 21–019
    security, 21–018
    statutory definition, 21–018
  foreign subsidiaries, 21–025
  gifts, 21–018
  guarantees, 21–018
  history of rule, 21–012—21–014
  indemnity, 21–018, 21–023
  Jenkins Committee, 21–013, 21–014
  larger purpose exception,
    definition, 21–029
    judicial interpretation, 21–029, 21–030
    meaning, 21–029
    narrow construction, 21–030
    purpose of assistance, 21–031
    reason and purpose distinguished, 21–030
    statutory basis, 21–026, 21–027
  loans, 21–018, 21–021
  minority shareholder interests, 21–041
  money lending institutions, 21–032
  officer of the company, 21–016
  penalties, 21–016
  practical operation, 21–042—21–044
  principal purpose exception, 21–026—21–028
  private companies,
    conditions for exemption, 21–035
    exemption, 21–034
    minority shreholder interests, 21–041
    procedure for exemption, 21–034
    special resolution, 21–039
    statutory declaration, 21–035—21–038

Financial assistance for purchase of own shares,—*cont.*
  private companies,—*cont.*
    timetable, 21–040
  prohibition,
    breach, 21–016
    purpose, 21–013
    statutory basis, 21–015
  public companies, 21–033
  purpose of prohibition, 21–013
  reduction in assets, 21–018, 21–022
  reform proposals, 21–042—21–044
  security, 21–018
  severance, 21–017
  trust, breach of, 21–017
Financial Intermediaries, Managers and Brokers Regulatory Association, 3–010
Financial reporting,
  PIA, 3–075
  SFA, 3–073
Financial resources rules,
  calculation, 3–063, 3–064
  capital, qualifying, 3–063
  core rule, 3–060
  determining, 3–064
  E.U. Directive, 3–064
  general rule, 3–060
  IMRO,
    application of rules, 3–067
    calculation, 3–069
    category of member, 3–067, 3–068
    exceptions, 3–066
    generally, 3–066
    gross capital requirement, 3–068, 3–069
    liquid capital requirement, 3–068, 3–070, 3–071
    returns, 3–071
  member, category of, 3–064
  monitoring, 3–064
  PIA, 3–074, 3–075
  purpose, 3–060, 3–062
  qualifying capital, 3–063
  reasons for, 3–062
  returns, 3–064
  risk, 3–064
  SFA, 3–071—3–073
  SROs, 3–065
  statement of principle, 3–060

Financial services regulation,
  advertising. *See* **Advertising**
  arranging deals, 2–020
  background to legislation, 2–002, 2–003
  carrying on investment business. *See* **Carrying on investment business**
  cold calling. *See* **Cold calling**
  collective investment schemes. *See* **Collective investment schemes**
  commencement, 2–011
  definition of investment, 1–008, 2–016, 2–017
  enforcement. *See* **Enforcement of financial services regulation**
  European influence, 2–008—2–010
  financial resources. *See* **Financial resources rules**
  framework, 2–011—2–014
  fraud prevention legislation, 2–004—2–006
  freedom of establishment, 2–010
  investment business. *See* **Investment business**
  investments,
    betting as, 2–017
    definition, 1–008, 2–016, 2–017
  jurisdiction, 2–047
  key concepts, 2–015 *et seq.*
  life insurance. *See* **Life insurance**
  overview of legislation, 2–001 *et seq.*, 3–001, 3–002
  range, 2–012
  risk, understanding. *See* **Risk**
  scope, 2–012
  Securities and Investment Board. *See* **SIB**
  SIB. *See* **SIB**
  suitability of investment. *See* **Suitability of investment**
  supervision of scheme, 2–013
  unit trusts. *See* **Unit trusts**
  unsolicited calls. *See* **Cold calling**
  White Paper on Financial Services in the United Kingdom, 2–007
Fines,
  OPRA, 6–029
  SFA, 4–063

535

Fisher Report, 11–039
FIU, 24–045
Forfeiture,
　occupational pensions, 7–088
Forgery,
　control of false instrument,
　　16–077
　copying a false instrument,
　　16–075
　custody of false instrument,
　　16–077
　discs, 16–072
　electronic documents, 16–072
　essence of, 16–071
　false, 16–074
　instrument, 16–072, 16–078
　intention, 16–072
　offence, 16–072
　penalties, 16–078
　prejudice, 16–072, 16–074
　preservation of information,
　　16–073
　statutory provisions, 16–072
　using a false instrument, 16–076
Foss v. Harbottle, rule in,
　derivative actions,
　　costs, 26–038
　　general rule, 26–037
　　indemnities, 26–038
　　liquidation, 26–040
　　ulterior purposes, 26–039
　effect of rule, 26–031
　exceptions to rule, 26–032
　fraud on a minority,
　　establishment of rule, 26–033
　　"fraud", 26–034
　　meaning, 26–033, 26–034
　meaning, 26–031
　propositions forming, 26–031
　unfair prejudice. *See* **Unfair prejudice**
　wrongdoer control, 26–035,
　　26–036
Fraud,
　prevention legislation,
　　2–004—2–006
　problems of prosecuting, 1–016
　witnesses, reluctant, 1–016
Fraudulent trading,
　active participation, 17–009
　aiding and abetting, 17–010

Fraudulent trading,—*cont.*
　carrying on of business,
　　17–005—17–008
　civil sanction, 26–057
　company, 17–002
　company receivers, 17–014
　company secretaries, 17–009
　conduct as part of business,
　　17–005—17–008
　controlling functions, 17–009
　Cork Committee, 17–002
　creditors, 17–013,
　　17–015—17–017, 26–058
　criminal offence, 17–003, 17–004
　development of law, 17–002
　director's liability, 26–059
　disqualification of directors,
　　22–27, 22–028
　elements of offence, 17–004
　establishing offence, 17–004
　example, 17–001
　fraudulent purpose, 17–018,
　　17–019
　individual, 17–002
　instructions of others, 17–010
　intent to defraud,
　　company receivers, 17–014
　　creditors, 17–013
　　definition, 17–012
　　generally, 17–011
　　meaning, 17–012
　　prejudice to others, 17–013
　　"to defraud", 17–013
　intent to defraud creditors, 26–058
　jury directions, 17–008
　managerial functions, 17–009
　participation, 17–009
　party to carrying on of business,
　　17–009, 17–010
　prosecutions, 17–001
　proving offence, 17–004
　salesmen, 17–009
　secondary parties, 17–010
　typical case, 17–001
　uses of offence, 17–001
Freedom of establishment,
　cold calling, 2–010
　financial services regulation,
　　2–010
Friendly Societies, 15–001
　authorisation, 10–011

Funding,
  Deposit Protection fund, 14–095
  ICS, 4–044—4–047
  OPRA, 6–019
  Pensions Compensation Board, 9–017
  PIA Ombudsman Bureau, 4–057
  SIB, 2–014
  SRO, 3–006

Gaming legislation, 2–017
Gifts,
  financial assistance for purchase of own shares, 21–018
GMP,
  buying back, 8–002
  contracting out, *See* **Contracting out**
Good faith, directors acting in, 26–008
Goode Report,
  See also **Occupational pensions**
  adoption of recommendations, 6–008
  appointment, 6–007
  background to, 6–007
  commissioning, 6–007
  function, 6–007
  Occupational Pensions Regulatory Authority, 6–016
  purpose, 6–007
  recommendations, 6–007
  response to recommendations, 6–008
  state pensions, 8–016
  surpluses, occupational pension scheme, 7–065
  trustees, occupational pensions, 7–003
Gower Report,
  balance in protection, 1–025
  commissioning, 2–006
  jurisdiction, 2046
  publication, 2–006
  purpose of review, 2–006
  recommendations, fraud prevention legislation, 2–006
Guaranteed minimum pensions,
  buying back, 8–002
  contracting out. *See* **Contracting out**

Guarantees,
  financial assistance for purchase of own shares, 21–018

Hampel Committee, 26–027
Harmonisation of financial services regulation, 2–009, 3–017
Harrods Bank, 14–101
Hodgson Committee, 23–001
Holding companies,
  parties to civil action, 30–009

ICS,
  commencement of scheme, 4–049
  courts' approach, 4–051
  cross contribution, 4–045
  establishment, 4–044
  extent of liabilities, 4–048
  function, 4–044
  funding, 4–044—4–047
  history of, 4–046
  levies, 4–045
  limiting compensation, 4–049
  operation, 4–044
  personal representatives, 4–050
  purpose, 4–044
  scope, 4–048—4–051
  statutory regulation, 4–044
IMAS, 12–017, 20–041
IMRO,
  advertising standards, 3–057
  authorisation, 3–012, 3–013
  categories of memeber, 3–067, 3–068
  client money, 3–035
  complaints, 4–060
  customer agreement, 3–050, 3–051
  financial resources rules. *See* **Financial resources rules**
  function, 3–012, 3–013
  mission statement, 3–012, 3–013
  monitoring, 4–018
  OPS assets regulated by, 3–013
  purpose, 3–012
  risk, 3–044
  suitability of investment, 3–039
Indemnity,
  financial assistance for purchase of own shares, 21–018, 21–023
Individual pension contract, 5–012

Inducing an investment,
creating a false or misleading
impression,
artificial devices, 20–050
defences, 20–056, 20–057
determining creation, 20–049
engaging in conduct, 20–052
examples, 20–050
"false or misleading
impression",
20–049—20–051
false price or value, 20–053
inducing another to act, 20–055
intent, 20–054
matched orders, 20–050
objectively incorrect, 20–049
price stabilsation rules, 20–057
scope of offence, 20–051
statutory provision, 20–048
wash sales, 20–050
creation of offences, 20–042
defences, creating a false or
misleading impression,
20–056, 20–057
dishonesty, 20–046. *See also* **Theft**
investment, 20–047
jurisdiction, 20–058
matched orders, 20–050
penalties, 20–059
practical operation, 20–060
price stabilisation rules, 20–57
problems, 20–060, 20–061
prosecutions, 20–061
recklessness, 20–045
scope of legislation, 20–042
several statements, 20–044
statutory provisions, 20–043
wash sales, 20–050
Industrial Tribunals,
dispute resolution of pensions,
9–020
Informants,
identity, 4–026
journalist, obtaining identity
from, 4–026
liability, 4–025
Information provision,
enforcement of financial services
regulation, 4–020, 4–021
insurance companies, by, 10–043,
10–044
OPRA, to, 6–033

Information provision,—*cont.*
RPB, 4–020
SIB requiring, 4–020, 4–021
SRO, 4–021
Injunctions,
advantages, 4–006
application, 4–008
conditions for grant, 4–006, 4–008
function, 4–006
knowingly concerned, 4–009
Mareva. *See* **Mareva injunctions**
OPRA, 6–031
payment into court, 4–007
provisions for granting, 4–006
purpose, 4–006
SIB application, 4–008
Insider dealing,
acquiring and disposing of
securities, statutory basis,
20–010, 20–011
background, 20–005—20–007
breach of confidence, 20–009
commission of offence, 20–010
confidence undermined by,
20–006
constructive trusts, 20–008
criminal sanctions, 20–008
criticisms, 20–036—20–041
dealing, 20–022
deals on and off market,
causal link, 20–023
definition of dealing, 2–022
requirement, 20–021
defences,
absence of intention, 20–26
available, 20–26
burden of proof, 20–027
good faith acting as market
maker, 20–29
market information, 20–030
market maker, 20–029
price stabilisation rules, 20–031
special, 20–029—20–031
statutory provisions, 20–028
derivatives, directors' dealings in,
20–020
Directive on, 20–006
directors, 20–009
disclosing inside information,
20–010, 20–011
effectiveness of legislation,
20–036—20–041

538

Insider dealing,—*cont.*
encouraging acquistion or disposal of securities,
companies, 20–012
statutory basis, 20–010, 20–011
fiduciary accountability, 20–009
firms, 20–012
forms of offence, 20–010
good faith acting as market maker, 20–029
"individual", 20–012
inside information,
definition, 20–15
E.C.Directive, 20–016
meaning, 20–015, 20–016
precise nature, 20–015, 20–016
price-affected securities, 20–015
specific nature, 20–015, 20–16
insider,
definition, 20–013
having information as an insider, 20–013, 20–014
source of information, 20–013, 20–014
inspections by SIB, 20–041
institution of proceedings, 20–033
Integrated Monitoring and Surveillance (IMAS), 20–041
introduction of offence, 20–004
jurisdiction, 20–034, 20–35
limited companies, 20–012
market information defence, 20–030
market maker, 20–029
meaning, 20–005
nature of, 20–005—20–007
offence, 20–010, 20–011
penalties, 20–032
price stabilisation rules, 20–031
price-affected securities, 20–015, 20–019, 20–020
professional intermediaries, 20–024
proof of offence, 20–010
public information,
confidentiality lost, 20–017
effect, 20–017
loss of confidentiality, 20–017
meaning, 20–017
publicly available data, 20–018
steps taken to obtain information, 20–018
reform proposals, 20–038

Insider dealing,—*cont.*
reported cases, 20–037
sanctions,
civil, 20–009
criminal, 20–008
scope of securities covered by, 20–019
secondary insider, 20–014
SIB investigation, 20–040
source of information, 20–13, 20–014
statutory regulation, 20–007
takeovers, 20–025
territorial scope, 20–035
unincorporated partnerships, 20–012
using information, 20–023
"victimless" crime, as, 20–006
Insolvency,
occupational pensions, contributions on, 8–042
Inspections,
DTI, 26–064—26–066
OPRA. *See* **OPRA**
PIA, 4–017
responsibility, 4–017
SFA, 4–019
SRO, 4–018
Insurance,
companies. *See* **Insurance companies liability,** 11–014
Insurance companies,
abstracts, 10–028
acceleration of information required, 10–042
accounts,
deposited documents, 10–028, 10–029
filing, 10–025
long-term business, 10–025
non-compliance with requirements, 10–026
preparation, 10–025
separate, 10–030
actuarial investigations, 10–041
actuary, requirement for, 10–027
advertisements, 10–047
annual statement of business, 10–025
assets,
custody, 10–039
maintenance in U.K., 10–038
auditor's report, 10–028

Insurance companies,—*cont.*
authorisation,
automatic, 10–021, 10–022
carrying on insurance business, 10–011—10–016
composite insurers, 10–019
exceptions, 10–011
false information, 10–018
Financial Services Act 1986, under, 10–021, 10–022
new composite insurers, 10–019
off-shore agents, 10–014
offences, 10–011
policy requirement, 10–016
requirement, 10–011
restricted, 10–017
Secretary of State, by, 10–017—10–019
unauthorised business, 10–012
unenforceability, 10–013
withdrawal, 10–020
balance sheets, 10–028
building societies, joint ventures with, 15–020
carrying on insurance business, 10–011—10–016
classification of business, 10–009, 10–010
composite insurers, 10–019
conduct of business,
advertisements, 10–047
cooling off period, 10–049
intermediaries, 10–048
withdrawal from transaction, 10–049
consolidation of legislation, 10–001
contracts,
misleading statements, 10–053—10–056
nature of, 10–003
regulated insurance companies, 10–050—10–052
controller, change of, 10–046
cooling off period, 10–049
custody of assets, 10–039
definition, 2–032
deposited documents, 10–028, 10–029
director, changes of, 10–046
filing accounts, 10–025

Insurance companies,—*cont.*
general business,
examples, 10–010
meaning, 10–009
importance of regulation, 10–002
information provision, 10–043, 10–044
"insurance business", 10–0024
intermediaries, 10–048
intervention by Secretary of State. *See* **Secretary of State** *below*
investments, requirement about, 10–037
key positions, changes in, 10–046
legislative control, 10–001 *et seq.*
limitation of premium income, 10–040
Lloyd's. *See* **Lloyd's**
long-term business,
accounts, 10–025
examples, 10–010
meaning, 10–009, 10–010
reinsurance, 10–010
maintenance of assets in U.K., 10–038
manager, change of, 10–046
misleading statements, 2–033, 10–053—10–056
new composite insurers, 10–019
notices to Secretary of State, 10–035
off-shore agents, 10–014
ombudsman. *See* **Insurance Ombudsman Bureau**
policyholder,
meaning, 10–008
protection, 10–045
production of documents, 10–043, 10–044
promotion of contracts, 2–033
protection of policy holders, 10–045
regulated,
activities restricted, 10–024
advertisements, 10–050
contracts, 10–050—10–052
definition, 10–023
generally, 2–032
"insurance business", 10–024
meaning, 10–023
restrictions, 10–024, 10–050
unenforceable contracts, 10–052
reinsurance, 10–010

Insurance companies,—*cont.*
  scheme of legislation,
    10–005—10–007
  Secretary of State,
    acceleration of information
      required, 10–042
    actuarial investigations, 10–041
    authorisation, 10–017—10–019
    considering exercising powers,
      10–036
    controller, change of, 10–046
    custody of assets, 10–039
    director, changes of, 10–046
    discretion, 10–033
    information provision to,
      10–043, 10–044
    intervention by,
      10–033—10–046
    investigation, 10–034
    investments, requirement about,
      10–037
    limitation of premium income,
      10–040
    maintenance of assets in U.K.,
      10–038
    manager, change of, 10–046
    notices to, 10–035
    powers, 10–033—10–046
    production of documents,
      10–043, 10–044
    protection of policy holders,
      10–015
    requirement about investments,
      10–037
  separate accounting, 10–030
  solvency requirement,
    calculation, 10–031
    E.C. Directive, 10–031
    meaning, 10–031
    non-compliance, 10–032
    short-term finance scheme,
      10–032
  statements, 10–025
  withdrawal, 10–020
    authorisation, 10–020
    transaction, from, 10–049
Insurance Ombudsman Bureau,
  complaints to, 10–057
  constitution, 10–058
  decisions, 10–058
  function, 10–057
  independence, 4–060

Insurance Ombudsman Bureau,—*cont.*
  judicial review, 10–058
  jurisdiction, 4–060
  membership of scheme, 10–057
  powers, 10–057
Integrated Monitoring and Surveillance (IMAS), 12–017, 20–041
Interdicts, 4–008
Interest in contracts, 19–003, 19–004
Interests, investor,
  balance in protecting, 1–025, 1–026
  European influence, 1–024
  international competiveness, 1–026
  property investment, 1–018—1–023
  re-active recognition, 1–018—1–016
  recognition, 1–010—1–023
  sources of law, 1–010—1–017
Intermediaries,
  insurance company, 10–048
  offer, 12–056
International competitiveness, 1–026
International Equity Market, 12–032
International Securities Self-Regulating Organisation,
  investment business exclusion, 2–026
Intervention powers,
  authorised person, prohibition on, 4–028
  collective investment schemes, 4–030
  conditions for exercise, 4–027
  RPB, 4–027
  scope, 4–027
  SIB, 4–027, 4–028
  SRO, 4–029
Investigations,
  companies. *See* **Company**
  costs, 4–024
  criminal conduct, proceeds of. *See* **Confisication of assets**
  DTI. *See* **DTI**
  evidential use, 4–024
  information provision, 4–024

Investigations,—*cont.*
  legal professional privilege, 4–024
  powers, 4–022, 4–023
  proceeds of criminal conduct. *See*
    Confiscation of assets
  purpose, 4–022
  RPB members, 4–023
  SIB powers, 4–022
  SRO members, 4–023
Investment,
  betting, 2–017
  definition, 1–003—1–009, 2–016, 2–017
  dictionary definition, 5
  meaning, 1–003
  occupational pensions. *See*
    Occupational pensions
  qualified definition, 1–004, 1–005
Investment business,
  advising on investments, 2–021
  arranging deals, 2–020
  carrying on in. *See* **Carrying on in investment business**
  collective investment scheme, 2–021
  corporate bodies, transactions between, 2–024
  dealing in investments, 2–019
  definition, 2–018—2–020
  employee's share scheme, 2–026
  excluded activities, 2–022—2–027
    corporate bodies, transactions between, 2–024
    employee's share scheme, 2–026
    International Securities Self-Regulating Organisation, 2–026
    joint ventures, 2–023
    media, advice in, 2–026
    non-investment business, 2–026
    overseas persons, 2–027
    own account dealings, 2–023
    permanent place of business in U.K., absence of, 2–027
    personal representatives' activities, 2–026
    publications , advice in, 2–026
    sale of bodies corporate, 2–026
    sale of goods, 2–025
    services' supply, 2–025
    trustee activities, 2–0126
  International Securities Self-Regulating Organisation, 2–026

Investment business,—*cont.*
  introduction of investor to, 2–020
  joint ventures, 2–023
  life insurance, 2–032, 2–033
  managing assets, 2–020
  media, advice in, 2–026
  non-investment business, 2–026
  overseas persons, 2–027
  own account dealings, 2–023
  permanent place of business in U.K., absence of, 2–027
  personal representatives' activities, 2–026
  publications, advice in, 2–026
  sale of bodies corporate, 2–026
  sale of goods, 2–025
  scope, 2–019, 2–029
  services' supply, 2–0125
  trustee activities, 2–026
Investment exchanges,
  overseas, 2–030
  recognition, 2–030
Investment income,
  meaning, 1–006
  surcharge, 1–006
Investment Management Regulatory Organisation. *See* **IMRO**
Investment Services Directive. *See* **ISD**
Investor,
  definition, 1–001, 1–003—1–005
  interests. *See* **Interests, investor**
Investors Compensation Scheme. *See* **ICS**
IOB. *See* **Insurance Ombudsman Bureau**
Irish Stock Exchange Limited, 12–009
Irrevocable letter of credit, 16–064
ISD,
  harmonisation through, 3–017
  implementation, 3–017
  scope, 3–017
Issue of securities. *See* **Securities**

Jenkins Committee, 21–013, 21–014
Johnson Matthey affair, 14–002
Joint tenancies, severance of, 1–020

Joint ventures,
 investment business exclusion, 2–023
Journalists,
 informant's identity, 4–026
Judicial review,
 Bank of England, 14–054, 14–055
 banking, 14–054—14–055
 decision not to prosecute. *See* **CPS; Serious Fraud Office**
 enforcement of financial services regulation, 4–041
 Insurance Ombudsman Bureau, 10–058
 Lloyd's, 11–051, 11–052
 Pensions Ombudsman. *See* **Pensions Ombudsman**
 PTM, 13–015—13–018
 Stock Exchange, 12–037, 12–044
Jurisdiction,
 concerns over, 2–046
 conspiracy, 18–021
 divorce cases, 8–017
 European Economic Area, 2–048
 financial services regulation, 2–047
 Gower report, 2–046
 inducing an investment, 20–058
 insider dealing, 20–034, 20–35
 Insurance Ombudsman Bureau, 4–060
 Investment Services Directive, 2–048
 Lloyd's Members' Ombudsman, 11–033
 off-shore problem, 2–046
 Pensions Ombudsman, 9–008
 PIA, 4–058
 theft cases, 16–079, 16–080
 trusts, 27–042
Just and equitable winding up,
 breakdown in mutual confidence, 26–055
 meaning, 26–053
 petitioning for, 26–053
 scope, 26–053
 unfair prejudice and, 26–056

Larceny, 16–001
Laundering money. *See* **Money laundering**

LAUTRO, 3–010
 advertising standards, 3–059
 risk, 3–047
 suitability of investment, 3–042
Legal professional privilege, 7–047, 9–019
 investigations, 4–024
Letter of credit, 16–064
Life Assurance and Unit Trust Regulatory Organisation, 3–010
Limitation periods,
 professional negligence, 29–028
Limited companies,
 background to legislative control, 2–003
Liquidators,
 carrying on investment business exclusion, 2–031
Listed institutions,
 carrying on investment business exclusion, 2–031
Listing,
 advertising of particulars, 2–044, 12–075—12–078
 agents, 12–061
 AIM. *See* **AIM**
 Alternative Investment Market. *See* **AIM**
 applicants, 12–012
 application,
  applicants, 12–012
  audited accounts, 12–048
  competent authority, to, 12–043, 12–045
  conditions for listing, 12–048
  consent of issuer, 12–045
  continuity of management, 12–048
  controlling shareholder, 12–048
  directors, 12–048
  incorporation requirement, 12–048
  notification of decision, 12–047
  refusal, 12–046
  securities, requirements of, 12–049
  trading record, 12–048
  vetting applications, 12–046
  working capital, 12–048
 application of Yellow Book rules, 12–041

Listing,—*cont.*
cancellation, 12–040, 12–050, 12–051
compliance with rules, 12–050
conditions for listing, 12–048
continuing obligations, 12–040
criteria for, 12–014
Department, 12–013
discontinuation, 12–050
E.C. Directives, 12–044
enforcement of obligations, 12–040
market makers, 12–057
methods of bringing securities to listing. *See* **Securities**
notification of decision, 12–047
Official List,
  admission, 12–042
  application. *See* **applications** *above*
  competent authority, 12–043
  conditions for admission, 12–042
  criteria for listing, 12–014
  first tier market, 12–012
  judicial review of decision, 12–044
  main market, as, 12–014
  power to make listing rules, 12–044
  refusal of admission, 12–044
particulars,
  advertising, 2–044, 12–075—12–078
  approval, 12–074
  circulation, 12–074
  compensation for false or misleading information, 12–069
  content, 12–064
  Directive, 12–063
  disclosure of information, 12–070—12–072
  E.C. Directive, 12–063
  false information, 12–069
  formal notice, 12–074
  misleading information, 12–069
  pre-publication vetting, 12–068
  preparation, 12–063
  publication, 12–074
  requirement, 12–063
  significant new matters, 12–073
  supplementary, 121–073

Listing,—*cont.*
particulars,—*cont.*
  vetting, 12–068
  place of, 12–038
  Quotations Committee, 12–051
  refusal of admission, 12–044
  requirements, 12–012, 12–038 *et seq.*
Rules. *See* **Yellow Book**
sanctions, 12–050, 12–051
securities, listed,
  See also **Securities**
  admission to list, 12–040
  continuing obligations, 12–040
  responsibility for admitting, 12–039
  suspension, 12–040, 12–050, 12–051
unlisted securities. *See* **AIM**
Yellow Book. *See* **Yellow Book**
Lloyd's,
annual accounting, 11–045
Appeal Tribunal,
  creation, 11–027
  establishment, 11–027
  requirement for, 11–027
Association of Lloyd's Members, 11–025
auditor's role, 11–045
authorisation, requirement, 11–015
baby syndicates, 11–040
Boards,
  Market, 11–025
  Regulatory. *See* **Regulatory Board** *below*
brokers,
  function, 11–013
  liability insurance, 11–014
  professional standards, 11–014
  requirements, 11–014
  underwriter and, 11–013
carrying on investment business
  exclusion, 2–031, 11–016
Central Fund, 11–026
Chairman, 11–018
core principles, 11–045
Corporation, 11–009
Council of,
  accounts, 11–019
  byelaws, purpose of, 11–019
  Chairman election, 11–018
  establishment, 11–017, 11–018

Lloyd's,—*cont.*
  Council of,—*cont.*
    external members, 11–018,
      11–019
    function, 11–018
    members, 11–018
    nomination of members, 11–018
    purpose, 11–018
    requirements, 11–018
    working members, 11–018
  crisis, 11–004
  Cromer Report, 11–002, 11–038
  disaster scenarios, 11–045
  Disciplinary Committee,
    acts of misconduct, 11–029
    basis of, 11–027
    misconduct, 11–029
    reporting misconduct, 11–032
    requirement for, 11–027
    sanctions, 11–030
    summary offences, 11–031
  divisions, 11–009
  DTI investigations, 11–022,
    11–023
  investigations into, 11–023
  Equitas. *See* **Equitas**
  errors and omissions insurance,
    11–045
  exemption, 11–016
  external Name, 11–011
  Fidentia, 11–008
  Financial Services Act 1986 and,
    11–016
  Fisher Report, 11–039
  fit and proper test, 11–015
  history, 11–006—11–008
  incorporation, 11–008
  investor, Name as, 11–003
  judicial review, 11–051, 11–052
  "Lloyd's News", 11–006
  losses of 1980's, 11–035—11–038
  marine disasters affecting, 11–035
  Members' Ombudsman,
    jurisdiction, 11–033
    role, 11–033
  membership,
    brokers. *See* brokers *above*
    fit and proper test, 11–015
    Names. *See* Names *below*
    underwriters, 11–010
  misconduct,
    meaning, 11–030
    reporting, 11–032

Lloyd's,—*cont.*
  Names,
    capital provided by, 11–001
    crisis, 11–004
    depositing shown capital,
      11–011
    external, 11–011
    investor, as, 11–003
    meaning, 11–001
    minimum capital requirment,
      11–011
    nature of, 11–011
    publication of annual
      information, 11–011
    register, 11–012
    requirements, 11–011
    risks, 11–002
    shares, 11–011
    shown capital, 11–011
    spreading risk, 11–011
    stop-loss policies, 11–011
    supervision of affairs, 11–011
    syndicates, 11–011
    types, 11–011
    unlimited liability, 11–001,
      11–011
    working, 11–011
  nature of, 11–037
  Neill Report, 11–040
  on-site investigation, 11–032
  origins, 11–006
  pressure for reform,
    11–041—11–043
  professional negligence,
    29–008—29–015
  reform proposals, 11–041—11–043
  register, 11–012
  registration of individuals, 11–045
  regulation, 11–005, 11–017
  Regulatory Board,
    creation, 11–020
    establishment, 11–020
    goal, 11–021
    membership, 11–020
    on-site investigation, 11–032
    responsibilities, 11–020, 11–021,
      11–024
    solvency assessment, 11–022
  Regulatory Plan, 11–044, 11–045
  RITC, 11–047
  shares, 11–011
  sound and prudent management
    criteria, 11–045

Lloyd's,—*cont.*
  stop-loss policies, 11–011
  structure, 11–009
  syndicates,
    baby, 11–040
    management, 11–001
    size, 11–001
  underwriters, 11–010
  working Name, 11–011
  working party report, 11–002
Loans,
  directors, to. *See* **Directors**
  financial assistance for purchase of own shares, 21–018, 21–021
Lump sums,
  death, on, 8–022
  pension commuted to, 8–021

Mareva injunctions,
  application, 31–003
  assets,
    delivery up, 31–013
    disclosure, 31–008
    foreign, 31–008
  bankers trust order, 31–009—31–012. *See also* **Self-incrimination**
  BCCI case, 31–005
  Brussels Convention, 31–006
  contempt of court, 4–014
  cross-examination. *See* **Cross-examination order**
  cross-undertakings in damages, 4–012
  defendants, 31–004
  delivery up of assets, 31–013
  disclosure of assets, 31–008
  effect, 31–002
  ex parte application, 31–003
  examples of use, 4–011, 4–012
  fear of physical violence, 31–059
  freedom of movement restrained, 31–014—31–016
  grant of, 31–004
  growth in, 31–009
  importance of, 31–008
  international cases, 31–006
  jurisdiction, 31–004
  meaning, 31–002
  Practice Direction, 31–026
  procedure, 31–026
  purpose, 31–002

Mareva injunctions,—*cont.*
  self incrimination, 31–036—31–040
  SIB application, 4–010
  summary judgment, 4–013
  undertakings, 31–005
  uses, 31–003
Market makers,
  registration, 12–021
  requirements for listing, 12–057
Market manipulation,
  background, 20–002—20–004
  development of law, 20–002—20–004
  generally, 2–038, 20–001
  inducing an investment. *See* **Inducing an investment**
  insider dealing. *See* **Insider dealing**
  introduction of legislation, 20–004
  United States legislation, 20–004
Matched orders, 20–050
Maxwell affair, 6–001, 6–005, 9–013
Media, advice in, 2–026
Member nominated trustees. *see* Trustees, occupational pensions
Merger,
  issue, 12–056
  Panel on Take-overs and mergers. *See* **PTM**
Minimum funding requirement,
  occupational pensions, 7–022—7–026, 7–041
  public service pension scheme, 8–047
Minimum trading requirements, AIM, 12–015
Minority shareholder interests,
  financial assistance for purchase of own shares, 21–041
  Foss v. Harbottle, rule in. *See* **Foss v. Harbottle**, rule in
  fraudulent trading, 26–057
  just and equitable winding up,
    breakdown in mutual confidence, 26–055
    meaning, 26–053
    petitioning for, 26–053
    scope, 26–053
    unfair prejudice and, 26–056
  Law Commission review, 26–030

INDEX

Minority shareholder interests,—*cont.*
scope of remedies, 26–029
unfair prejudice. *See* **Unfair prejudice**

Misleading statements,
See also **Market manipulation**
insurance companies, 2–033

Misrepresentation,
common law, 28–009
damages, 28–011
deceit as alternative, 28–012
difficulty in establishing, 28–009
disclosure, 28–013
excluding liability, 28–014
illustration, 28–014
innocent, 28–014
limits of remedy, 28–013
measure of damages, 28–011
obligations imposed, 28–011
onus of proof, 28–009
professional negligence and, 29–048—29–050
requirements, 28–011
scope of remedy, 28–013
statutory,
  bonus of proof, 28–009
  damages, 28–011
  disclosure, 28–013
  limits of remedy, 28–013
  measure of damages, 28–011
  obligations imposed, 28–011
  provisions, 28–010
  requirements, 28–011
  scope of remedy, 28–013

Money had and received,
development of law, 28–020
forgeries, 28–022, 28–023
fraud cases, 28–022
limited companies, 28–025
meaning, 28–020
modern formulation of law, 28–021
origins of law, 28–020
partners, 28–024, 28–025
practical uses, 28–028
rescission of contract, 28–027
restitutionary basis, 28–020—28–022
scope, 28–026
services, 28–026

Money laundering,
agitation stage, 24–001
acquisition, possession or use of proceeds,
  defences, 24–015—24–017
  employees, 24–017
  offence, 24–014
  penalties, 24–018
assisting another to retain the benefit of criminal conduct,
breach of confidence, 24–007—24–009
defences,
  burden of proof, 24–013
  consent of constable, 24–010
  disclosure to constable, 24–010
  employees, 24–012
  intention to disclose, 24–011
  knowledge absent, 24–011
  professional, reliance on, 24–013
  reasonable excuse, 24–011, 24–013
fines, 24–006
imprisonment, 24–006
offence, 24–004, 24–005
penalty, 24–006
proving, 24–005
reporting, 24–007—24–009
sanctions, 24–006
suspicion, 24–005
concealing proceeds,
  commission of offence, 24–020
  offence, 24–019
  penalties, 24–021
Directive, 24–002
drugs, 24–002
Financial Investigation Unit (FIU), 24–045
FIU, 24–045
identification procedures,
  applicants for business, 24–034, 24–035
  creation of system, 24–034
  electronic transfer of funds, 24–035
  exemptions, 24–038
  maintenance of system, 24–034
  postal transfer of funds, 24–036
  principal, of, 24–037
  satisfactory evidence, 24–039

INDEX

Money laundering,—*cont.*
  integration stage, 24–001
  internal procedures, 24–032, 24–033
  internal reporting procedures, 24–042
  international element, 24–001
  layering stage, 24–001
  meaning, 24–001
  National Criminal Intelligence Service Economic Crimes Unit, 24–045
  placement stage, 24–001
  possession of proceeds,
    defences, 24–015—24–017
    meaning, 24–014
    offence, 24–014
    penalties, 24–018
  practice, in, 24–045, 24–046
  re-integration stage, 24–001
  record keeping procedures, 24–040—24–042
  regulations, 24–003
    application of, 24–031
    commencement, 24–030
    identification procedures. *See* **identification procedures** *above*
    internal procedures, 24–032, 24–033
    internal reporting procedures, 24–042
    purpose, 24–030
    record keeping procedures, 24–040—24–042
    reporting procedures, 24–042
    supervisory authorities, 24–043, 24–044
  reporting procedures, 24–042
  stages, 24–001
  statutory provisions, 24–003
  supervisory authorities, 24–043, 24–044
  tackling, 24–002
  tipping off. *See* **Tipping off**
  transferring proceeds,
    commission of offence, 24–020
    disguising proceeds, offence, 24–019
    meaning, 24–020
    offence, 24–019
    penalties, 24–021

Money laundering,—*cont.*
  using property from proceeds,
    defences, 24–015—24–017
    employees, 24–017
    offence, 24–014
    penalties, 24–018
  Vienna Convention, 24–002
Money purchase schemes,
  compliance with requirements, 8–041
  contracting out for, 8–010, 8–011
  contributions schedule, 8–041
  dates for payments, 8–041
  definition, 8–038
  final salary benefit scheme distinguished, 8–037
  meaning, 8–005, 8–038
  minumum funding requirement, 8–040
  payment schedule, 8–041
  purpose, 8–005
  schedules,
    contributions, 7–034
    payments, 8–041
  statutory definiton, 8–038
Monitoring,
  IMRO, 4–018
  PIA, 4–017
  RPB, 4–016
  SFA, 4–018
  SRO, 4–015, 4–017, 4–018
Monopolies and Mergers Commission, 13–038, 13–039
Multiple share applications, 16–045

Names. *See* **Lloyd's**
National Criminal Intelligence Service Economic Crimes Unit, 24–045
Ne exeat regno, writ of, 31–015
Negligence claim,
  advice. *See* **Professional Negligence**
  banking, 14–098
Neill Report, 11–040
Nemo tenetur prodere seipsum, 31–029
Non-investment business, 2–026
Non-occupational schemes. *See* **Personal pensions**

INDEX

Obtaining property by deception,
deception, definiton of, 16–044
deliberate, 16–044
meaning, 16–043
mortgage advances,
  16–047—16–054
multiple share applications,
  16–045, 16–046
Preddy decision, 16–047—16–054
reckless, 16–044
share applications, 16–045, 16–046
statutory provision, 16–043
Occupational pensions,
actuary, 7–043
administration, 7–053
advisory service. *See* **OPAS**
alienability, 7–088
amendment,
  certification requirements,
    7–081, 7–082
  entitlement, 7–083
  Goode Committee, 7–079
  manner, 7–080
  methods, 7–080
  power, 7–079, 7–080
  requirement, 7–079
  restriction on power,
    7–080—7–083
ancillary provisions, 8–001 *et seq.*
Article 119, 8–026—8–035
assets,
  certification, 7–028
  valuation,
    certification, 7–028, 7–029
    further valuation required,
      7–029
    method, 7–027
    requirement, 7–027
    responsibility, 7–027
    standards, 7–030
auditor, 7–043
augmentation on winding up,
  7–088
background to legislation,
  6–001—6–006
benefits, 7–084
blowing whistle, 7–045—7–047
cash equivalent, right to, 7–073,
  7–074
certificate of value of assets,
  7–028, 7–029
changes in, 6–003

Occupational pensions,—*cont.*
communication obligations, 7–078
compensation. *See* **Pensions Compensation Board**
complexity of law, 6–006
confidence in management, 6–005
contracting out of SERPS, 6–004
contributions,
  determining rates, 7–031
  rates, 7–031
  schedule of, 7–031
contributions on insolvency,
  8–042
definition, 6–002
disclosure by trustees, 7–058
dispute resolution. *See* **Dispute resolution of pensions**
divorce. *See* **Divorce**
draft transfer value, 7–076
employer related investments,
  7–049, 7–050
entitlement, statement of, 7–075
equal treatment, 8–024—8–035
expenses of trustees, 7–061
forfeiture, 7–088
fund manager, 7–039
generally, 6–001
Goode Report. *See* **Goode Report**
guarantee date, 7–076
importance of regulation, 6–003
indemnities, 7–057
ineligibility to act as scheme
  auditors/actuaries, 7–056
insolvency, contributions on,
  8–042
investment,
  advice, 7–040, 7–041
  choosing, 7–041
  consultation of employer, 7–040
  delegation, 7–037, 7–039
  diversification, 7–041
  duty of care, 7–036
  employer consultation, 7–040
  fund manager, 7–039
  importance of proper, 7–035
  minimum funding
    requirements, 7–041
  non-compliance with statutory
    provisions, 7–035
  penalties, 7–040, 7–041
  principles, 7–040
  professional advisers. *See*
    Professional advisers

549

Occupational pensions,—*cont.*
  investment,—*cont.*
    prudently, duty to act, 7–038
    trustees' powers, 7–035
    vicarious liability, 7–039
    written statement of principles, 7–040
  investment business, 5–006
  legal advisers, 7–044
  Maxwell affair, 6–005
  minimum funding requirement, 7–022—7–026, 7–041
  modification of scheme,
    orders, 7–085
    public service pension schemes, 7–086
    resolution., 7–084
  modification of schemes, 7–079
  money purchase schemes, 7–034. *See also* **Money purchase schemes**
  Ombudsman. *See* **Pensions Ombudsman**
  OPAS. *See* **OPAS**
  OPRA. *See* **OPRA**
  opt-out,
    adverse, 5–011
    definition, 5–010
    guidelines, 5–008
    numbers, 5–008
    PIA Statement of Policy, 5–008
    quality of advice, 5–008
    review of past pensions, 5–008
  overseas schemes, 8–043
  payment of transfer vlaues., 7–077
  principles underlying regulation, 6–013
  professional advisers. *See* **Professional advisers**
  public service schemes. *See* **Public service pensions schemes**
  purpose of legislation, 6–013
  rates of contributions, 7–031
  receipts. *See* **Trustees, occupational pension**
  records, 7–055
  Regulatory Authority. *See* **OPRA**
  reporting to OPRA, 7–032
  resolution modifying scheme, 7–084
  salary related schemes, 8–039
  schedule of contributions, 7–031
  scheme of regulation, 6–013—6–015

Occupational pensions,—*cont.*
  self-investment,
    directions of court, 7–052
    employer related investments, 7–049, 7–050
    general rule, 7–049
    non-compliance with rules, 7–051
    restoring parties to previous position, 7–052
    restrictions, 7–049
    scope of regulations, 7–049
    unauthorised, 7–049
  separate bank accounts, 7–054
  serious under-provision, 7–033
  sex equality, 7–087
  statement of entitlement, 7–075, 7–076
  surpluses,
    causes, 7–066
    contribution level reduced, 7–067
    employer, payment to, 7–067—7–070
    Goode Committee proposal, 7–065
    growth in, 7–065
    ongoing scheme, 7–066
    payment to employer, 7–067—7–070
    reason for, 7–065
    reduction in levels, 7–067—7–070
    repayment, 7–067
    whistle blowing, 7–070
    winding up, 7–066
  transfer, 5–009
    values, 7–071, 7–072, 7–077
  trustees. *See* **Trustees, occupational pensions**
  under-provision, serious, 7–033
  valuation of assets,
    certification, 7–028
    further valuation required, 7–029
    methods, 7–027
    requirement, 7–027
    responsibility, 7–027
    standards, 7–030
  winding up,
    augmentation on, 7–088
    surpluses, 7–066

OFEX, 12–016
Offences,
See also **Criminal law**
advertising, 2–039
conspiracy. *See* **Conspiracy**
controller, failure to give notice of changes in, 14–050—14–0502
Europersons, 3–016
false information furnished, 10–018
false or misleading statements, insurance, 1–055
offer of securities, 12–105
Theft Act. *See* **Theft Act offences**
trustees, occupational pension, 7–064
unauthorised insurance business, 10–012
Offer of securities, 12–092, 12–093
Official receivers, 2–031
Ombudsman,
Building Societies, 15–031
insurance. *See* **Insurance Ombudsman**
Lloyd's Members,
jurisdiction, 11–033
role, 11–033
memorandum of understanding between, 5–021
pensions, 5–021. *See also* **Pensions Ombudsman**
PIA. *See* **Complaints**
OPAS,
availability, 9–004
case load, 9–005
level of complaints, 9–005
operation, 9–004
Pensions Ombudsman, referral to, 9–004
powers, 9–004
referral to, 9–003
staffing, 9–004
statistics, 9–005
subject matter of complaints, 9–005
OPB, 6–017
Open offer, 12–055
OPRA,
annual report, 6–019
appeals, 6–039
appointment of trustees, 6–028, 7–015

OPRA,—*cont.*
civil penalties,
fines, 6–029
injunctions, 6–031
restitution, 6–032
winding up power, 6–030
communications with, 7–078
compensation board levies, 6–019
conclusions, 6–040—6–045
disclosure of restricted information, 6–037
disqualification, 6–025—6–027
entry power, 6–034
establishment, 6–017
exercise of functions, 6–018
facilitating discharge of functions, 6–037
fines, 6–029
funding, 6–019
Goode Committee recommendations, 6–016
information gathering, 6–033
injunctions, 6–031
inspections,
entry power, 6–034
misappropriation of assets, 6–034
misuse of assets, 6–034
non-compliance with requirements, 6–035
obstruction, 6–035
offences, 6–035
power, 6–034
production of documents, 6–034
reports, 6–036
restricted information, 6–037
warrants, 6–034
levies, 6–019
membership, 6–018
obligations, 6–019
procedure, 6–018
production of documents, 6–034
prohibition orders, 6–020, 6–021
questioning decisions, 6–038
register of disqualification, 6–027
reporting to, 7–032
restitution, 6–032
restricted information, 6–037
review of decisions, 6–038
supervision by,
appointment of trustees, 6–028
disqualification, 6–025, 6–026

OPRA,—*cont.*
supervision by,—*cont.*
prohibition from being trustee, 6–024
prohibition orders, 6–020, 6–021
purpose, 6–022
register of disqualification, 6–027
removal of trustee, 6–023
suspension orders. *See* suspension orders *below*
suspension orders,
interim suspension, 6–022
maximum length, 6–022
notices, 6–023
prohibition from being trustee, 6–024
purpose, 6–022
removal of trustee, 6–023
revocation of order, 6–022
winding up power, 6–030
OPS. *See* **Occupational pensions**
Overdrafts,
theft, 16–023
Overseas investment exchanges,
carrying on investment business exclusion, 2–030
Overseas persons,
investment business exclusion, 2–027
Overseas schemes, 8–043
Own account dealings,
investment business exclusion, 2–023

Panel on Take-overs and mergers. *See* **PTM**
Particulars, listing. *See* **Listing**
Parties to civil action,
agency, 30–010—30–014
corporate liability, 30–002, 30–003
costs, 30–022
device to evade obligations, 30–006—30–008
directors,
agency, 30–010—30–014
contractual obligation, device to evade, 30–006—30–008
corporate liability, 30–002, 30–003
device to evade obligations, 30–006—30–008

Parties to civil action,—*cont.*
directors,—*cont.*
evading obligations, 30–006—30–008
fraud, 30–004, 30–005
holding companies, 30–009
legal obligation, device to evade, 30–006—30–008
personal liability, 30–002 *et seq.*
wrongful trading. *See* **Wrongful trading**
evading obligations, 30–006—30–008
fraud by directors, 30–004, 30–005
generally, 30–001
holding companies, 30–009
"lifting the corporate veil", 30–003
wrongful trading. *See* **Wrongful trading**
Payment into court, 4–007
Pecuniary investment,
definition, 1–007
Pensions,
compensation. *See* **Pensions Compensation Board**
contracting out. *See* **Contracting out**
individual pension contract, 5–012
non-occupational. *See* **Personal pensions**
occupational. *See* **Occupational pensions**
ombudsman, 5–021
Ombudsman. *See* **Pensions Ombudsman**
personal. *See* **Personal pensions**
public service. *See* **Public service pension schemes**
SERPS, 6–004
state, 8–002, 8–003
transfer, 5–009
Pensions Compensation Board,
administration, 9–013
amount of compensation, 9–016
applications for compensation, 9–015
distribution of surplus funds, 9–017
effect, 9–014
establishment, 9–013
false or misleading information provided to, 9–019

Pensions Compensation Board,—*cont.*
function, 9–013
funding, 9–017
Goode Committee recommendations, 9–013
information gathering, 9–019
interim payments, 9–016
legal professional privilege, 9–019
limitations, 9–018
Maxwell scandal, 9–013
offences, 9–019
penalties, 9–019
powers, 9–019
procedure, 9–015
purpose, 9–013
requirements for compensation, 9–014
review of decisions, 9–017
scope, 9–018
self-incrimination, 9–019
surplus funds, 9–017

Pensions Ombudsman,
ambit of complaints, 9–007
appointment, 9–013
basis, 9–006
case load, 9–007
fairness, 9–012
function, 9–006
judicial review of,
  availability, 9–010
  examples, 9–010—9–012
  fairness, 9–012
  improper exercise of powers, 9–011
jurisdiction, 9–008
maladministration investigated, 9–006
overlap with other Ombudsmen, 9–009
personal pensions, 9–009
powers, 9–006
statutory basis, 9–006
subject matter of complaint, 9–007

Personal Investment Authority. *See* **PIA**
rules, carrying out, 5–007

Personal pensions,
actuaries, whistle blowing by, 7–048
APP, 8–005
appropriate, 8–005
auditors, whistle blowing by, 7–048

Personal pensions,—*cont.*
authorisation, 5–003
importance, 5–001
individual pension contract, 5–012
investment advice, as, 5–004
member's rights, investment, as, 5–005
non-occupational schemes distinguished, 5–001
numbers, 5–002
ombudsman, 5–021
pensions Ombudsman, 9–009
quality of advice, 5–002
SIB Pension Review. *See* **SIB Pension Review**
whistle blowing, 7–048

Personal representatives,
activities, 2–026
ICS, 4–050

PIA,
adjusted capital requirements, 3–076
advertising standards, 3–058
client money, 3–037
complaints. *See* **Complaints**
customer agreement, 3–053, 3–054
financial reporting, 3–075
financial resources rules, 3–074, 3–075
focus of regulation, 3–010
function, 3–009
inspections, 4–017
investment business, 3–011
key feature document, 3–054
liquid capital requirements, 3–075
membership, categories, 3–074, 3–075
mission statement, 3–009
Ombudsman. *See* **Complaints**
pension regulation,
  FIMBRA rules adopted, 5–007
  responsibility for, 5–007
personal liability of members, 3–026
personal pension regulation. *See* **Personal pensions**
purpose, 3–009, 3–010
risk, 3–046, 3–047
role, 3–009, 3–010
types of investment business, 3–011

PINCs, 1–021

INDEX

Placing, 12–056
Policy holder,
  meaning, 10–008
  protection, 10–045
  Pre-emptive civil remedies. *See*
    Anton Piller order; Mareva
    injunction; self-incrimination;
    Summary judgment
Preddy decision, 16–047—16–054
Price stabilisation rules,
  inducing an investment, 20–57
  insider dealing, 20–031
  uses, 20–57
Proceeds of crime. *See*
  Confiscation of assets
Profesional investors,
  suitability of investment, 3–042
Professional advisers,
  occupational pensions schemes,
    actuary, 7–043
    appointment, 7–042
    auditor, 7–043
    blowing whistle, 7–045—7–047
    delegation of functions to,
      7–059
    function, 7–042
    legal advisers, 7–044
    legal professional privilege,
      7–047
    liability, 7–043, 7–044
    purpose, 7–042
    requirement, 7–042
    role, 7–042
    statutory monitoring role, 7–045
    whistle blowing, 7–045—7–047
    written report to OPRA, 7–046
Professional negligence,
  accounts,
    bidders, 29–039,
      29–041—29–043
    lenders, 29–040, 29–044
    shareholders, duty to, 29–037,
      29–038
  auditing standards, 29–046,
    29–047
  background, 29–002—29–004
  breach of contract and,
    29–048—29–050
  causation, 29–019
  contributory negligence, 29–027
  damage to property, 29–020

Professional negligence,—*cont.*
  development of law,
    29–005—29–015
  difficulties in establishing, 29–029,
    29–030
  duty of care, 29–005
  examples, 29–031—29–033
  exercise of skill and judgment,
    29–018
  forseeability, 29–020, 29–021
  general principle, 29–006
  generally, 29–001
  Hedley Byrne, 29–005—29–007
  ingredients of action,
    29–016—29–021
  limitation periods, 29–028
  Lloyd's Name, 29–008—29–015
  measure of damages,
    application of principles,
      29–023
    basic rule, 29–022—29–023
    forseeability of loss, 29–022
    loss of chance, 29–025—29–026
    profit projections, 29–024
  misrepresentation and,
    29–048—29–050
  practical problems, 29–029,
    29–030
  property damage, 29–020
  proximity, 29–016, 29–017
  pure economic loss, 29–020
  quasi-professional advisors,
    29–013
  realisation of reliance, 29–016
  reasonable forseeability, 29–020
  reliance, 29–016
  takeovers, 29–034—29–036
Profit forecasts,
  Code on Take-overs and Mergers,
    13–049
Prohibition orders,
  OPRA, 6–020, 6–021
Promotion,
  advertising. *See* **Advertising**
  control, 2–038
Property,
  investment. *See* **Property**
    investment
  nature, 1–004
  purpose of acquisition, 1–005
  species, 1–005
Property Income Certificates,
  1–021

554

Property investment,
court response to developments, 1–023
historical background, 1–019
interests, investor, 1–018—1–023
joint tenancies, 1–020
PINCs, 1–021
problems of, 1–021
Property Income Certificates, 1–021
recession in value, 1–022
SAPCOs, 1–021
Single Asset Property Company, 1–021
Single Property Ownership Trust, 1–021
SPOTs, 1–021

Prospectus,
advertising, 2–044
AIM, 12–089, 12–090
content,
doubt warning, 12–065
generally, 12–064
regulation, 12–065
required, 12–065
disclosure duty, 12–066
exemption, 12–063
form, 12–065—12–067
inaccuracies, 12–067
mandatory, 12–063
pre-publication vetting, 12–068
reasonable requirement, 12–066
requirement, 12–063
significant inaccuracies, 12–067
supplementary, 12–067, 12–091
vetting, 12–068

PTM,
administration of Code, 13–008
ambit of Code, 13–003
appeals, 13–062
background, 13–001—13–004
breach of Code, 13–012—13–014
Chairman, 13–008
City Code. *See* **Code on Take-overs and Mergers**
common law vacuum, 13–005
conclusions, 13–063—13–065
defamation, 13–019
definition of terms, 13–007
Directive, 13–006
effectiveness, 13–065

PTM,—*cont.*
enforcement of code, 13–002
establishment, 13–001
Europe, 13–006
Executive, 13–010, 13–011
function, 13–002, 13–004
future developments, 13–066
general principles, App 5
implementation of Code, 13–004
judicial review,
availability, 13–015—13–016
unavailability, 13–017, 13–018
levy, 12–029
liability of panel for defamation, 13–019
membership, 13–002, 13–008—13–011
offer, 13–007
offeree, 13–007
offeror, 13–007
performance of functions, 13–003
practical implementation of Code, 13–004
proposals, 13–001
purpose, 13–002, 13–004
reasons for establishing, 13–001
reform proposals, 13–066
representatives, 13–009
role, 13–004
sanctions, 13–012—13–014
spirit of Code, 13–004
Stock Exchange Rules and, 13–003, 13–013
substantial acquisition rules. *See* **Substantial acquisition rules**
supervisory function, 13–008
voluntary nature, 13–002

Public companies,
financial assistance for purchase of own shares, 21–033

Public service pension schemes,
application of, 8–046
definition, 8–045
disputes, 8–048
fast accrual schemes, 8–046
local government scheme, 8–047
meaning, 8–044
member nominated trustees, 8–047
minimum funding requirement, 8–047
modification, 7–086

Public service pension schemes,—*cont.*
pay as you go, 8–047
scope, 8–046
settlement of disputes, 8–048
statutory definition, 8–045
Publications, advice in, 2–026
Purchase of own shares,
basic rule, 21–002
breach of prohibition, 21–005
commission of offence, 21–005
company officers, 21–006
court order, 21–008
exceptions to principle, 21–008—21–011
financial assistance. *See* **Financial assistance for purchase of own shares**
general rule, 21–002
generally, 21–001
lifting corporate veil, 21–009
penalties, 21–007
principle, 21–03
prohibition, 21–002—21–007
rationale of law, 21–04
shadow directors, 21–006
statutory basis, 21–003
subsidiary companies, 21–009—21–011
summary trial, 21–007
target company, 21–009
triable either way offence, 21–007

Qualifying capital,
financial resources rules, 3–063
Quistclose trust, 27–008, 27–009
Quotations Committee, 12–051

Receipts,
trustees, occupational pensions. *See* **Trustees, occupational pensions**
Recognised Investment Exchange. *See* **RIE**
Recognised Professional Body. *See* **RPB**
Records,
occupational pensions, 7–055
Reform proposals,
building societies, 15–007, 15–032—15–034

Reform proposals,—*cont.*
conspiracy, 18–022
financial assistance for purchase of own shares, 21–042—21–044
insider dealing, 20–038
Lloyd's, 11–041—11–043
need for, 32–001—32–004
PTM, 13–066
scope of system, 32–002
Register,
authorisation, 3–002
disqualification orders, 6–027, 22–031
Lloyd's names, 11–012
OPRA, 6–027
SIB Central, 3–002
Regulated insurance companies. *See* **Insurance companies**
Reinsurance, 10–010
Remuneration,
directors, 19–002
Restitution orders,
availability, 23–052
contempt of court, 23–054
failure to comply, 23–054
knowingly concerned, 4–009
OPRA, 6–032
passive knowledge, 4–009
payment into court, 4–007
power to make, 4–007, 23–052
provisions for granting, 4–006
scope of power, 4–007
SIB application, 4–008
statutory basis, 23–052
types, 23–053
Restraint of assets orders. *See* **Confiscation of assets; Injunctions;** Restitution orders
Restraint orders. *See* **Confiscation of assets**
Returns, financial,
IMRO, 3–071
RIE,
carrying on investment business exclusion, 2–030
list of, App 1
Stock Exchange, 12–011
Rights issue,
definition, 12–053
holders, rights between, 12–054
pre-emption rights, 12–054

Rights issue,—*cont.*
  purpose, 12–053
Risk,
  customer agreement, 3–043, 3–044
  exceptions to requirement, 3–045
  FIMBRA, 3–046
  general rule, 3–043
  IMRO, 3–044
  LAUTRO, 3–047
  PIA, 3–046, 3–047
  private customers, 3–045
  SFA, 3–045
  SIB core rule, 3–043
  warning, 3–043, 3–044, Apps 14, 15
Risk Asset Ratio (RAR), 14–031, 14–032
Roskill Committee, 25–003, 25–004
Royal Brunei Airlines decision, 27–023, 27–024
RPB,
  authorisation, 3–014
  certificates issued by, 3–014
  complaints, 4–053
  function, 3–014
  information required for, 4–021
  intervention powers, 4–027
  investigation of members, 4–023
  list of, App 1
  member, 3–014
  membership, 2–014
  monitoring, 4–016
  purpose, 3–014
  recognition, 3–014
  role, 3–014

SAEF, 12–033
Sale of bodies corporate, 2–026
Sale of goods,
  investment business exclusion, 2–025
SAPCOs, 1–021
Schedule of contributions,
  money purchase schemes, 7–034
  occupational pensions, 7–031
Scotland,
  divorce, pensions on, 8–023
  interdicts, 4–008
SEAQ, 12–005, 12–033
SEATS, 12–033
Secret profits. *See* **Directors**

Securities,
  acquisition issue, 12–056
  AIM. *See* **AIM**
  Alternative Investment Market.*See* **AIM**
  bonus issue, 12–056
  capitalisation issue, 12–056
  cash, issues for, 12–056
  conditions for listing, 12–049
  disclosure,
    adviser's interests, 12–058
    issuer's, 12–070—12–072
  exempted offers, 12–094
  false or misleading statements,
    common law remedies, 12–104
    compensation, 12–099
    criminal offences, 12–105
    defences, 12–100, 12–102
    exemptions from liability, 12–100
    losses, 12–101
    remedies, 12–099—12–105
    statutory remedy, 12–099—12–103
  freely transferable, 12–049
  incorporation, conforming to law of place of, 12–049
  insider dealing. *See* **Insider dealing**
  intermediaries offer, 12–056
  issue,
    acquisition, 12–056
    bonus issue, 12–056
    capitalisation, 12–056
    cash, 12–056
    intermediaries offer, 12–056
    merger issue, 12–056
    placing, 12–056
    rights,
      definition, 12–053
      pre-emption rights, 12–054
      purpose, 12–053
      rights between holders, 12–054
    tender, offer by, 12–056
    vendor consideration issue, 12–056
  issuer's duty of diclosure, 12–070—12–072
  listing agents, 12–061
  listing particulars. *See* **Listing**
  listing requirements, 12–049

Securities,—*cont.*
  low value, 12–049
  market makers, 12–057
  market value, 12–049
  merger issue, 12–056
  methods of bringing to listing,
      12–053 *et seq.*
  offer of, 12–092, 12–093
  open offer, 12–055
  placing, 12–056
  pre-emption rights, 12–054
  prospectus. *See* **Prospectus**
  rights issue,
    definition, 12–053
    pre-emption rights, 12–054
    purpose, 12–053
    rights between holders, 12–054
  sponsors,
    appointment, 12–059
    authorised persons, 12–060
    competence, 12–060
    duty, 12–059
    identity, 12–059
    listing agents, 12–061
    Listing Rules, 12–059
    need for, 12–060
    purpose, 12–059
    requirements, 12–059
  tender, offer by, 12–056
  underwriting, 12–062
  value, 12–049
  vendor consideration issue,
      12–056
Securities and Futures Authority.
  See **SFA**
Securities and Investments Board.
  See **SIB**
Self regulatory organisations. *See*
  SRO
Self-incrimination,
  abrogation by statute,
    bankruptcy, 31–051
    business fraud, 31–052—31–054
    copyright, 31–050
    theft, 31–046—31–049
  adverse inference, 31–055
  Anton Piller orders, 31–034,
      31–041
  asserting privilege,
      31–030—31–035
  bankers trust orders,
    Bankers Books Evidence Act,
      31–043

Self-incrimination,—*cont.*
  bankers trust orders,—*cont.*
    generally, 31–042
    operation of privilege, 31–043
  bankruptcy, 31–051
  business fraud, 31–052—31–054
  claiming privilege,
      31–030—31–035
  companies, 31–0333
  confiscation orders, 23–011
  copyright, 31–050
  criticisms of privilege, 31–056
  development, 31–029
  DTI investigations,
    generally, 26–074
    inspections, 26–075
    relationship between, 26–074
  effect of asserting privilege,
      31–055—31–058
  European Convention for the
      Protection of Human Rights
      and Fundamental Freedoms,
      31–028, 31–053, 31–057
  importance, 31–027, 31–044,
      31–045
  judicial discretion, 31–031
  Mareva injunctions and, 31–034,
      31–036—31–040
  nemo tenetur prodere seipsum,
      31–029
  petty offences, 31–032
  privilege, 31–027—31–029
  spouses, 31–033
  test for, 31–031
  theft, 31–046—31–049
  understanding, 31–035
Serious Fraud Office,
  compulsory interview,
    inquisitorial nature, 25–005
    nature of powers, 25–005
    non-compliance offences,
        25–06—25–10
    powers, 25–005
  creation, 25–003, 25–004
  decision not to prosecute,
      reviewing,
    disciplinary proceeedings,
        25–026
    generally, 25–021, 25–0322
    implications of decision, 25–022
    jurisdiction of court, 25–023
    reaching decision, 25–022
  disclosure of information
      obtained, 25–012—25–020

INDEX

Serious Fraud Office,—*cont.*
  establishment, 25–003, 25–004
  generally, 25–001, 25–002
  information provision,
    disclosure of information
      obtained, 25–011—25–020
    inquisitorial nature of
      provisions, 25–006
    legal professional privilege,
      25–010
    non-compliance offences,
      25–006—25–010
    powers, 25–005
    refusal to produce, 25–010
    uses of information obtained,
      25–011—25–020
  Roskill Committee, 25–003,
    25–004
  witnesses, compulsion of, 25–005
SERPS,
  6–004. *See also* **Contracting out**
Services,
  dishonestly obtaining, 16–067,
    116–068
  supply, 2–0125
SFA,
  advertising standards, 3–058
  aims, 3–007
  authorisation, 3–008
  broad scope firms, 3–071
  categories of membership, 3–071
  client money, 3–036
  Consumer Arbitration Scheme,
    4–061
  customer agreement, 3–052
  financial reporting requirement,
    3–073
  financial resources rules,
    3–071—3–073
  function, 3–007
  inspection, 4–019
  membership, 3–008, 3–071, 3–072
  mission statement, 3–007
  monitoring, 4–018
  purpose, 3–007
  reporting requirements, 3–073
  risk, 3–045
  role, 3–007
  scope of duties, 3–008
  statistics, 3–008
  suitability of investment, 3–040
  tribunals, 4–034
  types of membership, 3–071

Shadow directors,
  disqualification, 22–033. *See also*
    Disqualification of directors
  meaning, 26–003
  purchase of own shares, 21–006
  wrongful trading, 30–020
SIB,
  authorisation. *See* **Authorisation**
  Central Register, 3–002
  codes of practice, 3–025
  Core Conduct of Business Rules.
    See **Core rules**
  core rules. *See* **Core rules**
  delegation of functions from
    Secretary of State, 2–013
  fees for funding, 2–014
  function, 2–013
  funding, 2–014
  ICS. *See* **ICS**
  information required by, 4–020,
    4–021
  injunction application, 4–008
  insider dealing investigations,
    20–041
  intervention powers, 4–027, 4–028
  investigations,
    powers, 4–022
    purpose, 4–022
  Investors Compensation Scheme.
    See **ICS**
  Mareva injunction application,
    4–010
  pension review. *See* **SIB Pension
    Review**
  powers, 2–013
  rationale of rules/principles, 1–026
  recognition of SROs, 2–013
  restitution order application,
    4–008
  risk, understanding, 3–043
  role, 2–014
  Secretary of State, delegation of
    functions, 2–013
  SROs. *See* **SRO**
  statement of principles. *See*
    Statement of principles
  Takeover Code, 3–020, App 3
SIB Pension Review, 5–014—5–020
  background, 5–014, 5–015
  impeded progress, 5–020
  judicial review and, 5–018

INDEX

SIB Pension Review,—cont.
  number of cases to be reviewed, 5–015
  objectives, 5–014
  priority groups, 5–017
  progress report, 5–017
  purpose, 5–014
  qualification for redress, 5–017
  remit, 5–014
  scale of problem, 5–015
  scope of review, 5–016
  subject matter, 5–016
Simple procedure. *See* **Confiscation of assets**
Single Asset Property Company, 1–021
Single Property Ownership Trust, 1–021
Solvency rules, 3–060
Sources of law,
  civil law, 1–011
  criminal law, 1–015, 1–016
  generally, 1–010
  non-statutory systems, 1–014
  statutory systems, 1–012, 1–013
Sponsors. *See* **Securities**
SPOTs, 1–021
SR,
  inspections, 4–017, 4–018
SRO,
  authorisation. *See* **Authorisation**
  core rules, 3–026—3–028
  creation, 1–026
  definition, 3–005
  effect of membership, 2–013
  existing, 3–006
  funding, 3–006
  information required from, 4–021
  intervention powers, 4–029
  investigation of members, 4–023
  Investment Management Regulatory Organisation. *See* **IMRO**
  membership, 2–013
  monitoring, 4–015
  numbers reduced, 3–006
  Personal Investment Authority. *See* **PIA**
  range, 3–006
  recognition by SIB, 2–013, 3–005
  relationship with members, 3–026

SRO,—cont.
  rule books,
    importance, 3–027
    purpose, 3–027
  Securities and Futures Authority. *See* **SFA**
  SIB recognition, 2–013
  simplification of system, 3–006
  tribunals, 4–035
  volume of rules created by, 1–026
Stabilising manager, 12–026
State pensions, 8–002, 8–003
  age, equalisation of, 8–036
  equalisation of age, 8–036
  Goode report, 8–016
Statement of principles,
  background to, 3–019—3–021
  client money, 3–030
  customer assets, 3–030
  financial resources rules, 3–060
  first tier of regulation, 3–019—3–021
  list of, App 3
  power to issue, 3–019
Statements,
  insurance companies, 10–025
Statutory obligation, breach of,
  common law actions, 4–065
  lack of remedies, 4–065
  possibility of action, 4–065
Stock Exchange,
  action for damages, 12–052
  acts, misleading, 12–023
  advice to correct erroneous statement, 12–031
  AIM. *See* **AIM**
  Alternative Investment Market. *See* **AIM**
  Alternative Trading Service (SEATS), 12–033
  artificial transactions, 12–023
  Automated Execution Facility, 12–03
  Automated Quotations, 12–005
  Big Bang, 12–005
  board of directors, 12–010
  charges,
    revenue, 12–028
    transactions, 12–027
  competent authority, 12–012, 12–043
  compliance with rules, 12–034—12–036

560

Stock Exchange,—*cont.*
  conditional transactions, 12–024
  conduct of business,
    acts, misleading, 12–023
    advice to correct erroneous
      statement, 12–031
    artificial transactions, 12–023
    charges, 12–027
    conditional transactions, 12–024
    conduct, misleading, 12–023
    contract notes, 12–022
    erroneous statement, advice to
      correct, 12–031
    false impression created, 12–023
    fictitious transactions, 12–023
    member firms' responsibility,
      12–030
    prohibited practices, 12–023
    prohibited transactions, 12–025
    PTM levy, 12–029
    reckless actions, 12–023
    revenue charges, 12–028
    stabilisation, 12–026
    suspended activities, 12–025
    transaction charges, 12–027
    unreasonable price differences,
      12–023
  conduct, misleading, 12–023
  contract notes, 12–022
  core rules, 12–019
  damages, action for, 12–052
  Deed of Settlement, 12–010
  discipline, 12–034—12–036
  Domestic Equity Market, 12–033
  electronic markets, 12–005
  erroneous statement, advice to
    correct, 12–031
  establishment, 12–002
  Europe, 12–007—12–009
  false impression created, 12–023
  fictitious transactions, 12–023
  Financial Services Act 1986,
    12–006
  first tier, 12–012
  history, 12–001, 12–002
  information requests, 12–034
  Integrated Monitoring and
    Surveillance (IMAS), 20–041
  Irish, 12–009
  judicial review, 12–037, 12–044
  liability, 12–052
  listing. *See* **Listing**

Stock Exchange,—*cont.*
  main market, 12–012
  manipulation of market, 12–004
  market makers,
    appeals, 12–021
    refusal of registration, 12–021
    registration, 12–021
    rules, 12–021
    withdrawal of registration,
      12–021
  market regulation department,
    function, 12–017
    IMAS, 12–017
    integrated monitoring and
      surveillance, 12–017
    methods, 12–017
    purpose, 12–017
  member firms' responsibility,
    12–030
  membership,
    applicants, 12–018
    requirements, 12–018
    responsibility, 12–030
    rules, 12–018
    suitability for, 12–018
  Memorandum and Articles of
    Association, 12–010
  need for regulation,
    12–003—12–005
  number of listed companies,
    12–001
  OFEX, 12–016
  Official List. *See* **Listing**
  "on exchange", 12–020
  original constitution, 12–010
  origins, 12–002
  performance of functions, 12–044
  prohibited practices, 12–023
  prohibited transactions, 12–025
  reckless actions, 12–023
  Recognised Investment Exchange,
    as, 12–011
  revenue charges, 12–028
  role, 12–001
  rules,
    compliance, 12–034—12–036
    conduct of business. *See*
      conduct of business *above*
    core rules, 12–019
    discipline, 12–034—12–036
    Domestic Equity Market,
      12–033

Stock Exchange,—*cont.*
rules,—*cont.*
International equity Market, 12–032
market makers, 12–021
membership, 12–018
SAEF, 12–033
SEAQ, 12–033
SEATS, 12–033
transactions, 12–020
SAEF, 12–03
SEAQ, 12–005, 12–033
SEATS, 12–033
second tier market, 12–015
SIB, answerable to, 12–011
stabilisation, 12–026
structure, 12–010—12–017
board of directors, 12–010
Memorandum and Articles of Association, 12–010
Recognised Investment Exchange, as, 12–011
suspended activities, 12–025
third tier, 12–016
three tiers, 12–014—12–016
transaction charges, 12–027
transactions, 12–020
unreasonable price differences, 12–023
Subrogation, 27–037
Subsidiary companies, 21–009—21–011
Substantial acquisition rules,
appeals, 13–062
background, 13–056
"dawn raids", 13–056
exemptions, 13–059
function, 13–057
general rule, 13–058
guidance noted, 13–057
interpretation, 13–057
introduction, 13–056
issue, 13–056
joint acts, 13–061
notification of acquisition, 13–060
purpose, 13–057
scope, 13–057—13–061
tender offers, 13–061
Suitability of investment,
advice of unsuitability, 3–041
breach of requirements, 3–038
complaints, 3–038
FIMBRA, 3–041

Suitability of investment,—*cont.*
general rule, 3–038
grounds for believing, 3–041
importance, 3–038
IMRO, 3–039
LAUTRO, 3–042
life policies, 3–042
PIA, 3–041, 3–042
professional investors, 3–042
safeguards, 3–038
scandals due to, 3–038
SFA, 3–040
written reasons for, 3–042
Summary judgment, 31–060—31–063
advantage, 31–060
availability, 31–060
defences, 31–062
evidence, 31–061
obtaining, 31–060, 31–061
purpose, 31–060
resisting application, 31–061
SIB use of procedure, 4–013
uses, 31–062
Surpluses. *See* **Occupational pensions**
Suspension,
authorisation, 3–004, 4–031—4–033
order. *See* **Suspension order**
Suspension order,
OPRA,
interim suspension, 6–022
maximum length, 6–022
notices, 6–023
prohibition from being trustee, 6–024
purpose, 6–022
revocation of order, 6–022

Takeover Code,
SIB, 3–020, App 3
Takeovers,
insider dealing, 20–025
Panel on Take-overs and mergers. *See* **PTM**
professional negligence, 29–034—29–036
Ten Commandments, 3–019. *See also* **SIB**

Tenancy in common,
joint tenancies severed into, 1–020
Tender, offer by, 12–056
Theft,
See also **Theft Act offences**
appropriation,
assumption of rights of owner, 16–010
chose in action, 16–018, 16–019
consent of owner, 16–010, 16–012
date of, 16–015
definition, 16–009
innocent agents, 16–020
misuse of investment money, 16–013—16–017
multiple assumptions of rights of owner, 16–021
preparatory acts, 16–011
statutory definition, 16–009
technical points, 16–016, 16–017
time of, 16–021
bailment, 16–033
Barlow Clowes affair, 16–036—16–040
belonging to another,
bailment, 16–033
Barlow Clowes affair, 16–036—16–040
corporation sole, 16–034, 16–036—16–040
definition, 16–034
establishing, 16–033
importance, 16–033
jury directions, 16–041
mistake, 16–034
statutory definition, 16–034
trust property, 16–034, 16–037—16–040
CHAPS, 16–028
cheques, 16–023
clearing house automated payment system order, 16–028
corporation sole, 16–034, 16–036—16–040
credit balances. See property *below*
definition, 16–005
directors, 16–008
dishonesty,
directors, 16–008
discovering owner of property, 16–007

Theft,—*cont.*
dishonesty,—*cont.*
honest belief in right to deprive, 16–007
importance of, 16–006
meaning, 16–006
test for, 16–006, 16–007
documents, 16–029, 16–030
electronic transfers, 16–028
elements, 16–005
identification of property, 16–031, 16–032
intangible property, 16–022
intention to permanently deprive, 16–042
jurisdiction of court, 16–079, 16–080
overdrafts, 16–023
permanently deprive, intention to, 16–042
proceeds of sale, 16–032
property,
CHAPS, 16–028
cheques, 16–023
chose in action, 16–025
clearing house automated payment system order, 16–028
credit balances,
chose in action, 16–025
false representations, 16–024
forgeries, 16–027
definition, 16–022
documents, 16–029, 16–030
electronic transfers, 16–028
identification, 16–031, 16–032
intangible, 16–022
meaning, 16–022
overdrafts, 16–023
statutory definition, 16–022
titled documents, 16–030
self-incrimination, 31–046—31–049
titled documents, 16–030
Theft Act offences,
abatement of liabilities, 16–069, 16–070
accounting. See **False accounting**
background to law, 16–001—16–004
civil law and, 16–083
conclusions, 16–081—16–083
counterfeiting. See **Forgery**

Theft Act offences,—*cont.*
deception, obtaining property by.
   See **Obtaining property by deception**
development of law,
   16–001—16–004
dishonesty,
   directors, 16–008
   meaning, 16–006
   test for, 16–006, 16–007
false accounting. *See* **False accounting**
forgery. *See* **Forgery**
jurisdiction, 16–079, 16–080
larceny, 16–001
Law Commission review, 16–003
liabilities, remission of, 16–069, 16–070
property by deception. *See* **Obtaining property by deception**
remission of liabilities, 16–069, 16–070
services, dishonestly obtaining, 16–067, 16–068
theft. *See* **Theft**
valuable securities. *See* **Valuable securities**

Three tiers of regulation,
   3–018—3–028

Tipping off,
   creation of offences, 24–022
   defences, 24–026—24–028
   offences, 24–022—24–025
   penalties, 24–029

Tracing,
   advantages of remedy, 27–030
   applications in investor fraud cases, 27–035
   availability, 27, 032
   Clayton's Case, rule in, 27–033
   common law right, 27–032
   constructive trustees,
      27–038—27–041
   equitable right, 27–032
   general principles,
      27–030—27–034
   identification of funds, 27–030
   insolvent banks, 27–036
   losing right, 27–032
   Maxwell case, 27–035

Tracing,—*cont.*
   mixed funds,
      bank accounts, 27–033
      other monies, 27–032
   nature of claim, 27–038
   non-existant fund, 27–035
   origins of law, 27–031
   overdrawn bank accounts, 27–035
   pre-misappropriation assets,
      27–037
   subrogation, 27–037

Trade unions,
   authorisation, 10–011

Trading,
   unauthorised. *See* **Unauthorised trading**

Transfer values,
   occupational pensions, 7–071, 7–072

Treaty of Rome,
   obligations, 2–008

Tribunals,
   Banking Appeals. *See* **Banking**
   disciplinary, 4–034, 4–035
   SFA, 4–034
   SRO, 4–035

Trustee,
   activities, 2–026
   bankruptcy, in, 2–031
   occupational pension schemes. *See* **Trustees, occupational pensions**

Trustees, occupational pensions,
   actuaries as, 7–012—7–014
   appointment, 6–028, 7–003
      member nominated trustees,
         7–006
      OPRA, by, 7–015
   associated persons, 7–014
   auditors as, 7–012—7–014
   automatic disqualification, 7–016, 7–017
   civil penalties, 7–057
   communications with OPRA,
      7–078
   conflicts of interest, 7–020, 7–021
   connected companies, 7–009
   connected persons, 7–014
   corporate, 7–009
   delegation,
      investment power, 7–039
      professional advisers, 7–059
   disclosure, 7–058

Trustees, occupational pensions,—*cont.*
disqualification, 6–025—6-028, 7–003
  acting as trustee while disqualified, 7–017
  automatic, 7–016, 7–017
  reasons, 7–016
  waiver, 7–017
duty of care, 7–036
eligibility, 7–002
employee trustees, protection for, 7–062
expenses, 7–061
fines, 7–057
Goode Committee recommendations, 7–003
indemnity, 7–057
ineligibility from acting, 7–013
investment,
  delegation, 7–037, 7–039
  duty of care, 7–036
  power, 7–035, 7–037
  prudently, duty to act, 7–038
  vicarious liability, 7–039
majority decisions,
  exceptions to rule, 7–018
  meaning, 7–018
  notice of meetings, 7–018
  requirement, 7–018
  super majority, 7–018
member nominated trustees,
  alternative route, 7–008, 7–011
  appointment, 7–006
  ceasing to be member, 7–006
  conflict of duties, 7–010
  duration of appointment, 7–006
  functions, 7–006
  implementation rules, 7–006
  introduction, 7–005
  limitations on role, 7–008
  numbers required, 7–006
  OPRA conferring functions, 7–007
  opt-out schemes, 7–008, 7–011
  problems with, 7–010
  prohibition form being, 7–011
  public service schemes, 8–047
  re-selection, 7–006
  removal, 7–006
  requirement, 7–006, 7–008
  specific functions conferred, 7–007

Trustees, occupational pensions,—*cont.*
member nominated trustees,—*cont.*
  time limits, 7–008
  vetoing candidate, 7–006
non-payment of deductions, 7–064
notice of meetings, 7–018
OPRA appointment, 7–015
professional advisers,
  appointment required, 7–059
  delegation to, 7–059
protection for employee trustees, 7–062
prudently, duty to act, 7–038
receipts,
  non-compliance, 7–063
  non-payment of deductions, 7–064
  offences, 7–064
  payments not made to members, 7–064
  requirement, 7–063
removal of member nominated trustees, 7–006
reporting obligations, 7–078
scheme auditors/actuaries,
  ineligibility to act as, 7–056
super majority, 7–018
suspension. *See* **Suspension orders**
vicarious liability, 7–039
Trusts,
application in investor context, 27–009—27–012
beneficiary, 27–006
common intention to create, 27–010
creation of relationship, 27–005
essence of relationship, 27–006
examples, 27–011, 27–012
implications of relationship, 27–008
importance of law, 27–001—27–004
impressed with trust, 27–002
investor's funds held on,
  Barlow Clowes case, 27–006
  contractual relationship, 27–005
  essence of relationship, 27–006
  nature of relationship, 27–005
  Quistclose trust, 27–008, 27–009
jurisdiction, 27–042

Trusts,—*cont.*
knowing receipt/assistance,
constructive trusts. *See*
Constructive trusts
definitions, 27–014
dishonest and fraudulent
design, 27–014
dishonesty, 27–019, 27–020
foundation of liability, 27–013
general principle, 27–013,
27–014
innocent acts of trustee, 27–022
participation, 27–014
potential liability, 27–014
preferred terminology, 27–018
Royal Brunei Airlines decision,
27–023—27–025
state of mind of trustee, 27–021,
27–022
occupational pension trustees. *See*
**Trustees, occupational
pensions**
procedural significance, 27–004
Quistclose trust, 27–008, 27–009
Royal Brunei Airlines decision,
27–023, 27–024
third party,
constructive trustee. *See*
Constructive trusts
involvement in misapplication
of funds, 27–003
tracing. *See* **Tracing**
trustees. *See* **Trustees**

Unauthorised trading,
civil sanction, 4–005
compensation, 4–005
criminal sanctions, 4–003, 4–004
defence, 4–003
example of prosecution, 4–004
general rule, 4–002
generally, 4–001
money, recovery of, 4–005
penalties, 4–003
property, recovery of, 4–005
recovery of property/money, 4–005
unenforceability of agreements,
4–005
Understanding risk. *See* **Risk**
Underwriting,
commissions, 12–062
meaning, 12–062
securities, 12–062

Undischarged bankrupt,
disqualification of directors,
22–029
Unfair prejudice,
applications, 26–042
buy-out orders, 26–052
definition, 26–043
generally, 26–029, 26–030
just and equitable winding up
and, 26–056
meaning, 26–043
petitioner's interest, 26–047
procedural rules, 26–042
quasi-partnerships, 26–046
rationale of law, 26–041
remedies,
buy-out orders, 26–052
range, 26–051
scope, 26–051
statutory, 26–051
rules, 26–042
scope, 26–044
shareholders' interests, 26–045
subject matter of complaint,
26–049
test, 26–048
Unit trusts,
authorisation,
applications, 2–036
procedure, 2–036
requirement, 2–036
revocation, 2–037
SIB, by, 2–036
Board of Trade investigation,
2–005
constitution, 2–037
continuation undesirable, 2–037
European Union, 2–036
fraud prevention, 2–004
intervention in, 2–037
investigation, 2–037
management, 2–037
manager, 2–036
overseas schemes, 2–036
revocation of authorisation, 2–037
United States,
market manipulation legislation,
20–004
Unlisted Securities Market (USM),
12–015, 12–079. *See also* **AIM**
Unsecured loans,
building societies, 15–019

INDEX

Unsolicited calls. *See* **Cold calling**
Using a false instrument, 16–076
USM, 12–015

Valuable securities,
  causation, 16–065
  CHAPS order, 16–064
  deception, 16–062, 16–065
  defacing, 16–062
  definition, 16–063
  destruction, 16–062
  dishonest destruction, 16–062
  electronic transfer, 16–064
  execution of document, 16–065
  intent to cause loss, 16–062
  irrevocable letter of credit, 16–064
  letter of credit, 16–064
  offences, 16–062
  view to gain, 16–062
Vendor consideration issue, 12–056
Vetting,
  listing particulars, 12–068
  prospectus, 12–068
Vienna Convention, 24–002

Warning notices,
  3–043, 3–044, Apps 14, 15
Wash sales, 20–050
Whistle blowing,
  actuaries, 7–045—7–048
  auditors, 7–045—7–048
  occupational pensions,
    7–045—7–047, 7–070
  personal pensions, 7–048
  surpluses, occupational pension
    scheme, 7–070

White Paper on Financial Services in the United Kingdom, 2–007
Winding up, 4–036
  occupational pension schemes, 7–066
  OPRA, by, 6–030
  supluses on, 7–066
Witnesses, reluctant, 1–016
Wrongful trading,
  background, 30–015
  Cork Committee, 30–016
  criteria, 30–016—30–018
  disqualification of directors,
    22–027, 22–028
  liability, 30–016
  liquidators, 30–021
  purpose of law, 30–019
  requirements, 30–016—30–018
  shadow directors, 30–020
  statutory provisions, 30–016
  test for, 30–016—30–018
  winding-up, 30–021

Yellow Book,
  application of rules, 12–041
  compliance with rules, 12–050
  enforcement, 12–050
  meaning, 12–012
  objectives, 12–041
  power to make, 12–044
  principles, 12–041
  sponsors, 12–059
  statutory basis, 12–012
  Stock Exchange power to make, 12–044